Lecture Notes in Artificial Intelligence 6320

Edited by R. Goebel, J. Siekmann, and W. Wahlster

Subseries of Lecture Notes in Computer Science

Fu Lee Wang   Hepu Deng   Yang Gao
Jingsheng Lei (Eds.)

Artificial Intelligence and Computational Intelligence

International Conference, AICI 2010
Sanya, China, October 23-24, 2010
Proceedings, Part II

 Springer

Series Editors

Randy Goebel, University of Alberta, Edmonton, Canada
Jörg Siekmann, University of Saarland, Saarbrücken, Germany
Wolfgang Wahlster, DFKI and University of Saarland, Saarbrücken, Germany

Volume Editors

Fu Lee Wang
Caritas Francis Hsu College
Department of Business Administration
18 Chui Ling Road, Tseung Kwan O, Hong Kong, China
E-mail: pwang@cihe.edu.hk

Hepu Deng
RMIT University
School of Business Information Technology
City Campus, 124 La Trobe Street, Melbourne, Victoria 3000, Australia
E-mail: hepu.deng@rmit.edu.au

Yang Gao
Nanjing University
Department of Computer Science
Nanjing 210093, China
E-mail: gaoy@nju.edu.cn

Jingsheng Lei
Nanjing University of Posts and Telecommunications
School of Computer
Nanjing 210003, China
E-mail: leijs@njupt.edu.cn

Library of Congress Control Number: 2010936499

CR Subject Classification (1998): I.2, F.1, J.3, F.2, K.4.4, D.2

LNCS Sublibrary: SL 7 – Artificial Intelligence

ISSN   0302-9743
ISBN-10   3-642-16526-5 Springer Berlin Heidelberg New York
ISBN-13   978-3-642-16526-9 Springer Berlin Heidelberg New York

springer.com

© Springer-Verlag Berlin Heidelberg 2010
Printed in Germany

Typesetting: Camera-ready by author, data conversion by Scientific Publishing Services, Chennai, India
Printed on acid-free paper   06/3180

Preface

The 2010 International Conference on Artificial Intelligence and Computational Intelligence (AICI 2010) was held October 23–24, 2010 in Sanya, China. The AICI 2010 received 1,216 submissions from 20 countries and regions. After rigorous reviews, 105 high-quality papers were selected for publication in the AICI 2010 proceedings. The acceptance rate was 8%.

The aim of AICI 2010 was to bring together researchers working in many different areas of artificial intelligence and computational intelligence to foster the exchange of new ideas and promote international collaborations. In addition to the large number of submitted papers and invited sessions, there were several internationally well-known keynote speakers.

On behalf of the Organizing Committee, we thank Hainan Province Institute of Computer and Qiongzhou University for its sponsorship and logistics support. We also thank the members of the Organizing Committee and the Program Committee for their hard work. We are very grateful to the keynote speakers, invited session organizers, session chairs, reviewers, and student helpers. Last but not least, we thank all the authors and participants for their great contributions that made this conference possible.

October 2010

Fu Lee Wang
Hepu Deng
Yang Gao
Jingsheng Lei

Organization

Organizing Committee

General Co-chairs

Qing Li   City University of Hong Kong, China
Mingrui Chen   Hainan University, China

Program Committee

Co-chairs

Hepu Deng   RMIT University, Australia
Yang Gao   Nanjing University, China

Local Arrangement

Chairs

Zhuang Li   Qiongzhou University, China

Proceedings

Co-chair

Fu Lee Wang   Caritas Francis Hsu College, China
Jingsheng Lei   Nanjing University of Posts and Telecommunications,
                             China

Publicity

Chair

Lanzhou Wang   China Jiliang University, China

Sponsorship

Chair

Zhiyu Zhou   Zhejiang Sci-Tech University, China

Program Committee

Adi Prananto	Swinburne University of Technology, Australia
Adil Bagirov	University of Ballarat, Australia
Ahmad Abareshi	RMIT University, Australia
Alemayehu Molla	RMIT University, Australia
Andrew Stranier	University of Ballarat, Australia
Andy Song	RMIT University, Australia
An-Feng Liu	Central South University, China
Arthur Tatnall	Victoria University, Australia
Bae Hyeon	Pusan National University, South Korea
Baoding Liu	Tsinghua University, China
Carmine Sellitto	Victoria University, Australia
Caroline Chan	Deakin University, Australia
CheolPark Soon	Chonbuk National University, South Korea
Chowdhury Morshed	Deakin University, Australia
Chung-Hsing Yeh	Monash University, Australia
Chunqiao Tao	South China University, China
Costa Marly	Federal University of Amazonas, Brazil
Craig Parker	Deakin University, Australia
Daowen Qiu	Zhong Shan University, China
Dat Tran	University of Canberra, Australia
Dengsheng Zhang	Monash University, Australia
Edmonds Lau	Swinburne University of Technology, Australia
Elspeth McKay	RMIT University, Australia
Eng Chew	University of Technology Sydney, Australia
Feilong Cao	China Jiliang University, China
Ferry Jie	RMIT University, Australia
Furutani Hiroshi	University of Miyazaki, Japan
Gour Karmakar	Monash University, Australia
Guojun Lu	Monash University, Australia
Heping Pan	University of Ballarat, Australia
Hossein Zadeh	RMIT University, Australia
Ian Sadler	Victoria University, Australia
Irene Zhang	Victoria University, Australia
Jamie Mustard	Deakin University, Australia
Jeff Ang Charles	Darwin University, Australia
Jennie Carroll	RMIT University, Australia
Jenny Zhang	RMIT University, Australia
Jian Zhou T	Tsinghua University, China
Jingqiang Wang	South China University, China
Jinjun Chen	Swinburne University of Technology, Australia
Joarder Kamruzzaman	Monash University, Australia
Kaile Su	Beijing University, China
Kankana Chakrabaty	University of New England, Australia
Konrad Peszynski	RMIT University, Australia
Kuoming Lin	Kainan University, Taiwan

Table of Contents – Part II

Applications of Computational Intelligence

Biomedical Informatics and Computation

Fuzzy Computation

Genetic Algorithms

Immune Computation

Information Security

Intelligent Agents and Systems

Nature Computation

Particle Swarm Optimization

Probabilistic Reasoning

Table of Contents – Part I

Data Mining and Knowledge Discovering

Distributed AI and Agents

Expert and Decision Support Systems

Fuzzy Logic and Soft Computing

Intelligent Information Fusion

Intelligent Scheduling

Intelligent Signal Processing

Machine Learning

Machine Vision

Multi-agent Systems

Natural Language Processing

Neural Networks

Pattern Recognition

Robotics

A New Fault Detection Method of Induction Motor

Chuanbo Wen[1,*] and Yun Liang[2]

[1] Electric Engineering School, Shanghai Dianji University,
Shanghai, China
[2] Electronic and information school, Shanghai Dianji University,
Shanghai, China
{wencb,liangy}@sdju.edu.cn

Abstract. According to the shortcoming that the Extended Kalman filter (EKF) method can only estimate the speed and rotor position of induction motors in time domain when it is used to diagnose the fault existed in induction motor. A new multi-scale default diagnosing method is developed by combining EKF and wavelet transform. By monitoring the voltages and currents of the stator, it is possible to estimate the speed and position on-line. The new filter combines the merit of EKF and wavelet, and it not only possesses the multiscale analysis capability both in time domain and frequency domain, but also has better estimation accuracy than traditional EKF. Computer simulation shows the effect of the new algorithm.

Keywords: Induction motor, multi-scale analysis, extended Kalman filter (EKF).

1 Introduction

In the fault diagnosis of induction motors, the information of the speed and rotor position of which is absolutely necessary. Because the price of speed sensorless is low and it can work in the complicated environment, the research of the technique of speed sensorless becomes more and more interest [1, 2].

Recently, some scholars pay attention to the methods such as model reference adaptive and rotate speed observer, however, these methods are partly affected by the motor parameters [3]. EKF is also used to estimate the speed and rotor position of induction motors, but it can only estimate the parameters in time domain [4, 5]. This paper develops a new method, which not only possesses the multiscale analysis capa-

---

* This work is supported by National Nature Science Foundation under Grant 60801048, Major Project of Shanghai National Programs for Fundamental Research under Grant 09JC1408000, Science and Technology Commission of Shanghai Municipality project under Grant 08DZ1200505, and Shanghai Municipal Commission of economy and informatization project under Grant 09A118.

F.L. Wang et al. (Eds.): AICI 2010, Part II, LNAI 6320, pp. 1–8, 2010.

bility both in time domain and frequency domain, but also has better estimation accuracy than traditional EKF.

2   Mathematical Model Description of Induction Motor

Let $x = \begin{bmatrix} i_{sd} & i_{sq} & \Psi_{rd} & \Psi_{rq} & \omega \end{bmatrix}^T$, the dynamic model of the voltage can be described in the d, q rotor frame as follows[5]:

$$\dot{x} = Ax + Bu \tag{1}$$

where

$$A = \begin{bmatrix} -1/T_s & 0 & L_m/(\sigma L_s T_r) & \omega L_m/(\sigma L_s L_r) & 0 \\ 0 & -1/T_s & -\omega L_m/(\sigma L_s L_r) & L_m/(\sigma L_s L_r T_r) & 0 \\ L_m/T_r & 0 & -1/T_r & -\omega & 0 \\ 0 & L_m/T_r & \omega & -1/T_r & 0 \\ 0 & 0 & 0 & 0 & 1 \end{bmatrix}, \ \sigma = 1 - L_m^2/(L_r L_s)$$

$$B = \begin{bmatrix} 1/(\sigma L_s) & 0 & 0 & 0 & 0 \\ 0 & 1/(\sigma L_s) & 0 & 0 & 0 \end{bmatrix}^T, \ T_r = 1/[R_s/(\sigma L_s) + (1-\sigma)/(\sigma T_r)] ,$$

R_s, L_s, L_r, L_m are the resistance of stator phase winding, the resistance of stator phase winding, inductance of stator winding, inductance of rotor winding and mutual inductor, respectively.

With discretization operator and adding system noise, the continuous system (1) becomes [6]:

$$x(k+1) = A_d(k)x(k) + B_d u(k) + w(k) \tag{2a}$$

For describing convenience, the input $u(k)$ is omitted, and the new state equation is

$$x(k+1) = A_d(k)x(k) + w(k) \tag{2b}$$

where

$$A_d = e^{AT} \approx \begin{bmatrix} 1-T/T_s & 0 & TL_m/(\sigma L_s T_r) & T\omega L_m/(\sigma L_s L_r) & 0 \\ 0 & 1-T/T_s & -T\omega L_m/(\sigma L_s L_r) & TL_m/(\sigma L_s L_r T_r) & 0 \\ TL_m/T_r & 0 & 1-T/T_r & -T\omega & 0 \\ 0 & TL_m/T_r & T\omega & 1-T/T_r & 0 \\ 0 & 0 & 0 & 0 & 1 \end{bmatrix}$$

The corresponding measurement equation is

$$z(k) = Cx(k) + v(k) \tag{3}$$

where

$$C = \begin{bmatrix} 1 & 0 & 0 & 0 & 0 \\ 0 & 1 & 0 & 0 & 0 \end{bmatrix}^{T}$$

The state described in (2b) will be blocked and suitable for wavelet transform, the length of each block is $M = q^{N-1}$ and the $m+1$-th block is

$$X(m+1) = \left[x^{T}(mM+1), x^{T}(mM+2), \cdots, x^{T}(mM+M) \right]^{T}$$

For $i = 1, 2, \cdots$, the recursive state of blocked state is

$$X(m+1,i) \doteq x(mM+i) = g_{i}(X(m,M), w(mM), w(mM+1), \cdots, w(mM+i-1)) \tag{4}$$

where g_i can be obtained from function f, $X(m+1,i) \doteq x(mM+i)$ is the i-th element of block $m+1$. According to (4), the $m+1$-th block can be described as

$$X(m+1) = \begin{bmatrix} g_1(X(m,M), w(mM)) \\ g_2(X(m,M), w(mM), w(mM+1)) \\ \vdots \\ g_M(X(m,M), w(mM), w(mM+1), \cdots, w(mM+M-1)) \end{bmatrix} \tag{5}$$
$$\doteq g(X(m,M), w(mM), w(mM+1), \cdots, w(mM+M-1))$$

The blocked measurement is

$$Z(m+1) = \overline{C}(m+1)X(m+1) + \overline{v}(m+1) \quad m = 0,1,2,\cdots \tag{6}$$

where

$$Z(m+1) = \left[z^{T}(mM+1), z^{T}(mM+2), \cdots, z^{T}(mM+M) \right]^{T}$$

$$\overline{C}(m+1) = diag\left[C(mM+1), C(mM+2), \cdots, C(mM+M) \right]$$

$$\overline{v}(m+1) = \left[v^{T}(mM+1), v^{T}(mM+2), \cdots, v^{T}(mM+M) \right]^{T}$$

3 Blocked Description of the System

For the signal sequence $x(i,k) \in V_i \subset (l^2(Z))^n$ ($k \in Z$) , which is obtained on scale i. Consider a subsequence with length $M = q^{i-1}$

$$X^{(i)}(m) = \left[x^{\mathrm{T}}(i,(m-1)M+1), x^{\mathrm{T}}(i,(m-1)M+2), \cdots, x^{\mathrm{T}}(i,(M)) \right]^{\mathrm{T}}$$

Denote it as

$$X_V^{(i)}(m) = X^{(i)}(m)$$

Let $\overline{H}_i$ and $\overline{G}_{r,i}$ represent the scale operator and wavelet operator of signal $x(i,k) \in V_i \subset l^2(Z)$, respectively, and the operator operated on signal $x(i,k) \in V_i \subset (l^2(Z))^n$ are

$$H_i = L_{i-1}^{\mathrm{T}} \mathrm{diag}\{\overline{H}_{i-1}, \cdots, \overline{H}_{i-1}\} L_i$$

$$G_{r,i} = L_{i-1}^{\mathrm{T}} \mathrm{diag}\{\overline{G}_{r,i-1}, \cdots, \overline{G}_{r,i-1}\} L_i$$

In above equations, the number of diagonal elements is n, L_i is linear operator used to translate X_m into a form suitable for wavelet transform [7,8].

The multiscale decomposition and reconstruction of $X_V^{(i)}(m)$, respectively, are

$$X_V^{(i)}(m) = H_i X_V^{(i+1)}(m), \quad L \le i \le N-1 \tag{7}$$

$$X_{r,D}^{(i)}(m) = G_{r,i} X_V^{(i+1)}(m), \quad r = 1,2,\cdots,q-1 \tag{8}$$

and

$$X_V^{(i+1)}(m) = H_i^* X_V^{(i)}(m) + \sum_{r=1}^{q-1} G_{r,i}^* X_{r,D}^{(i)}(m) \tag{9}$$

Denote

$$\gamma(m) = \left[(X_D^{(N-1)}(m))^{\mathrm{T}}, (X_D^{(N-2)}(m))^{\mathrm{T}}, \cdots; (X_D^{(L)}(m))^{\mathrm{T}}, (X_V^{(L)}(m))^{\mathrm{T}} \right]^{\mathrm{T}}$$

where

$$X_D^{(i)}(m) = \left[(X_{1,D}^{(i)}(m))^{\mathrm{T}}, (X_{2,D}^{(i)}(m))^{\mathrm{T}}, \cdots, (X_{q-1,D}^{(i)}(m))^{\mathrm{T}} \right]^{\mathrm{T}}$$

Also let

$$\gamma(m) = W_X X^{(N)}(m) \tag{10}$$

represents the multiscale decomposition of $X^{(N)}$, and

$$X^{(N)}(m) = W_X^* \gamma(m) \tag{11}$$

represents the reconstruction of $\gamma(m)$, where

$$W_X = \begin{bmatrix} G_{N-1} \\ G_{N-2}H_{N-1} \\ \vdots \\ G_L H_{L+1} H_{L+2} \cdots H_{N-1} \\ H_L H_{L+1} H_{L+2} \cdots H_{N-1} \end{bmatrix} \tag{12}$$

$G_i = \begin{bmatrix} G_{1,i}^T, G_{2,i}^T, \cdots, G_{q-1,i}^T \end{bmatrix}^T$ is the wavelet operator matrix, and W_X^* is the associate matrix of W_X, which satisfies

$$W_X^* W_X = I \tag{13}$$

where I is a identity matrix.

Operating the wavelet operator matrix (12) on both sides of (2b), and the state equation described both in time domain and frequency domain becomes

$$W_X X(m+1) = W_X g(X(m,M), w(mM), \cdots, w(mM+M-1))$$

i.e.

$$\gamma(m+1) = W_X g(X(m,M), w(mM), \cdots, w(mM+M-1)) \tag{14}$$

The measurement equation can also described as

$$Z(m+1) = C_w(m+1)\gamma(m+1) + \bar{v}(m+1) \tag{15}$$

where

$$C_w(m+1) = C(m+1)W^*$$

Equation (15) can also be rewritten as

$$Z(m+1,s) = C_w(m+1,s)\gamma(m+1) + \bar{v}(m+1,s) \quad s = 1,2,\cdots,M \tag{16}$$

where $Z(m+1,s) = z(mM+s)$ 、 $\bar{v}(m+1,s) = v(mM+s)$, $C_w(m,s)$ is the s-th row of matrix $C_w(m)$.

4 Multiscale Description of the System

With the blocked measurement equation (16), the blocked state (14) is estimated based on multiscale algorithm. We assume that the estimate $\hat{X}(m \mid m)$ of state $X(m)$ and its estimate error covariance $P_X(m \mid m)$ has been obtained, and the prediction and prediction error covariance of wavelet block $\gamma(m+1)$ are $\hat{\gamma}(m+1|m) = g(\hat{X}(m, M), 0, \cdots, 0)$ and $P_\gamma(m+1|m)$, respectively. Finally, when the last measurement $Z(m+1, M)$ is coming, the optimal estimate of $m+1$ -th block wavelet coefficient $\hat{\gamma}(m+1|m+1) \doteq \hat{\gamma}(m+1, M)$ and its estimate error covariance $P_\gamma(m+1 \mid m+1) \doteq P_\gamma(m+1, M)$ are obtained.

Using inverse wavelet transform (11), the optimal blocked state is

$$\hat{X}(m+1|m+1) = W_X^* \hat{\gamma}(m+1 \mid m+1) \tag{17}$$

and estimate error covariance is

$$P_X(m+1|m+1) = W_X^* P_\gamma(m+1 \mid m+1)W_X \tag{18}$$

5 Computer Simulation

This section presents the performance of the multiscale estimation algorithm. The parameters are $L_s = L_r = 0.168\,\mathrm{mH}$, $L_m = 0.147\,\mathrm{mH}$, $R_s = 2.015\,\Omega$, $J = 0.0026\mathrm{kg \cdot m^2}$, $p = 2$, n $= 1250\mathrm{r / min}$, $Q(k) = 1$ and $R(k) = 1$. In this section, the Haar wavelet are used and the state are rewritten with $M = 4$, $N = 3$ and $L = 1$.

The multiscale estimate algorithm and traditional EKF are used to estimate the speed and rotor position of induction motors, respectively. Simulation results show the situation of error based on two methods, which are presented in Figures 1 and 2.

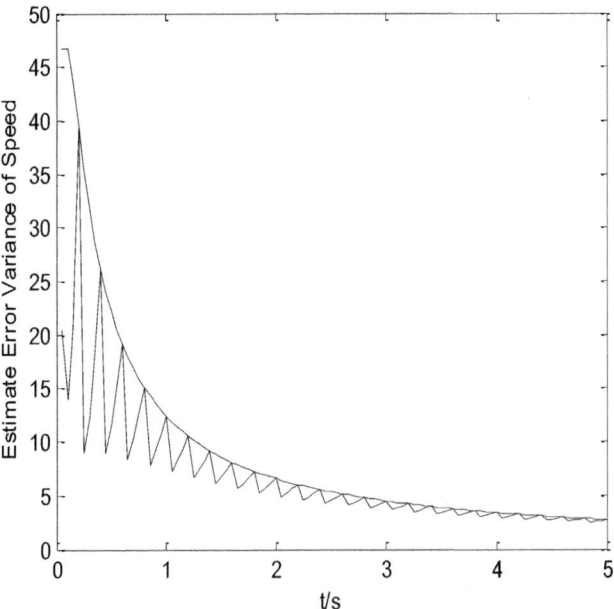

Fig. 1. Comparison of estimate error of motor speed based on two methods

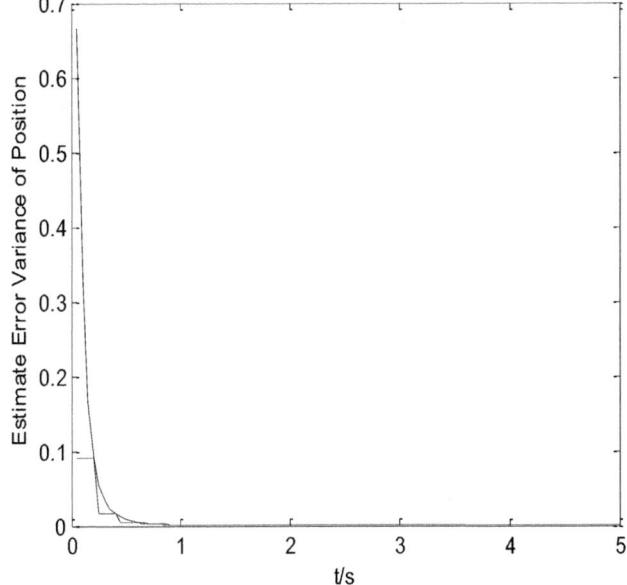

Fig. 2. Comparison of the estimate error of motor position based on two methods

In Figs. 1 and 2, real line and dashed line presented the estimate error from multis-cale algorithm and EKF respectively. We can see that the result of the former is smaller than that of the latter, which shows the advantage of new algorithm.

6 Conclusions

In this paper, a multiscale algorithm is developed to estimate the speed and rotor position of induction motors. New method combines the advantages of EKF and wavelet transform and obtain a better estimation result. The estimate process is online and real-time, and the simulation results show the advantage of new algorithm.

References

1. Zhanying, W.: Study of Induction Motor's Speed Sensorless Control Based on MATLAB. Micromotors 41(3), 75–77 (2008)
2. Tajima, H., Guidi, G., Umida, H.: Consideration about problems and solutions of speed estimations method and parameter turning for speed sensorless vector control of induction motor drives. IEEE Trans. Ind. Appl. 38(5), 1282–1292 (2002)
3. Shen, A.W., Li, T.: Rotor Resistance Identification in Speed Sensor-less Vector Control of Induction Motor. Micromotors 39(5), 6–9 (2006)
4. Guan, Y.J., Ni, X.L.: Application of Extended Kalman Filter for Speed Sensorless Vector Control on Induction Motor. Cont. Auto. 24(3), 87–88 (2008)
5. Masayuki, T., Takayuki, M.: Novel motors and controllers for high-performance electric vehicle with four in-wheel motors. IEEE Trans. Ind. Appl. 30, 1225–1233 (1994)
6. Jiang, J., Ji, Z.C.: Sensorless Vector Control of Induction Motor Based on EKF. Small and Special Machines 11, 37–40 (2005)
7. Debnath, L.: Wavelet Transforms and Time-Frequency Signal Analysis. Birkhuser, Boston (2001)
8. Daubechies: Ten lectures on wavelets. Society for industrial and Appl. Math., Philadephia (1992)

A Method to Identify Damage of Roof Truss under Static Load Using Genetic Algorithm

Ying Wang, Jianxin Liu, Fengying Shi, and Jun Xiao

College of Civil Engineering
Shanghai Normal University
Shanghai, P.R. China
wycyt2000@163.com

Abstract. In recent years, computational intelligence methods are widely used to solve problems in engineering structural field by more and more researchers. In this paper, a method based on genetic algorithm (GA) for identifying the damage in a roof truss under static loads has been developed. At first, the forward analysis based on the finite element model method clearly demonstrates that the damage of elements on a roof truss can result in a change of static axial strain. Then GA has been used to identify the location and the degree of structural damage. In this paper, damage in the structure is modeled as a reduction in the cross-sectional of the damaged element. The identification problem is formulated as a constrained optimization problem, which is solved using GA. Unlike the traditional mathematical methods, which guide the direction of hill climbing by the derivatives of objective functions, GA searches the problem domain by the objective functions itself at multiple points. The objective function is defined as the difference between the measured static strains and the analytically predicted strains obtained from a finite element model. By minimizing the objective function, the damage location and damage severity can be successfully identified. The static-based method uses only strain measurements at a few degrees of freedom as input to the identification procedure and no additional excitation is required. These features make the method ideally suited for long-term monitoring of large civil structures. The method proposed in this paper is demonstrated using a plane roof truss model, and the results fit well with the actual value.

Keywords: Genetic algorithm, Identification, Damage, Roof truss, Static strain.

1 Introduction

Computational intelligence methods, such as neural networks, genetic algorithms, and fuzzy logics, are highly adaptive methods originated from the laws of nature and biology. Unlike the mathematical methods, they are effective and robust in coping with uncertainty, insufficient information, and noise [1-5]. They can adapt themselves to the current environment, so they are able to find a near optimal solution no matter how much information is available. Actually, the more information is available, the better they can get. In real life, the biological systems have to make instantaneous

F.L. Wang et al. (Eds.): AICI 2010, Part II, LNAI 6320, pp. 9–15, 2010.

decisions with a limited amount of information. Therefore, computational intelligence methods use the same basic approaches as the biological system and consequently, the restriction of mathematical methods is no longer a necessary condition for finding the solution.

Genetic algorithm is a search method based on the philosophy of Darwin's theory of evolution [6]. Instead of finding the optimum from a single point in traditional mathematical methods, which may be stuck in the local optima, in GAs, a set of points, that is, a population of coded strings, is used to search for the optimal solution simultaneously. Three basic operators in simple genetic algorithms, reproduction, crossover, and mutation, are used to search for the optimal solution.

With the fast development of civil engineering in China, density of highways network improves constantly and the tall buildings are emerging constantly. But structural damages such as cracking, aging etc. to some degree during the structures' service life occur from time to time. Some invisible damages do not alert the engineering in time and may result in disastrous consequences and ultimately cause substantial loss of life and property. Therefore, it is important to master the health status of structures in service in time and to detect damages at the earliest possible stage.

In the past two decades, researchers have investigated ways of automating the process of identifying and assessing damage in civil structures. The objective of the identification of structural damage is to qualitative or quantitative description of the deterioration in physical structural system from the measured loads and the measured responses of the structure. Liu and Chian [7] developed a procedure for identifying the cross sectional areas of a truss using static strain measurements resulting from a series of concentrated forces. A closed-form solution was obtained for the truss. Chou and Ghaboussi [8] used a genetic algorithm to identify damage in a truss structure based on measured deflections. Shenton III, H. W. and Hu, X. [9] presented a method for damage identification using static strain measurements due to dead load based on genetic algorithm.

In this paper, an identification method in structural damage detection was formulated as an optimization problem, which is solved by using GA. The procedure of identification can be defined as a minimization problem. The optimum solution can be obtained effectively by using GA. By identifying the location and degree of the plane roof truss, the proposed method was verified.

2 Analytical Model

Although the proposed method in this paper is general and it can be applied to most types of structures in civil engineering, only roof truss is considered in this study. It is assumed that in the actual implementation of the proposed method, sensors have been placed on the roof before the damage occurs. The roof load is treated as a series of static nodal loads.

The gable roof truss model and its loads under consideration are shown in Fig. 1, and it has 13 elements. This structure is modeled as a plane truss. Fig. 2 is the finite element model of the plane truss.

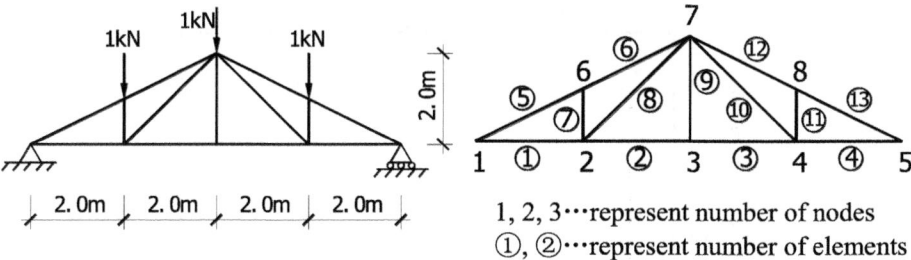

Fig. 1. Configuration and loads of plane roof truss

1, 2, 3···represent number of nodes
①, ②···represent number of elements

Fig. 2. Finite element model of plane roof truss

3   Forward Analysis

As many researchers [7,9-11] have pointed out that damage will result in a change of structural strain. In this study, the first step is to understand how the change is resulted in a roof truss when damage is introduced. Considering the roof truss model shown in Fig. 1, the Young's modulus is 2.07×10^{11}Pa, Poisson's ratio is 0.3, and the cross-section area is uniformly 1.0×10^{-2}m² under undamaged state. The damage is modeled as a reduction in the cross-section area of the damaged element. The damaged index α is defined as the ratio of damaged to undamaged cross-section area of the element.

Two different damage cases are considered. One in which there is only one element is damaged and the other is two elements are damaged simultaneously. In the first case, element 5 is assumed to be damaged, and the damage index α is 0.8 or 0.4. In the second case, element 5 and 10 are assumed to be damaged, the damage index a also is 0.8 or 0.4. The finite element method is used to solve the numerical model (the finite element model is shown in Fig.2) and the results are presented in Fig.3 and Fig.4 (α=1.0 means that no element is damaged).

Presented in Fig.3 is the axial strain distribution in the roof truss model for three damage situations (i.e. a=1.0, a=0.8 and a=0.4) at element 5. One can see from Fig.3 that the axial strain of element 5 does change due to the damage in either of the two damage cases. The effect of varying damage severity is also shown in Fig. 3. With the

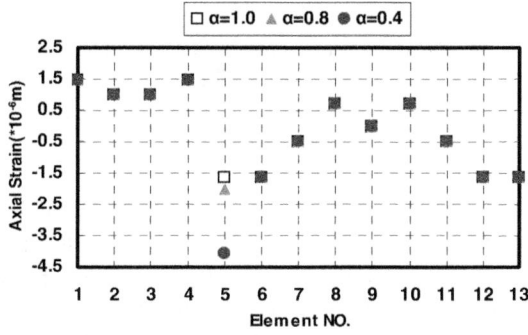

Fig. 3. The axial strain of roof truss with damage in element 5

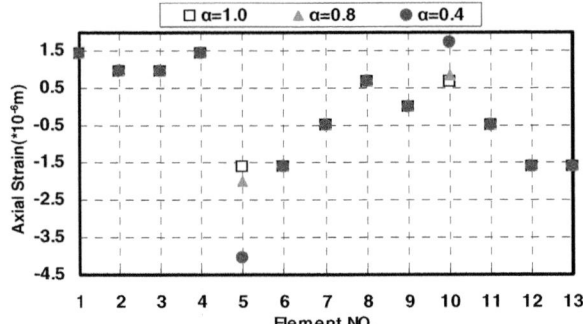

Fig. 4. The axial strain of roof truss with damage in element 5 and 10

increase of damage severity (a is smaller), the relative change in axial strain increases as well. The similar results can be observed in Fig. 4 in which two elements are damaged simultaneously. So, a conclusion can be obtained that the axial strain of roof truss model is a sensitive index of structural damage and should be able to be used to identify the location and severity of damage in the plane truss model. In the next section, a damage identification procedure is presented by solving inverse problem.

4   Formulation of Damage Identification as an Optimization Problem

The objective of the damage identification procedure is to determine the damage parameters (elements' No. and damage index) of the roof truss based on the known measurements (axial strain of elements), the known properties of the undamaged structure, and the known dead loads. Generally, the measurements are only made at a limited number of elements. So, it is a classical inverse problem to identify damage of structures based on incomplete measurements.

The inverse problem can be cast as a constrained optimization problem, in which the objective function to be minimized is defined by the output error between the measured and theoretical strains. This can be expressed as

$$\text{Minimize} \quad f(a,n) = \sum_{j=1}^{k} \left| \frac{\varepsilon_j^t - \varepsilon_j^m}{\varepsilon_j^m} \right| \tag{1}$$

subject to $n = 1, \cdots, N$

and $0 \leq a \leq 1$

in which ε_j^t and ε_j^m denote the theoretical strains and measured strains, respectively, k denotes the number of strain measurements, and N denotes the element numbers.

To solve the minimization problem of equation (1), a number of techniques could be used. Here a genetic algorithm has been adopted [12]. A genetic algorithm is a stochastic search technique based on the mechanism of natural selection and natural genetics. Unlike conventional deterministic search techniques, which operate on a single potential solution, a genetic algorithm operates on a set of potential solutions, called a population. Each element of the population is termed a chromosome and represents a possible solution to the problem. The chromosomes evolve through successive iterations, called generation. New chromosomes, called offspring, are created by either merging two chromosomes using a crossover operator or modifying a chromosome using a mutation operator. The new generation is formed by selecting some of the parents and some of the offspring. The selection of parents and offspring is based on a fitness evaluation. Chromosomes that yield a better fit have a higher probability of being selected. After several generations, the algorithm converges to the best chromosome, which hopefully represents the optimum or suboptimal solution to the problem. Other advantages of the genetic algorithm are that it does not use the derivative of the objective function, and it can handle continuous and discrete parameters simultaneously. In this paper, the genetic algorithm was implemented in Matlab [13].

5   Example Problem

The damage identification procedure was tested on a number of cases to study the validity of the procedure. A roof truss model is shown in Fig. 1, the finite element model of the damaged truss (Fig. 2) contains 13 elements and is subjected to the nodal loads. The damage identification procedure was tested by specifying a certain damage scenario (element, damage index), a finite element method based ANSYS [14] was then used to compute the static axial strain where the strain gages were located. Those strains were then used as input to the inverse problem to identify the damage parameters.

Three different damage cases are considered. In the first case element 5 is assumed to be damaged with the damage index of 0.6, i.e. the axial stiffness is reduced to 60% of the undamaged value. In the second case two elements 5 and 10 are assumed to be damaged and the damage indexes are assumed to be 0.8 uniformly. In the last case two elements 5 and 10 are assumed to be damaged and the damage indexes are 0.8 and 0.4 respectively. For each damage case, ten independent analyses are performed up to two hundred generations. The results are presented in terms of the average values as shown in Fig. 5 to Fig. 7.

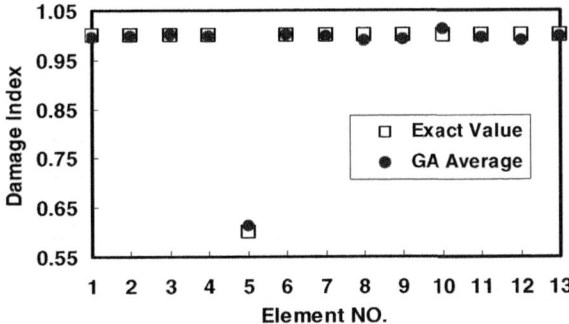

Fig. 5. Average identification results for case 1 using GA

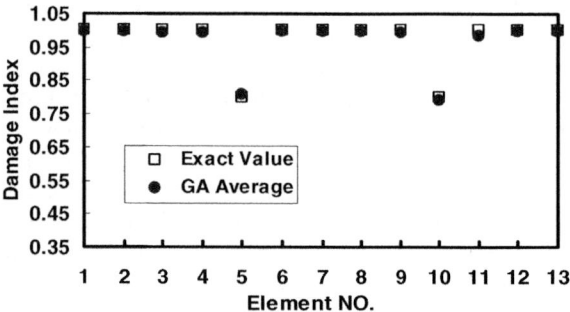

Fig. 6. Average identification results for case 2 using GA

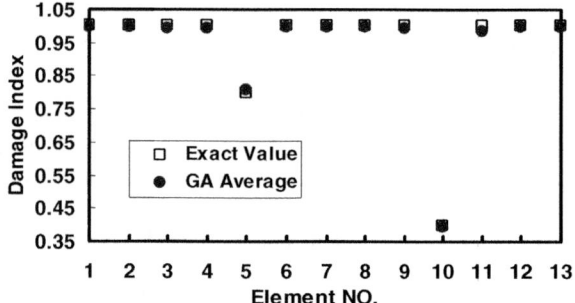

Fig. 7. Average identification results for case 3 using GA

Presented in Fig. 5 to Fig. 7 are the average identification results using GA for three damage cases. On the x axis are plotted element numbers and on the y axis is plotted damaged index. The square mark represents the actual damage scenario and the solid circle represents the identification results: the closer the circle is to the square mark, the better the prediction is. The results show that damage is successfully identified in all cases. Although, the location of damage is predicted very accurately in all cases, the error in the severity increases slightly with smaller damage index.

6 Conclusion

The forward analysis clearly demonstrates that the damage of elements on a roof truss model can result in a change of static axial strain. A method has been presented for identifying damage in roof truss under nodal dead loads. Damage is modeled as a reduction in the cross-section area of the damaged element. The damage is identified by minimizing the error between the theoretical and measured static strain in the roof truss. A finite element approach has been adopted for calculating the theoretical strains and a genetic algorithm has been used to solve the optimization problem. Results show that the damage identification procedure can successfully identify the damage locations and damage severity on the elements of the roof truss.

The effects of measurement noise and model error are important factors that must be considered with any damage identification procedure. They will be addressed in future studies.

Acknowledgment. The study presented in this paper was founded by the Project on Primary Scientific Research of Shanghai Normal University (No.SK201012 & No.SK201011), the Project on start-up Scientific Research of Shanghai Normal University (No.PL942) and the Key Innovation Project of Shanghai (No.09ZZ140). The authors would like to express their thanks and appreciation to the support organization.

References

1. Wang, Y., Zhao, R., Chen, Q., Lu, P., Shi, Z.: Research on the Prediction of Seismic Response for Bridges based on Neural Network. In: Proceedings of International Conference on Earthquake Engineering—the First Anniversary of Wenchuan Earthquake, pp. 456–459. Southwest Jiaotong University Press, Chengdu (2009)
2. Yu'ao, H., Xianzhong, H., Sheng, Z.: Predicting Seismic Response of Structures by Artificial Neural Networks. Transaction of Tianjin University 2(2), 36–39 (1996)
3. Zhaodong, X., Yapeng, S., Aiqun, L.: Neural Network Prediction for Seismic Response of Structure under the Levenberg-Marquardt Algorithm. Academic Journal of Xi'an Jiaotong University 15(1), 15–19 (2003)
4. Wang, Y., Zhao, R.: Damage Identification of Truss Bridge under Normal Traffic Loads. In: Proceedings of International Conference on Transportation Engineering 2007, vol. 2, pp. 2017–2022. ASCE (2007)
5. Kumar, S.: Neural Networks. Tsinghua University Press, Beijing (2006)
6. Guoliang, C., Xifa, W., Zhenquan, Z., Dongsheng, W.: Genetic Algorithm and its Application. Posts & telecom Press, Beijing (1996) (in chinese)
7. Liu, P.L., Chian, C.C.: Parametric identification of truss structures using static strains. Journal of Structural Engineering 123(7), 927–933 (1997)
8. Chou, J.H., Ghaboussi, J.: Genetic algorithm in structural damage detection. Computers and Structures 79(14), 1335–1353 (2001)
9. Shenton III, H.W., Hu, X.: Damage identification based on dead load redistribution: Methodology. Journal of Structural Engineering 132(8), 1254–1263 (2006)
10. Sanayei, M., Saletnik, M.J.: Parameter estimation of structures from static strain measurements I: Formulation. Journal of Structural Engineering 122(5), 555–562 (1996)
11. Sanayei, M., Saletnik, M.J.: Parameter estimation of structures from static strain measurements II: Error sensitivity analysis. Journal of Structural Engineering 122(5), 563–572 (1996)
12. Yingjie, L., Shanwen, Z., Jiwu, L., Chuangming, Z.: Matlab Genetic Algorithm Toolbox and its Application. Xidian University Press, Xi'an (2005) (in chinese)
13. User's guide: Genetic Algorithm and Direct Search Toolbox for Use with MATLAB, The MathWorks (2004)
14. Jingzhong, X.: The Application Example & Analysis of ANSYS. China Science Press, Beijing (2006) (in chinese)

Non-linear Improvement on Hydraulic Pump and Motor Models Based on Parameter Optimization Algorithms

Anlin Wang, Binnan Yue, Kaifei Jiang, and Xiaotian Li

School of Mechanical Engineering, Tongji University
Shanghai, 201804, P.R. China
wanganlin@online.sh.cn, Ventola1600@sina.com,
Kaifei.86@163.com, xiaotian3881@hotmail.com

Abstract. To solve the imprecise description of efficiency and improve the accuracy of the key hydraulic components models in complex operating conditions, the traditional hydraulic pump and motor model is discussed and improved. With the non-linear improvement and the parameter optimization algorithms, model parameters can be determined based on the experimental efficiency data of samples. Take a motor product sample for example, the efficiency distribution of the improved model is much closer to the experimental results than that of the traditional model. The mean value and the variance value of percentage error for the improved model are much smaller, and the error analysis proves that the improved model is much more suitable for the modeling in complex operating conditions.

Keywords: parameter optimization algorithms; non-linear improvement; complex operating conditions; hydraulic pump and motor; efficiency distribution.

1 Introduction

The application of walking hydraulic transmission for construction machinery products is increasingly widespread. Within the power matching problem of construction machinery, the efficiency of hydraulic pumps and hydraulic motors make an enormous difference to the performance of construction machinery. In traditional design, hydraulic drive walking systems are often mismatched in extreme operating conditions.

In order to achieve a reasonable power matching to solve the efficiency problems of hydraulic pump and motor in various operating conditions, dynamics modeling of construction machineries is necessary. Most of the studies about pumps and motors in the reference focus on the mathematical description [1] [2] [3] of swash plate dynamic characteristics, but less on description for the efficiency of the various conditions.

Some traditional efficiency computing models are mentioned in reference [4], but often described linearly and there aren't better methods for determining parameters of models, so these models are difficult to apply in products. The Bond Graph modeling

F.L. Wang et al. (Eds.): AICI 2010, Part II, LNAI 6320, pp. 16–23, 2010.

[5] uses resistive elements to respectively describe mechanical friction and internal leakage to reflect the efficiency.

This linear modeling faces the problem of insufficient accuracy and parameter determination for the complex non-linear characteristics of hydraulic components. Therefore, this paper focuses on the modeling improvement describing the efficiencies of models accurately, and seeks to determine the models parameters reasonably.

2 Efficiency Description of the Traditional Model

Bond Graph method is mainly used to describe the pump and motor models. The form of Bond Graph models is shown in Fig 1; the form of block diagram is shown in Fig 2.

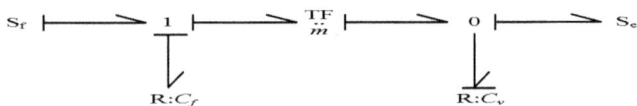

Fig. 1. Characteristics Bond Graph models of the pump and motor

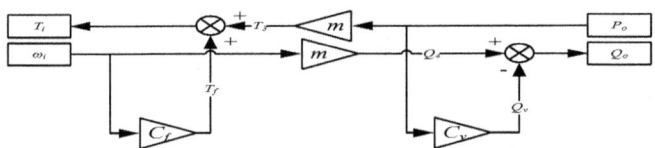

Fig. 2. Characteristics block diagram models of the pump and motor

Where T_i : Torque of mechanical revolution axis, ω_i : rotational speed of mechanical revolution axis, P_o : Hydraulic pressure, Q_o : hydraulic rate of flow , m : coefficient of converter; C_f : Value of resistive element; C_v : Value of resistive element. Here, coefficient of converter m is determined by pump displacement. The equations of resistive elements are enumerated as follows.

Friction torque of mechanical revolution axis can be written as

$$T_f = \omega_i C_f .$$ (1)

Where T_f is mechanical friction torque, ω_i is rotational speed of revolution axis, and C_f is friction factor, with the unit of $\frac{N \cdot m \cdot s}{rad}$.

Internal leakage rate of flow can be written as

$$Q_v = P_o C_v .$$ (2)

Where P_o is working pressure, Q_v is internal leakage flow, c_v is internal leakage coefficient, with the unit of $\frac{m^3}{s.Pa}$, C_f and C_v belongs to model parameters to be determined.

In the Bond Graph models of pump and motor, the resistive element on both sides of the converter respectively represents mechanical friction and internal leakage, thus models can reflect change of mechanical efficiency and volumetric efficiency in different operating conditions.

Models with linear resistance, which means the mechanical friction torque is proportional to rotational speed, and internal leakage flow is proportional to working pressure, the Iso-efficiency curve shows as a linear form. However, the efficiency distribution graph of existing pump and motor product samples shows that the Iso-efficiency curve appears as a curve form (see Fig.4).This shows that the actual pumps and motors have nonlinear characteristics, which makes the linear models are not accurate enough in extreme operating conditions.

3 Presentation of the Improved Model

The traditional Bond Graph model is improved nonlinearly, linear equations are replaced by quadratic equations, that means mechanical friction torque is proportional to the square of rotational speed and internal leakage flow is proportional to the square of working pressure. Then the initial static friction torque is added into the mechanical part of model (see in Fig. 3).

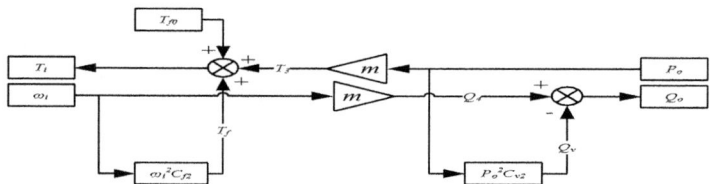

Fig. 3. Characteristics block diagram of improved models for the pump and motor

Then friction torque of mechanical revolution axis can be written as

$$T_f = \omega_i^2 C_{f2}$$ (3)

Where T_f is mechanical friction torque, ω_i is rotational speed of revolution axis, and C_{f2} is quadratic friction factor, with the unit of $\frac{N.m.s^2}{rad^2}$.

Internal leakage flow can be written as

$$Q_v = P_o^2 C_{v2}$$ (4)

Where P_o is working pressure, Q_v is Internal leakage flow, C_{v2} is quadratic internal leakage coefficient, with the unit of $\dfrac{m^3}{s.Pa^2}$.

The initial static friction torque is added to overcome the initial starting static friction of the bump and motor. The equation can be written as

$$T_i = T_3 + T_f + T_{f0}.$$ (5)

Where T_i is torque of mechanical revolution axis, T_3 is effectively transformed torque, T_{f0} is initial static friction torque, their expressions in the model refer to Fig. 3. Thus, C_{f2}, C_{v2} and T_{f0} are model parameters to be determined.

4   Comparisons between the Traditional Model and the Improved Model

4.1   Presentation of Optimization Algorithms for Parameters Determination

In practical engineering applications, the model parameters are difficult to determine. Manufacturers usually don't provide the required parameters C_f and C_v in bond graph model. However, the model parameters change with the efficiency of the pumps and motors in different operating conditions, and manufacturers can provide the efficiency distribution graph obtained by experiment in all working conditions. Taking Sauer-Danfoss 51-type Piston Motor for example, its efficiency distribution graph is shown in Fig. 4[6].

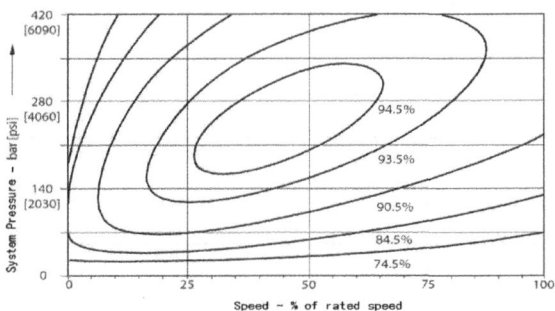

Fig. 4. Iso-efficiency curve distribution graph of Sauer-Danfoss 51-type Piston Motor

The required parameters C_f and C_v are related with mechanical efficiency and volumetric efficiency. Use the experimental data of efficiency distribution graph as the evaluation criteria, validate theoretical efficiency values and optimize the model parameters, then the model efficiency error is minimized after being calculated in various operating conditions. The optimization procedure is shown in Fig. 5.

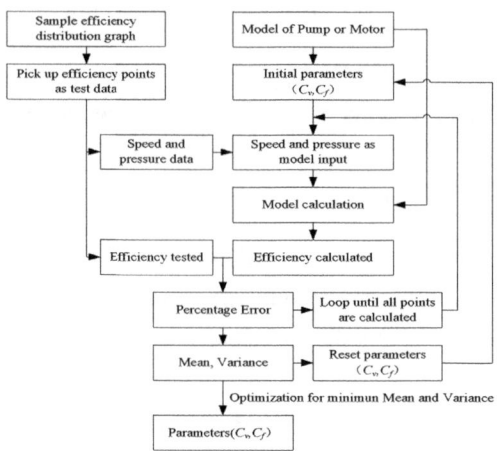

Fig. 5. Based on sample efficiency distribution graph, optimization procedure of model parameters determination

C_{f2}, C_{v2} and T_{f0} can also be chosen as optimization parameters, thus not only C_f and C_v are determined according to sample data, but also the new model parameters such as C_{f2}, C_{v2} and T_{f0} can be determined.

4.2 Comparison of Two Models

Taking a typical product for example, the two models are compared to prove the superiority of the improved model. Here is Sauer-Danfoss 51 Series 110 Piston Motor, the product parameters are shown in Table 1[6].

Table 1. Parameters of Sauer-Danfoss 51 Series 110 Piston Motor

Parameters of sample	value
displacement (cm2/r)	110
rated speed (rpm)	2800
maximum pressure (bar)	420

In order to optimize the model parameters, sampling points got from Iso-efficiency curve in efficiency distribution graph (see Fig. 4) are used as experimental data for optimizing as follows. In this paper, 137 points are calculated, among these points, 29 points are from 74.5% Iso-efficiency curve, 32 points from 84.5% ISO-efficiency curve, 30 points from 90.5% curve, 30 points from 93.5% curve, and 16 points from 94.5% curve.

4.2.1 Model Parameters Optimization
For the two kinds of models, comparison is making between sample experimental data and model calculation data, the optimization results are shown in Table 2.

Table 2. Optimization results of two kinds of models

Traditional models		Improved models	
Parameter	Improved value	parameter	Improved value
Friction coefficient / C_f	0.12	Quadratic friction coefficient/ C_{f2}	0.29
Internal leakage coefficient/ C_v	2.34×10^{-12}	Quadratic internal leakage coefficient / C_{v2}	5.03×10^{-20}
		Initial static friction torque / T_{f0}	12.6

All the coefficients here are in the International System of Units.

4.2.2 Comparison of Iso-efficiency Curves

Based on the parameters above, efficiency values can be calculated separately in different working conditions. The efficiency distribution graph is shown in Fig. 6.

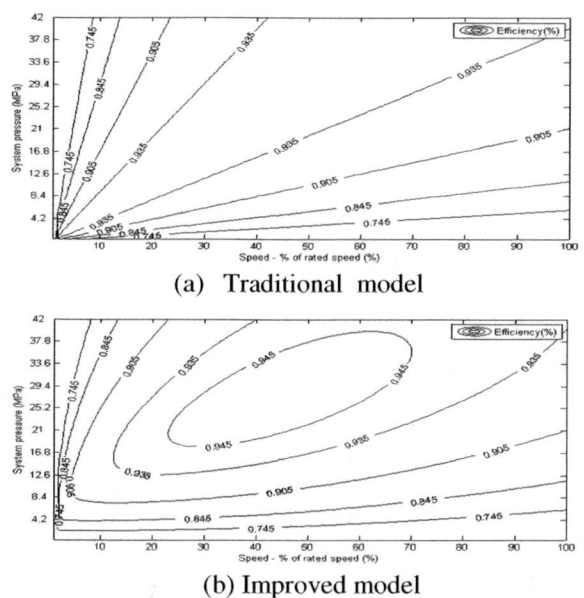

(a) Traditional model

(b) Improved model

Fig. 6. Iso-efficiency curves theoretical distribution graph for two kinds of models

As seen from Fig. 6, the Iso-efficiency curve of traditional model appears as a linear form and has a low similarity to Fig. 4. This is determined by the linear characteristic of the model. And the Iso-efficiency curve of improved model has obvious similarities to Fig. 4, so the improved model is more precise.

4.3 Comparison of Percentage Error Distribution

The comparison between the efficiencies of the experimental data and the model calculation is obtained based on samples, and percentage error distribution graphs of two kinds of models are drawn respectively (see Fig. 7).

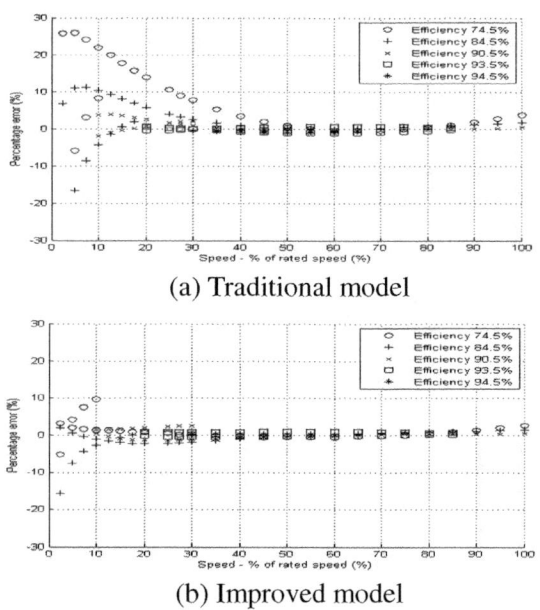

(a) Traditional model

(b) Improved model

Fig. 7. Percentage errors distribution of two models in the rotational speed operating conditions

As seen from Fig. 7, the horizontal axis is the rotational speed operating conditions, the vertical axis is a percentage error and different tracing points represent different efficiency operating points. The traditional model (see Fig.7 (a)) has small error in high-speed section, but has large error in extreme operating conditions such as high pressure and low-speed. However, the improved model reduces the error significantly in these extreme conditions. This shows that the improved model has better sphere of application and more advantages of modeling in complex operating conditions.

4.4 Statistics of Percentage Errors

After statistical analysis of data obtained from Fig. 7, the mean value and the variance of the percentage errors of two models can are obtained, which are shown in Table 3.

Table 3. Percentage error statistics of two models

Traditional model		Improved model	
Mean value	3.55%	Mean value	1.18%
Variance	0.005298	Variance	0.0004875

Statistics show that the improved model has smaller equalizing error value and variance, and model accuracy is improved on the whole.

4.5 Results Discussion

According to comparison of models above, conclusions can be drawn as follows

- By comparison between efficiency distribution graph (see Fig. 6) and sample experiment graph (see Fig. 4), it's known that the improved model has much better similarity than the traditional model.
- Percentage error distributions show that the traditional model has large error in extreme operating conditions and the improved model has better distribution.
- Compared to sample experimental results, the mean value of percentage error for traditional model is 3.55% and for improved model is 1.18%, the variance value for traditional model is 0.005298 and for improved model is 0.0004875.

It's shown that these efficiency distribution graphs have similarity with that of Sauer51-type motor. In this paper, although the pumps and motors of other manufacturers and other types haven't been studied by applying this model, the improved model can also describe these product samples accurately due to the certain commonality of this model, and optimization procedures are needed to optimize model parameters. However, because of complexity of practical products, the applicability of the model still needs further study.

5 Conclusions

In this paper, the traditional models of pump and motor are improved nonlinearly. The efficiency distribution graph of the improved model has better similarity with sample experimental graph than that of the traditional model. Compared to sample experimental results, the mean value of percentage error for the traditional model is 3.55% and for the improved model is 1.18%, the variance value for the traditional model is 0.005298 and for the improved model is 0.0004875. The error analysis proves that the improved model is more suitable for description of device modeling in complex operating conditions and the model accuracy is also improved.

References

1. Zhang, X., Cho, J., Nair, S.S.: Reduced order modeling of the dynamics of an indexing valve plate pump. In: The American Control Conference, Alaska, American, pp. 3595–3599 (2000)
2. Manring, N.D.: The control and containment forces on the swash plate of an axial piston pump utilizing a secondary swash-plate angle. In: The American Control Conference, Alaska, American, pp. 4837–4842 (2002)
3. Du, H.: Pressure Control with Power Limitation for Hydraulic Variable Displacement Piston Pumps. In: The American Control Conference, pp. 940–945 (2002)
4. Yao, H.: Hydraulic Dynamics and Control principles of Engineering Machinery. China Communication Press, Beijing (2006)
5. Wang, Z.: Bond Graph Theory and Its Application in System Dynamics. Harbin Engineering University Press, Harbin (2000)
6. Sauer: Series 51 Bent Axis Variable Displacement Motors Technical Information (2003)

Diurnal and Seasonal Changes in Stem Water Content of Single Yulan Magmolia Tree

Hailan Wang and Yandong Zhao

School of Technology, Beijing Forestry University,
100083 Beijing, China
{wanghailan,yandongzh}@bjfu.edu.cn

Abstract. In this paper the objective was to study diurnal and seasonal changes in Yulan Magmolia tree by SWR principle. Laboratory and field tests were performed. Laboratory calibration test was performed on two sapwood samples, which shows that the relation between the volumetric water content and the output voltage of SWR sensor was monotonic as the coefficients R^2 reached above 0.90.were periodically weighed on a balance. In field test, the diurnal and seasonal changes were monitored in natural Yulan Magmolia tree by SWR sensor for nearly 2 years. It indicated that seasonal variation of stem water content measured was 20% ~ 25%. A maximum in stem water content occurred in summer, then decreased in autumn, and reaching a minimum in winter, recovery is almost complete till next spring. The short-term (diurnal) variations were found 2% ~ 5%. The daily changes show that a decline in stem water content happened, and then recovered each day. At the same time, leaf water content and sap flow velocity were measured, which shows that diurnal leaf water potential has the similar curve with diurnal stem water content while sap flow velocity was reverse to stem water content.

Keywords: stem water content, SWR (Standing wave ratio), dielectrics, leaf water potential.

1 Introduction

Techniques available to monitor seasonal changes in the water content of the woody tissue in situ are limited. The traditional technique of taking increment cores is time-consuming, destructive, and can be prone to error due to movement of water out of the core during sampling. Gamma-ray attenuation, nuclear magnetic resonance, and more recently computer axial tomography are not readily available, are time-consuming to use and can pose a health risk to the operator[1],[2]. Values of $\Delta\theta$stem ranging approximately from 0.10 LL^{-1} to 0.40 LL $^{-1}$ have been reported[3],[4],[5]. Diurnal changes in θstem of 0.08 LL^{-1} were found in irrigated apple trees and in unirigated pines using γattenuation and gravimetric methods[5],[6]. Time domain reflectometry (TDR) is a relatively new technique which has seen widespread use for measuring soil water content[7]. To date there are few published reports of attempts to use TDR to monitor the status of water in tree stems. Short-term (diurnal) and long-term (seasonal) changes in θ stem by using TDR in natural groves of aspen, pinion,

F.L. Wang et al. (Eds.): AICI 2010, Part II, LNAI 6320, pp. 24–30, 2010.

cottonwood, and ponderosa, Constantz and Murphy[8] found absolute values of θ stem between 0.20 LL^{-1} and 0.70 LL^{-1}, with an annual change in moisture content between 15% to 70% depending on tree species, as well as soil and atmospheric conditions. Absolute values of θ stem as measured by TDR were in good correlation with gravimetric measurements of θstem as determined by weight loss [9],[10]. But as the TDR probe size decreases timing interval become very small and resolution becomes an increasing problem. The longer wave guides attenuate the signal, and the returning edge of the pulse will be undetectable.

In this paper, standing wave ratio (SWR) principle was used to monitor stem water content. The calibration equation was concluded in laboratory test and diurnal and seasonal variations were measured in filed test.

2   Techniques

In this paper, the sensor measuring stem water content was based on SWR (Standing Wave Ratio). This approach is to measure the electric constant. Because of its large dipole moment and ability to form hydrogen bonds, water has an extremely high dielectric constant (78.3 at 25°C) compared to most solids and liquids (3 to 10). Furthermore, the dielectric properties of pure water are fairly insensitive to temperature. Changes in the dielectric constant of a water-permeated medium, therefore, may result primarily from changes in the moisture content.

Our sensor consisted of a 100MHz RF (radio frequency) oscillator, two wave detectors, a transmission line and a 2-pin probe (50mm long, 3mm in diameter, and 30mm separation). According to Wullschleger's equation, stem water content can be derived from the output voltage of SWR sensor [11].

3   Material and Methods

The tests were performed in March 2008 on the campus in Beijing Forestry University in the southwestern Negev region (Latitude 39 ° 56 ', longitude 116 ° 17'). The main soil types for the tidal wetland soil texture for the loam. Climate is sub-humid warm with Arid windy spring, hot summer and rainy autumn, high dry and cold winter. To verify the feasibility of the SWR technology, one 5-yr-old Yulan Magmolia tree about 3m tall (with a diameter of 20cm) was chosen.

3.1   Calibration Tests

To address the empirical relation between the volumetric water content and the output voltage, two sapwood samples were cut from a freshly felled 18cm diameter Yulan Magmolia tree. The sapwood samples were ~20cm in length, cylindrical in shape, with volumes of ~ 1620cm^3. In this test, pair of stainless steel rods (50mm long, 3mm in diameter, and 30mm separation) was driven into parallel pilot holes drilled into woody parts of samples, and a data collector was used to measure the output voltage of the transmission line. The two sapwood samples were saturated and allow to gradually dry on a oven-drying at 60°C over one week. The samples were periodically placed in a closed container to encourage a more uniform moisture distribution within each sample, then they were weighed on a balance with a resolution of ±0.1g. This drying procedure yielded a relation between the sapwood water content and the output voltage of the transmission line.

3.2   Field Evaluation

Pair of stainless steel rods (5cm long, 0.03cm diameter, and 3cm separation) was driven into parallel pilot holes above 1m from the ground in Yulan Magmolia tree. SWR probe was installed to measure stem water content. Leaf water potential and sap flow velocity were measured by water potential system (PSψPRO) and SF-L sensor respectively. Sap flow gauge was put on 1.5m above the ground. Measurements were monitored every 2 hours from 8:00 to 16:00 in sunny days.

4   Results and Discussion

4.1   Calibration Test

Fig.1. shows the stem volumetric water content θ and the output voltage U_{AB} of the transmission line from the calibration test. It indicated that U_{AB} was increased as θ increased. In particular, for sample 1 equation of determination y = 0.6377x + 2.6014, and the coefficient of determination R^2 reached 0.9086; for sample 2 equation of determination y = 0.6486x + 2.6098, and the coefficient of determination R^2 reached 0.9268. from t test, it shows that no difference between the two samples using the single SWR sensor.

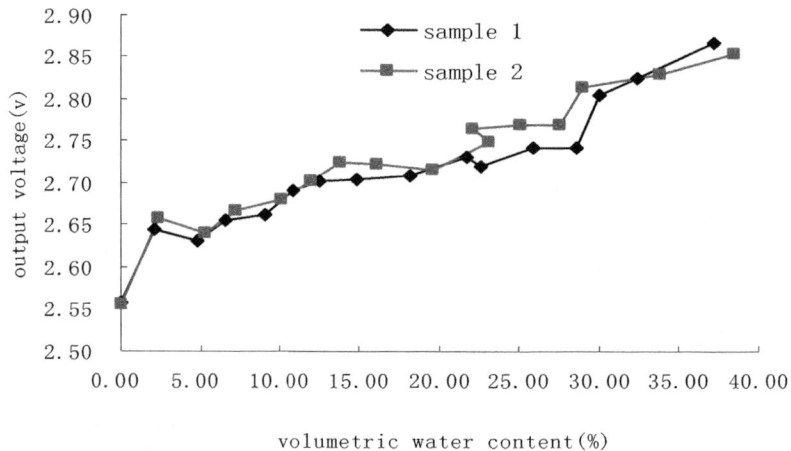

Fig. 1. Relationship between the electrode length and the output voltage

4.2   Field Evaluation

Diurnal variation. Fig.2. shows diurnal variation in stem water status in several sunny days which selected randomly in 2008. The data show clearly that a minimum

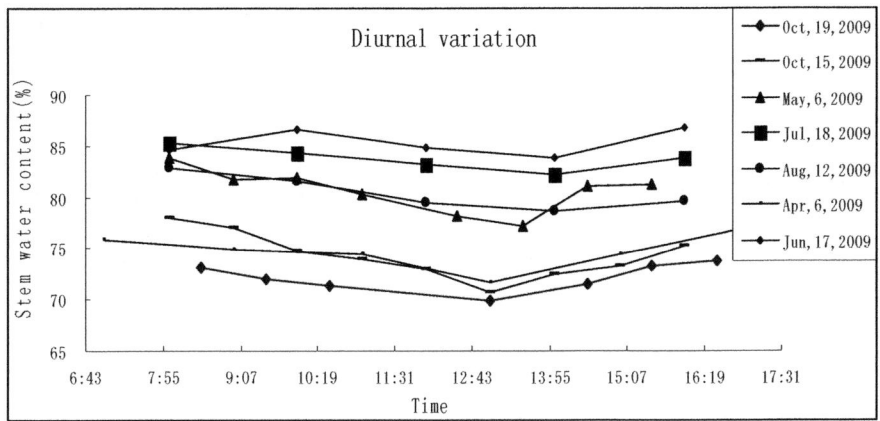

Fig. 2. Diurnal changes of stem water content

does occur at about 14:30 when transpiration rate is high and soil water reserves are depleted, recovery is happened after that. Absolute values in diurnal changes of stem water content ranged approximately from 5% to 2%. Similar data have been obtained by Brough et al., and Constantz and Murphy[5],[8].

Diurnal leaf water potential and stem water content during two consecutive days (on May 5 and 6, 2008) were presented in Fig.3. Diurnal leaf water potential has the similar curve with diurnal stem water content. With the bigger opening of the stomata of tree leaves and higher transpiration rate, the leaf water potential decreased. And a minimum was measured at about 14:00, after then it increased again.

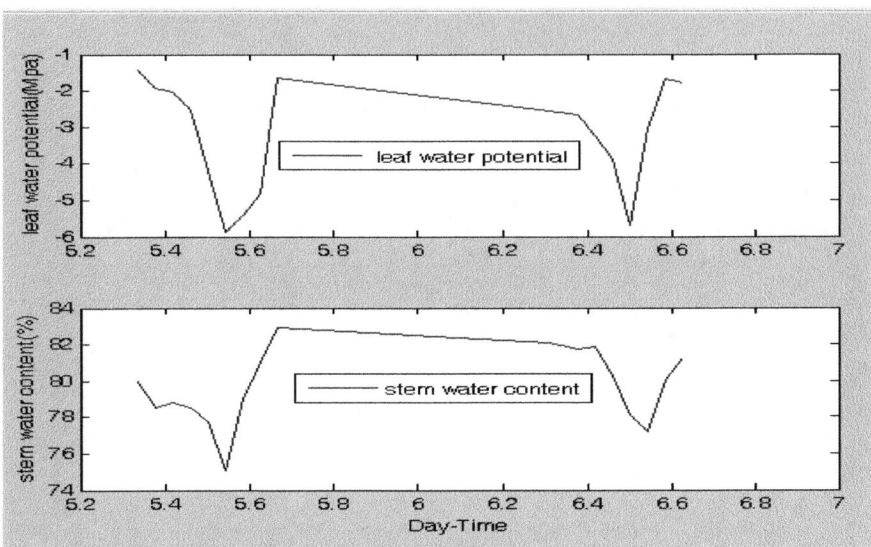

Fig. 3. Leaf water potential and stem water content from May 5 to 6, 2008

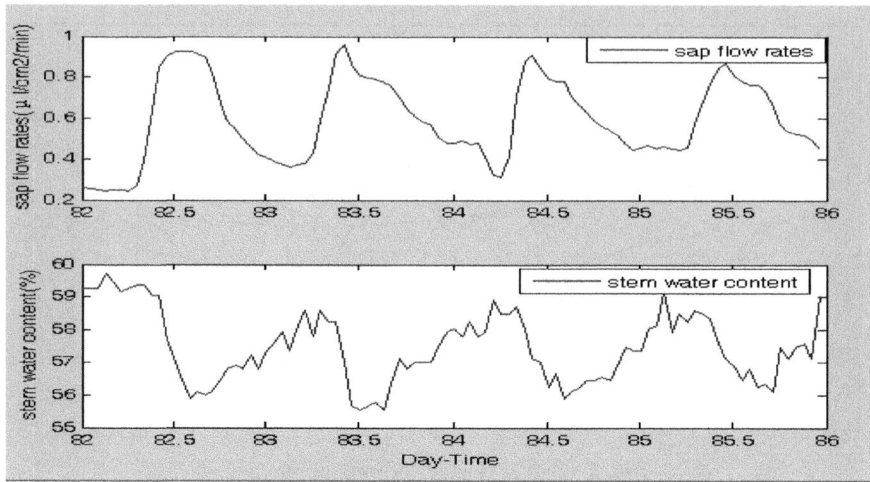

Fig. 4. Sap flow velocity and stem water content from Nov 22 to 25, 2008

Diurnal sap flow velocity and daily stem water content during four consecutive days (Nov 22 to 25,2008)were presented in Fig.4. Diurnal sap flow velocity has the relevant curve with diurnal stem water content. With the bigger opening of the stomata of tree leaves and higher transpiration rate, the sap flow velocity increased while stem water content decreased. And a maximum was measured at about 14:00, after then it decreased again.

Seasonal variation. The data in fig.5 show the observations which made from Mar 13,2008 to Nov 10,2009. The first 50 days' value was ignored to minimize the risk of

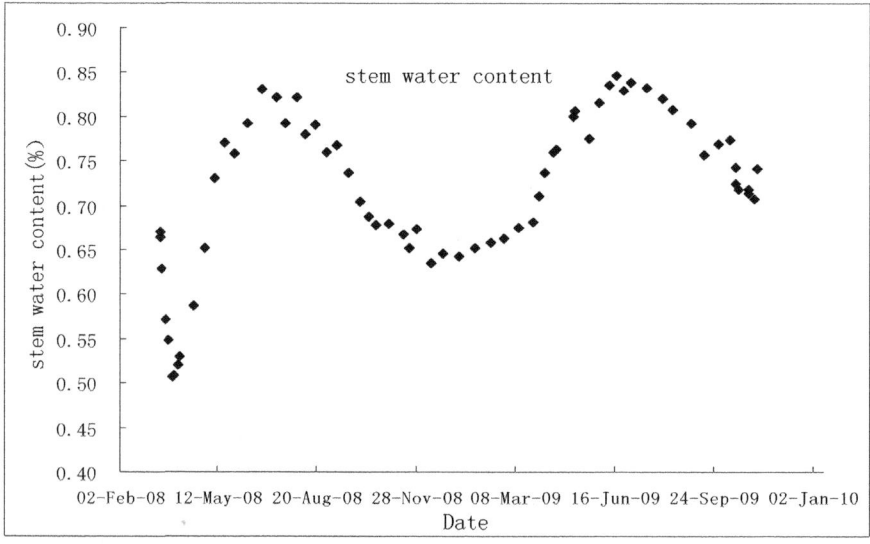

Fig. 5. Seasonal changes of stem water content

wound recovery effects[1]. It indicated that stem undergo seasonal variations in water content, ranged approximately 20% ~ 25%. These wide ranges are in agreement with similar water content distributions in stems of oaks and redwoods [8], in red maple and white oak [1], and in pines [2]. A maximum in stem water content did occur in summer, then decreased in autumn, and reaching a minimum in winter, recovery is almost complete till next spring.

5 Conclusion

In this paper, laboratory and field tests were made to verify the feasible and workable of SWR technology for monitoring stem water content. In laboratory calibration test shows that the relation between the volumetric water content and the output voltage of SWR sensor was monotonic as the coefficients R^2 reached above 0.90. Short-term (diurnal) changes of 5%~2% and long-term (seasonal) changes of 20%~25% were found in stem water content by using SWR in natural Yulan Magmolia tree. A decline in stem water content does occur each day morning⬚ recovery is almost complete in the afternoons. Similar data have been obtained by using TDR[5]. A maximum in stem water content did occur in summer, then decreased in autumn⬚ and reaching a minimum in winter. Diurnal leaf water potential has the similar curve with diurnal stem water content while sap flow velocity was reverse to stem water content.

Acknowledgments. This project was supported by Central University special fund basic research and operating expenses (No.BLYX200906). I express my gratitude to Vice-Prof Yandong Zhao for her guidance on this research project.

References

1. Wullschleger, S.D., Hanson, P.J., Todd, D.E.: Measuring stem water content in four deciduous hardwoods with a time-domain reflectometer. Tree Physiology 16, 809–815 (1996)
2. Irvine, J., Grace, J.: Non-destructive measurement of stem water content by time domain reflectometry using short probes. Jour. Exp. Botany 48(308), 813–818 (1997)
3. Nadler, A., Raveh, E.: Evaluation of TDR Use to Monitor Water Content in Stem of Lemon Trees and Soil and Their Response to Water Stress. SSSAJ 67(2), 437–448 (2003)
4. Edwards, W.R.N., Jarvis, P.G.: A method for measuring radial differences in water content of intact tree stems by attenuation of gamma radiation. Plant Cell and Environment 6, 255–260 (1983)
5. Brough, D.W., Jones, H.G., Grace, J.: Diurnal changes in water content of the stems of apple trees, as influenced by irrigation. Plant Cell and Environment 9, 1–7 (1986)
6. Byrne, G.F., Fenn, M.D., Burgar, M.I.: Nuclear magnetic resonance studies of water in tree sections. Agric. For. Meteorol. 38, 307–317 (1986)
7. Raschi, A., Tognetti, R., Ridder, H.W., Beres, C.: Water in the stems of sessile oak (Quercus petraea) assessed by computer tomography with concurrent measurements of sap velocity and ultrasound emission. Plant Cell Environ. 18, 545–554 (1995)

8. Constantz, J., Murphy, F.: Monitoring Moisture Storage in Trees Using Time Domain Reflectometry. Journal of Hydrology 119, 31–42 (1990)
9. Holbrook, N.M., Burns, M.J., Sinclair, T.R.: Frequency and Time-Domain Dielectric Measurements of Stem Water Content in the Arborescent Palm, Sabal Palmetto. Journal of Experimental Botany 43(246), 111–119 (1992)
10. Schiller, G., Cohen, Y.: Water regime of pine forest under a mediterranean climate. Agri. and For. Meter 74, 181–193 (1995)
11. Wang, H.L., Bai, C.X., Zhao, Y.D.: Experiment on the Probe Configuration of Stem Water Content Measuring Sensor. Transactions of the Chinese Society for Agricultural Machinery 1(40), 176–179 (2009)

Reliability Analysis on Wing Structures under the Gust Load

Xiaozhou Ning, Yunju Yan, Kangkang Qu, and Zhilao Li

School of Mechanics, Civil Engineering and Architecture,
Northwestern Polytechnical University, Xi'an, China
409236099@163.com

Abstract. Reliability analysis on the aircraft structures is an integrative study about the structural components and the endured force load on aircraft structures. Especially, the wing reliability is an important index of the aircraft reliability. The reliability of a wing structure model under gust load is analyzed by computer simulation in this paper using the Probability Finite Element Method (PFEM). The gust load, elastic modulus and yield strength are taken as input variables to simulate the reliability problem of the wing structures using the Monte Carlo method, and the influences of the input parameters on aircraft wing strength are obtained. This may provide a viable analysis method for the design and manufacture of an aircraft.

Keywords: Wing Structure, Gust load, Reliability.

1 Introduction

Aircraft strength Analysis is the assurance of its safety and reliability, which is also a very important step in the aircraft design. The wing structure is the complicated component of an aircraft and the undergone force in flight also is very complex. Wing is the most important component of an aircraft, so its strength analysis becomes into the key of the whole aircraft structure design. Because the strength analysis of a wing is involved in many complex factors, it is very difficult to calculate the reliability of the whole aircraft by analytical method. Luckily, with the development of the computer technology, it has become feasible to simulate the aircraft structures reliability through Monte Carlo gradually.

Ye et al. [1] briefly introduced the method of probabilistic design based on ANSYS, and it provided new thoughts for reliability analysis of other complicated structures; Wang et al. [2] had put forward a method for calculating crane structure reliability based on Monte-Carlo and finite element method; Fan et al. [3] used a reliability analysis method based upon Monte-Carlo to calculate the reliability of aircraft structures, and it has been preliminarily realized on computer.

In this paper, the stress reliability of a wing structure is studied using stochastic finite element method, which combined the parametric design of ANSYS software with Monte Carlo method. A wing structure is taken as the research model, in which the

F.L. Wang et al. (Eds.): AICI 2010, Part II, LNAI 6320, pp. 31–37, 2010.

vertically uniform load is exerted to simulate the gust load, and the strength reliability analysis of the wing structure is carried out based on the specific statistical distribution.

2 Theory of Structural Reliability

The reliability of engineering structures is usually governed by many factors, such as the effect of acted loads, material properties, geometric parameters and the accuracy of calculation model, etc. When ones deal with the analysis and design of structural reliability, these relevant factors can be considered as the basic variable X_1, X_2 ;$\cdots X_n$, and they should meet the structural features requirement. The function $Z = g(X_1, X_2, \cdots X_n)$, which is controlled by the variables of describing structure status is called as the structural function, of course, some basic variables can also be combined into an integrated variable, for example, the effect of acted loads is combined into a comprehensive action effects S, the diversified enduring abilities of the structure and material are combined into an integrated resistance R, thus the structure function can be written as $Z = R - S$.

One can evaluate the health status according to the value of the structural function Z, that is

$Z = R - S > 0$ shows that the structure is at the reliable state,

$Z = R - S < 0$ indicates that the structure is invalid or damaged, and

$Z = R - S = 0$ denotes that the structure is at the limit state.

The structural limit state will be described by the limit state equation. Obviously, for different structural designs, the performance function is different, and its corresponding limit state equation also is different in form and content. However, as long as the action effects S and the structural resistance R are given, the various types of limit state equations can still be expressed as the general formula $Z = g(X_1, X_2, ..., X_n) = 0$.

3 Monte Carlo Method

Monte Carlo is a numerical simulation method, which can solve the practical engineering problems related to random variable. Numerical simulation of the random variable is equivalent to an experiment, so Monte Carlo is also called statistical experiment method. In ANSYS software the Monte Carlo method is divided into three types: Direct Sampling method, Latin Hypercube method and of User defined method. Latin Hypercube method is more efficient than Direct Sampling method. Simulation times of Latin Hypercube method are usually 20%-40% less than Direct Sampling method to produce the same results.

Monte Carlo method is of the wide applications. As long as model is accurate and the simulation times enough, the result will be deemed credible. The good performance of modern computer provides a hardware foundation for the Monte Carlo method. Since many hypotheses and the systematic errors introduced in other reliability analysis methods are difficult to achieve in mathematics, Monte Carlo simulation is the only means to verify the correctness of the reliability results currently.

4   Reliability Analysis of a Wing Structures

A Wing structural model is shown as Fig. 1, the AB side is completely clamped, the wing length is $length = 800mm$. The uniform load $P = 3000N/m^2$ is exerted on the upper surface to simulate the vertical gust load. The material yield strength is $\sigma_s = 4e6MPa$, material density is $DENS = 7.8e-6kg/mm$, elastic modulus $E = 2.1e8MPa$, and they all obey Gaussian distribution. Besides, the Poisson's ratio $\mu = 0.3$.

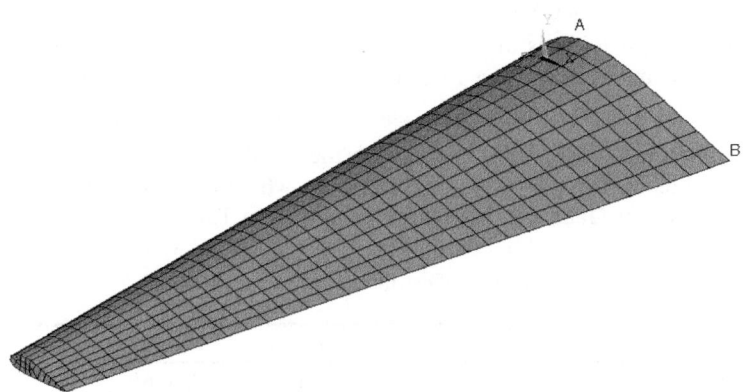

Fig. 1. Wing structural finite element mode

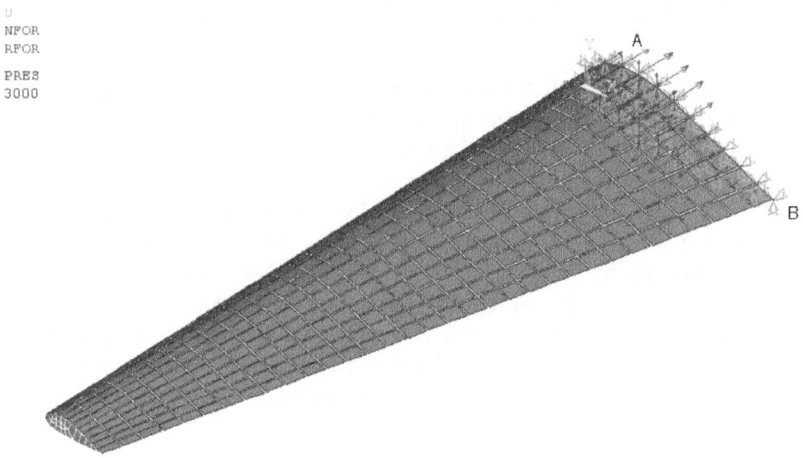

Fig. 2. The exerted load on the model

According to the stress-strength theory, the wing stress in flight does not allow to exceed the yield strength, therefore, the wing structural failure criteria can be expressed as

$$\sigma_{max} \geq \sigma_s .$$ (1)

where σ_{max} is the maximum equivalent stress of wing structures occurred during flight, and σ_s is the yield strength of the structural materials. Therefore, the limit state function for the structure will be

$$g(X) = \sigma_s - \sigma_{max} .$$ (2)

Thereinto, the $g(X) \leq 0$ is failure state, so the wing reliability can be expressed as the probability of $g(X) \geq 0$.

In the strength analysis of wing structures, the elastic modulus, yield strength, material density and vertical gust load are all taken as random input variables, and the value of $g(X) = \sigma_s - \sigma_{max}$ is regarded as the output variable. We adopted the random sampling of the 1000 times to do the reliability analysis for the given structural model using Latin Hypercube method, in which the required input variables are assumed to follow Gaussian distribution as shown in Table 1.

Table 1. Distribution of input variables

Random variable	Symbols	Distribution	Mean	Standard Deviation
Density/Kg/mm3	DENS	Gaussian	7.8e-6	7.8e-5
Load/N/ m2	P	Gaussian	3000	300
Elastic modulus /MPa	E	Gaussian	2.1e8	2.1e6
Yield strength /MPa	S	Gaussian	4e6	4e5

The sampling process of the maximum equivalent stress is shown in Fig. 3. The two red curves in figure indicate the average value of the sampling process, obviously, its average is convergent. This shows that, when the simulation times are enough, the curve will tend to a stable value. The red lines are upper and lower limits of confidence interval. The probability that the sample points fall inside is 95%, and this means the confidence level is 95%. The blue line indicates the mean change in the sampling process. View from the analysis process, with the increase of simulation experimental times, the accuracy of simulation results is well improved. The value of the cumulative distribution function at any point is equal to the probability value of the data under this point, and the cumulative distribution function tends to 1 as shown in. Fig. 4, this is well consistent with the relevant concepts of probability theory.

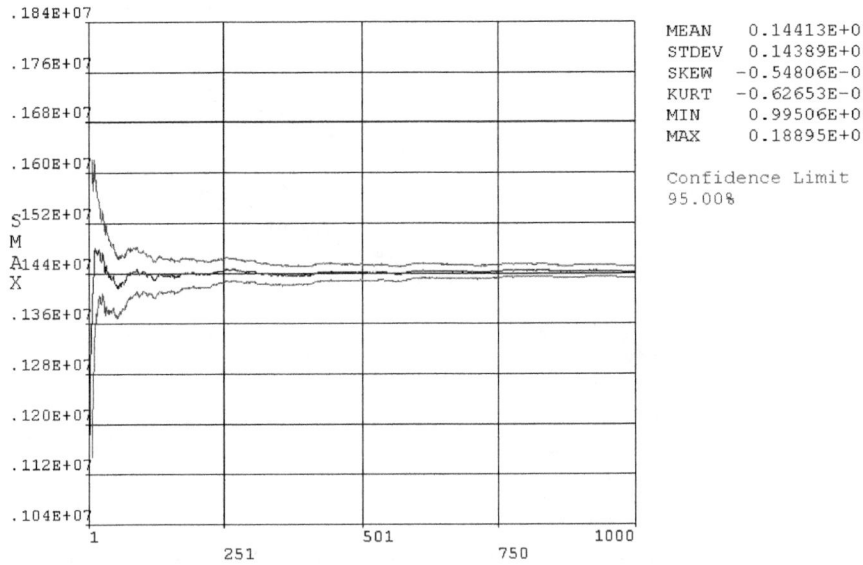

Fig. 3. Sampling of the maximum equivalent stress

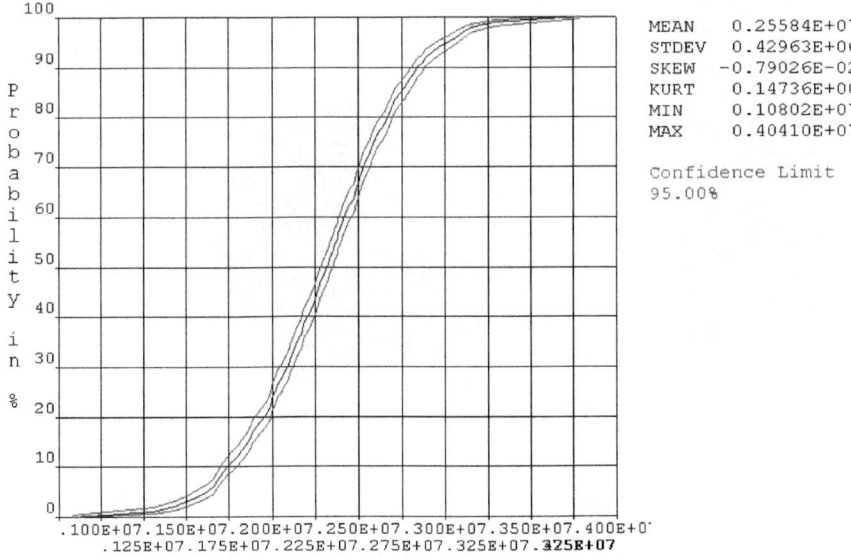

Fig. 4. Cumulative function distribution of maximum stress

It's known from the equivalent stress cloud showed in Fig. 5 that the maximum stress of the wing structure is 1.47e6MPa under vertical gust load, and it is much less than the material strength limit 4e6MP, so the researched wing structure is safe. The stress of the wing root is the most concentrated, and also it is the most vulnerable.

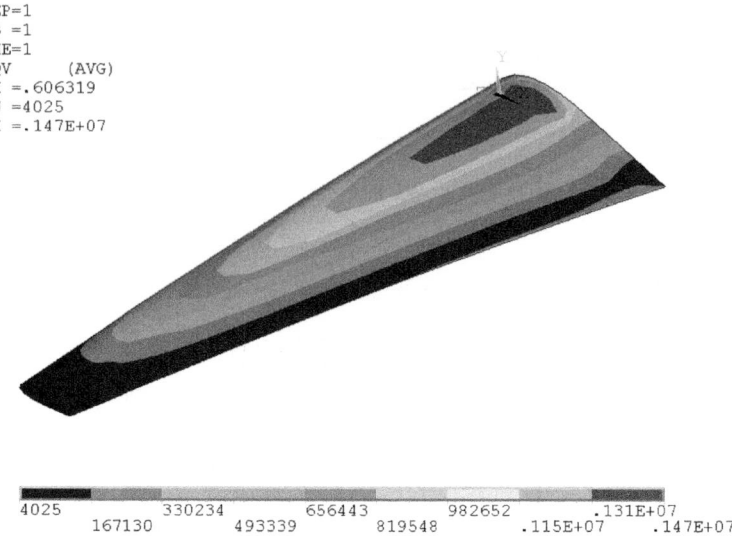

```
STEP=1
SUB =1
TIME=1
SEQV     (AVG)
DMX =.606319
SMN =4025
SMX =.147E+07
```

```
4025          330234         656443         982652        .131E+07
     167130         493339         819548        .115E+07       .147E+07
```

Fig. 5. Equivalent stress cloud chart of wing structure

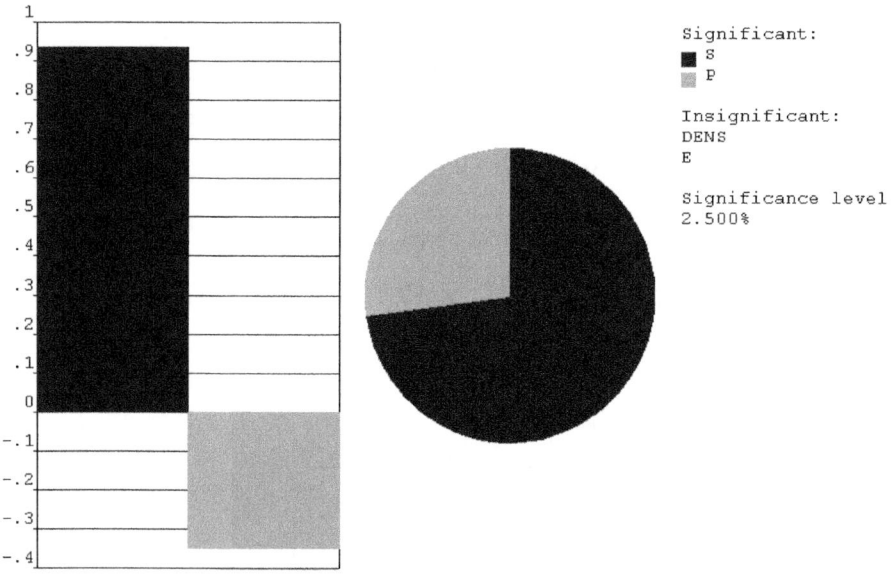

Fig. 6. Result based on sensitivity analysis

Therefore, the stress concentration in the wing root should try to be reduced in the design and manufacture for ensuring the safety of aircraft flight. Sensitivity analysis showed that, in the effect factors on the wing strength reliability from various parameters, the influences of the vertical gust load and material yield limit on the wing strength reliability is the greatest, so two factors should be given more attention in the design and manufacturing process of a wing structure.

5 Conclusions

Probability analysis function has successfully been used to do the strength reliability analysis of wing structures with Monte Carlo method in this paper. The reliability of structure stress, probability distribution, the sensitivity of design variables and other information can be obtained. Results indicated that the parameters extent of wing strength is very visually. This can provide an important basis for the design and optimization of structural parameters. The researches also showed that, the combination of finite element method with the reliability theory can provide a new feasible reliability analysis for complex structures.

References

1. Ye, Y., Hao, Y.H., Zhang, C.H.: Structure reliability analysis in ANSYS. Mechanical Engineering and Automation 6, 63–35 (2004)
2. Wang, Q., Liu, G., Wen, J.L.: Reliability of crane structure based on Monte-Carlo and Finite Element method. Journal of Wuhan University of Technology (Transportation Science & Engineering) 27, 702–704 (2003)
3. Fan, H.T., Chen, X.H., Wang, H.: Reliability Analysis of Aircraft Structures Based upon Monte-Carlo Method. Aircraft Design 29(3), 6–8 (2009)
4. Gao, J., Luo, Q.F., Che, W.: Theory of Monte-Carlo method and implementation in ANSYS. Journal of Qingdao Technological University 29(4), 18–22 (2008)
5. Peng, C.L., Ai, H.N., Liu, Q.S.: Reliable analysis for pressure vessel based on ANSYS. Nuclear Power Engineering 30(1), 109–111 (2009)
6. Zhu, D.F., Chen, J.K., Guo, Z.X.: Summary on structure reliability analysis methods. China Rural Water and Hydropower 8, 47–49 (2002)
7. Qi, H., Wang, X.P.: Modeling and Simulation. Tsinghua University Press, Beijing (2004)

Prediction Interval on Spacecraft Telemetry Data Based on Modified Block Bootstrap Method

Jiahui Luan, Jian Tang, and Chen Lu

School of Reliability and System Engineering, Beihang University,
100191 Beijing, China
tjstone12345@163.com

Abstract. In spacecraft telemetry data prediction field, unknown residual distribution and great volatility of predicted value have hampered traditional prediction interval methods to follow forecast trend and give high-precision intervals. Hence, modified Block Bootstrap prediction interval Method is proposed in this paper. Contrast to traditional method, this method can enhance accuracy of non-stationary time series data prediction interval for its data sampling frequency can be adjusted by data character. In the end, an example is given to show the validity and practicality of this method.

Keywords: block bootstrap, telemetry data, prediction interval, spacecraft.

1 Introduction

Studies of spacecraft failure prediction techniques mainly concentrated on prediction algorithms and theory based on telemetry data [1, 2]. These prediction techniques can only predict a series of single-point value without confidence interval; at the same time, spacecraft state parameters are always impacted by its complex operating environment, so that single-value prediction methods failed to meet actual project needs. Therefore, since 1990s, international studies on prediction interval technology developed rapidly [3-6]. However, application in space field is less. What is more, most existing methods are focused on prediction residual distribution known scenarios [7, 8] and few studies on unknown residual distribution that often encounter in practical engineering. Thus, study on interval prediction of unknown residual distribution is valuable.

In spacecraft telemetry data prediction field, unknown residual distribution and great volatility of predicted value have hampered traditional prediction interval methods to follow forecast trend and give high-precision intervals. Hence, Modified Block Bootstrap prediction interval Method is proposed in this paper. Sampling frequency can be adjusted by data's character in this method in order to fit prediction real time and high accuracy demand. The method is also applied to calculate HY-1B telemetry data's prediction interval and the practical value of this method is also demonstrated.

F.L. Wang et al. (Eds.): AICI 2010, Part II, LNAI 6320, pp. 38–44, 2010.

2   Block Bootstrap Method Idea

Block Bootstrap method is an improved Bootstrap method. Bootstrap method is a statistical method that proposed by Efron (1979). This method does not need sample distribution or extra new sample information, but only use duplicated samples that resampled from original data and statistics to estimate overall distribution character [9].

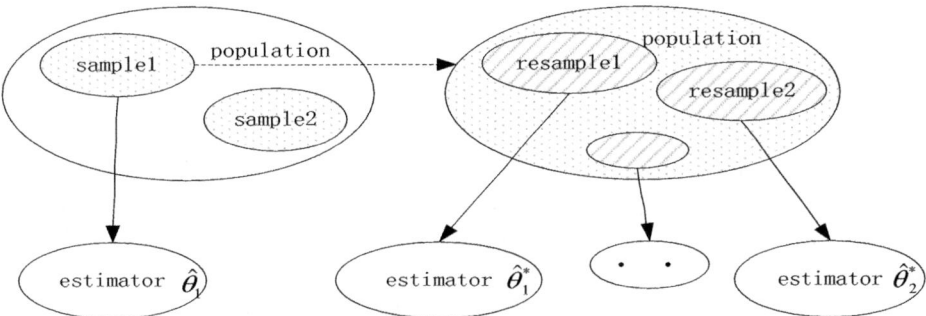

Fig. 1. Bootstrap idea schematic diagram

Bootstrap method efforts better to i.i.d data, but gains larger error when it used to deal with time series data. This is mainly because bootstrap samples are extracted from original data by point repeated sampling, which destroys the data structure [10]. Therefore, Hall (1985) proposed block Bootstrap idea firstly (Figure 2). Namely, use data block to maximum reserve data features, and then Bootstrap sampling step is applied to each block.

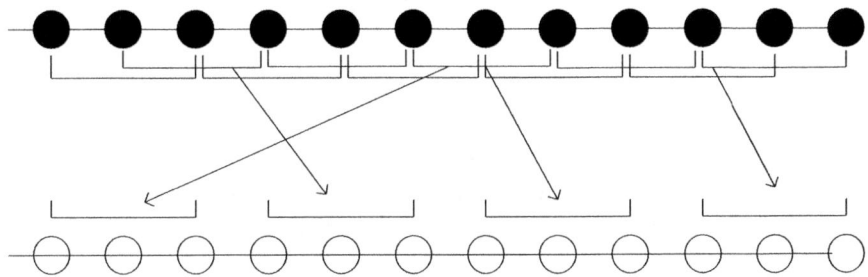

Fig. 2. Block Bootstrap Method idea sketch

Figure 2 black circle indicates original time series. The white circle represent by the sequence generated by block Bootstrap sampling. KÜnsch (1989) gave a complete description of the Block Bootstrap steps. However, the Block Bootstrap method is also deficient for sample frequency cannot be adjusted according to data character, especially to mutational data, which mainly affects prediction interval accuracy.

3   Modified-Block Bootstrap Method

3.1   Basic Idea

Data sampling frequency self-adjusting method is given in this paper to modify original Block Bootstrap for that sample frequency cannot be adjusted according to data characteristics. That is, calculate block data fluctuation ratio firstly

$$D_i = \frac{\max(Y_t) - \min(Y_t)}{l},$$

$\max(Y_t)$ represents maximum value of data block, $\min(Y_t)$ represents minimum value of data block, l represents data block length. Then calculate the ratio of neighbor data blocks fluctuation ratio D_i/D_{i+1}. If $D_i/D_{i+1} > 1$, the (i+1)th data block resample times adjusted to be num=M/(Di/Di+1) in order to improve prediction interval accuracy by obtaining more accurate data character.

3.2   Modified Block Bootstrap Prediction Interval Procedure

Consider a serial continuous prediction vector

$$Y_t = (X_{t-m+1}, \cdots, X_t), \quad t = m,...,n \tag{1}$$

Modified Block Bootstrap interval prediction procedure as following:

a)   Construct block-resample on the basis of these vectorized predictions. Build overlapping blocks of consecutive vectors firstly

$$(Y_m, \cdots, Y_{m+l-1}),$$
$$(Y_{m+1}, \cdots, Y_{m+l}),$$
$$\cdots,$$
$$(Y_{n-l+1}, \cdots, Y_n).$$

where $l \in N$ is the block length parameter, generally, $l = n^{1/3}$ (n means sample size). For simplicity, assume data blocks number k meet the condition $n - m + 1 = kl$, $k \in N$. Then, resample K blocks independently with replacement.

$$Y_{s_1+1}, \cdots, Y_{s_1+l},$$
$$Y_{s_2+1}, \cdots, Y_{s_2+l},$$
$$\cdots,$$
$$Y_{s_k+1}, \cdots, Y_{s_k+l}. \tag{2}$$

where the block-starting points s_1, ... , s_k are i.i.d. If the number of blocks n-m+1 is not a multiple of l, we resample $k = \frac{n-m+1}{l} + 1$ blocks but use only a portion of the

Kth block to get n-m+1 resampled m-vectors in total. These resampled blocks of m-vectors in (2) could be named as block bootstrap sample;

b) Bootstrap M times from the K data blocks, so we get M bootstrap replicated block samples Y_t^* ;

c) Calculate fluctuation rate Di of each replicated block samples Y_t^* , then resample N times bootstrap samples from replicated block samples Y_t^* $M\big/{Di}$ times, calculate estimated standard deviation $\overset{\wedge}{se}(\hat{Y}_t^*)$ of replicated block samples Y_t^* .

d) Calculate statistic $Z^* = \dfrac{\hat{Y}_t^* - \hat{Y}_t}{\overset{\wedge}{se}(\hat{Y}_t^*)}$ for each bootstrap replicated block samples Y_t^* , $\hat{Y}_t$

is mean value of block data.

e) Calculate sub-site value of α , $\#\{Z^* < \hat{t}(\alpha)\}\big/(M/D_i) = \alpha$.

f) Obtain prediction value's modified bootstrap interval $(\hat{Y}_t - \hat{t}^{(1-\alpha)} \bullet \overset{\wedge}{se}, \hat{Y}_t - \hat{t}^{(1-\alpha)} \bullet \overset{\wedge}{se})$.

4 Simulation Illustration

Modified-Bootstrap Method is applied to HY-1B satellite power system telemetry data's prediction. We use part of HY-1B satellite battery final discharge pressure that predicted by modified probabilistic neural network [11], as table 1.

Table 1. Part prediction data of HY-1B battery final discharge pressure

NO.	Value	NO.	Value	NO.	Value	NO.	Value
1	22.0967	17	22.0185	33	21.9080	49	21.8192
2	22.1511	18	21.9801	34	21.9170	50	21.8070
3	22.2013	19	21.9426	35	21.9256	51	21.7949
4	22.2458	20	21.9078	36	21.9328	52	21.7834
5	22.2796	21	21.8790	37	21.9373	53	21.7732
6	22.2953	22	21.8613	38	21.9366	54	21.7651
7	22.2967	23	21.8521	39	21.9320	55	21.7587
8	22.2879	24	21.8485	40	21.9248	56	21.7534
9	22.2712	25	21.8495	41	21.9154	57	21.7491
10	22.2507	26	21.8526	42	21.9050	58	21.7454
11	22.2261	27	21.8578	43	21.8936	59	21.7423
12	22.1962	28	21.8658	44	21.8810	60	21.7399
13	22.1629	29	21.8750	45	21.8679	61	21.73781

Table 1. (*Continued*)

14	22.1277	30	21.8838	46	21.8553	62	21.7085
15	22.0911	31	21.8923	47	21.843	63	21.70339
16	22.0550	32	21.9002	48	21.8310	64	21.69622

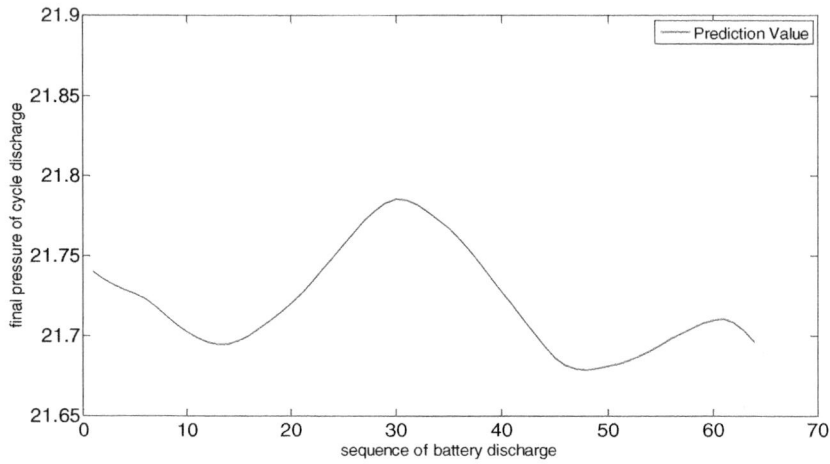

Fig. 3. HY - 1B final discharge pressure predict curve

Before interval analysis of these prediction data, parameter value should be set firstly. According to empirical formula, each block length $l = n^{1/3} = 64^{1/3} = 4$. So the total data block number k=16, sample time M=200, set confidence degree c=95%. Interval prediction curve as Fig.4(b).

Table 2. Data block fluctuation rate

D1	D2	D3	D4	D5	D6	D7
1.99	0.23	0.74	1.03	10.52	0.38	1.05
D8	D9	D10	D11	D12	D1 3	D14
7.34	0.20	0.45	0.97	1.05	1.91	2.12

Prediction interval results as shown in Figure 4. From this figure, we can see that the accuracy of prediction interval curve that get by Modified Bootstrap method is much higher. This means that the Modified Bootstrap Method is able to give higher precision prediction interval of the final discharge voltage pressure prediction data.

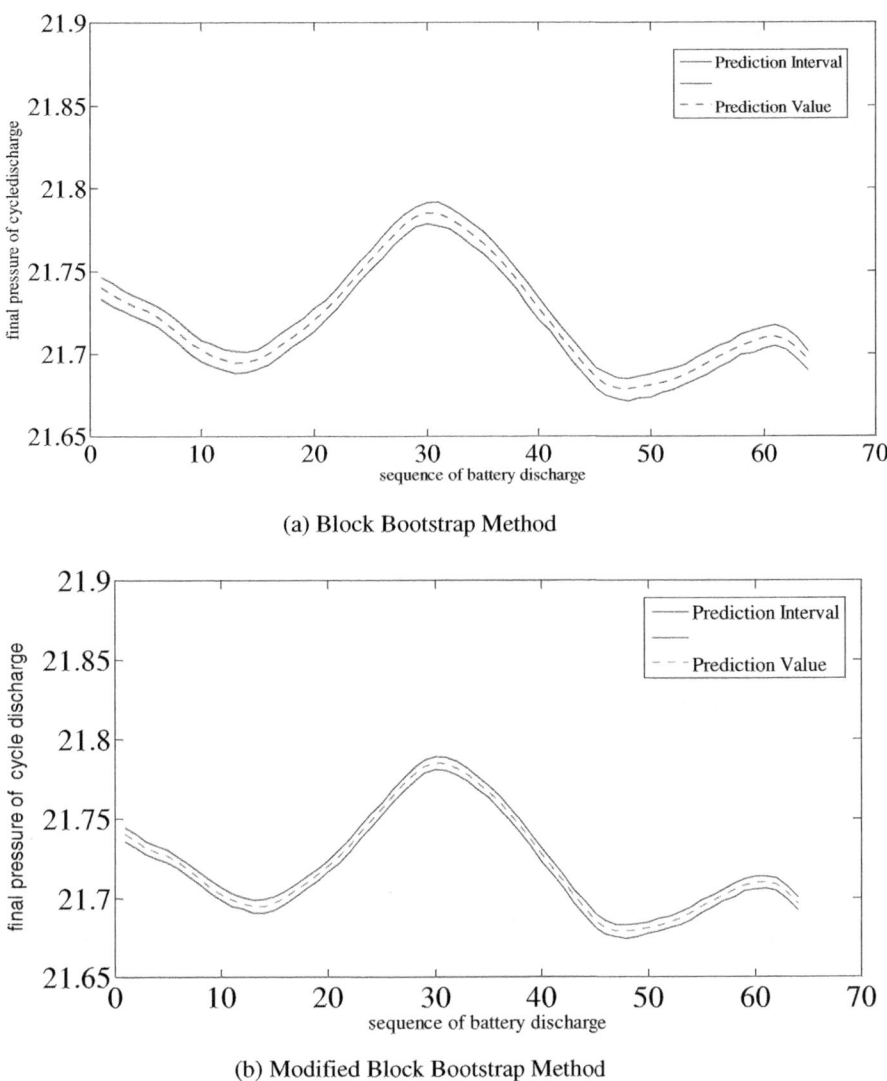

(a) Block Bootstrap Method

(b) Modified Block Bootstrap Method

Fig. 4. Prediction interval curve of final discharge pressure at 95% confidence degree of HY-1B

5 Conclusion

Simulation results, compared to traditional Block Bootstrap method, shows modified method shorten the prediction interval length, which improves the accuracy of prediction interval and is in favor of aerospace experts judging the operational status of satellite. This was a further illustration that the modified method both retained the advantage of original Bootstrap method and enhanced data characteristics adaptive capacity of traditional method.

Acknowledgments. This research is supported by the 863 program of China (Grant No.2007AA04Z431), the National Natural Science Foundation of China (Grant No. 50705005) and Technology Foundation Program of National Defense (Grant No. Z132010B004). The author is also grateful to the reviewers for their valuable suggestions for this paper.

References

1. Cottrell, M., Gaubert, P., et al.: Fault prediction in aircraft engines using self-organizing maps. LNCS, vol. 5629, pp. 37–44. Springer, Heidelberg (2009)
2. Xianyong, J., Mingqing, X., Leigang, H., Wei, L.: Prognostic of an aerial equipment based on PNN forecast model. Computer Measurement & Control, 12 (2009)
3. Kim, J.H.: Bootstrap prediction intervals for autoregression using asymptotically mean-unbiased estimators. International Journal of Forecasting 20(1), 85–97 (2004)
4. Jiahui, L., Chen, L.: The modified PNN prediction interval for spacecraft data. In: 2008 Congress on Image and Signal Processing, CISP 2008, vol. 5, pp. 121–126 (2008)
5. Ahmadi, J., MirMostafaee, S.M.T.K.: MirMostafaee Prediction intervals for future records and order statistics coming from two parameter exponential distribution. Statistics & Probability Letters 79(7), 977–983 (2009)
6. Guo, C., Jia, Z.: Research on parameters and forecasting interval of support vector regression model to small sample. Acta Metrologica Sinica 1 (2008)
7. Olive, D.J.: Prediction intervals for regression models. Computational Statistics & Data Analysis 51(6), 3115–3122 (2007)
8. Weiguang, A., Zhenming, S., Hui, Z.: Reserch on prediction interval technology in applying to spacecraft data processing. Journal of Astronautics 27 (2006)
9. Efron, B., Tibshirani, R.: An introduction to the Bootstrap. Chapman and Hall, London (1993)
10. Alonso, A.M., Pena, D., Romo: Introducing model uncertainty by moving blocks bootstrap. Statistical Papers 47, 167–179 (2006)
11. Laifa, T., Jiahui, L., Chen, L.: Prediction on moonlet powers system data based on modified probability neural network. In: Proc. IEEE Symp. International Conference on Reliability, Maintainability and Safety (ICRMS 2009), pp. 864–867. IEEE Press, Los Alamitos (July 2009)

Application of Sleep Scheduling Mechanism in Three-Dimensional Environment

Tongneng He[1] and Peijun Chen[2]

[1] Director of Electronic Information and Intelligent Systems Research Institute,
[2] Graduate student of Detection Technology and Automation,
Zhejiang University of Technology, Hangzhou, China
htn@zjut.edu.cn, Peijun995@163.com

Abstract. To study the issues of network coverage and network of life in the three-dimensional geographical environment, the cross deployment strategies and random deployment strategies were adopted, and random-sleep dissemination algorithm based on the dynamic neighbors' nodes information was used to study the regional coverage, node coverage and the network life under these two strategies. The experiment results show that, after using random-sleep dissemination algorithm based on the dynamic neighbors nodes information, the effect of the regional coverage throughout the region changes little, the network life extends about 1.1 times when there are enough nodes.

Keywords: wireless sensor network, scheduling mechanism, 3-D.

1 Introduction

Wireless sensor network is mainly made up of the sensor nodes, sensor gateway and host machine. Remote users can collect required data and information, also control the sensor network through the Internet, show in **Fig. 1**. When the wireless sensor network is working, the nodes are at the state of Work or Hibernation. For convenience, the node working state is generally divided into two types: Activity and Sleep. On one hand, at the state of Activity, nodes are in charge of perception, communication, calculation; On the other hand, at the state of Sleep, nodes do nothing, energy consumption is the least.

Scheduling of the sensor nodes, the entire scheduling cycle is divided into serial equal cycles T, show in **Fig. 2**. At the beginning of each cycle T, each node's state is determined by scheduling algorithm. Nodes which are scheduled to execute start to work, others remain in the state of sleep. Using the scheduling mechanism, it can reduce the number of activity nodes, achieves the purpose of saving energy, prolongs the entire network life.

Now, there are two ways to study the existing three-dimensional wireless sensor networks: ① The conclusions of two-dimensional directly have been extended to three-dimensional[2-3]; ② The three-dimensional issues are reduced to two-dimensional plane to solve. However, performance using these processes is not good, for most problems cann't be solved by applying extension and constraint. Network coverage,

F.L. Wang et al. (Eds.): AICI 2010, Part II, LNAI 6320, pp. 45–51, 2010.
© Springer-Verlag Berlin Heidelberg 2010

connectivity, topology control and deployment are fundamentally issues for wireless sensor network, further, in term of these issues, difficulty and complexity in calculating in three-dimensional is more than in two-dimensional. So, it needs new theory and new method, different from traditional two-dimensional wireless sensor network, to study three-dimensional wireless sensor network.

This article studys on the coverage and scheduling mechanism for three-dimensional network, analysises the influence on network life through adopting cross deployment strategies and random deployment strategies in three-dimensional region.

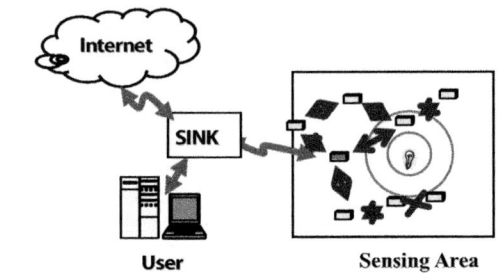

Fig. 1. System framework of WSN

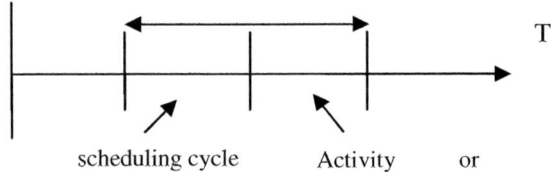

Fig. 2. State chart of node scheduling

2   Relation Work

2.1   Perceptual Model of Sensor Node

In order to achieve surveillance, each node transfers real signals into electrical signals, then transmits them to users. Accuracy of perceive signals of nodes is related with distance, directivity and uncertainty[5]. According to these condition, perceptual model has three types: binary perceptual model, exponent perceptual model and mixed perceptual model.

The principle of binary perceptual model is simple. If the object exits in the perceived radius r_0 of the node, then the object is perceived, or else isn't perceived. Node perceptual model as follow:

$$O(p_s,q) = \begin{cases} 1; & d(p_s,q) \le r_0 \\ 0; & else \end{cases} \tag{1}$$

where p_s is location of sensor node , q is the object location, and $d(p_s,q)$ is Euclidean distance between node and object.

Exponent perceptual model is more complex than binary perceptual model. The signals sent from sensor node vary along with variation of distance. Node perceptual model as follow:

$$O(p_s,q) = \begin{cases} \dfrac{\rho}{d(p_s,q)^\alpha}; & r_0 \leq d(p_s,q) \leq r \\ 0 \quad ; & else \end{cases} \qquad (2)$$

where ρ is arithmetic number determined from sensor model; r_0 is the minimum distance threshold[6].

Compared with Exponent perceptual model and binary perceptual model, mixed perceptual model[7] is more close to perceptual model of real sensor node. Beside, r_c is distance threshold, when the object is in radius of threshold r_c, intensity of perception is 1, then object is out of threshold r_c, Variation of intensity is along with distance increment. Mixed perceptual model as follow:

$$O(p_s,q) = \begin{cases} 1 & ; \quad 0 \leq d(p_s,q) < r_c \\ \dfrac{\rho}{d(p_s,q)^\alpha} & ; \quad r_c \leq d(p_s,q) \leq r \\ 0 & ; \quad else \end{cases} \qquad (3)$$

2.2 Coverage Model

The purpose of wireless sensor network application is to monitor special geographical district. Coverage model mainly involves two aspects: area coverage and point coverage. Ratio of covered district area and total district area is calculated to indicate the district coverage, and ratio of redundancy node number and total node number is calculated to indicate point coverage [8].

3 Sensor Deploying Strategy

3.1 Random Deploying Strategy

When supervised area is so large, such as forest, mountainous, etc. It is so difficulty to deploy sensor nodes artificially at these distract, it generally adopt random deploying strategy. Using this strategy, it doesn't need the detailed node location, places nodes randomly. Although it is easy to deploy nodes, random deploying strategy has some obvious weakness compared with artificial deployed strategy, such as nodes unevenly distributed, nodes cannot be judged good or bad after deployment.

3.2   Cross Deployment Strategy

This deployment strategy is designed based on the characteristic of wireless sensor network. Because nodes which close to sink nodes cost more energy than other nodes. These nodes not only percept and transmit themselves data, but also transmit other nodes' data. In order to prolong the network life, it must protect the nodes which close to sink node.

The method of cross deployment is that, at the time of deployment, geographical district is divided into two direction: horizontal and longitudinal, then forms cross sharp. Meanwhile, sensor nodes are separated into two section: one section is horizontally deployed, the other section is longitudinal deployed. This research takes an 1 km * 1 km three-dimensional district model. The district is segmented by n of parallel lines, according to horizontal and longitudinal direction. Then the length of parallel lines determines the space of two neighbor nodes, and generates bias through Gaussian distribution at every step, the purpose of bias is to make the result of deployment strategy more close to reality, because there are some factors, such as wind, unfairness ground, in real world, these could not accurate.

With this strategy, the number of nodes at each parallel lines isn't the same as others. Only a little portion of nodes are placed far away the center, the majority are placed nearby the center, such as around sink node. In simulation, the number of node at some parallel lines are the same, except two middle parallel lines.

3.3   Sleep Scheduling Mechanism

Adopting cross deployment strategy, the node density is high at the centre district, these nodes are always at state of activity at the same time, so collected data would be excessiveness.; the other side, as channel competition between nodes in same area, it brings about many packet collisions[9]. To prolong the network life, reduce packet collision, this study adopt sleep deployment algorithm based on the dynamic neighbors nodes information.

4   Simulation

The three-dimensional simulation model in this simulation is download from SRTM ftp, the size is 1 km*1 km, supposed that perceptual radius of sensor node r_c =25m, and this study adopts mixed perceptual model to detect performance of deployment strategy, show in **Fig. 3**.

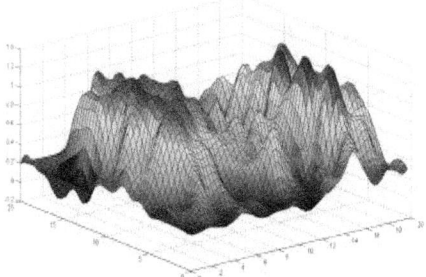

Fig. 3. Three-dimensional regional model

4.1   Result of without Sleep Scheduling Mechanism

From result of simulation in **Fig.4**, it can conclude random deployment strategy is better than cross deployment strategy in performance on coverage at situation of without sleep scheduling. Because at cross deployment strategy, the density is high nearby the sink node, it takes a lot of excessiveness, the density is low far away the sink node, the coverage effect is not good.

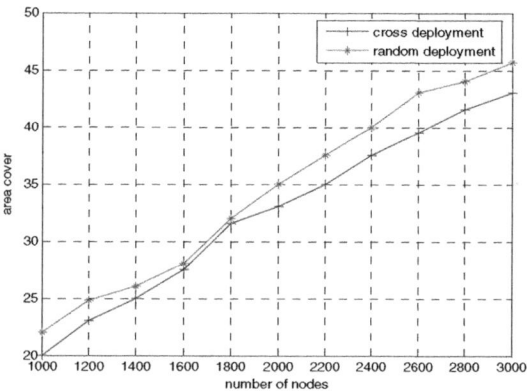

Fig. 4. Effect contrast of the regional coverage

Under the same condition, along with node number increases, the node coverage also improves. Compared with both strategy, coverage at cross deployment strategy is better than at random deployment strategy, this is because at the cross deployment strategy, central node number is more than random deployment strategy, show in **Fig. 5**.

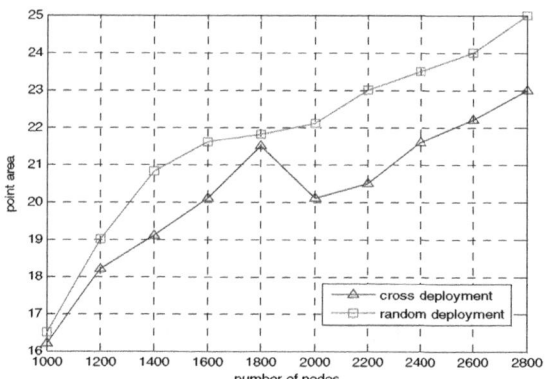

Fig. 5. Effect contrast of nodes cover

4.2   Result of Sleep Scheduling Mechanism

Show in **Fig. 7**, on the condition that the model has lots of nodes, the coverage with random sleep scheduling mechanism based on dynamic neighbors' nodes information is the same as one without this mechanism.

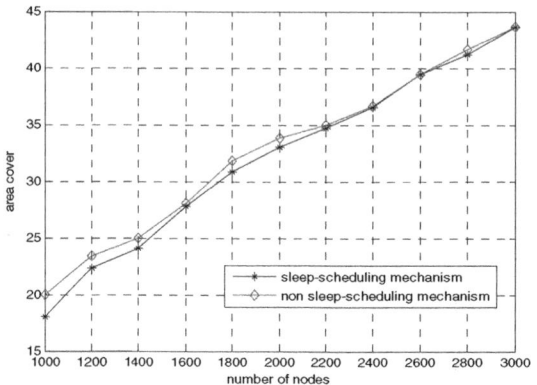

Fig. 6. Cover effect contrast under scheduling of with and without sleep

Compared models with and without sleep scheduling mechanism, number of survival node in the network is showed in **Fig. 7**. It is obvious that, at the same period, survival number with sleep scheduling mechanism is more, and the network life is extends about 1.1 times.

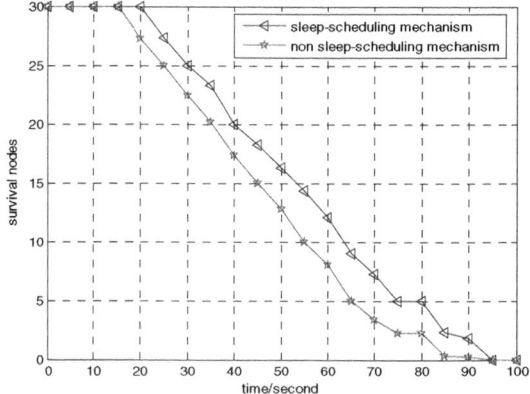

Fig. 7. Number of live node

5   Conclusion

This paper mainly talks about some current researches on wireless sensor network, then studys and simulates the coverage and scheduling at three-dimensional district model adopting cross deployment strategy and random deployment strategy, with and without sleep scheduling mechanism. It can conclude from the result of simulation that the coverage of random deployment strategy is better than cross deployment strategy; after adopting sleep scheduling mechanism, the life of cross deployment strategy is extend about 1.1 times, and survival nodes number is more than without sleep scheduling mechanism.

This study algorithms and deployment strategy has been verified under simulation environment, but more idealistic, in practical application there will be certain gaps.So, late work will be on the basis of further analysis of this improvement.

References

1. Tian, D., Georganas, N.D.: A coverage-preserving Node Scheduling Scheme for Large Wireless Sensor Networks. In: Pro. 1st ACM Int' l. Workshop on Wireless Sensor Networks and Applications, pp. 132–141. ACM Press, New York (2002)
2. Verdone, R.: A Statistical Analysis of Wireless Connectivity in Three Dimension. In: IEEE International Conference Communications (ICC 2005), pp. 3207–3210. IEEE Press, New York (2005)
3. Bahramgiri, M., Hajiaghayi, M., Mirrokniv, S.: Fault-tolerant and 3-dimensional Distributed topology Control Algorithm in Wireless Multi-hop Networks. In: IEEE international Conference on Computer Communications and Networks (ICCCN 2002), Miami, pp. 179–188 (2002)
4. Huang, C.F., Tseng, Y.C., Lo, L.G.: The coverage Problem in Three-dimensional Wireless Sensor Network. In: IEEE GLOBECOM, pp. 3182–3186. IEEE Press, Dallas (2004)
5. Karl, H., Willig, A.: Protocols and Architectures for Wireless Sensor Networks. Wiley, Chichester (2005)
6. Zhao, F., Guibas, L.: Wireless Sensor Networks-An information Processing Approach. Elsevier, Morgan Kaufman, Amsterdam (2004)
7. Elfes, A.: Occupancy Grids: A stochastic Spatial Representation for Active Robot Perception. Autonomous Mobile Robots: Perception, Mapping and Navigation, 60–70 (1991)
8. Liu, B., Townsley, D.: A study of Coverage of Large-scale Sensor Network. In: IEEE International Conference on Mobile Ad-hoc and Sensor Systems, pp. 475–483. IEEE, Florida (2004)
9. Wang, Z., Yan, L., Hu, F.: Wireless sensor network theory and its application. University of Aeronautics and Astronautics Press, Beijing (2007)
10. He, C., Shi, G., Liao, M.: Sensor network nodes in random sleep scheduling algorithm research and implementation. Computer Engineering 33(8), 115–117 (2007)
11. National Geophysical Data Center. Global Land One-kilometer Base Elevation Retrieved[EB/OL] (2007-08-22), http://www.ngdc.noaa.gov/mgg/fliers/globe-dem.html
12. Qi, N., Han, B., Li, P.: Intelligent Transportation System Applications of Wireless Sensor Networks. Electrical and Mechanical Engineering 24(10), 85–87 (2007)

Dimensions of E-commerce Benefits as Perceived by Businesses

Xibao Zhang

Department of International Economics and Trade, Qingdao University
xibao.zhang@qdu.edu.cn

Abstract. In this study the underlying dimensions of e-commerce benefits as perceived by businesses are investigated. Statistical analysis of empirical data from a questionnaire survey of managers of Chinese businesses resulted in three meaningful e-commerce benefits dimensions being uncovered. They are the Market, Efficiency, and Quality dimensions, which represent what companies perceive as business aspects where they can derive benefits by adopting e-commerce. In addition, the limitations of this study and directions for future research are discussed.

Keywords: electronic commerce, benefits, Chinese businesses, marketing dimension, efficiency dimension, quality dimension.

1 Introduction

The benefits of e-commerce to business have been widely discussed. On the theoretical side, [1] proposed three areas in which e-commerce can bring benefits to businesses, namely, customer relations, dealing with suppliers, and internal company operations. Reference [2] pointed out that e-commerce can help a firm improve, transform, and define its business operations, thereby generating business value. Specifically, they theorized that there are ten components to the business value system of electronic commerce, namely, product promotion, new sales channel, direct savings, time to market, customer service, brand or corporate image, technological learning and organizational laboratory, customer relationship, new product capabilities, and new business model, upon which propositions were postulated. Reference [3] put forth 15 specific benefits of e-commerce. In addition, [4] devised a 10-item construct for measuring transactional efficiency benefits of IS projects. According to [5], the benefits of e-commerce can be categorized into four groups, External/internal communication expenses, Revenues, Tangible benefits, and Intangible benefits, which altogether include 17 specific benefits. Reference [6], on the other hand, proposed a business model for e-commerce that includes three streams, the value stream, the revenue stream, and the logistics stream.

On the empirical side, there have been several studies that focus on e-commerce benefits to businesses. These studies produced similar findings. Reference [7] carried out an exploratory study on use of the Internet by small New Zealand firms. They found that the top-rated benefits as reported by the respondents are: 'Improved information gathering', 'Availability of expertise regardless of location', 'Better service

F.L. Wang et al. (Eds.): AICI 2010, Part II, LNAI 6320, pp. 52–57, 2010.

and support from suppliers', 'Increased productivity', 'Better awareness of business environment', 'Ability to reach international markets', 'Faster and more flexible delivery from suppliers'. Results from [8] show that the top five most important Internet usage drivers as reported by their Australian respondents are: 'Direct and indirect advertising', 'Low cost communication', 'Easy access to potential customers', 'Company image enhancement', and 'Form and extend business networks', while those cited by their UK respondents include 'External e-mail', 'Casual browsing for information', 'Searching for Web pages addresses', 'Information research', 'Advertising/promoting the business', and 'Linking to a professional body'. The most valuable attributes of e-commerce reported by [9] include 'Save time to look for resources', 'Obtain useful expertise from the Net', 'Savings in communication costs', and 'Better company image'. Reference [10] found that Dutch firms derive 'border-crossing' benefits, i.e., 'Distance related barriers disappear' and 'Continuous advertising all around the world', from the Internet. In addition, 'Improvement in company image', 'Increased sales', 'Effectiveness in collecting information, and 'Increased customer satisfaction' are also major benefits cited by their respondents. The top five benefits of e-commerce revealed in the study by [11] include 'Cheaper/more efficient communication', 'Improved customer service', 'Cheaper research', 'Improved image', and 'Access to global markets'.

Such diversity in both the conceptual constructs and empirical measures of e-commerce benefits reflects the overwhelming impact of the Internet in transforming business activities and processes. These benefits, however, have been proposed or identified by the researchers, and may not necessarily represent what businesses perceive as the benefits of e-commerce. In other words, there is lack of research on business perceptions of e-commerce benefits, especially dimensions underlying the specific benefits proposed or identified in previous research. In this vein, [12] carried out factor analysis on ten transactional efficiency indicators put forth by [4], which resulted in four factors, namely, Communication, System development, Personnel, and Capital. Therefore, the purpose of this paper is to find out if there are any theoretically meaningful underlying constructs or dimensions of e-commerce benefits from a business perspective.

2 Methodology

The empirical data of this study come from a questionnaire survey of Chinese managers. The first question of the questionnaire asks respondents to indicate firm size, which is broken into five categories on an ordinal scale of 1 through 5: 1 (employing 1-5 people), 2 (6-20 employees), 3 (21-50 employees), 4 (51-200 employees), and 5 (over 200 employees). Respondents were then asked to pick top five e-commerce benefits from a list of twelve: Goods to market faster, Cheaper/more efficient communications, Access to global markets, Lower transaction costs, Improved customer service, Increased sales (greater customer base), Cheaper research (ease of access to vital business information), Financial benefits derived from use of Internet outweigh cost of implementation, Cheaper product promotion (on-line brochures etc.), Improved image (being seen as innovative and technologically apt), Shorter payment cycles, Improved product quality (through ease of research). The lists of e-commerce benefits were adapted from [11]. The questionnaire was administered to a sample of students in executive training classes in Qingdao, China. The students were asked to participate in the survey, and those who agreed were further instructed on how to complete the questionnaire. A total of 68 usable responses were colleted. The collected data were then entered into a Microsoft Excel file and analyzed with SPSS.

The specific SPSS procedure used is CATPCA (categorical principal component analysis) so as to find out if there are any theoretically meaningful underlying constructs or dimensions. CATPCA is a type of principal components analysis that includes nonlinear optimal scaling, and is suited not only for categorical data, but also for ordinal and nominal multivariate data [13]. The raw data were converted to ordinal ranking on a five-point scale, with 5 the most important, and 1 the least important. The items that were not picked within the top five were given a value of 0, and treated as missing data in the subsequent analysis.

3   Results and Discussion

The sample is skewed toward large firms, with 51 firms (75.00% of the sample) employing over 200 people; there are another 12 firms (17.65%) with 51-200 employees, and the remaining 5 firms (7.35%) employing 21-50 people.

As Table 1 shows, the top five benefits as measured by the number of cases reported as one of the top five benefits by the respondents are Goods to market faster, Cheaper/more efficient communication, Improved customer service, Increased sales, and Improved image. Among these top five benefits, Improved image ranks first in terms of average and median (3.58, 4, respectively), followed by Increased sales (3.15, 3, respectively), Improved customer service (3.03, 3, respectively), Goods to market faster (2.25, 2, respectively), and Cheaper/more efficient communication (2.13, 2, respectively).

These top five benefits are similar to findings by others, including [7], [8], [9], [10], and [11]. For example, [14] found seven best e-commerce benefits in their empirical study: Improve customer services, Speed up business/administrative process, Increase communication with customers, Facilitate communication around the organization, Simplify ordering process, Share knowledge around the organization, and Create competitive advantage. Improved image as perceived by Chinese businesses to be the number one benefit associated with Internet use may well reflect the well-known Chinese cultural preoccupation with face, or Mianzi.

The CATPCA procedure resulted in three meaningful dimensions (Tables 2 and 3). The first dimension can be called the Marketing dimension, with Goods to market faster, Improved customer service, Increased sales, and Cheaper/more efficient communication as its principal components. Dimension 2, on the other hand, can be termed the Efficiency dimension, with Cheaper/more efficient communication, Financial benefits derived from use of Internet outweigh cost of implementation, Cheaper product promotion, and Shorter payment cycles as its principal components. The last dimension can be considered as the Quality dimension because it includes Improved product quality as its major components, even though Lower transaction costs, Financial benefits derived from use of Internet outweigh cost of implementation, and Cheaper product promotion also have fairly large loadings on this dimension.

Table 1. Top Five Benefits as Perceived by Chinese Firms

Benefits	N[a]	Mean[b]	Median[b]
Goods to market faster	40	2.25	2
Cheaper/more efficient communication	40	2.13	2
Access to global markets	24	2.21	3.5
Lower transaction costs	18	3.33	3.5
Improved customer service	36	3.03	3
Increased sales	27	3.15	3
Cheaper research	20	2.85	3
Financial benefits derived from use of Internet outweigh cost of implementation	10	3.10	3
Cheaper product promotion	12	3.50	4
Improved image	33	3.58	4
Shorter payment cycles	10	3.90	4.5
Improved product quality	10	3.90	4

a. Number of cases reported as one of top five benefits.
b. Values calculated from cases reported as one of top
   five benefits

The appearance of some efficiency benefits in the Marketing and Quality dimensions shows the business perception of efficiency gains through Internet use as the underlying driver of Internet-related competitive advantages. For example, Cheaper/more efficient communication can arguably lead to marketing advantages because businesses can communicate more often, more easily, and more efficiently with their customers and potential customers on the Internet.

Reference [5] proposed four groups of e-commerce benefits: External/Internal communication expenses, Revenues, Tangible benefits, and Intangible benefits. The Efficiency dimension as revealed in this study corresponds with [5]'s External/Internal communication expenses, which includes items in communications cost reduction, and Tangible benefits, which includes items that lead to cost reduction in areas other than communications. In addition, the Marketing dimension is similar to [5]'s Revenues group of benefits. The Quality dimension seems to be an aspect of e-commerce benefits to businesses that [5] did not propose.

The CATPCA dimensions of this study are not directly comparable to [12]'s four factors. They carried out factor analysis on ten transactional efficiency indicators put forth by [4]. And the four factors uncovered, namely, Communication, System development, Personnel, and Capital, can be considered as being related to the efficiency dimension of this study.

Table 2. Model Summary

Dimension	Cronbach's Alpha	Variance Accounted For Total (Eigenvalue)
1	.874	5.019
2	.823	4.067
3	.808	3.861
Total	1.007[a]	12.947

a. Total Cronbach's Alpha is based on the total Eigenvalue.

Table 3. Component Loadings

	Dimension		
	1	2	3
Goods to market faster	.892	-.432	-.212
Cheaper/more efficient communication	.799	.770	-.088
Access to global markets	-.939	-.167	-.614
Lower transaction costs	.363	-.861	.567
Improved customer service	.784	.002	-.143
Increased sales	.433	-.448	-.246
Cheaper research	-.661	-.030	.135
Financial benefits derived from use of Internet outweigh cost of implementation	-.085	.987	.638
Cheaper product promotion	-.194	.898	.521
Improved image	-1.040	-.450	.071
Shorter payment cycles	-.327	.539	-1.079
Improved product quality	-.314	-.212	1.078

4   Limitations and Directions for Future Research

This study represents an effort in identifying underlying dimensions of e-commerce benefits as perceived by Chinese businesses. It is notable that of the myriad benefits put forth by academics and/or identified by practitioners, three meaningful underlying dimensions have been uncovered in this study. The value of these dimensions, of course, is that they can be used in future research so as to simplify theoretical deliberations. The specific benefits, on the other hand, should be used as indicators for measuring these dimensions.

Apparently the twelve specific benefits that have been used to collect raw data in this study have a strong bearing on the dimensions subsequently uncovered. Of course these benefits do not constitute an exhaustive list. One direction for future research is to include more benefits, which could well lead to more meaningful underlying dimensions to be discovered. In addition, [15] distinguished between the intermediate effects and final effects e-commerce has on businesses. The twelve specific benefits, and hence the resulting dimensions, include those in both groups. Therefore, in future research attempts should be made to separately study benefits in these two groups, which could well lead to more meaningful findings.

References

1. Cronin, M.J.: Doing More Business on the Internet. Van Nostrand Reinhold, New York (1995)
2. Bloch, M., Pigneur, Y., Segev, A.: On the Road of Electronic Commerce – A Business Value Framework. Gaining Competitive Advantage and Some Research Issues (1996), http://inforge.unil.ch/yp/Pub/ROAD_EC/EC.HTM
3. Lederer, A.L., Mirchandani, D.A., Sims, K.: Electronic Commerce: A Strategic Application? In: Proceedings of the 1996 ACM SIGCPR/SIGMIS Conference on computer personnel research. ACM Press, New York (1996)
4. Mirani, R., Lederer, A.L.: An Instrument for Assessing the Organizational Benefits of IS Projects. Decision Sciences 29(4), 803–838 (1998)
5. Currie, W.: The Global Information Society. Wiley, Chichester (2000)
6. Mahadevan, B.: Business Models for Internet Based E-Commerce. California Management Review 42(4), 55–69 (2000)
7. Abell, W., Lim, L.: Business Use of the Internet in New Zealand: An Exploratory Study (1996), http://ausweb.scu.edu.au/aw96/business/abell/paper.htm
8. Poon, S., Strom, J.: Small Businesses' Use of the Internet: Some Realities (1997), http://www.isoc.org/inet97/proceedings/C2/C2_1.HTM
9. Poon, S., Swatman, P.: A Longitudinal Study of Expectations in Small Business Internet Commerce, http://www.uni-koblenz.de/~swatmanp/pdfs/poon.bled98.pdf
10. Walczuch, R., Van Braven, G., Lundgren, H.: Internet Adoption Barriers for Small Firms in The Netherlands. European Management Journal 18(5), 561–572 (2000)
11. Moussi, C., Davey, B.: Level of Internet Use by Victorian Manufacturing Firms. School of Business Information Technology Working Paper Series, 1/2000 (2000) ISBN: 086459061X
12. Kaefer, F., Bendoly, E.: Measuring the Impact of Organizational Constraints on the Success of Business-to-Business E-Commerce Efforts: A Transactional Focus. Information & Management 41(5), 529–541 (2004)
13. Meulman, J.J., Van der Kooij, A.J., Heiser, W.J.: Principal Components Analysis with Nonlinear Optimal Scaling Transformations for Ordinal and Nominal Data. In: Kaplan, D. (ed.) The Sage Handbook of Quantitative Methodology for the Social Sciences. Sage Publications, Thousand Oaks, California (2004)
14. Piris, L., Fitzgerald, G., Serrano, A.: Strategic Motivators and Expected Benefits from E-Commerce in Traditional Organizations. International Journal of Information Management 24, 489–506 (2004)
15. Mustaffa, S., Beaumont, N.: The Effect of Electronic Commerce on Small Australian Enterprises. Technovation 24(2), 85–95 (2004)

Nonlinear Analysis of a Hybrid Optimal Velocity Model with Relative Velocity for Traffic Flow[*]

Tao Liu[1,2] and Lei Jia[2]

[1] College of Electric Information and Control Engineering,
Shandong Institute of Light Industry, Jinan, Shandong Province, China
[2] School of Control Science and Engineering, Shandong University,
Jinan, Shandong Province, China
liutaobaby@163.com

Abstract. An extension of an optimal velocity model with the relative velocity is analyzed. From the nonlinear analysis, the propagating kink solution for traffic jams is obtained. The fundamental diagram and the relation between the headway and the delay time are examined by numerical simulation. We find that the result from the nonlinear analysis is in good agreement with that obtained from the numerical simulation.

Keywords: optimal velocity model, relative velocity, nonlinear analysis.

1 Introduction

Traffic flow problems have been given much attention for decades. It is important to study traffic flow dynamics of transportation. Various traffic models have been proposed and studied[1-19]. Toward a realistic model, which explains the traffic flow dynamics, the optimal velocity model was proposed by Bando[1]. Nagatani [2] put forward an extended optimal velocity model including the vehicle interaction with the next vehicle ahead (i.e., the next-nearest-neighboring interaction). Xue [3] proposed a lattice model of optimized traffic flow with the consideration of the optimal current with the next-nearest-neighboring interaction. After that Ge et al. [4] considered arbitrary number of sites ahead. Lenz et al. [5] constructed a model that a driver can receive the moving information about many vehicles ahead of him/her. In 2004, Hasebe et al. proposed an extended optimal velocity model applied to cooperative driving control system by considering any arbitrary number of vehicles that precede [6], and we called it forward looking optimal velocity model. They found that there exist a certain set of parameters that make traffic flow "more stable" in this model. Ge et al.[7] continued to investigate the dynamic behavior near the critical point of the model.

---

[*] Project supported by the National Natural Science Foundation of China (Grant NO.60674062), Natural Science Foundation of Shandong Province(Grant NO..ZR2009GM032), Independent Innovation Foundation of Shandong University, IIFSDU(Grant NO..2009TS046).

F.L. Wang et al. (Eds.): AICI 2010, Part II, LNAI 6320, pp. 58–63, 2010.

The above models are related to the forward looking effect, but only few models studied the backward looking effect, such as the models proposed by Nakayama et al.[8] and Hasebe et al.[9]. We think it is reasonable to take the backward looking effect into account. In 2006, Ge et al.[10] proposed an extended car following model with the consideration of arbitrary number of vehicles ahead and one vehicle following on a single-lane highway.

2 Model

In the original OV model[1], the acceleration of the n-th vehicle at time t is determined by the difference between the actual velocity and an optimal velocity, which depends on the headway to the car in the front. The optimal velocity equation is

$$\ddot{x}_n(t) = \alpha[V(\Delta x_n(t)) - \dot{x}_n(t)] \tag{1}$$

where α is the sensitivity of a driver, $\Delta x_n(t) = x_{n+1}(t) - x_n(t)$ is the headway, and $V(\Delta x_n(t))$ is the optimal velocity function, $V(\Delta x_n(t)) = \alpha \tanh(\Delta x_n(t) - \beta) + \gamma$.

An extension of an optimal velocity model was proposed by Nakayama which is called the backward looking OV(BL-OV)model[2]. In this model, a driver looks at the following car as well as the preceding car at the same time. The equation is

$$\ddot{x}_n(t) = \alpha[V_F(\Delta x_n(t)) + V_B(\Delta x_{n-1}(t)) - \dot{x}_n(t)] \tag{2}$$

where $V_F(\Delta x_n(t))$ is the OV function for forward looking that plays the same role as $V_B(\Delta x_n(t))$ in Eq.(1). $V_B(\Delta x_{n-1}(t))$ is the OV function for backward looking, which is a function of the headway of the following car. We find that the above models did not consider the relative velocity. We will consider a traffic flow model described by

$$\ddot{x}_n(t) = \alpha[(1 - p)V_F(\Delta x_n(t)) \\ + pV_B(\Delta x_{n-1}(t)) - \dot{x}_n(t)] + \lambda \alpha \Delta v_n(t) \tag{3}$$

where P is a constant standing for the relation between the two OV functions, and we set p from 0~0.5 which permitted that the forward looking play dominant role in the model; λ is a constant ranging from 0~1; $\Delta v_n(t) = dx_{n+1}(t)/dt - dx_n(t)/dt$, and $dx_{n+1}(t)/dt$ indicates the velocity of the (n+1)th vehicle at time t;

The two OV functions were given in [4] respectively as[8]

$$V_F(\Delta x_n(t)) = \alpha \tanh(\Delta x_n(t) - \beta) + \gamma \\ V_B(\Delta x_{n-1}(t)) = -(\alpha \tanh(\Delta x_{n-1}(t) - \beta) + \gamma) \tag{4}$$

3 Nonlinear Analysis

We consider the slowly varying behavior for small wave number k near the critical point. We introduce slow scales for space variable n and time variable t and define slow variable X and T as follows

$$X = \varepsilon(n + bt) \quad \text{and} \quad T = \varepsilon^3 t \quad 0 < \varepsilon \le 1 \tag{5}$$

where b is a constant to be determined. We set the headway as

$$\Delta x_n(t) = h_c + \varepsilon R(X, T) \tag{6}$$

Where $R(X, T)$ is a function to be determined. By expanding to the fifth order of ε and using Eq.(5), we obtain the following nonlinear partial differential equation:

$$\alpha \varepsilon^2 (b - V') \partial_X R + \varepsilon^3 \left(b^2 - \frac{\alpha}{2} V' - \lambda \alpha b \right) \partial_X^2 R + \varepsilon_4 \left[\alpha \partial_T R - (\frac{V'}{6} + \frac{b}{2} \lambda) \alpha \partial_X^3 R - \frac{V'''}{6} \alpha \partial_X R^3 \right]$$

$$+ \varepsilon^5 \left[(2b - \lambda \alpha) \partial_T \partial_X R - (\frac{b}{6} \lambda \alpha - \frac{\alpha V'}{24}) \partial_X^4 R - \frac{V'''}{12} \alpha \partial_X^2 R^3 \right] = 0 \tag{7}$$

where

$$V' = \frac{d[(1-p)V_F(\Delta x) + pV_B(\Delta x)]}{d\Delta x} \bigg|_{\Delta x = h_c}$$

$$V''' = \frac{d^3[(1-p)V_F(\Delta x) + pV_B(\Delta x)]}{d\Delta x^3} \bigg|_{\Delta x = h_c}$$

Taking $b = V'$, we can eliminate the second order terms of ε from Eq.(7). We consider the neighborhood of the critical point τ_c, such that

$$\tau/\tau_c = 1 + \varepsilon^2 \tag{8}$$

Where $\tau_c = \dfrac{1 + 2\lambda}{V'(h_c)}$. Then Eq.(7) can be rewritten as

$$\varepsilon_4 \left[\partial_T R - \frac{1+3\lambda}{6} V \partial_X^3 R - \frac{V'''}{6} \partial_X R^3 \right] + O(\varepsilon) = 0 \tag{9}$$

To derive the regularized equation, we make a transformation for Eq.(9), as follows:

$$T' = \frac{1+3\lambda}{6} V'T$$

and

$$R = \left[-\frac{1+3\lambda}{V'''} V' \right]^{1/2} R' \tag{10}$$

Then, Eq.(9) can be rewritten as the following equation

$$\partial_{T'}R' - \partial_X^3 R' - \partial_X R'^3 + O(\varepsilon) = 0 \tag{11}$$

If we ignore the perturbed term $O(\varepsilon)$. The kink solution of this equation is

$$R_0'(X, T') = \sqrt{c}\, \tanh\sqrt{\tfrac{c}{2}}(X - cT') \tag{12}$$

Where c is the propagation speed of the kink wave. This speed is determined by the $O(\varepsilon)$ term, it is necessary to imply the solvability condition satisfied by $R_0'(X, T')$[2]

$$\left(R_0', M\left[R_0'\right]\right) = \int_{-\infty}^{\infty} dX R_0'(X, T') M\left[R_0'(X, T')\right] = 0 \tag{13}$$

Where

$$M[R_0'] = c_1 \partial_X^2 R' + \frac{c_2}{2}\partial_X^4 R' - \frac{c_3}{2}\partial_X^2 R'^3$$

$$c_1 = \frac{\lambda}{1 + 3\lambda}, \quad c_2 = \frac{1}{1 + 3\lambda}, \quad c_3 = 1$$

By performing the integration, we obtain the selected propagation speed $c = 2\lambda/5 + 9\lambda$. Thus, we have derived the solution of the modified KDV equation, that is

$$R(X, T) = \left[-\frac{2(1 + 3\lambda)}{3V'''}V'c\right]^{1/2} \tanh\sqrt{\frac{c}{2}}\left(X - \frac{1 + 3\lambda}{6}V'cT\right) \tag{14}$$

The amplitude of the kink solution is given by

$$A = \left[\frac{1 + 3\lambda}{3}c\left(\frac{\alpha_c}{\alpha} - 1\right)\right]^{1/2}$$

with $\tag{15}$

$$\alpha_c = \tau_c^{-1}$$

The kink wave solution represents the coexisting phase, which consists of the freely moving phase with low density and the congested phase with high density. The headway of the freely moving phase is $\Delta x = h_c + A$, and that of the congested phase is $\Delta x = h_c - A$, based on which we can depict the coexisting curves in the parameterized space $(\Delta x, \alpha)$.

4 Simulation

Finally, we examine their relation between the headway and the delay time for various values of p. In the congested region, stop-and-go states appear. We can obtain the relation between the headway and the inverse of the delay time numerically. Numerical results are plotted in figure 1 for the cases of p=0 and 0.1 as an example. The theoretical curve is drawn as a solid curve.

We find that the result obtained from the nonlinear analysis is in good agreement with the simulation result near the critical point.

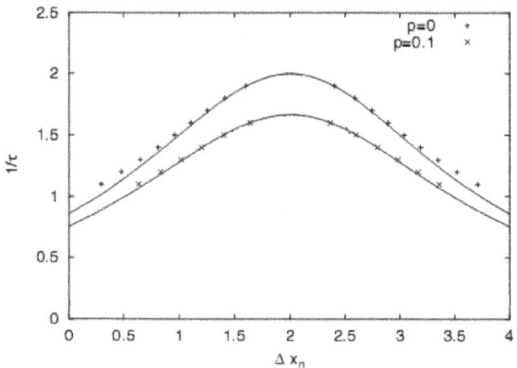

Fig. 1. The relation between the headway and $1/\tau$ for the cases of p=0 and 0.1.

5   Conclusions

An optimal velocity model with the relative velocity was proposed to describe the motion of the vehicle on a single lane highway in this paper. The traffic behavior has investigated analytically with this model by the use of the nonlinear wave analysis. Nonlinear analysis of the model shows that the traffic congestion is described by the MKdV equation at the critical point. The propagating kink solution and the relation between the headway and the delay time are obtained. We found that the analytical result is in good agreement with the numerical simulation near the critical point.

References

1. Bando, M., Hasebe, K., Nakayama, A., Shibata, A., Sugiyama, Y.: Phys. Rev. E 51, 1035 (1995)
2. Nagatani, T.: Phys. Rev. E 60, 6395 (1999)
3. Xue, Y.: Acta Physica Sinica 53, 25 (2004)
4. Ge, H.X., Dai, S.Q., Xue, Y., Dong, L.Y.: Phys. Rev. E 71, 066119 (2005)
5. Lenz, H., Wagner, C.K., Sollacher, R.: Eur. Phys. J. B 7, 331 (1998)
6. Hasebe, K., Nakayama, A., Sugiyama, Y.: Phys. Rev. E 69, 017103 (2004)
7. Ge, H.X., Dai, S.Q., Dong, L.Y., Xue, Y.: Phys. Rev. E 70, 066134 (2004)
8. Nakayama, A., Sugiyama, Y., Hasebe, K.: Phys. Rev. E 65, 016112 (2001)
9. Hasebe, K., Nakayama, A., Sugiyama, Y.: Phys. Rev. E 68, 026102 (2003)
10. Ge, H.X., Zhu, H.B., Dai, S.Q.: Phys. J. B 54, 503–507 (2006)
11. Wang, T., Gao, Z.Y., Zhao, X.M.: Acta Phys. Sin. 55, 634 (2006) (in chinese)
12. Li, Z.P., Liu, Y.C.: Chin. Phys. 15, 1570 (2006)

13. Han, X.L., Jiang, C.Y., Ge, H.X., Dai, S.Q.: Acta Phys. Sin. 56, 4383 (2007) (in chinese)
14. Telesca, L., Lovallo, M.: Physica A 387, 3299 (2008)
15. Jiang, R., Hu, M.B., Jia, B., Wang, R., Wu, Q.S.: Transportmetrica 4(1), 51 (2008)
16. Zhu, W.-X., Jia, L.: International Journal of Modern Physics C 19(9), 1321–1335 (2008)
17. Zhu, W.-X., Liu, Y.-C.: Journal of Shanghai Jiaotong University (English Edition) 13(2), 166–170 (2008)
18. Zhu, W.-X., Jia, L.: Communications in Theoretical Physics 50(2), 505–510 (2008)
19. Xue, y., Dong, l.-y., Yuan, y.-w., Dai, s.-q.: Commun.Theor. Phys(Beijing,China) 38, 230–234 (2002)

Insertion Force of Acupuncture for
a Computer Training System

Ren Kanehira[1], Weiping Yang[2],
Hirohisa Narita[1], and Hideo Fujimoto[3]

[1] FUJITA Health University, 1-98 Dengakugakubo, Kutsukake-cho,
Toyoake, Aichi, 470-1192, Japan
[2] Aichi Shukutoku University, Nagoya, Japan
[3] Nagoya Institute of Technology, Nagoya, Japan
kanehira@fujita-hu.ac.jp, wpyang@asu.aasa.ac.jp,
fujimoto@vier.mech.nitech.ac.jp

Abstract. In this study, a training computer simulation system for acupuncture training was proposed for the purpose of a quantitative characterization of the traditional oriental technique. A system using a force measuring device was constructed to record and analyze the basic data of insertion force. The index of insertion force was decided, and fundamental data for the development of such a computer simulation system of acupuncture training was obtained.

Keywords: Acupuncture, Computer Training system, Insertion force, Quantification of technique.

1 Introduction

Acupuncture is such to cure or keep the human body healthy by stimulating related acu-points. Acupuncture was originated from ancient China with the typical Chinese thinking and special philosophy. Though there still remain some unresolved questions, the oriental medicine has been more and more accepted by the world for its miraculous effect, particularly to diseases which are difficulty to the west medicine to treat. Acupuncture among the traditional oriental medical treatments has the merit of high efficiency with almost no harmful side-effects. The effectiveness of it has been re-realized in recent years, and promotions are also carried on worldwide. Acupuncture was well recognized in Japan from the past with widespread clinics and even some universities majoring in acupuncture. With an increasing attention and widespread of acupuncture activities, the need for acupuncture education is also increased [1-3].

In consideration of such an increasing trend, however, it is hardly satisfactory in the field of acupuncture training. Acupuncture is such to looking firstly for the acu-point along the meridian distributed in a 3D style on the human body, and to insert the needle using hands with precise force adjustment [4]. It is known to be very difficult in the conventional training method to understand the 3D position of an acupoint using a textbook showing only 2D pictures, and such techniques as the precise

F.L. Wang et al. (Eds.): AICI 2010, Part II, LNAI 6320, pp. 64–70, 2010.

adjustment of speed and force for an insertion are usually obtained by watching the motion of an expertise doctor.

It is mostly important in acupuncture to become highly skilled by training with repeated practice. However, such practice can hardly be done on a real human body, which may always be accompanied with pain and misery.

In our research for solving around acupuncture education problems, we have proposed a training system using the computer simulation technology [5,6], in which a 3D human body model with acu-points for positioning and a real-timely true-false judgment [7], and the ability of teaching of insertion angle [8], the measurement and training of insertion speed [9,10], have been studied and developed. Figure 1 shows the acupuncture process and the flow of our research focus points.

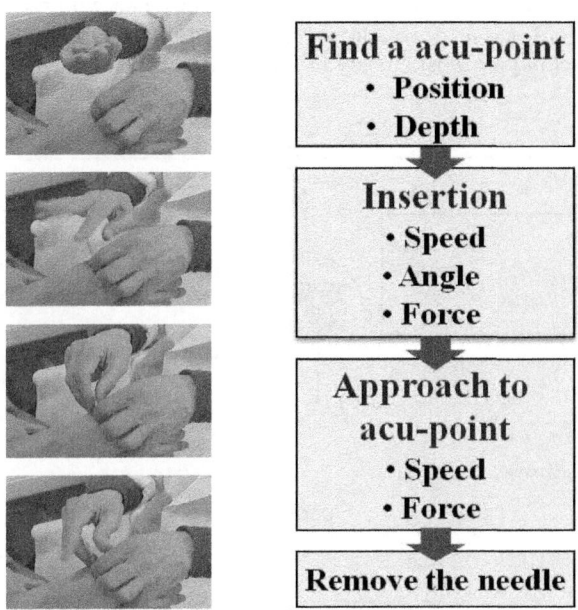

Fig. 1. Acupuncture process & Research Focus points

In the development of the training system, it has been pointed out that the quantified index to the training of acupuncture is important, and for this purpose that the system should be developed with real time true-false judgment. As one of the series studies carried out by us, this paper tried to solve the problem in the insertion force, which is to hold the needle and insert it into the skin having an acupoint with precise adjustment of force, speed, and angle. Here we define the "insertion" action is to beat the needle handle 4-5 (*mm*) into the skin after looking out the right acu-position. Upon an insertion, the insertion forces of expert doctor were measured and the index of insertion force was decided. The characterized results were applied to make quantified indexes for the construction of a training device and system.

2 Proposed System

2.1 Construction of the System

The final purpose of the system is to make a training of the whole process in acupuncture possible, including the learning of basic theory and the mastering of the acupuncture technique. A human acu-points model is firstly created within the VR space, and then the necessary software for training is constructed. Figure 2 shows the construction of the proposed acupuncture training computer system. The system is constructed by a head-mount display (HMD), a 3-dimension sensor, a computer, and other training devices made by us. Information on the position and attitude of trainees is detected from the head sensor, and from the information the field of view is calculated in the computer and output from the HMD. With the HMD on head, the trainees can get a 3D view of the human acu-points model and are then trained with real presences. Further with the use of a force feedback device developed in our lab., it is possible to learn the acupuncture techniques most closely to the practice.

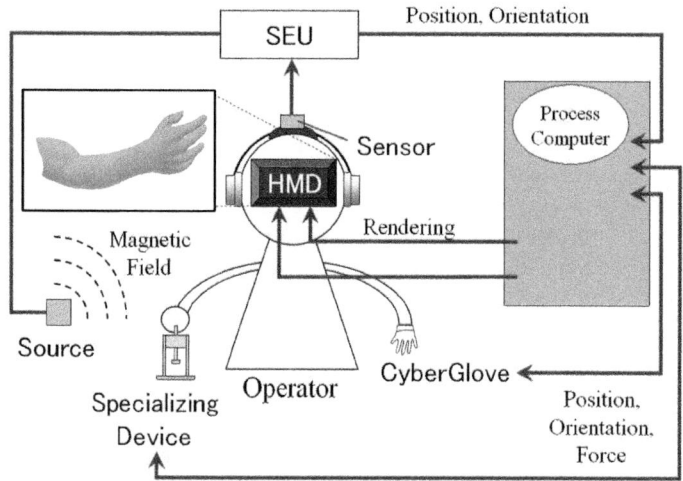

Fig. 2. Construction of the system

2.2 Learning and Training of Acupuncture

Acupuncture is a medical treatment using acupuncture needle to stimulate the acu-points of body according to different symptoms. An acu-point is the point on the body receiving the needle and proper stimulus. So acupuncture has techniques of not only holding and insertion, but also those of stinging, trail, whirl as shown in Figure 3, according to different symptoms. It is further required for good healing to use different techniques such as the stinging angle, the speed, and the depth upon different acu-points for each symptom. Therefore, it is especially important to be trained by repeated practice.

The proposed system can be roughly divided into two parts. One is the software for teaching and explanation of the sequence of basic theory, case prehension, treatment policy, acu-points combination and handling. Another part, and the most important one

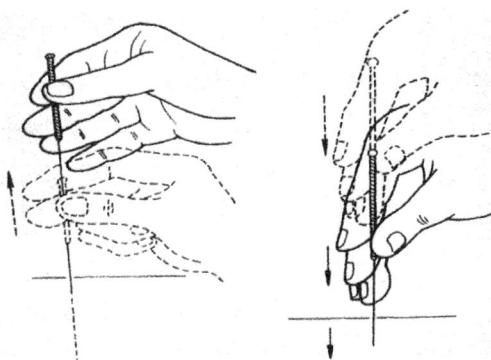

Fig. 3. Needle therapy

in the system, is the development of the training system with the force feedback with a precise response to the acu-point model [11]. Firstly, information of operation forces from experienced doctors are measured and stored in the computer as a training index.

3 Measurement of the Tapping Force in Insertion

A device for the measurement of the insertion force during stinging was made. The device was applied to both doctor and intern for practice operation. It is considered that quantitative values for a good acupuncture treatment with proper tapping force can be obtained by comparing the measurement results from the teacher and the trainee.

3.1 The System

The insertion force along the insertion direction was measured with the system in Figure 4.

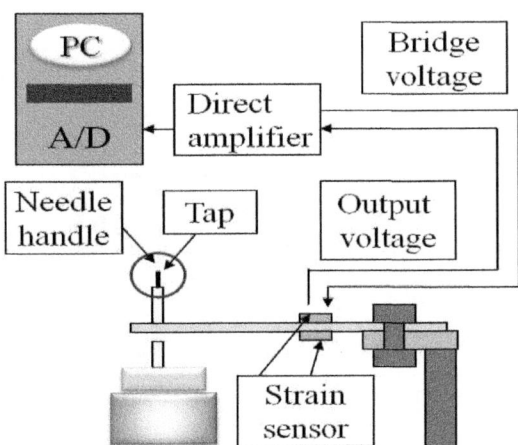

Fig. 4. Measurement device

The system is composed of a cantilever bridge with 4 strain sensors attached on a aluminum sheet. Real needle and tube were used in the tapping part, and an acrylic pipe covered with skin gel was used as a support for the human hand.

3.2 Measurement

The tapping force was measured with the above system. Experiment was done in Institute of Oriental Medicine located in Chikusa-ku, Nagoya, Japan. A total number of 12 persons, including 5 of the experienced doctor and 7 of trainees were asked to join the experiment.

Measurement was done for each person after 1 minute practice time. Then measurement was started with one person to tapping 6 times, in each time he was given a 10 second time to start tapping freely on his willing.

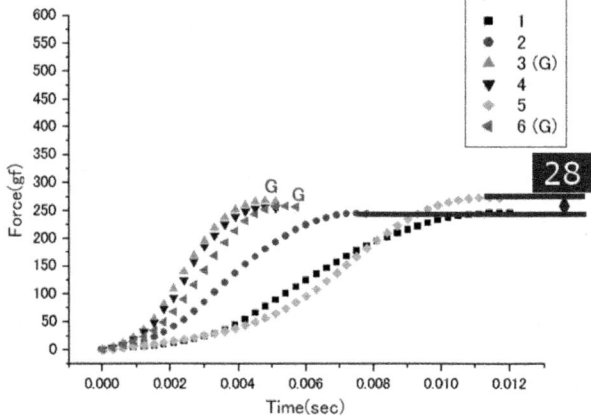

Fig. 5. Results of intern

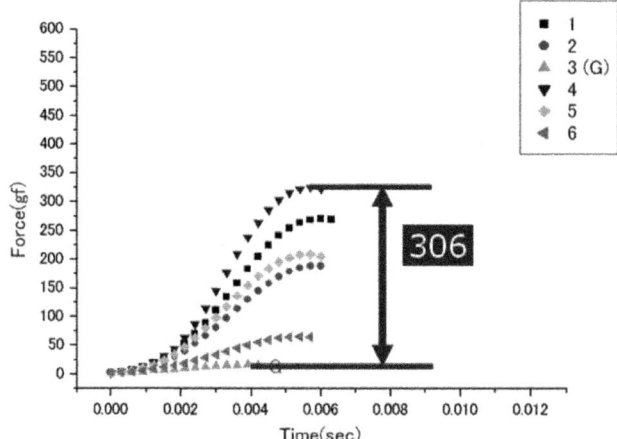

Fig. 6. Results of expert

The results of tapping force vs tapping time were plotted in Figure 5 for the experienced, and Figure 6 for the trainees, as the representatives of the average for the 6 tries. It can be seen that the difference in tapping force from the experienced doctor is apparently much less (28gf) than the trainees (306gf). The 2 figures indicate clearly the fact that the experienced doctor carry out much stable insertion than the trainees, and the system quantitatively tell the difference.

3.3   Determination of the Standard Tapping Force

A proper value of 260gf was obtained after analyzing the experiment results. This value can then be applied as the standard tapping force of insertion as the index used in the system to judge real-timely an insertion training process.

4   Conclusions

The research for the development of a training system for a quantitative indexing of insertion force in acupuncture has been done. The measurement device and system enabling the measuring and training of insert force were developed. The insertion force was recorded as an index and displayed to the trainee to allow a real time true-false judgment. The trainee knows instantly the training effect at once which is very much helpful to the improvement of the technique. Further study and experiments are considered to be done towards an improved one capable of the measurement of the stinging force information and giving a more satisfactory teaching and evaluation for acupuncture training.

Acknowledgments

This research was done with the financial support from the JSPS Grant-in-Aid for Scientific Research(C).

References

1. Mori, H.: Initiation of acupuncture, pp. 8–14. IDO-NO-NIPPON SHA INC. (1971) (in japanese)
2. Oriental Medicine College Association: Textbook writing subcommittee, Outline of meridian and acu-points, pp. 4–12. IDO-NO-NIPPON SHA INC. (1992) (in japanese)
3. Meiji University of Oriental Medicine, http://www.meiji-u.ac.jp/
4. Sugiyama, I.: Manual of acupuncture, pp.13–21. Gensosha, Inc. (2003) (in japanese)
5. Chen, L., Atsumi, H., Fujimoto, H.: A computer training system for acupuncture with force feedback. In: Proceedings of the First International Conference on Complex Medical Engineering, pp. 245–248 (2005)
6. Chen, L., Natsuaki, R., Atsumi, H., Shoda, A., Yagihashi, M., Fujimoto, H.: Development of an Acupuncture Educational Training System. In: Proceedings of Complex Medical Engineering, CME 2006, pp. 102–105 (2006) (in japanese)

7. Kanehira, R., Shoda, A., Yagihashi, M., Narita, H., Fujimoto, H.: Development of an acupuncture training system using virtual reality technology. In: Proceedings of 5th FSKD, pp. 665–668. IEEE Press, Los Alamitos (2008)
8. Kanehira, R., Yang, W., Tateishi, M., Yagihashi, M., Narita, H., Fujimoto, H.: Insertion angle teaching for an acupuncture training system. In: Proceedings of CSEDU 2009, pp. 281–284. IEEE Press, Los Alamitos (2009)
9. Chen, L., Atsumi, H., Yagihashi, M., Mizuno, F., Narita, H., Fujimoto, H.: Basic experiment for analysis of acupuncture technique. In: Proceedings of 6th EUROSIM, pp. 1–6. ELES Press (2007)
10. Kanehira, R., Yang, W., Shoda, A., Narita, H., Fujimoto, H.: Indexing of insertion speed for acupuncture training system. In: Proceedings of HCI 2009, pp. 692–696. IEEE Press, Los Alamitos (2009)
11. Kanehira, R., Yang, W., Narita, H., Shoda, A., Fujimoto, H.: Insertion training with computer acupuncture education system. In: Proceedings of 17th International Conference on Computers in Education, pp. 41–45 (2009)

Classifying Motor Imagery EEG Signals by Iterative Channel Elimination according to Compound Weight

Lin He, Zhenghui Gu, Yuanqing Li, and Zhuliang Yu

South China University of Technology, College of Automation Science and Engineering,
Wushan R.D. 384, Guangzhou 510640, China
{helin,zhgu,auyqli,zlyu}@scut.edu.cn

Abstract. There often exist redundant channels in EEG signal collection which deteriorate the classification accuracy. In this paper, a classification method which can deal with redundant channels, as well as redundant CSP features, is presented for motor imagery task. Our method utilizes CSP filter and margin maximization with linear programming to update a compound weight that enables iterative channel elimination and the update of the following linear classification. Theoretical analysis and experimental results show the effectiveness of our method to solve redundancy of channels and CSP features simultaneously when classifying motor imagery EEG data.

Keywords: Motor imagery, compound weight, CSP feature, channel elimination, linear programming.

1 Introduction

Brain computer interface (BCI) allows an individual to send messages or commands to the external world, without passing through the brain's normal motor output pathways of peripheral nerves and muscles [1]. Several types of BCI system have been developed so far, one of which is Motor imagery based BCI utilizing electroencephalogram (EEG) signal. Related studies have showed that when one perform motor imagination, his mu and beta rhythms are found to reveal event-related synchronization and desynchronization (ERS/ERD) over sensorimotor cortex just like when he actually does the motor tasks [1]. Common spatial pattern (CSP) is a highly successful and commonly used method for feature extraction in motor imagery EEG signals[1][2]. It searches optimal spatial projection for discriminate ERD/ERS topologies in different tasks. However, there are some problems when we apply CSP feature for classification. Motor imagery for a specific task occurs within a restricted region in brain. Hence, it is a usual case that not all channels contribute to classification in real BCI systems. On the other hand, not all the CSP features, the number of which is equal to that of channels, are beneficial to discrimination.

This paper presents a classification method by iterative channel elimination with compound weights which can deal with the redundant of the channels and CSP features simultaneously. It can be done robustly in the absence of a prior knowledge about the spatial distribution of brain activity and the number of CSP features. The results of experiment verify the effectiveness of this method.

F.L. Wang et al. (Eds.): AICI 2010, Part II, LNAI 6320, pp. 71–78, 2010.

2 CSP Feature Extraction

2.1 CSP Feature

CSP feature maximizes the difference of variances of the filtered EEG signals in two different classes [1][3]. Let $C \times C$ matrix $\mathbf{\Gamma}_1$ and $\mathbf{\Gamma}_2$ be covariance matrices corresponding to two classes of C channels EEG data. Based on the symmetry of these two matrices, the following equation can be deduced [3]

$$(\mathbf{U\Lambda}^{-\frac{1}{2}}\mathbf{V})^{T}(\mathbf{\Gamma}_1 + \mathbf{\Gamma}_2)\mathbf{U\Lambda}^{-\frac{1}{2}}\mathbf{V} = \mathbf{I} \tag{1}$$

where $\mathbf{U\Lambda}^{-\frac{1}{2}}$ is the whiten transforming matrix corresponding to $\mathbf{\Gamma}_1 + \mathbf{\Gamma}_2$ with its first row being non-negative, $\mathbf{V}$ is the common eigenvector matrix of $(\mathbf{U\Lambda}^{-\frac{1}{2}})^{T}\mathbf{\Gamma}_1(\mathbf{U\Lambda}^{-\frac{1}{2}})$ and $(\mathbf{U\Lambda}^{-\frac{1}{2}})^{T}\mathbf{\Gamma}_1(\mathbf{U\Lambda}^{-\frac{1}{2}})$. For the test EEG data $\mathbf{X} \in \mathbf{R}^{C \times M}$ where M is the number of test samples, we obtain the CSP feature vector of $\mathbf{X}$ as

$$\mathbf{x}_{csp} = \frac{diag((\mathbf{U\Lambda}^{-\frac{1}{2}}\mathbf{V})^{T}\mathbf{X}\mathbf{X}^{T}(\mathbf{U\Lambda}^{-\frac{1}{2}}\mathbf{V}))}{sum(diag((\mathbf{U\Lambda}^{-\frac{1}{2}}\mathbf{V})^{T}\mathbf{X}\mathbf{X}^{T}(\mathbf{U\Lambda}^{-\frac{1}{2}}\mathbf{V})))} \tag{2}$$

In order to make the distribution of CSP normal, we can transform $\mathbf{x}_{csp}$ to logarithmic value.

CSP feature extraction can also be explained in the framework of Rayleigh coefficient maximization [3], i.e.

$$\max J(\mathbf{w}) = \frac{\mathbf{w}^{T}(\mathbf{\Gamma}_1 - \mathbf{\Gamma}_2)\mathbf{w}}{\mathbf{w}^{T}(\mathbf{\Gamma}_1 + \mathbf{\Gamma}_2)\mathbf{w}} \tag{3}$$

where J is value of the Rayleigh coefficient. The solution of (3) can be obtained by solving the following generalized eigen problem

$$(\mathbf{\Gamma}_1 - \mathbf{\Gamma}_2)\mathbf{w} = \lambda(\mathbf{\Gamma}_1 + \mathbf{\Gamma}_2)\mathbf{w} \tag{4}$$

Where λ is the generalized eigenvalue.

2.2 Singularity from CAR Preprocessing in CSP Feature Extraction

Common average reference (CAR) is an effective preprocessing method for EEG classification [3], which is utilized to remove artifact and noise. Let $\mathbf{X} = (\mathbf{x}_1^{T}, \mathbf{x}_2^{T}, ..., \mathbf{x}_C^{T}) \in \mathbf{R}^{C \times M}$ and $\mathbf{Y} = (\mathbf{y}_1^{T}, \mathbf{y}_2^{T}, ..., \mathbf{y}_C^{T}) \in \mathbf{R}^{C \times M}$ represent the EEG signal and CAR processed EEG signal, respectively, we have

$$\sum_{i=1}^{C} \mathbf{y}_i = \sum_{i=1}^{C} (\mathbf{x}_i - \frac{1}{C} \sum_{j=1}^{C} \mathbf{x}_j) = 0 \tag{5}$$

i.e., rows of $\mathbf{Y}$ is linear dependent. Furthermore, we can obtain that the row rank of $\mathbf{Y}$ is $C-1$ easily.

Usually, another preprocessing step before CSP filtering is frequency filtering which leads to extraction of component related to the subject's intent. If assuming the this filtering corresponds to a linear transformation, we have

$$Rank_{col}(\mathbf{YF}) \leq \min(Rank_{col}(\mathbf{Y}), Rank_{col}(\mathbf{F})) < C \tag{6}$$

where $Rank_{col}(\cdot)$ denotes the column rank of a matrix. We can have $Rank_{col}(\mathbf{YF}) = C-1$ easily. Accordingly, if we utilize the data processed with CAR and frequency filtering in CSP filtering, $\mathbf{\Gamma}_1 + \mathbf{\Gamma}_2$ is singular which leads to computation instability. To avoid this problem, we eliminate a channel with low discriminability for different class before CSP filtering.

3   Classification with Iterative Channel Elimination

CSP features are directly related to classification, while EEG signals from C channels are not directly. However, the channel redundancy of EEG signals will lead to deviation of the CSP features. In order to depict the channel redundancies relative to classification, we quantify the channel importance for classification as shown in subsection 3.1.

3.1   Compound Weight Evaluating Channel Importance

In the formulation of CSP feature, $M \times M$ matrix $\mathbf{U\Lambda}^{-\frac{1}{2}}\mathbf{V}$ corresponds to M spatial filters mapping preprocessed data to a M dimension pattern space. In fact, a spatial filter represents a group of weights which presents the contribution of data of every channel to the corresponding CSP feature. Hence, contributions of data from all channels relative to CSP feature vector can be measured by

$$\mathbf{D}_{CSP} = \mathbf{U\Lambda}^{-\frac{1}{2}}\mathbf{V} \tag{7}$$

Let $\mathbf{w}_{CSP}$ be the weight vector of a certain linear classifier with respect to CSP features, we can quantify the contributions of all channels to this classifier as compound weights defined by

$$\mathbf{D}_{chan} = \left| \mathbf{D}_{CSP}\mathbf{w}_{CSP} \right| = \left| \mathbf{U\Lambda}^{-\frac{1}{2}}\mathbf{V}\mathbf{w}_{CSP} \right| \tag{8}$$

where $| \, . \, |$ denotes calculating the absolute values of each entry of the vector. The value of the ith entry of $\mathbf{D}_{chan}$ measures the contribution of data from ith channel to the class label.

3.2 Formulation of Removing Channel Redundancy and CSP Feature Redundancy

Minimizing zero norm is utilized to eliminate the redundancy of channels and that of CSP features in our method. If we consider the channel importance evaluated by compound weight and adopt linear classifier with bounded empirical risk, removing the redundancies of channels and that of CSP features is an problem of multi-objective optimization [5] as follows

$$min \quad \| \mathbf{D}_{chan} \|_0, \quad \|\mathbf{w}_{CSP}\|_0 + \alpha \sum_{i=1}^{N} \xi_i \tag{9}$$

$$s.t. \quad y_i (\mathbf{w}_{CSP} \mathbf{x}_{CSP} + b) \geq 1 - \xi_i \quad (\xi_i \geq 0, i = 1, 2, ..., N) \tag{10}$$

$$(\mathbf{\Gamma}_1 - \mathbf{\Gamma}_2) \mathbf{w}_{chan,i} = \lambda_i (\mathbf{\Gamma}_1 + \mathbf{\Gamma}_2) \mathbf{w}_{chan,i} \quad (i = 1, 2, ..., C) \tag{11}$$

$$\mathbf{D}_{chan} = \mathbf{U} \mathbf{\Lambda}^{-\frac{1}{2}} \mathbf{V} \mathbf{w}_{CSP} \quad (\mathbf{w}_{CSP} = (\mathbf{w}_{chan,1}, \mathbf{w}_{chan,2}, ..., \mathbf{w}_{chan,C})) \tag{12}$$

where α is the regularization parameter, N is the number of CSP samples.

Unfortunately, solving zero norm minimization is usually NP hard [4] and a convex approximation can be introduced via replacing the zero norm with one norm of the weight [4]. Such approximation transforms $\|\mathbf{w}_{CSP}\|_0 + \alpha \sum_{i=1}^{N} \xi_i$ in (9) and (10) into a procedure of margin maximization with linear programming [6][7] as follows

$$\begin{aligned} \min_{\mathbf{w},b} \quad & \|\mathbf{w}\|_1 + \alpha \sum_{i=1}^{N} \xi_i \\ s.t. \quad & y_i (\mathbf{w}^T \mathbf{x}_i + b) \geq 1 - \xi_i \\ & \xi_i \geq 0, i = 1, 2, ..., N \end{aligned} \tag{13}$$

On the other hand, the optimization problem mentioned in (9)-(12) is a problem of multi-objective optimization and $\|\mathbf{w}_{CSP}\|_0$ is closely related to $\| \mathbf{D}_{chan} \|_0$. Therefore, such an optimization problem is not easy or direct to solve even if (13) is adopted. Alternatively, we conduct an iterative procedure involving updating of a compound weight based and margin maximization with linear programming to approach suboptimal solution of this optimization problem.

3.3 Algorithm

Our iterative algorithm is as follows
Step 1 Preprocessing:
         Step 1.1 CAR filtering data $\mathbf{X}$ from all N channel and eliminating a channel whose *a priori* discriminability is small;
         Step 1.2 Band-pass filtering;

Step 2 Spatial filter and CSP feature update:

Step 2.1 Calculate spatial filter matrix $\mathbf{U\Lambda}^{-\frac{1}{2}}\mathbf{V} = [\mathbf{s}_1, \mathbf{s}_2, ..., \mathbf{s}_{N_R}]$ in (1) utilizing data from available N_R channels;

Step 2.2 Calculate CSP features $\mathbf{x}_{CSP} = (\mathbf{x}_{CSP,1}, ..., \mathbf{x}_{CSP,N_R})$ utilizing (2);

Step 3 CSP feature normalization;

Step 4 Compound weight update:

Step 4.1 Weight-of-CSP-feature update: Calculate the weight of CSP features through linear programming formulated in (14). The regularization parameter α is determined by cross validation;

Step 4.2 Calculate the absolute value of the sum of N_R spatial filters weighted by Weight-of-CSP-feature as shown in (9);

Step 5 Eliminate N_E channels whose corresponding compound weights are smallest in N_R channels. The number of left channels is updated as N_R;

Step 6 If $|N_R - N_P| \le \gamma$, where N_P is the channels number corresponding to the optimal channel subset determined via cross-validation and γ is a predefined threshold, then return to step 2. Otherwise, end the iteration;

4 Data Analysis

In our data analysis, we use the data set IVa of BCI competition III [3] to evaluate our algorithm. For each subject, the collected EEG signals is from 118 channels and for two class task. EEG signals of subject "al" and "aw" in mu rhythm is used. The eliminated channel in preprocessing steps 1.2 mention in subsection 3.4 is channel I2.

For EEG data of subject "al", there are 224 trials as training set and 56 trials as test set. The parameter α in (14) and the eliminated channels 117- N_P were determined by 5-fold cross validation as 0.081 and 78, respectively. Fig. 1 shows the average classification accuracies versus the different number of eliminated channel over the 5 folds on training set when α is set as 0.081. From this figure, the optimal number of channels to be eliminated is 78, i.e. the remaining 39 channels are most effective to the classification. Fig. 2 shows the classification accuracies versus the different number of eliminated channel on test set with the α =0.081, classification accuracy achieve 0.9821 when the number of selected channels is 39. Fig. 3 illustrates the corresponding 39 most effective channels marked by circles.

For EEG data of subject "aw", there are 56 trials as training set and 224 trials as test set. The parameter α and the number of eliminated channels are determined by 5-fold cross validation are 0.071 and 108, respectively. Fig. 4 shows result of cross validation. Fig. 5 shows the result on test set with selected parameters, classification accuracy achieves 0.8437. Fig. 6 illustrates 9 most effective channels.

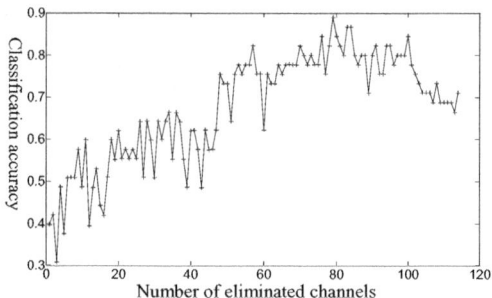

Fig. 1. Average classification accuracies versus the different number of eliminated channel over the 5 folds on training set for subject al

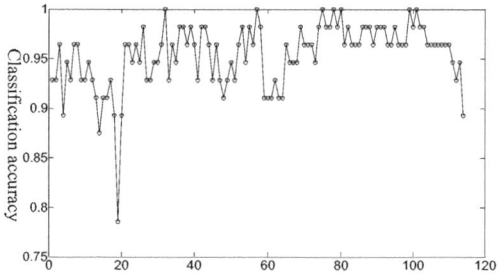

Fig. 2. Classification accuracies versus the different number of eliminated channel with the selected parameters for subject al

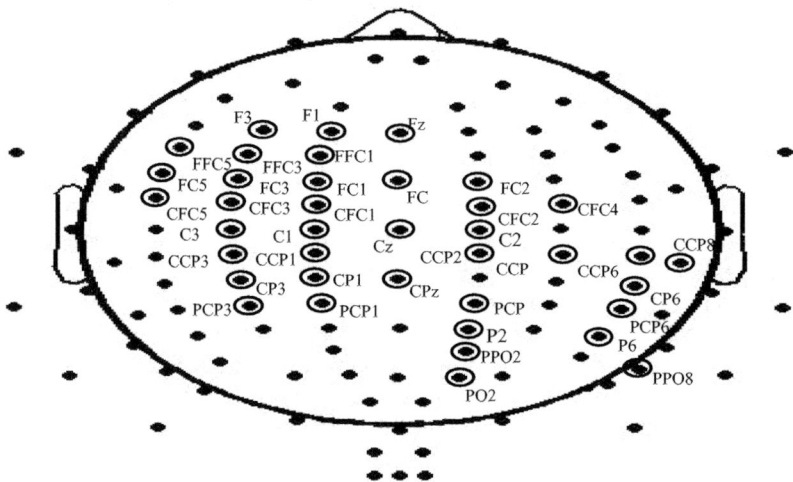

Fig. 3. Most effective channel subset for subject al

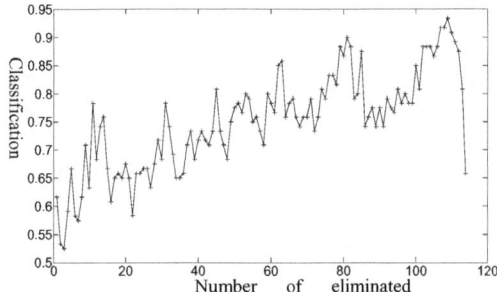

Fig. 4. Classification accuracies versus the different numbers of eliminated channel over the 5 folds on training set for subject aw

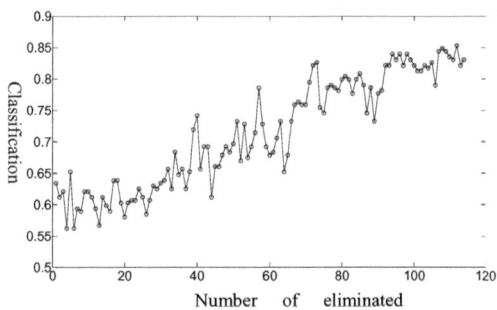

Fig. 5. Classification accuracies versus the different numbers of eliminated channels with the selected parameters for subject aw

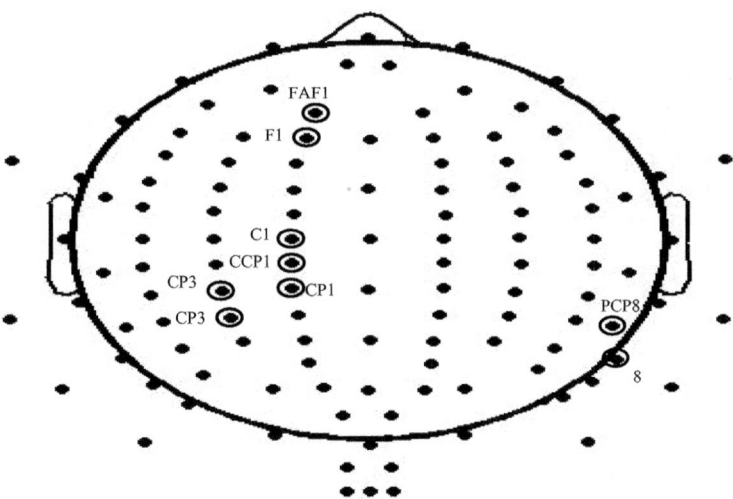

Fig. 6. Most effective channel subset for subject aw

5 Conclusion

In this paper, a classification method which can deal with redundant channels, as well as redundant CSP features, is presented for motor imagery task. Our method utilizes CSP filters and margin maximization with linear programming to update a compound weight that enables iterative channel elimination and the updating of the following linear classifying. Theoretical analysis and experimental results show the effectiveness of our method for classifying motor imagery EEG data while there are redundancy of channels and CSP features.

Acknowledgments. This work is supported by National Nature Science Foundation of China under Grant 60825306 and 60802068, Specialized Research Foundation for the Doctoral Program of Higher Education of China under Grant 200805611063 and 20090172120039, and Guangdong Nature Science Foundation under Grant 9251064101000012, 8451064101000498 and 9451064101002925, the Program for New Century Excellent Talents in University under Grants NCET-10-0370, the Fundamental Research Funds for the Central Universities, SCUT under Grants 2009ZZ0055.

References

1. Wu, W., Gao, X.R., Hong, B., et al.: Classifying Single-Trail EEG During Motor Imagery by Iterative Spatio-Spectral Patterns Learning (ISSPL). IEEE Trans. on Biomedical Engineering 55(6), 1733–1743 (2008)
2. Lal, T.N., Schroder, M., Hinterberger, T., et al.: Support Vector Channel Selection in BCI. IEEE Trans. on Biomedical Engineering 51(6), 1003–1010 (2004)
3. Li, Y.Q., Guan, C.T.: Joint Feature Re-extraction and Classification Using an Iteration. Machine Learning 71, 33–53 (2008)
4. Li, Y.Q., Cichocki, A., Amari, S.: Analysis of Sparse Representation and Blind Source Separation. Neural Computation 16(6), 1193–1234 (2004)
5. Boyd, S., Vandenberghe, L.: Convex Optimization. Cambridge Press, London (2004)
6. Zhu, J., Rosset, S., Hastie, T., Tibshirani, R.: 1-norm Support Vector Machines. In: NIPS, pp. 49–56 (2004)
7. Guo, G.D., Dyer, C.R.: Simultaneous Feature Selection and Classifier Training via Linear Programming: A Case Study for Face Expression Recognition. In: CVPR, vol. 1, pp. 346–352 (2003)

Automatic Reference Selection for Quantitative EEG Component Interpretation: Cross Spectrum Analysis Based on Bipolar EEG

Bei Wang[1], Xingyu Wang[1], Akio Ikeda[2], Takashi Nagamine[3], Hiroshi Shibasaki[4], Takenao Sugi[5], and Masatoshi Nakamura[6]

[1] Key Laboratory of Advanced Control and Optimization for Chemical Processes, Ministry of Education, School of Information Science and Engineering, East China University of Science and Technology, Shanghai 200237, China
beiwang@ecust.edu.cn, xywang@ecust.edu.cn
[2] Department of Neurology, Kyoto University, Kyoto 606-8501, Japan
akio@kuhp.kyoto-u.ac.jp
[3] Department of System Neuroscience, Sapporo Medical University, Hokkaido 060-8556, Japan
nagamine@sapmed.ac.jp
[4] Takeda General Hospital, Kyoto 601-1495, Japan
shib@kuhp.kyoto-u.ac.jp
[5] Department of Electrical and Electronic Engineering, Saga University, Saga 840-8502, Japan
sugi@cc.saga-u.ac.jp
[6] Research Institute of Systems Control Institute for Advanced Research and Education, Saga University, Saga 840-0047, Japan
nakamura@cc.saga-u.ac.jp

Abstract. Automatic Electroencephalography (EEG) interpretation system had been developed as an important tool for the inspection of brain diseases. In this study, an automatic reference selection technique was developed to obtain the appropriate derivation for EEG components interpretation. The cross spectrum of bipolar EEG was adopted to detect the phase reversal among the EEG channels covering the scalp of head. Appropriate reference was selected automatically based on the detected phase reversal. Finally, a referential derivation was constructed. The distribution of EEG components was analyzed based on the constructed referential derivation to evaluate the effectiveness of selected reference for quantitative EEG component interpretation.

Keywords: Bipolar EEG, Cross spectrum, Phase reversal, Reference selection, Quantitative interpretation.

1 Introduction

Electroencephalography (EEG) is the recording of electrical activity along the scalp produced by the neurons within the brain. EEG has important diagnostic applications

F.L. Wang et al. (Eds.): AICI 2010, Part II, LNAI 6320, pp. 79–86, 2010.

in brain diseases. In clinics, short term recording of background EEG was adopted for visual inspection to evaluate the abnormalities. Automatic EEG interpretation technique had been developed for decades to free the clinicians from the laborious work of visual inspection [1]-[3]. An automatic integrative interpretation system of awake background EEG according to the Electroencephalographers (EEGer)' knowledge had been developed by some of the authors and been successfully applied in real clinics [4] [5].

With the development of recording technique, digital EEG record was popularly used instead of analog EEG record. Previously, EEGer inspected the EEG by combining ear-lobe referential derivation and bipolar derivation. Currently, the usage of digital EEG record made EEGer having possibilities to inspect the EEG by any derivation. The advantages of digital EEG recording technique were considered to be efficiently integrated with the automatic interpretation system for modern clinical application. Therefore, 'which the appropriate reference is' became a hot topic in the field of clinical neurophysiology.

In this study, we were investigating on the appropriate reference to construct the EEG derivation adaptively to the actual EEG data. An automatic reference selection technique was developed. The ultimate purpose was to improve the accuracy of automatic quantitative EEG interpretation system for clinical application. Several parameters were calculated according to the cross spectrum of bipolar EEG to identify the phase reversal among the EEG channels covering the scalp of head. The appropriate reference was determined based on the detected phase reversal. The distribution of EEG components was analyzed by using the constructed new referential derivation. The result was compared with the ear-lobe referential EEG to evaluate the effectiveness of selected reference for quantitative EEG component interpretation.

2 Method

2.1 Data Acquisition

The EEG data was recorded at Kyoto University, Japan. Each data included 19 EEG channels at Fp_1, F_3, C_3, P_3, O_1, Fp_2, F_4, C_4, P_4, O_2, F_7, T_3, T_5, F_8, T_4, T_6, F_Z, C_Z and P_Z, based on International 10-20 System. The electrodes at the two ear-lobes were A_1 and A_2. The recording was done with the time constant of 0.3 s, the high cut filter of 120 Hz and a sensitivity of 0.5 cm/50μV. The sampling rate was 100 Hz for all the channels. The long EEG record was divided into consecutive segments of 5 s long each for automatic interpretation.

2.2 Cross Spectrum of Bipolar EEG

The flowchart of whole technique was illustrated in Fig. 1. The 5 s long EEG waveforms under bipolar derivations were obtained by the differences of the amplitude of two conjoint electrodes. The cross spectrums in horizontal and vertical direction were obtained for one electrode based on bipolar EEG. The peak frequency was detected firstly in each cross spectrum. Secondly, coherence and phase were calculated around the peak frequency. Finally, criteria were defined to compare the obtained parameters with thresholds,

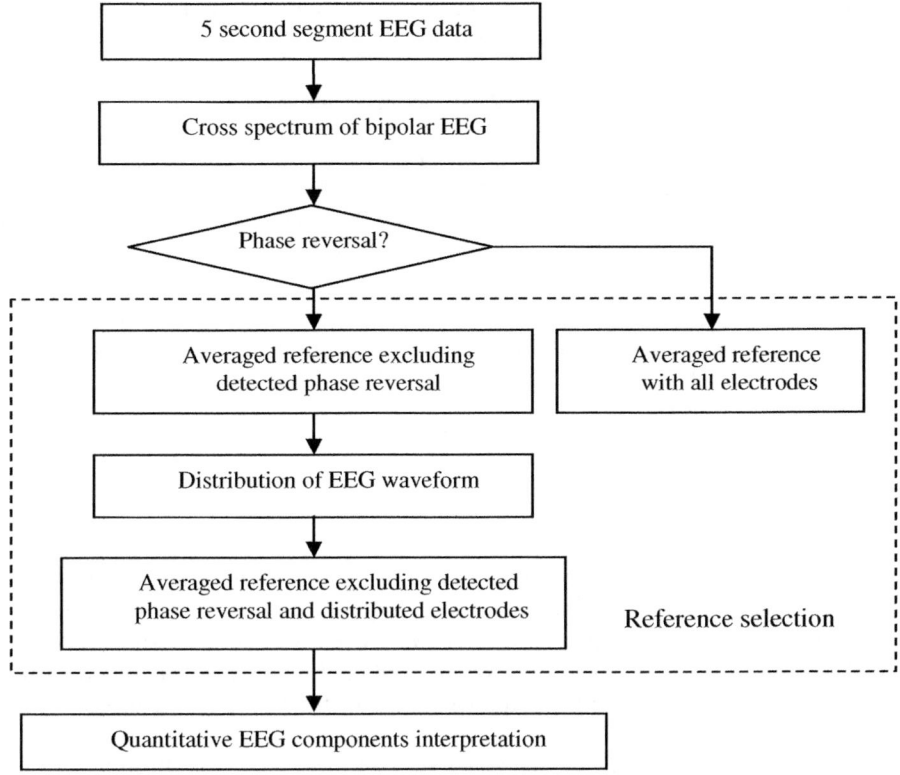

Fig. 1. Flow chart

$$\begin{cases} \mid f_1 - f_2 \mid < 0.5 Hz \\ r_1 > 0.7, r_2 > 0.7 \\ \mid \phi_1 \mid > 150°, \mid \phi_2 \mid > 150° \end{cases} \qquad (1)$$

where the footnote of 1 and 2 indicated the two cross spectrums. When all of the three criteria were satisfied, phase reversal was detected at the central electrode of two cross spectrums.

2.3 Cross Spectrum of Bipolar EEG

Appropriate derivation was referred to the referential derivation with common reference. An iterative method was adopted to find out the distributed electrodes. The marked block in Fig. 1 illustrated the algorithm of automatic reference selection.

The phase reversal result was firstly checked. When the phase reversal was detected, the related electrodes were determined as focal area. A common reference was defined by the average of all the electrodes besides focal electrode. Otherwise, the common reference was the average of all the electrodes. Secondly, the distribution of peak frequency components was analyzed. The electrodes which had higher amplitude were determined as the distributed area. Finally, the electrodes selected to make the common reference were determined by the average of the remainder electrodes excluding the focal and distributed electrodes.

2.4 Quantitative EEG Components Interpretation

Background EEG was mainly interpreted by consisted frequency components (δ: 0.5-4 Hz; θ: 4-8 Hz; α: 8-13 Hz; β: 13-25 Hz). The distribution of those frequency components was evaluated quantitatively by the amplitude. The amplitude of the frequency components around the peak frequency was calculated,

$$A = 4\sqrt{S} \tag{2}$$

where S was the amount of the power. The definition of amplitude was based on Markov EEG amplitude model.

3 Results

3.1 Phase Reversal Detection

The EEG recording of one subject was analyzed in detail. The subject was a patient in Kyoto Hospital suffered by brain diseases. The skull of this subject was also partially defected at the right hemisphere. The recorded EEG waveforms were inspected by a qualified EEGer. The visual inspection showed continuous rhythmic and/or irregular slow waves on the right hemisphere. The shape of the irregular waveform was sharp and the amplitude was high.

The cross spectrum utilized for phase reversal detection was illustrated in Fig. 2. The bipolar EEG waveforms around T_4 were given. In Fig. 2, the above two trails were the EEG waveforms under bipolar derivation in vertical direction. Another two trails were under bipolar derivation in horizontal direction.

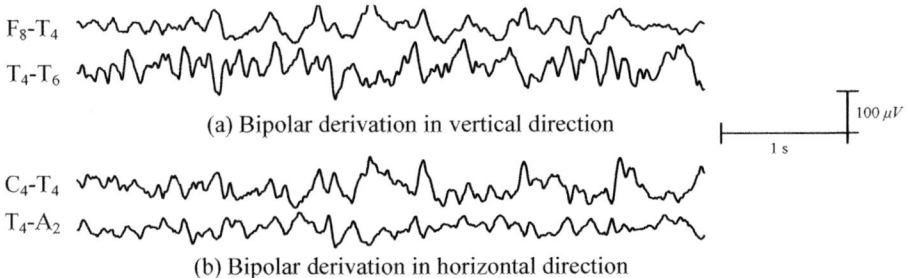

Fig. 2. Bipolar EEGs related to T4

The phase reversal in the original bipolar EEG data can be observed through the waveforms. In the vertical direction, the waveform shape in F_8-T_4 and T_4-T_6 contained some slow components which showed reversed phase. In the horizontal direction, similar reversed shape can be observed.

Table 1. Parameters for focus estimation

Cross spectrum	Peak	Coherence	Phase
C_4-T_4, T_4-A_2	1.95 Hz	0.96	-161.6 °
F_8-T_4, T_4-T_6	1.95 Hz	0.85	-156.2 °

In Table 1, the related parameters of two obtained cross spectrum were given. The first column indicated the bipolar EEGs for cross spectrum analysis. The parameter values were shown in the other columns. The detected peaks in both cross spectrum were the same. The parameters values were satisfied with the criteria. Finally, phase reversal was detected at T_4.

3.2 Quantitative EEG Component Interpretation

For this subject, the focal area was determined at T_4 according to the phase reversal result. Another two electrodes F_8 and T_6 near T_4 were determined as the distributed area. Those electrodes were excluded to obtain the common average reference for EEG component interpretation.

The quantitative EEG component interpretation was processed under the new referential derivation by comparing with the ear-lobe referential derivation in Fig. 3 and Fig. 4. The EEG waveforms were shown in (a) and the amplitudes of peak frequency for all the channels were given in (b).

In Fig. 3, the EEG waveform was under the ear-lobe referential derivation. It was difficult to identify the irregular slow wave. The ear-lobe A_2 was activated. In (a), all the channel data with A_2 reference were contaminated with artifacts of ear-lobe

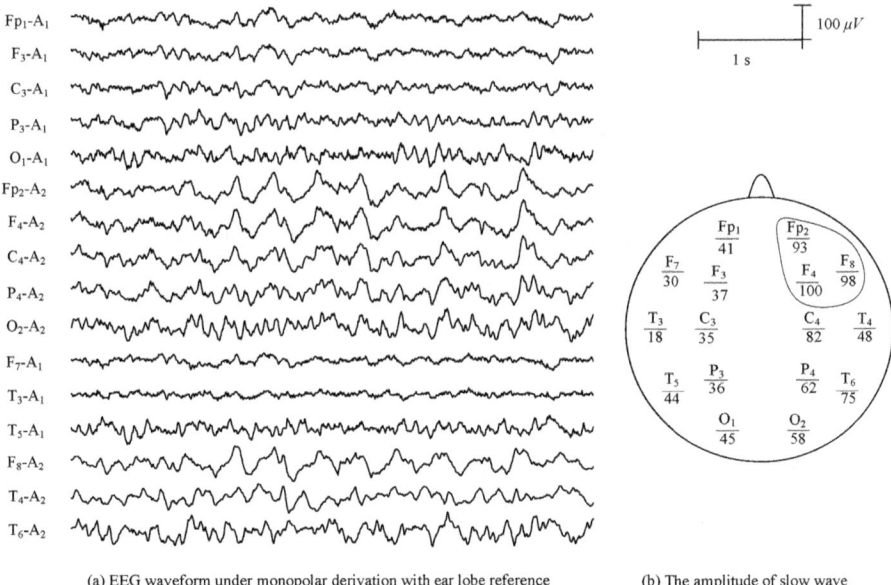

(a) EEG waveform under monopolar derivation with ear lobe reference   (b) The amplitude of slow wave

Fig. 3. Ear-lobe referential EEG and the distribution of slow wave

activation. Similar shape can be observed in those channels. The related amplitude of slow wave component was given in (b). Through the value of amplitudes, Fp_2, F_4 and F_8 had rather large amplitude. The evaluation result was inconsistent with the visual inspection. Therefore, the artifact of ear-lobe activation affected to find out the correct distribution of EEG components for quantitative interpretation.

In Fig. 4, the EEG waveform was under the new referential derivation. Through the time series in (a), the ear-lobe artifact was disappeared. There were high voltage sharp slow wave occurred in the anterior area. The related amplitude of slow wave component was calculated and shown in (b). The maximum value was at T_4. The electrodes F_8 and T_6 near T_4 were also higher than other electrodes. It can be concluded that there were irregular slow wave occurred at the area which was marked in (b). The result of quantitative interpretation of slow wave was consistent with the visual inspection. Therefore, the new constructed referential derivation with appropriate selected reference can avoid the artifact and obtain correct distribution of EEG components.

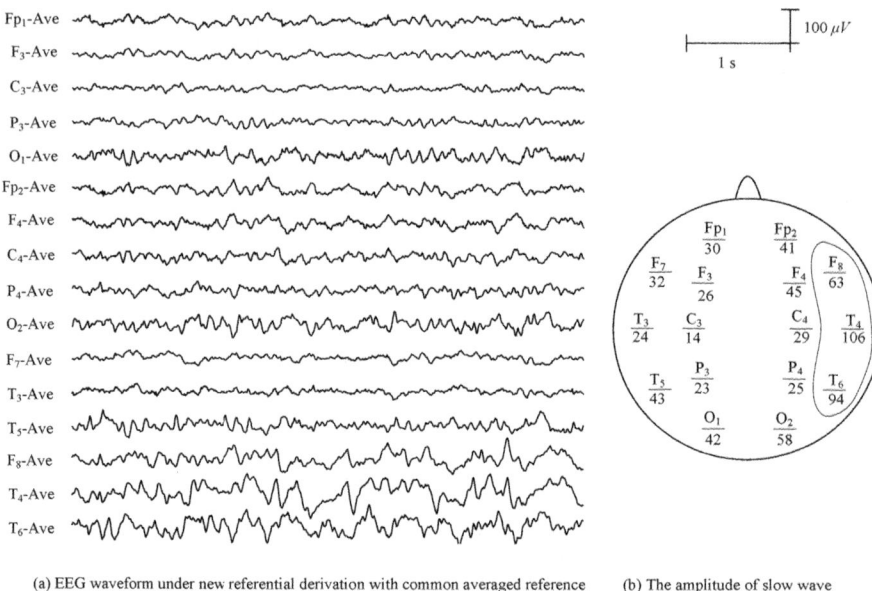

(a) EEG waveform under new referential derivation with common averaged reference   (b) The amplitude of slow wave

Fig. 4. New referential EEG and the distribution of slow wave

4   Discussion

4.1   Bipolar EEG

Ear-lobe referential derivation with ear-lobe reference was usually adopted to interpret the distribution of EEG components. The EEG data of test subject was contaminated by ear-lobe activation artifact. The Ear-lobe referential EEG data were affected with artifacts. Additionally, the partially defected skull caused large amplitude in the right hemisphere. Those increased the difficulty for correct inspection of affected area by brain diseases. Mis-interpretation was happen for this subject by using Ear-lobe referential derivation. It was necessary to find out an appropriate reference to obtain the correct distribution of EEG components.

Bipolar derivation was recorded by the difference between two conjoint electrodes. It was adopted to inspect the phase reversal. In this study, the phase reversal analysis result according to the cross spectrum of bipolar EEG was utilized to determine the appropriate common reference. The constructed new referential derivation can avoid the artifact contamination problem. Even for the subject with partial defect of skull, it can obtain the correct distribution of EEG components for quantitative interpretation.

4.2 Automatic Quantitative EEG Interpretation

The developed automatic integrative interpretation system by some of the authors for awake background EEG had been used for real clinical application for years. The performance of the automatic interpretation system had been improved gradually by using appropriate technique dealing with actual problem in real clinics.

In this study, the appropriate reference selection technique was developed based on the cross spectrum of bipolar EEG. The main purpose of bipolar EEG was to improve the accuracy of automatic quantitative interpretation. An iterative method was utilized in current technique to be excluded the electrodes in focal and distributed area. The constructed new derivation under averaged reference highlighted the distributed channels which were caused by brain diseases. The automatic quantitative EEG component interpretation result was consistent with the visual inspection by EEGer. The developed technique was usable for the automatic EEG interpretation system.

4.3 Clinical Application

With the development of digital EEG recording technique, the EEG waveforms under different derivation can be obtained easily. The EEG recording from real clinics may contained complex factors from internal (personal conditions, such as diseases) and external sides (environment conditions, such as artifacts). Therefore, the appropriate reference selection technique which was helpful for clinical inspection would be an important topic for investigation.

The developed technique has application significance for real clinics. It avoided the artifact contamination problem from external environment and highlighted the affected area caused by internal diseases. For further study, the investigation on more data from real clinics was important to evaluate the effectiveness of presented automatic reference selection technique.

5 Conclusion

An automatic reference selection technique according to the cross spectrum of bipolar EEG was presented. The developed technique constructed an averaged referential derivation which was adaptive to the focal and distributed area related to brain diseases. It improved the performance of automatic EEG interpretation system for clinical application.

Acknowledgments. This study is supported by Nation Nature Science Foundation of China 60674089, Shanghai Leading Academic Discipline Project B504, and Fundamental Research Funds for the Central Universities WH0914028.

References

1. Cooley, J.W., Tukey, J.W.: An algorithm for the machine calculation of complex Fourier series. Math. Comput. 19, 297–301 (1965)
2. Gotman, J.: Practical use of computer-assisted EEG interpretation in epilepsy. J. Clin. Neurophysiol. 2, 251–265 (1985)
3. Lopes da Silva, F.: A critical review of clinical applications of topographic mapping of brain potentials. J. Clin. Neurophysiol. 7, 535–551 (1990)
4. Nakamura, M., Shibasaki, H., Imajoh, K., Nishida, S., Neshige, R., Ikeda, A.: Automatic EEG interpretation: a new computer-assisted system for the automatic integrative interpretation of awake background EEG. Electroenceph. Clin. Neurophysiol. 82, 423–431 (1992)
5. Nakamura, M., Sugi, T., Ikeda, A., Kakigi, R., Shibasaki, H.: Clinical application of automatic integrative interpretation of awake background EEG: quantitative interpretation, report making, and detection of artifacts and reduced vigilance level. Electroenceph. Clin. Neurophysiol. 98, 103–112 (1996)

Mixed Numerical Integral Algorithm for Deformation Simulation of Soft Tissues

Hui Liang[*] and Ming Yong Shi

Communication University of China, Beijing, China
lianghui@cuc.edu.cn

Abstract. A novel mixed numerical integral algorithm is proposed for the deformation simulation of soft tissues in virtual surgery system. First, a Mass-Spring System is built as the soft tissue's kinetic model. And then, a mixed numerical integral algorithm is derived to solve the model's deformation differential equations. At the end of the paper, results are presented as examples, which validate the effectiveness of our algorithm in improving simulation performance by reducing complexity and enhancing accuracy.

Keywords: virtual surgery system; deformation simulation; mixed numerical integral algorithm.

1 Introduction

To enhance the realism and immergence of the virtual operation environment, the accurate simulation for deformable soft tissues appears to be an essential element of a virtual surgery system. The Euler's method together with its modified methods and Runge-Kutta method are the most commonly used numerical integral methods in virtual surgery simulation. The Euler methods are simple methods of solving ODE (Ordinary Differential Equation), particularly suitable for quick programming because of their great simplicity, although their accuracy is not high. Runge-Kutta method is quite competitive for its very high accuracy, but with a higher computation complexity. We propose a novel mixed numerical integral algorithm by combining with Euler's method and Runge-Kutta method and using these two methods in different collision simulation phases respectively to improve the simulation performance by making a good balance between complexity and accuracy.

2 Related Work

2.1 Collision Detection Methods

Deformable collision detection is an essential component in interactive virtual surgery simulation. Hierarchy-bounding volume methods including the Axis-Aligned Bounding

---

[*] Supported by the Project of State Administration of Radio Film and Television (SARFT) under Grant No. 2007-07.

F.L. Wang et al. (Eds.): AICI 2010, Part II, LNAI 6320, pp. 87–97, 2010.

Box (AABB [1]), the Sphere-Bounding Box (SBB [2]) and the Oriented Bounding Box (OBB [3]), are commonly used in collision detection.

Typically for a simulated environment consisting of multiple moving objects, the collision detection techniques based on a hierarchy-bounding volumes representation of objects, separate the collision procedure in two phases: the "broad phase" where collision culling is performed to reduce the number of pair wise tests which are far from a possible collision, and the "narrow phase" where the pairs of objects in proximity are checked for collision.

2.2 Numerical Integral Algorithms

The physically-based deformable model of soft tissue results in a system of equations which cannot be solved analytically; therefore, a numerical integration method need to be used in virtual surgery simulation. The discretization of the deformable object by using the mechanical laws usually produces a system of ordinary differential equations that has to be solved numerically along time evolution [4].

Explicit integration methods are the simplest methods to solve the differential equations by using the system state information at current time step to calculate the future system state information at next time step. The examples of explicit integration methods are Euler, Midpoint, and Runge-Kutta method. The simulation error per step of the Euler's method is $o(h^2)$ which is proportional to h^2. The forth order of Runge-Kutta method (the classical Runge-Kutta method), an explicit four-step formula, is a popular method of integration to achieve a high accuracy but also with a high complexity, and its simulation error is $o(h^5)$.

3   Mixed Numerical Integral Algorithm for Soft Tissue Deformation Simulation

Since the implementation of efficient numerical integration method is the key for efficient simulation, our new mixed numerical integral algorithm tries to enhance the simulation realism by making a good balance between the simulation accuracy and computing complexity, and increases speed without sacrificing accuracy.

3.1   The Idea

As mentioned previously, a typical collision detection procedure consists of the "broad phase" and "narrow phase": one for quickly excluding the pair between which collision can not happened and the other for explicitly tests intersections between the rest pairs to identify accurate collisions.

By adopting a maybe not accurate enough but simple integration method-the Euler's method for example, in the "broad phase" through which there is no need to simulate in a precise manner, and a complex but more accurate integration method-the Runge-Kutta method for example, in the "narrow phase" where the complexity simulation is more crucial, we take both the advantages of the two commonly used integration methods and put forward the mixed numerical integral algorithm as follows:

The "broad phase" consists on descendant tests from the lower resolution (the root bounding volume of the hierarchical tree) to the higher representation of surface objects (the bounding volumes covering all possible colliding mesh facets). In this phase, large subsets of facets of the object surfaces that are far from a possible collision will be quickly discarded and the simulation accuracy seems not so essential. So we can simply use a large time step Euler's method to solve the deformation equations to reduce integration time and pursue the great efficiency and speed.

If once a bounding volume intersection at the higher resolution is found, the "narrow" phase explicitly tests intersections between the corresponding polygons to identify accurate collisions. As the slowly-varying phase in the simulation procedure, the "narrow" phase will introduce the corresponding collision response and then the virtual soft tissue deformation will happen, due to its interaction with the virtual surgical instruments, such as pulling, pressing, cutting and stretching. Compared with the first detection phase, in this accurate detection phase, the realism and accuracy of simulation is obviously more important, so we should implement a more precise method-such as the Runge-Kutta method, to achieve a higher accuracy.

On the basis of the analysis above, the mixed numerical integral algorithm would be concluded as follows:

- Step 1: Use Euler's method in the beginning of the virtual surgery simulation
- Step 2: Execute the "broad phase" detection circularly until collision happened and then enter Step3
- Step 3: Use classical Runge-Kutta method instead of Euler's method for the accuracy deformation simulation
- Step 4: When the instruments left soft tissues, reuse Euler's method instead of Runge-Kutta method

Repeat Step 1 to Step 4 for simulation integration until the whole simulation procedure finished.

3.2 Solution of the Mixed Numerical Integral Algorithm

In this section, we will build a Mass-Spring System as the kinetic deformable model for the virtual soft tissue and then give the derivation and solution of the mixed numerical integral algorithm for the model's deformation simulation.

Mass-Spring System for Soft Tissue

There are two commonly used methods as the kinetic model for deformable tissues in virtual surgery system: Finite Element Method (FEM) [5] and Mass-Spring System (MMS) [6]. In this paper, our motivation to use MMS as the kinetic model for deformation simulation is derived from the cognition that MMS is more efficient, simple and suitable over FEM for deforming bodies with large displacements and local elastic deformations [7~9].

We designed a triangular Mass-Spring model and its nodes, also the mass points, n_i, n_j and n_k, are connected by damped springs. The deformation of soft tissues is expressed through the compression and tensile between springs. And the damping forces are attached to both the mass points and the springs. Fig.1 presents two essential parts of

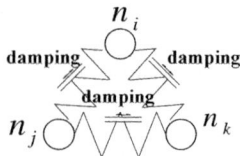

Fig. 1. Mass-Spring Model

the unit: the elastic equipment and the damper. The former generates elasticity force proportional to the alteration of the springs' length, and the latter engenders damping force proportional to the velocity of mass points.

The dynamics of the nodes in the Mass-Spring System is governed by the Newton's law of motion. The nodal displacement of the i th node due to the internal and external force is given by

$$m_i \mathbf{a}_i + \mathbf{f}_i^{\text{int}}(\mathbf{u}_i, \mathbf{v}_i) = \mathbf{f}_i^{\text{ext}} \tag{1}$$

Where m_i and $\mathbf{u}_i$ are, respectively, the mass and displacement of node i, $\mathbf{f}_i^{\text{int}}$ and $\mathbf{f}_i^{\text{ext}}$ are respectively the internal and external force. The acceleration vector of node i is calculated as $\mathbf{a}_i = \mathbf{u}_i''$ and velocity vector is $\mathbf{v}_i = \mathbf{u}_i'$.

The internal force $\mathbf{f}_i^{\text{int}}$ is obtained from the elasticity force $\mathbf{f}_i^s$ and damping force $\mathbf{f}_i^d$ when the Mass-Spring model deformation happens:

$$\mathbf{f}_i^{\text{int}} = \mathbf{f}_i^s + \mathbf{f}_i^d \tag{2}$$

The elasticity force $\mathbf{f}_i^s$

$$\mathbf{f}_i^s = \sum k_{ij} \left[l_{ij} \left(1 - \frac{l_{ij}^0}{\|l_{ij}\|} \right) \right] \tag{3}$$

Where k_{ij} is the elasticity coefficient of the spring between node i and its adjacent node j; l_{ij} is the distance vector between node i and j, l_{ij}^0 represents the initial distance.

Supposing that the current position coordinates of node i is $\mathbf{p}_i$ and initial position is $\mathbf{p}_i^0$, we can get

$$l_{ij} = \mathbf{P}_i - \mathbf{P}_j$$

And

$$l_{ij}^0 = \mathbf{P}_i^0 - \mathbf{P}_j^0$$

The damping force $\mathbf{f}_i^d$:

$$\mathbf{f}_i^d = r_i^d \mathbf{v}_i + \sum r_{ij} \left\| (\mathbf{v}_i - \mathbf{v}_j) \cdot \frac{l_{ij}}{\|l_{ij}\|} \right\| \cdot \frac{l_{ij}}{\|l_{ij}\|} \tag{4}$$

Where r_i^d and r_{ij} are respectively the damping coefficient of node i and damping co-efficient of the spring between node i and j, and $\mathbf{v}_i$ is the velocity of node i. We then can get:

$$\mathbf{v}_i = \mathbf{P}_i^{'}$$
$$\mathbf{v}_j = \mathbf{P}_j^{'}$$

Using equation (3) and equation (4), equation (1) is solved as follows:

$$m_i \mathbf{a}_i + \sum k_{ij} \left[l_{ij} \left(1 - \frac{l_{ij}^0}{\|l_{ij}\|} \right) \right] + r_i^d \mathbf{v}_i + \sum r_{ij} \left\| (\mathbf{v}_i - \mathbf{v}_j) \cdot \frac{l_{ij}}{\|l_{ij}\|} \right\| \cdot \frac{l_{ij}}{\|l_{ij}\|} = \mathbf{f}_i^{\text{ext}}$$

Since the acceleration vector of node i is $\mathbf{a}_i = \mathbf{u}_i^{''}$ and its velocity vector is $\mathbf{v}_i = \mathbf{u}_i^{'}$, equation (1) can be farther solved.

And then, the kinetic equation of node i can be finally represented as:

$$m_i \mathbf{u}_i^{''} + \sum k_{ij} \left[l_{ij} \left(1 - \frac{l_{ij}^0}{\|l_{ij}\|} \right) \right] + r_i^d \mathbf{u}_i^{'} + \sum r_{ij} \left\| (\mathbf{u}_i^{'} - \mathbf{u}_j^{'}) \cdot \frac{l_{ij}}{\|l_{ij}\|} \right\| \cdot \frac{l_{ij}}{\|l_{ij}\|} = \mathbf{f}_i^{\text{ext}} \tag{5}$$

Solution of the Integration
Combining with equation (1) and equation (2), we can get

$$m_i \mathbf{a}_i + \mathbf{f}_i^s + \mathbf{f}_i^d = \mathbf{f}_i^{\text{ext}}$$

Given $\mathbf{a}_i = \mathbf{u}_i^{''}$ and $\mathbf{v}_i = \mathbf{u}_i^{'}$, differentiating the equation above with respect to time yields

$$\begin{cases} \dfrac{d}{dt} \mathbf{u}_i(t) = \mathbf{v}_i(t) \\[2mm] \dfrac{d}{dt} \mathbf{v}_i(t) = \dfrac{\mathbf{f}_i^{\text{ext}} - \mathbf{f}_i^s - \mathbf{f}_i^d}{m_i} \end{cases} \tag{6}$$

Because of the arbitrariness of the node i, for simplification, $\mathbf{u}_i$ is rewritten as u and given the initial displacement $u(t_0) = u_0$ and the initial velocity

$\dfrac{du}{dt}\Big|_{t=t_0} = u'(t_0) = u_0'$ at the beginning of the simulation, the further differential equations can be then derived as follows:

$$
\begin{cases}
\dfrac{d^2u}{dt^2} - \dfrac{f_i^{\text{ext}} - f_i^s - f_i^d}{m_i} = 0 \\[2mm]
u'(t_0) = u_0' \\[1mm]
u(t_0) = u_0
\end{cases}
\tag{7}
$$

Equations (7) can also be rewritten as the derivative formation:

$$
\begin{cases}
y'' - \dfrac{f_i^{\text{ext}} - f_i^s - f_i^d}{m_i} = 0 \\[2mm]
y(x_0) = y_0 \\[1mm]
y'(x_0) = y_0'
\end{cases}
\tag{8}
$$

Where y represents the displacement instead of u and x instead of time t.

First, we convert the above second-order equations form into a first order equations form:

$$
\begin{cases}
y' = z \\[2mm]
z' = \dfrac{f_i^{\text{ext}} - f_i^s - f_i^d}{m_i} \\[2mm]
y(x_0) = y_0 \\[1mm]
z(x_0) = z_0
\end{cases}
\tag{9}
$$

With the simple substitution

$$
z = y'
$$

Next, we use the Euler's method and classical Runge-Kutta method as the numerical integration method respectively to solve equations (9).

The Euler's method solution
Given the Euler formula:

$$
y_{i+1} = y_i + hf(x_i, y_i) \quad (i = 0,1,2,...,n-1)
$$

Set the time step as h_E and solve equations (9), then we can get the Euler's method numerical solution:

$$
\begin{cases}
y_{n+1} = y_n + h_E z \\
z_{n+1} = z_n + h_E \dfrac{\mathbf{f}_i^{\text{ext}} - \mathbf{f}_i^{s} - \mathbf{f}_i^{d}}{m_i}
\end{cases}
\tag{10}
$$

The classical Runge-Kutta method solution

Set the time step as h_R and use the classical Runge-Kutta formula to solve equations (9), we can get the Runge-Kutta Method numerical solution:

$$
\begin{cases}
y_{n+1} = y_n + \dfrac{h_R}{6}(K_1 + 2K_2 + 2K_3 + K_4) \\[2mm]
z_{n+1} = z_n + \dfrac{h_R}{6}(L_1 + 2L_2 + 2L_3 + L_4)
\end{cases}
$$

Where

$$
\begin{cases}
K_1 = z_n, L_1 = f(x_n, y_n, z_n) \\[2mm]
K_2 = z_n + \dfrac{h_R}{2}L_1, L_2 = f(x_{n+\frac{1}{2}}, y_n + \dfrac{h_R}{2}k_1, z_n + \dfrac{h_R}{2}L_1) \\[2mm]
K_3 = z_n + \dfrac{h_R}{2}L_2, L_3 = f(x_{n+\frac{1}{2}}, y_n + \dfrac{h_R}{2}k_2, z_n + \dfrac{h_R}{2}L_2) \\[2mm]
K_4 = z_n + h_R L_3, L_4 = f(x_{n+1}, y_n + h_R k_3, z_n + h_R L_3)
\end{cases}
$$

By eliminating the variables K_1, K_2, K_3, K_4, the above equations can be further simplified as follows:

$$
\begin{cases}
y_{n+1} = y_n + h z_n + \dfrac{h_R^2}{6}(L_1 + L_2 + L_3) \\[2mm]
z_{n+1} = z_n + \dfrac{h_R}{6}(L_1 + 2L_2 + 2L_3 + L_4)
\end{cases}
\tag{11}
$$

Where

$$
\begin{cases}
L_1 = f(x_n, y_n, z_n) \\[2mm]
L_2 = f(x_{n+\frac{1}{2}}, y_n + \dfrac{h_R}{2}z_n, z_n + \dfrac{h_R}{2}L_1) \\[2mm]
L_3 = f(x_{n+\frac{1}{2}}, y_n + \dfrac{h_R}{2}z_n + \dfrac{h_R^2}{4}L_1, z_n + \dfrac{h_R}{2}L_2) \\[2mm]
L_4 = f(x_{n+1}, y_n + h_R z_n + \dfrac{h_R^2}{2}L_2, z_n + h_R L_3)
\end{cases}
$$

3.3 Workflow of Programming Algorithm

The programming workflow chart of our algorithm is shown as Fig2.

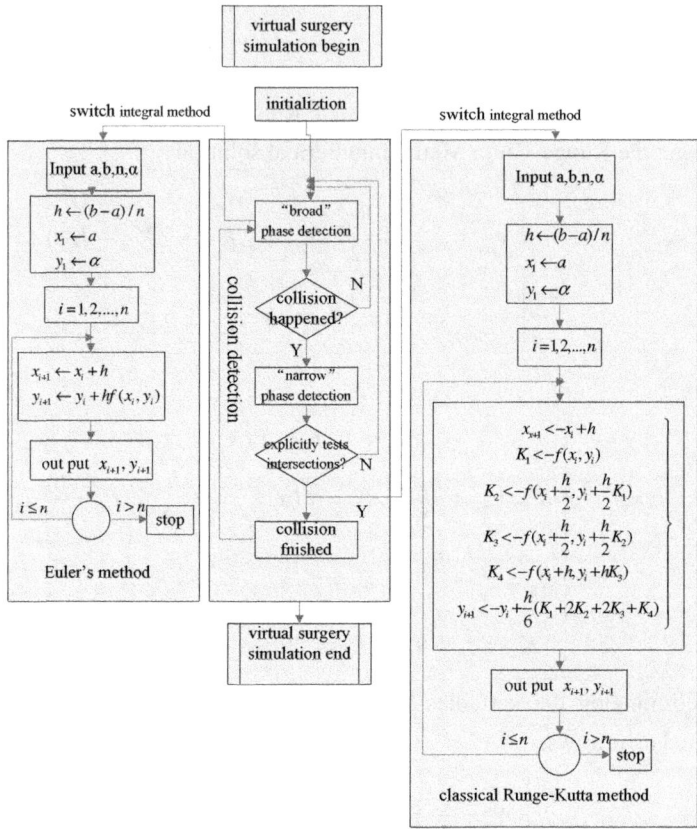

Fig. 2. The Programming Workflow Chart

4 Experiment and Discussion

The experiment is done in a DELL workstation with 2.66GHz Intel Pentium Dual CPU, 2GB DDR3 memory and 256M NVIDIA Quadro NVS 290 graphic card and the operation system is Windows XP Professional. The virtual surgery simulation system is developed using the OpenGL library in IDE VC++.NET 2008. We use Mass-Spring System to model a liver with 181 nodes, 1330 triangles and 596 tetrahedrons. The elasticity coefficient is set as 4500; the damping coefficient is 5, and mass is distributed on each node averagely.

In the experiment, one end of the virtual liver model is fixed and the other end is pulled by mouse which is used to simulate the separating pliers. A realistic deformation procedure can be observed shown as Fig 3.

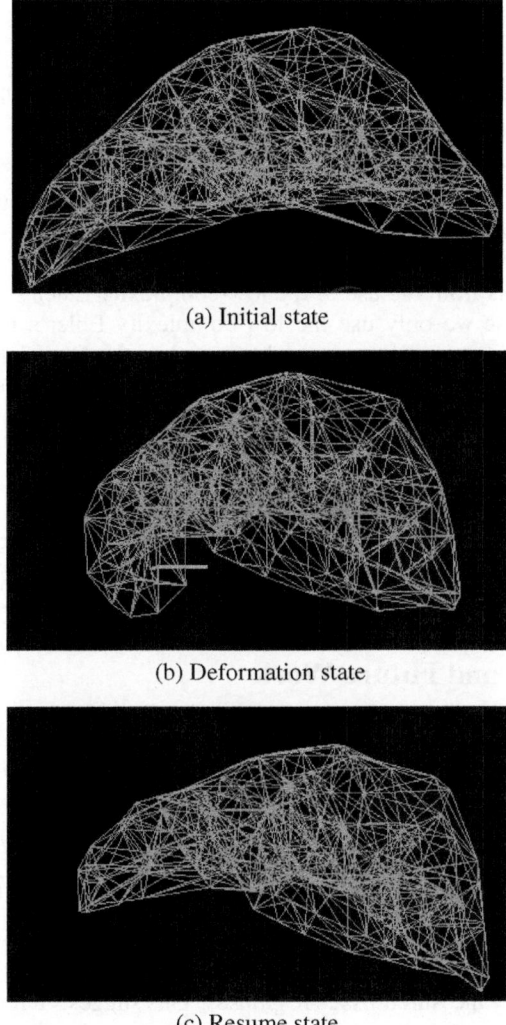

(a) Initial state

(b) Deformation state

(c) Resume state

Fig. 3. Deformation procedure of the liver model

In the initial simulation phase of virtual surgery simulation, we use Euler's method and the time step h_E is set as 0.02s; when accurate collisions is identified, we use classical Runge-Kutta method instead of Euler's method and the time step h_R is set as 0.1s. We finally find that the integral times consumed by the two methods are very similar but the Runge-Kutta method does not achieve a high accuracy as be respected because of the large time step. When set by a smaller time step, the Runge-Kutta method shows a higher accuracy for simulation, but also compared with a higher complexity inevitably. This can be explained approximately by analyzing as follows:

In our experiment, the local truncation error for the Euler's method is $R_E = C_1 \times 10^{-2}$ while for the classical Runge-Kutta method, the local truncation error is $R_R = C_2 \times 10^{-5}$, where C_1, C_2 both are constants and with the approximate order of magnitude. So we get $R_E \gg R_R$.

To validate the efficiency of our method, we adopt both the classical Runge-Kutta method and our mixed numerical integral algorithm to simulate the liver model's deformation and record the assumed computation time. The result is showed in Table 1. It can be seen from the table that our algorithm consumes less computation time per update, which profits from the use of the low-complexity Euler's method in the "broad phase". And because we only use the low-complexity Euler's method in the "broad phase" and still use Runge-Kutta method to simulate the liver deformation procedure, we enhance the computation speed and achieve high accuracy at the same time. At next step, we plan to adopt different models and different configuration parameters for the simulation test to get more experiment data.

Table 1. Computation time(second) per update

	Classical Runge-Kutta method	Our algorithm
Computation time	0.021	0.015

5 Conclusions and Future Work

The proposed mixed numerical integral algorithm provides a novel integral method for the simulation of the soft tissues deformation. It is computationally efficient and easy to implement since the solution is provided as well as the programming workflow. From our experiments, we can see that our algorithm works well compared with the commonly used integral method.

Our algorithm can simulate the true kinetic behavior of a specific soft tissue only if appropriate algorithm variables are available, such as the time step h_E and h_R. It is resorted to estimations through interactive parameter adjustments, by making comparison to the experimentally measured tissue responses. This suggests a further investigation on the development of an effective scheme to extract the variables-the time step for example, automatically by calibrating with the measured responses of specific tissues.

References

1. Held, M., Klosowski, J.T., Mitehell, J.S.B.: Evaluation of Collision Detection Methods for VirtualReality Fly-Throughs. In: Proc. Seventh Canadian Conefrence on Computational Geometry, pp. 205–210 (February 1995)
2. Hubbard, P.M.: Approximating polyhedra with spheres for time-critical collision detection. ACM Transaction on Graphics 15(3), 179–210 (1996)
3. Gottsehalk, S., Lin, M.C., Manoeha, D.: OBBTrees: A Hierarchical Structure for Rapid Interference Detection. In: Proc. SIGGRAPH 1996, ACM Computer Graphics, pp. 171–180 (1996)

4. Natsupakpong, S., Cavusoglu, M.C.: Comparison of Numerical Integration Methods for Simulation of Physically-Based Deformable Object Models in Surgical Simulation. In: Proc. the 12th Annual National Symposium on Computational Science and Engineering: AN-SCSE12, Ubon Rajathanee, Thailand, March 27-29 (2008)
5. Huang, S.-h., Wang, B.-l., Research Progress on Simulation of Deformable Objects Using Finite Elements Model. Journal of System Simulation 19(22) (2007)
6. Lloyd, B.A., Székely, G., Harders, M.: Identification of spring parameters for deformable object simulation. IEEE Transactions on Visualization and Computer Graphics 13, 1081–1094 (2007)
7. Mollemans, W., Schutyser, F., Cleynenbreugel, J.V., Suetens, P.: Fast Soft Tissue Deformation with Tetrahedral Mass SpringModel for Maxillofacial Surgery Planning Systems. In: Barillot, C., Haynor, D.R., Hellier, P. (eds.) MICCAI 2004. LNCS, vol. 3217, pp. 371–379. Springer, Heidelberg (2004)
8. Zhang, S., Gu, L., Huang, P., Xu, J.: Real-Time Simulation of Deformable Soft Tissue Based on Mass-Spring and Medial Representation. In: Liu, Y., Jiang, T.-Z., Zhang, C. (eds.) CVBIA 2005. LNCS, vol. 3765, pp. 419–426. Springer, Heidelberg (2005)
9. Mollemans, W., Schutyser, F., Cleynenbreugel, J.V., Suetens, P.: Tetrahedral mass spring model for fast soft tissue deformation. In: Proc. International Symposium on Surgery Simulation and Soft Tissue Modeling, pp. 145.1 (2003)

Multiple Sequence Alignment Based on ABC_SA

Xiaojun Xu and Xiujuan Lei

College of Computer Science Shaanxi Normal University
Xi'an, Shaanxi Province, China, 710062
{hbxuxiaojun,xjlei168}@163.com

Abstract. In this paper, we apply the artificial bee colony (ABC) and its improving format to solve multiple sequence alignment (MSA) problem. The improved method named ABC_SA, which is presented to prevent algorithm from sliding into local optimum through introducing Metropolis acceptance criteria into ABC's searching process. The results of simulation experiment demonstrate that ABC_SA algorithm is able to settle multiple sequence alignment effectively by increasing the food source's diversity and is able to converge at global optimal alignment.

Keywords: Multiple Sequence Alignment (MSA), Artificial Bee Colony (ABC), Metropolis Acceptance Criteria, ABC_SA.

1 Introduction

Multiple sequence alignment (MSA) is a crucial problem in bioinformatics. It can be useful for structure prediction, phylogenetic analysis and polymerase chain reaction (PCR) primer design. The alignment results reflect the similarity relation and biological characteristics of sequences. Unfortunately, finding an accurate multiple sequence alignment has been shown NP-hard [1]. Therefore several methods were proposed which can be grouped in four great classes. The first class includes exact methods which use a generalization of Needleman algorithm [2] in order to align all the sequences simultaneously. Their main shortcoming is their complexity which becomes even more critical with the increase of the number of sequences. The second class contains methods based on a progressive approach [3], which builds up multiple sequence alignment gradually by aligning the closest pair of sequences first and successively adding in the more distant ones. It is easy to trap into the local minima and consequently they can lead to poor quality solutions. The third class covers methods [4] based on graph theory of which the main representative is the partial order alignment. Then, the iterative methods of the forth class were showed to be promising. The basic idea is to start with an initial alignment including all the sequences and then iteratively refines it through a series of suitable refinements called iterations. The main iterative methods consist of SA [5], GA [6], PSO [7] and so on. However, the performance of above mentioned methods solving MSA is not ideal. ABC [8] was firstly proposed in 2005 and it has not been applied in this area. In this paper, we apply the ABC algorithm and its improving format to solve MSA problem. The improved method named ABC_SA, which is presented to prevent algorithm from falling into stagnation through

F.L. Wang et al. (Eds.): AICI 2010, Part II, LNAI 6320, pp. 98–105, 2010.

introducing Metropolis acceptance criteria into ABC's searching process. The consequences of simulation experiment indicate the ABC_SA performs better in solving MSA.

2 Multiple Sequence Alignment

2.1 The Mathematical Model of Multiple Sequence Alignment

A biological sequences of which the length is l is a string consists of l characters that are collected from a finite alphabet Σ. In terms of DNA sequence, Σ contains four characters which respectively represent four different kinds of nucleotides. In terms of protein sequence, Σ contains twenty characters which respectively represent twenty different kinds of amino acid. Given a group of sequences which comprised of $n(n \geq 2)$ sequence $S = (s_1, s_2, ..., s_n)$, where $s_i = s_{i1}s_{i2}......s_{il_i}$, $1 \leq i \leq n$, $s_{ij} \in \Sigma$, $1 \leq j \leq l_i$, l_i is equal to the length of i-th sequence. Then an alignment about S can be defined as a matrix $A = (a_{ij})$, where $1 \leq i \leq n$, $1 \leq j \leq l$, $\max(l_i) \leq l \leq \sum_{i=1}^{n} l_i$ and the characteristics of A are as follows: (1) $a_{ij} \in \Sigma \cup \{-\}$, where the symbol $\{-\}$ denotes a gap; (2) The i-th sequence of A is identical with the i-th of S when the gaps are deleted; (3) There is no row formed by only $\{-\}$ in matrix A.

2.2 Objective Function of Multiple Sequence Alignment

The common objective functions of multiple sequence alignment refer to Sum-of-Pairs (SP) [9] function and Coffee function [10]. We select SPS function based on SP as evaluation criteria. Supposed there are N sequences to be aligned, and the aligned length is L, c_{ij} is j-th letter of i-th sequence, then the score of j-th row of all N sequences can be defined as $SP(j)$.

$$SP(j) = \sum_{i=1}^{N-1} \sum_{k=1}^{N} p(c_{ij}, c_{kj}) \tag{1}$$

Where

$$p(c_{ij}, c_{kj}) = \begin{cases} +1 \ (c_{ij} = c_{kj} \ and \ c_{ij}, c_{kj} \in \Sigma) \\ 0 \ \ (c_{ij} \neq c_{kj} \ and \ c_{ij}, c_{kj} \in \Sigma) \\ 0 \ \ (c_{ij} = '-' \ or \ c_{kj} = '-') \\ 0 \ \ (c_{ij} = '-' \ and \ c_{kj} = '-') \end{cases} \tag{2}$$

So, the final score of A is

$$SUM(A) = \sum_{j=1}^{L} SP(j) \tag{3}$$

If the aligned sequences come from the standard database, for example Balibase1.0, there is certainly a standard alignment $A - S\tan d$, so we can get a relative score SPS,

$$SPS = \frac{SUM(A)}{SUM(A - S\tan d)} \qquad (4)$$

Then we estimate A using SPS.

3 Algorithm Description

3.1 Artificial Bee Colony Algorithm (ABC)

ABC algorithm which simulates the intelligent foraging behavior of honey bee swarms was proposed by Karaboga in 2005 [8]. The model of ABC consists of four factors: food source, employed bees, onlookers, and scout bees.

Food source: the value of a food source depends on many factors such as its richness or concentration of its energy and so on. When solving MSA based on ABC, the position of a food source represents a possible alignment which is assessed by formula (4). The value of SPS is higher, the alignment is better.

Employed bees: they are associated with a particular food source which they are currently exploiting or are "employed" at. They carry with them information about this particular source. At the same time, an employed bee produces a modification on the position in her memory depending on the local information and tests the value of the new source. Because MSA is a special and discrete problem, the mean of modifying is different from that in reference [8]. We define it as following:

Proposed there are N sequences in food source A, the length of which is l_A and the length of i-*th* sequence without gap is l_i, then a new food source B is got by randomly breaking $l_A - l_j$ gaps in a random sequence $j(1 \le j \le N)$. If the SPS score of B is higher than that of A, the bee memorizes the position of B instead of A. Otherwise it keeps the position of A. If a position of food source can not be improved further through a pre-determined number of cycles called "limit", then that food source is assumed to be abandoned. The bee whose food source has been exhausted becomes a scout.

Onlookers: they are waiting in the nest and establishing a food source through the information shared by employed bees. An artificial onlooker bee chooses a food source depending on the probability values associated with that food source. Assumed there are M food sources, the probability of i-th food source selected by onlooker is $p(i)$.

$$P(i) = \frac{f(i)}{\sum\limits_{j=1}^{M} f(j)} \qquad (5)$$

And $f(i)$ is the SPS score of i-th food source. There is a greater probability of onlookers choosing more profitable sources.

Scouts: they are searching the environment surrounding the nest for new food sources randomly.

3.2 ABC_SA Algorithm

In the process of solving MSA, ABC may not get a global optimizer alignment. After analyzing, the shortcoming happens in the random search process of scouts.

Hypothesized the food source A has not been promoted for "limit" cycles, so it should be abandoned. The relative employed bee turns to a scout which immediately finds a new food source B instead of A. If the property of B is lower than that of A, the algorithm cannot arrive the global optimizer solution. In order to settle this problem, we introduce Metropolis acceptance criteria into the searching process of scouts. Whether to accept B is decided by the following rule 1.

Rule 1: if $f(B) > f(A)$, B is accepted;
    Else, calculate

$$P = \exp(\frac{f(A) - f(B)}{T\_cur})$$ (6)

If $P > rand$, then B is accepted;

So, the algorithm not only reserves the global optimizer but also increases the food source's diversity through adding a worse food source to scout according to a small probability. And the main step of the ABC_SA is given below:

STEP 1: Initialize the number size of bee *popsize*, the maximal cycle max *it*, the initial temperature T_ini, the terminal temperature T_end, annealing parameter *alpha* and so on. Set $iter = 1$, $T\_cur = T\_ini$

STEP 2: Calculate the fitness of each food source according to formula (4), record the position of the best food source. And the first half of the colony consists of the employed artificial bees and the second half includes the onlookers. For every food source, there is only one employed bee. In other words, the number of employed bees is equal to the number of food sources around the hive.

STEP 3: Produce the new solution of the employed bees and onlookers.

STEP 4: Produce the new solution of the scouts according to rule 1.

STEP 5: $iter = iter + 1$, $T\_cur = alpha * T\_cur$

STEP 6: Output the best alignment if the termination condition is met. Otherwise turn to Step2.

4 Key Problems

4.1 Encoding Method of the Food Source

We prefer two dimension matrix encoding method after analyzing the features of MSA. Supposed there are N sequences to be aligned, and the respective length of each sequence is $l_1, l_2, ..., l_N$ and the aligned length L is between l_{max} and $1.2 * l_{max}$, so we should generate a one-dimensional vector ∂_i as a set of which the element is a random permutation of the integers from 1 to $L - l_i$. Then the encoding of the food source may be expressed as $\beta = [\partial_1, \partial_2, ..., \partial_N]$ showed in example 1.

Example 1. There are three sequences s_1, s_2, s_3 to be aligned, and $s_1 = ydgeilyqskrf$, $s_2 = adesvynpgn$, $s_3 = ydepikqser$. So a possible food source is signified as $\beta = [\partial_1, \partial_2, \partial_3]$, where $\partial_1 = [2,8,13]$, $\partial_2 = [1,4,8,11,14]$, $\partial_3 = [2,4,9,13]$.

4.2 The Alignment Corresponding to Encoding Food Source

For sequence $s = ydgeilyqskrf$, presumed the set of inserted gaps is $\partial = (1,4,7)$, we get a new sequence $s' = \_yd\_ge\_ilyqskrf$ after inserting gaps into s. In terms of example 1, the homologous alignment is displayed as follow example 2.

Example 2. An alignment of s_1, s_2, s_3

```
y_dgeil_yqsk_rf
_ad_esv_yn_pg_n
y_d_etpi_kqs_er
```

5   Simulation Results and Discussion

In the simulation process, ABC_SA was applied for finding the alignment of multiple sequences from BAliBASE1.0 for the evaluation of MSA programs. The BAli-BASE1.0 multiple alignments were constructed by manual comparison of structure and are validated by structure-superposition algorithms. Thus, the alignments are unlikely to be biased toward any specific multiple alignment method [11]. In order to evaluate the performance of the ABC_SA algorithm, we select nine sequences with different lengths and different similarities from BAliBASE1.0.

We compare the results obtained by ABC_SA approach with those by genetic algorithm (GA) (6), particle swarm algorithm (PSO) (7), artificial bee colony (ABC) (8) and simulated annealing (SA) (5). In ABC_SA algorithm, the predetermined number is $\lim it = 5/10/10$ which indicates the number $\lim it$ for short, medium and long sequences are respective 5, 10 and 10, the annealing parameter is $alpha = 0.95/0.97/0.99$. Experimental results further indicate that our approach performs better than above approaches. The parameters setting are showed in Table 1. Table 2 displays the characters of nine testing sequences.

Table 1. The parameters setting of five algorithms

Algorithm	P_{cro}	P_{mut}	α	β	Limit	T_ini	T_end	alpha	Popsize	Maxiter
GA	0.6	0.05	—	—	—	—	—	—	20	600/1000/1200
PSO	—	—	0.8	0.8	—	—	—	—	20	600/1000/1200
ABC	—	—	—	—	5/10/10	—	—	—	20	600/1000/1200
SA	—	—	—	—	—	10000	0.0001	0.95/0.97/0.99	20	600/1000/1200
ABC_SA	—	—	—	—	5/10/10	10000	0.0001	0.95/0.97/0.99	20	600/1000/1200

5.1 Simulation Results

In the simulation studies, for each group sequences to be aligned, the algorithm runs for ten times. And the comparative results of the best, mean and worst alignment of the investigated algorithm are presented in table 3, table 4 and table 5 for short, medium and

Table 2. The characters of nine testing sequence

Types	Name	Number	(Longest, Shortest)	Identity
Short	SH3	5	(80,49)	<25%
	451 c	5	(70,87)	20%-40%
	lkrn	5	(66,82)	>35%
Medium	kinase	5	(263,276)	<25%
	lpii	4	(247,259)	20%-40%
	5ptp	5	(222,245)	>35%
Long	lajsA	4	(358,387)	<25%
	glg	5	(438,486)	20%-40%
	ltaq	5	(806,928)	>35%

Table 3. The comparative results for short sequences

Sequence Name	Algorithm	Average	Best	Worst
SH3	GA	0.6090	0.6829	0.5463
	PSO	0.6444	0.6543	0.6296
	ABC	0.6895	0.7654	0.6543
	SA	0.6694	0.7037	0.6420
	ABC_SA	0.8824	0.8976	0.8634
451c	GA	0.5141	0.5398	0.4891
	PSO	0.6252	0.6407	0.6116
	ABC	0.5369	0.5652	0.5144
	SA	0.5137	0.5543	0.4746
	ABC_SA	0.5493	0.5833	0.5326
lkrn	GA	0.7455	0.8065	0.6921
	PSO	0.7120	0.7331	0.7008
	ABC	0.7956	0.8168	0.7732
	SA	0.7546	0.8412	0.6784
	ABC_SA	0.8227	0.8587	0.7889

Table 4. The comparative results for medium sequences

Sequence Name	Algorithm	Average	Best	Worst
kinase	GA	0.3508	0.3620	0.3453
	PSO	0.4848	0.5065	0.4765
	ABC	0.4951	0.5272	0.4765
	SA	0.4776	0.4915	0.4620
	ABC_SA	0.5024	0.5247	0.4877
lpii	GA	0.3317	0.3440	0.3244
	PSO	0.3813	0.4117	0.3529
	ABC	0.3825	0.4292	0.3682
	SA	0.3382	0.3511	0.3279
	ABC_SA	0.4541	0.4690	0.4426
5ptp	GA	0.3792	0.4334	0.3579
	PSO	0.2626	0.2725	0.2507
	ABC	0.4178	0.4480	0.4036
	SA	0.4164	0.4367	0.4019
	ABC_SA	0.4462	0.4596	0.4291

Table 5. The comparative results for long sequences

Sequence Name	Algorithm	Average	Best	Worst
lajsA	GA	0.3646	0.3719	0.3548
	PSO	0.5819	0.5903	0.5645
	ABC	0.5819	0.5936	0.5741
	SA	0.5683	0.5801	0.5573
	ABC_SA	0.5983	0.6181	0.5839
glg	GA	0.3738	0.3824	0.3648
	PSO	0.3987	0.4154	0.3828
	ABC	0.4040	0.4254	0.3857
	SA	0.3512	0.3642	0.3357
	ABC_SA	0.4645	0.4764	0.4558
ltaq	GA	0.2500	0.2644	0.2441
	PSO	0.2533	0.2588	0.2484
	ABC	0.3051	0.3133	0.2983
	SA	0.2569	0.2615	0.2520
	ABC_SA	0.3127	0.3194	0.3043

long sequence respectively. You can also see the curves of convergence from figure 1 to figure 4 which reveal the speed of convergence along with the increase of iteration.

From table 3, it is clearly to be seen that the ABC_SA algorithm can solve MSA with effect in which the length of sequences is short. The comparative results for SH3 are remarkable. The accuracy of average obtained by ABC_SA is bigger than that obtained by other four approaches as well as the accuracy of best and worst. When it comes to sequence 451c and lkrn, we receive the same verdict as it to SH3. Table 4 shows the simulation result about medium sequences which contain kinase, lpii and 5ptp. As we have seen, ABC_SA algorithm takes up the leading position among all above five algorithms. Table 5 presents the comparative results of long sequences. The length of long sequence is much longer than medium and short sequence. So settling long sequence alignment needs much time which is the reason why we set the maximum iterative number is 1200. From table 5, we can conclude the performance of ABC_SA is as well as it of ABC, but is more excellent than other three approaches.

Fig 1 to Fig 4 respectively displays the curves of convergence of sequence SH3, 451c, lpii and glg. In these figures, the bold line expresses the convergence rate of ABC_SA algorithm, and the other four lines express the rate of SA, ABC, GA and PSO. Like we see, the bold line is not only higher than others, but also it stays in a stable value. In other words, ABC_SA algorithm can both get a greater alignment and take less time when solving sequence alignment.

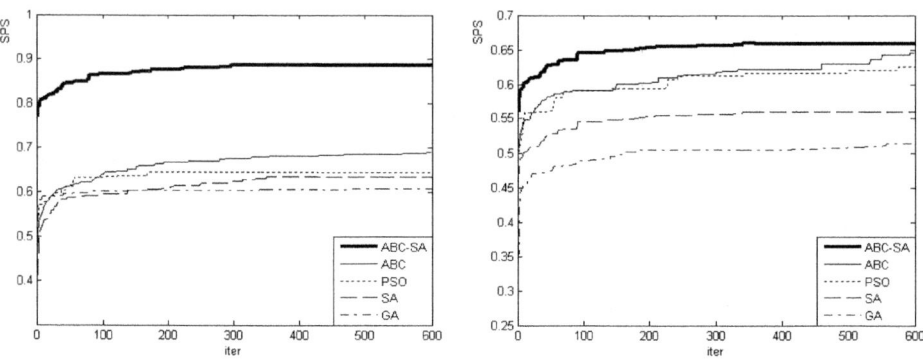

Fig. 1. The curves of convergence for SH3   **Fig. 2.** The curves of convergence for 451c

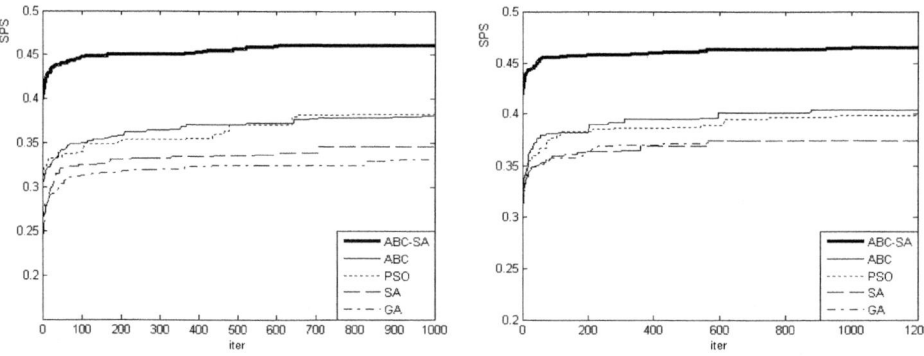

Fig. 3. The curves of convergence for lpii   **Fig. 4.** The curves of convergence for glg

Consequently, the ABC_SA algorithm which merges the Metropolis acceptance criteria into basic ABC, has the superiority of both ABC and SA. So the algorithm reserves the global optimizer as well as increases the food source's diversity through adding a worse food source to scout according to a small probability decided by rule 1. All these strategies encourage the exploration process and make the algorithm performs better. Furthermore, the simulation results all demonstrate the validity.

6 Conclusion

We put up with multiple sequence alignment successfully based on ABC, for the sake of improving the performance of ABC, a new algorithm ABC_SA is proposed by introducing metropolis acceptance criteria into ABC. In the way that was expected ABC_SA perform better than GA, PSO, ABC, SA. However, the accuracy rate of alignment gained by ABC_SA is different from that of alignment from Balibase1.0. There are two drawbacks in ABC_SA algorithm. One is that the alignment is worse than that from Balibase1.0 which needed enhance. The other is that the number of parameter in ABC_SA is too much, each of which has big influence on algorithm. So the next task is to overcome the both problems.

Acknowledgement. This work was supported by the Natural Science Foundation of Shaanxi Province of China (2010JQ8034) and the Fundamental Research Funds for the Central Universities, Shaanxi Normal University (2009020016).

References

1. Lei, X.j., Sun, J.j., Ma, Q.z.: Multiple sequence alignment based on chaotic PSO. In: Advances in Computation and Intelligence: 4th International Symposium on Intelligence Computation and Application, pp. 351–360 (2009)
2. Needleman, S.B., Wunsch, C.D.: A general method applicable to the search for similarities in the amino acid sequence of two proteins. Journal of Molecular Biology, 569–571 (1970)
3. Feng, D.F., Doolittle, R.F.: Progressive sequence alignment as a prerequisite to correct phylognentic trees. Journal of Molecular Biology, 351–360 (1987)
4. Huo, H.W., Xiao, Z.W.: A Multiple Alignment Approach for DNA Sequences Based on the Maximum Weighted Path Algorithms. Journal of Software, 185–195 (2007)
5. Kim, J., Pramanik, S., Chung, M.J.: Multiple sequence alignment using simulated annealing. Computer applications in bioscience, 419–426 (1994)
6. Horng, J.T., Wu, L.C., Lin, C.M., Yang, B.H.: A genetic algorithm for multiple sequence alignment. Soft Computing - A Fusion of Foundations. Methodologies and Applications, 407–420 (2005)
7. Lei, C.W., Ruan, J.H.: A particle swarm optimization algorithm for finding DNA sequence motifs. In: IEEE Bioinformatics and Biomeidcine Workshops, pp. 166–173 (2008)
8. Karaboga, D.: An idea based on honey bee swarm for numerical optimization. Technical Report-TR06, Erciyes University, Engineering Faculty, Computer Engineering Department (2005)
9. Thompson, J.D., Plewniak, F., Poch, O.: A comprehensive comparison of multiple sequence alignment programs. Nucleic Acid Research, 2682–2690 (1999)
10. Notredame, C., Holm, L., Higgins, D.G.: COFFEE: An objective functions for multiple sequence alignments. Bioinformatics, 407–422 (1998)
11. Zhang, M., Fang, W.W., Zhang, J.H., Chi, Z.X.: MSAID: multiple sequence alignment based on a measure of information discrepancy. Computational Biology and Chemistry, pp.175–181 (2005)

TDMA Grouping Based RFID Network Planning Using Hybrid Differential Evolution Algorithm

Xiang Gao[1] and Ying Gao[2]

[1] Department of Computer Science and Engineering,
Hong Kong University of Science and Technology,
cs_gxx@ust.hk
[2] School of Computer Science and Educational Software,
Guang Zhou University
falcongao@21cn.com

Abstract. With the fast development of Radio Frequency Identification (RFID) technology, RFID network has been applied in different aspects of logistic management. How to effectively deploy the readers becomes a crucial problem in RFID network planning. The planning is related to a complicated optimization problem and interference elimination between readers. To find a good solution in the optimization problem effectively, we introduced Differential Evolution algorithm. To minimize the interference between the readers, we applied TDMA on the network and proposed two methods to group the readers. The first method is a modified version of Differential Evolution algorithm. Since part of the problem domain is binary while the searching space of the Differential Evolution algorithm is in a real domain, we modified the mutation rule of the Differential Evolution algorithm so that it can support binary parameters. The other way is to transform the problem into a graph and apply a maximum cut heuristic on it. The experimental result shows that both methods are effective.

Keywords: RFID Network Planning, TDMA, Differential Evolution Algorithm, Binary Encoding, Maximum Cut.

1   Introduction

A RFID system is composed with two major parts, the readers and tags. A reader keeps sending signal to its neighborhood and if a tag nearby receives the signal, it echoes a signal back to the reader with its unique identifier. The reader detects the tag by recognizing the identifier. In most of the practical logistic management systems, an array of RFID readers work together to form an RFID network which can achieve a larger coverage. RFID network has been applied in inventory control and warehouse management for many years but how to effectively deploy readers still remains to be a problem.

F.L. Wang et al. (Eds.): AICI 2010, Part II, LNAI 6320, pp. 106–113, 2010.
© Springer-Verlag Berlin Heidelberg 2010

RFID network planing has the following characteristics: [1]

- **Multi-objective**: There are many goals to be considered in the problem. For example, the coverage, interference, economy cost.
- **Non-linear**: The fitness function or the objective function is non-linear.
- **High dimensional**: For each reader, there are many parameters (position, angle, emitting power, etc) need to be determined during setting up. If more readers need to be deployed, the dimension of the search space will be higher.
- **Strong coupling**: There is strong interaction between different variables.

Due to these characteristics of RFID network planning, traditional optimization methods are not suitable for this problem. Additionally, the interference problem in RFID network needs to be considered carefully. A dense allocation of readers will lead to a high interference while a sparse one will lead to low coverage.

To solve the interference problem, redundant reader removal and channel access schemes are usually applied. A redundant reader removal method in [2] provided a solution to eliminate redundant readers but it does not guarantee the coverage of the planning area. The most popular and convenient channel access scheme is TDMA as it does not require hardware support. TDMA is a way to support channel access by dividing signal into different time slots and assign them to different channels. Shin et al [3] introduced a dynamic frame size TDMA to deal with reader interference. However, that paper did not discuss how to group the readers efficiently. Researchers had proposed various kinds of algorithms like simulated annealing [4] [5] to solve cellular network planning which is similar to RFID network planning. However, RFID network do not support handover and collision detection. Base on these limitations, Guan et al [6] introduced a genetic algorithm using discrete model and hierarchical encoding. Yang et al[7] later analyzed different selection methods and incorporated controlled elitism in his paper. Although Genetic Algorithm is simple and easy to implement, it is not perfect for optimizing over a continuous domain.

In this paper, Differential Evolution algorithm [8] is used to solve the RFID network optimization problem and TDMA grouping is introduced to solve the interference problem between readers. To optimize the effectiveness of TDMA grouping, two methods are proposed. The first one is a modified version of Differential Evolution algorithm which supports binary encoding. The other one convert the problem into a graph and uses a maximum heuristic to optimize the grouping. Both versions of the algorithm are applied to a simplified RFID network planing model and the experiment result indicates that both of them can find a good solution effectively.

2   RFID Network Planning Modeling

Our model is partially adopted from Guan's paper[6] and Yang's paper[7]. The advancement is that the new model is extended by allowing readers to be placed in any place. Assume we have a $M \times N$ room with obstacle (walls or large metal objects that can block signal) in it, a number of testing RFID tags are evenly distributed in the area that needs a signal coverage. For a RFID reader i, its **detection range** R is a function proportional to its **emitting power** P. That is $R_i = f(P_i)$. We simplify the model by claiming that if the distance between a tag and a reader i is smaller than R_i and there is no obstacle between them, then the tag can receive the signal sent by the reader. If a tag can receive the signal sent by exactly one reader, we say that the tag is detected by the reader. However, if a tag can receive the signal sent by more than one reader, it usually cannot respond to either of the readers because of the nature of passive RFID tags. We say that the tag is interfered.

For each of the readers to be deployed in a plan, we need to consider following parameters:

- (X, Y): The position of the reader in the room, where $X \in [0, M]$ and $Y \in [0, N]$.
- P: The emitting power of the reader. $P \in [MinPower, MaxPower]$.
- G: The group of the reader in the TDMA scheme. $G \in [0, N]$ (where integer N is the number of groups in the system).

Fig. 1 shows how TDMA works. Reader A, B and C are nearly readers so if we do not apply TDMA, they will interfere with each other. With TDMA, reader A and B are assigned to group 0 while reader C is assigned to group 1. At time slot t where $t\%2 = 0$, readers in group 0 are allowed to emit signal. It is similar for the readers in group 1. So only reader A and B (both in group 0) will interfere with each other since they always emit signal together. Reader C will not interfere with A or B because they are in different groups and emit signal at different time.

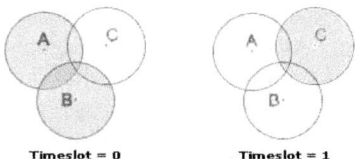

Fig. 1. Basic idea of using Time Division Multiple Access

3   Differential Evolution Algorithm

We can consider a plan $\mathbf{x}$ as a vector or a point in the solution space. Given a fitness function, the Differential Evolution Algorithm tries to find an optimal solution of $fitness(\mathbf{x})$ in the solution space. The algorithm keeps a set of candidate solutions S. For each $\mathbf{x_i} \in S$, we use mutation and crossover rule to generate $\mathbf{y_i}$ and replace $\mathbf{x_i}$ with $\mathbf{y_i}$ if $\mathbf{y_i}$ is a better solution.

The mutation process is randomly choosing three distinct points x_{p1}, x_{p2}, x_{p3} from the current set S and generating the mutated point using the mutation rule: $\hat{\mathbf{x}}_\mathbf{i} = \mathbf{x_{p1}} + F(\mathbf{x_{p2}} - \mathbf{x_{p3}})$ where $\mathbf{x_{p1}}$ is the base point, F is the scaling factor of the difference between points $\mathbf{x_{p2}}$ and $\mathbf{x_{p3}}$. In the original paper of Differential

Evolution Algorithm, F is a uniform random value in $[0, 2]$ according to Storn's paper[8]. If any component of mutated point $\hat{\mathbf{x}}_{\mathbf{i}}^{\mathbf{j}}$ does not satisfy the constraints, the mutation process should be repeated.

The trial point $\mathbf{y_i}$ is generated from the original point $\mathbf{x_i}$ and the mutated point $\hat{\mathbf{x}}_{\mathbf{i}}$ by using the crossover rule:

$$y_i^j = \begin{cases} \hat{x}_i^j, & if \ R^j \le C_R \ or \ j = I_i \\ x_i^j, & if \ R^j > C_R \ and \ j \ne I_i \end{cases} \tag{1}$$

where j represents the j'th component of the point. I_i is a randomly chosen integer from $\{1, 2....N\}$ and R^j is a uniform random number from $[0, 1]$. The parameter C_R controls whether the trial point is more similar to the original point or the mutated point. When $C_R > 0.5$, more components of the trial point are coming from the mutated point, otherwise, more components are derived from the original point.

Finally, the two points $\mathbf{x_i}$ and $\mathbf{y_i}$ are compared by the fitness function and the one with higher fitness value can stay in the candidate set S. We do this for every point $\mathbf{x_i}$ in the set S and after one iteration, points in S are partially replaced by new points generated by mutation and crossover. If we consider S as a generation, we are actually using S to generate a new generation. We stop this process until certain condition is met.

4   Applying DE on RFID Network Planning

We first introduce a fitness function which is for measuring the goodness of a plan. In this model, the fitness function is a weighted summation of cost, interference and coverage:

$$f = w_{cost} \times (B - N \times P) + w_c \times \frac{\# \ DetectedTags}{\# \ TotalTags} + w_i \times \frac{\# \ InterferedTags}{\# \ TotalTags} \tag{2}$$

where B is the budget, N is the number of readers and P is the unit price of reader.

4.1   Hybrid Encoding

To support both real parameters and binary parameters, the hybrid encoding is adopted here. A plan $\mathbf{x}$ with n readers can be expressed as a vector $\mathbf{x} = \{X_1, ...X_n, Y_1, ...Y_n, P_1, ...P_n; G_1, ...G_n\}$ where X_1, Y_1, P_1 and G_1 are the x-coordinate, y-coordinate, emitting power and group of reader 1. Note that $X_1, ...X_n, Y_1, ...Y_n, P_1, ...P_n$ are all real value parameters so we can use them directly in the differential evolution algorithm. Since the group should be binary encoded, two solutions are proposed. The first solution is a modified version of Differential Evolution Algorithm that support binary encoding. The second one turns the grouping problem to the maximum cut problem and a simple heuristic is introduced to solve it.

4.2   Solution One: Modified Differential Evolution Algorithm

For the binary encoding problem, we try to replace the real number operator to binary ones. The subtraction in the mutation rule is to take the difference between the two vectors $\mathbf{x_{p2}}$ and $\mathbf{x_{p3}}$. So in our modified version, we change it to "exclusive or" since in essence "exclusive or" also takes the difference of binary values. F is now a random integer in $\{-1, 1\}$. When $F = 1$, the mutation expression turns to $\hat{\mathbf{x}}_\mathbf{i} = \mathbf{x_{p1}} + (\mathbf{x_{p2}} - \mathbf{x_{p3}})$; When $F = -1$, the mutation expression turns to $\hat{\mathbf{x}}_\mathbf{i} = \mathbf{x_{p1}} - (\mathbf{x_{p2}} - \mathbf{x_{p3}})$. The binary plus is defined as "complement of exclusive or". The entire binary mutation expression is:

$$\hat{\mathbf{x}}_\mathbf{i} = \begin{cases} \sim (\mathbf{x_{p1}} \wedge (\mathbf{x_{p2}} \wedge \mathbf{x_{p3}})), \ if \ F = 1 \\ \mathbf{x_{p1}} \wedge (\mathbf{x_{p2}} \wedge \mathbf{x_{p3}}), \ if \ F = -1 \end{cases} \tag{3}$$

where $\wedge$ is the operator for exclusive or and $\sim$ is the operator for complement. The algorithm that supports hybrid encoding can be described as:

Require: Map of planning area, Constraints of parameters
Ensure: A good feasible plan
 1: Randomly initialize a set of plans S
 2: **while** Convergence requirement is not meet **do**
 3:    **for** each plan $\mathbf{x_i} \in S$ **do**
 4:       Randomly choose 3 other distinct plan in S
 5:       Mutate the real valued parameters using the original DE mutation rule
 6:       Mutate the binary parameters using the binary mutation rule
 7:       $y_i = \mathrm{crossover}(\hat{\mathbf{x}}_\mathbf{i}, \mathbf{x_i})$
 8:       **if** $fitness(\mathbf{y_i}) > fitness(\mathbf{x_i})$ **then**
 9:          Replace $\mathbf{x_i}$ with $\mathbf{y_i}$
10:       **else**
11:          Keep the original $\mathbf{x_i}$ in set S
12:       **end if**
13:    **end for**
14: **end while**
15: Output the best plan in the set S

4.3   Solution Two: Maximum Cut Heuristic

Besides modifying the mutation rule, we proposed an alternative way to optimize the binary part of the plan. The idea is to transform the plan into a graph and find a maximum cut on the graph. Since TDMA guarantees that readers in different group will not interfere each other, we can find a good group arrangement to minimize the interference level. This is equivalent to the complement of maximum cut problem in graph theory. We can convert a plan to a graph in the following way: Every reader in the plan is mapped to a vertex in the graph; If two readers' detection range overlaps, there is an edge between the corresponding vertices and the area of the overlapped detection range is the weight of the edge.

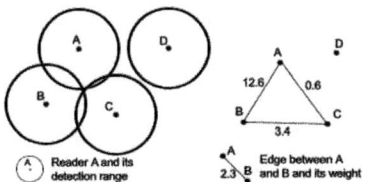

Fig. 2. Transform a Plan into a Graph

Fig. 2 shows how to transform a plan into a graph. Reader A, B and C are close and their detection range overlap so they are mutually connected in the graph. The size of the overlapping area is the weight of the edge. Reader D do not have any common detection range with other readers. So it is an isolated vertex in the transformed graph.

A **cut** of a graph is a partition of all vertices into two disjoint vertex sets. The **size of the cut** is the weight of the edges that ends in different vertex sets. A **maximum cut** is the cut whose weight is not smaller than any other cut in the graph. Finding a grouping with minimum interference is actually equivalent to finding a maximum cut in the corresponding graph because the complement of the maximum cut is the grouping with minimum interference. Finding a maximum cut in a general graph is NP-hard but there exists some fast heuristic for finding a good solution in the graph. One of them is the 0.5-approximation algorithm. We try to incorporate the idea of this algorithm into our Differential Evolution algorithm to enhance the performance. After the crossover step of each iteration, the largest weight edge ends in the complement of the maximum cut was found out. Since both the end points of the edge are in the same group, we randomly choose one and move it to the other group. If this reduces the interference level, we finalize the change, otherwise, we revert the change. The algorithm can be described as following:

Require: Map of planning area, Constraints of parameters
Ensure: A good feasible plan
1: Randomly initialize a set of plans S
2: **while** Convergence requirement is not meet **do**
3:   **for** each plan $\mathbf{x_i} \in S$ **do**
4:     Randomly choose 3 other distinct plan in S
5:     For parameters other than grouping: $\hat{\mathbf{x}}_i = \mathbf{x_{p1}} + F(\mathbf{x_{p2}} + \mathbf{x_{p3}})$
6:     $\mathbf{y_i} = \text{crossover}(\hat{\mathbf{x}}_i, \mathbf{x_i})$
7:     Find the largest weight edge (a, b) in the complement of the original cut in plan $\mathbf{y_i}$
8:     Move a or b into the other group
9:     **if** $fitness(Original\ \mathbf{y_i}) > fitness(\mathbf{y_i})$ **then**
10:      Revert the change
11:    **end if**
12:    **if** $fitness(\mathbf{y_i}) > fitness(\mathbf{x_i})$ **then**
13:      Replace $\mathbf{x_i}$ with $\mathbf{y_i}$

14:      **else**
15:          Keep the original x_i in set S
16:      **end if**
17:    **end for**
18: **end while**
19: Output the best plan in the set S

5   Experiment

Both versions of the algorithm are implemented using Java. We simulated a planning area which corresponds to a $20m \times 20m$ warehouse. The northern part of the warehouse is relatively empty while the southern part is divided into more rooms. Intuitively, more readers should be deployed in the southern part to achieve a higher coverage. The detection range $R \in [2.5m, 3.5m]$ is tunable by adjusting the emitting power. Readers are divided into two groups for TDMA. Mutation parameter is $F \in [-0.2, 0.2]$ (For real-value parameters) and $F \in -1, 1$ (For binary parameters). The crossover rate $CR = 0.5$ and the number of individuals in the population is 20. Fig. 3 shows how the best plan in the candidate set S evolves when we use the maximum cut heuristic. The initial plan randomly allocates the parameters of the readers. After several iterations, more readers are allocated to the southern part because there are more obstacles. Nearby readers in the northern part are assigned to different groups to avoid interference. The coverage of the best plan is also increasing from 62.70 percent to 91.75 percent.

We compared the modified Differential Evolution version and the maximum cut heuristic version. Both versions are executed 50 times and at each time 1000 iterations. The average running time for the one using binary encoding and the one using maximum heuristic are 169,851ms and 184,236ms respectively. However, the one with maximum cut heuristic outperforms the one using binary encoding in terms of coverage in terms of coverage. The coverage for the one with binary encoding is 89.26 percent while the coverage for the one using maximum cut heuristic is 92.15 percent. The extra time spent in the maximum cut heuristic is the time for finding the largest weight edge in the adjacency list. So there is a trade off here. Since the planning problem does not require a very fast execution time, it is worthwhile to spend more time for a better output.

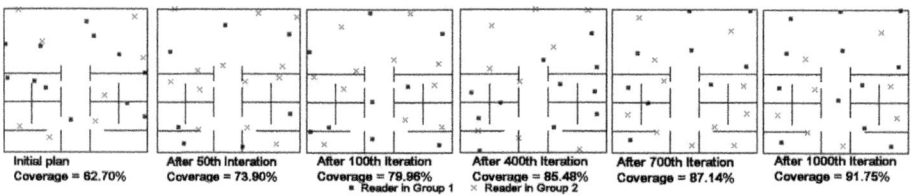

Initial plan
Coverage = 62.70%

After 50th Interation
Coverage = 73.90%

After 100th Iteration
Coverage = 78.96%
• Reader in Group 1

After 400th Iteration
Coverage = 85.48%
× Reader in Group 2

After 700th Iteration
Coverage = 87.14%

After 1000th Iteration
Coverage = 91.75%

Fig. 3. Best Plan After Each Iteration

6   Conclusion

In this paper, we discussed how to apply Differential Evolution Algorithm on RFID network planning problem so that a good solution could be found in the high dimensional search space. TDMA is used to reduce interference between readers and we proposed two methods to group the readers. One simple and effective method is the modified version of Differential Evolution Algorithm which supports binary encoding. The other one which use a maximum cut heuristic is complicated but has a better performance. By our comparative experiment, both methods work well and the one with maximum cut heuristic outperform the modified version of Differential Evolution Algorithm. In the future, we will focus on modeling the problem in 3-dimensional and consider backscatter signal in the simulation.

References

1. Chen, H., Zhu, Y.: RFID Networks Planning Using Evolutionary Algorithms and Swarm Intelligence. Wireless Communications, Networking and Mobile Computing (2008)
2. Carbunar, B., Ramanathan, M.K., Koyuturk, M., Hoffmann, C., Grama, A.: Redundant-Reader Elimination in RFID Systems. In: Sensor and Ad Hoc Communications and Networks (2005); Taxonomy and survey of RFID anti-collision protocols. Computer Communications (2006)
3. Shin, K.C., Park, S.B., Jo, G.S.: Enhanced TDMA Based Anti-Collision Algorithm with a Dynamic Frame Size Adjustment Strategy for Mobile RFID Readers. Sensors (September 2009)
4. Kannan, A.A., Mao, G., Vucetic, B.: Simulated Annealing based Wireless Sensor Network Localization. Journal of Computers 1(2) (May 2006)
5. Jin, S., Zhou, M., Wu, A.S.: Sensor Network Optimization Using a Genetic Algorithm. In: 7th World Multiconference on Systemics, Cybernetics and Informatics (2003)
6. Guan, Q., Liu, Y., Yang, Y., Yu, W.: Genetic Approach for Network Planning in the RFID Systems. In: Sixth International Conference on Intelligent Systems Design and Applications
7. Yang, Y., Wu, Y., Xia, M., Qin, Z.: A RFID Network Planning Method Based on Genetic Algorithm. In: 2009 International Conference on Networks Security, Wireless Communications and Trusted Computing (2009)
8. Storn, R., Price, K.: Differential Evolution - A simple and efficient adaptive scheme for global optimization over continuous spaces. Technical Report TR-95-012, International Computer Science Institute, Berkeley (1995)

An Improved PSO-SVM Approach for Multi-faults Diagnosis of Satellite Reaction Wheel

Di Hu, Yunfeng Dong, and Ali Sarosh

School of Astronautics BeiHang University, 37 Xueyuan Road, Haidian district,
100191, Beijing, China
hudibuaa@yahoo.cn, sinosat@buaa.edu.cn,
alisarosh@sa.buaa.edu.cn

Abstract. Diagnosis of reaction wheel faults is very significant to ensure long-term stable satellite attitude control system operation. Support vector machine (SVM) is a new machine learning method based on statistical learning theory, which can solve the classification problem of small sampling, non-linearity and high dimensionality. However, it is difficult to select suitable parameters of SVM. Particle Swarm Optimization (PSO) is a new optimization method, which is motivated by social behavior of bird flocking. The optimization method not only has strong global search capability, but is also very simple to apply. However, PSO algorithms are still not mature enough for handling some of the more complicated problems as the one posed by SVM. Therefore an improved PSO algorithm is proposed and applied in parameter optimization of support vector machine as IPSO-SVM. The characteristics of satellite dynamic control process include three typical reaction wheel failures. Here an IPSO-SVM is used in fault diagnosis and compared with neural network-based diagnostic methods. Simulation results show that the improved PSO can effectively avoid the premature phenomenon; it can also optimize the SVM parameters, and achieve higher diagnostic accuracy than artificial neural network-based diagnostic methods.

Keywords: Improved Particle Swarm Optimization, Support Vector Machine, Reaction Wheel, Satellite Attitude Control System, Artificial Neural Network, Fault diagnosis.

1 Introduction

Satellite system is a highly complex, highly integrated and high-cost system. As scientific tasks increase, there is an attendant increase in the demand for longer life and high reliability of satellite systems. Characteristics and distribution failures of on-orbit satellites were researched in Literature [1]. During the life cycle of a satellite, the frequency of failures of attitude and orbit control system remains fairly high. Especially for the high-orbit satellite, which have longer lifetime, and use reaction wheels as actuators for the attitude control system [2]. Therefore, the problem posed is how to diagnose the reaction wheel's faulty conditions during on-orbit operation, and then propose the effective measures to improve its basic conditions so as to ensure longer

F.L. Wang et al. (Eds.): AICI 2010, Part II, LNAI 6320, pp. 114–123, 2010.

life and high reliability operations of the satellite. Currently, fault tree [3], dynamic neural network [4] and data mining [5] are used for fault diagnosis of reaction wheels.

In 1995 Kennedy and Eberhart proposed the PSO optimization algorithm, based as the predatory behavior of birds [6]. It was further improved into global optimized particle swarm optimization [7] and so on. The algorithm has been used in many fields because of its simplicity and good search capability.

Support Vector Machine (SVM) [8] proposed by Vapnik is a minimum structural risk theory for a small sample. It is characterized by good generalization ability. Since aerospace is limited by the conditions of telemetry and other systems, the collected data is also very limited. Therefore, the need for processing a small sample and good generalization is of great significance. LS-SVM method was proposed by Suykens in [9]. As compared with standard SVM method, which uses equality constraints, the LS-SVM method utilizes inequality constraints, and the second norm of the error becomes the optimization goal of the loss function thus transforming the solution of the two time planning problem into linear equations.

At present, many scholars use PSO to optimize SVM parameters, and have a number of fruitful researches in the application of PSO-SVM. For example, literature [10] proposed applying PSO-SVM into fault diagnosis of turbo pump rotor to greater advantage than Genetic Algorithm (GA) and/or SVM. In Literature [11] Chaos PSO is applied to optimize the parameter of support vector machine and classify multiple faults. However as yet there exists no major research whereby PSO-SVM is applied in fault diagnosis of reaction wheel.

Three typical fault modes including reaction wheel motor current failure, increase of friction torque and increase of back electromotive force (BEMF) are researched in accordance with reaction wheel fault characteristics in the attitude control system (ACS) that utilizes reaction wheels for attitude control. Here support vector machines (SVM) is used to classify and identify fault signal characteristics. The SVM parameters are then optimized by improved PSO in sample training. Simulation results show that the proposed method can effectively diagnose a variety of reaction wheel failure modes, and has better accuracy than neural network diagnosis method.

2 Basic Principles

2.1 PSO and Its Improvement

Standard particle swarm optimization is an optimization algorithm that initializes position and velocity of a group of particles in solution space. The particles location represents the solution of the required function. The particles speed determines the particle flight direction and distance. Fitness describes the particles calculation in this optimal function. The local optimal solution and the global optimal solution can be evaluated by solving the fitness of each particle. Assume that there are m particles to form a community in a D dimension target search space. The position of ith particle is expressed as vector $\mathbf{X}(x_1, x_2, ..., x_D)$, and flight speed is expressed as $\mathbf{V}(v_1, v_2, ..., v_D)$. Each particle updates itself by tracking the two "best positions". One position is the best place that the particle currently finds, namely the local optimal solution (pbest), and the other is the best place that is found in all particles of the group, namely the global optimal solution (gbest). gbest is the best value in the pbest. For the kth iteration, each particle changes according to (1), (2).

$$v_{ij}(k + 1) = w*v_{ij}(k) + c_1*rand()(pbest_{ij} - x_{ij}(k)) + c_2 rand()(gbest_j + x_{ij}(k)). \tag{1}$$

$$x_{ij}(k + 1) = x_{ij}(k) + v_{ij}(k + 1). \tag{2}$$

In expression (1), (2), $i = 1, 2, ..., m$ expresses m particles, $j = 1, 2, ..., D$ expresses particles dimension, $v_{ij}(k)$ is the j-dimensional component of flight velocity vector that particle i forms in the kth iteration; $x_{ij}(k)$ is the j-dimensional component of position vector that that particle i forms in the kth iteration; $pbest_{ij}$ is the j-dimensional component of the particle's best position pbest for particle i, $gbest_j$ is the j-dimensional component of global best position (gbest); c_1, c_2 is learning factor; rand() is a random function to generate random number in [0,1]. Standard particle swarm algorithm adopts a fixed inertia weight. Literature [12] believes that inertia weight should be adjusted.

When the particles are closer and closer to the global optimum, the inertia weight should be smaller, this also means that speed adjustment is smaller, and hence could be more stable. Proofs are given in the literature. It verifies that the linear inertia weight can achieve good results. This paper directly uses findings of literature [10]. For linear inertia weight refer equation (3), w is the inertia weight, and is nonnegative.

$$w = w_{max} - (w_{max} - w_{min})/iter_{max} * iter . \tag{3}$$

Where, w_{max}, w_{min} are the maximum and minimum inertial weights; $iter, iter_{max}$ are the current iteration number and maximum iteration numbers.

The standard particle swarm algorithm is improved to avoid the premature phenomena from occurring. This implies namely sorting the particles according to fitness after the speed is updated each time, directly removing half of the particles that have low fitness, regenerating half of the particles according to the current global optimal solution. In this way, the new generation of particles involved in evolution is:

$$Nextgeneration = sortrows(fitness); \tag{4}$$

$$Nextgeneration-Position(N/2 + 1 : N) = gbest + randn *range/2; \tag{5}$$

$$Nextgeneration-Velocity(N/2 + 1 : N) = gbest + randn *range/2. \tag{6}$$

where, Nextgeneration is particle sorted according to fitness, Nextgeneration-P osition(N=2+1 : N) is position of the latter half of sorted particles, gbest is the current global best solution, randn is random number with mean 0 and variance 1. range is particle search range.

2.2 SVM

The detailed introduction of SVM is given in the reference [13]. The kernel function is significant in the process of SVM algorithm needed to construct hyper-planes.

Suitable kernel function can be chosen to realize linear classification after some nonlinear transformation, and computation of load that does not increase.

Different kernel functions will produce different SVM algorithms. The RBF kernel function is chosen to produce SVM in this paper.

RBF kernel function

$$K(X; Y) = \exp\{-(X - Y)^2/\sigma^2)\}. \tag{7}$$

SVM is a dual Classification algorithm, and is not appropriate for multi-class situation. Some researchers provide different improved algorithms. One of them is the "1-vs-1" algorithm which was provided by Kressel [14]. The "1-vs-1" algorithm constructs all possible dual class classifier within the K classes. Every dual class classifier uses two classes to train in the training samples. So it needs $K*(K-1)/2$ dual class classifiers. The multi-dual-class classifiers judge the data comprehensively during identification.

In the fault diagnosis process, the error class may bring enormous loss. Considering the features of fault class, the Decision Directed Acyclic (DDAG) [15] is used, which is an improved "1-vs-1" algorithm.

2.3 Fault Diagnosis Steps

In this section, the basic step of IPSO-SVM algorithm is described as follows:

1) Collect the different models of reaction wheel at different times, and classify as training sample and test sample data.

2) Initialize a swarm with N particles.

3) Compute the particles' fitness; initialize the particle's local best and global best point.

4) Compute particle weight, update the particle's velocity and position according to their respective formulae, and update the local best and global best points.

5) Sort the particles with fitness function, this implies deleting half of the particles having lower fitness and then reserving the other half with higher fitness level. The current global optimized solution will then produce a new half of the particles composed of a new swarm generation.

6) Compute the fitness function of new generation of swarm particles. If it fits the process is exited else the algorithm returns to step 4.

7) load the diagnosis data and use the train support vectors to diagnose the data, and hence return the diagnosis result.

The train data is used for support vectors learning, whereby every parameter is decided by particles' position. The train support vectors are used to diagnose the test data and the diagnosis accuracy represents the particle's fitness.

3 Satellite Reaction Wheel Control System

The main purpose of the attitude control subsystem (ACS), which is commonly considered as momentum management system, is to orientate the main structure of the satellite at desired angle within required accuracy [8]. As the satellite runs on-orbit,

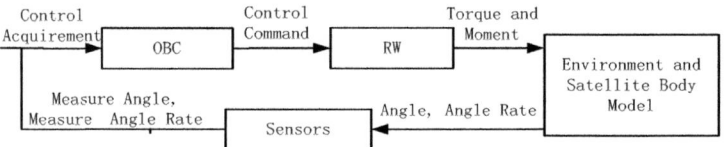

Fig. 1. A type of ACS function diagram

according to the system design's operation life, the ACS adopts the reaction wheel as the actuator in the normal mode. Fig. 1 represents function diagram of ACS model using a 'feedback control' loop. The data of reaction wheel is downloaded from the telemetry channel, including rotor current telemetry, wheel speed telemetry and bearing temperature telemetry. Therefore corresponding fault information is acquired from only a small amount of telemetric data to make diagnosis, thus providing evidence for the on-orbit management of reaction wheel.

As Fig. 1 shows, the On-Board-Computer (OBC) calculates command voltage, (according to the measured angle and angle rate) from the sensor data, to control the Reaction Wheels' (RW) output torque and moment acting on the satellite body. The environment model is then used to compute the environment disturbance torque. Finally the satellite body model is used to compute the dynamics and its kinematics. After it has acted, the satellite body model outputs current attitude angle and attitude angle rate to the sensors which are used to measure the angle and angle rate, using Gyros and Earth sensors or Star tracer etc.

4   Reaction Wheel Fault Diagnosis

4.1   Fault Mode Analysis

Various faults of reaction wheels used for attitude control will occur because it operates for a long period. The fault modes include friction increase, rotor current failure, and back electromotive force (BEMF) increase, together with normal mode, to constitute the four kinds of modes. The paper uses limited simulated telemetric data, such as rotor current and speed, to analyze four modes of the reaction wheels.

Friction Increase: The increased in friction leads to increase of reaction wheel friction torque this occurs as a result of lubricant failure or bearing wear.

Fig. 2 shows data of rotor current and speed as the friction torque increases. It can be seen from the figure that as friction torque increases, the rotor current increases and a slight change in speed occurs. As a part of ACS, the reaction wheel is controlled by OBC. This fault leads to a change in desired attitude angle, the OBC then outputs the command to control the wheel, which could lead to sudden up-surge in the rotor current. When rotor current reaches its maximum limit, the generated torque can no longer overcome the friction torque, and the satellite will go out of control.

Rotor Current Failure: In this mode the reaction wheel rotor current suddenly disappears because of line faults or any other failures, hence the current is zero.

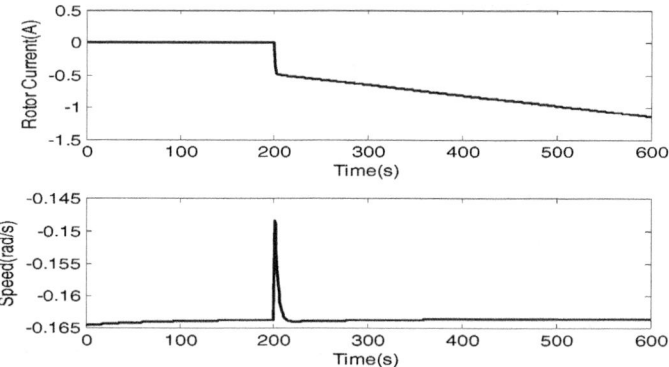

Fig. 2. The Rotor Current and Speed Data as the Friction Increasing

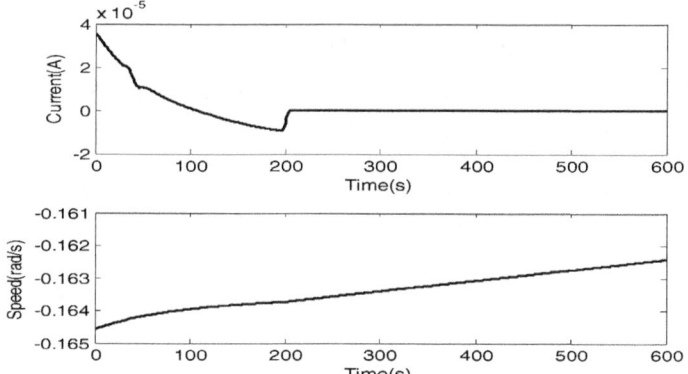

Fig. 3. The Rotor Current and Speed Data as the Rotor Current Failure

Fig. 3 shows the data of rotor current and speed for the case of rotor current failure. The fault happens at 200 seconds and the rotor current drops to zero. The speed reduces under the action of the friction torque; it then generates momentum that has the opposite effect on the satellite. If the faults exist for a long time, the satellite would go out of control.

Back Electro-Motive Force (BEMF): Its increment results from transient surge in reaction wheels circuit or hardware level failure in the rotor driver unit which leads to sudden increase in back-EMF to maximum control voltage.

Fig. 4 is time-domain graph of rotor current and speed data for the case of back electromotive force increase. As seen from the figure, after the event of back-EMF increase, a variation may occur in rotor current and speed. But eventually rotor current returns to normal, and a certain speed will always be maintained. This is because BEMF will have the effect of offsetting the attitude control system by a certain fix value, this is in accordance with instruction to control attitude. The variation will generate sway of the satellite and add other uncertainties, and the energy consumption of the entire satellite will increase.

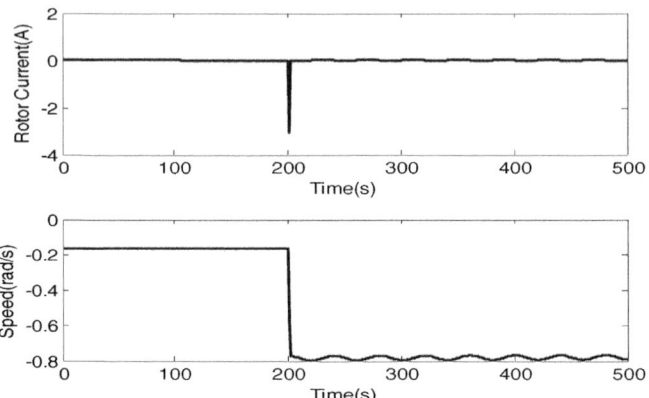

Fig. 4. The Rotor Current and Speed Data as Back Electromotive Force (BEMF) Increasing

4.2 SVM Parameters Optimized by PSO

Data is collected for each failure mode samples. An improved PSO is used to optimize the SVM that picks up support vectors. The fault classification accuracy of each particle's fitness is expressed as a percentage.

In training data friction-increase is defined as the first class, BEMF as the second class, rotor current failure as the third class, normal mode as the forth class.

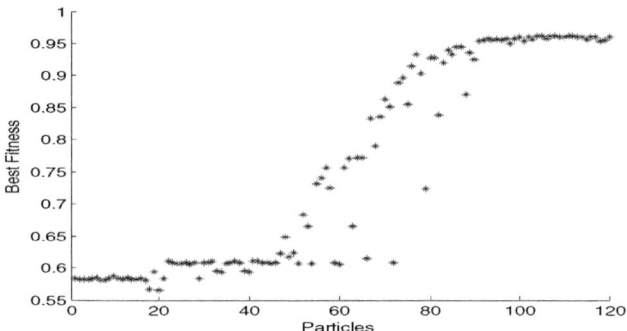

Fig. 5. Particle Fitness Trend

Fig. 5 shows the trend of particles fitness. At first the class accuracy is not high, for standard particle swarm optimization algorithm, the first generation's 20 particles are trapped into the local best solution, and the accuracy is just 0.58. For the improved PSO, fitness changes appear better at the second generation. And from the third generation, the particles escape from the local best solution. As shown in the figure, the train class accuracy archives at 0.95 at the fifth generation.

4.3 Fault Diagnosis

After control system is stable, friction increasing faults are injected at the 200th second and the fault continues for 100 seconds. Rotor current faults are injected at the 300th

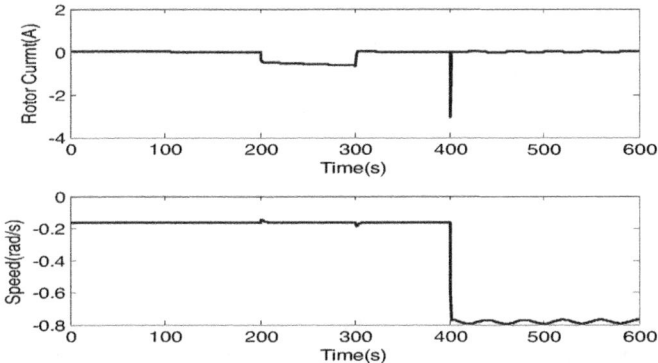

Fig. 6. Rotor Current and Speed Data as Injected Three Faults

second and the fault continues for 100 seconds. BEMF faults are injected at the 400th second. Only one fault occurs at the same time.

Fig.6 shows the rotor current and speed data when the three faults are injected. From the figure, it transpires that the injected fault had the same feature as the fault analysis.

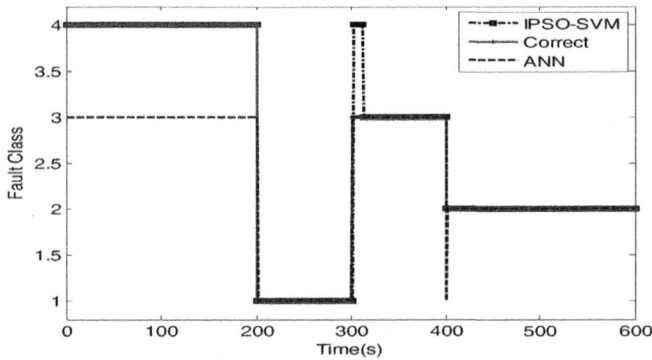

Fig. 7. Fault Diagnosis by IPSO-SVM, Artificial Neural Network (ANN) and the Correct Class

Fig.7 shows the IPSO-SVM, Artificial Neural Network (ANN) fault diagnosis and comparison with the correct class. The figure shows that the SVM has a very good diagnostic ability for independent faults. As seen from the figure, the SVM diagnoses the model as the fourth class normal mode for the first 200 seconds, first class friction-increasing mode for 200-300 seconds, third class current failure for 300-400 seconds, and the second class BEMF for 400-600 seconds. The IPSO-SVM diagnosis result is similar to the injected faults and the accuracy is 0.98. At the same time, the IPSO-SVM diagnosis result of above-mentioned fault modes is compared with faults diagnosis using artificial neural network (ANN). The result is also shown in the fig.7. The class definition is the same. ANN diagnoses the mode as the third class for the first 200 seconds and 300-400 seconds, and the first class for 200-300 seconds, the second class for 400-600 seconds, and as first class for a small data at 400 seconds. The diagnosis accuracy is only 0.6633. It shows that the diagnostic accuracy of ANN is far less than that of IPSO-SVM.

5 Conclusion

The paper analyzes the three types of fault modes of reaction wheel which acts as a actuator in a satellite attitude control system. An improved PSO for SVM parameters optimization is presented, and applied to the reaction wheel fault diagnosis. It can be seen from the result that the improved PSO overcomes the premature shortage for SVM training. The simulated results show that IPSO can serve as a promising method for training SVM. When compared with ANN, the IPSO-SVM exhibits far better performance.

References

1. Tafazoli, M.: A study of on-orbit spacecraft failures. Acta Astronautica 64, 195–205 (2009)
2. Geng, L.-H., Xiao, D.-Y., Wang, Q., et al.: Attitude control model identification of on-orbit satellites actuated by reaction wheels. Acta Astronautica 66, 714–721 (2010)
3. Barua, A., Sinha, P., Khorasani, K., et al.: A novel fault tree approach for identifying potentiall causes of satellite reaction wheel failure. In: Proceedings of the 2005 IEEE Conference on Control applications Toronto, Canada (August 2005)
4. Li, Z.Q., Ma, L., Khorasani, K.: A dynamic neural network based reaction wheel fault diagnosis for satellites. In: 2006 International Joint Conference on Neural Networks, Sheraton Vancouver wall centre hotel, Vancouver, Canada (July 2006)
5. Zhou, J., Liu, Q., Jin, G., et al.: Reliability Modeling for Momentum Wheel based on Data Mining of failure-Physics. In: 2010 Third Internatinal Conference on Knowledge Discovery and Data Mining, pp. 115–118. IEEE, Los Alamitos (2010)
6. Eberhart, R.C., Kennedy, J.: A New Optimizer Using Particle Swarm Theory. In: Proc. of the 6th Int'l. Symp. on Micro Machine and Human Science, Nagoya, Japan, pp. 39–43 (1995)
7. Ali, M.M., Kaelo, P.: Improved particle swarm algorithms for global optimization. Applied mathematics and computation 196, 578–593 (2008)
8. Vapnik, V.N.: The Nature of statistical Learning Theory. Springer, New York (1995)
9. Suykens, J.A.K., Vandewalle, J.: Least Squares Support Vector Machine Classifiers. Neural Processing Letters 3, 293–300 (1999)
10. Yuan, S.-F., Chu, F.-L.: Fault diagnositics based on particle swarm optimisation and support vector machines. Mechanical Systems and Signal Processing 21, 1787–1798 (2007)
11. Tang, X., Zhuang, L., Cai, J., et al.: Multi-fault classification based on support vector machine trained by chaos particle swarm optimization. Knowledge based systems (2010) (article in press)

12. Shi, Y.H., Eberhart, R.C.: Empirical study of particle swarm optimization. In: Proc. of Congress on Evolution Computation, pp. 1945–1950 (1999)
13. Zhao, H.-b., Yin, S.: Geomechanical parameters identification by particle swarm optimization and support vector machine. Applied mathematical modeling 33, 3997–4012 (2009)
14. Kressel, U.: Pairwise classification and support vector machines. In: Scholkopf, B., et al. (eds.) Advances in kernel Methods-Support vector learning, pp. 255–268. MIT Press, Cambridge (1999)
15. Platt, J., Cristianini, N., Shawe-Taylor, J.: Large margin dags for multiclass classification. In: Advances in Neural Information Processing Systems, vol. 12, pp. 547–553. MIT Press, Cambridge (2000)

Research of Long-Term Runoff Forecast Based on Support Vector Machine Method

Yong Peng and Zhi-chun Xue

Hydraulic Engineering Institute, Dalian University of Technology, Dalian, China
pyongcuidi@163.com

Abstract. Using the global optimization properties of Particle Swarm Optimization(PSO) to carry out parameter identification of support vector machine(SVM). Before the particle swarm search for parameters, exponential transform the parameters first to make intervals [0, 1] and [1, infinity] have the same search probability. Fitness function of PSO as generalization ability of support vector machine model to be the standard, at the same time discussed the minimum error of testing samples and leave-one-out method to the SVM learning method promotion ability. Finally taking the data of monthly runoff of Yichang station in Yangtze River as an example, respectively using the ARMA model, seasonal ARIMA model, BP neural network model and the SVM model that have built to simulate forecasting, the result shows the validity of the model.

Keywords: long-term runoff forecasting, parameter identification, PSO, SVM.

1 Introduction

Long-term hydrological forecasting has the longer forecasting period, enable people to take early measures to co-ordinate arrangements in resolving conflicts of flood control and drought control, sectors of water storage water disposal and water use, to obtain the maximum benefit. There are many models of medium and long-term hydrological forecasting, and have be widely used in research of hydrological and water resources, playing a very important role in solving the science problems of hydrological and water resources. Among them, machine learning is an important direction of hydrological forecasting, the realization method can mainly be divided into three types:

(1) Classical statistical estimation methods, such as ARMA models, however this model has serious limitation, first of all, it need to know the distribution form of sample, which takes a very high price; also, traditional statistical study the asymptotic theory when the sample size tend to infinity, while the actual number of sample is limited.

(2) Experience non-linear methods such as artificial neural network [1]. This method builds a non-linear model by using the given samples, overcoming difficulties of traditional parameter estimation method. But this approach lacks a unified mathematical theory.

F.L. Wang et al. (Eds.): AICI 2010, Part II, LNAI 6320, pp. 124–133, 2010.

(3) Support vector machine [2-4]. Statistical learning theory(SLT) is a theory which study the machine learning regulation especially in small sample situations, statistical inference rules under the theoretical system not only consider the request for asymptotic performance, but also pursuit of getting the best results in the existing limited information condition, Support vector machine is built based on the VC dimension theory of statistical learning theory and principle of structural risk minimization, according to the limited information of sample to explore the best compromise between complexity and learning ability of model, in order to obtain the best generalization ability.

As the theory of SLT and SVM method is still in the developing stage, they are not perfect in many aspects, such as: ① Many theories only have theoretical significance, have not yet realized in the actual algorithm currently; ② Besides, there are not yet general methods for VC dimensional analysis of actual learning machine; ③ there are still no rationale of choosing the appropriate kernel function according to the specific problems in the SVM method; ④ identification of parameters C and kernel function parameters. The article focus on ④, put PSO into use of parameter identification problems of SVM by some index transform, and then put the model that have optimized into practice of medium and long-term runoff forecasting.

2 SVM Parameter Identification Based on PSO

2.1 Theory of Regression Support Vector Machine [5]

Give a training set

$$x = \{(x_1, y_1), (x_2, y_2), \cdots (x_l, y_l)\} \subset R^n \times R \qquad (1)$$

Using non-linear Map ϕ mapping the data to High-dimensional feature space, where linear regression proceed

$$f(x) = <w, \phi(x)> +b, \quad w, x \in R^n, \ b \in R \qquad (2)$$

Optimal regression function is minimization and regularity of risk functional by some constraint conditions

$$\frac{1}{2}\|w\|^2 + C \cdot \frac{1}{l} \cdot \sum_{i=1}^{l} L_\varepsilon(y_i, f(x_i)) \qquad (3)$$

In this equation: the first term called rule of entry, the second called empirical risk functional, they can be determined by different loss function, constant $C > 0$ is used to control the punishment level to sample which beyond the error ε. Using the ε-insensitive loss functional

$$L_\varepsilon(y_i, f(x_i)) = \max\{0, |y_i - f(x_i)| - \varepsilon\} \qquad (4)$$

To $L_\varepsilon(y_i, f(x_i))$, if the modulus of deviation between estimated output $f(x_i)$ and expected output y_i is less than ε, it is equal to 0; Otherwise, it equals to the result that modulus of deviation minus ε, by introducing non-negative slack variables ξ_i^* and ξ_i, the risk functional of minimization and regularization can be Re-described as :

$$\min \quad \frac{1}{2}\|w\|^2 + C\sum_{i=1}^{l}(\xi_i^* + \xi_i) \tag{5}$$

$$\text{subject to} \quad \begin{cases} y_i - <w,\phi(x_i)> -b \leq \varepsilon + \xi_i \\ <w,\phi(x_i)> +b - y_i \leq \varepsilon + \xi_i^* \\ \xi_i, \xi_i^* \geq 0 \end{cases} \tag{6}$$

This is a quadratic optimization problem, the dual problem is:

$$\max \quad W(\alpha_i, \alpha_i^*) = -\frac{1}{2}\sum_{i=1}^{l}\sum_{j=1}^{l}(\alpha_i - \alpha_i^*)(\alpha_j - \alpha_j^*) < x_i, x_j >$$

$$-\varepsilon\sum_{i=1}^{l}(\alpha_i + \alpha_i^*) + \sum_{i=1}^{l}y_i(\alpha_i - \alpha_i^*) \tag{7}$$

$$\text{subject to} \quad \sum_{i=1}^{l}(\alpha_i - \alpha_i^*) = 0 \quad \text{and} \quad 0 \leq \alpha_i, \alpha_i^* \leq C \tag{8}$$

Solving this quadratic optimization the value of α can be obtained, the expression of w is:

$$w = \sum_{i=1}^{l}(\alpha_i - \alpha_i^*)\phi(x_i) \tag{9}$$

$$f(x) = \sum_{i=1}^{l}(\alpha_i - \alpha_i^*) < \phi(x_i), \phi(x) > +b \tag{10}$$

The Support Vector Machine theory just take the high dimensional space's Dot products operations $K(x_i, x) < \phi(x_i), \phi(x) >$ into consideration, $K(x_i, x)$ is called kernel function. The conventional kernel function is :① Linear kernel function $< x, x_i >$, ② Polynomial kernel function, ③ RBF kernel function $\exp(-\sigma\|x - x_i\|^2)$, ④Sigmoid kernel function: $\tanh(b < x, x_i > +c)$. The article chose RBF kernel function.

2.2 Principle of PSO

In the search process of PSO, each particle simultaneously close to two points in the solution space, the first point is the optimal solution of all particles in the whole particle which could achieved In the course of ages by searching g^{best} ; Another point is the optimal solution p^{best}, which each particle could obtained by themselves in the courses of age by searching. Every particle means a point in the n dimensional space, $x_i = [x_{i1}, x_{i2}, \cdots, x_{in}]$ means the i particle ($x_i = [C_i, \sigma_i, \varepsilon_i]$ when searching for SVM parameters), the individual optimal solution of the i particle is expressed as $p_i^{best} = [p_{i1}, p_{i2}, \cdots, p_{in}]$, global optimal solution can be expressed as $g^{best} = [g_1, g_2, \cdots, g_n]$, while the k times correction of x_i is expressed to be $v_i^k = [v_{i1}^k, v_{i2}^k, \cdots, v_{in}^k]$, the formulation is:

$$v_{id}^k = w_i \cdot v_{id}^{k-1} + c_1 \cdot rand_1 \cdot (p_{id}^{k-1} - x_{id}^{k-1}) + c_2 \cdot rand_2 \cdot (g_d^{k-1} - x_{id}^{k-1}) \tag{11}$$

$$x_{id}^k = x_{id}^{k-1} + v_{id}^k \tag{12}$$

In this equation: $i = 1, 2, \cdots, m$, $d = 1, 2, \cdots, n$, m is the particle number of particle swarm, n is the dimensional of solution vector; c_1 and c_2 is learning factor, Kennedy and Eberhart [6] suggested $c_1 = c_2 = 2$; $rand_1$ and $rand_2$ are two individual nonce in between [0,1]; w_i is the Momentum coefficient which linear decrease with iterative algorithm; $v_{id} \in [-v_d^{max}, v_d^{max}]$ and v_d^{max} decided the search accuracy of particles in the d dimensional of solution space.

2.3 Parameter Identification Steps

RBF kernel function SVM have 3 parameters need to be decided: C, ε and σ. Explore the best parameter is a parameter identification problem of SVM model. In the article, the rapid global optimization characteristics of particle swarm are used to search for parameters, which can decrease the aimlessness of trial and improve the prediction accuracy of the model. On account of the possibility of parameter C, ε and σ located in the interval [0,1] is quite large, if searched directly, the probability of interval [0,1] could be selected would be lower, so the article making parameters exponential transformed before search, cause interval [0,1] and [1, ∞] to have the same search probability [7]. Steps of identification SVM parameters based on PSO is as follows:

(1) Initialization setting of SVM, the setting including group size, iterations, maximum allowable particle velocity v_d^{max}, randomly given initial particle x_i^0 and particle initial velocity v_i^0, One of the particle vector represents a support vector machine model, The elements of particle vectors corresponding support vector machines parameters C, ε and σ.

(2) The corresponding parameters of particle vector decided the model of SVM, calculate the fitness value of each particle, to reflect the promotion predictability of SVM model. Fitness function has the following three forms:

① Taking the minimum error between actual value and forecasting value of training sample to be the objective function, the form is not good. Because the research of Keerthi [8] shows that to a C which is big enough, when $\sigma \to \infty$, RBF kernel function SVM can simulate and train samples at very high accuracy, however, the test sample does not have any generalization ability; When $\sigma \to 0$, RBF kernel function SVM can simulate all the training samples to be a number.

② Taking the minimum error between actual value and forecasting value of forecasting sample to be the objective function[7,9], under this form, just ensure higher generalization ability of forecast samples, but can not guarantee the model has a high generalization ability, the expression is:

$$F = \frac{1}{m} \sum_{i=1}^{m} |[y_i - f(z_i)]/y_i| \tag{13}$$

In this equation, m is the prediction sample number, z_i is the i input value of SVM, y_i is the measured value of the i forecast sample.

③ Maximize generalization ability of the model is aimed to be objective function. Using the leave one out method can estimate the learning method generalization ability of SVM[10]. When estimate use the leave one out method, first of all leave a sample to be tested from the training set, then to train forecast model using the other training models, at last, predict samples to be tested in the training set.

Let f^i to express the forecasting model get from the remaining training sample after leave the i sample, $f^i(z_i)$ express forecasting of the i sample using the model, $y_i - f^i(z_i)$ expresses the forecasting error of leave-one method, so the estimation of leave-one method to the learning method promotion ability would be:

$$F = \frac{1}{k} \sum_{i=1}^{k} |[y_i - f^i(z_i)]/y_i| \tag{14}$$

In the equation, k is the number of training sample, z_i is the i input value of SVM, y_i is the i training sample measured value, $f^i(z_i)$ is the i training sample predictive value.

(3) Compare the fitness function value $F(x_i)$ which calculated by the equation (13) or (14) with personal optimal value $F(p_i^{best})$, if $F(x_i) < F(p_i^{best})$, so $F(p_i^{best}) = F(x_i)$, $p_i^{best} = x_i$.

(4) Compare the fitness value $F(p_i^{best})$ of each particle with the best fitness value $F(g^{best})$ of all particles, if $F(p_i^{best}) < F(g^{best})$, then $F(g^{best}) = F(p_i^{best})$, $g^{best} = p_i^{best}$.

(5) Deciding whether the maximum number of iterations has come true, if not, a new round of calculation would be executed, to move the particles by equation (11) and (12), the new particles would produced, return to step(2), or the calculation will over.

3 Actual Application

3.1 Construction Situation

52(1890.1~1941.12) years' average monthly runoff data of Yichang hydrographic station of Yangtze river was collected. The first 49(1890.1-1938.12) years' data can be served as training data, the later 3(1939.1-1941.12) years' data used to forecasting test. In order to test the forecasting effect of SVM, the article simulation predict the original sequence of monthly runoff respectively use the ARMA model, seasonal ARIMA model and BP neural network model, and choose their average modulus of relative error as the evaluation index. For the seasonal ARIMA model, first of all, getting stationary series by difference at the cycle $\omega=12$, then to establish ARMA model for the stationary series that has got. For the BP neural network model, input nodes is 12; taking a hidden layer, using "trial and error" to determine hidden nodes.

3.2 Determine the Range of Parameter

Process of average monthly runoff make up the no-linear time-series $X=\{x_1,x_2,\cdots,x_N\}$, forecasting the no-linear runoff-series, just to find the relationship between the flow at time $i+p$ and the flow $x_{i+1},x_{i+2},\cdots,x_{i+p-1}$, the first p (as the coefficient of autocorrelation of average monthly runoff process will be maximum when the lag time is 12 month, so take $p=12$) minutes, that's means $x_{i+p}=f(x_{i+1},x_{i+2},\cdots,x_{i+p-1})$, f is a non-linear function, expression the relationship between runoff-time-series. f can learn from runoff time series of $N-p$ group by SVM, the model can be expressed by $f(x)=\sum_{i=1}^{k}(\alpha_i-\alpha_i^*)K(x,x_i)+b$, the parameter α_i,α_i^*,b can acquired by C,σ,ε, which get by PSO. SVM training algorithm takes the training algorithm minimizing sequence [11].

Interval's decision of C,σ,ε based on considerations as follow:

First to determine the range of σ. From the kernel function $\exp(-\sigma\|x-x_i\|^2)$ it can be seen that the size of σ is entirely depending on $\|x-x_i\|^2$. So in actual applications, as long as the value of σ much smaller than the minimum distance between training samples, the effect $\sigma\to0$ can be achieved; as well, when the value of σ much larger than the maximum distance between training samples, the effect $\sigma\to\infty$ will get. Based on the consideration, the search space of σ determined on trail is [$\min(\|x-x_i\|^2)/20$, $\max(\|x-x_i\|^2)\times20$]. For the Yichang station's training data $\min(\|x-x_i\|^2)$ =5.895×10-3, $\max(\|x-x_i\|^2)$ =3.934, so $\sigma\in[2.947\times10^{-4},78.680]$ and at last $\sigma\in[10^{-4},10^2]$.

Then to determine the range of C. When constructing the classification of surface equation, the penalty factor C will be used to set a term to value of Lagrange multipliers α, it can be seen in formula (8). When C exceeds a certain value, it will lose the binding effect on the value of α, experience risk and generation capacity almost have no change at this time. Therefore taken the following heuristic to determine maximum of C: first give a small C, named C_t, using it to train SVM and get a group α_i, $i = 1,2,\cdots,k$, where k is the total number of training samples, let $C^* = \max(\alpha_i)$. If $C^* < C_t$, take C_t as the maximum of C. Or, change a larger C_t to train SVM, until the result of C^* much smaller than C_t. In this way, search space $[0, C_t]$ of C will get. For the training data of Yichang station, $C_t = 10000$, so $C \in [0,10^4]$. As a result of having made exponential transformed for parameter before search, and the exponential transform of 0 is ∞, so $C \in [10^{-5},10^4]$ as a matter of experience.

At last, determine the range of ε. Because the input of SVM is normalized in between of interval $[0,1]$ before training samples, so the range of ε would be $[0,1]$, that's means $\varepsilon \in [0,1]$.

The range of SVM model parameter is: $C \in [10^{-5},10^4]$, $\sigma \in [10^{-4},10^2]$ and $\varepsilon \in [0,1]$; Correspondingly the search range of PSO is: $C \in [-5,4]$, $\sigma \in [-4,2]$ and $\varepsilon \in [0,1]$. When training SVM model by PSO, initial parameter should be set by references [12]: learning factor $c_1 = c_2 = 2$, maximum velocity $v_1^{\max} = v_2^{\max} = v_3^{\max} = 0.1$, maximum iteration $T = 50$, particle number is 20, momentum coefficient $w_1^t = w_2^t = w_3^t = 0.9 - t*0.5/T$, in this formula t is present iteration.

3.3   The Results of Calculation and Analysis

The result of simulation forecasting shown in table 1 and figure 1, SVM$_1$ express the SVM model which taking promotion ability maximization of forecasting sample to be the objective, the training set sample number of the model is 576, sample number of testing set is 36; SVM$_2$ express the SVM model which taking generation ability maximization of the model to be objective estimated by using the leave one out method, testing set would be the training set itself, sample number is 576. As can be seen from Table 1: Simulation accuracy on training data of the two SVM models is improved in different degrees than ARMA, ARIMA and ANN, forecast accuracy is about the same with ARIMA and ANN, but higher than the forecast accuracy of ARMA.

As can be seen from calculation result of the example: ① Both kinds of SVM models achieved good simulation forecast effect. ② Forecast accuracy of SVM$_1$ is higher than of SVM$_2$ that's because SVM$_1$ is obtained by target optimization at forecast error minimization of testing sample, that's means the forecast error is minimum by using SVM$_1$, so it's reasonable that the forecast accuracy of SVM$_1$ is higher than the forecast accuracy of SVM$_2$. ③ SVM model and ANN model is about the same simulation accuracy, but model building process of ANN has many difficulties, such as the hidden layer nodes is difficult to determine, the same with iterations, promotion ability is not easy to estimate and so on; While SVM model can achieve the better simulation forecast accuracy just need taking promotion ability maximization to be targets optimize parameters C, ε and Kernel parameter. ④ Simulation forecast accuracy of ARIMA model get the better effect as well, that's because time series after

Table 1. Performance indices of ARMA, ARIMA, ANN and SVM in Yichang station

Module name	Module parameter	Simulation error	Forecast error
SVM$_1$ (Objective is to minimize the sample error of prediction)	$C = 0.247$ $\sigma = 1.736$ $\varepsilon = 9.220 \times 10^{-3}$	12.8%	12.8%
SVM$_2$ (Leave-one method and $F = 14.7\%$)	$C = 0.350$ $\sigma = 1.168$ $\varepsilon = 0.0015$	12.4%	13.7%
Simple ARMA model	ARMA(9,6)	15.5%	14.5%
Seasonal ARIMA model	ARIMA(1,1,13)$_{12}$	14.5%	13.4%
Neural network model(nodes number of each layer)	12-4-1	14.3%	13.0%

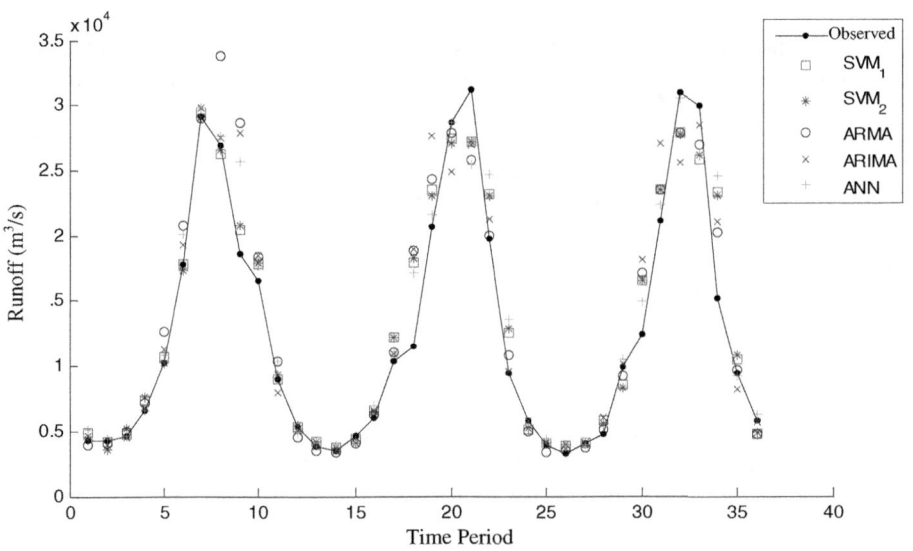

Fig. 1. ARMA, ARIMA ANN, and SVM forecasted and observed flow during validation period

difference become relatively stationary, which come up to application condition of ARMA model better. ⑤ All of simulation forecast accuracy of SVM model, ARIMA model and ANN model is better than ARMA model's, that's because ARMA model mostly fit to stable time series, while monthly runoff time series is unstable, so the bad calculation result is reasonable.

4 Summary

Through the paper we come to some understanding as follow: (1) SVM is based on the learning method of Statistical Learning Theory, it's unnecessary to know the relationship between dependent variable and independent variable when building models, very complex nonlinear relationship between dependent variable and independent variable can be obtained by studying the samples; Meanwhile, it based on the principle of structural risk minimization, and having well extrapolation. (2) Parameters C, σ, ε of SVM have great affect to forecast effectiveness, it's necessary to optimize them by using Optimization Algorithm, in this way we can reduce the aimlessness of trial and improve forecast accuracy. (3) Optimization Algorithm PSO is sample and easy and rapid convergence, we can get a well forecast effect by using the model parameters of SVM obtained through PSO rapid convergence.

Using "leave one out method" to estimate the learning method promotion ability of SVM can build a higher forecasting accuracy model on the basis of the original data. But estimation efficiency of the Algorithm is lower, a sample need to be studied and forecasted both once. As the number of sample is increasing, calculating increase rapidly. So finding a promotion ability simulation method of faster and high accuracy is our future work.

Acknowledgments. As the number of research group, all authors thank Prof. Zhou Hui-cheng and other group numbers. They help us deduce the equations, and even check the grammars of this paper. This article is Supported by "Open Research Fund of State Key Laboratory of Hydrology-Water Resources and Hydraulic Engineering, Hohai University" (2009490211), "National Nature Science Foundation" (50909012,50979011), The Research Foundation of "Key Laboratory for Engineering of Disaster Prevention and Mitigation of Liaoning Province" (DPMKL2008001) and "The Fundamental Research Funds for the Central Universities".

References

1. Huang, W., Xu, B., Chan-Hilton, A.: Forecasting flows in Apalachicola River using neural networks. Hydrological Processes 18(13), 2545–2564 (2004)
2. Wen, J., Liu, T.-q., Li, X.-y.: On-line Identification of Coherent Generator Using Optimized LS-SVM. Proceedings of the Chinese Society for Electrical Engineering 28(25), 80–85 (2008)
3. Liu, Q.-b., Zhang, B.-h., Wang, K.: Research on SA-SVM methods for price forecasting. Power System Protection and Control 36(22), 34–39 (2008)
4. Li, D.-z., Wang, Z.: Modeling of Biomass Gasification Process Based on Least Squares SVM. Journal of System Simulation 21(3), 629–633 (2009)
5. Smola, A.J., Schoelkopf, B.: A tutorial on support vector regression. Statistics and Computing (14), 199–222 (2004)
6. Kennedy, J., Eberhart, R.: Particle swarm optimization. In: Proc. IEEE Int. Conf. on Neural Networks, Perth, pp. 1942–1948 (1995)
7. Lin, J.-y., Cheng, C.-t.: Application of support vector machine method to long-term runoff forecast. Journal of Hydraulic Engineering 37(6), 681–686 (2006)

8. Keerthi, S.S., Lin, C.J.: Asymptotic behaviors of support vector machines with Gaussian kernel. Neural computation (15), 1667–1689 (2003)
9. Yang, X., Ji, Y.-b., Tian, X.: Parameters Selection of SVM Based on Genetic Algorithm. Journal of Liaoning University of Petrol Eum & Chemical Technology 24(1), 54–58 (2004)
10. Dong, C.-x., Yang, S.-q., Rao, X.: Comparison in Generalization Performance of Support Vector Machine Algorithms. Journal of Circuits and Systems 9(4), 86–91 (2004)
11. Fan, R.-E., Chen, P.-H., Lin, C.-J.: Working Set Selection Using Second Order Information for Training Support Vector Machines. Journal of Machine Learning Research (6), 1889–1918 (2005)
12. Yuhui, S., Eberhart, R.: Empirical study of particle swarm optimization. In: Proc of the Congress on Evolutionary Computation, Washington, DC, pp. 1945–1950 (1999)

Application of Latin Hypercube Sampling in the Immune Genetic Algorithm for Solving the Maximum Clique Problem

Zhou Benda and Chen Minghua

Dept. of Mathematics & Physics West Anhui University Lu'an, China
bendazhou@wxc.edu.cn

Abstract. Based on Latin Hypercube Sampling method, the crossover operation in GA is redesigned; combined with immune mechanism, chromosome concentration is defined and clonal selection strategy is designed, thus an Immune Genetic Algorithm is given based on Latin Hypercube Sampling for solving the Maximum Clique Problem in this paper. The examples shows the new algorithm in solution quality, convergence speed, and other indicators is better than the classical genetic algorithm and good point set genetic algorithm. On the other hand, the new algorithm is not inferior to such classical algorithms as dynamic local search, and it got better solutions to some examples.

Keywords: Maximum Clique Problem(MCP), Genetic Algorithm (GA), Latin Hypercube Sampling(LHS), Artificial Immune Systems(AIS), Immune Genetic Algorithm based on Latin Hypercube Sampling(LIGA).

1 Introduction

A clique is a complete subgraph of graph G. A maximal clique of G is a clique which is not included in any others. A greatest clique of G is a maximal clique which has the most vertices. Maximum Clique Problem (MCP) [1] is to find the greatest clique of G for a given graph. By reason of wide application of many aspects, such as market analysis, bioinformation, and so on [2] , it is certain that MPC has abundant theoretical and practical value. Traditional deterministic algorithm can't solve MCP effectively on account of it's typical NP-hard characters. As an intelligent and overall optimization algorithm, Genetic Algorithm [3] is suitable for solving MCP. However, GA is deficient in keeping population diversity, such as capability failure, prematurity, time consuming, low success rate, and so on.

Paper[4] points out that the essence of GA is a random searching technique with directed guidance. The principle of guidance is guiding to those families which have higher fitness schema as their ancestors. Paper[5] designed a new cross operation by using good-point set [5]. theories in order to improve the efficiency of GA. But when the number n of good point is selected, the good-point set is determined. Thus, the set has no randomness, and is not a sampling which is simply based on statistics. Therefore, it has great effects on the whole search capability of GA. Paper [6-8] gives methods of Latin Hypercube Sampling (LHS) and points out the Latin Hypercube Sampling

F.L. Wang et al. (Eds.): AICI 2010, Part II, LNAI 6320, pp. 134–141, 2010.

is a stratified sampling. As the uniform design sampling is a statistical sampling, the randomness and spread of uniformity of each sample are better than the good point set. Therefore, in terms of using the Latin Hypercube Sampling method to design the crossover, the GA will have a stronger search capability. The ease of running into prematurity of GA is also an aspect that influences its effect, but clonal selection operators Artificial Immune System simulate antibody strategy based on concentration, it can keep population diversity very well.[9-11]. Using the methods of defining and calculating the similarities and concentrations among antibodies in Artificial Immune System, we can calculate similarities and concentrations of chromosomes in GA, and make clonal selection based on concentrations, thus improves the exploiting ability of GA.

Combining genetic with immunity mechanism, this paper presents an immune genetic algorithm based on Latin Hypercube Sampling for solving the maximal clique problem. To prove the validity of the new algorithm, we carry out some computer simulation for the sake of the standard testing examples offered by DIMACS. [12] database. Results show that the new algorithm is superior to simple GA and "good-point set" GA, and it is also superior to DLS-MC[1] , QUALEX[1] We could get better solutions to some examples.

2 Genetic Operator and Chromosomes Concentration

2.1 Chromosome Code

In view of characteristic of MCP, we use binary encoding $x=[x_1, x_2, \ldots, x_n]$, if vertex i is in clique S, then $x_i=1$, otherwise $x_i=0$. For example, $x=[01011101]$ represents the clique S of vertex set $V=\{1,2,3,4,5,6,7,8\}$, and vertices 2,4,5,6,8 are in S.

2.2 Fitness Function

We define fitness function $g(x)$ as follows: if $x=[x_1, x_2, \ldots, x_n]$ is a legal chromosome, then, $g(x)=\sum_1^n x_i$ otherwise, $g(x)=0$.

2.3 The Crosser Based on Latin Hypercube Sampling, LHS Crossover

Do LHS crossover to two chromosomes A_1 and A_2 selected from chromosome pool according to roulette. $A_1=(a_1^1, a_2^1, \ldots, a_l^1)$, $A_2=(a_1^2, a_2^2, \ldots, a_l^2)$ and $J=\{i| a_i^1 \neq a_i^2\}$. Suppose the first i components of A_1 and A_2 are different and the back $l-t$ ones are same. Let schema:
$$H = \{(x_1, x_2, \cdots, x_n) | i \in J, x_i = *; i \notin J, x_i = a_i^1\}.$$

Intercross A_1 and A_2 (either one-point crossover or multiple-point crossover), their descendants are surely belong to H, LHS cross operation is to find out good samples on H using LHS methods. In the maximal clique problems, we compare chromosomes A_1 and A_2, then make a note of locations of different values (suppose the number is t) in J, let the corresponding schema be H. The different locations form a t-dimension cube, denoted by H', then do LHS on H', that is, do LHS interlace operations to select n points on t-dimension cube $C=[0,1]^t$, just as follows:

(1) Divides interval $[0,1]$ into n inter-cell, i said that with the i-th inter-cell $(\dfrac{i-1}{n},\dfrac{i}{n}]$;

(2) Let $(\pi_{1j},\pi_{2j},...,\pi_{nj})^T$ represents a random permutation of n inter-cells in the j-th dimensional coordinates;

(3) Let $\pi=(\pi_{ij})_{n\times t}$, and then $\pi=(\pi_{ij})_{n\times t}$ is a stochastic matrix of order $n\times t$;

(4) Let $C=(c_{ij})_{n\times t}$, where $c_{ij}=(\pi_{ij}+u_{ij}-0.5)/n$ $i=1,2,...,n$, u_{ij} is samples uniformly distributed on interval $[-0.5,0.5]$, and u_{ij} is independent of π_{ij}, $j=1,2,...,t$.

Let the k-th chromosome $b^{(k)}=(\ b_1^k, b_2^k,..., b_l^k\ )$ among the crossing garneted n descendants, where

$$b_m^k = \begin{cases} a_m^1 & m \notin J \\ <x_{kj}> & m=t_j \in J, 1\leq j \leq t \end{cases}$$

for $1\leq k\leq n$, $1\leq m\leq l$. Notation $<a>$ means that if the decimal part of a is lesser than 0.5, then $<a>=0$; otherwise $<a>=1$.

Among the generating n descendants, we select one (or several) which have the maximal adaptive value as the descendants after crossover. Above interlace operation is called LHS interlace operation.

2.4 Mutation

Select chromosome A and random integer $1\leq i\leq l$, chromosome $A=(a_1,a_2,a_l)$ changes into $B=(a_1,a_2,...,a_{i-1},b_i,a_{i+1},...,a_l)$, where $b_i=\bar{a}_i$.

2.5 Chromosomes Concentration and Expectations of Survival Probability

Methods of computing similarities and concentrations of antibodies are numerous in Immune Algorithm, such as based on entropy of information, Euclidean distance and binary Hamming distance. But the methods based on entropy of information can't reflect faithfully the similarities and concentrations between binary-code antibodies. For discontinuous functions and functions with large range of variations, these methods also can't define truly the similarities and concentrations between antibodies and they are slow in running[11]. In addition, bioinformatics tells us that different gene digits have different fuctions. For example, vertices with different degrees have different weights in corresponding digits. According to the characteristics of MCP binary coding, we endow with different weight for different gene digits, use weighted Hamming distance to computer the similarities of chromosomes and determine deeply chromosomes concentrations and expectation of survival probability.

Suppose the length of each chromosome in binary-coded population with size N is l.

Definition 1 (weighted Hamming Distance). Let chromosomes $A_1=(\ a_1^1, a_2^1,..., a_l^1\ )$ and $A_2=(\ a_1^2,a_2^2,..., a_l^2\ )$, where $a_i^k \in \{0,1\}$, then define weighted Hamming Distance between A_1 and A_2 as: $H(A_1, A_2) = \sum_{k=1}^{l} w_k |a_k^1 - a_k^2|$, where w_k is the weight of k-th gene. It is the percentage of the vertex degree in the sum of all vertex degree in this paper.

Definition 2(similarities between chromosomes). Suppose g_1 and g_2 are the fitness values of two chromosomes A_1 and A_2 respectively, for given constants $r>0$ and $m>0$, if $H(A_1, A_2) < r$ and $|g_1 - g_2| < m$, the A_1 and A_2 are called similitude.

Definition 3(chromosomes concentration). The number n_i of chromosomes similar to chromosomes A_i (or A_i itself) in population is called the concentration of A_i.

Definition 4(expectation of survival probability). Expectations of survival probability of chromosome A_i is defined as: $p_i = g_i / (n_i \sum_{i=1}^{N} g_i)$.

By definition 4, we know that expectation of survival probability is proportional to fitness value and is directly proportional to concentration, this insures either convergence rate of the algorithm or variety of chromosomes.

3 An Immune Genetic Algorithm Based on Latin Hypercube Sampling, LIGA

3.1 Repair

Use selection, crossover and mutation on chromosomes, search solution space. The generating solutions after these actions are not always the feasible solutions. So we design the correcting algorithm, just as follows:

Step 1. Judge the legality of the chromosomes, legal then stop, and output the chromosomes, if not, go to step 2.

Step 2. Traverse the chromosomes based on adjacency matrix, find out the adjacency matrix of corresponding subgraph.

Step 3. Delete the vertices with minimal degrees in the subgraph, go to step 1.

3.2 An Immune Genetic Algorithm Based on Latin Hypercube Sampling, LIGA

Give cross probability p_c and mutation probability p_m, and then LIGA is:

Step 1. Use weighted Hamming distance to compute the chromosomes concentration, expectation of survival probability and fitness value, and then make clonal selection based on expectations of survival probability.

Step 2. Select two chromosomes under roulette use probability p_c to do interlace operations based on Latin Hypercube Sampling.

Step 3. Use probability p_m to do mutation operation.

Step 4 . Do correcting operation to the generating chromosomes.

Step 5. Put the gained chromosomes into chromosome pool, compute fitness value and concentration of each chromosome. Suppose the capacity of the pool is fixed, when the number of the chromosomes exceeds the capacity, delete those chromosomes which have small fitness value and large concentrations.

Step 6. Proceed above operations to T-th generation (T is a given constant), during the process. Make a note of the chromosomes that have the largest fitness value, they are the expected chromosomes, and then decode them to get optimum solution.

4 Solving Maximal Clique Problem Using LIGA

To prove the efficiency of the LIGA, we use SGA, GGA and LIGA respectively under the same condition, and adopt MATALB 7.0 computing plat from to emulate the standard examples provided by DIMACSPP [11]. Compare with paper [1] as follows:

Table 1. Experimental result of GA, GGA and LIGA

Problem	DLS-MC	QUA-LEX	Alg	Best	Ave	σ	Tave	Sr
c-fat 200-1	12	12	SGA	12	11.75	0.44	2.03	75
			GGA	12	11.93	0.26	0.92	93
			LIGA	12	12	0	1.54	100
c-fat 200-2	24	24	SGA	24	21.78	1.22	3.39	9
			GGA	24	23.64	1.04	3.39	27
			LIGA	24	24	0	1.64	100
c-fat 200-5	58	58	SGA	56	54.63	2.09	5.78	6
			GGA	58	57.4	0.82	5.02	58
			LIGA	58	58	0	1.43	100
c-fat 500-1	14	14	SGA	14	13.34	0.61	42.52	41
			GGA	14	13.48	0.54	43.02	50
			LIGA	14	14	0	32.29	100
c-fat 500-10	126	126	SGA	121	105.55	7.76	67.64	1
			GGA	100	89.00	3.01	60.65	1
			LIGA	126	126	0	35.74	100
c-fat 500-2	26	26	SGA	26	22.90	1.37	45.90	3
			GGA	26	24.22	1.24	46.23	18
			LIGA	26	26	0	35.74	100
c-fat 500-5	64	64	SGA	64	53.51	5.08	51.64	1
			GGA	64	60.56	2.70	52.44	9
			LIGA	64	63.82	0.38	36.98	82
Hamming 10-4	40	36	SGA	32	31.40	0.52	1019.9	28
			GGA	33	32.00	0.47	1038.8	31
			LIGA	40	40	0	979.33	100

Table 1. (*Continued*)

			SGA	508	502.4	1.50	1852.5	68
Hamming 10-2	512	512	GGA	510	506.3	1.38	1550.2	82
			LIGA	512	512	0	1209.8	100
			SGA	32	32	0	1.89	100
Hamming 6-2	32	32	GGA	32	32	0	1.71	100
			LIGA	32	32	0	1.24	100
			SGA	4	4	0	0.27	100
Hamming 6-4	4	4	GGA	4	4	0	0.27	100
			LIGA	4	4	0	0.25	100
			SGA	123	108.14	9.52	21.48	2
Hamming 8-2	128	128	GGA	104	95.08	3.94	27.14	1
			LIGA	128	128	0	20.79	100
			SGA	16	15.08	0.64	3.67	25
Hamming 8-4	16	16	GGA	16	15.50	0.56	4.01	53
			LIGA	16	16	0	3.36	100
			SGA	8	8	0	0.67	100
Johnson 16-2-4	8	8	GGA	8	8	0	0.71	100
			LIGA	8	8	0	0.67	100
			SGA	16	15.51	0.50	45.68	51
Johnson 32-2-4	16	16	GGA	16	15.89	0.20	46.18	96
			LIGA	16	16	0	39.65	100
			SGA	4	4	0	0.13	100
Johnson 8-2-4	4	4	GGA	4	4	0	0.13	100
			LIGA	4	4	0	0.12	100
			SGA	14	13.99	0.1	1.69	99
Johnson 8-4-4	14	14	GGA	14	14	0	1.29	100
			LIGA	14	14	0	0.29	100
			SGA	11	9.96	0.45	3.04	1
Keller4	11	11	GGA	11	10.04	0.47	3.12	2
			LIGA	12	11.97	0.17	2.92	97

To avoid randomicity of GA, we compute 100 times on the same machine to each standard example, and note the following results: ① the best solution gained by 100 times operations (denoted by Best); ② the average value and standard deviation of the gained solutions (denoted by *Ave* and σ); ③ the average spending time on finding the best solution (denoted by Tave); ④ success rate with finding out the best solutions (denoted by sr).

Above table shows that the solutions gained by LIGA is not inferior to [1], and LIGA can seek out completely the best solutions to complex Hamming 10-2 and Hamming 10-4. Furthermore, to "Keller 4", LIGA gained the solutions superior to [1]; SGA and GGA can only get the solutions partly. Moreover, LIGA is superior to SGA and GGA on Ave, and so to search capability, convergence rate, etc.

5   Conclusions

As we know, the interlace operations of any GA is to find out a descendant with higher fitness in its family. Existing operations can only ensure the gained descendants which can be contained in the family above, but their search capability is deficient. The descendants which gained through a good-point method can represent the behaviors of their families, but the stationing of good-point set has directivity. When the number n is selected, elements in the set are determined, and this influences the global search capability of the method. However, LHS crossover can overcome the deficiency and the gained samples have random distribution. So it can take all grids. This makes the generating solutions represent the properties of solution space. In addition, combined immunologic mechanism with artificial immune system, we introduce chromosomes concentration and expectations of survival probability. Meanwhile using clonal selection to chromosomes can avoid the deficiency of GA keeping population diversity and give attention to local and global search capabilities of the algorithm.

References

1. Pullan, W., Hoos, H.H.: Dynamic Local Search for the Maximum Clique Problem. Journal of Artificial Intelligence Research 25, 159–185 (2006)
2. Singh, A., Gupta, A.K.: A hybrid heuristic for the maximum clique problem. Journal of Heuristics 12, 5–22 (2006)
3. Balas, E., Niehaus, W.: Optimized Crossover-Based Genetic Algorithms for the Maximum Cardinality and Maximum Weight Clique Problems. Journal of Heuristics 4, 107–122 (1998)
4. Zhang, L., Zhang, B.: Research on the Mechanism of Genetic Algorithms. Journal of Software 7, 945–952 (2000) (chinese)
5. Zhang, L., Zhang, B.: Good point set based genetic algorithm. Chinese Journal of Computers 9, 917–922 (2001) (chinese)
6. Chen, M.-h., Ren, Z., Zhou, B.-d.: Solving 2-way graph partitioning problem using genetic algorithm based on latin hypercube sampling. Control Theory & Applications 8, 927–930 (2009) (chinese)
7. Stein, M.: Large sample properties of simulations using Latin hypercube sampling. Technometrics 2, 143–151 (1987)

8. Owen, A.B.: A central limit theorem for Latin hypercube sampling. Journal of the Royal Statistical Society 54(B), 541–551 (1992)
9. Stepney, et al.: Conceptual Frameworks for Artificial Immune Systems. Journal of Unconventional computing 1 (2005)
10. Li, Z., Cheng, J.: Immune good- point set genetic algorithm. Computer Engineering and Applications 28, 37–40 (2007) (chinese)
11. Bin, J.: Basic Research on Artificial Immune Algorithm and Its Application, Central South University (March 2008) (chinese)
12. [EB/OL] (2009-07-15), `ftp://dimacs.rutgers.edu/pub/challeng/`

The Selection of Sales Managers in Enterprises by Fuzzy Multi-criteria Decision-Making

Yu-Jie Wang[1], Chao-Shun Kao[2], and Li-Jen Liu[3]

[1] Department of Shipping and Transportation Management,
National Penghu University, Penghu 880, Taiwan, ROC
[2] Department of International Business Management,
Lan Yang Institute of Technology, I Lan 261, Taiwan, ROC
cskao@mail.fit.edu.tw
[3] Department of Shipping and Transportation Management,
National Penghu University, Penghu 880, Taiwan, ROC

Abstract. The sales manager selection is very important for human resource planning of enterprises because it directly affects their service quality. That is to say, an appropriate sales manager is able to improve communication and provide necessary services for customers. Thus, sale ability of an enterprise will be increased by appropriate sales managers. To select appropriate sales managers easily and quickly, we utilize a fuzzy multi-criteria decision-making(FMCDM) method called fuzzy TOPSIS to solve the selection problem in enterprises. Fuzzy TOPSIS is an extension of TOPSIS under fuzzy environment, and TOPSIS is one of famous multi-criteria decision-making(MCDM) methods under certain environment. By fuzzy TOPSIS, an optimal sales manager is easily found from lots of candidates. Besides, selection criteria of the FMCDM method will be also evaluation standards of sales managers' ability after worked in the enterprise.

1 Introduction

In enterprises, one of critical decision-making issues is to select sales managers for improving service quality of themselves. Since the selection practically takes varied factors[1-4,6,9,11-27] being evaluation criteria into consideration, such as communication skill, determination, energy, patience and professionalism, etc, the selection problem belongs to multi-criteria decision-making (MCDM) ones[1-4,6,9,11-27]. Generally, MCDM problems are modeled as follows:

$$G = \begin{bmatrix} G_{11} & G_{12} & \cdots & G_{1n} \\ G_{21} & G_{22} & \cdots & G_{2n} \\ \vdots & \vdots & \cdots & \vdots \\ G_{m1} & G_{m2} & \cdots & G_{mn} \end{bmatrix} \text{ and } W = [W_1, W_2, ..., W_n], \text{ where } G_{ij} \text{ is the performance}$$

rating of ith alternative on jth criterion, and W_j is the weight of jth criterion.

F.L. Wang et al. (Eds.): AICI 2010, Part II, LNAI 6320, pp. 142–151, 2010.

Commonly, the MCDM problems are classified into classical MCDM ones[9,13,16] and fuzzy multi-criteria decision-making (FMCDM) ones[1-4,6,11,12,14,15,17-27]. In the classical MCDM problems, evaluation ratings and criteria weights are expressed by crisp numbers. On the other hand, evaluation ratings and criteria weights estimated on imprecision, subjectivity or vagueness belong to the FMCDM problems. The ratings and weights are often presented by linguistic terms[7,10] and transformed into fuzzy numbers[28-30]. For instance, the evaluation ratings are assessed by linguistic terms: very poor(VP), poor(P), medium poor(MP), fair(F), medium good (MG), good(G) and very good(VG), and the criteria weights are evaluated by linguistic terms: very low (VL), low(L), medium(M), high(H) and very high(VH). Obviously, the selection problem of sales managers is one of FMCDM problems.

Some past researchers extended MCDM methods under fuzzy environment to solve FMCDM problems, such as Chen, Liang, Raj and Kumar[4,20,22]. Chen[4] extended TOPSIS[13], being one of famous MCDM methods, into a FMCDM one. Liang, Raj and Kumar[20,22] utilized maximizing and minimizing sets[5] to rank a set of approximate trapezoidal fuzzy numbers in FMCDM. Practically, there were some drawbacks in their works. To avoid above limitations, we use fuzzy TOPSIS[27] to select sales managers in enterprises.

2 Mathematical Preliminaries

In this section, we review basic notions of fuzzy sets[28-30].

Definition 2.1. Let U be a universe set. A fuzzy set A of U is defined as a membership function $\mu_A(x) \rightarrow [0,1]$, where $\mu_A(x)$, $\forall x \in U$, indicates the degree of x in A.

Definition 2.2. The $\alpha - cut$ of a fuzzy set A is a crisp set $A_\alpha = \{x | \mu_A(x) \geq \alpha\}$.

Definition 2.3. The support of a fuzzy set A is a crisp set $Supp(A) = \{x | \mu_A(x) > 0\}$.

Definition 2.4. A fuzzy subset A of U is normal iff $\sup_{x \in U} \mu_A(x) = 1$.

Definition 2.5. A fuzzy subset A of U is convex iff $\mu_A(\lambda x + (1-\lambda)y) \geq (\mu_A(x) \wedge \mu_A(y))$, $\forall x, y \in U$, $\forall \lambda \in [0,1]$, where $\wedge$ denotes the minimum operator.

Definition 2.6. A fuzzy set A is a fuzzy number iff A is both normal and convex on U.

Definition 2.7. A triangular fuzzy number X is displayed by a triplet (a,b,c) and the membership function[28-30] is defined as

$$\mu_X(x) = \begin{cases} (x-a)/(b-a), & a \leq x < b, \\ 1, & x = b, \\ (c-x)/(c-b), & b < x \leq c, \\ 0, & otherwise. \end{cases}$$

Definition 2.8. Let $X_1 = (a_1, b_1, c_1)$ and $X_2 = (a_2, b_2, c_2)$ be two triangular fuzzy numbers. The addition $\oplus$ of the two fuzzy numbers by extension principle is

$$X_1 \oplus X_2 = (a_1, b_1, c_1) \oplus (a_2, b_2, c_2) = (a_1 + a_2, b_1 + b_2, c_1 + c_2).$$

Definition 2.9. The multiplication $\otimes$ of X_1 and a real number t is defined as

$$t \otimes X_1 = t \otimes (a_1, b_1, c_1) = (ta_1, tb_1, tc_1).$$

Definition 2.10. Let $S = \{X_1, X_2, ..., X_n\}$ indicate a set consisting of n triangular fuzzy numbers, where $X_j = (a_j, b_j, c_j) \in S$, $j = 1, 2, ..., n$. Then normalized fuzzy number $\tilde{X}_j$ of X_j is defined as follows:

(i) $\tilde{x}_j = x_j$ as S is the set consisting of linguistic[7,10], ordinal or qualitative ratings which are expressed by fuzzy numbers in the interval of [0,1];

(ii) $\tilde{x}_j = (\dfrac{a^-}{c_j}, \dfrac{a^-}{b_j}, \dfrac{a^-}{a_j})$ as S is the set composed of cost ratings;

(iii) $\tilde{x}_j = (\dfrac{a_j}{c^+}, \dfrac{b_j}{c^+}, \dfrac{c_j}{c^+})$ as S is the set consisting of benefit ratings;

where $a^- = \min_{1 \le j \le n}\{a_j\}$ and $c^+ = \max_{1 \le j \le n}\{c_j\}$.

Definition 2.11. Let $\succeq$ indicate a binary relation between triangular fuzzy numbers. Assume $X_1 = (a_1, b_1, c_1)$ and $X_2 = (a_2, b_2, c_2)$ to be two triangular fuzzy numbers. Then $X_1 \succeq X_2$ iff $a_1 \ge a_2$, $b_1 \ge b_2$, $c_1 \ge c_2$.

Lemma 2.1. $\succeq$ is a partial ordering relation[8,27] between triangular fuzzy numbers.

Definition 2.12. Let MIN and MAX [27] be two operators in a set of triangular fuzzy numbers $\{X_1, X_2, ..., X_n\}$, where $X_j = (a_j, b_j, c_j)$, $j = 1, 2, ..., n$. Define

$$MIN\{X_1, X_2, ..., X_n\} = MIN_{1 \le j \le n}\{X_j\} = X^- = (a^-, b^-, c^-),$$

$$MAX\{X_1, X_2, ..., X_n\} = MAX_{1 \le j \le n}\{X_j\} = X^+ = (a^+, b^+, c^+),$$

where $a^- = \min_{1 \le j \le n}\{a_j\}$, $b^- = \min_{1 \le j \le n}\{b_j\}$, $c^- = \min_{1 \le j \le n}\{c_j\}$, $a^+ = \max_{1 \le j \le n}\{a_j\}$, $b^+ = \max_{1 \le j \le n}\{b_j\}$ and $c^+ = \max_{1 \le j \le n}\{c_j\}$.

Lemma 2.2. $X_t \succeq MIN_{1 \le j \le n}\{X_j\}$ and $MAX_{1 \le j \le n}\{X_j\} \succeq X_t$, where $t = 1, 2, ..., n$.

Definition 2.13. Let $X_1 = (a_1, b_1, c_1)$ and $X_2 = (a_2, b_2, c_2)$ be two triangular fuzzy numbers. The distance measure function[4] of the two fuzzy numbers is defined as

$$d(X_1, X_2) = \sqrt{\dfrac{1}{3}[(a_1 - a_2)^2 + (b_1 - b_2)^2 + (c_1 - c_2)^2]}.$$

3 The Fuzzy TOPSIS Method

In this paper, the fuzzy TOPSIS method proposed by Wang et al.[27] is used to solve a selection problem of sales managers in enterprises. In this problem, $A_1, A_2, ..., A_m$ are candidates(feasible alternatives) assessed by experts $E_1, E_2, ..., E_h$ based on criteria $C_1, C_2, ..., C_n$. Let $G_{ijk} = (p_{ijk}, q_{ijk}, r_{ijk})$ be the performance rating given by E_k to A_i on C_j , where $i = 1, 2, ..., m$; $j = 1, 2, ..., n$; $k = 1, 2, ..., h$. Additionally, $G_{ij} = (p_{ij}, q_{ij}, r_{ij})$ presents the performance rating of A_i on C_j , where $i = 1, 2, ..., m$; $j = 1, 2, ..., n$. Let

$$G_{ij} = (p_{ij}, q_{ij}, r_{ij}) = (\frac{1}{h}) \otimes (G_{ij1} \oplus G_{ij2} \oplus ... \oplus G_{ijh}), \tag{1}$$

where $p_{ij} = \frac{1}{h} \sum_{k=1}^{h} p_{ijk}$, $q_{ij} = \frac{1}{h} \sum_{k=1}^{h} q_{ijk}$, $r_{ij} = \frac{1}{h} \sum_{k=1}^{h} r_{ijk}$, for $i = 1, 2, ..., m$; $j = 1, 2, ..., n$.

Then $\tilde{G}_{ij}$ is assumed to be normalized value of G_{ij}, and the $\tilde{G}_{ij}$ will be classified into three situations.

(i) $\tilde{G}_{ij} = G_{ij}$ as G_{ij} is evaluated by linguistic, ordinal or qualitative terms, and presented by triangular fuzzy numbers in the interval of [0,1].

(ii) $\tilde{G}_{ij} = (\frac{p_j^-}{r_{ij}}, \frac{p_j^-}{q_{ij}}, \frac{p_j^-}{p_{ij}})$ as G_{ij} belongs to cost criteria, for $p_j^- = \min_i \{p_{ij}\}$, $\forall j$.

(iii) $\tilde{G}_{ij} = (\frac{p_{ij}}{r_j^+}, \frac{q_{ij}}{r_j^+}, \frac{r_{ij}}{r_j^+})$ as G_{ij} belongs to benefit criteria, for $r_j^+ = \max_i \{r_{ij}\}$, $\forall j$. (2)

In addition, $W_{jk} = (u_{jk}, v_{jk}, z_{jk})$ represents the weight of C_j evaluated by E_k , where $j = 1, 2, ..., n$; $k = 1, 2, ..., h$. Let $W_j = (u_j, v_j, z_j)$ be the weight of C_j , where $j = 1, 2, ..., n$. Define

$$W_j = (u_j, v_j, z_j) = (\frac{1}{h}) \otimes (W_{j1} \oplus W_{j2} \oplus ... \oplus W_{jh}), \tag{3}$$

where $u_j = \frac{1}{h} \sum_{k=1}^{h} u_{jk}$, $v_j = \frac{1}{h} \sum_{k=1}^{h} v_{jk}$, $z_j = \frac{1}{h} \sum_{k=1}^{h} z_{jk}$, for $j = 1, 2, ..., n$.

Further, group fuzzy decision matrix and related weights are constructed as similar as the MCDM model in section 1.

Assume that negative extreme solution A^- and positive extreme solution A^+ on n criteria are obtained by MIN and MAX operations. Thus

$$A^- = [\tilde{G}_1^-, \tilde{G}_2^-, ..., \tilde{G}_n^-] \quad \text{and} \tag{4}$$

$$A^+ = [\tilde{G}_1^+, \tilde{G}_2^+, ..., \tilde{G}_n^+],\tag{5}$$

where $\tilde{G}_j^- = MIN_{1 \leq i \leq m}\{\tilde{G}_{ij}\}$ and $\tilde{G}_j^+ = MAX_{1 \leq i \leq m}\{\tilde{G}_{ij}\}$.

Let $d(\tilde{G}_{ij}, \tilde{G}_j^-)$ indicate the distance from $\tilde{G}_{ij}$ to $\tilde{G}_j^-$, and $d(\tilde{G}_{ij}, \tilde{G}_j^+)$ denote the distance from $\tilde{G}_{ij}$ to $\tilde{G}_j^+$, where $j = 1,2,...,n$. With $d(\tilde{G}_{ij}, \tilde{G}_j^-)$, $d(\tilde{G}_{ij}, \tilde{G}_j^+)$ and W_j, we assume D_i^- and D_i^+ to be respectively weighted distances form alternative A_i to A^- and A^+. Define

$$D_i^- = (W_1 \otimes d(\tilde{G}_{i1}, \tilde{G}_1^-)) \oplus (W_2 \otimes d(\tilde{G}_{i2}, \tilde{G}_2^-)) \oplus ... \oplus (W_n \otimes d(\tilde{G}_{in}, \tilde{G}_n^-))\tag{6}$$

and

$$D_i^+ = (W_1 \otimes d(\tilde{G}_{i1}, \tilde{G}_1^+)) \oplus (W_2 \otimes d(\tilde{G}_{i2}, \tilde{G}_2^+)) \oplus ... \oplus (W_n \otimes d(\tilde{G}_{in}, \tilde{G}_n^+)),\tag{7}$$

for $i = 1,2,...,m$.

$[D_i^-, D_i^+]$ denotes a weighted distance vector composed of distances A_i to A^- and A^+. Then negative extreme vector $[MIN_{1 \leq i \leq m}\{D_i^-\}, MAX_{1 \leq i \leq m}\{D_i^+\}]$ and positive extreme vector $[MAX_{1 \leq i \leq m}\{D_i^-\}, MIN_{1 \leq i \leq m}\{D_i^+\}]$ of $[D_i^-, D_i^+]$ can be computed.

Let A_i^- and A_i^+ respectively indicate the distances from $[D_i^-, D_i^+]$ to $[MIN_{1 \leq i \leq m}\{D_i^-\}, MAX_{1 \leq i \leq m}\{D_i^+\}]$ and $[MAX_{1 \leq i \leq m}\{D_i^-\}, MIN_{1 \leq i \leq m}\{D_i^+\}]$. Define

$$A_i^- = d(D_i^-, MIN_{1 \leq i \leq m}\{D_i^-\}) + d(D_i^+, MAX_{1 \leq i \leq m}\{D_i^+\})\tag{8}$$

and

$$A_i^+ = d(D_i^-, MAX_{1 \leq i \leq m}\{D_i^-\}) + d(D_i^+, MIN_{1 \leq i \leq m}\{D_i^+\}),\tag{9}$$

for $i = 1,2,...,m$.

Finally, A_i^* is relative closeness coefficient of A_i. Define

$$A_i^* = \frac{A_i^-}{A_i^- + A_i^+}, \text{ for } i = 1,2,...,m.\tag{10}$$

Obviously, $0 \leq A_i^* \leq 1$. An alternative is closer to the positive extreme solution and farther from the negative extreme solution as its closeness coefficient approaches 1. Oppositely, an alternative is closer to the negative extreme solution and farther from the positive extreme solution as its closeness coefficient approaches 0. Once all alternatives' closeness coefficients are obtained, their ranking order is determined.

4 An Numerical Example for the Selection of Sales Managers

Assume that a company desires to find a new sales manager from lots of interviewees for improving service quality. Four experts E_1, E_2, E_3 and E_4 are employed to assess the selection problem. Through initial evaluation, the experts suppose that A_1, A_2 and A_3 to be short-listed candidates. They evaluate the three candidates(i.e. feasible alternatives) based on five criteria: communication skill(C1), determination(C2), energy(C3), patience(C4), and professionalism(C5).

The following linguistic terms and corresponded fuzzy numbers are employed to express ratings and weights respectively shown in Table 1 and Table 2.

Table 1. The linguistic terms and corresponded fuzzy numbers of ratings

Linguistic terms	Fuzzy numbers
Very poor (VP)	(0, 0, 0.2)
Poor (P)	(0, 0.2, 0.4)
Medium poor (MP)	(0.2, 0.4, 0.5)
Fair (F)	(0.4, 0.5, 0.6)
Medium good (MG)	(0.5, 0.6, 0.8)
Good (G)	(0.6, 0.8, 1)
Very good (VG)	(0.8, 1, 1)

Table 2. The linguistic terms and corresponded fuzzy numbers of weights

Linguistic terms	Fuzzy numbers
Very low (VL)	(0,0, 0.3)
Low (L)	(0, 0.3, 0.5)
Medium (M)	(0.3, 0.5, 0.7)
High (H)	(0.5, 0.7, 1)
Very high (VH)	(0.7, 1, 1)

Based on entries of Table 1 and Table 2, linguistic ratings and weights are employed by the experts to assess the three candidates on the five criteria. Then group fuzzy decision matrix computed by (1) is shown in Table 3 and average weights of criteria obtained by (3) are in Table 4.

Table 3. The group fuzzy decision matrix

	A_1	A_2	A_3
C1	(0.6,0.75,0.9)	(0.65,0.85,1)	(0.45,0.55,0.7)
C2	(0.675,0.85,0.95)	(0.425,0.525,0.65)	(0.75,0.95,1)
C3	(0.475,0.575,0.75)	(0.75,0.95,1)	(0.525,0.65,0.85)
C4	(0.625,0.8,0.95)	(0.6,0.75,0.9)	(0.65,0.85,1)
C5	(0.7,0.9,1)	(0.575,0.75,0.95)	(0.6,0.75,0.9)

Table 4. The average weights

Weight	Importance
W1	(0.5, 0.725, 0.925)
W2	(0.4, 0.6, 0.85)
W3	(0.5, 0.725, 0.925)
W4	(0.4, 0.6, 0.85)
W5	(0.275, 0.5, 0.725)

Through entries of Table 3, we can obtain normalized fuzzy decision matrix in the Table 5. Obviously, entries of Table 5 are just the same as the entries of Table 3 in the example. Then negative extreme solution and positive extreme solution of the three alternatives derived by MIN and MAX operations are shown in Table 6.

Table 5. The normalized fuzzy decision matrix

	A_1	A_2	A_3
C1	(0.6,0.75,0.9)	(0.65,0.85,1)	(0.45,0.55,0.7)
C2	(0.675,0.85,0.95)	(0.45,0.525,0.65)	(0.75,0.95,1)
C3	(0.475,0.575,0.75)	(0.75,0.95,1)	(0.525,0.65,0.85)
C4	(0.625,0.8,0.95)	(0.6,0.75,0.9)	(0.65,0.85,1)
C5	(0.7,0.9,1)	(0.575,0.75,0.95)	(0.6,0.75,0.9)

Table 6. The negative and positive extreme solutions of alternatives on criteria

	Negative extreme solution	Positive extreme solution
C1	(0.45,0.55,0.7)	(0.65,0.85,1)
C2	(0.45,0.525,0.65)	(0.75,0.95,)
C3	(0.475,0.575, 0.75)	(0.75,0.95,1)
C4	(0.6,0.75,0.9)	(0.65,0.85,1)
C5	(0.575,0.75,0.9)	(0.7, 0.9, 1)

Based on entries of Table 5 and Table 6, $d(\tilde{G}_{ij}, \tilde{G}^-)$ is derived in Table 7, for $i=1,2,3; \ j=1,2,\ldots,5$. $d(\tilde{G}_{ij}, \tilde{G}^+)$ is obtained by similar computation in Table 8, for $i=1,2,3; \ j=1,2,\ldots,5$.

Table 7. The distance from alternatives to the negative extreme solution on criteria

	A_1	A_2	A_3
C1	0.1848	0.2708	0
C2	0.2865	0	0.3620
C3	0	0.3048	0.0777
C4	0.0433	0	0.0866
C5	0.1267	0.0289	0.0144

Table 8. The distance from alternatives to the positive extreme solution on criteria

	A_1	A_2	A_3
C1	0.0866	0	0.2708
C2	0.0777	0.3620	0
C3	0.3048	0	0.2332
C4	0.0433	0.0866	0
C5	0	0.1164	0.1190

Through entries of Table 4 and Table 7, the weighted distances from alternatives to the negative extreme solution computed by (6) are expressed in Table 9. Based on entries of Table 4 and Table 8, the weighted distances from alternatives to the positive extreme solution obtained by (7) are presented in Table 10.

Table 9. The weighted distances form alternatives to the negative extreme solution

	The weighted distances
D_1^-	(0.2592, 0.3952, 0.5431)
D_2^-	(0.2958, 0.4318, 0.5534)
D_3^-	(0.2223, 0.3327, 0.4637)

Table 10. The weighted distances form alternatives o the positive extreme solution

	The weighted distances
D_1^+	(0.2441, 0.3564, 0.4649)
D_2^+	(0.2114, 0.3273, 0.4657)
D_3^+	(0.2847, 0.4249, 0.5525)

By *MIN* and *MAX* operations on entries of Table 9 and Table 10,

$MIN_{1\leq i\leq 3}\{D_i^-\}=(0.2223, 0.3327, 0.4637)$,

$MAX_{1\leq i\leq 3}\{D_i^-\}=(0.2958, 0.4318, 0.5534)$,

$MIN_{1\leq i\leq 3}\{D_i^+\}=(0.2114, 0.3273, 0.4649)$

and

$MAX_{1 \le i \le 3}\{D_i^+\} = (0.2847, 0.4249, 0.5525)$.

Then distance from $[D_i^-, D_i^+]$ to negative extreme vector $[MIN_{1 \le i \le 3}\{D_i^-\}, MAX_{1 \le i \le 3}\{D_i^+\}]$ and distance from $[D_i^-, D_i^+]$ to positive extreme vector $[MAX_{1 \le i \le 3}\{D_i^-\}, MIN_{1 \le i \le 3}\{D_i^+\}]$ respectively derived by (8) and (9) are displayed in Table 11 and Table 12, for $i = 1, 2, 3$.

Table 11. The distance values from weighted vectors to negative extreme vector

	The distance values
A_1^-	0.1305
A_2^-	0.1745
A_3^-	0

Table 12. The distance values from weighted vectors to positive extreme vector

	The distance values
A_1^+	0.0557
A_2^+	0.0004
A_3^+	0.1747

Finally, relative closeness coefficient of A_i obtained by (10) is shown in Table 13, for $i = 1, 2, 3$.

Table 13. The relative closeness coefficients

	The closeness coefficients
A_1	0.7009
A_2	0.9976
A_3	0

The integrated indices can be represented by the above closeness coefficients, i.e. A_1: 0.7009, A_2: 0.9976 and A_3: 0. The rank order based on the indices will be $A_2 > A_1 > A_3$. Thus A_2 is the best sales manager.

5 Conclusions

In this paper, we utilize a FMCDM method called fuzzy TOPSIS to select sales managers in enterprises. The FMCDM method enables experts to evaluate candidates by linguistic terms, hence vagueness messages will be encompassed in the selection problem of sales managers. In addition, the FMCDM method provides extreme values by MAX and MIN operators on distinct criteria beside the integrated indices, so the experts can evaluate candidates on different perspectives they desired.

References

1. Bellman, R.E., Zadeh, L.A.: Decision-making in a fuzzy environment. Management Sciences 17, 141–164 (1970)
2. Boender, C.G.E., de Graan, J.G., Lootsma, F.A.: Multi-attribute decision analysis with fuzzy pairwise comparisons. Fuzzy Sets and Systems 29, 133–143 (1989)
3. Chang, Y.H., Yeh, C.H.: A survey analysis of service quality for domestic airlines. European Journal of Operational Research 139, 166–177 (2002)
4. Chen, C.T.: Extensions to the TOPSIS for group decision-making under fuzzy environment. Fuzzy Sets and Systems 114, 1–9 (2000)
5. Chen, S.H.: Ranking fuzzy numbers with maximizing set and minimizing set. Fuzzy sets and Systems 3, 113–129 (1985)
6. Chen, S.J., Hwang, C.L.: Fuzzy multiple attribute decision making methods and application. Lecture Notes in Economics and Mathematical Systems. Springer, New York (1992)
7. Delgado, M., Verdegay, J.L., Vila, M.A.: Linguistic decision-making models. International Journal of Intelligent System 7, 479–492 (1992)
8. Epp, S.S.: Discrete Mathematics with Applications. Wadsworth, California (1990)
9. Feng, C.M., Wang, R.T.: Performance evaluation for airlines including the consideration of financial ratios. Journal of Air Transport Management 6, 133–142 (2000)
10. Herrera, F., Herrera-Viedma, E., Verdegay, J.L.: A model of consensus in group decision decision making under linguistic assessments. Fuzzy Sets and Systems 78, 73–87 (1996)
11. Hsu, H.M., Chen, C.T.: Aggregation of fuzzy opinions under group decision making. Fuzzy Sets and Systems 79, 279–285 (1996)
12. Hsu, H.M., Chen, C.T.: Fuzzy credibility relation method for multiple criteria decision-making problems. Information Sciences 96, 79–91 (1997)
13. Hwang, C.L., Yoon, K.: Multiple Attribute Decision Making: Methods and Application. Springer, New York (1981)
14. Jain, R.: A procedure for multi-aspect decision making using fuzzy sets. The International Journal of Systems Sciences 8, 1–7 (1978)
15. Kacprzyk, J., Fedrizzi, M., Nurmi, H.: Group decision making and consensus under fuzzy preferences and fuzzy majority. Fuzzy Sets and Systems 49, 21–31 (1992)
16. Keeney, R., Raiffa, H.: Decision with Multiple Objective: Preference and Value Tradeoffs. Wiley, New York (1976)
17. Lee, H.S.: Optimal consensus of fuzzy opinions under group decision making environment. In: 1999 IEEE International Conference on Systems, Man and Cybernetics, Tokyo, Japan (1999)
18. Lee, H.S.: A fuzzy multi-criteria decision making model for the selection of the distribution center. In: Wang, L., Chen, K., S. Ong, Y. (eds.) ICNC 2005. LNCS(LNAI), vol. 3612, pp. 1290–1299. Springer, Heidelberg (2005)
19. Lee, H.S.: On fuzzy preference relation in group decision making. International Journal of Computer Mathematics 82, 133–140 (2005)
20. Liang, G.S.: Fuzzy MCDM based on ideal and anti-ideal concepts. European Journal of Operational Research 112, 682–691 (1999)
21. Nurmi, H.: Approaches to collect decision making with fuzzy preference relations. Fuzzy Sets and Systems 6, 249–259 (1981)
22. Raj, P.A., Kumar, D.N.: Ranking alternatives with fuzzy weights using maximizing set and minimizing set. Fuzzy Sets and Systems 105, 365–375 (1999)
23. Tanino, T.: Fuzzy preference in group decision making. Fuzzy Sets and Systems 12, 117–131 (1984)

24. Tsaur, S.H., Chang, T.Y., Yen, C.H.: The evaluation of airline service quality by fuzzy MCDM. Tourism Management 23, 107–115 (2002)
25. Wang, Y.J., Kao, C.S.: Applying fuzzy multiple-criteria decision-making method to select the distribution center. In: The 4th International Conference on Fuzzy Systems and Knowledge Discovery (FSKD 2007), Haikou, China (2007)
26. Wang, Y.J., Lee, H.S.: Generalizing TOPSIS for fuzzy multiple-criteria group decision-making. Computers and Mathematics with Applications 53, 1762–1772 (2007)
27. Wang, Y.J., Lee, H.S., Lin, K.: Fuzzy TOPSIS for multi-criteria decision-making. International Mathematical Journal 3, 367–379 (2003)
28. Zadeh, L.A.: Fuzzy sets. Information and Control 8, 338–353 (1965)
29. Zimmermann, H.J.: Fuzzy Set: Decision Making and Expert System. Kluwer, Boston (1987)
30. Zimmermann, H.J.: Fuzzy Set Theory – And Its Application, 2nd edn. Kluwer, Boston (1991)

Towards the Impact of the Random Sequence on Genetic Algorithms

Yongtao Yu[1] and Xiangzhong Xu[2]

[1] Naval Academy of Armament, Mailbox 1303-17, Beijing, China
[2] Academy of Armored Force Engineering, No. 21 Dujiakan, Fengtai District, Beijing, China
y_yt128@yahoo.com.cn
xuxz02@21cn.com

Abstract. The impact of the random sequence on Genetic Algorithms (GAs) is rarely discussed in the community so far. The requirements of GAs for Pseudo Random Number Generators (PRNGs) are analyzed, and a series of numerical experiments of Genetic Algorithm and Direct Search Toolbox computing three different kinds of typical test functions are conducted. An estimate of solution accuracy for each test function is included when six standard PRNGs on MATLAB are applied respectively. A ranking is attempted based on the estimated solution absolute/relative error. It concludes that the effect of PRNGs on GAs varies with the test function; that generally speaking, modern PRNGs outperform traditional ones, and that the seed also has a deep impact on GAs. The research results will be beneficial to stipulate proper principle of PRNGs selection criteria for GAs.

Keywords: GAs, PRNGs, stochastic methods, accuracy.

1 Introduction

Genetic algorithms (GAs) are categorized as stochastic methods and global search heuristics, and used in computing to find approximate solutions to optimization and search problems. GAs use techniques inspired by evolutionary biology such as inheritance, selection, crossover, and mutation. The four components that are nondeterministic and use randomization in GAs are initialization, reproduction, crossover, and mutation. That is, Pseudo Random Number Generators (PRNGs) have great impact on GAs.

So far, tremendous studies have been conducted on the following basic and critical problems in both theoretical and application domains, such as code representation, fitness function, genetic operators, controlling parameters selection, convergence analysis, parallel computing with GAs, and many fruitful results have been achieved. At the same time, while statisticians are generally aware of potential problems with PRNGs, the GAs community often is not. As a result, the impact of the random sequence on genetic algorithms has not gained enough attention and is rarely researched.

F.L. Wang et al. (Eds.): AICI 2010, Part II, LNAI 6320, pp. 152–159, 2010.

The scope of this paper will be to highlight the effect of PRNGs on the outcome of Genetic Algorithm and Direct Search Toolbox. Six PRNGs provided on MATLAB will be substituted as the parent population. A comparison of the solution accuracy of the test functions is conducted. An estimate of accuracy is included for each test function. A ranking of the PRNGs is attempted based on the estimated solution absolute/relative error.

The rest of this paper is organized as follows: Section 2 analyzes the requirements of GAs for PRNGs in brief. In Section 3, six standard PRNGs on MATLAB are given. In Section 4, a series of numerical experiments are conducted and the impact of PRNGs on GAs is analyzed. The conclusion appears in Section 5.

2 Requirements of GAs for PRNGs

2.1 The Building Block Hypothesis

Genetic algorithms are relatively simple to implement. The theoretical underpinning is the building block hypothesis (BBH), which consists of [1]:

(1) A description of an abstract adaptive mechanism that performs adaptation by identifying and recombining "building blocks", i.e. low order, low defining-length schemata with above average fitness.

(2) A hypothesis that a genetic algorithm performs adaptation by implicitly and efficiently implementing this abstract adaptive mechanism.

Reference [2] describes the abstract adaptive mechanism as follows:

(1) Short, low order, and highly fit schemata are sampled, recombined [crossed over], and resampled to form strings of potentially higher fitness. In a way, by working with these particular schemata [the building blocks], we have reduced the complexity of our problem; instead of building high-performance strings by trying every conceivable combination, we construct better and better strings from the best partial solutions of past samplings.

(2) Just as a child creates magnificent fortresses through the arrangement of simple blocks of wood [building blocks], so does a genetic algorithm seek near optimal performance through the juxtaposition of short, low-order, high-performance schemata, or building blocks.

2.2 Requirements of GAs for PRNGs

A reliable PRNG is a basic and essential ingredient for any stochastic methods. As also, the Building Block Hypothesis depends highly on the quality of uniform random sequences used for producing initial population, and using the genetic operators. To achieve good figure of merit [3] [4], the pseudo random sequence should possess the following features:

(1) Independence. A good deal of research has gone into pseudo-random number theory, and modern algorithms for generating pseudo-random numbers are so good that each number drawn must be statistically independent of the others.

(2) Uniform distribution. Every random number is one that is drawn from a set of possible values, each of which is equally probable. A sequence of real-valued random variables, $u_0, u_1, u_2, \cdots$, are i.i.d. U(0, 1) if and only if for all integers $i \geq 0$ and $n > 0$, the vector $u_{i,n} = (u_{i+1}, u_{i+2}, \cdots, u_{i+n})$ is uniformly distributed over the n-dimensional unit hypercube $(0, 1)^n$. Of course, this cannot hold for PRNGs because any vector of n successive values produced by the generator must belong to

$$\Psi_n = \left\{ (u_0, \cdots, u_{n-1}) : s_0 \in S \right\} .$$
(1)

which is the finite set of all vectors of n successive output values that can be produced, from all possible initial states [5].

(3) Long period. PRNGs are typically periodic, which means the sequence will eventually repeat itself. While periodicity is hardly ever a desirable characteristic, modern PRNGs have periods that are so long that they can be ignored for most practical purposes.

(4) Multiple stream and substream support. In the circumstance of parallel computing with GAs, besides the huge period, the PRNGs should support multiple streams and substream [6].

3   Standard PRNGs on MATLAB

Genetic Algorithm and Direct Search Toolbox software in MATLAB v7.7.0.471 (R2008b) extends the optimization capabilities in MATLAB and Optimization Toolbox (GAOT) products, and is the handy and powerful tool for GAs, simulated annealing, and direct search. The available generator algorithms and their properties are given in the following table (Table 1).

Table 1. The standard PRNGs on common MATLAB

No.	Keyword	Generator	Multiple Streams and Substream Support	Approximate Period In Full Precision
1	mt19937ar	Mersenne twister	NO	$2^{19936}-1$
2	mcg16807	Multiplicative congruential generator	NO	$2^{31}-2$
3	mlfg6331_64	Multiplicative lagged Fibonacci generator	YES	2^{124}
4	mrg32k3a	Combined multiple recursive generator	YES	2^{127}
5	shr3cong	Shift-register generator summed with linear congruential generator	NO	2^{64}
6	swb2712	Modified subtract with borrow generator	NO	2^{1492}

In the following chapter, the impact of different PRNGs on GAs will be tested.

4   Impact of Random Sequences on GAs

To evaluate the test problems (many of which are violently fluctuating, i.e., containing many local minima), several numerical experiments are performed and some results are presented to analyze the impact of PRNGs on GAs.

4.1 Test Functions

Since the usefulness of a particular generator depends on its usage, without loss of generality, the following several different kinds of test functions are employed throughout the paper. They are among the most frequently used functions to test performance of mathematical optimization algorithms.

Test function 1: A unimodal one variable problem. Using a test problem obtained from the GAs playground [7] (short for TF1), the goal is to find x' in the closed interval from -3 to 3 that minimizes

$$f(x) = x^4 - 12x^3 + 15x^2 + 56x - 60 \ . \tag{2}$$

The known solution is found at $x' = -0.8702$ resulting in a function value of $fval' = -88.891568$.

Test function 2: A multimodal one variable problem with one global minimum. Using a test problem provided by Goldberg [2] (short for TF2), the goal is to find x' in the closed interval from -2 to 1 that minimizes

$$f(x) = -1.0 - x\sin(10\pi x) \ . \tag{3}$$

The known solution is found at $x' = -1.8508$ resulting in a function value of $fval' = -2.850227$. Note that there are many local minima.

Test function 3: A multimodal two variable problem with one global minimum. Using the Rosenbrock function [8] (short for TF3), which is defined by

$$f(x, y) = (1 - x)^2 + 100(y - x^2)^2 \ . \tag{4}$$

It has a global minimum at $(x', y') = (1,1)$ where $fval' = f(x', y') = 0$. A different coefficient of the second term is sometimes given, but this does not affect the position of the global minimum. It is a non-convex function and the global minimum is inside a long, narrow, parabolic shaped flat valley. It is also known as Rosenbrock's valley or Rosenbrock's banana function. To find the valley is trivial, however to converge to the global minimum is difficult.

4.2 Stopping Criteria and Tolerance

In all the computations, the stopping criteria options are maintained as default values in Genetic Algorithm and Direct Search Toolbox software, except that the option 'TolFun' is set to 1.0000e-20.

4.3 Some Results

Following are the results using the six different PRNGs as the parent population with different seeds for TF1, TF2 and TF3.

The Influence of PRNGs Algorithms. When these PRNGs are all seeded to 1, the search results for TF1, TF2 and TF3 are listed in Table 2, Table 3, Table 4, respectively:

Table 2. Search results for TF1 (seed=1)

PRNGs	x	fval	Relative Error (%)	Ranking
mt19937ar	-0.870205	-88.891568	0.000575	2
mcg16807	-0.870116	-88.891568	0.009653	6
mlfg6331_64	-0.870201	-88.891568	0.000115	1
mrg32k3a	-0.870180	-88.891568	0.002298	3
shr3cong	-0.870177	-88.891568	0.002643	4
swb2712	-0.870169	-88.891568	0.003562	5

As the function values are all almost the same, the relative error is computed by $|(x - x')/x'| \times 100$, and the performances of PRNGs are based on the ranked comparison of relative error.

It is clear from the table that the global minimum was found in all cases. Further, the relative error is less than 0.01% in all cases. Based on the relative error, the ranking of the generators is: mlfg6331_64, mt19937ar, mrg32k3a, shr3cong, swb2712, and mcg16807.

Table 3. Search results for TF2 (seed=1)

PRNGs	x	fval	Relative Error (%)	Ranking
mt19937ar	-1.650601	-2.650307	7.014178	3
mcg16807	0.851167	-1.850595	35.07201	4
mlfg6331_64	-1.850591	-2.850272	0.001579	1
mrg32k3a	-1.850527	-2.850273	0.001614	2
shr3cong	0.851161	-1.850595	35.07201	5
swb2712	0.851241	-1.850594	35.07205	6

Here, the relative error is computed by $|(fval - fval')/fval'| \times 100$, and the performances of PRNGs are based on the ranked comparison of relative error.

It is clear from the table that the global minimum was only successfully found by the generators, mlfg6331_64 and mrg32k3a. Further, the relative error is less than 0.005% in these two cases. However, the generator, mt19937ar, found second minimum, and the other PRNGs are lost in local minima. Thus, the ranking of the generators is: mlfg6331_64, mrg32k3a, mt19937ar, mcg16807, shr3cong, and swb2712.

Table 4. Search results for TF3 (seed=1)

PRNGs	x	y	fval	Absolute Error	Ranking
mt19937ar	0.9503	0.9045	0.0027	0.0027	1
mcg16807	1.2091	1.4695	0.0495	0.0495	4
mlfg6331_64	0.9652	0.9203	0.0141	0.0141	3
mrg32k3a	0.9297	0.8671	0.0057	0.0057	2
shr3cong	0.7349	0.5400	0.0703	0.0703	5
swb2712	0.6000	0.3660	0.1636	0.1636	6

As the global minimum is 0, the absolute error is taken as the index for the ranking of PRNGs. Based on the absolute error, the ranking of the generators is: mt19937ar, mrg32k3a, mlfg6331_64, mcg16807, shr3cong, and swb2712.

The Influence of the Seed. When these PRNGs are all seeded to 12345, the search results for TF1, TF2 and TF3 are listed in Table 5, Table 6, Table 7, respectively:

Table 5. Search results for TF1 (seed=12345)

PRNGs	x	fval	Relative Error (%)	Ranking
mt19937ar	-0.870118	-88.891568	0.009423	6
mcg16807	-0.870124	-88.891568	0.008734	5
mlfg6331_64	-0.870160	-88.891568	0.004597	2
mrg32k3a	-0.870156	-88.891567	0.005056	3
shr3cong	-0.870143	-88.891568	0.00655	4
swb2712	-0.870171	-88.891568	0.003333	1

The relative error is computed in a way similar to Table 2. It is clear from the table that the global minimum was found in all cases. Further, the relative error is less than 0.01% in all cases. Based on the relative error, the ranking of the generators is: swb2712, mlfg6331_64, mrg32k3a, shr3cong, mcg16807, mt19937ar.

Table 6. Search results for TF2 (seed=12345)

PRNGs	x	fval	Relative Error (%)	Ranking
mt19937ar	0.851179	-1.850595	35.07201	2
mcg16807	0.851195	-1.850595	35.07201	3
mlfg6331_64	-0.651607	-1.650777	42.08261	6
mrg32k3a	-0.851249	-1.850594	35.07205	5
shr3cong	0.851169	-1.850595	35.07201	4
swb2712	-1.650578	-2.650305	7.014248	1

It is clear from the table that all the PRNGs fail to find the global minimum. According to the relative error, the ranking of the generators is: swb2712, mt19937ar, mcg16807, shr3cong, mrg32k3a, and mlfg6331_64.

Table 7. Search results for TF3 (seed=12345)

PRNGs	x	y	fval	Absolute Error	Ranking
mt19937ar	1.1261	1.2585	0.0254	0.0254	3
mcg16807	1.2045	1.4627	0.0561	0.0561	6
mlfg6331_64	1.0107	1.0156	0.0036	0.0036	1
mrg32k3a	0.7769	0.5985	0.0523	0.0523	5
shr3cong	1.1467	1.3119	0.0225	0.0225	2
swb2712	0.8275	0.6799	0.0321	0.0321	4

It is clear from the table that the global minimum was found in all cases. Based on the absolute error, the ranking of the generators is: mlfg6331_64, shr3cong, mt19937ar, swb2712, mrg32k3a, mcg16807.

Rankings of PRNGs. The comparison of the rankings of the PRNGs for the three test functions when seeded to 1 and 12345 are given in Table 8 and Table 9 respectively.

Table 8. Comparison of rankings for each generator based on test functions(seed=1)

PRNGs	TF1	TF2	TF3	Overall Ranking
mt19937ar	2	3	1	2
mcg16807	6	4	4	4
mlfg6331_64	1	1	3	1
mrg32k3a	3	2	2	3
shr3cong	4	5	5	4
swb2712	5	6	6	6

Based on the average rank for the entire test functions, the generators when seeded to 1 are ranked overall as mlfg6331_64, mt19937ar, mrg32k3a, shr3cong and mcg16807 (tied), and swb2712.

Table 9. Comparison of rankings for each generator based on test functions(seed=12345)

PRNGs	TF1	TF2	TF3	Overall Ranking
mt19937ar	6	2	3	4
mcg16807	5	3	6	6
mlfg6331_64	2	6	1	2
mrg32k3a	3	5	5	5
shr3cong	4	4	2	3
swb2712	1	1	4	1

Based on the average rank for the entire test functions, the generators when seeded to 12345 are ranked overall as swb2712, mlfg6331_64, shr3cong, mt19937ar, mrg32k3a, and mcg16807.

5   Conclusions

Different PRNGs cause different levels of GAs performance (both better and worse) depending on the test function. However, it can be seen from Table 8 and Table 9 that mlfg6331_64 and the default generator on MATLAB, viz. mt19937ar has remarkable performances in most cases, and surely, mcg16807 are an outdated alternative. Generally speaking, modern PRNGs outperform traditional ones.

The usefulness of GAs with a particular generator depends on the complexity of the test function. For a unimodal one variable problem, all GAs can successfully find the global minima with rather high accuracy; as for a multimodal one variable problem with one global minimum, some GAs with traditional PRNGs may be lost in local minima.

Having said that the effect of PRNGs on GAs depends on the test function, the seed also has a deep impact on GAs. The PRNGs may fail to find the global minima in some cases. This is especially the case for swb2712, which ranks first and last when seeded differently.

The convergence of GAs is usually slower than traditional techniques, such as Newton-Raphson and conjugate gradient techniques (both of which are derivative based). This is because of the constant testing of suboptimal solutions. Further, the solution will only be an estimate versus an exact answer.

In further research, quasi-random number sequences as the parent population (specifically Sobol and Niederreiter) may be used to improve the final objective function value and the number of generations used, and the comparison of different effect between pseudo- and quasi-random number generators will be performed later.

References

[1] Holland, J.H.: Adaptation in Natural and Artificial Systems. University of Michigan Press, Ann Arbor (1975)
[2] Goldberg, D.E.: Genetic Algorithms in Search, Optimization and Machine Learning. Kluwer Academic Publishers, Boston (1989)
[3] Marasaglia, G.: Random Numbers Fall Mainly in the Planes. Proc. Nat. Acad. Sci. U.S.A. 12, 25–28 (1968)
[4] Entacher, K.: Bad Subsequences of Well-Known Linear Congruential Pseudorandom Number Generators. ACM Transactions on Modeling and Computer Simulation 7, 61–70 (1998)
[5] Ecuyer, P.L.: Random Number Generation. In: Handbook of Computational Statistics. Springer, Berlin (2004)
[6] Zeigler, B.P., Kim, J.: Asynchronous Genetic Algorithms on Parallel Computers. In: 5th International Conference on Genetic Algorithms, pp. 75–83. Morgan Kaufmann Publishers, San Francisco (1991)
[7] GAs Playground,
http://www.aridolan.com/ofiles/ga/gaa/gaa.aspx#Examples
[8] Lagarias, J.C., Reeds, J.A., Wright, M.H., Wright, P.E.: Convergence Properties of the Nelder-Mead Simplex Method in Low Dimensions. SIAM Journal of Optimization 9, 112–147 (1998)

A New Pairwise Comparison Based Method of Ranking LR-fuzzy Numbers

Mingxin Zhang and Fusheng Yu

School of Mathematical Sciences, Beijing Normal University
Laboratory of Mathematics and Complex Systems, Ministry of Education
Beijing 100875, China
monica0516@163.com, yufusheng@263.net

Abstract. This paper aims to rank LR-fuzzy numbers (LR-fns) by the pairwise comparison based method. Different from the existing methods, our method uses the information contained in each LR-fn to get a consistent total order. In detail, since an LR-fn may not be absolutely larger or smaller than another, this paper proposes the concept of dominant degree to quantify how much one LR-fn is larger and smaller than another. From the dominant degrees, we construct a pairwise comparison matrix based on which a consistent ranking is got. Meanwhile, the ranking result is transitive and consistent, and agrees with our intuition. Examples and comparison with existing methods show the good performance of our method.

Keywords: fuzzy numbers; ranking; pairwise comparison; dominant degree.

1 Introduction

Ranking fuzzy numbers is a hot topic. It is related to some problems in the real life, such as risk analysis, decision making, socioeconomic systems, etc.[5,8,10]. A lot of ranking methods have been proposed. Most methods design some ranking indexes to help ranking. Wang and Kerre[4] classified the ranking indexes into three categories. The first two often used categories [2,3,4,9,10,11] both map each fuzzy number to a real number and decide the order of fuzzy numbers by the order of the corresponding real numbers. The difference between these two categories is whether a reference set is used. Although these methods can rank fuzzy numbers and get a total order, they may sometimes loss the information contained in fuzzy numbers.

In order to get a total order of a set of fuzzy numbers, some scholars [7,12] proposed a ranking method by pairwise comparison with a given index. But the order made by these methods may not satisfy transitivity. Furthermore some scholars combined these pairwise comparison results by calculating how many times one fuzzy number is less than other ones [10]. These method seemed to map each fuzzy number to one integer, and a total order is got according to the order of the corresponding integers. However, only considering the times that one given fuzzy number is less than others seems to be incomplete and not discriminative enough. When two fuzzy numbers have the same times that less than others, then how to determine the order of

F.L. Wang et al. (Eds.): AICI 2010, Part II, LNAI 6320, pp. 160–167, 2010.

them? What's more, whether a fuzzy number is less than others is decided by the comparing index, so these methods are subjective at some extent. In our opinion, it is better to consider the degrees that how much one fuzzy number is smaller and larger than another respectively and then get a total order by these degrees.

For this purpose, a new pairwise comparison based ranking method is proposed in this paper. It first constructs a pairwise comparison matrix, and then with consistency considered, gives the total order. The objects to be ranked in this paper are restricted to LR-fns(LR-fn) only.

The remainder of this paper is organized as follows. Section 2 introduces fuzzy numbers and the pairwise comparison based ranking method. Section 3 discuss the comparison based on the definition of dominant degrees. The details of the pairwise comparison based ranking method are shown in Section 4. Comparisons with exiting methods are given in Section 5. Section 6 concludes this paper.

2 Preliminaries

Definition 1. The support and kernel of a fuzzy number A are defined as

$$\text{Supp}(A) = \{x \mid x \in X, A(x) > 0\} \text{ and } \text{Ker}(A) = \{x \mid x \in X, A(x) = 1\}.$$

Definition 2. The membership function of an LR-fn A is defined as

$$A(x) = \begin{cases} L((m-x)/(m-a)) & \text{if } x < m \\ 1 & \text{if } x \in [m,n] \\ R((x-n)/(b-n)) & \text{if } x > n \end{cases}$$

where $a \leq m \leq n \leq b$, L and R are decreasing functions defined in $[0,+\infty)$ and satisfy that $L(0) = R(0) = 1$ and $L(x), R(x) \in [0,1]$. A fuzzy number A can be simply denoted as $(a, m, n, b)_{LR}$. L, R are called left branch and right branch respectively [1, 2, 3].

When comparing more than two objects, if the pairwise comparisons don't satisfy the transitivity, a total order may be hard to give. For example, when we talk about some people's enthusiasm, we may get the judgment that "John is more enthusiastic than Bob and Bob is more enthusiastic than Tom. However, it seems that Tom is more enthusiastic than John." How to give a total order is worthy of discussion.

In order to give a total order, the pairwise comparison based ranking method is studied in [1]. It is applicable to the complex and fuzzy problems in the real life. In this method, a pairwise comparison matrix is first build to describe how much one is prior to the other, and then the ranked first element prior to the others consistently is given for a given threshold. The ranked second till ranked last elements are given in similar process. At last, the total order is got.

3 Comparison between Two LR-fns

The main idea of this part is not to give an index for getting a conclusion whether an LR-fn A is larger than another LR-fn B or not. Our purpose is to give the dominant degree quantifying the degree A is larger than B.

3.1 Dominant Degrees

Definition 4. Suppose A, B are LR-fns, a function D: $F(X) \times F(X)$ [0,1] is called a dominant degree between LR-fns, if it satisfies the following four conditions:

(1) $D(A,B)=1 \Leftrightarrow A>B \Leftrightarrow \forall \lambda, A_\lambda^+ > B_\lambda^+, A_\lambda^- > B_\lambda^-$;

(2) $D(A,B)+D(B,A)=1$; (3)$D(A, \varnothing)=1$; (4)$D(A,A)=0$

In this definition, $\varnothing$ stands for an empty set, A_λ^- and A_λ^+ are the left and the right endpoints of the λ-cut of A. $D(A,B)$ means the degree that A is larger than B, while $D(B,A)$ means the degree that B is larger than A.

According to the above definition, we present here one kind of dominant degree. It is based on the shapes of membership functions and the areas surrounded by them. Denote $S(A,B)$ as the total areas representing that A is larger than B. Then, we have

$$D(A,B)=S(A,B)/(S(A,B)+S(B,A))$$

$$D(B,A)=S(B,A)/(S(A,B)+S(B,A)).$$

Actually, $S(A,B)$ and $S(B,A)$ are equivalent to the values of the Hamming distances $d_H(\max(A,B),B)$ and $d_H(\max(A,B),A)$ respectively in Kerre's method[12]. The Geometric meaning of $S(A,B)$ is the sum of the area which is the top right part of the right branch of B and covered by the membership function of A (e.g. S_4 in Fig.1), and the area which is the top left part of the left branch of A and covered by the membership function of B (e.g. S_1 in Fig.1). The Geometric meaning of $S(B,A)$ is the sum of the area which is the top right part of the right branch of A and covered by the membership function of B (e.g. S_3 in Fig.1), and the area which is the top left part of the left branch of B and covered by the membership function of A (e.g. S_2 in Fig.1).

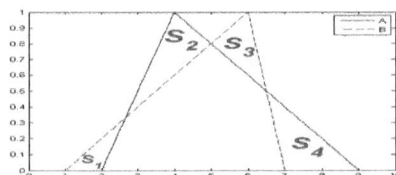

Fig. 1. An example to illustrate the definitions of two dominant degrees

The ideas of this kind of definition are based on the following three points. First, if only consider the kernels, the larger the kernel is, the larger this LR-fn is. Second, if only consider the right branch, the larger the value is, the larger this fuzzy number is. The first two points are easy to understand. Third, with the left branch only considered, if a fuzzy number has larger values, then it is more relevant to the elements which are smaller than the kernel in the universe set, and it means this fuzzy number is farther from the right-hand side of the horizontal axis, so this fuzzy number is smaller than the other.

In Fig.1, based on the last two points, it is easy to know that S_1 and S_4 both represent that A is larger than B. In S_2, the function values that A has in part of its left branch and part of its right branch are larger than those that B has in its left branch. In this case we notice that $Ker(B)>Ker(A)$, that is, B tends to stand for a larger number. So we think that S_2 represents that B is larger than A. Similarly S_3 also represents that B is larger than A. Then in Fig.1, $S(A,B)=S_1+S_4$ and $S(B,A)=S_2+S_3$, so $D(A,B)$ and $D(B,A)$ are easy to be calculated. Obviously $D(A,B)$ and $D(B,A)$ are relative degrees and the sum of them is equal to 1.

At the end, there's still one point to be added. When comparing two LR-fns A and B, we can draw the conclusion that A and B are equal iff $S(A,B)=0$ and $S(B,A)=0$.

3.2 Rationality of the Definition of Dominant Degree

In order to show the rationality of the definitions above, we adopt them to the cases when the two fuzzy numbers are degenerated as interval numbers or real numbers.

Given two interval numbers $A=[m_1,n_1]$ and $B=[m_2,n_2]$, there are three situations of their values as shown in Fig.2.

In Fig.2(a), A and B are non-overlapped. According to our method, $S(A,B)=0$ and $S(B,A)=n_2-m_2+n_1-m_1$, so $D(A,B)=0$ and $D(B,A)=1$.In Fig.2(b), A and B are overlapped. According to our method, $S(A,B)=0$ and $S(B,A)=n_2-n_1+m_2-m_1$, so $D(A,B)=0$ and $D(B,A)=1$. In Fig.2(c), A is included by B. According to our method, $S(A,B)=m_1-m_2$ and $S(B,A)=n_2-n_1$, so $D(A,B)=(m_1-m_2)/(n_2-n_1+m_1-m_2)$ and $D(B,A)=1-D(A,B)$.

The comparing conclusions of Fig.2(a) and (b) are the same as the theory of interval number[1]. The comparing conclusion of Fig.2(c) extends the original theory because it not only gives the degree $D(A,B)$ but also gives the degree $D(B,A)$. It can help understand the problem more comprehensively. Suppose A and B are two real numbers. In our method, if $A>B$, $D(A,B)=1$ and $D(B,A)=0$; if $A=B$, $S(A,B)=0$ and $S(B,A)=0$, so we can also get the conclusion that $A=B$.

In a word, our definitions are adaptive to compare two interval numbers or real numbers, so our method is reasonable.

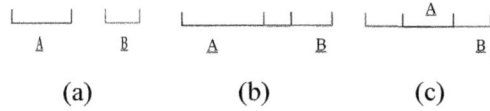

Fig. 2. Cases of the values of two interval numbers

4 Total Order of a Set of LR-fns

In Section 3, we have given the definition of dominant degree. In this section, we will construct the pairwise comparison matrix by these dominant degrees and illustrate the pairwise comparison based ranking method to get a total order of a set of LR-fns.

4.1 Pairwise Comparison Based Ranking Method

In the Preliminaries, we have introduced the idea and the basic steps of the pairwise comparison based ranking method. As noted in that section, first we need to construct a pairwise comparison matrix R. The (i, j) element in R denoted as r_{ij} is a real number of $[0,1]$, satisfying $r_{ij}+r_{ji}=1$, where $i{\neq}j$. It represents the dominance of the ith element to the jth element in the set of the compared objects.

According to the definition of dominant degree in Section 3, we can give $D(A_i, A_j)$. It represents the degree that how much A_i is larger than A_j and its value is in $[0,1]$. What's more, $D(A_i,A_j)+D(A_j,A_i)=1$. Then it is easy to construct a pairwise comparison matrix based on $D(A_i,A_j)$ and $D(A_j,A_i)$, by taking $D(A_i, A_j)$ as the element r_{ij} of R .

From the pairwise comparison matrix constructed above, we can get the total order of these LR-fns. In order to determine the LR-fn which is ranked first, we just need to find out the infimum of each row with the element in the diagonal excluded in R and then select the largest one of these infimums. We call this process the "largest infimum process". The row index of the selected largest corresponds to the largest LR-fn. Then delete the row and the column that respectively corresponds to the chosen largest LR-fn. Continue the "largest infimum process" and the "delete process" until the total ranking is got. We illustrate these steps in Example 1.

Example 1. Given 12 trapezoidal fuzzy numbers(see Fig.3): $A_1=(0,2,4,9)$, $A_2=(1,3,6,8)$, $A_3=(4,4.5,6,7.5)$, $A_4=(5,6,6,8)$, $A_5=(3,5,6,7)$, $A_6=(2,3,3,9)$, $A_7=(1,4,6,7)$, $A_8=(5,6,7,10)$, $A_9=(3.5,5,7,8.5)$, $A_{10}=(0,3,6,8)$, $A_{11}=(4,7,7,8)$, $A_{12}=(3,6,6,9)$.

$$R=\begin{pmatrix}
0 & 0.0909 & 0.0784 & 0.0357 & 0.1296 & 0.25 & 0.2 & 0 & 0.0081 & 0.125 & 0.027 & 0 \\
0.9091 & 0 & 0.1 & 0 & 0.2 & 0.6429 & 0.5 & 0 & 0 & 1 & 0 & 0 \\
0.9216 & 0.9 & 0 & 0 & 0.875 & 0.9058 & 1 & 0 & 0.1 & 0.9167 & 0 & 0.1429 \\
0.9643 & 1 & 1 & 0 & 1 & 0.9578 & 1 & 0 & 0.625 & 1 & 0.3225 & 0.6667 \\
0.8704 & 0.8 & 0.125 & 0 & 0 & 0.8261 & 1 & 0 & 0 & 0.8333 & 0 & 0 \\
0.75 & 0.3571 & 0.0942 & 0.0422 & 0.1739 & 0 & 0.3849 & 0 & 0.0092 & 0.5 & 0.0342 & 0 \\
0.8 & 0.5 & 0 & 0 & 0 & 0.6151 & 0 & 0 & 0 & 0.6667 & 0 & 0 \\
1 & 1 & 1 & 1 & 1 & 1 & 1 & 0 & 1 & 1 & 0.8333 & 1 \\
0.9919 & 1 & 0.9 & 0.375 & 1 & 0.9908 & 1 & 0 & 0 & 1 & 0.1667 & 0.5 \\
0.875 & 0 & 0.0833 & 0 & 0.1667 & 0.5 & 0.3333 & 0 & 0 & 0 & 0 & 0 \\
0.973 & 1 & 1 & 0.6875 & 1 & 0.9658 & 1 & 0.1667 & 0.8333 & 1 & 0 & 0.8125 \\
1 & 1 & 0.8571 & 0.3333 & 1 & 1 & 1 & 0 & 0.5 & 1 & 0.1875 & 0
\end{pmatrix}$$

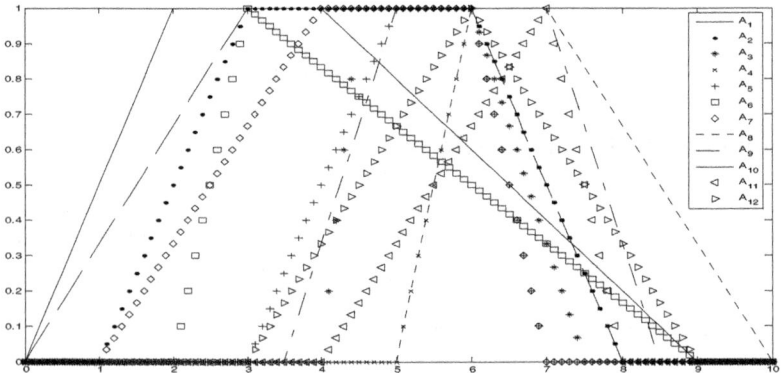

Fig. 3. 12 LR-fns in Example 3

Based on our definition of dominant degree introduced in Section 3, a pairwise comparison matrix R is got as above.

In order to get the fuzzy number to be ranked first, firstly implement the "largest infimum process". The infimum of each row (exclude the element in the diagonal) is 0, 0, 0, 0, 0, 0, 0, 0.8333, 0, 0, 0.1667 and 0 respectively. The largest of these infimum s is 0.8333 and it is on the 8th row in R, so the fuzzy number to be ranked first is A_8. Delete the 8th row and the 8th column in R and continue the "largest infimum process". We see that 0.6875 is the largest infimum in this step and it is on the 11th row, so A_{11} is ranked second. Go on with these steps and we can get a total order.

4.2   Remarks

Example 1 shows how the pairwise comparison based method is used to give a total order of a set of LR-fns. Different from the methods which map each fuzzy number to an index of real number, our method makes fully use of the information contained in each fuzzy number. On the other hand, compared with the other methods for determining the total order [7,10], our method proposed in this paper considers the degrees that how much one fuzzy number is larger and smaller than another respectively. So the total order from this method is more acceptable and more consistent to human's intuition.

Further attention should be paid to the situation when there are more than one "largest infimum" in the "infimum-largest process". In this case, we consider that the LR-fns corresponding to the rows of these largest infimums are not comparable, i.e. the total order of a set of LR-fns may be a partial order. This means the method proposed in this paper is close to the nature of ranking fuzzy numbers and it is softer for solving the problems in the real life.

In Example 1, we can get the first three numbers are A_8, A_{11} and A_4. When we want to choose the 4th fuzzy number, it is found that the largest "infimum" is 0.5 and it appears on both the 9th row and the 12th row. It means that A_9 and A_{12} are not comparable. They are both smaller than A_8, A_{11} and A_4 and both larger than the remaining seven fuzzy numbers. We can think that A_9 and A_{12} are in the same grade but they are not comparable. Go on with the ranking steps and we can find that the situation of being not comparable still appears.

The notation '~' represents the relationship that two LR-fns are not comparable. As stated above, we have $A_9{\sim}A_{12}$. When the ranking steps are finished, we can see that the total order of these 12 trapezoidal fuzzy numbers is

$$A_8 \succ A_{11} \succ A_4 \succ A_9{\sim}A_{12} \succ A_3 \succ A_5 \succ A_2{\sim}A_7 \succ A_6{\sim}A_{10} \succ A_1.$$

Different from the "absolutely larger than" notation ('>'), the notation '$\succ$' used here means consistently larger than. It is decided by the relationship of all the fuzzy numbers being ranked.

From Example 1, we can see that when we use the pairwise comparison based ranking method proposed in this paper, we can have a consistent total order of a set of LR-fns. Although there may be some pairs of fuzzy numbers that are not comparable, we can have an overall understanding of the total order and know that which grade each fuzzy number is probably in. This is useful especially when there are many fuzzy numbers to be ranked.

5 Comparison

In this section, we compare the result of our method with some existing methods. Considering the methods in [2], [3], [7] and [10], we have the comparisons as follows:

Table 1. Comparisons of Different Ranking Methods

Wang and Lee's method[2]	$A_8>A_{11}>A_4>A_9=A_{12}>A_3>A_5>A_6>A_2>A_7>A_{10}>A_1$
Asady's method[3]	$A_8\succ A_{11}\succ A_4\succ A_9\approx A_{12}\succ A_3\succ A_5\succ A_2\succ A_7\succ A_6\succ A_{10}\succ A_1$
Gao and Wang's method[7]	$A_8>A_4>A_{11}>A_9=A_{12}>A_3>A_5>A_2>A_7>A_6=A_{10}>A_1$
Setnes and Cross's method	$A_8>A_{11}>A_4>A_9>A_{12}>A_3>A_5>A_2>A_7>A_6>A_{10}>A_1$
Our method	$A_8\succ A_{11}\succ A_4\succ A_9\sim A_{12}\succ A_3\succ A_5\succ A_2\sim A_7\succ A_6\sim A_{10}\succ A_1$

In Table 1, the notation '=' used in [2] means identical, while the same notation used in [7] just means that the total possibility degree that the former fuzzy number is smaller than the latter one is the same as the degree that the former one is larger than the latter one, and it is not to represent that they are identical. The notation '$\succ$' used in [3] and the notation '>' used in [2, 7, 10] represent that the former fuzzy number is larger than the latter one, and '$\approx$' used in [3] means identical. In our method, the notation '~' is to represent the relationship that two LR-fns are not comparable and '$\succ$' means that the former fuzzy number is larger than the latter one with consideration of the relationship of all the fuzzy numbers.

From the comparisons, we can see that the order given by our method is almost the same as other methods. What's more, when comparing A_2, A_7, A_6 and A_{10}, our method concludes that the pair of A_2 and A_7 and the pair of A_6 and A_{10} are not comparable. It is much softer when dealing with real problems and consistent to human's intuition.

6 Conclusions

In this paper, we first review the methods of ranking fuzzy numbers. Some drawbacks, such as loss of information, lack of transitivity, discrimination and consistency, are pointed out. This motives us to propose a better method to rank fuzzy numbers more objectively and consistently.

For this propose, we give a new concept of dominant degree. The dominant degree quantifies the degree that one LR-fn is larger or smaller than another. From these dominant degrees of the ranked fuzzy numbers, a pairwise comparison matrix is constructed to accomplish the ranking of the given fuzzy numbers.

There are two advantages of our proposed method proposed. First, the definition of the dominant degree is trying to make full use of the objective information in each LR-fn. Secondly, the pairwise comparison based ranking method helps to get a consistent ranking. Especially when there are more than two LR-fns, the method in this paper is more applicable and more consistent to human's intuition.

The objects to be ranked in this paper are restricted to LR-fns. In the future, we can try to generalize this method to rank generalized fuzzy numbers. What's more, the definition of the dominant degree used in this paper is based on the kernels and the left and the right branches of LR-fns. Other definition methods should be studied.

Acknowledgments

Support from Project 60775032 and Project 10971243 supported by National Natural Science Foundation of China (NSFC) is gratefully acknowledged. The research is also sponsored by priority discipline of Beijing Normal University.

References

1. Luo, C.Z.: The Foundation of Fuzzy Set Thoery. Beijing Normal University, Beijing (2005)
2. Wang, Y.-J., Lee, H.-S.: The revised method of ranking fuzzy numbers with an area between the centroid and original points. Computers and Mathematics with Applications 5, 2033–2042 (2008)
3. Asady, B.: The revised method of ranking LR fuzzy number based on deviation degree. Expert Systems with Applications 37, 5056–5060 (2010)
4. Wang, X., Kerre, E.E.: Reasonable properties for the ordering of fuzzyquantities(I). Fuzzy Sets and Systems 118, 375–385 (2001)
5. Lazzerini, B., Mkrtchyan, L.: Ranking of generalized fuzzy numbers and its application to risk analysis. In: The Second Asia-Pacific Conference on Computational Intelligence and Industrial Applications, vol. 1, pp. 249–252. IEEE Press, Los Alamitos (2009)
6. Jiao, B., Lian, Z., Qunxian, C.: A Method of Ranking Fuzzy Numbers in Decision-making Problems. In: The Sixth International Conference on Fuzzy Systems and Knowledge Discovery, vol. 6, pp. 40–44. IEEE Press, Los Alamitos (2009)
7. Gao, X., Wang, G.: A New Method for Ranking Fuzzy Numbers-Endpoint Method. In: The Sixth International Conference on Fuzzy Systems and Knowledge Discovery, vol. 5, pp. 145–149. IEEE Press, Los Alamitos (2009)
8. Lee, J.H., Hyung, L.K.: A Method for Ranking Fuzzily Fuzzy Numbers. In: The Ninth IEEE International Conference on Fuzzy Systems, vol. 1, pp. 71–76. IEEE Press, Los Alamitos (2000)
9. Deng, H.: A Discriminative Analysis of Approaches to Ranking Fuzzy Numbers in Fuzzy Decision Making. In: The Fourth International Conference on Fuzzy Systems and Knowledge Discovery, vol. 1, pp. 22–27. IEEE Press, Los Alamitos (2007)
10. Setnes, M., Cross, V.: Compatibility-Based Ranking of Fuzzy Numbers. In: The Annual Meeting of the North American Fuzzy Information Processing Society, pp. 305–310 (1997)
11. Li, R.: Fuzzy Multiple Criteria Decision Making Theory and Applications. Science Press, Beijing (2002) (in chinese)
12. Kerre, E.E.: The use of fuzzy sets theory in electrocardiological diagnostics. In: Gupta, M.M., Sanchez, E. (eds.) Approximate Reasoning in Decision Analysis, pp. 277–282. NorthHolland, Amsterdam (1982)

A Fuzzy Assessment Model for Traffic Safety in City: A Case Study in China

Zhizhong Zhao[1], Boxian Fu[2], and Ning Zhang[3]

[1] Department of Transportation Engineering, Tongji University, Shanghai, China
[2] handong Luqiao Construction Co,Ltd, Jinan, China
[3] Dezhou Highway Bureau, Dezhou, China
11asc@163.com

Abstract. According to the principle of theory combining with practice, pre-liminary indicators of road safety evaluation are selected by integrating the characteristics of road traffic safety in China. On the basis of preliminary indi-cators, evaluation index system of traffic safety is constructed from three re-spects: accident rate, accident severity and the improved level of safety man-agement. Considering the fuzziness, dependence and interaction of assessing indices, we applied the fuzzy method to assess traffic safety, and the evaluation and grading criteria for different indexes were presented. Finally, the practical value of the evaluation system and the evaluation model proposed in this study were proved by case study. Furthermore, the results of the study may provide reference for the traffic management departments.

Keywords: Traffic safety, Assessment index, Fuzzy method.

1 Introduction

The problems with respect to public traffic safety in cities of China are increasingly outstanding. Although the number of accidents in China stopped to increase and began to fall from 2003, the number of deaths still was in a high level[1]. Therefore, road safety issue is still worth causing high attention for governments and related depart-ments. Thus, it is needed to carry on systematic analysis the effectiveness of road traffic safety management, and develop an effective method to assess the traffic safety status.

Traffic safety managements have received wide ranges of concerns, leading to considerable achievements by previous research works. There are several conventional such evaluation methods as the Analytic Hierarchy Process method [2], Classical Set Theory [3], Gray Clustering Method [1], and Neural Network method [4]. Although each of these methods possesses individual merits, further improvements are required for objectivity, comprehensiveness, and fuzziness. The interior of the road traffic safety system is extremely complicated, and influence factors are numerous and every factor is fuzzy. Fortunately, fuzzy theory can solve the problem of fuzziness in the complex system. Application of fuzzy theory in fields such as water quality [5], habitat suit-ability[6], shows the reliability of this theory.

F.L. Wang et al. (Eds.): AICI 2010, Part II, LNAI 6320, pp. 168–174, 2010.

Considering fuzziness in traffic safety evaluation, we apply the fuzzy theory to assess the traffic safety in this study. The evaluation and grading criteria for different indexes were presented, and the comprehensive evaluation method for traffic safety based on fuzzy mathematics was proposed. Finally, we take two cities as the case study, to assess the traffic safety status by using the model proposed here.

2 Fuzzy Set Theory

Zadeh (1965) introduced fuzzy sets which specify uncertainty by membership functions, and have been widely used in a range of disciplines to analyze real-world phenomena[5,7]. In the development of fuzzy sets theory, Zadeh successfully introduced fuzzy sets, fuzzy systems, fuzzy logic, linguistic variable and approximate reasoning, fuzzy logic and soft computing in words, and the generalized theory of uncertainty. The description of fuzzy theory formulas are shown in [5].

In the fuzzy set theory, a fuzzy set is a class of objects with a continuum of grades of membership. Such a set is characterized by a membership characteristic or function which assigns to each object a grade of membership varying between zero and one. To define a fuzzy set; let X={x} denote a space of points, with x denoting a generic element of X. Then a fuzzy set A in X is a set of ordered pairs of: $X = \{[x, \mu_A(x)]\}$, $x \in X$, $\mu_A(x)$ is the grade of membership of x in A. Thus if $\mu_A(x)$ takes on values in space M (termed the membership space), then A is essentially a function from A to M. The function $\mu_A : X \rightarrow M$ which defines A is called the membership function of A. For simplicity, M is the interval [0, 1], with grades 0 and 1, respectively representing non-membership and full-membership in a fuzzy set.

3 Fuzzy Comprehensive Evaluation Model for Traffic Safety

3.1 Description Of Fuzzy Comprehensive Assessment Method

The method presented in this study is a combination of a fuzzy comprehensive evaluation method and the Analytic Hierarchy Process (AHP). This method is capable of providing an integrated suitability index. The following gives a description about the assessment model based on a fuzzy comprehensive evaluation method.

Assuming that the affecting factors for traffic safety assessment are A1, A2, A3,…,An and the importance of every index is divided into m degrees. Their weights are $a_1, a_2, \ldots a_n$, noted by $\underset{\sim}{A} = (\alpha_1, a_2; \cdots, \alpha_n)$ the membership matrix of index, can be expressed by equation(1)[8]:

$$\underset{\sim}{R} = \begin{pmatrix} \gamma_{11} & \gamma_{12} & \cdots & \gamma_{1m} \\ \gamma_{21} & \gamma_{22} & \cdots & \gamma_{2m} \\ \cdots & \cdots & \cdots & \cdots \\ \gamma_{n1} & \gamma_{n2} & \cdots & \gamma_{nm} \end{pmatrix}_{n \times m} \tag{1}$$

The comprehensive assessment result can be expressed by equation (2):

$$\underset{\sim}{C} = \underset{\sim}{A} \circ \underset{\sim}{R} = \left\{ b_1, b_2, \cdots, b_n \right\} \tag{2}$$

When there are many indexes, the number of factors in A will be more and the weights of factors classified will be finer. This leads to a too little comprehensive assessment value. With more factors, this problem will become more obvious. So the affecting factors can be divided into several levels according to their parallel or result-reason relationship to construct a multi-level comprehensive assessment model. These steps are explained as follows:

(a) The factor set U is first divided into subsets $U_1, U_2, \cdots, U_s$ (where $\sum_{i=1}^{s} U_i = U$).

And then let $U_k = \left\{ u_{k2}, u_{k3}, \cdots, u_{kn_j} \right\}$ (k = 1 2 ; $\cdots$, s)

(where $\sum_{k=1}^{s} n_k = n$), n is the number of affecting factors.

(b) For every U_k, it can be assessed by the first-level model

For assessment sector $V = \left\{ v_1, v_2, \cdots, v_m \right\}$, the weight $\underset{\sim}{A}_k^1 = (\alpha_1^1, \alpha_2^1, \alpha_3^1; \cdots, \alpha_n^1)$

(where $\sum_{i=1}^{n_k} \alpha_{km} = 1, \quad m = 1, 2, \cdots, n_k$), the assessment matrix of single factor R, the assessment value by the first-level model can be expressed by equation (3)

$$\underset{\sim}{C}_k^1 = \underset{\sim}{A}_k^1 \circ \underset{\sim}{R}_k^1 = \left(b_{k1}^1, \cdots, b_{kn}^1 \right) \quad, \quad k = 1, 2, \cdots, S \tag{3}$$

(c) Then each subset U_k can be deemed as a new factor, its single factor assessment can be expressed by equation (4)

$$\underset{\sim}{R}_k^2 = \begin{bmatrix} \underset{\sim}{C}_1^1 \\ \underset{\sim}{C}_2^1 \\ \vdots \\ \underset{\sim}{C}_s^1 \end{bmatrix} = \left[b_k^1 \right]_{s \times m} \tag{4}$$

where U_k is single factor assessment matrix of $U = \left\{ u_1, u_2, \cdots, u_s \right\}$; $\underset{\sim}{C}_k^1$ is single factor assessment U_k, as a part of U, can reflect some properties of U. Then its weight can be determined according to its importance, that is $\underset{\sim}{A}_k^2 = \left(\alpha_1^2, \alpha_2^2, \cdots, \alpha_s^2 \right)$.

For second-level comprehensive assessment: $\underset{\sim}{C}_k^2 = \underset{\sim}{A}_k^2 \circ \underset{\sim}{R}_k^2$.

According to the reality, the multi-time comprehensive assessment can be finished through many times, cycle. The last comprehensive assessment will be $\underset{\sim}{C} = \underset{\sim}{A} \circ \underset{\sim}{R}$.

(d) According to the eigenvalue h= (1, 2, …, m), Traffic Safety (TS) value can be expressed by the equation (5)

$$TS = H(u) = hC^{T} \tag{5}$$

3.2 Assessment Index System for Traffic Safety

Establishment of a reasonable evaluation index system is the basis of road traffic safety evaluation model. The evaluation index system should be followed in scientificalness, comparability, and operability etc. On the basis of comprehensive analysis on the role of road traffic safety management facilities in road traffic safety management, and extensively consultation of the expert advices, a evaluation system with single goal layer, 3 rule layers, and 9 defined indexes is developed based on the results of present research. Table 1 shows the traffic safety evaluation index system.

The weights of indexes shown in Table 1 are determined by analytic hierarchy process (AHP) [9], which has been widely used to process weight.

For Traffic Safety comprehensive evaluation : $A = (0.41, 0.36, 0.23)$;

For Accident rate: $A_1^1 = (0.67, 0.33)$;

For Accident severity: $A_2^1 = (0.71, 0.29)$;

For The improved level of safety management: $A_3^1 = (0.19, 0.27, 0.29, 0.12, 0.13)$.

Table 1. Evaluation index system of traffic safety

Objective layer	Rule layer	Index layer
Traffic safety	Accident rate (A_1)	Accidents per 10 thousand vehicles(A_{11})
		Beginners's accidents(A_{12})
	Accident severity(A_2)	Deaths per 10 thousand vehicles (A_{21})
		Rate of hurt with death (A_{22})
	The improved level of safety management (A_3)	Safety investment rate (A_{31})
		Treatment rate of places with more accidents (A_{32})
		Solving rate of accidents escape (A_{33})
		Treatment rate with simple procedure (A_{34})
		The death rate of decline (A_{35})

3.3 Degree Classification of Index and Membership Function

According to the characteristics of traffic safety, based on the domestic and foreign study results [1-4], the inter-zone of factors which belong to certain degree are listed in Table 2. The degree of affecting factors belong to certain class is determined through fuzzy theory. The triangle function is selected as membership function. As sketched in Fig. 1, when the membership degree is 1, it means that one factor completely belongs to one evaluation grade. The membership degree 0 means that one factor does not belong to one evaluation grade. The membership degree, in [0, 1], means that it is partially belonging to one evaluation grade.

Table 2. Degree classification of Traffic safety evaluation indexes

Index	Very high	High	medium	Low	Very low
Accidents per 10 thousand vehicles(A_{11})	< 80	80-120	120-160	160-200	> 200
Aeginners's accidents(A_{12})	< 30	30-35	35-40	40-45	> 45
Deaths per 10 thousand vehicles (A_{21})	< 8	8-12	12-16	16-20	> 20
Rate of hurt with death (A_{22})	< 13	13-17	17-21	21-25	> 25
Safety investment rate (A_{31})	> 20	16-20	12-16	8-12	< 8
Treatment rate of places with more accidents (A_{32})	> 90	80-90	70-80	60-70	< 60
solving rate of accidents escape (A_{33})	> 70	60-70	50-60	40-50	< 40
Treatment rate with simple procedure (A_{34})	> 85	80-85	75-80	70-75	< 70
The death rate of decline (A_{35})	<-7.6	-7.6-1.8	-1.8-4.0	4.0-9.8	> 9.8

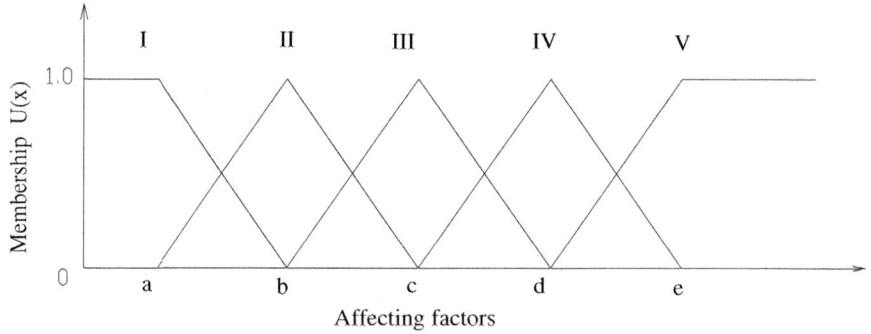

Fig. 1. Sketch of membership function

4   Application

In this study, using the values of assessnent indices of City A and B in Table 3, step by step application of the model is implemented. The results listed in Table 4. One can obtain from Table 4 that the degree of traffic safety of City A and B is 2.050, 3.625. Traffic safety level for City A, therefore falls in grade 2–3, much closer to grade 2. And the traffic safety level for City B, falls in grade 3–4, much closer to grade 4.

Table 3. Indices values for traffic safety of City A and B

City	A_{11}	A12	A_{21}	A_{22}	A_{31}	A_{32}	A_{33}	A_{34}	A_{35}
A	96.3	26.1	9.2	17.5	18.2	75.0	45.0	82.5	-3.5
B	151.2	40.8	15.1	22.3	8.2	62.1	35.6	70.2	8.1

Table 4. Assessment values of traffic fasety for two cities

City	Membership vector value					Ranking feature value
A	0.216	0.584	0.133	0.067	0	2.050
B	0	0	0.499	0.376	0.124	3.625

5 Discussion and Conclusion

To evaluate the traffic safety level of the road traffic safety management comprehensively, objectively and accurately, the problem is concerned to many complex and uncertain factors. Althogh there are many methods to assess the traffic safety state, the evaluation values can not reflect the real situation fully because of infromation-omitting in assessing process.

This paper applied the fuzzy mathematics theory to evaluate the road traffic safety. The resuts of two cities show that traffic safety level of City A is higher than that of City B. The traffic safety of City A is close to grade 2, which means the high safety level, while City B is close to grade 4, low safety level. He et al (2010) assessed the traffic safety status for the two cities by using the gray clustering method[1]. The results of the both methods reach good agreement. Also, the grade ranges were obtained by the proposed method in this study. Considering the fuzziness, the dependence and interaction of assessing indices, the evalution product based on the fuzzy theory can discern the traffic safety level more effectively than other methods.

The index selection and degree classification of traffic safety play very impotant roles in traffic safety evaluation implementment. In this study, the index selection and its degree classification presented here, may need to be tested with more cases in the future.

Acknowledgment

This project was supported by the National Western Highway Project of China (200731849026). We also gratefully acknowledge the contributions by Wang Yuankun and Ma Huiqun. The efforts of the field technicians are also very much appreciated.

References

1. He, M., Guo, X., Chen, Y.: Application of Improved Gray Clustering Method in Urban Traffic Safety Assessment. Journal of Transport Information and Safet. 28(1), 104–107 (2010)
2. Liu, T., Guo, Q.: Traffic safety assessment by AHP method. Hei Long Jiang Jiao Tong 4, 152–153 (2009)

3. Jianhua, P.: Index System of Urnban Road Safety Evaluation and Method Research. Aeijing Science and Technology University Master degree thesis (2006)
4. Wenjie, H.: Research on the Evaluation of City Road Traffic Safety based on BP Artificial Network. Science Technology and Engineering 18, 5607–5609 (2009)
5. Wang, D., Singh, V.P., Zhu, Y.: Hybrid fuzzy and optimal modeling for water quality evaluation. Water Resour. Res. 43, 5415 (2007), doi:10.1029/2006WR005490
6. Wang, Y.K., Xia, Z.Q.: Fuzzy comprehensive evaluation model for Chinese sturgeon habitat suitability in the Yangtze River. In: Proc. Int. Conf. Fuzzy Syst. Knowl. Discov., vol. 3, pp. 565–569 (2008)
7. Zadeh, L.A.: Fuzzy sets. Inf. Control. 8(3), 338–353 (1965)
8. Wanduo, W.: Fuzzy mathematics and its application on computer. Electronic Press, China (1988)
9. Qiao, H., Yuan, R., Yangzi, L.: Application of uncertain type of AHP to condition assessment of cable-stayed bridges. Journal of Southeast University (English Edition) 23(4), 599–603 (2007)

An Optimization Model of Site Batch Plant Layout for Infrastructure Project

Kwan-Chew Ng[1,*], Jing Li[2], Chen-Xi Shi[1], and Qian Li[1]

[1] School of Management Science and Engineering, Nanjing University, Nanjing, China
[2] School of Engineering, Nanjing Agricultural University, Nanjing, China

Abstract. Construction site layout is crucial to any project and has a significant impact on the economy, quality, schedule, and other aspects of the project. Especially for infrastructure construction project, the layout planning of site temporary batch plant is one of the key factors for assessing on complexity scales and project performances. The poorer the site batch plant layout planning, the more increasing the project complexity (risks) and the greater the construction cost raised. Generally, the site batch plant layout problem has been solved through the experiences of site management team, using more or less sophisticated numerical model, but mostly the final decision made by the leader who responsible for the site management taking much more consideration of the design conditions and the site spatial constrained. Therefore, the site batch plant layout has always been considered in complying with maximization principles. That is, individual contractor is often required to build his own batch plants for servicing his own project only according to its contract clauses. This construction management strategy has caused to a large waste of resources and much low productivity of the operated plants. The purpose of this paper applies genetic algorithms and computing techniques to develop an optimal model in order to search an optimal solution to the site batch plant layout in the planning stage, and combine with the practical contracting strategies to design feasible construction management plan for enhancement of site management and improvement of concrete quality, as well as minimizing the total construction costs. The GA's model was developed and applied to specific project located in Taiwan. The usefulness of the model was proven through by the practical operation of the project.

Keywords: Site Layout; Optimization; Genetic Algorithms.

1 Introduction and Background

In general, construction site temporary facility layout planning (CSTFLP) can be viewed as a complex optimization problem and it is one of the crucial factors impacting the performance of the project, such as optimization for location and number of batch plant built of infrastructure construction project. Site batch plant is one of the

---

* Corresponding author: Kwan-Chew Ng (known as Kuang-Chiu Huang);
  Tel.:+8613584096143, +886921900345; E-mail: kwanchew_ng@hotmail.com

F.L. Wang et al. (Eds.): AICI 2010, Part II, LNAI 6320, pp. 175–184, 2010.

temporary site facilities most affecting quality and performance of infrastructure project, especially in highway project. Unfortunately, causing by client's lack of knowledge and experience, most clients are reluctant to take CSTFLP into consideration in the design phase, and the perception of "leave it to the contractor", CSTFLP is often not planned by design engineers as coordination of CSTFLP will raise the increment of engineering labor-hours [3]. Furthermore, owing to the peculiarities of the construction project, activities within the construction site are commonly much high dynamic and uncertain. Although many variables affect project performance, but for infrastructure construction project, site temporary facility layout planning which is the most impacting factor for evaluation of the project time and cost [8] as well as safety, particularly in more dynamic and complex infrastructure construction project located at outskirt and rural area.

Concrete is one of the basic structural materials for the infrastructure construction project. It is a mixture of cement, sand, aggregate, admixtures and water. Use of concrete and its cementations (volcanic) constituents, such as pozzuolanic ash, has been made since the days of the Greeks, the Romans, and possibly earlier ancient civilizations. However the intensive start use of concrete is marked in early nineteen century [15]. Thereafter, considerable progress developed in the art and science of reinforced and pre-stressed concrete analysis, design, and construction has resulted in large demand of concrete material. Moreover, quality and cost of concrete material have become crucial factors of project performance. These factors have resulted in development of ready-mixed concrete (RMC) with the purposes for cost-down and quality improvement. It was first introduced into the construction industry in the early 20th century and has been ever seen widely employed.

RMC is produced by a batch plant according to the designed specification for specific project. RMC is unlike some other products that can be manufactured in advance and stored before order made. It has a rapid hydration and solidification in nature once started mixing. Hence, in order to control the quality of the project, RMC must be placed within 1.5 hours after being produced by the site batch plant, which constrains service area of the site batch plant also. Generally, it is produced at the time that the project manager requires the delivery [4].

The natures of ready-mixed concrete as well as the peculiarities of infrastructure construction project have resulted in increasing project complexity (risks). Apparently, the site layout planning of temporary batch plant is one of the key factors for assessing on complexity scales and project performances. Furthermore, the objective of the site batch plant layout is to determine adequate number of site batch plant and allocate them to the predetermined location in order to control quality of concrete and lower total construction cost. Traditional practices of project manager for the site layout planning of temporary batch plant often maximizes the number and the capacity of the batch plant building nearby to support their construction activities without considering total construction costs. And these requirements are generally written in contract clauses. Additionally, some of the optimization issue of site batch plant layout has been solved through the experiences of site management team, using more or less sophisticated numerical model, but the final decision mostly made by the project manager who responsible for the site management taking much more consideration of the design conditions and the site spatial constrained. These are the most conservative risks management currently used. Consequently, these construction management strategies have caused to a large waste of resources and much low productivity of the operated plants.

The optimal site batch plant layout involves determining the sufficient number of the site batch plant and positioning it to a set of predetermined locations, and also selecting the most economical vehicle type and fleet size to perform the concrete works in order to achieve planned schedule and quality required, while complying with contract clauses and layout constraints. This is a time-consuming and difficult problem as there are numerous probable solutions [21], and also an evident NP feature. The purpose of this paper applies genetic algorithms and computing techniques to develop an optimal model in order to search an optimal solution to the site batch plant layout in the planning stage, and combine with the practical contracting strategies to design feasible construction management plan for enhancement of site management and improvement of concrete quality, as well as minimizing the total construction costs. The paper is organized as follow, site batch plant layout problem and current management strategies practice are described in section one. Related literatures are discussed in the immediately following section. The proposed model is formulated in the third section and a case study of the proposed model is illustrated in the forth section. Lastly, the conclusion is drawn.

2   Related Literatures Review

Taking site temporary facility layout planning (STFLP) during design stage can have a significant impact on the efficiency of site management and the project performance, mainly for site batch plant of highway construction project. A feasible site temporary facility layout plan of batch plant can: (i) minimize travel time; (ii) raise quality; (iii) increase productivity; and (iv) improve safety, and hence lower total construction cost and time. But, recently site investigates and interviews with superintendents and site managers, demonstrate that site temporary facility layout planning is often disregarded in the planning phase of construction projects [17].

Construction site batch plant layout is a dynamic and complex problem as the constantly changing nature of a project. Moreover, temporary facility layout planning is also a nonlinear and discrete system. This makes it different from static optimization such as the layout of industrial factories. Hence, the optimization problem becomes practically important and theoretically challenging. Since the early 1960s, the optimization problem has been analyzed extensively in the industrial engineering (IE) and operational research (OR) communities. Optimization models have been developed specifically for the construction domain as the dynamic and complex nature of construction sites. Early models were based solely on mathematical optimization techniques and successful in laying out only a single or a limited number of facilities. The aim of the model is to minimized handling costs on site which is often stated to what mathematicians term ''objective functions''. This objective function is then optimized under problem-specific constraints to figure out the needed site layout. An example is the optimization model of Warszawski and Peer [20] to place storage facilities and construction equipment on the site, with the objective of minimizing transportation, maintenance, and installation costs. Another example is the model of Rodriguez-Ramos and Francis [16] to locate a crane within a construction site. However, most traditional mathematical models implemented as black-box systems, and such models do not provide the practitioner and project manager with any means to get insight into the process. The project manager's intervention is not allowed to make intuitive change in order to lead to a feasible solution. It is opposed and proved unsuitable for STFLP.

The second methodology termed as heuristic approach or knowledge-based system has been used to solve larger size problems of site layout. Hamiani [7] and Tommelein [18], for example, used a rule-based system to place temporary facilities on site, one at a time, through a constraint-satisfaction search. Cheng [2] also used a similar knowledge-based approach linked to a geographic information system (GIS) to provide a dynamic layout solution. Sadeghpour, et al. [17] proposed a CAD-based model to solve construction site layout problem as CAD-based model could offer an intuitive understanding of the overall construction site layout planning. In general, heuristic solutions attempt to satisfy spatial relationships among facilities and have been reported to produce good but not optimal solutions [22].

Artificial intelligence (AI) system is the third optimization techniques has been developed and widely applied recently. The main advantage of AI methods lies in their ability to deal with inexact, incomplete, and/or ill-structured problems. Yeh [21], for example, used a simulated annealing neural network to find an optimal site lay out by having a set of predefined facilities continuously exchange their positions within a predetermined set of locations on the site until a layout of minimum cost is obtained. In addition, Lam et al. [13] applied continuous dynamic searching scheme to conduct the max-min ant system algorithm, which is one of the ant colony optimization algorithms, to solve the dynamic construction site layout planning problem under the two congruent objective functions of minimizing safety concerns and decreasing construction cost. Many researchers [1, 5, 6, 9, 10, 11, 12, 14, 19, 23] have used the powerful random-search capabilities of genetic algorithms (GAs) to search for optimal solutions. Generally speaking, genetic algorithms base on random sampling and maintain a population of solutions in order to avoid being trapped in a local optimal solution. Mimicking the role of mutation of an organism's DNA, the algorithm periodically makes changes or mutations in one or more members of the population, yielding a new candidate solution. Genetic algorithms for site layout have many capabilities, including handling construction sites and temporary facilities with different shapes and accommodating various physical constraints. GAs are powerful in solving complex non-smooth construction site layout problems. However, numerous studies have reported the merits of the GA approach in large-scale complicated site layout problems.

3   The Proposed Model

The optimal site batch plant layout problem involves determining the sufficient number of the site batch plant and positioning it to a set of predetermined locations, and also relates to the quantities of concrete required from the plant to the site. Therefore, the objective of the site batch plant layout problem is to minimize the total construction cost (TC) of batch plants built and operation. The cost function is defined as in (1)

$$\min f(X) = \sum_{i=1}^{n} \sum_{j=1}^{m} c_{ij} y_{ij} D_j x_i + \sum_{i=1}^{n} x_i c_s \qquad (1)$$

Where $X = \{x_1, x_2, ..., x_n\}$, if location x_i is selected for site batch plant built, hence, $x_i = 1$, if not $x_i = 0$; c_{ij} is the unit cost of concrete transportation between batch plant i and site j, and D_j is the required quantities of site j. c_s is the buildup cost of each batch plant; in equation (1),

$$y_{ij} = \max\{t_{max} - d_{ij} / v, 0\} / (t_{max} - d_{ij} / v) \qquad (2)$$

where t_{max} is the maximum time allowed for transportation of concrete, d_{ij} is the distance between batch plant i and site j, and v is the average speed of the truck for concrete transportation. From equation (2), if the concrete transportation time greater than t_{max}, hence $y_{ij} = 0$, if not, $y_{ij} = 1$, additionally the constraint for each demand area only serviced by one batch plant is set as $\sum\limits_{j=1}^{m} y_{ij} = 1$.

Based on previous papers studied, the genetic algorithm is employed to the proposed model. By setting a set of binary string with length n called a chromosome as representing one possible solution of the site batch plant layout, the gene i of the chromosome shows as "1" indicating the location where the batch plant is built, and "0" meaning that the location is not placed. Such as, the chromosome $\{0,0,1,1,0,0\}$ shows the third and forth locations are selected among six potential locations for building required batch plant. The fitness function of the proposed model is given by

$$F(X) = M - \min f(X) \qquad (3)$$

Where, M is the much bigger numeric number compares to the total cost, the bigger the fitness of the chromosome is derived the lower total cost of the batch plant. The objective of the algorithm is to search the set of biggest fitness of the chromosome.

The proposed model nature is survival of the fittest procedure. Fitter chromosomes survive, while weaker ones perish. Chromosome survives to the next generation and produces off-spring based on its relative fitness by simulating the natural selection mechanism. The proportionate selection is employed to the algorithm, i.e. each individual is selected for next generation according to the probability of the proportional individual fitness. In the population comprised with k_p chromosomes, the probability of chromosome k selected for next generation is calculated by

$$F(X_k) / \sum\limits_{k=1}^{k_p} F(X_k) \, .$$

Crossover is the procedure of exchanging information of both parent chromosomes and making up offspring with mixed genes. The single-point crossover operator is employed in the algorithm. Chromosomes are picked randomly from the population to be parents and subjected to crossover operator.

In order to prevent the loss of good genes after crossover continuously employing for some generations, a random mutation operator is designed for the algorithm. The operator then randomly chooses a gene from the chromosome of the population by a smaller probability of mutation and swaps it with its inverse gene in the chromosome. The probability uses the default settings of JGAP[*].

4 Application of the Model

The project selected for the case study is an infrastructure project located at the middle of Taiwan. The project with a total length of 37.6 km demands a total ready-mixed concrete quantity of 1,786,500 m3. The combination of the project is structured with 19 percent of earthworks, 70 percent of bridgeworks and 11 percent of tunnel structure. The budget of the project is 33 billion NTD, and the duration is 5 years, construction commenced at 2004. The layout of the project is shown as figure 1.

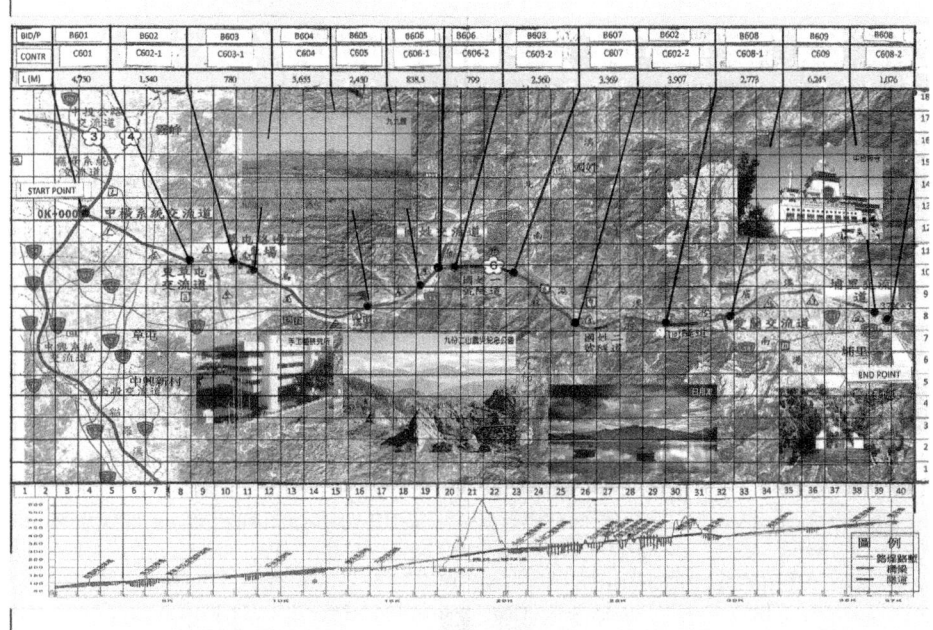

Fig. 1. The No.6 highway located in the middle of Taiwan

As an initial part of this work, the engineers and construction personnel were investigated the site to find out the most suitable locations for building site batch plant. There are 11 locations determined according to spatial and transportation constraints. For facilitating formulation of the proposed model, the project is divided into 18 sections, and the demand of the concrete is calculated accordingly. The predetermined locations for building site batch plant and the divided sections of the project are shown in Table 1.

---

[*] http://en.wikipedia.org/wiki/Genetic_algorithm

Table 1. The Distance between predetermined locations and subsections of the project

	1	2	3	4	5	6	7	8	9	10	11	Demand (m3)
1	4	16.5	6	11	12.5	11.5	8.5	32.5	37.5	38	44.5	64125
2	6	15	4.5	9.5	11	10	7	31	36	36.5	43	64125
3	8	13	4	7.5	9	8	5	29	34	34.5	41	32513
4	10	15	6	5.5	7	6	3	27	32	32.5	39	20773
5	10	17	6	9.5	9	10	5	29	34	34.5	41	32513
6	12	17	8	7.5	5	4	1	25	30	30.5	37	111697
7	14	19	9	5.5	3	6	2	23	28	28.5	35	111697
8	17	22	12	2	3	9	10	20	25	26.5	32	204647
9	18.5	23.5	13.5	3.5	4.5	9	11.5	18.5	23.5	25	30.5	44062
10	22	25	15	5	6	10.5	13	17	22	22.5	29	265639
11	30	35	25	15	16	20.5	23	3	8	9.5	15	65782
12	33	38	28	18	19	23.5	26	0.5	5	6.5	12	144368
13	35	40	30	20	21	25.5	28	2.5	3	4.5	10	75863
14	37	42	32	22	23	27.5	30	4.5	5	2.5	8	75863
15	40	45	35	25	26	30.5	33	7.5	8	2.5	5	122368
16	43	48	38	28	29	33.5	36	10.3	11	5.5	6	100963
17	45	50	40	30	31	35.5	38	12.5	13	7.5	8	100963
18	47	52	42	32	33	37.7	40	14.5	5	9.5	10	148550

In Table 1, the row represents the 18's concrete demand sections, and the column represents predetermined locations of site batch plant. The intersect of the matrix represents the distance of site access road between the concrete demand section and the predetermined location (d_{ij}), but the last column represents the design concrete quantities of the 18 demand sections (D_j). For complying the quality specification of ready-mixed concrete , the transportation time is constrained within 1.5 hours t_{max}), and the average speed of the truck for transporting RMC from the site batch plant to specific concrete demand area is controlled in 40km/hr (v) . It is clearly determined that each concrete demand area can be serviced by at least one of the site batch plant. The objective of this study is applied genetic algorithm to search an optimal number of site batch plant to be built and position them to adequate predetermined locations, also determine service area of each site batch plant.

From the investigation of the project, the installation cost (included an used batch machine, transportation , assembly and disassembly of batch machine, supporting facilities etc) of an used site batch plant is about 15,000,000 New Taiwan Dollar(NTD), the rental of land used is about 60,000 NTD/year, and the average rental of the concrete truck is given as 30 NTD/ m³(c_{ij} =30). The period of the site batch needed is set as 3 years, hence, the cost of building up a site batch plant is c_s =15,000,000+60,000*3=15,180,000 NTD.

As formulation of the proposed model shown in previous section, there are 11 pre-determined locations for the optimization of site batch plant layout problem. Hence, the length of the chromosome is assigned as 11, a constant value of M is assumed as 910800000, and the size of population (k_p) is set to 20, the rest of parameters are derived from the default settings of the system. Due to the natures of the project, the fitness of the chromosome is evaluated by nearest (shortest distance) principle. That is, if the concrete demand area is serviced by more than one site batch plant, then the nearest one is assigned.

A model was developed by using JAVA program links up JGAP3.4.4 on a personal computer as the implementation of the GA system. After 500's periodic operations, the GA algorithms were converged and an optimal solution was derived. The optimal fitness value is 611462925, corresponding total cost is 910800000 − 611462925 = 299337075, and corresponding chromosome is {0, 0, 1, 0, 1, 0, 1, 1, 0, 1, 0}. The optimal layout result is indicated in Table 2.

Table 2. Optimal Layout Result of No.6 of Highway Located In The Middle of Taiwan

	No.3 Predetermined Location	No.5 Predetermined Location	No.7 Predetermined Location	No.8 Predetermined Location	No.10 Predetermined Location
1	serviced				
2	serviced				
3	serviced				
4			serviced		
5			serviced		
6			serviced		
7			serviced		
8		serviced			
9		serviced			
10		serviced			
11				serviced	
12				serviced	
13				serviced	
14					serviced
15					serviced
16					serviced
17					serviced
18					serviced

In Table 2 indicated that there are five site batch plant built at no.3, no.5, no.7, no.8, no.10 of the predetermined location, and the each site batch plant serviced to its specific concrete demand area of the project. Obviously, the site batch plants were installed to rest on construction schedule manifesting the lowest construction cost of the project.

5 Conclusion

This paper has studied the actual operation of site batch plant layout problem for infrastructure project in Taiwan area. Optimization of site batch plant layout problem has an evident NP feature, which is a nonlinear and discrete system. Hence, optimization site batch layout employing scientific model is difficult and laborious. For this reason, layout engineers often resort to using heuristics to reduce their search only for acceptable solutions. The number and capacity of site batch plant are often designed by maximization principle, and the site batch plant is built as close as to site area to support construction activities without considering total construction costs also. This is the most conservative construction practices currently used. Consequently, this operation of site batch plant layout has caused to a large waste of resources and much low productivity of the operated plants. This paper then demonstrated the application of GA algorithm can robustly search the optimal site batch plant layout and the proposed model was proven by the case study in reducing the total construction cost.

Today, in China, infrastructure construction projects are usually becoming huge in size, involving much more interdisciplinary fields and increasing in complexity. Since international economics crisis, the government has expanded the investment in infrastructure construction in order to stimulate local economics. The expansion of the development has resulted huge demand of building site batch plant in China. Hence, the proposed model can be employed for the optimization of site batch plant layout to infrastructure project of China in order to decrease waste of resources, also energy saving and emission reduction.

In future research, extensive tests will be conducted to proof the usefulness of the model in dealing with site batch plant layout problems with larger sizes and dynamic of infrastructure project. In addition, studies will be needed to compare the robustness and performance of the GA algorithm with other scientific approaches employed in solving site temporary facilities layout problems.

Acknowledgements

The authors would like to acknowledge the contribution of Kao-Tuan Chua from NEEB, Second District Engineering Office (Taiwan) and Sinotech Engineering Consultants for providing the No.6 highway of Taiwan construction site case study. The authors would also like to thank Bao-Ru Cheng from Ho Chang International Co. for providing the costs data of site batch plant operation and appreciation is extended to Join Engineering Consultants and Bureau of High Speed Rail, Mass Rapid Engineering Office for their inspiring comments and suggestions.

This research was supported by the NSFC (National Natural Science Foundation of China) key program under Grant 70731002.

References

1. AbouRizk, S.M., Zhou, F., AL-Battaineh, H.: Optimisation of construction site layout using a hybrid simulation-based system. Simulation Modeling Practice and Theory 17, 348–363 (2009)

2. Cheng, M.Y.: Automated site layout of temporary construction facilities using geographic information systems (GIS). Ph.D. thesis, University of Texas, Austin, TX (1992)
3. Cheng, M.Y., O'Connor, J.T.: Arc Site: Enhanced GIS for construction site layout. J. Constr. Eng. Manage. 122(4), 329–336 (1996)
4. Feng, C., Cheng, T., Wu, H.: Optimizing the schedule of dispatching RMC trucks through genetic algorithms. Automation in Construction 13, 327–340 (2004)
5. Elbeltagi, E., Hegazy, T., Eldosouky, A.: Dynamic Layout of Construction Temporary Facilities Considering Safety. Journal of Construction Engineering and Management 130(4), 534–541 (2004)
6. Osman, H.M., Georgy, G.E., Ibrahi, M.E.: A hybrid CAD-based construction site layout planning system using genetic algorithms. Automation in Construction 12, 749–764 (2003)
7. Hamiani, A.: CONSITE: A knowledge-based expert system framework for construction site layout, Ph.D. thesis, University of Texas, Austin, TX (1987)
8. Hamiani, A., Popescu, G.: CONSITE: A knowledge-based expert system for site layout Computing in Civil Engineering. In: Will, K.M. (ed.) Microcomputers to supercomputers, pp. 248–256. ASCE, New York (1988)
9. Hegazy, T., Elbeltagi, E.: EvoSite: An evolution-based model for site layout planning. Journal of Computing in Civil Engineering, ASCE 13(3), 198–206 (1999)
10. Elbeltagi, E., Hegazy, T.: A Hybrid AI-Based System for Site Layout Planning in Construction. Computer-Aided Civil and Infrastructure Engineering 16, 79–93 (2001)
11. Li, H., Love, P.: Site-level facilities layout using genetic algorithms. Journal of Computing in Civil Engineering, ASCE 12(4), 227–231 (1998)
12. Li, H., Love, P.: Genetic search for solving construction site-level unequal-area facility layout problems. Automation in Construction 9(2), 217–226 (2000)
13. Ning, X., Lam, K.C., Lam, M.C.K.: Dynamic construction site layout planning using max-min ant system. Automation in Construction 19, 55–65 (2010)
14. Mawdesley, M.J., Al-jibouri, S.H., Yang, H.: Genetic algorithms for construction site layout in project planning. J. Const. Eng. Manage, ASCE 128(5), 418–426 (2002)
15. Nawy, E.G.: Reinforced Concrete: A fundamental approach. Prentice-Hall, Englewood Cliffs (1984)
16. Rodriguez-Ramos, W.E., Francis, R.L.: Single crane location optimization. Journal of Construction Division, ASCE 109(4), 387–397 (1983)
17. Sadeghpour, F., Moselhi, O., Alkass, S.: A CAD-based model for site planning. Automation in Construction 13, 701–715 (2004)
18. Tommelein, I.D., Levitt, R.E., Hayes-Roth, B.: SightPlan for site layout. Journal of Construction Engineering and Management, ASCE 118(4), 749–766 (1992)
19. Tam, C.M., Tong, T.K., Chan, W.K.: Genetic algorithm for optimizing supply locations around tower crane. J. Constr. Eng. Manag., ASCE 127(4), 315–321 (2001)
20. Warszawski, A., Peer, S.: Optimizing the location of facilities on a building site. Operational Research Quarterly 24(1), 35–44 (1973)
21. Yeh, I.-C.: Construction-site layout using annealed neural network. ASCE Journal of Computing in Civil Engineering 9(3), 201–208 (1995)
22. Zouein, P.P.: MoveSchedule: A planning tool for scheduling space use on construction sites. Ph.D. thesis, University of Michigan, Ann Arbor, MI (1995)
23. Zouein, P.P., Tommelien, I.D.: Dynamic layout planning using a hybrid incremental solution method. J. Constr. Eng. Manag., ASCE 125, 400–408 (1999)

Damping Search Algorithm for Multi-objective Optimization Problems

Jia Ji[1], Jinhua Peng[1], and Xinchao Zhao[2]

[1] School of Software Engineering,
Beijing University of Posts and Telecommunications, Beijing 102209, China
jijia07byr@yahoo.cn
[2] Department of Mathematics, School of Sciences,
Beijing University of Posts and Telecommunications, Beijing 100876, China
xcmmrc@gmail.com

Abstract. An algorithm based on damped vibration for multi-objective optimization problems is proposed in this paper. This algorithm makes use of the concept of damped vibration to do local search to find optimal solutions. The concept of Pareto Dominance is used to determine whether a solution is optimal. Meanwhile, the use of many random vibrators and the randomness of the initial maximum displacement ensure that the solutions are global. Simulation results show that the damping search algorithm is efficient in finding more solutions and also have good convergence and solution diversity.

Keywords: multi-objective optimization; damping search algorithm; damped vibration; Pareto optimal solution.

1 Introduction

Problems with multiple objectives are common in real life and they are widely used in scientific research and engineering practice. In most of these problems there are several conflicting objectives to be optimized, that is, it's difficult to make them reach maximum or minimum simultaneously. So, in such problems, there are more than one global optimal solutions. Instead, there exists a series of optimal solutions, called Pareto optimal set[1].

Over the last few decades, many algorithms have been developed, such as genetic algorithm[2] and differential algorithm[3]. Among many research focus, Multi-Object Evolutionary Algorithm (MOEA) has caused great concern and it solves the problem effectively in a unique way. One of the most representative MOEAs is the Non-Dominate Sorting Genetic Algorithm 2, NSGA2[4] and SPEA II[5]. Another well-known algorithm is the Multi-Objective Particle Swarm Optimization, MOP-SO[6] which is based on the Particle Swarm Optimization algorithm proposed by Kennedy and Eberhart in 1995[7].

An algorithm based on damped vibration for multi-objective optimization problems (DSA)is proposed in this paper. The algorithm uses the vibrator's damped vibration to do local search and to find the optimal solutions and make these solutions

F.L. Wang et al. (Eds.): AICI 2010, Part II, LNAI 6320, pp. 185–192, 2010.

the equilibrium positions for the next vibrations. We use the concept of Pareto dominance to update the external set that stores the global optimal solutions. The proposed algorithm shows good convergence, solution diversity and computation efficiency and is an effective way to solve the multi-objective problems.

The remainder of the paper is organized as follows: Section 2 gives the background of our algorithm. Section 3 describes the algorithm in detail. Section 4 gives the experimental results and compares it with MOPOS and NSGA2. Finally, in section 5, we give the conclusions.

2   Background

2.1   The Multi-objective Problem

The general Multi-objective problem can be defined as follows[8]:

Def. 1 (multi-objective problem)

$$\min \ f(x) \ = \ (f_1(x), f_2(x), \dots, f_k(x)) \tag{1}$$

$$\text{s.t.} \ \ g_i(x) \leq 0 \quad i = 1, 2, \dots, m \tag{2}$$

$$h_i(x) = 0 \quad i = 1, 2, \dots, s \tag{3}$$

where $x = [x_1, x_2, \dots x_n]^T$ is the decision vector, $f_k(x)$ is the kth objective function, $g_i(x) \leq 0$ is the inequality constraint and $h_i(x) = 0$ is the equality constraint.

Def. 2 (Pareto dominance): Decision variable u is said to dominate v if and only if $f_i(u) \leq f_i(v)$ where $i = 1,2,\dots,k$, and there exists at least one i that satisfies $f_i(u) < f_i(v)$.

Def. 3 (Pareto Optimality) A point $x^* \in \Omega$ is Pareto optimal if and only if there isn't another point $x \in \Omega$ that satisfies (1) $f_i(x) \leq f_i(x^*)$ where $i = 1,2,\dots,k$ and (2) there exists at least one $i \in \{1,2,\dots,k\}$ that satisfies $f_i(x) < f_i(x^*)$.

Def. 4 (Pareto Optimal Set) The set of all the Pareto optimal solutions for the multi-objective problems are called Pareto Optimal Set.

2.2   Damped Vibration[9]

As friction and media resistance of the outside world are always there, spring oscillator or simple pendulum has to overcome this resistance in its vibration process. Thus, the amplitude will be gradually reduced and the vibration will be completely stopped. This kind of vibration is called damped vibration whose amplitude is getting smaller and smaller.

The following is the displacement-time map of damped vibration.

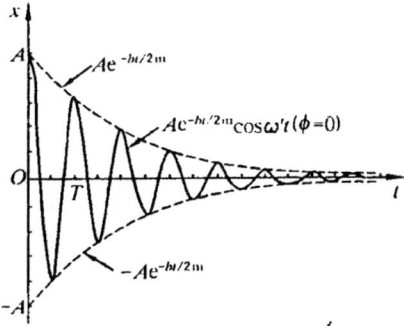

Fig. 1. Displacement-time map of damped vibration

We only choose the maximum displacement of each cycle as the position of the oscillator in our algorithm. It satisfies the formula $x_n = x_0 + (-1)^n Ae^{-\beta(n-1)}$, $n = 1,2,3 \dots$; x_0 is the equilibrium position.

3 Damping Search Algorithm for Multi-objective Optimization Problems

3.1 Why to Propose DSA Algorithm

For any algorithm, they can only find some Pareto solutions who are very close to the true optimal fronts. Because of this, the possibility is large to find better solutions in the neighborhood of the Pareto solutions that have been found. In response to this feature, the damping search algorithm is proposed, which is denoted as DSA.

From Figure 1, we can see that O is the current optimal point. According to the curve, points which are far away from O can also be searched, but the interval is large. The closer a point is to O, the smaller the interval is. Thus, solutions in the neighborhood of O can be found and controlled within a certain precision. Furthermore, optimal solutions that are not close to O can also been found.

3.2 Algorithm Description in Detail

The damping search algorithm is based on the phenomena of damped vibration in nature. The spring oscillator's amplitude is reduced so that it can only vibrate between the initial maximum displacements and finally completely stopped at the equilibrium position. We use this to find the optimal solutions and then make these solutions equilibrium positions of the next oscillators. By using the concept of Pareto dominance we update the external set continually subsequently. Finally we will get the global optimal solutions. The main steps of this algorithm are as follows.

DSA Algorithm:

Step 1. Initialize: Generate m oscillators randomly, that is, for each oscillator, the equilibrium position x_{i0} and the maximum displacement A_{im} are randomly generated, $i = 1,2, \dots m$.. There is an external set storing the global optimal solutions. Also, each oscillator has its own internal set that stores the global optimal solutions found by it.

Step 2. Vibrate: For each oscillator, generate the position x_{in} according to the formula $x_{in} = x_{i0} + (-1)^n Ae^{-\beta(n-1)}$, $n = 1,2,3 \dots ; i = 1,2,3, \dots m$. Compare x_{in} with solutions in the external set. If x_{in} dominate some solutions in the set, remove these solutions and store x_{in} in this set and the corresponding internal set. If we can't determine whether x_{in} dominates a solution, just store x_{in} in the set and the corresponding internal set. Otherwise, take no action. Vibrate until the termination condition is met. That is, the precision condition is met.

Step 3. Generate new oscillators: For each element in the internal set, if neither of the position just before or after it is in the set, make this element the equilibrium position and generate a new oscillator with a random maximum displacement. If the position just before it is in the set, generate a new oscillator with the equilibrium position at the midpoint of these two positions and the maximum displacement half the distance between these two points.

Loop step 2 and step 3 until it ends. A timer is used to stop the algorithm in special situations where the algorithm cannot stop itself.

4   Experimental Results and Algorithmic Analysis

As the Pareto solutions of multi-objective optimization problems have convex, non-convex, continuous and discontinuous characteristics, we select several functions for testing. In addition, we analyze the algorithm in its convergence, distribution and computing efficiency.

4.1   Algorithmic Setup

In our algorithm, the initial number of oscillators is 10 and they are randomly generated. The adjacent precision d is 0.1, and the search cycle T is 1. The damping coefficient can be adjusted during the experiment.

4.2   Experimental Comparison

Test function 1:

SCH function:

$$\min \ f(x) = \{f_1(x), f_2(x)\} \tag{4}$$

$$s.\,t. \ x \in [-10,10] \tag{5}$$

$$\text{where } f_1(x) = x^2, f_2(x) = (x - 2)^2 \tag{6}$$

This function was proposed by schaffer[4]. Using the NSGA-II to solve it, not many solutions are found, as illustrated below:

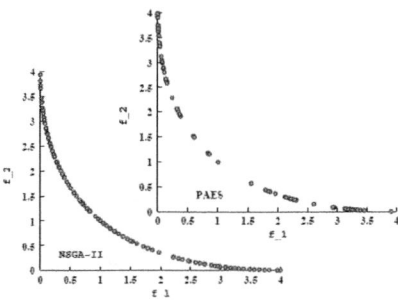

Fig. 2. Pareto curve for test function 1 with NSGA-II

However, using the DSA twice to solve it, we get the following figures.

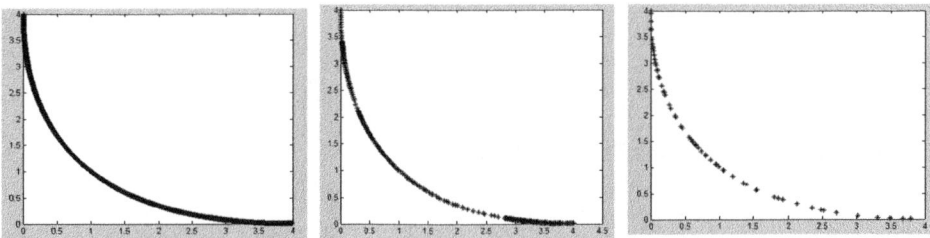

Fig. 3. Pareto curve for function 1 with DSA, where $\beta\beta = 0.003, d = 0.1$ $\beta\beta = 0.03, d = 0.1$ and $\beta\beta = 0.15, d = 0.1$ respectively

We see that the obtained results are very dense and have a good distribution. With a small number of iterations, it gets good result: 3117 solutions respectively.

This algorithm can also adjust the damping coefficient and stopping precision according to the required intensity to get satisfactory results, as shown above:

Test function 2:

$$\min \ f(x) = \{f_1(x), f_2(x)\} \tag{7}$$

$$\text{s. t. } \ x \in [-5,10] \tag{8}$$

$$\text{where } f_1(x) = \begin{cases} -x, \text{if } x \leq 1 \\ -2 + x, \text{if } 1 < x \leq 3 \\ 4 - x, \text{if } 3 < x < 4 \\ -4 + x, \text{if } x \geq 4 \end{cases}, f_2(x) = (x - 5)^2 \tag{9}$$

NSGA-II solution[10] and DSA solution:

This test function tests discrete Pareto solutions. Obviously, our algorithm can adjust some parameters flexibly so that a more accurate distribution of Pareto solutions is got. Compared with NSGA-II, our algorithm has a broader applicability, better flexibility and accuracy.

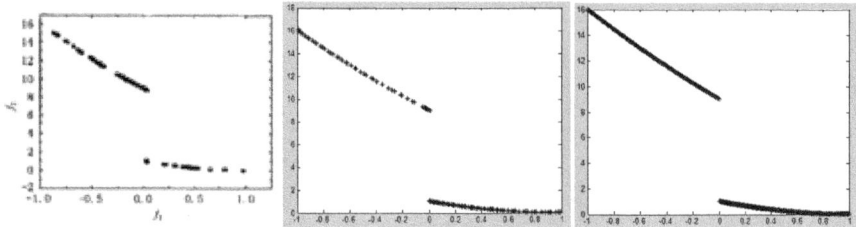

Fig. 4. Pareto curve for function 2 with NSGA-II and DSA, where $\beta\beta = 0.03, d = 0.1$ and $\beta\beta = 0.003, d = 0.1$ respectively

Test function 3:

$$\min\ f(x) = \{f_1(x), f_2(x)\} \tag{10}$$

$$s.t. x \in [-5,10] \tag{11}$$

where $f_1(x,y) = (x^2 + y^2)^{\frac{1}{8}}, f_2(x,y) = [(x - 0.5)^2 + (y - 0.5)^2] \tag{12}$

NSGA-II solution[10] and DSA solution:

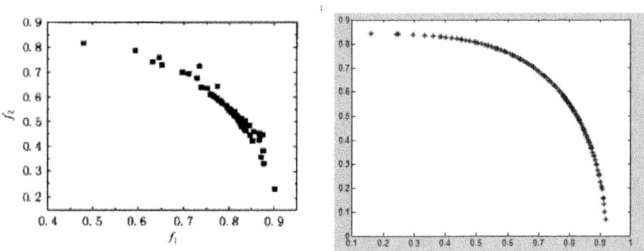

Fig. 5. Pareto curve for function 3 with NSGA-II and DSA, where β $\beta = 0.03, d = 0.1$

From the figures above, we see that our algorithm is much better. And till now, the number of initial points we use is less than 10. When more initial points are used, both the accuracy and distribution will be better.

Test function 4

ZDT-1:

$$\min\ f_1(x) = x_1 \tag{13}$$

$$\min f_2(x) = g(x)\left[1 - \sqrt{\frac{x_1}{g(x)}}\right] \tag{14}$$

$$g(x) = 1 + \frac{9(\sum_{i=2}^{n} x_i)}{n - 1}, n = 30 \tag{15}$$

NSGA-II solution[10] and DSA solution:

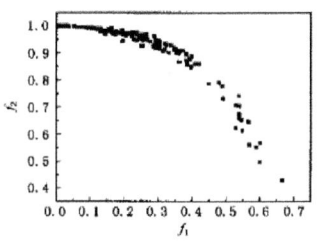 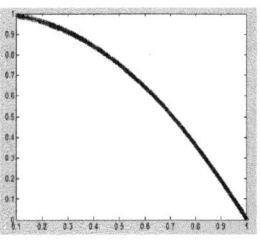

Fig. 6. Pareto curve for function 4 with NSGA-II and DSA, where $\beta = 0.03, d = 0.1$

4.3 Algorithm Comparison

For DSA, choosing β=0.003, d=0.1 and executing it 30 times independently using γ measurement and Δ measurement respectively, we get the mean and variance.

The following are the comparison results with NSGA-II algorithms:

Table 1. Comparison results of the mean and variance using γ measurement

		ZDT-1	ZDT-2	ZDT-3	ZDT-4	ZDT-6
DSA	mean	**0.007131**	**0.002184**	**0.003816**	**0.000459**	**0.091627**
	Variance	**0.000009**	**0.000003**	**0.000001**	**0.000001**	**0.012954**
NSGA-II	mean	0.033482	0.072391	0.114500	0.513053	0.296564
	Variance	0.004750	0.031689	0.007940	0.118460	0.013135

Table 2. Comparison results of the mean and variance using Δ measurement

		ZDT-1	ZDT-2	ZDT-3	ZDT-4	ZDT-6
DSA	mean	**0.011130**	**0.015629**	**0.140738**	**0.000060**	**0.085543**
	Variance	**0.000056**	**0.000007**	**0.000005**	**0.000003**	**0.002497**
NSGA-II	mean	0.390307	0.430776	0.738540	0.702612	0.668025
	Variance	0.001876	0.004721	0.019706	0.064648	0.009923

5 Conclusion

The damping search algorithm (DSA) is proposed and implemented in this paper which is based on the damped vibration. Experimental results show that this algorithm has better convergence, distribution and computing efficiency compared with some well-known algorithms, NSGA-II[4]. This algorithm also illustrates a broader applicability, better flexibility and accuracy.

By analyzing the experiments and the inherent nature of the algorithm, we find the main contribution of DSA for such a good performance:

First, Both the equilibrium position and the maximum displacement are random. This ensures that we can find the locations of the Pareto solutions as much as possible and it also ensures certain coverage.

Second. The maximum displacement can be random or fixed, and the recursion of the fixed method is controlled by accuracy and the damping coefficient. Thus, the distribution is good.

Third, the damped vibration is symmetrical. Because of this, Pareto solutions can be quickly found and symmetric distribution of the solutions is ensured. Thus, a better distribution is ensured.

Acknowledgement. This paper is supported by "the Fundamental Research Funds for the Central Universities (BUPT2009RC0701)" of China and School of Software Engineering, Beijing University of Posts and Telecommunications.

References

[1]   Coello Coello, C.A.: A Comprehensive survey of evolutionary based multi-objective optimization techniques (March 1999)

[2]   Zeng, W.-f., Yan, L., Wang, Z.-b.: Genetic programming model based on multiobjective optimization in fund's assignment. Computer Engineering and Design 28(7) (2007)

[3]   Abbass, H.A., Sarker, R., Newton, C.: PDE: Apareto-frontier differential evolution approach for multiobjective optimization problems (2001)

[4]   Deb, K., Agrawal, S., Pratap, A.: A Fast and Elitist Multiobjective Genetic Algorithm: NSGA-ll (February 2002)

[5]   Chen, Q., Xiong, S., Liu, H.: Evolutionary multi-objective optimization algorithm based on global crowding diversity maintenance strategy. ACM, New York (2009)

[6]   Goello Coello, C.A., Lechuga, M.S.: MOPSO:A Proposal for Multiple Objective Particle Swarm Optimization (2002)

[7]   Eberhart, R., Kennedy, J.: A New Optimizer Using Particle Swarm Theory (1995)

[8]   Cagnina, L., Esquivel, S., Coello Coello, C.A.: A Particle Swarm Optimizer for Multi-Objective Optimization. Jouranl of Computer Science and Technology 5(4) (2005)

[9]   Jiang, S.: Cycle of vibration damping. Physics Teacher 25(1) (2004)

[10] Zhang, L.-b., Zhou, C.-g., Ma, M., Liu, X.-h.: Solutions of Multi-Objective Optimization Problems Based on Particle Swarm Optimization. Journal of Computer Research and Development 41(7) (2004)

[11] Lin, C., Li-cheng, J., Yu-heng, S.: Orthogonal Immune Clone Particle Swarm Algorithm on Multiobjective Optimization. Journal of Electronics & Information Technology 30(10) (2008)

Pruned Genetic Algorithm

Seyyed Mahdi Hedjazi and Samane Sadat Marjani

Dept. of Software Engineering,
Islamic Azad University Tehran North Branch of Iran
Tehran, Iran
mahdi_hedjazi@yahoo.com, sm_marjani@yahoo.com

Abstract. Genetic algorithm is known as one of the ways of resolving complicated problems and optimization issues. This algorithm works based on a search space and in this space it'd seeking for the optimum answer. In this algorithm, there exist agents and gorges which expand the search space with no logical reason. We can find the measures which take us away from the optimal answer by observing the trend of changes, and it can apply the changes in a way that increases the speed of reaching the answers. It's obvious these changes must be as much as they don't add time complexity or memory load to the system.

In this paper, we represent a mechanism as a pruning operator in order to reach the answer more quickly and make it work optimal by omitting the inappropriate measures and purposeful decrease of search space.

Keywords: Genetic algorithm, search space, optimization, mutation, pruning.

1 Introduction

Genetic Algorithm is known as a way of resolving complicated problems in which reaching the answers needs non-deterministic polynomial time. This algorithm is used in different problems and industries. In theoretical discussions, well-known problems such as knapsack, graph coloring, dynamic programming [1], greedy algorithms [2] and etc. are resolvable by this algorithm, and in practical discussions, resolving the statistical problems for complicated statistical societies such as exchange, designating and measuring the unreachable contents, image processing [3], timing, etc. [4, 5] is performed or optimized with this algorithm. This algorithm is considered as a way of optimization based on search [6], and we try to recover and speedup to reach the results by mixing this algorithm with other aspects and the discussions of artificial intelligence such as fuzzy logic and neural network, and in this way the range of applying genetic algorithm increases.

Random assignment of value is a discussion which gives the genetic algorithm a high time order and complexity. In this algorithm, the starting point of search is provided randomly and continuously tries to approach the answer by random search in a searching space.

In this paper, there has been effort to control the assignments of values purposefully in the genetic algorithm and to prune the results in a way that decreases the time to reach the answers and the amount of occupied memory.

F.L. Wang et al. (Eds.): AICI 2010, Part II, LNAI 6320, pp. 193–200, 2010.

2   A Look at Genetic Algorithm

In genetic algorithm, existing parameters in problem are encoded in genome and chromosome. Genome is the smallest element of genetic algorithm. Chromosome is formed by a sequence of genomes. A generation creates by putting together distinct amounts of chromosomes. The amount of chromosomes of a generation is called population. Each chromosome is examined with fitness function and its value is gained in terms of its proper answer. Genetic algorithm works in this way that forms genome and chromosome randomly and creates a generation by putting them together; and from the previous generation chromosomes which are called the parents, next generation chromosomes, called children, creates. Genetic algorithm examines the new chromosomes and again creates the next generation to approach the answer or reach it.

For creation of next generations, there are operators of which algorithm uses to either provide next generation or make the next generation more advanced in compare to the previous one. These operators are selection, crossover and mutation.

Selection operator selects the parents randomly but with different possibility (on the base of resultant amount of fitness function for each chromosome) for the creation of the next generation. The chosen parents produce the next generation children using cross over operator. A parameter called the possibility of crossover chooses which child comes from which parent. We use mutation operator to prevent convergence of the answers toward one undesirable number (local maximums). In this operation some chromosomes change randomly among the created children based on a possibility called possibility of mutation. This algorithm and production of generations continues to the point that the answers become convergent, or to reach the appropriate answer [7]. The routine trend of performing genetic algorithm is shown in the fig 1.

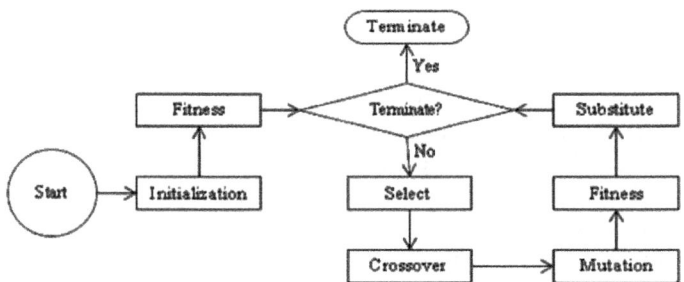

Fig. 1. Flowchart of Simple genetic algorithm

3   Exploring the Speedup in Genetic Algorithm

Different agents are effective in optimizing genetic algorithm. Population, complexity of selection, mutation, crossover, possibility of crossover, possibility of mutation, etc. are the agents which affect on the result. We can explore the effect of each one of these on genetic algorithm and it's not in the scope of our discussions.

Random amount created for this algorithm which may take away the results from the true answers, is an element which causes waste of time in genetic algorithm and it waists lots of time till reaches to the point in which chromosomes contain desirable amounts.

The idea of this paper has formed from pruning and placement of appropriate amounts in genetic algorithm. It means we try to take away the amounts which are not appropriate for the answer from population to get the considered answer more quickly.

4   Pruning and Placing the Values in the Genetic Algorithm

Based on this idea, we should design a mechanism which creates some changes in some courses of genetic algorithm to purposefully control the trend of creation of population which is randomly performed in genetic algorithm. This change takes place in order to prevent waiting of time in reaching the local maximums and deleting inappropriate chromosomes which can occur in two steps; in the time of initial creation of the generation and in the time of mutation.

Performing these changes, an operator called "pruning", whose duty is to prevent inappropriate amounts into the genomes, adds to the genetic algorithm. In fig 2, we display the trend of performing the pruned genetic algorithm.

As mentioned earlier, one of the operations of genetic algorithm is to resolve the complicated problems. Problems such as N-queen, knapsack, graph coloring, etc. are of these. In all these problems there are values which we know don't helping us reach the answer. For example in knapsack the values which are excessively designated, are inappropriate values and during initialization we can forget about them.

For different problems, we should define different pruning operators. Pruning operator should remove values which are not appropriate with least complexity. In fact, for using pruning operator, we must define a suitable pruning function for considered problem.

4.1   Pruning during Initialization

According the trend of genetic algorithm, initial creation of the generation is one of the most important phases. As the algorithm is due to using this generation, if this generation stays away from the answers, it takes a lot of time to clear the effects of inappropriate answers.

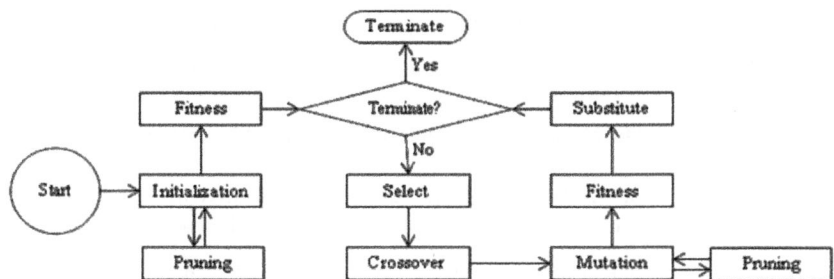

Fig. 2. Flowchart of Pruned genetic algorithm

The better the initialization, the closer starting point in the search space to the goal point, and we should walk a shorter way to reach the goal.

So it's better during appointment of value for the genomes of the chromosomes of this generation to prevent from value appointment for the values which are not appropriate.

4.2 Pruning during Mutation

In many circumstances, mutation is a proper element in approaching the answer but because the value chosen for replacement of genome is randomly chosen, in this section also do value appointment in case the selected value is not appropriate, using the same logic explained.

5   The Conditions of Using Pruning Operator

The idea of this paper is to add a pruning operator to genetic algorithm, so that with deletion of inappropriate values from search space, we can decrease time to reach the answer and the amount of created data. Now the raised question is that in which circumstances using pruning operator results in recovery? To answer this question, we should examine the 2 following aspects: Time order of pruning operator and the pruned area by the pruning operator.

5.1 Time Order of Pruning Operator

Genetic algorithm contains two parts, initialization and reproduction.

The time order of initialization, according to a coefficient of the number of genomes in each chromosome that called "Npopulation" and the number of chromosomes of each generation that called "Nchromosome",

$$Initialization = O(Npopulation * Nchromosome) \tag{1}$$

In case of using pruning operator, it would change in this way.

$$Initialization = O(Npopulation * Nchromosome * Npruning) \tag{2}$$

In this formula "Npruning" is related by Pruning function time order.
The time order of reproduction is closely related to the search space.

$$Reproduction = O(Nsearchspace * Nchromosome * Nchromosome) \tag{3}$$

In this formula "Nsearchsapce" is related by search space that we search for the optimum.

In case of using time order pruning operator, this operator will be added to the time order, but the search space decreases and this time the search space would be different.

$$Reproduction = O((Nsearchspace / Z) * Nchromosome * Nchromosome * \\ Npruning) \tag{4}$$

In addition to explained parameters in previous formula, Z is reduced ratio of search space.

Considering these changes which result in genetic algorithm time order, we conclude the time order of this operator is related to the amount of pruning on the search space, and in case of excessive pruning, it's costly beneficent to use other algorithms. All parameters explained in previous formula.

$$
\text{Npruning} = \begin{cases} Z & , Z <= \text{Npopulation} * \text{Nchromosome} \\ \text{Npopulation} * \text{Nchromosome} & , Z > \text{Npopulation} * \text{Nchromosome} \end{cases} \tag{5}
$$

5.2 The Pruned Area by Pruning Operator

Regarding the gained time order for pruned genetic algorithm, it's evident that the pruned area has a role in the structure of this operator. On one hand if the pruned area is small, first the resultant effect in the algorithm time is trivial, and second, finding a structure for this operator which would be performed even with low time order is difficult. One the other hand, in case the pruned area is much more, in fact there creates an algorithm which can move toward the proper answer without using genetic algorithm, and in fact without limiting the search space of this genetic algorithm, this search space has been directed to a subset of genetic algorithm, and because these changes are in the innermost loops of genetic algorithm, increasing the time order of this operator makes the time order of the whole algorithm very much more than expected.

Considering what mentioned above, it's evident in order to use pruning operator we should pay close attention to the area which is pruned by this operator, because high time order for this operator makes even genetic algorithm to lose its normal speed.

In sum we should care to this point that pruning operator is not a solution for finding the answer, but a solution for optimizing genetic algorithm and deleting inappropriate data.

In fact, when pruned area is very small or very large, using pruning operator is not a logical choose.

6 Exploring the Results of Pruned Genetic Algorithm

In order to explore the amount of improvement and the appropriateness of the pruned genetic algorithm, there is a test case for observing the trend of changes. In such a test, algorithmic complications are created by programming techniques. In this sample test, the genome is a complete number less than 10, and the optimal result is to reach a chromosome whose whole genomes are the maximum possible. For example if the chromosome contains 10 genomes, the desirable state is the one in which the sum of these 10 genomes becomes 100. In this test Npopulation is 100 and Nchromosome is 100. Before adding the pruning operator to the genetic algorithm, we record the gained properties from performing simple genetic algorithm on this sample test in order to compare with the next performances. Because in the genetic algorithm search is performed randomly in search space, the time of performance and tow performance generations of this algorithm are different, and for this sample test has been performed several times to create a range for these parameters which is represented in table 1.

Table 1. Calculation time and the number of reproduced generation in performing sample test with simple genetic algorithm.

No	Calculation time (second)	Generations Number
1	49.70	2397
2	49.47	2407
3	42.68	2044

Now we add pruning operator to our test case. Algorithmic complications for pruning operator are created by programming techniques. Table2 is the results of performing pruned genetic algorithm in three conditions. In First condition, we don't consider the numbers less than two as improper. In this manner the search space from 10^{10} decreases to 8^{10} and Nprunning would be $(10/8)^{10}$.

In second condition, the pruning operator is adjusted in a way that the numbers less than 5 are considered inappropriate. In this condition the search space reduces from 10^{10} to 5^{10} and Npruning would be 2^{10}; and in third condition, the numbers less than 8 are improper in pruning operator. In this condition the search space decreases from 10^{10} to 2^{10} and considering the mentioned formula number5, Npruning would be 10000.

In second test (4th and 5th column in table2), we can see the time order has decreased and reproduction of generations also has decreased which leads to intelligence level decrease; regarding the explanations in parts 5.2, in first test (2nd and 3rd column in table2), we can see because the pruned area is very less, there is no considerable improvement, and also due to smallness of Npruning, the changes resulting from time

Table 2. Time of calculation and reproduction of generation in test sample with different Npruning and with pruned genetic algorithm

Npruning / Time Order	$(10/8)^{10}$		2^{10}		10000	
	Calculation time (second)	Generations Number	Calculation time (second)	Generations Number	Calculation time (second)	Generations Number
1	40.76	1496	27.39	910	16.81	422
Log N	44.84	1613	27.43	902	19.71	526
N	43.37	1562	31.78	999	22.76	414
N * Log N	42.39	1558	31.53	966	44.78	471
N^2	53.14	1952	538.76	773	Up to 10000	

overflow are less and it doesn't affect significantly on the time of performing the whole algorithm; but in third test (6th , 7th column in table2), this change would be very useful only if the possibility of pruning the search space is created by low time order. But regarding the great volume of the pruned space, this is unlikely. Also due to largess of Npruning, the range resulting from time overflow is very much to the amount that decreases greatly the normal speed of genetic algorithm.

7 Conclusion

To create a mechanism with the purpose of omitting the inappropriate random elements in genetic algorithm has a great role in optimizing this algorithm which is mentioned in this paper as "pruning operator", but this omission should be performed with proper analyze and purposefully in order not to overflow the system and also there be a result of these changes and for this purpose, we investigated conditions resulting in desired solution. Since this operator performs jointly with mutation at inner loops of genetic algorithm, the higher order of this operator may lead to dysfunction of the algorithm. Therefore, if the overflow of the operator is pre-analyzed using formulae introduced in this paper, pruning operator is an appropriate mechanism to speed up the process for reaching the solution and reduces the volume of data produced as well as the memory required for storage of the data.

In fact, the pruned genetic algorithm may be considered for improving of the genetic algorithm, this measure is taken by omission of the useless data. Its best application is the time that the area of the useless data has logical ratio with the total search space and pruning operator has suitable complexity.

References

[1] Amini, A.A., Tehrani, S., Weymouth, T.E.: Using dynamic programming for minimizing the energy of active contours in the presence of hard constraints. In: Proceedings of 2nd International Conference on Computer Vision, pp. 95–99 (1988)
[2] Williams, D., Shah, M.: A fast algorithm for active contours and curvature estimation. Proceedings of computer vision, graphics and image processing on image understanding 55(1), 14–26 (1992)
[3] Holland, J.: Adoption in natural and artificial systems, p. 211. The MIT Press, Cambridge (1975)
[4] Papadakis, S.E., Tzionas, P., Kaburlasos, V.G., Theocharis, J.B.: A genetic based approach to the type I structure identification. Informatica 16(3), 365–382 (2005)
[5] Misevicius, A.: Experiments with hybrid genetic algorithm for the grey pattern problem. Informatica 17(2), 237–258 (2005)
[6] Tsang, P.W.M., Au, A.T.S.: A genetic algorithm for projective invariant object recognition. In: Conference Proceedings, 1996 IEEE TENCON: Digital Signal Processing Applications, pp. 58–63 (1996)
[7] Mitchell, M.: An introduction to genetic algorithms, p. 208. The MIT Press, Cambridge (1996)
[8] Schwefel, H.P., Rudolph, G.: Contemporary evolution strategies. Advances in artificial life, 893–907 (1995)

[9] Senaratna, N.I.: Genetic Algorithms: The Crossover – Mutation Debate, Bachelor. University of Colombo (2005)

[10] Spears, W.M.: Crossover or Mutation? In: Proceedings of Foundations of Genetic Algorithms Workshop, pp. 221–237 (1991)

[11] Marsili Libelli, S., Alba, P.: Adaptive mutation in genetic algorithms, Soft Computing - A Fusion of Foundations. Methodologies and Applications

[12] Muthu, S.R., Rajaram, R.: Performance Study of Mutation Operator in Genetic Algorithms on Anticipatory Scheduling. In: Conference on Computational Intelligence and Multimedia Applications (2007)

A New Computational Algorithm for Solving Periodic Sevendiagonal Linear Systems

Xiao-Lin Lin and Ji-Teng Jia

Faculty of Science, Shaanxi University of Science & Technology,
Xi'an 710021, P.R. China
linxl@sust.edu.cn
lavenderjjt@163.com

Abstract. Many issues in engineering computation and practical application that ultimately boil down to a matrix computation. And different applications will lead to some of the special sparse structure of the matrix computation. A modified chasing method has been proposed to solve the sevendiagonal linear equations in this paper firstly. By using this method, the condition that each principal minor sequence of coefficient matrix must nonzero is unnecessary. At the same time, we present a new computational algorithm for solving periodic sevendiagonal linear systems. An example is given in order to illustrate the algorithm.

Keywords: Periodic sevendiagonal equation, Linear systems, LU decomposition, Chasing method, Computer algebra systems (CAS).

1 Introduction

As a mathematical abstraction or idealization, linear systems having penta-diagonal or sevendiagonal coefficient matrices find important applications in automatic control theory, signal processing, and telecommunications, etc. For example, the propagation medium for wireless communication systems can often be modeled by linear systems [1,2]. Therefore, to design a rapid and stable numerical algorithm for solving linear system by employing the special structure features of these coefficient matrices will be of great significance [3]-[6],[11,12].

In this paper, our main objective is to develop an efficient algorithm for solving periodic sevendiagonal linear systems of the form:

$$PX = Y \ . \tag{1.1}$$

where

F.L. Wang et al. (Eds.): AICI 2010, Part II, LNAI 6320, pp. 201–208, 2010.
© Springer-Verlag Berlin Heidelberg 2010

$$P = \begin{pmatrix} d_1 & a_1 & A_1 & q_1 & 0 & \cdots & \cdots & \cdots & 0 & b_1 \\ b_2 & d_2 & a_2 & A_2 & q_2 & \ddots & \cdots & \cdots & \cdots & 0 \\ B_3 & b_3 & d_3 & a_3 & A_3 & q_3 & \ddots & & & \vdots \\ Q_4 & B_4 & b_4 & d_4 & a_4 & A_4 & q_4 & \ddots & & \vdots \\ 0 & \ddots & \ddots & \ddots & \ddots & \ddots & \ddots & \ddots & \ddots & \vdots \\ \vdots & \ddots & \ddots & \ddots & \ddots & \ddots & \ddots & \ddots & \ddots & 0 \\ \vdots & & \ddots & \ddots & \ddots & \ddots & \ddots & \ddots & \ddots & q_{n-3} \\ \vdots & & & \ddots & \ddots & \ddots & \ddots & \ddots & \ddots & A_{n-2} \\ 0 & & & & \ddots & Q_{n-1} & B_{n-1} & b_{n-1} & d_{n-1} & a_{n-1} \\ a_n & 0 & \cdots & \cdots & \cdots & 0 & Q_n & B_n & b_n & d_n \end{pmatrix} \tag{1.2}$$

$$X = (x_1, x_2, \ldots, x_n)^T, Y = (y_1, y_2, \ldots, y_n)^T. \tag{1.3}$$

To achieve this goal we are going to modify the classic chasing method and extend the numerical algorithm given in [7] to remove all cases for which the numerical algorithm fails. A $n \times n$ periodic sevendiagonal matrix P of the form (1.2) can be stored in 7n memory locations by using seven vectors $q = (q_1, q_2, \ldots, q_{n-3}, 0, 0, 0), A = (A_1, A_2, \ldots, A_{n-2}, 0, 0), a = (a_1, a_2, \ldots, a_n), d = (d_1, d_2, \ldots, d_n), b = (b_1, b_2, \ldots, b_n), B = (0, 0, B_3, \ldots, B_n), Q = (0, 0, 0, Q_4, \ldots, Q_n)$. The algorithm is suited for implementation using computer algebra systems (CAS) such as Mathematics, Macsyma, Matlab and Maple.

The work is organized as follows: In Section 2, main results and an algorithm for solving periodic sevendiagonal linear equations are presented. An illustrative example is given in Section 3. In Section 4, a conclusion is given.

2   Main Results

In this section, we are going to formulate a new computational algorithm for solving periodic sevendiagonal linear systems of the form (1.1). To the best of our knowledge, the LU factorization [8] of the matrix P in (1.2) exists if $c_i \neq 0$ for each $i = 1, 2, \ldots, n$, that is

$$P = LU . \tag{2.1}$$

where

$$L = \begin{pmatrix} 1 & 0 & \cdots\cdots & \cdots & \cdots & \cdots & \cdots & 0 \\ f_2 & 1 & \ddots & & & & & \vdots \\ g_3 & f_3 & 1 & \ddots & & & & \vdots \\ l_4 & g_4 & f_4 & 1 & \ddots & & & \vdots \\ 0 & \ddots & \ddots & \ddots & \ddots & \ddots & & \vdots \\ \vdots & \ddots & \ddots & \ddots & \ddots & \ddots & \ddots & \vdots \\ \vdots & & \ddots & \ddots & \ddots & \ddots & \ddots & \vdots \\ & & & \ddots & \ddots & \ddots & \ddots & \ddots \\ 0 & \cdots\cdots & 0 & l_{n-1} & g_{n-1} & f_{n-1} & 1 & 0 \\ h_1 & h_2 & \cdots\cdots & h_{n-4} & h_{n-3} & h_{n-2} & h_{n-1} & 1 \end{pmatrix} \quad (2.2)$$

$$U = \begin{pmatrix} c_1 & e_1 & s_1 & q_1 & \cdots & \cdots & \cdots & \cdots & \cdots & v_1 \\ 0 & c_2 & e_2 & s_2 & q_2 & & & & & v_2 \\ \vdots & \ddots & c_3 & e_3 & s_3 & q_3 & & & & v_3 \\ \vdots & & \ddots & \ddots & \ddots & \ddots & \ddots & & & \vdots \\ \vdots & & & \ddots & \ddots & \ddots & \ddots & \ddots & & \vdots \\ \vdots & & & & \ddots & c_{n-4} & e_{n-4} & s_{n-4} & q_{n-4} & v_{n-4} \\ \vdots & & & & & \ddots & c_{n-3} & e_{n-3} & s_{n-3} & v_{n-3} \\ \vdots & & & & & & \ddots & c_{n-2} & e_{n-2} & v_{n-2} \\ \vdots & & & & & & & \ddots & c_{n-1} & v_{n-1} \\ 0 & \cdots\cdots & \cdots & \cdots & \cdots & & & 0 & & c_n \end{pmatrix} \quad (2.3)$$

From (2.1)-(2.3) we get

$$c_i = \begin{cases} d_1 & \text{if } i = 1 \\ d_2 - f_2 e_1 & \text{if } i = 2 \\ d_3 - f_3 e_2 - g_3 s_1 & \text{if } i = 3 \\ d_i - f_i e_{i-1} - g_i s_{i-2} - l_i q_{i-3} & \text{if } i = 4, 5, \ldots, n-1 \\ d_n - \sum\limits_{i=1}^{n-1} h_i v_i & \text{if } i = n \end{cases} \quad (2.4)$$

$$
v_i = \begin{cases}
b_1 & \text{if } i = 1 \\
-f_2 v_1 & \text{if } i = 2 \\
-g_3 v_1 - f_3 v_2 & \text{if } i = 3 \\
-l_i v_{i-3} - g_i v_{i-2} - f_i v_{i-1} & \text{if } i = 4, 5, \ldots, n-4 \\
q_{n-3} - l_{n-3} v_{n-6} - g_{n-3} v_{n-5} - f_{n-3} v_{n-4} & \text{if } i = n-3 \\
A_{n-2} - l_{n-2} v_{n-5} - g_{n-2} v_{n-4} - f_{n-2} v_{n-3} & \text{if } i = n-2 \\
a_{n-1} - l_{n-1} v_{n-4} - g_{n-1} v_{n-3} - f_{n-1} v_{n-2} & \text{if } i = n-1
\end{cases} \quad (2.5)
$$

$$
h_i = \begin{cases}
\frac{a_n}{c_1} & \text{if } i = 1 \\
-k_2 h_1 & \text{if } i = 2 \\
-r_3 h_1 - k_3 h_2 & \text{if } i = 3 \\
-p_i h_{i-3} - r_i h_{i-2} - k_i h_{i-1} & \text{if } i = 4, 5, \ldots, n-4 \\
l_n - p_{n-3} h_{n-6} - r_{n-3} h_{n-5} - k_{n-3} h_{n-4} & \text{if } i = n-3 \\
m_n - p_{n-2} h_{n-5} - r_{n-2} h_{n-4} - k_{n-2} h_{n-3} & \text{if } i = n-2 \\
o_n - p_{n-1} h_{n-4} - r_{n-1} h_{n-3} - k_{n-1} h_{n-2} & \text{if } i = n-1
\end{cases} \quad (2.6)
$$

$$
e_i = \begin{cases}
a_1 & \text{if } i = 1 \\
a_2 - f_2 s_1 & \text{if } i = 2 \\
a_i - g_i q_{i-2} - f_i s_{i-1} & \text{if } i = 3, \ldots, n-2
\end{cases} \quad (2.7)
$$

$$
f_i = \begin{cases}
\frac{b_2}{c_1} & \text{if } i = 2 \\
o_3 - g_3 k_2 & \text{if } i = 3 \\
o_i - l_i r_{i-1} - g_i k_{i-1} & \text{if } i = 4, \ldots, n-1
\end{cases} \quad (2.8)
$$

$$
g_i = \begin{cases}
\frac{B_3}{c_1} & \text{if } i = 3 \\
m_i - l_i k_{i-2} & \text{if } i = 4, \ldots, n-1
\end{cases} \quad (2.9)
$$

$$
l_i = \frac{Q_i}{c_{i-3}}, \quad i = 4, \ldots, n. \quad (2.10)
$$

$$
s_i = \begin{cases}
A_1 & \text{if } i = 1 \\
A_i - f_i q_{i-1} & \text{if } i = 2, \ldots, n-3
\end{cases} \quad (2.11)
$$

where

$$
p_i = \frac{q_{i-3}}{c_i}, \quad i = 4, \ldots, n-1. \quad (2.12)
$$

$$r_i = \frac{s_{i-2}}{c_i}, \ i = 3, \ldots, n-1 \ . \tag{2.13}$$

$$k_i = \frac{e_{i-1}}{c_i}, \ i = 2, \ldots, n-1 \ . \tag{2.14}$$

$$m_i = \frac{B_i}{c_{i-2}}, \ i = 4, \ldots, n \ . \tag{2.15}$$

$$o_i = \frac{b_i}{c_{i-1}}, \ i = 3, \ldots, n \ . \tag{2.16}$$

We also have

$$\det(P) = \prod_{i=1}^{n} c_i \ . \tag{2.17}$$

At this point it is worth to mention that we shall use a generalized Doolittle LU factorization [9] for the matrix P. Such LU factorization always exists even if $c_i = 0$ for some $i = 1, 2, \ldots, n$ or even if P is a singular matrix. It depends on at most one parameter which can be treated as a symbolic name whose actual value is 0.

Now, we are ready to construct the algorithm for solving periodic sevendiagonal linear equations. Assume that the matrix P in (1.2) is nonsingular.

2.1   Algorithm

To find the solution of periodic sevendiagonal linear equations (1.1) by using the relations (2.4)-(2.16).

INPUT: Order of the matrix n and the components $Q_i, B_i, b_i, d_i, a_i, A_i, q_i, i = 1, 2, \ldots, n.(Q_1 = Q_2 = Q_3 = B_1 = B_2 = A_{n-1} = A_n = q_{n-2} = q_{n-1} = q_n = 0).$

OUTPUT: Vector $X = (x_1, x_2, \ldots, x_n)^T$.

Step1: Set $c_1 = d_1$, if $c_1 = 0$ then $c_1 = t$ end if, $f_2 = \frac{b_2}{c_1}, s_1 = A_1, e_1 = a_1, v_1 = b_1, h_1 = \frac{a_n}{c_1}, c_2 = d_2 - f_2 e_1$, if $c_2 = 0$ then $c_2 = t$ end if, $k_2 = \frac{e_1}{c_2}, s_2 = A_2 - f_2 q_1, e_2 = a_2 - f_2 s_1, v_2 = -f_2 v_1, h_2 = -k_2 h_1, g_3 = \frac{B_3}{c_1}, o_3 = \frac{b_3}{c_2}, f_3 = o_3 - g_3 k_2, c_3 = d_3 - f_3 e_2 - g_3 s_1$, if $c_3 = 0$ then $c_3 = t$ end if, $k_3 = \frac{e_2}{c_3}, r_3 = \frac{s_1}{c_3}, s_3 = A_3 - f_3 q_2, e_3 = a_3 - g_3 q_1 - f_3 q_2, v_3 = -g_3 v_1 - f_3 v_2, h_3 = -r_3 h_1 - k_3 h_2.$

Step2: For $i = 4, 5, \ldots, n-4$ do
$l_i = \frac{Q_i}{c_{i-3}}, m_i = \frac{B_i}{c_{i-2}}, o_i = \frac{b_i}{c_{i-1}}, g_i = m_i - l_i k_{i-2}, f_i = o_i - l_i r_{i-1} - g_i k_{i-1}, s_i = A_i - f_i q_{i-1}, e_i = a_i - g_i q_{i-2} - f_i s_{i-1}, c_i = d_i - f_i e_{i-1} - g_i s_{i-2} - l_i q_{i-3}$, if $c_i = 0$ then $c_i = t$ end if, $p_i = \frac{q_{i-3}}{c_i}, r_i = \frac{s_{i-2}}{c_i}, k_i = \frac{e_{i-1}}{c_i}, v_i = -l_i v_{i-3} - g_i v_{i-2} - f_i v_{i-1}, h_i = -p_i h_{i-3} - r_i h_{i-2} - k_i h_{i-1}$ End do.

Step3: Set $l_{n-3} = \frac{Q_{n-3}}{c_{n-6}}, m_{n-3} = \frac{B_{n-3}}{c_{n-5}}, o_{n-3} = \frac{b_{n-3}}{c_{n-4}}, g_{n-3} = m_{n-3} - l_{n-3} k_{n-5}, f_{n-3} = o_{n-3} - l_{n-3} r_{n-4} - g_{n-3} k_{n-4}, s_{n-3} = A_{n-3} - f_{n-3} q_{n-4}, e_{n-3} = a_{n-3} - g_{n-3} q_{n-5} - f_{n-3} s_{n-4}, c_{n-3} = d_{n-3} - f_{n-3} e_{n-4} - g_{n-3} s_{n-5} - l_{n-3} q_{n-6}$; if $c_{n-3} = 0$

then $c_{n-3} = t$ end if, $p_{n-3} = \frac{q_{n-6}}{c_{n-3}}, r_{n-3} = \frac{s_{n-5}}{c_{n-3}}, k_{n-3} = \frac{e_{n-4}}{c_{n-3}}, l_{n-2} = \frac{Q_{n-2}}{c_{n-5}},$
$m_{n-2} = \frac{B_{n-2}}{c_{n-4}}, o_{n-2} = \frac{b_{n-2}}{c_{n-3}}, g_{n-2} = m_{n-2} - l_{n-2}k_{n-4}, f_{n-2} = o_{n-2} - l_{n-2}r_{n-3} -$
$g_{n-2}k_{n-3}, e_{n-2} = a_{n-2} - g_{n-2}q_{n-4} - f_{n-2}s_{n-3}, c_{n-2} = d_{n-2} - f_{n-2}e_{n-3} -$
$g_{n-2}s_{n-4} - l_{n-2}q_{n-5},$ if $c_{n-2} = 0$ then $c_{n-2} = t$ end if, $p_{n-2} = \frac{q_{n-5}}{c_{n-2}}, r_{n-2} =$
$\frac{s_{n-4}}{c_{n-2}}, k_{n-2} = \frac{e_{n-3}}{c_{n-2}}, l_{n-1} = \frac{Q_{n-1}}{c_{n-4}}, m_{n-1} = \frac{B_{n-1}}{c_{n-3}}, o_{n-1} = \frac{b_{n-1}}{c_{n-2}}, g_{n-1}$
$= m_{n-1} - l_{n-1}k_{n-3}, f_{n-1} = o_{n-1} - l_{n-1}r_{n-2} - g_{n-1}k_{n-2}, c_{n-1} = d_{n-1} - f_{n-1}e_{n-2} -$
$g_{n-1}s_{n-3} - l_{n-1}q_{n-4},$ if $c_{n-1} = 0$ then $c_{n-1} = t$ end if, $o_n = \frac{b_n}{c_{n-1}}, p_{n-1} =$
$\frac{q_{n-4}}{c_{n-1}}, r_{n-1} = \frac{s_{n-3}}{c_{n-1}}, k_{n-1} = \frac{e_{n-2}}{c_{n-1}}, v_{n-3} = q_{n-3} - l_{n-3}v_{n-6} - g_{n-3}v_{n-5} - f_{n-3}v_{n-4},$
$v_{n-2} = A_{n-2} - l_{n-2}v_{n-5} - g_{n-2}v_{n-4} - f_{n-2}v_{n-3}, v_{n-1} = a_{n-1} - l_{n-1}v_{n-4} -$
$g_{n-1}v_{n-3} - f_{n-1}v_{n-2}, h_{n-3} = l_n - p_{n-3}h_{n-6} - r_{n-3}h_{n-5} - k_{n-3}h_{n-4}, h_{n-2} =$
$m_n - p_{n-2}h_{n-5} - r_{n-2}h_{n-4} - k_{n-2}h_{n-3}, h_{n-1} = o_n - p_{n-1}h_{n-4} - r_{n-1}h_{n-3} -$
$k_{n-1}h_{n-2}, c_n = d_n - \sum_{i=1}^{n-1} h_i v_i$ if $c_n = 0$ then $c_n = t$ end if.

Step4: Set $z_1 = y_1, z_2 = y_2 - f_2 z_1, z_3 = y_3 - g_3 z_1 - f_3 z_2.$

Step5: For $i = 4, 5, \ldots, n-1$ do
$$z_i = y_i - l_i z_{i-3} - g_i z_{i-2} - f_i z_{i-1}.$$

Step6: Compute $z_n = y_n - \sum_{i=1}^{n-1} h_i z_i.$

Step7: Compute the solution vector $X = (x_1, x_2, \ldots, x_n)^T$ using

$$x_n = \frac{z_n}{c_n}, x_{n-1} = \frac{z_{n-1} - v_{n-1}x_n}{c_{n-1}}, x_{n-2} = \frac{z_{n-2} - e_{n-2}x_{n-1} - v_{n-2}x_n}{c_{n-2}},$$

$$x_{n-3} = \frac{z_{n-3} - e_{n-3}x_{n-2} - s_{n-3}x_{n-1} - v_{n-3}x_n}{c_{n-3}}$$

for $i = 4, 5, \ldots, 1$ do

$$x_i = \frac{z_i - e_i x_{i+1} - s_i x_{i+2} - q_i x_{i+3} - v_i x_n}{c_i}$$

End do
End do.

Step8: Substitute the actual value $t = 0$ in all expressions to obtain $x_i, i = 1, 2, \ldots, n.$

2.2   Remark

If we add the following choice to the algorithm above:

(1) : $c_i \neq 0, i = 1, 2, \ldots, n.$
(2) : $q_i = 0, i = 1, 2, \ldots, n-3.$
(3) : $Q_i = 0, i = 4, 5, \ldots, n.$

We can obtain the **KPENTA** algorithm in [7]. At this point, it means our algorithm can not only solve the sevendiagonal linear equations, but also remove all cases for which the **KPENTA** algorithm fails.

3   An Illustrative Example

In this section we are going to give an illustrative example. Consider the 10×10 periodic sevendiagonal linear equations $PX = Y$ given by

$$
\begin{pmatrix}
1 & 1 & -1 & 0 & 0 & 0 & 0 & 0 & 0 & 1 \\
1 & 1 & 2 & -1 & 1 & 0 & 0 & 0 & 0 & 0 \\
-1 & 2 & 1 & 1 & 2 & 1 & 0 & 0 & 0 & 0 \\
1 & 1 & -1 & -1 & 1 & 1 & 0 & 0 & 0 & 0 \\
0 & -1 & 1 & 1 & 1 & 1 & 1 & 0 & 0 & 0 \\
0 & 0 & 0 & -1 & -1 & -1 & 1 & 0 & 1 & 0 \\
0 & 0 & 0 & 1 & 1 & 2 & 1 & 0 & 0 & 0 \\
0 & 0 & 0 & 0 & 0 & 1 & 1 & 0 & -1 & 1 \\
0 & 0 & 0 & 0 & 0 & 1 & 1 & -1 & 0 & 1 \\
2 & 0 & 0 & 0 & 0 & 0 & 1 & 1 & 0 & 1
\end{pmatrix}
\begin{pmatrix}
x_1 \\ x_2 \\ x_3 \\ x_4 \\ x_5 \\ x_6 \\ x_7 \\ x_8 \\ x_9 \\ x_{10}
\end{pmatrix}
=
\begin{pmatrix}
1 \\ -1 \\ 3 \\ 4 \\ 7 \\ -1 \\ 10 \\ 6 \\ 4 \\ 6
\end{pmatrix}
$$

By applying Algorithm 2.2, we get

$$(c_1, c_2, c_3, c_4, c_5, c_6, c_7, c_8, c_9, c_{10}) = (1, t, -\tfrac{9}{t}, -1, \tfrac{t+9}{3}, -\tfrac{2t}{3t+27}, \tfrac{7t+45}{2t}, t, -\tfrac{2t^2+27t+63}{7t^2+45t},$$
$$\tfrac{2t^2-4t+18}{2t^2+27t+63})$$

$$(v_1, v_2, v_3, v_4, v_5, v_6, v_7, v_8, v_9) = (1, -1, \tfrac{t+3}{t}, -1, -1, \tfrac{t+3}{t+9}, \tfrac{3t+9}{2t}, \tfrac{10t+54}{7t+45}, \tfrac{10t^2+64t+54}{7t^2+45t})$$

$$(h_1, h_2, h_3, h_4, h_5, h_6, h_7, h_8, h_9) = (2, -\tfrac{2}{t}, -\tfrac{2t+6}{9}, -\tfrac{2t+12}{9}, \tfrac{2t+6}{t+9}, 2, -\tfrac{6t}{7t+45}, \tfrac{1}{t},$$
$$-\tfrac{t^2+63}{2t^2+27t+63}) \text{ (Step 1-3)}.$$

$$(z_1, z_2, z_3, z_4, z_5, z_6, z_7, z_8, z_9, z_{10}) = (1, -2, \tfrac{4t+6}{t}, 3, \tfrac{7t+126}{9}, \tfrac{2t+144}{3t+27}, \tfrac{10t+72}{t}, \tfrac{9-t}{7t+45},$$
$$-\tfrac{15t^2+82t-9}{7t^2+45t}, -\tfrac{t^2-31t+18}{2t^2+27t+63}) \quad \text{(Step 4-6)}.$$

$$(x_1, x_2, x_3, x_4, x_5, x_6, x_7, x_8, x_9, x_{10})^T = (\tfrac{7t^2-13t+18}{2t^2-4t+18}, -\tfrac{6t}{t^2-2t+9}, \tfrac{2t^2+5t-9}{t^2-2t+9}, \tfrac{3t^2-13t+18}{2t^2-4t+18},$$
$$-\tfrac{t^2+2t-9}{t^2-2t+9}, \tfrac{5t^2+5t+18}{t^2-2t+9}, -\tfrac{t^2+43t-72}{2t^2-4t+18}, \tfrac{7t+9}{t^2-2t+9}, \tfrac{5t^2+20t-9}{t^2-2t+9}, -\tfrac{t^2-31t+18}{2t^2-4t+18})^T_{t=0} \qquad \text{(Step7)}.$$

$$(x_1, x_2, x_3, x_4, x_5, x_6, x_7, x_8, x_9, x_{10})^T = (1, 0, -1, 1, 1, 2, 4, 1, -1, -1)^T \quad \text{(Step8)}.$$

Also we can obtain the determinant of coefficient matrix P by using (2.17):

$$
det(P) = (\prod_{i=1}^{10} c_i)_{t=0} = (2t^2 - 4t + 18)_{t=0} = 18 \ .
$$

4   Conclusion

In this work, a modified chasing method has been constructed. It does not require any constraints on the elements of the matrix of the form (1.2). Numerical experiments show the algorithm described in this paper is very effective and stable. The recent algorithm presented in [7],[10] are special cases of the new algorithm.

References

1. Allen III, M.B., Isaacson, E.L.: Numerical Analysis for Applied Science. Wiley-Interscience, John Wiley & Sons (1997)
2. Chen, M.: On the solution of circulant linear systems. SIAM J. Numer. Anal. 24, 668–683 (1987)

3. Rao, S.S.: Applied Numerical Methods for Engineers and Scientists, Upper Saddle River, New Jersey (2002)
4. Batista, M.: A cyclic block-tridiagonal solver. Adv. Eng. Software 37(2), 69–74 (2006)
5. Wei, Y.M., Diao, H.A.: On group of singular Toeplitz matrices. Linear Algebra Appl. 399, 109–123 (2005)
6. Chawla, M., Khazal, R.R.: A parallel elimination method for periodic tri-diagonal systems. Int. J. Comput. Math. 79(4), 473–484 (2002)
7. Karawia, A.A.: A computational algorithm for solving periodic pentadiagonal linear systems. Appl. Math. Comput. 174, 613–618 (2006)
8. Zhao, X.L., Huang, T.Z.: On the inverse of a general pentadiagonal matrix. Appl. Math. Comput. 202, 639–646 (2008)
9. El-Mikkawy, M.E.A., Rahmo, E.D.: A new recursive algorithm for inverting general periodic pentadiagonal and anti-pentadiagonal matrices. Appl. Math. Comput. 207, 164–170 (2009)
10. El-Mikkawy, M.E.A.: A new computational algorithm for solving periodic tridiagonal linear systems. Appl. Math. Comput. 161, 691–696 (2005)
11. Lin, X.L., Jiang, Y.L.: QR decomposition and algorithm for unitary symmetric matrix. Chinese Journal of Computers 28, 817–822 (2005)
12. Lin, X.L., Jiang, Y.L.: Numerical algorithm for constructing Lyapunov functions of polynomial diffrential system. Appl. Math. Comput. 1-2, 247–262 (2009)

Local Weighted LS-SVM Online Modeling and the Application in Continuous Processes[*]

Lijuan Li, Hui Yu, Jun Liu, and Shi Zhang

College of Automation and Electrical Engineering,
Nanjing University of Technology, Nanjing, 210009, China
ljli@njut.edu.cn

Abstract. For continuous processes, the global LSSVM always gives good prediction for testing data located in the neighborhood of dense training data but incompetent for these in the sparse part. To solve the problem, the paper proposed a local weighted LSSVM method in the online modeling of continuous processes. At each period, only the samples similar to the current input are added into the training set and the obtained model is just for predicting the current output. To distinguish the importance of the training data, weight is defined to each data according to the Euclidean distances between the training data and testing data. The presented algorithm is applied in pH neutralization process and the result shows the excellent performance of the presented algorithm in precision and predicting time.

1 Introduction

Support Vector Machine (SVM) [1,2] has drawn much attention in classification and regression problems. Least Squares Support Vector Machine (LSSVM) [3] is a modified version of SVM in which analytical solutions can be obtained by solving linear equations instead of a quadratic programming (QP) problem. While the least squares version incorporates all training data to produce the result, the traditional SVM selects some of them (the support vectors) that are important in the regression. This sparseness of traditional SVM can also be reached with LSSVM by applying a pruning method [4] which omits the sample with the smallest approximation error in the previous pass. However, De Kruif *et al* consider the choice for this selection is suboptimal and present an alternative procedure that selects the sample that will introduce the smallest approximation error when it is omitted in the next pass of the approximation [5]. In [6], a new criterion is proposed to select data points that introduce least changes to a dual objective function.

The sparse LSSVM algorithms above are off-line iterative ones and requires huge computation, which prevents the application in actual application. An online sparse LSSVM algorithm is proposed in [7], which deletes the similarity

[*] This work was supported by the Jiansu Province Natural Science Fund(BK2009356), Jiansu Provincial university Natural Science Fund(09KJB51000) and Youth Found of Nanjing University of Technology.

F.L. Wang et al. (Eds.): AICI 2010, Part II, LNAI 6320, pp. 209–217, 2010.

in training data based on projection method so as to reduce computation and enhance generalizing ability. Contrarily, aiming at online modeling of batch processes, reference [8] presents a local LSSVM(LLSSVM) that selects the neighbor data of new input into training set.

In this paper, a local weighted LSSVM (LW-LSSVM) is proposed to solve online modeling of continuous processes. For continuous processes, the samples maybe scatteredly distribute in a rather wide range due to the fluctuation of operating conditions. The samples in the steady operation are dense in the sample set while these are sparse in the irregular running conditions. The global LSSVM always gives good prediction for these inputs located in the neighborhood of dense samples but incompetent for these in the sparse part. The main idea of LW-LSSVM is that similar input produces similar output, and only the samples similar to testing sample are selected for training to give accurate prediction. At each sampling period, the Euclidean distance between the new data to be predicted and each data in sample set is computed and the data with smaller distance are selected into training set. At the same time, the data participate training at different weights that is determined by the corresponding Euclidean distances. The data with smaller Euclidean distance is consider more important in current prediction and is given larger weight, vice versa. The presented algorithm is applied in the online modeling of pH neutralization process. The result indicates that the LW-LSSVM can obtain higher precision and less prediction time than the global LSSVM.

2 Local Weighted LSSVM

2.1 Local Learning

Standard LSSVM is a global learning algorithm in which all the samples are included to train the model. Due to plenty of information, the model has higher generalization ability. However, in some case, samples are nonuniformly distributed in the training set. For example, the samples are dense in steady operation while sparse in irregular running state for continuous processes. For global LSSVM method, the model has higher precision for testing data located in the neighborhood of dense training data and has lower precision for these in the sparse part. So, we introduce the local learning theory into LSSVM in this work expecting to obtain better results for all the testing data. Not using all the samples to train the LSSVM model and predict all the output in the future, the Local LSSVM trains the LSSVM model by selecting samples similar to the current input at each sampling time and predicts only the current output. Namely, the local LSSVM model is just for predicting one output at each sampling time and at next sampling time the model is renewed according to the next input for predicting the new output.

Suppose the sample set $S = \{(\boldsymbol{x}_i, y_i)\}_{i=1}^{N}$. For a new input $\boldsymbol{x}_p$, the similar samples are selected from S to form the training set $T = \{(\boldsymbol{x}_i, y_i)\}_{i=1}^{M}(M \leq N)$ and the corresponding LSSVM model is used to predict the new output y_p. In our work, the Euclidean distance between the new input $\boldsymbol{x}_p$ and each samples $\boldsymbol{x}_i|_{i=1}^{N}$ in S

$$d_i = \|\boldsymbol{x}_p - \boldsymbol{x}_i\| \tag{1}$$

is defined as the similarity criterion. Obviously, the smaller Euclidean distance d_i denotes more neighbouring to the new input $\boldsymbol{x}_p$ and corresponding samples are selected into the training set.

An important problem in local learning is to determine the appropriate neighborhood of the new input $\boldsymbol{x}_p$. Too narrow neighborhood would lead to too little samples in training set and exhibit weak generalization ability. Contrarily, too broad neighborhood would cause too many disperse samples in training set and obviously inaccurate prediction. Moreover, too many training data would increase the computation burden for the matrix inversion is included in the training process and the dimension of the matrix just equal to the number of training data. In actual application, the following method can be used to determine the neighborhood,

1. fixed size of training set;
2. a proportion of the sample set;
3. by the threshold of Euclidean distance.

For continuous processes, the newly sampled data can be added into the sample set constantly for the later prediction, thus the sample set increasingly becomes larger and the later training data can be selected in more larger sample set.

2.2 Local Weighted LSSVM

In local learning theory, the samples with relatively smaller Euclidean distance are selected to train the LSSVM model and they make the same contribution to the training. However, due to different Euclidean distances, the degrees of similarity to the new input are not just the same in the training set. Therefore, it is proposed in this paper that the data trains the LSSVM model at different weights determined by corresponding Euclidean distances. The data with smaller Euclidean distance play more important roles in the training and are given larger weights. The weight can be defined as linear function

$$s_i = 1 - (1 - \delta)\frac{d_i - d_{\min}}{d_{\max} - d_{\min}} \tag{2}$$

or exponential function

$$s_i = \exp(-d_i') \tag{3}$$

where d_i is the Euclidean distance between the ith training data $\boldsymbol{x}_i$ the new input $\boldsymbol{x}_p$, d_i' is normalized value of d_i, $d_{\min}$ is the minimum of $\{d_i\}_{i=1}^{M}$ and $d_{\max}$ is the maximum of $\{d_i\}_{i=1}^{M}$, δ is the preset minimal weight.

The weight s_i of each training data is introduced into LSSVM and the local weighted LSSVM(LW-LSSVM) is formed. Suppose a given regression data set $\{(\boldsymbol{x}_i, y_i)\}_{i=1}^{N}$, where N is the total number of training data pairs, $\boldsymbol{x}_i \in \mathcal{R}^n$ is the input variable and $y_i \in \mathcal{R}$ is the output variable. The nonlinear mapping function is $\varphi(\boldsymbol{x}_i)$. In the feature space we take the form

$$y(\boldsymbol{x}) = \boldsymbol{w}^T \varphi(\boldsymbol{x}) + b \quad \text{with} \quad \boldsymbol{w} \in \mathcal{Z}, b \in \mathcal{R} \tag{4}$$

to estimate the unknown function, where vector $\boldsymbol{w}$ and scalar b are the parameters to be identified.

The optimization problem is defined as follows,

$$\min_{\boldsymbol{w},e} J(\boldsymbol{w}, \boldsymbol{e}) = \frac{1}{2}\boldsymbol{w}^T \boldsymbol{w} + \frac{\gamma}{2}\sum_{i=1}^{M} s_i e_i^2 \quad \gamma > 0 \tag{5}$$

$$\text{subject to} \quad y_i = \boldsymbol{w}^T \varphi(\boldsymbol{x}_i) + b + e_i \quad i = 1, 2, \ldots, M \tag{6}$$

where e_i is the error between actual output and predictive output of the ith data, M is the number of training data selected from the total N data.

The LSSVM model can be given by

$$y(\boldsymbol{x}) = \sum_{i=1}^{N} \alpha_i K(\boldsymbol{x}, \boldsymbol{x}_i) + b \tag{7}$$

where $\alpha_i \in \mathcal{R}$ $(i = 1, 2, \ldots, N)$ are Lagrange multipliers, $K(\boldsymbol{x}, \boldsymbol{x}_i)$ $(i = 1, 2, \ldots, N)$ are any kernel functions satisfying the Mercer condition [9]. The model parameters $\alpha_i \in \mathcal{R}$ $(i = 1, 2, \ldots, M)$ and b can be obtained from the equation

$$\begin{bmatrix} b \\ \boldsymbol{\alpha} \end{bmatrix} = \begin{bmatrix} \boldsymbol{0} & \boldsymbol{1}^T \\ \boldsymbol{1} & \boldsymbol{\Omega} + \gamma \boldsymbol{S}^{-1} \end{bmatrix}^{-1} \begin{bmatrix} 0 \\ \boldsymbol{Y} \end{bmatrix} \tag{8}$$

where $\boldsymbol{Y} = [y_1\ y_2\ \cdots\ y_M]^T$, $\boldsymbol{\alpha} = [\alpha_1\ \alpha_2\ \cdots\ \alpha_M]^T$, $\boldsymbol{1} = [1\ 1\ \cdots\ 1]^T$, $S = \text{diag}\{s_1, \ldots, s_M\}$ and $\boldsymbol{\Omega}$ is a $M \times M$ symmetric matrix

$$\boldsymbol{\Omega}_{ij} = \varphi(\boldsymbol{x}_i)^T \varphi(\boldsymbol{x}_j) = K(\boldsymbol{x}_i, \boldsymbol{x}_j) \quad i, j = 1, 2, \ldots, M. \tag{9}$$

2.3 Algorithm Analysis

The participated training data not in the neighborhood of testing point are the key factors of model precision. By selecting training data with smaller Euclidean distance, the LW-LSSVM algorithm excludes those factors and thus the model precision is improved.

By introducing the weights in the objective function of optimization, each training data make different proportion according to the similarity to testing point. So, the modeling precision is increased further.

In (8), matrix inversion is included in the solving process of LSSVM, which is a time-consuming work. Compared with the computation of global LSSVM, Euclidean distances and weights of each training data should be computed first in LW-LSSVM. But, these computation are arithmetical calculations and not time-consuming. Conversely, the dimension of matrix is reduced greatly by excluding large number of training data in LW-LSSVM, which can save much more training time. So, LW-LSSVM is also more excellent than global LSSVM in training time.

2.4   Procedure of LW-LSSVM for Continuous Processes

For a continuous processes, the procedure of LW-LSSVM outlines as follows,

1. Initialization. Sample enough input and output data to form the initial sample set $S = \{(x_i, y_i)\}_{i=1}^{N_0}$, select optimal γ, parameter in Kernel function and appropriate size of training set;
2. For new sampling time $k + 1$, sample the new input x_{k+1}, compute the Euclidean distance $d_i(i = 1, \ldots, k)$ between x_{k+1} and $x_i(i = 1, \ldots, k)$ in sample set S by (1), select a proportion of the samples with smaller d_i to form the training set $T = \{(x_i, y_i)\}_{i=1}^{M}$, compute corresponding weight $s_i(i = 1, \ldots, M)$ by (2) or (3);
3. Train the LSSVM model by (8) using the training set $T = \{(x_i, y_i)\}_{i=1}^{M}$ and $s_i(i = 1, \ldots, M)$ got in 2, predict the current output y_{k+1};
4. Add the new sample $\{x_{k+1}, y_{k+1}\}$ into sample set $S = \{(x_i, y_i)\}_{i=1}^{k+1}$, $k \leftarrow k + 1$, go to 2;

3   Experiments

We applied the presented LW-LSSVM strategy in the simulation of pH neutralizing process, which is a weak acid-strong base system and with strong nonlinearity, especially in the vicinity of pH= 9.

The physical model of a pH process in a continuously stirred tank reactor (CSTR) consists of two parts, a linear dynamical part followed by a nonlinear static part[10]. The dynamical model is given by

$$\begin{cases} V\dfrac{dw_a}{dt} = F_a C_a - (F_a + F_b)w_a \\ V\dfrac{dw_b}{dt} = F_b C_b - (F_a + F_b)w_b \end{cases} \tag{10}$$

where F_a and F_b denote the inlet flow-rate of acid and base (cm^3/min), respectively, C_a and C_b are the inlet concentrations of acid and base (mol/l), the volume of the content in the reactor is denoted by the constant $V(cm^3)$, w_a and w_b are the concentrations of acid and base after the process of dynamical model (mol/l). Simultaneously w_a and w_b are the inputs of the static model

$$w_b + 10^{-y} - 10^{y-14} - \frac{w_a}{1 + 10^{pK_a - y}} = 0 \tag{11}$$

where y is the pH value of the effluent, K_a is the dissociation constant of the acetic acid with $K_a = 1.76 \times 10^{-5}$ and $pK_a = -\log_{10} K_a$.

Acid flow-rate F_a and base flow-rate F_b are the inputs of the system, and pH value y of the effluent is the output. The simulating system uses the physical model with the parameter values given in Table 1. The input F_a is the sum of a fixed value $81(cm^3/min)$ plus a periodically distributed signal ranging in the interval [-8.1, +8.1], and F_b is the sum of a fixed value 515 (cm^3/min) plus a

Table 1. Parameter Values Used in pH Neutralizing Model

Parameter	Nominal Value
C_a	0.32mol/l
C_b	0.05mol/l
V	1000cm^3
$w_a(0)$	0.0435mol/l
$w_b(0)$	0.0432mol/l

periodically distributed signal ranging in the interval [-51.5, +51.5]. The output y is polluted by a noise with zero mean and a variance of 0.01. The sampling period is 1min. The data are normalized before applying the algorithm.

Radial Basis Function (RBF)

$$K(\boldsymbol{x}, \boldsymbol{x}_i) = \exp\{-\|\boldsymbol{x} - \boldsymbol{x}_i\|_2^2/\sigma^2\} \tag{12}$$

with $\sigma = 0.04$ is chosen as the kernel function in the experiment. Another parameters $\gamma = 10$ is fixed on for the simulation after optimization. The size of training set and minimal weight are set to $M = 80$ and $\delta = 0.001$, respectively.

Fig.1 shows the predictive results for 500min with exponential weight LW-LSSVM where Yy is the actual output of system and Ym is the predictive value. Fig.2 shows the predictive results for the same samples by global LSSVM. Comparing Fig.1 to Fig.2, it is obvious that LW-LSSVM model with exponential weight can predict the output more accurately.

To compare the prediction ability of different method, the following parameters are used as the approximate performance index [11].

(1) Standard Error of Prediction(SEP)

$$\text{SEP} = \sqrt{\frac{\sum_{i=1}^{N}(Yy_i - Ym_i)^2}{N}} \tag{13}$$

where Yy is the vector of actual output, Ym is the predictive output, and N is the length of Yy. The smaller SEP denotes higher predicting precision.

(2) Multiple Correlation Coefficient R^2

$$\text{R}^2 = 1 - \frac{\sum_{i=1}^{N}(Yy_i - Ym_i)^2}{\sum_{i=1}^{N}(Yy_i - \overline{Yy})^2} \tag{14}$$

where $\overline{Yy}$ is the mean of Yy. R^2 is in the interval [0,1] and the value more near to 1 denotes stronger relevance of Yy and Ym.

The comparison of SEP, R^2 and running time of several LSSVM method is shown in Table 2 where constant weight means that the weights are all set to 1, *i.e.* non-weighted local LSSVM. The application of sparse recursive LSSVM algorithm in [7] is also listed in Table 2.

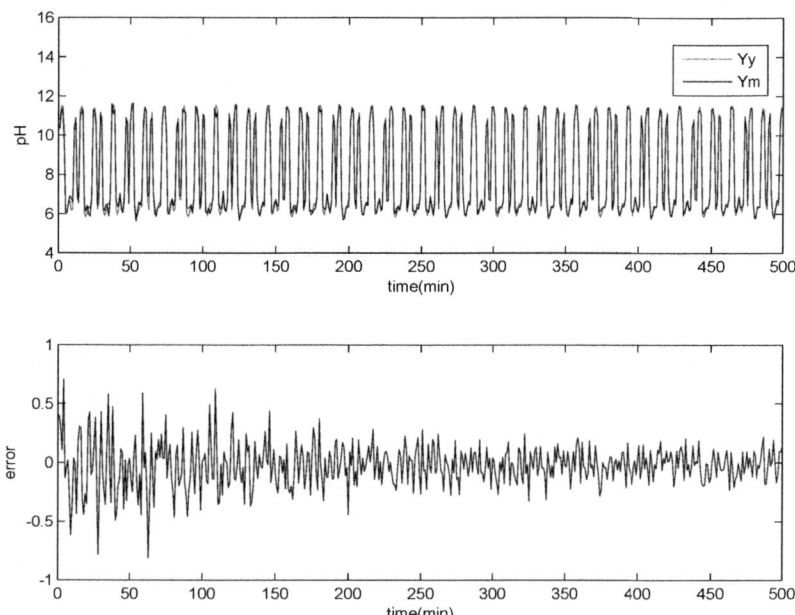

Fig. 1. Simulation of pH process with exponential weight LW-LSSVM method

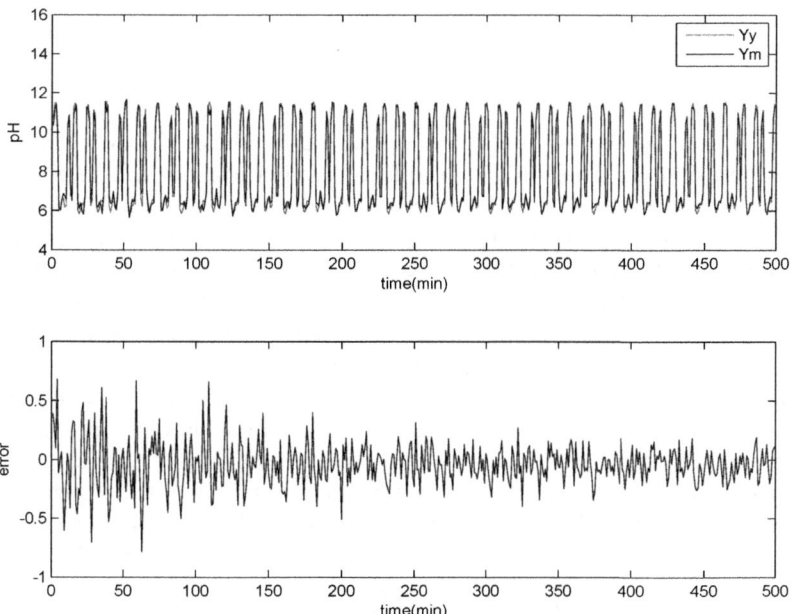

Fig. 2. Simulation of pH process with global LSSVM method

Table 2. Comparison of several LSSVM algorithms in pH process

		SEP	R^2	time(s)
	global LSSVM	0.1924	0.9931	556
LW-LSSVM	exponential weight	0.1862	0.9936	30
	linear weight	**0.1841**	**0.9937**	53
	constant weight	0.1849	**0.9937**	42
sparse LSSVM	140 support vectors	0.2991	0.9833	**3**
	222 support vectors	0.2261	0.9904	8

Observing Table 2, we can get the following conclusions:

(1) The index SEP, R^2 and running time of LW-LSSVM are all superior to global LSSVM. The precision indexes of LW-LSSVM are a little better than global LSSVM, while the running time are much smaller than global LSSVM. Moreover, the running time of global LSSVM would increase with the increase of samples. Therefore, the proposed LW-LSSVM method has the advantages both in precision and predicting time, especially the predicting time.

(2) Comparing to sparse recursive LSSVM method, the LW-LSSVM algorithm also exhibits obvious advantage in precision. But the running time of LW-LSSVM with just 80 training data is longer than that of sparse recursive one with more training data. The reason lies in that, the LW-LSSVM algorithm can not use the recursive formula to compute the model parameters but must compute the inversion of matrix for the irregular training data variant when model renews.

4   Conclusions

For continuous processes, the samples maybe non-uniformly distribute in a rather wide range due to the fluctuation of operating conditions. The samples in the steady operation are dense in the sample set while these are sparse in the irregular running conditions. The global LSSVM always gives good prediction for these inputs located in the neighborhood of dense samples but incompetent for these in the sparse part. To solve the problem, the paper proposed a local weighted LSSVM method in the online modeling of continuous processes. At each period, only the samples similar to the current input are added into the training set and the obtained model is just for predicting the current output. Due to the training data are in the neighborhood of testing data, the prediction is more precise than in global LSSVM. At the same time, the elimination of some samples from adding into the training set also make the computation decreased.

To distinguish the importance of the training data, weight are defined to each data according to the Euclidean distances between the training data and testing data. In this way, the training data participate the learning at different weights according to the similarity to the testing data.

The presented LW-LSSVM algorithm is applied in pH neutralization process. The result shows the excellent performance of the presented algorithm in precision and predicting time.

References

1. Vapnik, V.: The nature of statistical learning theory. Springer, Heidelberg (1995)
2. Vapnik, V.: Statistical learning theory. John Wiley, New York (1998)
3. Suykens, J.A.K., Vandewalle, J.: Least squares support vector machine classifiers. Neural Processing Letters 9, 293–300 (1999)
4. Suykens, J.A.K., Lukas, L., Vandewalle, J.: Sparse approximation using least squares support vector machines. In: Proceeding of IEEE International Symposium on Circuits and Systems, pp. 757–760. IEEE Press, Lausanne (2000)
5. de Kruif, B.J., de Vries, T.J.A.: Pruning error minimization in least squares support vector machines. IEEE Transaction on neural networks 14, 696–702 (2003)
6. Zeng, X., wenChen, X.: Smo-based pruning methods for sparse least squares support vector machines. IEEE Transaction on neural networks 16, 1541–1546 (2005)
7. Li, L., Su, H., Chu, J.: Sparse representation based on projection in least squares support vector machines. Control Theory and Application 7, 163–168 (2009)
8. Liu, Y., Wang, H., Li, P.: Local least squares support vector regression with application to online modeling for batch processes. Journal of Chemical Industry and Engineering (China) 58, 2846–2851 (2007)
9. Smola, A.J., Schökopf, B.: A tutorial on support vector regression, http://www.neurocolt.com/tech_reps/1998/98030.ps.gz
10. Nie, J.H., Loh, A.P., Hang, C.C.: Modeling ph neutralization process using fuzzy-neutral approaches. Fuzzy set and systems 78, 5–22 (1996)
11. Chen, M., Cheng, J., Liu, X.: Determination of Alkaloids of Coptis chinensis by Spectral Analysis Based on Local Fitting Principal Component Regression. Acta Chimica Sinica 61, 1623–1627 (2003)

A Cellular Automata Based Crowd Behavior Model

D. Wang[1], N.M. Kwok[1], Xiuping Jia[2], and F. Li[2]

[1] School of Mechanical and Manufacturing Engineering
[2] School of Engineering and Information Technology, University College
The University of New South Wales, Australia
{dalong.wang,nmkwok}@unsw.edu.au, x.jia@adfa.edu.au,
lifeng504@yahoo.com.cn

Abstract. This paper presents a Cellular Automata (CA) based crowd behavior model which mimics movements of humans in an indoor environment. Because of the increasing population in modern cities, the understanding of crowd behavior in the urban environment has become a crucial issue in emergency management. In the proposed crowd behavior model, pedestrians are confined to move in a cellular space where their movements are determined by their own status and the surrounding environment characteristics. A pedestrian's behavior is constructed from several attributes: including the "walking toward goal" behavior, "collision and congestion avoidance" behavior, "grouping" behavior and path smoothness. Simulations have been carried out with a crowd consisting of thirty pedestrians in an indoor environment to validate the model.

1 Introduction

This research focuses on the modeling of crowd behavior subject to stimulations and constraints in an urban environment. There are frequent occasions that people assemble in massive numbers as a crowd in their daily livings, e.g., during sport events, festivals or even in a demonstration. This brings a need to further understand crowd behavior for better crowd management in massive gatherings. One of the largest areas where crowd behaviors have been modeled is in crowd evacuation simulations, where studies are conducted on movements of a large number of people in enclosed areas like stadiums, shopping complexes and large buildings [1] - [5].

Existing crowd behavior modeling methodologies can be categorized into two main groups, namely, macroscopic approaches and microscopic approaches. Macroscopic approaches deal with the crowd behavior problem from a global point of view. The entire crowd is modeled as a flow whose properties can be defined by a collection of physics-based phenomena [6][7]. Pedestrians are treated as part of the flow instead of as individual entities, thus details of individual's behavior in the process may not be precisely represented.

In microscopic approaches, crowd behaviors are studied by considering the behaviors of individual pedestrians and their interactions with the environment. One popular approach is the social force model, which is inspired partly by the concept of Potential Field Method [8][9]. In the social force model, an individual's movement is

F.L. Wang et al. (Eds.): AICI 2010, Part II, LNAI 6320, pp. 218–225, 2010.
© Springer-Verlag Berlin Heidelberg 2010

influenced by other pedestrians and environmental obstacles [10]. This model has also been applied in video surveillance to detect and localize abnormal behaviors [11]. In addition, swarm intelligence techniques such as the Particle Swarm Optimization (PSO) algorithm has also been adopted in the crowd simulation in [1][12].

The purpose of the current research is to develop a CA-based crowd behavior model in an indoor environment. Pedestrians considered in this approach are placed in a cellular space. The probability of traveling to a neighboring cell is evaluated by cost functions which take into account the distances to the goals, influences from other pedestrians and obstacles, grouping behavior and movement smoothness. A feasible cell with the minimum cost will be selected as the pedestrian's next position.

The rest of this paper is organized as follows: Section 2 describes the CA-based crowd behavior model in detail. Section 3 tests the proposed approach with simulations consisting of thirty pedestrians in an indoor environment. Section 4 concludes this paper and suggests future research directions.

2   Crowd Behavior Model

2.1   Cellular Automata Model

In this paper, we consider human movement in a two-dimensional space. The space is divided into a number of equal sized cells. In each time instance, a pedestrian is supposed to move from his/her current location to one of the neighboring cells. The cell's size is $0.5m \times 0.5m$ and obeys the Moore neighbors definition. In the cellular space, each cell has one of the following states: a) occupied by obstacles, b) occupied by

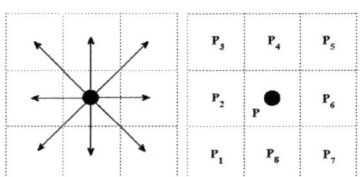

Fig. 1. Possible directions

a person, c) empty. Consider the cellular space shown in Fig. 1, in which a pedestrian is located at P. The possible next position will be selected from its eight neighboring cells denoted by $P_i, i = 1,2,...8$. The cost functions used to evaluate the occupancy states of these cells are developed on the basis of the pedestrian's own states and influences by other pedestrians and the surrounding environment.

2.2   Crowd Model

Pedestrian movements are difficult to model, especially when there are a large number of people existing in an environment. In most of the time a pedestrian moves towards a desired goal position. During their movements to their goals, pedestrians show behaviors like collision avoidance, congestion avoidance and group formation. Starting from this deduction, we propose a crowd behavior model which takes into account factors including the "walking toward goal" behavior, the "collision avoidance and congestion avoidance" behavior, the "grouping" behavior and motion path smoothness.

2.2.1 Walking Toward Goal

The "walking toward goal" behavior determines the way how a pedestrian walks towards a desired destination, e.g., an outlet of a building or end of a road. This behavior is defined by choosing candidate cells which will reduce the distance from the pedestrian to his/her goal. We define two cost functions: the first one is a function of the distance between the pedestrian and the goal, the second one is a function of the pedestrian's current orientation with respect to the goal. The reason underlying is quite straightforward, as illustrated in Fig. 2.

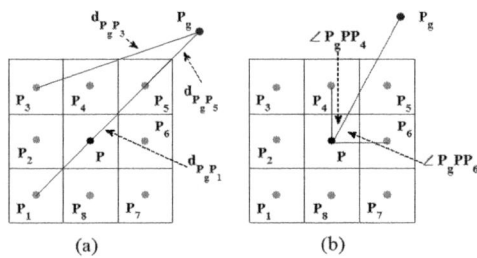

Fig. 2. Walking toward goal: (a) distance (b) orientation

In Fig. 2 (a), a pedestrian is located at point P and the goal is shown by P_g. The positions of neighboring cells, or in other words, candidate cells, are denoted by P_i, $i = 1,2,\ldots 8$. The distances from P_g to P_i are denoted by $d_{P_g P_i}$. A cost function is formulated so that a cell closer to the goal will have a higher chance to be selected:

$$f_{gd_i} = k_{gd} / d_{P_g P_i}; \quad i = 1,2\ldots 8 \tag{1}$$

where f_{gd_i} denotes the influence of distance from a candidate cell to goal. $d_{P_g P_i}$ is the distance between the candidate cell and the pedestrian's goal. k_{gd} is a factor which determines the influence of $d_{P_g P_i}$. Note that $d_{P_g P_i}$ may be very large when the pedestrian is far from the goal. Since the candidate cells are closely located to each other, the difference between the corresponding $d_{P_g P_i}$ remains small. In fact, the maximum difference is $2\sqrt{2}$ times of cell length, as the case of $d_{P_g P_5}$ and $d_{P_g P_1}$ shown in Fig. 2 (a).

The angle of a candidate orientation relative to the direction to the goal is also taken into consideration, as shown in Fig. 2 (b). A cost function is defined as below:

$$f_{ga_i} = k_{ga} |\angle P_g P P_i|; \quad i = 1,2\ldots 8 \tag{2}$$

where $\angle P_g P P_i$ is the angle between the candidate orientation and goal direction with $-\pi \le \angle P_g P P_i < \pi$. k_{ga} is a factor which determines the influence of this angle. f_{ga_i} denotes the influence of the angular difference. In the case shown in Fig. 2 (b), $|\angle P_g P P_4| < |\angle P_g P P_6|$, so P_4 has a larger probability to be selected than P_6.

2.2.2 Collision Avoidance and Congestion Avoidance

When a human moves towards his goal, he must avoid possible collisions with either other people or environmental obstacles. Moreover, a human tends to avoid congested conditions. In this approach, the influence of other people and obstacles is taken into consideration by assigning corresponding cost functions. It is reasonable to assume that a human only reacts to human and obstacles within a certain distance and neglects human and obstacles which are far away. Note that human reactions to obstacles vary from case to case, but an individual's reaction distance in a certain environment can be assumed to be constant.

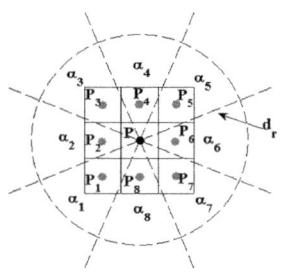

Fig. 3. Reaction range

Obstacles are treated as a set of obstacle points. The influence of an obstacle point P_o to a person located at P should decrease when the distance between the human and the obstacle point (denoted by d_{P_oP}) increases, as defined by the following equation:

$$f_o = \begin{cases} k_o/d_{P_oP}; & if\ d_{P_oP} < d_r \\ 0; & otherwises \end{cases} \tag{3}$$

where f_o is the influence of an obstacle point to the pedestrian. d_{P_oP} is the distance between the obstacle point and this person. k_o is a factor which determines the influence of this obstacle point to this person. d_r denotes the pedestrian's reaction distance and is a constant.

Similarly, the influence from another pedestrian at location P_a to this person is given by:

$$f_p = \begin{cases} k_p/d_{P_aP}; & if\ d_{P_aP} < d_r \\ 0; & otherwises \end{cases} \tag{4}$$

where f_p is the influence of a pedestrian to this human. d_{P_aP} is the distance from the pedestrian to this person. k_p is a factor which determines the influence of other pedestrians. d_r denotes a pedestrian's reaction distance.

We assume that a human's reaction range is a circle with a radius of d_r. To evaluate the influence of other pedestrians and environmental obstacles, we divide the reaction range into eight sectors evenly, as shown in Fig. 3. Each sector covers a span of $45°$, the center of a candidate cell is located on the intersection of angular bisectors.

We define that for candidate cell P_i, the collision avoidance and congestion avoidance function (f_{cc_i}) is a sum of influence from all humans and environmental obstacles which are in the area of sector α_i.

$$f_{cc_i} = \sum\nolimits_{\alpha_i} f_o + \sum\nolimits_{\alpha_i} f_p; \quad i = 1, 2 \ldots 8 \tag{5}$$

2.2.3 Grouping

Pedestrians often form into groups in their movements with friends and family members. People from the same group maintain short distances, which are different to the case that pedestrians from different groups tend to keep away from each other. Taking the "grouping" behavior into consideration, (4) and (5) are modified as followings:

$$f_p^* = \begin{cases} f_p; & \text{if pedestrians at } P_a \text{ and } P \text{ are not from same group} \\ 0; & \text{otherwises} \end{cases} \tag{6}$$

$$f_{cc_i}^* = \sum\nolimits_{\alpha_i} f_o + \sum\nolimits_{\alpha_i} f_p^*; \quad i = 1, 2 \ldots 8 \tag{7}$$

When group numbers are apart from each other, they tend to move closer. Based on this fact, for two pedestrians P_j and P_k from the same group, a grouping cost function is defined by:

$$f_{a_{jk}} = \begin{cases} k_a \big(d_{P_j P_k} - d_a \big); & \text{if } d_{P_j P_k} > d_a \\ 0; & \text{otherwises} \end{cases} \tag{8}$$

where $f_{a_{jk}}$ is the grouping cost between pedestrians P_j and P_k. $d_{P_j P_k}$ is the distance between two pedestrians. k_a is a factor which determines the amplitude of grouping cost and d_a denotes the minimum action distance of grouping cost.

For each sector, the influence of "grouping" behavior to a human is then given by:

$$f_{gr_i} = \sum\nolimits_{\alpha_i} f_{a_{jk}}; \quad i = 1, 2 \ldots 8 \tag{9}$$

2.2.4 Path Smoothness

Since it is not desirable that a pedestrian changes his/her movement direction suddenly, we take the orientation alteration as a measurement of path smoothness. We define that a human's orientation is given by the vector from its location to next destination cell. The change in orientation between two steps is given by:

$$f_{oa} = k_{oa} \big| \theta_{t+1_i} - \theta_t \big|; \quad i = 1, 2 \ldots 8 \tag{10}$$

where θ_{t+1_i} is the human's moving direction if he/she travels from the current location to the candidate cell i at time $t+1$ in the next step. θ_t is the human's current movement direction. k_{oa} is a scaling factor.

2.2.5 Motion Determination

Given the above components, we define the cost function to evaluate that the candidate cells will be reached in the next instance of time as:

$$f_{\text{cost}_i} = f_{gd_i} + f_{ga_i} + f_{cc_i}^* + f_{gr_i} + f_{oa_i}; \quad i \in N \tag{11}$$

where N is a set of feasible candidate cells which are not occupied by other pedestrians or obstacles. The candidate cell with minimum cost is then selected as the pedestrian's next position. With this cost function, a pedestrian is capable of walking toward his/her destination while avoiding collision and congestion. If there is no feasible cell, the pedestrian will stay at his/her current position.

3 Case Studies

Simulations have been carried out using the presented crowd model in an indoor environment shown in Fig. 4 (a). There are two corridors connecting to the hall. A rectangle obstacle is placed in the middle of this environment. A total of 30 pedestrians are simulated. Their initial positions and desired destinations are denoted by numbers in Fig. 4 (a). Pedestrians 1 to 10 start from the left side of the hall and walk towards right. Their initial positions are denoted by numerical indicators in green. Pedestrians 11 to 20 walk from right to left. Their initial positions are denoted by numbers in magenta at the right side of hall. Pedestrians 21 to 25 form a group (Group A) and move from the bottom corridor to the corridor at the top right corner. Their initial positions are indicated by numbers in blue. Pedestrians 26 to 30 are supposed to travel from the corridor at the top right to the corridor at the bottom. They form Group B and are shown with numbers in red. The desired destinations of all pedestrians are shown by their numbers with black color. Note that in all figures illustrated in this section, the unit of X and Y axes are unit cell length, i.e. 0.5m. The parameters used in the simulations are set as: $k_{gd} = 5$, $k_{ga} = 1$, $k_o = 25$, $k_p = 3$, $k_a = -0.1$, $d_r = 20$, $d_a = 0$, $k_{oa} = 1$.

The simulation process is illustrated in Fig. 4. The locations of the numbers are used to denote the positions of pedestrians in the environment. To be specific, the positions of pedestrians 1 to 10, pedestrians 11 to 20, pedestrians 21 to 25 and pedestrians 26 to 30 are shown by numbers with green, magenta, blue and red, respectively.

After the simulation begins, pedestrians leave their start points and move towards their goals, as shown in Fig. 4 (b) for the situation in iteration 10. It is observed that pedestrians 1 to 20 keep relatively large distances from each other while distances between pedestrians from the same group, 21 to 25 of Group A and 26 to 30 of Group B, are relatively small. As simulation continues, pedestrians approach the central area of the hall, Fig. 4 (c). Because of the rectangular obstacle in the middle, pedestrians change their moving directions and try to avoid collisions with the obstacles and other pedestrians. Group A and B meet in the area with X axis between [30, 40] and Y axis between [20, 30].

Figure 4 (d) shows the status of iteration 25. Pedestrians from the left side of hall passed the obstacle and are moving towards their goals. Pedestrians 13, 18 and 20 from right side are moving at the bottom side of the obstacle. Pedestrian 12 is going to move towards the bottom side of the obstacle. Pedestrians 11, 14 to 17, and 19 move along the top side of the obstacle. Group A and B pass each other successfully.

In Fig. 4 (e), all pedestrians are moving towards their goals. The simulation process finishes at iteration 52. All pedestrians arrive at their goals successfully. The resultant paths are given in Fig. 4 (f). Paths of pedestrians 1 to 10, 11 to 20, 21 to 25 (Group A) and 26 to 30 (Group B) are shown by lines with green, magenta, blue and red, respectively. The destinations of pedestrians are denoted by numbers in black.

In general, simulated pedestrians with the proposed crowd behavior model are capable of avoiding collision and congestion with obstacles and other pedestrians. For groups consisting of several members, the distances between their members are kept relatively small and do not disperse in the crowded traffic conditions.

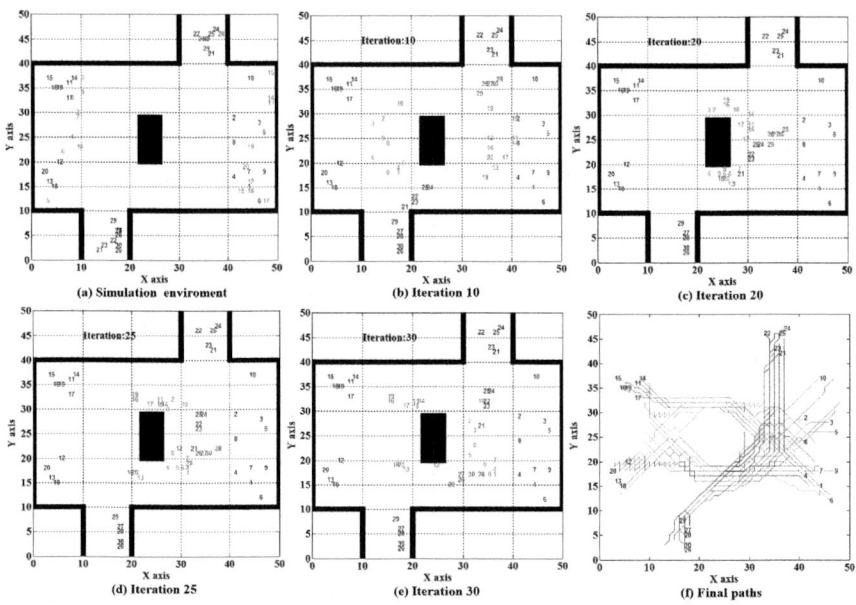

Fig. 4. Simulation snapshots and the final path

4   Conclusions and Future Work

A Cellular Automata based crowd behavior model has been presented in this paper. The pedestrians move in a cellular space. Cost functions are designed to evaluate a pedestrian's Moore neighboring cells taking into account of individual and group interactions with others and the environment. A feasible cell with minimum cost is then selected as this pedestrian's next position. Simulations are carried out in an indoor environment with thirty pedestrians. It is shown that this model is capable of mimicking crowd movement phenomenon in which they tend to avoid collisions with obstacles and other pedestrians while walking toward their destinations. Future work will include a decision making mechanism with transition probabilities to better represent pedestrian motions.

References

1. Fang, G., Kwok, N.M., Ha, Q.P.: Swarm interaction-based simulation of occupant evacuation. In: Proceedings of the Pacific-Asia Workshop on Computational Intelligence and Industrial Application (PACIIA 2008), December 19-20, vol. 2, pp. 329–333 (2008)
2. Was, J.: Cellular automata model of pedestrian dynamics for normal and evacuation conditions. In: Proceedings of the 5th International Conference on Intelligent Systems Design and Applications (ISDA 2005), September 8-10, pp. 154–159 (2005)
3. Jiang, L., Chen, J., Zhan, W.: A crowd evacuation simulation model based on 2.5-dimension cellular automaton. In: Proceedings of the IEEE International Conference on Virtual Environments, Human-Computer Interfaces and Measurements Systems (VECIMS 2009), May 11-13, pp. 90–95 (2009)
4. Sarmady, S., Haron, F., Talib, A.: Modeling groups of pedestrians in least effort crowd movements using cellular automata. In: Proceedings of the Third Asia International Conference on Modelling and Simulation (AMS 2009), May 25-29, pp. 520–525 (2009)
5. Kirchner, A., Schadschneider, A.: Simulation of evacuation processes using a bionics-inspired cellular automaton model for pedestrian dynamics. Physica A 312(1-2), 260–276 (2002)
6. Hughes, R.L.: A continuum theory for the flow of pedestrians. Transportation Research Part B: Methodological 36(6), 507–535 (2002)
7. Hughes, R.L.: The flow of human crowds. Annual Review of Fluid Mechanics 35(35), 169–182
8. Khatib, O.: Real-time obstacle avoidance for manipulators and mobile robots. International Journal of Robotics Research 5, 90–98 (1986)
9. Wang, D., Liu, D., Dissanayake, G.: A variable speed force field method for multi-robot collaboration. In: Proceedings of the IEEE/RSJ International Conference on Intelligent Robots and Systems (IROS 2006), Beijing, China, pp. 2697–2702 (2006)
10. Helbing, D., Molnar, P.: Social force model for pedestrian dynamics. Physical Review E 51, 4282–4286 (1995)
11. Mehran, R., Oyama, A., Shah, M.: Abnormal crowd behavior detection using social force model. In: Proceedings of the IEEE Conference on Computer Vision and Pattern Recognition (CVPR 2009), June 20-25, pp. 935–942 (2009)
12. Lin, Y., Chen, Y.: Crowd control with swarm intelligence. In: Proceedings of the IEEE Congress on Evolutionary Computation (CEC 2007), September 25-28, pp. 3321–3328 (2007)

A Novel Watermark Technique for Relational Databases

Hazem El-Bakry and Mohamed Hamada

Mannsura Univ., Egypt
Helbakry20@yahoo.com
Aizu University, Japan
mhamada2000@gmail.com

Abstract. In this paper, a new approach for protecting the ownership of relational database is presented. Such approach is applied for protecting both textual and numerical data. This is done by adding only one hidden record with a secret function. For each attribute, the value of this function depends on the data stored in all other records. Therefore, this technique is more powerful against any attacks or modifications such as deleting or updating cell values. Furthermore, the problems associated with the work in literature are solved. For example, there is no need for additional storage area as required when adding additional columns especially with large databases. In addition, in case of protecting data by adding columns, we need to add a number of columns equal to the number of data types to be protected. Here, only one record is sufficient to protect all types of data. Moreover, there is a possibility to use a different function for each field results in more robustness. Finally, the proposed technique does not have any other requirements or restrictions on either database design or database administration.

Keywords: Relational Database, Copyright Protection, Digital Watermarking.

1 Introduction

The copyright protection inserts evidence into the digital objects without lossless of its quality. Whenever, the copyright of a digital object is in question, this information is extracted to identify the right full owner. Digital watermarking is the solution of embedding information in multimedia data. There are many techniques used to protect copyrights [18].

Digital contents in the form of text document, still images motion picture, and music etc. are widely used in normal life nowadays. With the rapid grown of internet users, it boots up transaction rates (file sharing, distribution or change). Trend goes up dramatically and continues growing everyday due to convenient and easy to access. It is, hence, copyright protection becomes more concerned to all content owners [1-2].

Watermark is an open problem that aimed to one goal. This goal is how to insert [error/ mark/ data/ formula/ evidence/ so on] associated with a secret key known only by the data owner in order to prove the ownership of the data without lossless of its quality.

In order to evaluate any watermark system, the following requirements are generally considered in prior: (i) Readability: A watermark should convey as much information

F.L. Wang et al. (Eds.): AICI 2010, Part II, LNAI 6320, pp. 226–232, 2010.

as possible, statistically detectable, enough to identify ownership and copyright unambiguously, (ii) Security: Only authorized users access to the watermark data, (iii) Imperceptibility: The embedding process should not introduce any perceptible artifacts into original image and not degrade the perceive quality of image, and (iv) Robustness: The watermark should be able to withstand various attacks while can be detected in the extraction process.

In general, watermark is small, hidden perturbations in the database used as an evidence of its origin. Inserting mark into original data used to demonstrate the ownership. Watermark should not significantly affect the quality of original data and should not be able to destroy easily. The goal is to identify pirated copies of original data. Watermarking does not prevent copying, but it deters illegal copying by providing a means of establishing the ownership of a redistributed copy. There are more approaches and algorithms available for image, audio and video but the new is how to introduce a new approach serve the relational databases?

Agrawal et al. introduce a watermarking technique for numerical data [1]. This technique dependent on a secret key, uses markers to locate tuples to hide watermark bits, hides watermark bits in the least significant bits. Also Sion et al. introduce a watermark technique for numerical data [2]. This technique is dependent on a secret key, instead of primary key uses the most significant bits of the normalized data set, divides the data set into partitions using markers, and varies the partition statistics to hide watermark bits.

Relational database was selected because it is common and was created before. Watermarking for values of selected attributes in tuples of relational database, it must be small to be tolerated [3,4].

This paper is organized as follows: The problem statement is described in section II, Section III presents the proposed technique and discusses the evaluation of this novel technique.

2 Watermarking for Databases

Watermarking of relational databases is very important point for the researches; because the free databases available on the internet websites are published without copyrights protection and the future will exploding problems. If the database contains very important data; then the problem will be how to add watermark to the numerical or textual data in relational database. This should be performed without affecting the usefulness and the quality of the data.

The goal is how to insert intended error /mark /data /formula/ evidence associated with secret key known only by the data owner in order to prove the ownership of the data without lossless of its quality [5,6]. Fig.1 shows a typical watermark model for any relational database. Watermark W is embedded into the relational database I with a secret key k, the watermarked relational database IW later pass through a distribution channel (computer network, internet, etc.), which are simulated under several kinds of common attacks. The watermarked database after attack IW, with the same secret key, will then extracted in order to recover the original watermark data W [4-10].

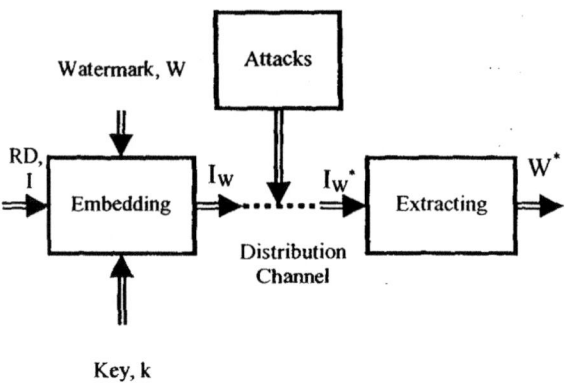

Fig. 1. Typical Watermark System Model

3 The Proposed Technique

Generally, the proposed technique relies on changing database schema; which is the model of database contents, thus the structure of the data will be changed by adding a new record (altering the table) relies on the original data in each field of the relational databse. The function used in constructing the new record as well as the secret key known only by the data owner. In general, the function used in protecting this relational database is locked via a predefined secret key. The proposed technique can be summarized in the following steps:

1. Get the relational table from the desired database; which must be numeric values.
2. For each field, adding a new calculated record based on the data stored in other records with a secret function $f(.)$.
3. Generate the secret function $f(.)$; which depends on the numeric values of the other cells in the current field in an encrypted structure.
4. Apply this function to the remaining fields in the table; thus an extra record has been created and added to the original database table.
5. Protect the calculated column from attack with a protection KEY known only to the data owner.
6. The added record may be hidden to malicious.

In general, the proposed technique can be used to protect the ownership of the relational database that contains only numeric values. This novel technique adds only one hidden record with a secret function. Not only that but also locking this calculated row from any attacks or changes such as deleting or updating. The advantages of the proposed technique are:

1. The proposed technique is available for any relational database.
2. No delay and no additional time required till the normal calculation end.
3. Allowable for any update such as adding rows and changing the values of the columns.
4. Not allowable for deleting the hidden records because it was locked with a secret key known only by the data owner.
5. The values in the hidden record are known only by the data owner [14-16].

6. Furthermore, there is a possibility to use a different function for each field results in more robustness.
7. Moreover, there is no need for additional storage area as required when adding additional columns as described in [18].

The relational database in Table 1 is the North wind database used for many applications because it was mostly published on the internet and common in different Microsoft applications. Table 2 presents the watermarked relational database. The algorithm has been practically summarized in the following:

(i) selecting any numerical table such as Table 1
(ii) adding a new record; its value relies on the data stored in other records by unknown functions, For example:

$$Key = STD(Cells)+Max(Cells)- Min(Cells)\pm Q \qquad (1)$$

where, STD is the standard deviation, and Q is a constant value.
(iii) Applying the function for all columns as shown in Table 2.

Table 1. The original relational database

Stock No.	Jan.	Feb.	Mar.	Apr.	May	June	July	Aug.	Sep.	Oct.	Nov.	Dec.
125970	1400	1100	981	882	794	752	654	773	809	980	3045	19000
212569	2400	1721	1414	1191	983	825	731	653	723	790	1400	5000
389123	1800	1200	890	670	550	450	400	410	402	450	1200	16000
400314	3000	2400	1800	1500	1200	900	700	650	1670	2500	6000	15000
400339	4300		2600	1800	1600	1550	895	700	750	900	8000	24000
400345	5000	3500	2800	2300	1700	1400	1000	900	1600	3300	12000	20000
400455	1200	900	800	500	399	345	300	175	760	1500	5500	17000
400876	3000	2400	1500	1500	1300	1100	900	867	923	1100	4000	32000
400999	3000	1500	1000	900	750	700	400	350	500	1100	3000	12000
888652	1234	900	821	701	689	621	545	421	495	550	4200	12000

Table 2. The watermarked relational database

Stock No.	Jan.	Feb.	Mar.	Apr.	May	June	July	Aug.	Sep.	Oct.	Nov.	Dec.
125970	1400	1100	981	882	794	752	654	773	809	980	3045	19000
212569	2400	1721	1414	1191	983	825	731	653	723	790	1400	5000
389123	1800	1200	890	670	550	450	400	410	402	450	1200	16000
400314	3000	2400	1800	1500	1200	900	700	650	1670	2500	6000	15000
400339	4300		2600	1800	1600	1550	895	700	750	900	8000	24000
400345	5000	3500	2800	2300	1700	1400	1000	900	1600	3300	12000	20000
400455	1200	900	800	500	399	345	300	175	760	1500	5500	17000
400876	3000	2400	1500	1500	1300	1100	900	867	923	1100	4000	32000
400999	3000	1500	1000	900	750	700	400	350	500	1100	3000	12000
888652	1234	900	821	701	689	621	545	421	495	550	4200	12000
564646	3433	2062	1340	994	1298	1362	553	715	1714	2167	5235	14200

(iv) Hide the calculated record and export the table with the new added record

(v) lock the entire table with a protection key known only to the data owner that deter the copying and changing the values of cells.

Another example is listed in Table 3. It combines different types of data. The same principles are applied to numerical The final result is shown in Table 4. A code for each character is given as listed in Table 5. The secret formula is calculated as follows:

$$\beta = \frac{\sum_{i=1}^{n} \alpha_i \sum_{j=1}^{\alpha_i} \rho_j}{n} \tag{2}$$

where, α is the number of characters per word, ρ is the character code, n is the number of words, and β is the secret key.

Table 3. The original relational database

Emp_ID	Emp_Name	Address	Birth Date	Salary
2324	Ahmed	Mansoura	17/11/1987	2320
4547	Nagi	Tanta	22/02/1989	1344
6549	Sameh	Cairo	12/12/1987	2456
7653	Kamel	Sudan	10/08/1986	1233
8975	Alaa	Cairo	04/10/1981	2356

Table 4. The watermarked relational database

Emp_ID	Emp_Name	Address	Birth Date	Salary
2324	Ahmed	Mansoura	17/11/1987	2320
4547	Nagi	Tanta	22/02/1989	1344
6549	Sameh	Cairo	12/12/1987	2456
7653	Kamel	Sudan	10/08/1986	1233
8975	Alaa	Cairo	04/10/1981	2356
5661	Tamer	Banha	01/19/1994	2164

Table 5. Alphabetic Character Coding

Character	Code (ρ)	Character	Code (ρ)
A	1	N	14
B	2	O	15
C	3	P	16
D	4	Q	17
E	5	R	18
F	6	S	19
G	7	T	20
H	8	U	21
I	9	V	22
J	10	W	23
K	11	X	24
L	12	Y	25
M	13	Z	26

The resulted Emp_name and address can be concluded as shown in Table 6.

Table 6. The computed secret key and its corresponding Emp_name and address

Secret key (β)	Emp_Name	Address
1:50	Mohamed	Sinai
51:100	Ali	Talkha
101:150	Hassan	Sandoub
151:200	Tamer	Banha
201:250	Shaker	El-Baramoon

4 Conclusions

A novel digital watermarking technique for relational database has been presented. The proposed technique has provided a very high degree of reliability and protection of relation database with the aid of the user predefined function; which inserts an additional hidden record to available relational database. This technique has many advantages over existing techniques. First, it is available for any relational database. Second, it does not require any additional time because the calculations required for the new record are done off line. Third, it is not possible to delete the hidden record because it has been locked with a secret key known only by the data owner. The values in the hidden record are known only by the data owner. Furthermore, the problems associated with the work in literature are solved. For example, there is no need for additional storage area as required when adding additional columns especially with large databases. In addition, in case of protecting data by adding columns, we need for to add a number of columns equal to the number of data types to be protected. Here, one record is sufficient to protect all types of data. Moreover, there is a possibility to use a different function for each field results in more robustness. Finally, the proposed technique does not have any other requirements or restrictions on either database design or database administration.

References

[1] Temi, C., Somsak, C., Lasakul, A.: A Robust Image Watermarking Using Multiresolution Analysis of Wavelet. In: Proceeding of ISCIT (2000)
[2] Collberg, C.S., Thomborson, C.: Watermarking, Tamper-Proofing, and Obfuscation-Tools for Software Protection. Technical Report 200003, University of Arizona (February 2000)
[3] Gross-Amblard, D.: Query-Preserve Watermarking of Relational Databases and XML Documents. In: PODS 2003: Proceedings of the 22nd ACM SIGMODSIGACT- SIGART Symposium on Principles of Database Systems, pp. 191–201. ACM Press, New York (2003)
[4] Digital Signatures in Relational Database Applications GRANDKELL systems INC. (2007), http://www.gradkell.com
[5] Cox, I.J., Miller, M.L.: A review of watermarking and the importance of perceptual modeling. In: Proc. of Electronic Imaging (February 1997)

[6] Cox, I., Bloom, J., Miller, M.: Digital Watermarking. Morgan Kaufinann, San Francisco (2001)

[7] Kiernan, J., Agrawal, R.: Watermarking Relational Databases. In: Proc. 28th International Conference on Very Large Databases VLDB (2002)

[8] Boney, L., Tewfik, A.H., Hamdy, K.N.: Digital watermarks for audio signals. In: International Conference on Multimedia Computing and Systems, Hiroshima, Japan (June 1996)

[9] Atallah, M., Wagstaff, S.: Watermarking with quadratic residues. In: Proc. Of IS&T/SPIE Conference on Security and Watermarking of Multimedia Contents (January 1999)

[10] Atallah, M., Raskin, V., Hempelman, C., Karahan, M., Sion, R., Triezenberg, K., Topkara, U.: Natural Language Watermarking and Tamper-proofing. In: The Fifth International Information Hiding Workshop, Florida, USA (2002)

[11] Hsieh, M.-S., Tseng, D.-C., Huang, Y.H.: Hiding Digital Watermarking Using Multiresolution Wavelet Transform. IEEE Trans. on Industrial Electronics 48(5) (October 2001)

[12] Shehab, M., Bertino, E., Ghafoor, A.: Watermarking Relational Databases Using Optimization Based Techniques, CERIAS Tech Report- (2006)

[13] Sion, R., Atallah, M., Fellow, IEEE, Prabhakar, S.: Rights Protection for Relational Data. IEEE Trans. on Knowledge and Data Engineering 16(6) (June 2004)

[14] Sion, R., Atallah, M., Prabhakar, S.: Rights Protection for Relational Data. IEEE Transactions on Knowledge and Data Engineering 16(6) (June 2004)

[15] Benjamin, S., Schwartz, B., Cole, R.: Accuracy of ACARS wind and temperature observations determined by collocation. Weather and Forecasting 14, 1032–1038 (1999)

[16] Bender, W., Gruhl, D., Morimoto, N.: Techniques for data hiding. In: Proc. of the SPIE. Storage and Retrieval for Image and Video Databases III, vol. 2420, pp. 164–173 (1995)

[17] Li, Y., Swarup, V., Jajodia, S.: Fingerprinting Relational Databases: Schemes and Specialties. IEEE Transactions on Dependable and Secure Computing 02(1), 34–45 (2005)

[18] Gamal, G.H., Rashad, M.Z., Mohamed, M.A.: A Simple Watermark Technique for Relational Database. Mansoura Journal for Computer Science and Information Systems 4(4) (January 2008)

A Cell-Phone Based Brain-Computer Interface for Communication in Daily Life

Yu-Te Wang, Yijun Wang, and Tzyy-Ping Jung

Swartz Center for Computational Neuroscience, Institute for Neural Computational
University of California, San Diego
La Jolla, CA, USA
{yute,yijun,jung}@sccn.ucsd.edu

Abstract. Moving a brain-computer interface from a laboratory demonstration to real-life applications poses severe challenges to the BCI community. Recently, with advances in the biomedical sciences and electronic technologies, the development of a mobile and online BCI has obtained increasing attention in the past decade. A mobile and wireless BCI based on customized Electroencephalogram recording and signal processing modules has the advantage of ultimate portability, wearability and usability. This study integrates a mobile and wireless EEG system and a signal-process platform based on a Bluetooth-enabled cell-phone into a truly wearable BCI. Its implications for BCI were demonstrated through a case study in which the cell-phone was programmed to assess steady-state, visual-evoked potentials in response to flickering visual stimuli to make a phone call directly. The results of this study on ten normal healthy volunteers suggested that the proposed BCI system enabled EEG monitoring and on-line processing of unconstrained subjects in real-world environments.

Keywords: Brain-computer interface (BCI), Electroencephalogram (EEG), Steady-state Visual-evoked potentials (SSVEP), Wireless data transmission.

1 Introduction

Brain-computer interface (BCI) systems acquire electroencephalography (EEG) signals from the human brain and translate them into digital commands which can be recognized and processed on a computer or computers using advanced algorithms [1]. BCIs can provide a new interface for the users suffering from motor disabilities to control assistive devices such as wheelchairs. Over the past two decades, different features of EEG signals such as mu/beta rhythms, event-related P300 potentials, and visual evoked potentials (VEP) have been used in BCI studies. Among these different BCI regimes, the VEP-based BCI has obtained increasing attention due to its advantages including high information transfer rate (ITR), little user training, low user variation, and ease of use [2].

Steady-state visual evoked potential (SSVEP) is the electrical response of the brain to the flickering visual stimulus at a repetition rate higher than 6 Hz [3]. The SSVEP is characterized by an increase in amplitude at the stimulus frequency, which makes it

F.L. Wang et al. (Eds.): AICI 2010, Part II, LNAI 6320, pp. 233–240, 2010.

possible to detect the stimulus frequency based on the measurement of SSVEPs. The frequency coding approach has been widely used in SSVEP-based BCI systems [4]-[9]. In such a system, each visual target is flickering at a different frequency. The system can recognize the gaze target of the user by detecting the dominant frequency of the SSVEP. Although robustness of the system performance has been demonstrated in many laboratory studies, moving this BCI system from a laboratory demonstration to real-life applications still poses severe challenges to the BCI community [9]. To design a practical BCI system, the following issues need to be addressed: (1) ease of use, (2) reliable system performance, (3) low-cost hardware and software. Recently, with advances in the biomedical sciences and electronic technologies, the development of a mobile and online BCI has been put on the agenda [10].

In real-life applications, BCI systems should not use a bulky, wired EEG acquisition device and signal processing platform [11]. Using these devices will not only uncomfortable and inconvenient for the users, but will also affect their ability to perform routine tasks in real life. Furthermore, signal processing of BCI systems should be in real-time instead of off-line analysis. Several studies have demonstrated the use of portable devices for BCIs [12]-[17]. Lin et al. [12] proposed a portable BCI system that can acquire and analyze EEG signals with a custom DSP module for real-time monitoring. Shyu et al. [17] proposed a system to combine an EEG acquisition circuit with an FPGA-based real-time signal processer. To the best of our knowledge, a cell-phone-based online BCI platform has not been reported.

This study aimed to integrate a wearable and wireless EEG system [12] with a mobile phone to implement an SSVEP-based BCI. The system consists of a four-channel biosignal acquisition/amplification module, a wireless transmission module, and a Bluetooth-enabled cell-phone. This study also demonstrates its implications in a case study in which wearers' EEG signals were used to directly make a phone call. Real-time data processing was implemented and carried out on a regular cell-phone. In a normal office environment, an average information transfer rate (ITR) of 28.47 bits/min was obtained from ten healthy subjects.

2   Methods

2.1   System Hardware Diagram

A typical VEP-based BCI that uses frequency coding consists of three parts: visual stimulator, EEG recording device, and signal processing unit [2]. The basic scheme of the proposed mobile and wireless BCI system is shown in Fig. 1. The hardware of this system consists mainly of three major components: a stimulator, an EEG acquisition unit and a mobile cell-phone.

The visual stimulator comprises a 21-inch CRT monitor (140Hz refresh rate 800x600 screen resolution) with a 4 x 3 stimulus matrix constituting a virtual telephone keypad which includes digits 0-9, BACKSPACE and ENTER. The stimulus frequencies ranged from 9Hz to 11.75Hz with an interval of 0.25Hz between two consecutive digits. The stimulus program was developed in Microsoft Visual C++ using the Microsoft DirectX 9.0 framework.

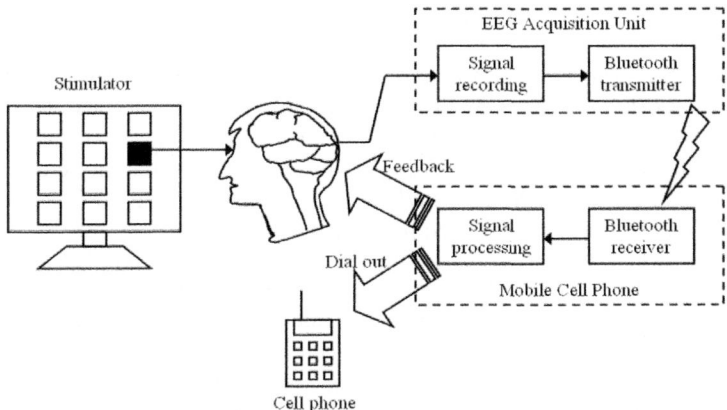

Fig. 1. System diagram of mobile and wireless BCI

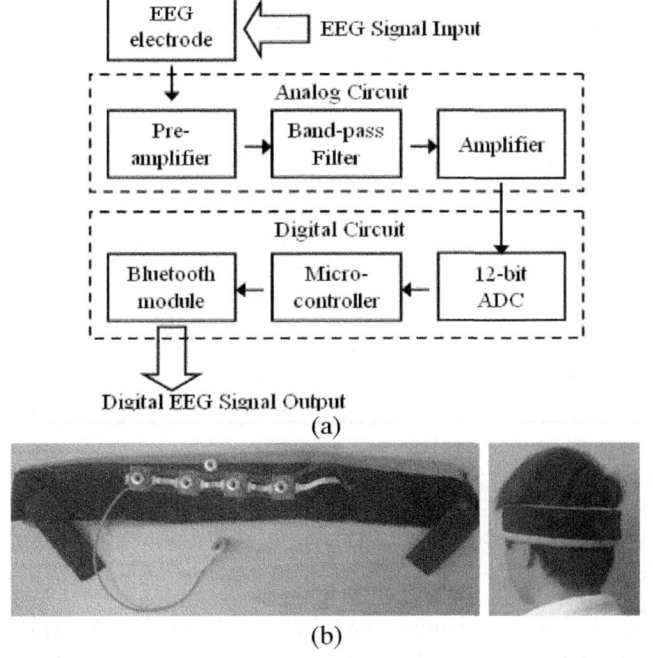

Fig. 2. (a) Block diagram of the EEG acquisition unit, (b) an EEG headband with an embedded data acquisition and wireless telemetry unit

The EEG acquisition unit is a 4-channel wearable bio-signal acquisition unit. Fig. 2(a) shows the data flow of EEG acquisition unit [11]. EEG signals were amplified (8,000x) by instrumentation amplifiers, Band-pass filtered (0.01-50 Hz), and digitized by analog-to-digital converters (ADC) with a 12-bit resolution. To reduce the number of wires for high-density recordings, the power, clocks, and measured signals were daisy-chained from one node to another with bit-serial outputs. That is, adjacent nodes (electrodes) are connected together to (1) share the power, reference voltage, and ADC clocks, and (2) daisy-chain the digital outputs. Next, TI MSP430 was used as a controller to digitize EEG signals using ADC via serial peripheral interface with a sampling rate of 128Hz. The digitized EEG signals were then transmitted to a data receiver such as a cell-phone via a Bluetooth module. In this study, Bluetooth module BM0203 was used. The whole circuit was integrated into a headband (Fig. 2(b)). The specifications of the EEG acquisition unit are listed in Table 1.

Data processing unit was realized using a Nokia N97 (Nokia Inc.) cell-phone. A J2ME program developed in Borland JBuilder2005 and Wireless Development Kit 2.2 were installed to perform online procedures including (1) displaying EEG signals in time-domain or frequency-domain on the screen, (2) band-pass filtering, (3) estimating power spectrum of the VEP using fast Fourier transform (FFT), (4) presenting auditory feedback to the user, and (5) phone dialing. The resolution of the 3.5-in touch screen of the phone is 640 x 360 pixels.

Table 1. Specification of EEG acquisition unit

Type	Example
Channel Number	4
System Voltage	3V
Gain	8,000
Bandwidth	0.01~50 Hz
ADC Resolution	12bits
Output Current	29.5mA
Battery	Lithium 3.7V 450mAh 15~33hr
Full Scale Input Range	577μV
Sampling	128Hz
Input Impedance	greater than 10MΩ
Common Mode Rejection Ratio	77dB
System Voltage	88dB
Gain	18mm x 20mm, 25mm x 40mm

2.2 System Software Design

When the program is launched, the connection to the EEG acquisition unit would be automatically established in a few seconds. The EEG raw data are transferred, plotted, and updated every second on the screen. Since the sampling rate is 128 Hz, the screen displays about 4-sec of data at any given time. Fig. 3(a) shows a snapshot of the screen of the cell-phone while it was plotting the raw EEG data in the time-domain. Users can switch the way of displaying from time-domain to frequency-domain by pressing the "shift" + "0" button at the same time. Under the frequency-domain display mode, the power spectral density of each channel will be plotted on the screen and updated every second, as shown in Fig. 3(b). An auditory and visual feedback would be presented to the user once the dominant frequency of the SSVEP is detected by the program. For example, when number 1 was detected by the system, the digit "1" would be shown at the bottom of the screen and "ONE" would be said at the same time.

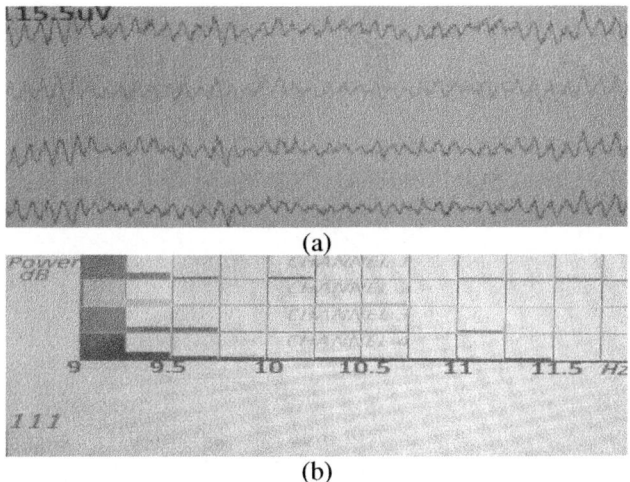

Fig. 3. Screen snapshots of the cell-phone's GUI: (a) A time-domain display of the 4-channel EEG, (b) Estimated power spectral density of the EEG when number '1' was attended.

Fig. 4 shows the flow chart of the program. First, the program initiates a connection to the EEG acquisition unit. Next, four-channel raw EEG data are band-pass filtered at 8-20 Hz, and then plotted on the screen every second. The display can be switched to the power spectrum display mode by pressing "shift" + "0" buttons simultaneously, as shown in Fig. 3. A 512-point FFT is applied to the EEG data using a 4-sec. moving window advancing at 1-sec. steps for each channel. To improve the reliability, a target is detected only when the same dominant frequency is detected in two consecutive windows (at time k, and k+1 seconds, k≥4). The subjects are instructed to shift their gaze to the next target (digit) flashed on the screen once they are cued by the auditory feedback.

2.3 BCI Experiment Design

Ten volunteers with normal or corrected to normal vision participated in this experiment. The experiment was run in a typical office room. Subjects were seated in a comfortable chair at a distance of about 60 cm to the screen. Four electrodes on the EEG headband were placed around the O1/O2 area, all referred to a forehead midline electrode.

At the beginning of the experiment, each subject was asked to gaze at some specific digits to confirm the wireless connection between the EEG headband and the cell-phone. Based on the power spectra of the EEG data, the channel with the highest signal-to-noise ratio was selected for online target detection. The test session began after a couple of short practice session. The task was to input a 10-digit phone number: 123 456 7890, followed by an ENTER key to dial the number. Incorrect key detection could be removed by a gaze shift to the "BACKSPACE" key. The percentage accuracy and ITR [1] were used to evaluate the performance of the cell-phone based BCI.

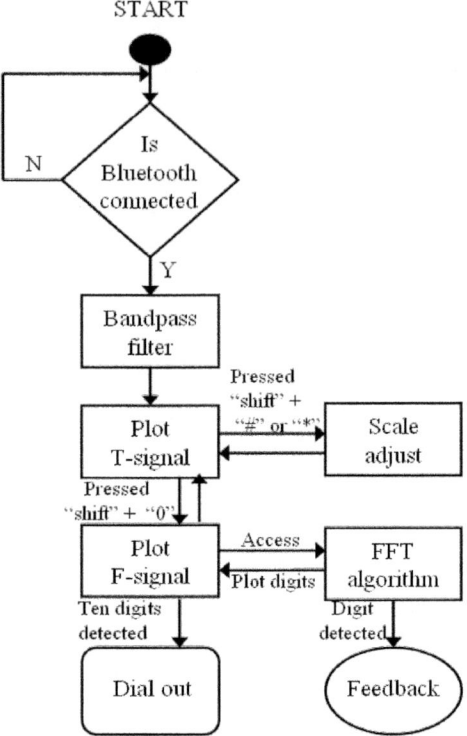

Fig. 4. The flow chart of the program coded on the cell-phone. T-signal refers to the time-domain display, and F-signal refers to the frequency-domain display.

3 Results

Table 2 shows the results of the EEG-based phone-dialing experiments. All subjects completed the EEG-based phone-dialing task with an average accuracy of 95.9±7.4%,

Table 2. Online test results of 10 subjects

Subject	Input length	Time(sec.)	Accuracy (%)	ITR
Y.T.	11	72	100	32.86
C.	11	72	100	32.86
A.	19	164	78.9	14.67
Y.B.	11	73	100	32.4
T.P.	17	131	82.4	17.6
T.	11	67	100	35.31
W.	11	72	100	32.86
B.	13	93	92.3	20.41
F.	11	79	100	29.95
D.	11	66	100	35.85
Mean	12.6	88.9	95.9	28.47

and an average time of 88.9 seconds. 7 subjects successfully inputted 11 targets without any error. The average ITR was 28.47 ± 7.8 bits/min, which was comparable to other VEP BCIs implemented on a high-end personal computer [4].

4 Conclusions and Discussion

This study detailed the design, development, and testing of a truly mobile and wireless BCI for communication in daily life. A lightweight, battery-powered, and wireless EEG headband was used to acquire and transmit EEG data of unconstrained subjects in real-world environments. The acquired EEG data were received by a regular cell-phone through Bluetooth. Signal-processing algorithms and graphic-user interface were developed and tested to make a phone call based on the SSVEPs in responses to frequency-encoded visual stimuli. The results of this study concluded that all of the participants, with no or little practicing, could make phone calls through this SSVEP-based BCI system in a natural environment.

Despite such successes, there is room for improvement. Future directions include: (1) the use of dry EEG electrodes over the scalp locations covered with hairs to avoid skin preparation and the use of conductive gels; and (2) the use of multi-channel EEG signals to enhance the accuracy and ITR of the BCI [18], as opposed to manually selecting a single channel from the recordings.

It is worth noting that, in the current study, the cell-phone was programmed to assess wearers' SSVEPs for making a phone call, but it can actually be programmed to function in ways appropriate for other BCI applications. In essence, this study is just a demonstration of a cell-phone based platform technology that can enable and/or facilitate numerous BCI applications in real-world environments.

Acknowledgments. This work is supported by a gift from Abraxis Bioscience Inc.

References

1. Wolpaw, J.R., Birbaumer, N., McFarland, D.J., Pfurtscheller, G., Vaughan, T.M.: Brain-computer interfaces for communication and control. Clin. Neurophysiol. 113(6), 767–791 (2002)
2. Wang, Y.J., Gao, X.R., Hong, B., Jia, C., Gao, S.: Brain-computer interfaces based on visual evoked potentials - Feasibility of practical system designs. IEEE Eng. Med. Biol. 27, 64–71 (2008)
3. Regan, D.: Human Brain Electrophysiology: Evoked Potentials and Evoked Magnetic Fields in Science and Medicine. Elsevier, New York (1989)
4. Cheng, M., Gao, X.R., Gao, S.G., Xu, D.F.: Design and implementation of a brain-computer interface with high transfer rates. IEEE T. Bio-Med. Eng. 49, 1181–1186 (2002)
5. Wang, Y., Wang, R.P., Gao, X.R., Hong, B., Gao, S.K.: A practical VEP-based brain-computer interface. IEEE Tr. Neur. Sys. Rehab. 14(2), 234–239 (2006)
6. Valbuena, D., Cyriacks, M., Friman, O., Volosyak, I., Graser, A.: Brain-computer interface for high-level control of rehabilitation robotic systems. In: 10th IEEE Int. Conf. Rehab. Robot., pp. 619–625 (2007)

7. Jia, C., Xu, H.L., Hong, B., Gao, X.R., Zhang, Z.G., Gao, S.K.: A human computer interface using SSVEP-based BCI technology. In: Schmorrow, D.D., Reeves, L.M. (eds.) HCII 2007 and FAC 2007. LNCS (LNAI), vol. 4565, pp. 113–119. Springer, Heidelberg (2007)
8. Muller-Putz, G.R., Pfurtscheller, G.: Control of an electrical prosthesis with an SSVEP-based BCI. IEEE T. Biomed. Eng. 55(1), 361–364 (2008)
9. Wang, Y., Gao, X., Hong, B., Gao, S.: Practical designs of brain-computer interfaces based on the modulation of EEG rhythms. In: Graimann, B., Pfurtscheller, G. (eds.) Invasive and Non-Invasive Brain-Computer Interfaces. Springer, Heidelberg (2009)
10. Lin, C.T., Ko, L.W., Chiou, J.C., Duann, J.R., Chiu, T.W., Huang, R.S., Liang, S.F., Jung, T.P.: A noninvasive prosthetic platform using mobile and wireless EEG. Proc. IEEE 96(7), 1167–1183 (2008)
11. Lin, C.T., Ko, L.W., Chang, M.H., Duann, J.R., Chen, J.Y., Su, T.P., Jung, T.P.: Review of Wireless and Wearable Electroencephalogram Systems and Brain-Computer Interfaces - A Mini-Review. Gerontology 56, 112–119 (2010)
12. Lin, C.T., Chen, Y.C., Chiu, T.T., Ko, L.W., Liang, S.F., Hsieh, H.Y., Hsu, S.H., Duan, J.R.: Development of Wireless Brain Computer Interface With Embedded Multitask Scheduling and its Application on Real-Time Driver's Drowsiness Detection and Warning. IEEE T. Biomed. Eng. 55, 1582–1591 (2008)
13. Gao, X.R., Xu, D.F., Cheng, M., Gao, S.K.: A BCI-based environmental controller for the motion-disabled. IEEE T. Neur. Sys. Reh. 11, 137–140 (2003)
14. Edlinger, G., Krausz, G., Laundl, F., Niedermayer, I., Guger, C.: Architectures of laboratory-PC and mobile pocket PC brain-computer interfaces. In: Proc. 2nd Int. IEEE EMBS Conf. Neural Eng., Arlington, VA, pp. 120–123 (2005)
15. Whitchurch, K., Ashok, B.H., Kumaar, R.V., Sarukesi, K., Varadan, V.K.: Wireless system for long term EEG monitoring of absence epilepsy. Biomed. Appl. Micro. Nanoeng. 4937, 343–349 (2002)
16. Obeid, Nicolelis, M.A.L., Wolf, P.D.: A multichannel telemetry system for signal unit neural recording. J. Neurosci. Methods 133, 33–38 (2003)
17. Shyu, K.K., Lee, P.L., Lee, M.H., Lin, M.H., Lai, R.J., Chiu, Y.J.: Development of a Low-Cost FPGA-Based SSVEP BCI Multimedia Control System. IEEE T. Biomed. Circ. S, 4125–132 (2010)
18. Bin, G.Y., Gao, X.R., Yan, Z., Hong, B., Gao, S.K.: An online multi-channel SSVEP-based brain-computer interface using a canonical correlation analysis method. J. Neural. Eng. 6 (2009)

DCISL: Dynamic Control Integration Script Language

Qingshan Li[1], Lei Wang[1], Hua Chu[1], and Shaojie Mao[2]

[1] Software Engineering Institute, Xidian Univ., Xi'an, China, 710071
[2] Key Laboratory of Science and Technology for National Defense of C4ISR Technology,
Nanjing, 210007
{qshli,lwang,hchu,sjmao}@mail.xidian.edu.cn

Abstract. This paper studies a script language DCISL for the dynamic control integration of the MAS (Multi-Agent System), which is used to describe the integration rules based on service flow. With the analysis of MAS-related language elements and combination of formalized description method and structure tool, this paper provides the definition of DCISL and realization of DCISL interpreter. DCISL uses the way of unifying the logistic definition and separating the physical realization to describe the MAS integration rules. Through the script interpreter, the integration rules between service agents which are described in DCISL are mapped into behavior logic between service agents, and by using the interpreting mechanism of the script interpreter, the dynamic script switch is realized. Through the interpreter within the service agents, the integration rules within the agents which are described in DCISL are mapped into the behavior logic between function agents, and according to the contract net protocol, the service agents interact with CMB (Common Message Blackboard) to realize the dynamic bid inviting. Ultimately, the experiment shows that the agents can run independently according to the integration logic based on the integration rules which are described in DCISL and eventually realizes the cooperation between agents and the dynamic integration control of agents system by using of the script switch and bid inviting mechanism.

Keywords: Script language; Service flow; System integration; Dynamic integration.

1 Introduction

With the emergence and development of Agent research, MAS is a practical idea to solve the communication, coordination and management between each isolated application system, so as to achieve the purpose of system integration. In ABS (Agent-Based System), each member of Agent often has incomplete information and problem solving ability. To solve complex problems, they were flexibly and dynamically integrated in accordance with the logical rules as a separate "MAS". Every Agent completes their respective work according to logical rules, achieves the interaction of ability between the Agents, and completes the complex task. Such process is the Agent System Integration. And the logical rules which reflect the order of the implementation of each Agent were known as Agent System Integration Rules.

F.L. Wang et al. (Eds.): AICI 2010, Part II, LNAI 6320, pp. 241–248, 2010.

Integration rules are customized and described by scripting language, analyzed by script parser, and distributed by script interpreter. However, in reality, the integration needs are constantly changing. Different needs have different integration rules to correspond them. So they need a scripting language to support the ever-changing of integration rules without affecting the operation of their systems. There are existing scripting languages, such as Python, Perl, Ruby, BPEL, etc. Issues need a scripting language, based services-based integration rules, have language elements to support MAS structure and dynamic control integrated, and describe the integration rules among and within Agents. However the above scripting language can not meet the needs.

In order to meet the needs of issue, this paper defines a dynamic control integration language DCISL, which adopts the approach unified in logic and separate in physical to define ABS integration rules. Integration developers, based on DCISL, can describe the integration rules between the service Agents and map them to the Service Agent logic of behavioral change by the once-interpretation and multi-operation explanation mechanism of script interpreter; and they can describe the integration rules within the service Agents and map them to function Agent behavioral change by the mechanism of Agent. Finally Agent system integration task was completed flexibly and dynamically.

2   Script-Based Control Strategy for Dynamic Integration

2.1   Service Integration Rules

Formation of service integration rules were shown in Fig.1. Aiming at business analysis, we extract a series of business processes, from which each service is took out to store and model unrelated process model. After users extract integration needs, integration developers come to integration logic by logically abstracting those needs. According to integration logic, services are integrated to the service process to form the executable process model of service-related. Then process model are mapped to script.

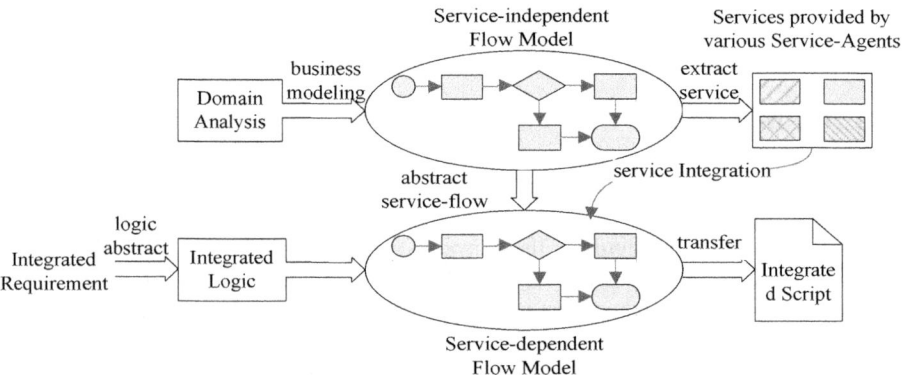

Fig. 1. Service-based Integrated Model

2.2 Script-Based Dynamic Integration

Script-based integration strategy is once-interpretation and multi-implementation. Relations between Agents, gained by interpreting integration script only once, are distributed to the Agents participating in the integration. Participants of integration take integration rules as their own knowledge to control the Collaboration with other. It was shown in Fig.2. Script integration describes the collaboration between tasks A, B, C, D which decompose from integration needs. By inquiring CRC, we can get Agent a, Agent b, Agent c, Agent d which complete tasks A, B, C, D respectively. After using script interpreter to explain script, we can obtain the following task collaborative relations: A→B, A→C, B→D, C→D. Then the generated integration rules are distributed to their corresponding Agent. When Agents received their corresponding rules, they will complete integration needs autonomously in accordance with the collaborative relations in Fig. 2.

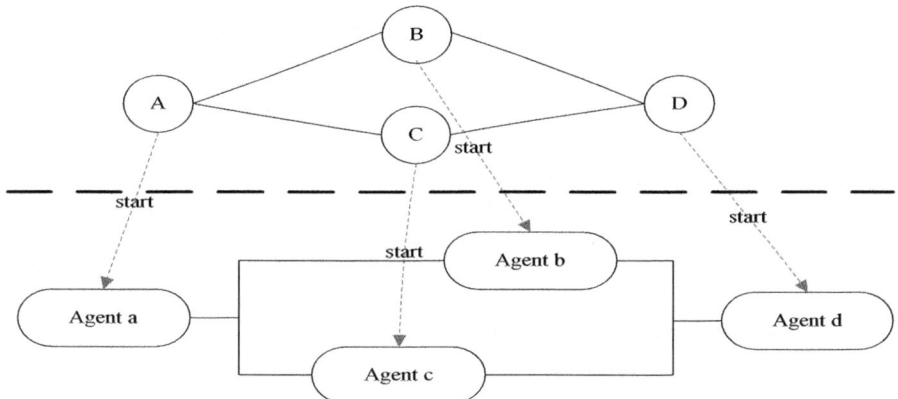

Fig. 2. Integration script mapping

3 Design of DCISL

3.1 DCISL Overall Design

DCISL adopts the approach unified in logic and separate in physical achievement. It uses a language DCISL in logic and adopts two processes in the physical achievement to achieve in accordance with the control object of the script. Between service Agents, using the script editor to write scripts, using the lexical syntax analyzers and script parser to convert script to integrated control commands, service Agents send these commands to their corresponding service Agents; Fig.3 is the structure of DCISL.

3.2 Grammar of DCISL

A complete integration rules within service Agents based on DCISL includes two parts: statement and rule definition. The part of statement (INIT_SECTION) mainly state the variables necessary in rule definition; and the part of rule definition (CONTROL_SECTION) focuses on the definition of interaction logic between Agents.

```
expression_statement and declaration_statement.
expression_statement→function;
function→identifier   OPEN_PAR   CLOSE_PAR              (1)
| identifier OPEN_PAR   paramlist   CLOSE_PAR ;
paramlist→_expression                                  (2)
| paramlist COMMA _expression ;
_expression→simple_expression
          | identifier DOT identifier
| OPEN_PAR _expression CLOSE_PAR
|_expression EQUAL _expression
 | _expression N_EQUAL _epression
| function  ;
```

The expression statement mainly describes the function call statement of the DCISL language. Production (1) describes the grammar structure of function operation; Production (2) is the parameter list of function, including a list of sub-tasks and logical expressions. The `declaration_statement` mainly defines the variables needed in the definition of control integration rule and gives them initial statement.

3.3 Design of DCISL Parser and Interpreter

When parsing Script file, the DCISL parser automatically establishes two grammar trees. Firstly, according to the definition of all sub-tasks in the part of TASK_SECTION, the DCISL parser establishes one task-tree; secondly, according to the execution logic of all sub-tasks that is defined in the part of RULE_SECTION, the DCISL parser establishes one rule-tree. Two grammar trees have uniform node structure, and its definition is shown as follows:

```
struct Node{
int type;            //type of this node
char *value;         //value of this node
struct Node *child;   //point to its first child
struct Node *brother; //point to its brother
struct Node *secchild; //point to its second child
struct Node *father;  //point to its pre-node
... ...
};
```

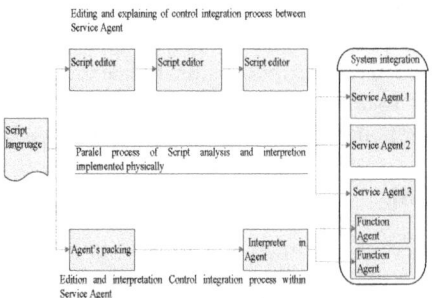

Fig. 3. System Structure of DCISL

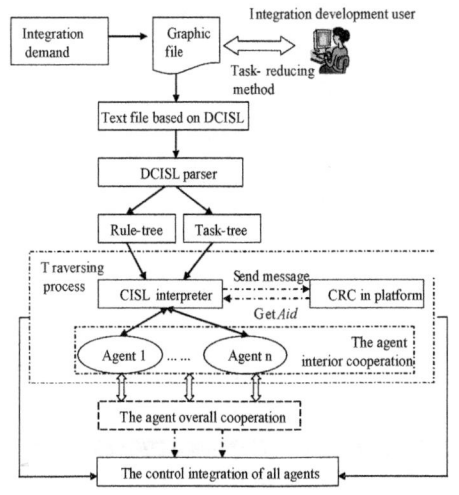

Fig. 4. The Analysis and interpretation mechanism of DCIS

Fig. 5. The control integration process within *InputGatherService* Agent

The premise of interpretation is that the text file (*.txt) has been parsed to intermediate XML document and it does not have any morphology mistakes and grammar mistakes. Interpretation of the DCISL file is one process of traversing all nodes of two grammar trees, and it starts from the first node of rule-tree and extracts the corresponding capacity name and interactive information that is pre-information and post-information. In terms of the value of each rule-tree node, it carries out inquiries to the CRC. If the corresponding Agent exists, it will be informed to join in the implementation of integrated tasks. When the Agent of this node completes its tasks, the tasks and data will be transferred to a successive Agent. If the corresponding Agent does not exist, the Agent will send tenders to the CMB until an Agent which can complete the task is added.

4 Experiment and Analysis

4.1 Integration Example Based on DCISL

We took the integration of five modules as the integration goal to be tested. These modules belong to BCDSS and they are independent, and they include the Radar module, Infrared module, InputGather module, Handler module and Show module. Firstly, we utilize the agent packing tool to wrap these modules as Service agents and Function agents, define the control integration process within Service Agents which was shown in Fig.5, and then these agents were registered in the control platform. Then we decomposed the integration goal into five independent sub-tasks: RadarTask, InfraredTask, InputGatherTask, HandlerTask and ShowTask. Secondly, we defined the integration rule in the DCISL Text editor which was shown in Fig.6; then, we saved this text rule as "test.txt". Thirdly, we used the DCISL parser to check our integration rule of between service Agents, and generate the intermediate file as "test.xml". The partial integration rule was shown as follows:

```
TASK_SECTION  //the definition part of all sub-tasks
TASK RadarTask  // the sub-tasks name definition
 CAPABILITY MCRadar//the MC definition
END_TASK //the end symbol of RadarTask definition
...      ... ... //definition of other sub-tasks
RULE_SECTION //the rule definition of all sub-tasks
LOOP    //all sub-tasks will be executed circularly
[EXECUTE RadarTask] //execution of RadarTask
AND //RadarTask and InfraredTask are coordinate
[ EXECUTE InfraredTask ]
      EXECUTE    IGTask    //execution of IGTask
... ... ...
END_LOOP //the end symbol of loop definition
END_SCRIPT //the end symbol of all definition
```

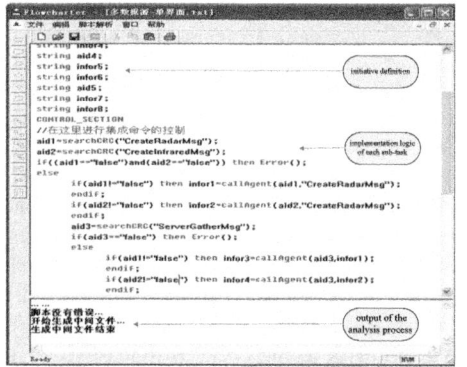

Fig. 6. The integration rule

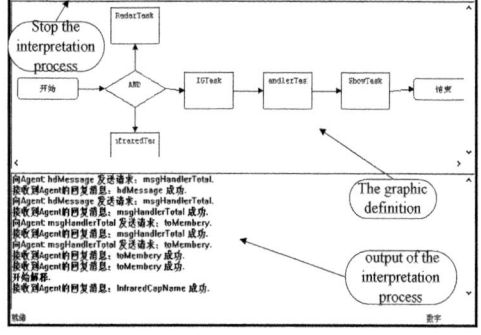

Fig. 7. The DCISL interpretation process

Then, we opened the DCISL interpreter, loaded and interpreted the XML file "test.xml". The integration rule defined in the intermediate file could act on each agent, and its interpretation process was shown in Fig.7. When the interpretation process is successful, we could get the integration result that was shown in Figure4.4. At this time, the agent cooperation was realized, and the Radar agent and the Infrared agent respectively detected their targets and then transmitted their information to other agents. Finally, these information were shown in the screen.

4.2   The Contrast between DCISL and MXML

DCISL and MXML are both used to define the integration rule of agent system. In view of the integration process that uses DCISL to define the integration rule and the integration process that uses MXML to define the integration rule, we did two contrasts in the fact of the completion efficiency and the communication rate.

Firstly, according to the BCDSS, we made one contrast of the completion efficiency of sub-tasks. To each agent, it needs some time to complete its sub-task, so the completion efficiency of sub-tasks is defined as the ratio of quality to time. In

BCDSS, one sub-task can be completed on time or not. In this case, we just calculated the efficiency of sub-tasks (*V*) finished successfully, the quality (*Q*) is 1 and the efficiency value is the reciprocal of time (*T*) that could be defined as: $V=1/T$. Fig.8 shows the contrast of DCISL and the traditional MXML in the fact of the completion efficiency of sub-tasks. The sub-task number increases from 1 to 10.

Fig.9 shows that, when finishing the same Sub-tasks, the time of the traditional MXML takes is more than that of the DCISL. With the increment of the ST number, MXML requires more and more time spending. The reason is that, in the MXML, each agent needs continually check its operation premise that is defined in the integration logic based on XML. And it is necessary to analyze the return message to determine its operation.

Secondly, we made one contrast of the communication rate. The time of communication among agents per second is defined as the communication rate (*V*), and it can be defined as $V=m/t$, and m is the communication number and t is the time. The contrast of MXML and DCISL in the fact of the communication rate can be shown in Fig. 9, and the sub-tasks number increases from 1 to 20.

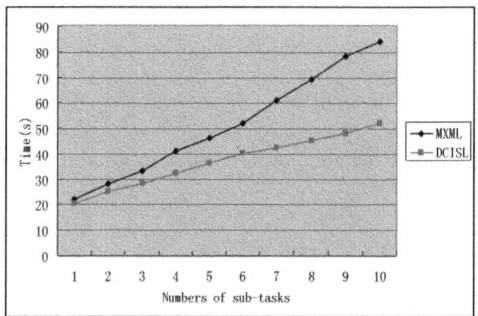

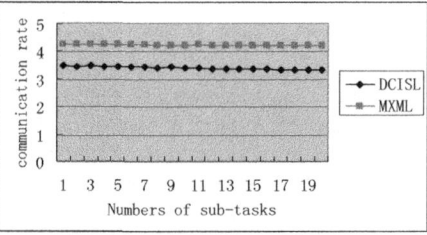

Fig. 9. The contrast of MXML and DCISL in the fact of the communication rate

Fig. 8. The contrast of DCISL and MXML in the fact of the completion efficiency of sub-tasks

The above contrast shows, when finishing the same sub-tasks, the communication rate of DCISL is less than that of the traditional MXML, and the difference becomes obvious with the increase of sub-tasks. This result proves that, with the increment of ST number, MXML needs more communications to realize its integration goal. Thus, the integration that uses MXML to define the integration rule needs more system spending and DCISL has great efficiency.

5   Conclusion

For the dynamic integration demand of Agent System, in this paper DCISL language used for ABS control integration is designed, the text script editing and the script editing visual environment was realized to edit integrated rules, and also the script language parser and interpreter was realized. The thinking of service flow and capacity hierarchical were applied to the process of Agent System's integration. A close coupling between integrated rules based on the definition controlling integrated scripting language and integrated Agent module is produced. And the use of scripting dynamic switching and dynamic bidding makes processing all dynamic situations realized, thereby makes the explanation of implementation more efficiently, stability and reliable and easier for integrated developing users to use.

Acknowledgment

This work is supported by the Defense Pre-Research Project of the 'Eleventh Five-Year-Plan' of China under contract number 513060401 and the Fund of C4ISR National Defense Science and Technology Key LAB under contract number 9140C8301011001, In addition, it is supported by the 'Fundamental Research Funds for the Central Universities'.

References

1. Hu, S., Qingshan, L.: ICSL: A scripting language used for intelligent control on simulation entity. Control and Decision 20 (2005)
2. Hendler, J., Metzeger, R.: Putting it all together-the control of Agent-based systems program. IEEE Intelligent Systems and their applications 14 (March 1999)
3. Tambe, M., Pynadath, D., Chauvat, N.: Building dynamic Agent organizations in cyberspace. IEEE Internet Computing 4(2), 65–73 (2000)
4. Wekman, K.: Using negotiation and coordination systems. In: Proceeding of 12th International Joint Conference on Artificial Intelligence, pp. 187–198 (1991)
5. Maximilien, E.M., Singh, M.P.: Agent-based architecture for autonomic web service selection. In: Proc. of the 1st International Workshop on Web Services and Agent Based Engineering, Sydney, Australia (July 2003)
6. Kuo, J.Y.: A Document-driven Agent-based Approach for Business Process Management. Information and Software Technology 46, 373–382 (2004)
7. Liang, W.Y., Huang, C.C.: The Agent-based Collaboration Information System of Product Development. International Journal of Information Management 22, 211–224 (2002)
8. Boudriga, N., Obaidat, M.: Intelligent Agents on the Web: A Review. Computing in Science and Engineering, 35–42 (July/August 2004)
9. Trappey, A.J.C., Trappey, C.V., Lin, F.T.L.: Automated Silicon Intellectual Property Trade Using Mobile Agent Technology. Robotics and CIM 22, 189–202 (2006)
10. Gao, P., Chen, C., Pan, Y.H.: One AOP Programming Language and Its Realization. In: Proc. of the 5th China Artificial Intelligence (October 1998)

Mapping Multi-view Architecture Products to Multi-agent Software Architecture Style

Zhongxue Li, Haiming Zhong, and Xike Wang

Dept. of Logistic Information Engineering, Logistic Engineering University,
Chongqing, China, 401311
lzxcq@sina.com, zhm614@sina.com, wxkwxkwang@163.com

Abstract. Multi-view architecture products describe the requirement connotation of complex information system explicitly and reflect the essence of problem domain. Agent organization gives a good idea in solving problem domain in course of its integrated and intelligent. This paper takes the DOD AF operational view products for example to combine with their merits. After the formalized expression of operational view products relating to organization abstract model, some mapping rules to mapping operational view products to organization abstract model were suggested. Then using the social network analysis method, a way of mapping organization abstract model to multi-agent software architecture style according to Pearson correlation coefficients was set up. In the end, an example was set up to validate the feasibility of this approach. This work can integrate the system requirements and multi-agent software architecture. It shortened the gap between system's top-design and its implementation, at the same time, it improved the system adaptability.

Keywords: multi-view architecture products, agent organization, software architecture style, mapping.

1 Introduction

Multi-view architecture provides a standardized expression language and unified description methods for the developing of complex information system. It offers a feasible method to solve complex problems and ensures the system's top design, which is beneficial to the interconnection, intercommunication and interoperation between complex information systems. Multi-view architecture products mainly focus on the organization and the structure of system. They can ensure a comprehensive and consistent top-level framework and provide guidance for the developing of complex information system. Multi-view architecture products mainly describe system's problem domain, while the agent technology provides a good solution for the problem domain. However, in practice, with the increasing of the degree of system complexity and the number of agent, the coordination of agent system becomes more difficult. To understand multi-agent system from the perspective of software architecture, which recognizes multi-agent system as a new style of software architecture[1] [2], it is conducive to solve the problem domain.

F.L. Wang et al. (Eds.): AICI 2010, Part II, LNAI 6320, pp. 249–258, 2010.

Multi-view architecture products can be used as the starting point to obtain the system requirements. To build the system with multi-view architecture products and implement the system with agent technology, this method ensures the integration efficiency and better adaptability of system. At present, there is little research on building the information system which combines with multi-view architecture products and agent organization. Some scholars proposed to use the multi-view architecture products in the agent-based modeling and simulation systems[3][4]. It extracts relevant data from architecture products to build individual agent by analyzing the relations between architecture products and the attributes of agent in the simulation platform. However, this work is limited to establishment of the data link between the architecture products and individual agent. The influence that architecture products take on the construction to agent-based system is not truly reflected. Therefore, research on the mapping multi-view architecture products to multi-agent software architecture style, in essence, is how to build multi-agent system with architecture products. To establish the relations between architecture products and agent-based system, it integrates architecture technology and agent technology in the construction of system. Take the DoD AF for example, this paper mainly studies mapping operational view products to multi-agent software architecture which provides a new way of building complex information systems.

2   Formal Description of Operational View Products

In order to standardize the description of operational view products and improve the accuracy, completeness as well as understandability of the description, OV-1, OV-2, OV-4 and OV-6a are complementary defined based on the existing formulations[5]. With the enrichment of data entities associated with architecture products, it can more clearly reflect their intrinsic properties.

Definition 1, High-level operational concept graphic,

$HOCG ::= < Mission, BPs, HOCs, Orgs, Res >$, where Mission denotes the set of operational missions that is a non-empty finite set. Operational missions can be divided into several operational goals. The fulfillment of operational missions depends on the implementation of operational goals. $Mission ::= \{ON\_Goals\}$. Bps shows the set of business process. HOCs shows the high-level operational idea which outlines a series concept of operational tasks. $HOC ::= < Tasks, Task\_Executors, Task\_Orders, Task\_Interactions >$, where $Tasks$ represents the set of operational tasks. Task_Executors represent the executor of operational tasks. The executor is usually an operational unit. Task_Executors $\subseteq$ Orgs. Task_Orders represents the sequence of tasks to complete operational missions. Task_Interactions represents the interactions between tasks and tasks, tasks and resources, tasks and the external systems. Org shows the set of organizations which complete the operational tasks. Res shows the resources required to complete operational tasks.

Definition 2. Operational node connectivity description,

$ONCD ::=< ONs, NLs, \sigma_{ON} >$. ONs represents the set of operational node that is a non-empty finite set. NLs represents the set of needlines. $NLs \subseteq ONs \times ONs$,$0<|NLs|<+\infty$. $NL \in NLs$. NL represents an orderly even from an operational node to another node. $\sigma_{ON} : ONs \to 2^{ONs}$. It represents the level of decomposition relations between nodes which is a parent-child relationship. The attributes of operational node includes:

$ON ::= \{ON \_ Name, ON \_ Type, ON \_ Goal, ON \_ Function, ON \_ Activities, \ ON \_ Org[, other \_ performances]\}$

ON_Name describes the name of operational node. ON_Type represents the type of operational node(internal node or external node). ON_Goal represents the set of goals which are accomplished by operational node. ON_Function represents the operational function that is finished by operational node. ON_Activities represents the set of operational activity that are implemented by operational node. ON_Org represents the organizations that operational node belongs to. other_performances represents the other attributes of operational node.

Definition 3. Organizational relationships chart, $CO ::=< C \_ Orgs, Org \_ Re >$

(1) C_Org represents the set of organizations that is a non-empty finite set. $0 <| C \_ Orgs |< +\infty$ .The attributes of organizational entity are:

$C \_ Org ::= \{Org \_ ID, Org \_ Name, Org \_ Type, Org \_ Roles, Org \_ Re s[, other \_ performances]\}$

ON_ID , ON_Name and ON_Type separately show the exclusive identification, name and type of the organization. Org_Roles represents the set of roles contained by organization. Org_Res represents the resources occupied by organization.

(2) Org_Re represents the relationship between organizations which is an orderly even from an organization to another organization. The attributes of organization are:

$Org \_ Re ::= \{Re\_ ID, Re\_ Name, Re\_ Type, From \_ Organization, \ To \_ Organization[, other \_ performances]\}$

Re_ID , Re_Name and Re_Type separately show the exclusive identification, name and type of the organization relationship. From_Organization and To_Organization separately show the source organization and the out organization which constitutes the organization relationship. The type of organization relationship mainly includes the command relationship, supervise relationship and cooperate relationship. $Re\_ Type ::= \{Command, Supervise, Cooperate\}$

Definition 4. Operational rules description

$$OR ::=< Mission \_ Rule, ON \_ Rule, OA \_ Rule[, other \_ Rule] >$$

Mission_Rule represents operational rules relating to operational mission which include regulations, operational guidelines and rules of war. Mission_Rule is the most basic and common rules of the system. ON_Rule represents operational rules relating to operational node. These rules make constraints on the connection and the state transition of operational node. OA_Rule represents operational rules relating to operational activity. These rules make constraints on the transition conditions and the transition way of operational activity. Other_Rule represents the other operational rules.

3   Mapping the Operational View Products to Organization Abstract Model

Operational view products can be used as the starting point to obtain the system requirements. In this paper, the organization requirements of multi-agent system can be obtained by them firstly, then it realizes mapping multi-agent system requirements to multi-agent software architecture style. The organization requirements of multi-agent system can be described by organization abstract model. Organization abstract model can be modeled by some abstract concepts of organization.

3.1   Organization Abstract Model

From the organizational point of view, the structure and behavior characteristics of multi-agent system can be described from a higher level with the help of some abstract concepts of organization. The developing methods of multi-agent system based on organization abstract, such as AALAADIN, Gaia, Tropos and AGR, use some abstract concepts of organization to model the system. These abstract concepts of organization include role, group, organization rule and organization pattern. These methods usually develop multi-agent system in accordance with the steps from the requirements analysis to system design. After the comprehensive comparison of these methods, this paper proposes to build an astract model in the analysis phase of system development, which is modeled by role, group and organization structure. The model which is modeled by these abstract concepts of organization and their relationship is usually called organization abstract model. Organization abstract model describes the different level of system requirement. And it also contains other abstract concepts of organization. For example, organization rules are decomposed which are defined as their properties.

Organization abstract model takes the role as the view point. And it analyzes and designs multi-agent system from the perspective of role. Role can effectively communicate with the real world and agent-based system because of its social characteristic. It can also serves as a link between real world and systems. Thus, to analyze the role and its attributes in the analysis phase of system development specify the behavior and attributes of agent in the agent-based system. And it also establishes the foundation for designing agent-based system. Describing the system requirements with organization abstract model makes it closer to real world requirement and easier for the management, analysis and design of system.

Definition 5. Role is an abstract of the combiner of responsibility, function and behavior in the organization. It is the basic unit for the construction of organization structure. It can be represented as:

$Role ::= < R\_ID, G\_S, R\_GOAL, R\_ACT, R\_ABILITY, R\_CONSTRAINT >$,where:

R_ID is the exclusive identification of role. A role in an organization is unique.

G_S represents the group which a role belongs to. For a non-empty role, it must belong to a group. A group is constituted by at least two roles.

R_Goal is a set of role goal that is a non-empty finite set. Goal means some expectation of the role. Role expects to implement some events or to achieve specific state through the activities. Role goal represents the responsibility for the role which is the main reason to define roles. And role goal is the result of the decomposition of group goal. The summation of role goal in a group is the group goal.

R _ *ABILITY* represents the set of plan ability for role. The plan ability shows that role can give a plan to accomplish a goal. A plan is consisted of a series of role goal or behavior, so each goal can accomplished by a series of goal or behavior.

R _ *ACT* represents the behavior ability for role. The behavior ability shows the behavior that can be implemented by role. The behavior ability is the inherent ability of role. The fulfillment of a role goal can be achieved by the role behavior or the co-operation between roles.

R _ *CONSTRAINT* is a set of role constraint that is a non-empty finite set. The role constraint is a specification for the role behavior. And it is also the main reason for co-operation or conflict resolution between roles. Role constraint can not be empty ,otherwise it shows the role behavior will exist without any constraints. Or it shows the role has no connection with other roles. The phenomena will not exist in the real world.

Definition 6. Group structure is a set of roles which has the common goal, same responsibility or high interactions.

$$G \_ S ::=< G \_ ID, G \_ GOAL, ROLE, R \_ RELATION, G \_ CONSTRAINT >$$

G _ *ID* is the exclusive identification of group structure that specifies a group structure.

G _ *GOAL* is a set of group structure goal that is a non-empty finite set. Group structure goal is the result of the decomposition of organization structure goal. The summation of group structure goal is the organization structure goal.

ROLE is a set of non-empty role. Group structure is constituted by at least two roles. If a group structure contains only one role, the group structure will transform into a role.

R _ *RELATION* is a set of relationships between roles in a group structure, including the command and control relations, peer relations, communication relations, inheritance and dependency relations.

G _ *CONSTRAINT* is a set of constraints for group structure that is a non-empty finite set. The constraints for group structure are the common restriction of the role behavior. These constraints standardize the rule of role behavior in the group structure.

Definition 7. Organization structure is a set of group structure which can work together to accomplish the common goal.

$$O \_ S ::=< O \_ ID, O \_ GOAL, G \_ S, G \_ RELATION, O \_ CONSTRAINT >$$

O _ *ID* is the unique identification of organization structure that specifies an organization structure.

O _ *GOAL* is a non-empty set of organization structure goal. Organization structure goal is the reason for the existence of group structure. With the decomposition of organization structure goal, the topology of organization structure can be ascertained.

G _ *S* is a non empty set of group structure. Group structure is the basic unit to constitute organization structure. An organization structure contains at least one group structure. When organization structure contains a single group structure, the organization structure will transform into a group structure.

G _ *RELATION* represents the relationships between group structures in the organization. It mainly includes two kinds of relations, aggregation relations and communication relations.

There is a recursion relation between role, group and organization structure from their definitions. Multiple roles constitute a group. Multiple groups constitute an organization structure. When group contains only a single role, it will transform into a role. The group goal becomes role goal. The constraints for group become the constraint of role. Similarly, when organization structure contains a single group, the organization structure will transform into a group. The attributes of organization structure transform into the attributes of group. So the relationship between role, group and organization structure can be recognized equivalent.

3.2 Mapping Operational View Products to Organization Abstract Model

Complex information system is composed of several organizations based on the perspective of organization. From the view of abstraction, the system is equivalent to an organization structure. Organization structure is the highest level of abstraction in the organization abstract model. Operational view products reflect the business requirement of the system. The establishment of operational node is based on the missions or operational tasks. These nodes are virtual nodes or logical nodes. Each node will accomplish specific operational task and operational function. Through the relationship between operational node and system node, we find that operational node can be implemented by one or more system. To build the system with agent technology, the system will be composed of several agents. So the similarity in structure and function exists in operational node and group structure.

Mapping rule 1-a: Operational node ON in OV-2 mapping into group structure G_S.

Mapping rule 1-b: Operational goal ON_Goal in OV-2 mapping into the set of group structure goal.

Mapping rule 2: Operational goal contained by operational missions in OV-1 mapping into organization structure goal O_GOAL.

O_GOAL is the summation of the goals of top-level operational nodes. It can be described as $O \_ GOAL \equiv \bigcup\limits_{k=1}^{n} ON \_ Goal$, n represents the number of top-level operational nodes.

Mapping rule 3: The relationships between operational nodes in OV-2 and OV-3 mapping into the relationships between group structures G_RELATION.

The typical relationships between operational nodes are the aggregation relationship and communication relationship. When a node decomposes to several sub-nodes, these nodes show a parent-child relationship. There is an aggregation relationship between the parent node and the child node. In addition, the other relationship between operational nodes is communication relationship. That indicates the information exchange exist between different operational nodes. According to mapping rule 3, the communication relationship between operational nodes can map into the relationship between group structures.

Mapping rule 4-a: Mission_Rule in OV-6a mapping into O_CONSTRAINT which belongs to organization structure.

Mission_Rule is the most basic rule of the system. It is also the common rule needed by the system. Theses rules can map into the constraint for organization structure.

The corresponding relations between operational view products and organization structure can be seen in Figure 1.

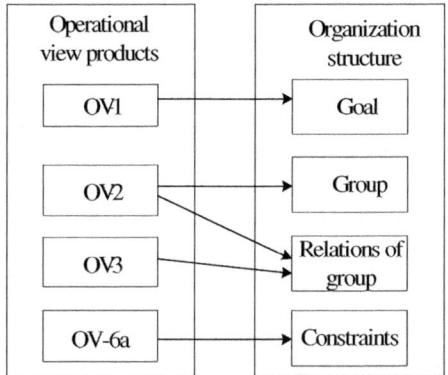

Fig. 1. Corresponding relations between operational view products and organization structure

According to the definition of group structure, it is a set of roles which has the common goal and constraints. The summation of role goal is the organization structure goal. Therefore, we can determine the role goal and their relationships based on the decomposition principle of goal. As shown in Figure 2.

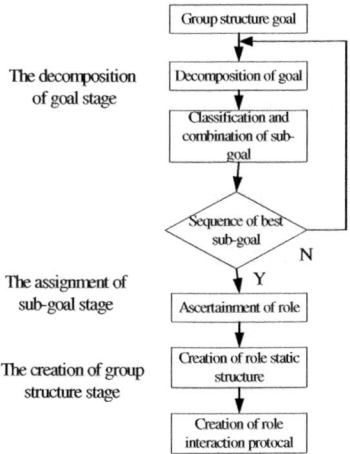

Fig. 2. The decomposing process of the goal of group

The creation of the role in a group is divided into three stages, the decomposition of goal stage, the assignment of sub-goal stage and the creation of group stage. Following these steps we can determine role and dynamic interaction relationship between roles. After that, organization abstract model of multi-agent system can be obtained.

4 Mapping Organization Abstract Model to Multi-agent Software Organization

Abstract model is a recursive model which is formed by role, group and organization structure. The smallest unit is role. Role has strong social characteristic and they can interact with each other. The interaction between roles directly determines the interaction behavior, thus affecting the overall behavior of the system. Organization abstract model can be seen as a social network composed by the role. Using social network analysis in organizational system is feasible[6].

4.1 Social Network Analysis of Architecture Style

Social network analysis comes from the human sociology. Network refers to the associations. Social network can simply posed as the structure of social relations. Social network represents a structure relationship which can reflect the social relations between actors. Social network analysis is a set of norms and methods to analysis the structure of social relations and their attributes. It mainly analyzes the structure of relations and their properties formed by different social units(individuals, groups or social) [7]. Pearson correlation coefficients are used to analyze the relations of social network. The formula is[8]:

$$r = \frac{n\sum XY - \sum X \sum Y}{\sqrt{[n\sum X^2 - (\sum X)^2][n\sum Y^2 - (\sum Y)^2]}} \tag{1}$$

Pearson correlation coefficients can be used to measure the correlation between variables. Here we use it to measure the degree of similarity between variables. X, Y is separately a vector matrix. N is the dimension of the vector matrix.

In order to compare the degree of correlation, the correlation coefficients can be divided to five grades. The value begins from -1.0 to +1.0, seen in Table 1.

Table 1. Interpretation of the correlation coefficients

-1.0 to -0.7	(--)	Strong negative correlation
-0.7 to -0.3	(-)	Partial negative correlation
-0.3 to +0.3	( )	Little or no correlation
+0.3 to +0.7	(+)	Partially positive correlation
+0.7 to +1.0	(++)	Strong positive correlation

4.2 An Example of Mapping

Structure-in-5 style, pyramid style and joint venture style are the typical multi-agent software architecture style[9]. Architecture style is formed by the components. There are interactions between components too. These components form a social network. Therefore, organization abstract model can map into multi-agent software architecture style using the social network analysis based on the structural similarity. There is a recursive relation between role, group and organization structure. Take a group for example. Figure 3 is a role interaction graph of group structure. Figure 4 shows the joint-venture style.

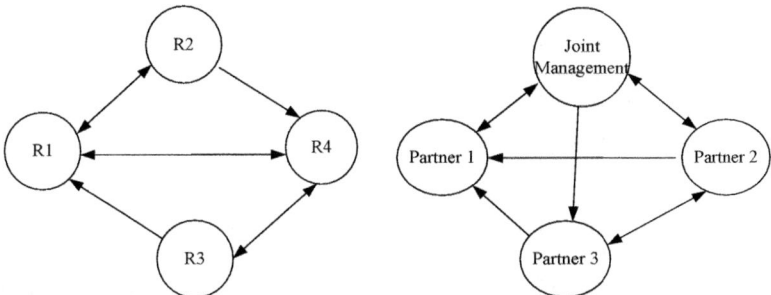

Fig. 3. Role interaction graph   **Fig. 4.** Joint Venture Style

The vector matrix can be obtained by the interactions between roles or components. Two cases will be considered separately, out-degree and in-degree, because of the bidirectional interaction between roles or components. According to the Pearson correlation coefficient, the analytic results are shown in Table 2 and Table 3.

Table 2. The correlation coefficient matrix based on out-degree

	Joint management	Partner 1	Partner 2	Partner 3
R1	0.6666	-0.4082	0.6666	0.1666
R2	-0.1666	0.6123	0.6666	-0.6666
R3	-0.1666	0.6123	0.6666	-0.6666
R4	-0.1666	0.6123	-0.1666	0.1666

Table 3. The correlation coefficient matrix based on in-degree

	Joint management	Partner 1	Partner 2	Partner 3
R1	0.6666	0.1666	-0.1666	-0.1666
R2	-0.4082	0.4082	0.6123	0.6123
R3	-0.4082	0.4082	0.6123	-0.4082
R4	0.6666	0.1666	-0.1666	0.6666

Integrating the analytic results of Table 2 and Table 3, the correlation between role and component can be obtained according to the principle of Table 1. The final result is shown in Table 4.

Table 4. The correlation matrix based between roles and components

	Joint management	Partner 1	Partner 2	Partner 3
R1	++	-		
R2	-	+	+	-
R3	-	+	+	-
R4		+		+

In order to map the role to component one by one, the conclusion are:
R1 is related to Joint management.
R2 is related to Partner 2.
R3 is related to Partner 1.
R4 is related to Partner 3.

Therefore, R1, R2, R3 and R4 can map into Joint management, Partner 2, Partner 1, Partner 3 separately. These roles are organized according to software architecture style. The software architecture will satisfy the requirements of complex information system

5   Conclusion

Research on the mapping operational view products of DoD AF to multi-agent software architecture style, it provides the possibility to integrate architecture technology and agent technology in the building of complex information system. Using this method in the system development, it can ensure the requirements and interconnection, intercommunication and interoperation of complex information system. It can also make sure the system has good ability of dynamic and adaptability to meet the actual needs.

References

1. Shehory, O.: Software architecture attributes of MAS. In: Ciancarini, P., Wooldridge, M.J. (eds.) AOSE 2000. LNCS, vol. 1957, pp. 77–90. Springer, Heidelberg (2001)
2. Kolp, M., Giorgini, P.: Multi-agent architectures as organizational structures. Autonomous Agent Multi-Agent 13(1), 3–25 (2006)
3. Zinn, A.W.: The use of integrated Architectures to Support Agent Based Simulation: An Initial Investigation, Department of the Air Force Air University, U.S, pp. 2–69 (2004)
4. De Stefano, G.V.: Agent Based Simulation SEAS Evaluation of DODAF Architecture. Department of the Air Force Air University, U.S (2004)
5. Aimin, L., Li, H., Xueshan, L.: Design on Architecture Products of C4ISR. Journal of National University of Defense Technology 28(5), 133–136 (2006)
6. Zack, M.H.: Researching organizational system using social network analysis. In: Proc of the 33rd Hawaii International conference on system sciences, Maui, Hawaii. IEEE, Los Alamitos (2000)
7. Tiankui, J.: Social Network Analysis: Theory, Methods and Application, pp. 41–45. Beijing Normal University Press, Beijing (2009)
8. Pearson Correlation Coefficient in Microsoft Excel (June 2005), http://www .bized.ac.uk/timeweb/crunching/crunch_relate_illus.htm#excelexp
9. Manuel, K., Mylopoulos, J.: Architecture styles for information systems: an organizational perspective. Dept. of Computer Science, University of Toronto, Tropos working Paper (January 2001), http://www.cs.toronto.edu/mkolp/tropos

ID-Based Authenticated Multi-group Keys Agreement Scheme for Computing Grid[*]

Xiaofeng Wang and Shangping Wang

Xi'an University of Technology, Xi'an, Shaanxi, 710048, P.R. China
xfwang66@sina.com.cn

Abstract. It has became a new active topic in grid security research fields that authentication and keys agreement between heterogeneous and dynamic grid nodes which belong to different trust domains. In this paper, an ID-based authenticated multi-group keys agreement scheme is proposed from bilinear pairings. Proposed scheme provides mutual authentication method for users that belong to different trust domains, and it employs shared password evolvement authentication mechanism that generates one-time passwords for every session. Moreover, our scheme overcomes limitations existed in some existing pairings-based authentication protocol, in which, special Hash functions are necessary. Proposed scheme can be used to generate session keys for large-scale distributed heterogeneous and dynamic grid resource.

Keywords: Computing grid, Identity authentication, Key agreement, Password evolvement.

1 Introduction

Grid [1,2] (grid computing, computational grid) is a important information technology that has developed rapidly in recent years. It is a high-performance distributed computing environment consisted of heterogeneous computers and resources that are distributed in geography. Such environment has an excellent data-processing capacity, also faced with a severe security challenge. Grid computing will not only encounter security issues such as authentication, access control, integrity, confidentiality, non-repudiation and so on, but also face unprecedented security challenges because of the large-scale distributed heterogeneous and dynamic resource increases its complexity. Grid system has the characteristics of both distributed system and parallel computing system, but is different from them because of the heterogeneous and the dynamic. Parallel computing involves hundreds of computers that belong to different trust domains. Large-scale computational resources lead to the failure to establish direct trust relationship between grid nodes. In addition, heterogeneous and dynamic characteristics require using resources in multiple management domains, dynamic resource request, complex communications structures and excellent performance and so on,

---

[*] This work was supported by the National Natural Science Foundation of China under Grant no.61075007 and no.61074077"; the Natural Science Foundation Research Plan of Shaanxi Province of China under Grant no.08JK382 and no.2009JM8004-5.

F.L. Wang et al. (Eds.): AICI 2010, Part II, LNAI 6320, pp. 259–266, 2010.

which makes it difficult to establish immovable trust relationship between grid nodes. Therefore, in addition to traditional security issues, grid security should also support authorization and key agreement between different trust domains[3,4,5].

In the past, the research on grid security is mainly focused on the certificate-based public key infrastructure (PKI), such as Globus grid security infrastructure GSI [6]. Such a system requires large capacity storage space and computing cost to generate, store, verify, revoke and manage users' public key certificates, which is impractical or impracticable for distributed heterogeneous grid environment. Recent researches show that an efficient substitute of the certificate-based PKI is Identity-based (ID-based) public key cryptography. The ID-based public key systems allow the public key of a user can be easily and publicly computed from a string associated with its identity. This characteristic avoids the necessity of using certificates.

As a pioneer, Shamir proposed the Identity-based public key cryptography [7] firstly in 1984. In subsequent 20 years, there aren't specific practical scheme until Boneh et al. [8] constructed the first identity-based encryption scheme from weil pairing. In recent years, ID-based cryptography is gradually being used to design grid security schemes [9,10,11,12,13]. However, ID-based public key systems have two inherent flaws. Firstly, there must have a global trusted party, referred to as the Private Key Generator (PKG), to generate and distribute users' private keys. This is impractical or impracticable for the grid environment because it involves vast distributed resources. Secondly, ID-based cryptography schemes from pairings would use some special hash functions, these hash functions are often probability and low efficiency. Although some results [14,15] have discussed on the structure of such Hash functions, but so far, there is not efficient polynomial-time algorithm on such a Hash function has been constructed [16].

With regard to using ID-based cryptography to design key agreement schemes, there are many schemes have been proposed [13,17,18,19]. However, using ID-based cryptography to design the grid security frameworks and key agreement protocols is started from Lim's work [9] and Mao's work [10]. In this paper, an ID-based authenticated multi-group keys agreement scheme is proposed from bilinear pairings. The contributions of this paper are as follows:

(1) Our scheme worked at a multi-group mode, and provides mutual authentication method for users that belong to different trust domains, which can be used to generate session keys for large-scale distributed heterogeneous and dynamic grid system.

(2) Our scheme employs shared password evolution authentication mechanism, which generates one-time password for every session. The passwords have two functions, the first is to authenticate identities and private keys of users; the other is to encrypt mutual information as symmetrical keys.

2   Bilinear Pairings and Gap Diffie-Hellman Group

(1) Bilinear pairings

Let q be a prime with l bits length. Let G_1 be a cyclic additive group generated by P whose order is q. Let G_2 be a cyclic multiplicative group of same order q. We assume that the discrete logarithm problems in both G_1 and G_2 are hard. A bilinear pairing is a map $\hat{e} : G_1 \times G_1 \to G_2$ with the following properties:

① Bilinear: For any $aP,bP \in G_1$, $\hat{e}(aP,bP) = \hat{e}(P,P)^{ab}$, where $a,b \in Z_q^*$. For any $P,Q,R \in G_1$, $\hat{e}(P+Q,R) = \hat{e}(P,R) \cdot \hat{e}(Q,R)$, $\hat{e}(P+Q,R) = \hat{e}(P,R) \cdot \hat{e}(Q,R)$.

② Non-degenerate: Existing $P,Q \in G_1$, such that $\hat{e}(P,Q) \neq 1$.

③ Computability: There is an efficient algorithm to compute $\hat{e}(P,Q)$.

(2) Gap Diffie-Hellman group (GDH)

① Computational Diffie-Hellman Problem (CDHP): Given $aP,bP \in G_1$, $a,b \in Z_q^*$, to compute abP.

② Determinal Diffie-Hellman Problem (DDHP): Given $aP,bP,cP \in G_1$, $a,b,c \in Z_q^*$, to decide whether $c = ab \bmod q$, if so, (P,aP,bP,cP) is called a valid Diffie-Hellman quaternion.

Definition 1. G_1 is called a GDH group if DDHP can be solved in polynomial time, but there is no polynomial time algorithm to solve CDHP on G_1 with non-negligible probability.

For more details of such a group and the bilinear pairings see [20]. An efficient method to solve DDHP [21]: assumption there is a bilinear map $\hat{e}$, then (P,aP,bP,cP) is a valid Diffie-Hellman quaternion $\Leftrightarrow$ $\hat{e}(aP,bP) = \hat{e}(P,cP)$.

3 ID-Based Authenticated Key Agreement Protocol and Our Construction

3.1 The General Definition of ID-Based Authenticated Key Agreement Protocol

Assumption there are n nodes $\{U_1,U_2,...,U_n\}$ in the system, they are in the same trust domain and share same PKG. An ID-based authenticated key agreement protocol is defined as follows:

Definition 2. An ID-based authenticated key agreement protocol is composed of five algorithms: Setup(1^k), keyExt($\cdot$), ID-KeyAuth($\cdot$), KeyAgreement($\cdot$), KeyConfirmat($\cdot$).

(1) Setup(1^k): the PKG takes as input a security parameter k, returns the master secret key and public key sk/pk and common system parameters cp.

(2) KeyExt($\cdot$): extracting node's secret keys. $U_i (1 \leq i \leq n)$ submits its identity ID_i and authenticates it to PKG, PKG computes its public key PK_i and secret key SK_i, and sends SK_i to the U_i via a secure channel.

(3) ID-keyAuth($\cdot$): authenticating node's identity and associated private keys. To take as input the U_i's identity ID_i, output 1 or 0. U_i's private key is valid if and only if the algorithm returns to 1.

(4) KeyAgreement($\cdot$): generating session key. To takes as input each node's key share during the j-th session, and output the session key K_j.

(5) KeyConfirmat($\cdot$): confirming whether generated session key K_j is unique. To takes as input the session key K_j, and node's identity set $L=(ID_1,ID_2,...,ID_n)$, output 1or 0. It is valid if and only if the algorithm returns to 1.

3.2 Our Construction

Assuming there are n nodes in m different trust domains, and there are open communication channels between any two nodes. Let $PKG_1,...,PKG_m$ denote PKG of each trust domain, respectively, let $L = (ID_{n_0}^1,...,ID_{n_1}^1,ID_{n_1+1}^2,...,ID_{n_2}^2,...,ID_{n_{m-1}+1}^m,...,ID_{n_m}^m)$ denote identities set. We divide nodes into m groups $\{(U_{n_0}^1,...,U_{n_1}^1),(U_{n_1+1}^2,...,U_{n_2}^2),...,(U_{n_{m-1}+1}^m,...,U_{n_m}^m)\}$ $(n_0=1,n_m=n)$ according to the trust domains. All nodes want to establish shared session keys.

Let G_1, G_2 be groups defined in section 2.1, and $\hat{e}: G_1 \times G_1 \to G_2$ be bilinear map with properties in section 2.1. Define cryptographic hash function $H: \{0,1\}^* \to Z_q^*$, and two one-way functions: $f_1(\cdot): Z_q^* \to Z_q^*$, $f_2(\cdot): G_1 \to G_1$.

(1) Setup (1^k)

PKG_t ($1 \le t \le m$) chooses $s_t \in_R Z_q^*$ as its private key, set $Pub_t = s_t P$ as its public-key, system parameters are $cp = (G_1, G_2, q, P, \hat{e}, H, f_1(\cdot), f_2(\cdot), Pub_1,...,Pub_m)$.

(2) Private key Extraction: UkeyGen(1^k)

① Every node $U_i^t \in \{(U_1^1,...,U_{n_1}^1),(U_{n_1+1}^2,...,U_{n_2}^2),...,(U_{n_{m-1}+1}^m,...,U_n^m)\}$ requests two shared initialization passwords $PW_0^1 \in Z_q^*$ and $PW_0^2 \in G_1$ in advance.

② Every node U_i^t ($1 \le i \le n, 1 \le t \le m$) submits and authenticates its identity ID_i^t to PKG_t ($1 \le t \le m$), PKG_t computes its private key [23] $S_i^t = \dfrac{1}{s_t + H(ID_i^t)} P$, and sends it to U_i^t via a secure channel. U_i should update its key after period of T_i. For simplicity, we do not discuss this problem here. (In fact, S_i^t is a T.Okamoto signature [23].)

(3) Identity-key Authentication: ID-keyAuth (ID_i^t, PW_j^1, PW_j^2)

In order to guarantee the authenticity of node's identity and reliability of node's private key, each node must authenticate other node's identity and corresponding private key before every session key agreement.

Before j-th ($j=1,2,...$) session, every node U_i^t ($1 \le i \le n, 1 \le t \le m$) authenticates other node's identity and corresponding private key as follows:

① U_i^t compute: $PW_j^1 = f_1(PW_{j-1}^1)$, $PW_j^2 = f_2(PW_{j-1}^2)$, $R_{ji}^t = PW_j^1 \cdot S_i^t = \dfrac{PW_j^1}{s_t + H(ID_i^t)} P$,

$Z_{ji}^t = R_{ji}^t \oplus PW_j^2$, broadcast (ID_i^t, Z_{ji}^t) and erases PW_{j-1}^1, PW_{j-1}^2.

② After receives (ID_i^t, Z_{ji}^t) $(i \ne u, t \ne v)$, U_u^v computes $PW_j^1 = f_1(PW_{j-1}^1)$, $PW_j^2 = f_2(PW_{j-1}^2)$, and checks $\hat{e}(Z_{ji}^t \oplus PW_j^2, H(ID_i^t)P + Pub_t) = \hat{e}(P,P)^{PW_j^1}$, continues protocol if all verification equations hold, else, terminates protocol.

Discussion: It is obvious that the function of password PW_j^1 is the same as shared information of all nodes, which can authenticate nodes' identities and corresponding private keys; the function of password PW_j^2 is the same as a symmetrical key to encrypt mutual information between nodes, which can guarantees the information integrality. The security of the passwords is guaranteed by the evolutionary mechanism. The advantage of the password evolutionary mechanism is to guarantee freshness of passwords, thus, even if a attacker obtained some previous password, it is unable to obtain any information about current key agreement, so long as it don't know how many times that passwords have been evolved. One-way functions $f_1(\cdot)$ and $f_2(\cdot)$ guarantee that the attacker can obtain nothing about the last passwords PW_{j-1}^1 and PW_{j-1}^2 from current passwords PW_j^1 and PW_j^2.

(4) Key Agreement: KeyAgreement $(PW_j^2, V_{j_i}^t, ID_i^t)$

If all verification equations hold in step (3), nodes compute shared session key as follows: in j-th session key agreement, U_i^t chooses $x_{j_i}^t \in_R Z_p^*$, computes $V_{j_i}^t = x_{j_i}^t S_i^t \oplus PW_j^2$ as its secret share, broadcast $V_{j_i}^t$, then computes its session key:

$$K_j = \prod_{t=1}^m (\prod_{i=n_{t-1}}^{n_t} \hat{e}((V_{j_i}^t \oplus PW_j^2), (H(ID_i^t)P + Pub_t))) = \hat{e}(P,P)^{\sum_{t=1}^m (\sum_{i=n_{t-1}}^{n_t} x_{j_i}^t)} .$$

where, $n_0 = 1, n_m = n$.

(5) Session Key Confirmation: KeyConfirm(PW_j^1, K_j, L **)**

Considering j-th **session** key agreement, every node $U_i^t \in \{(U_1^1,...,U_{n_1}^1),(U_{n_1+1}^2,...,U_{n_2}^2),...,(U_{n_{m-1}+1}^m,...,U_n^m)\}$ computes and publishes the MAC code: $MAC_{ij}^t = H(PW_j^1, K_j, L)$, then compares MAC_{ij}^t with MAC_{uj}^v ($1 \le u \le n$, $u \ne i$, $1 \le v \le m$, $v \ne t$), the latter are received from other nodes. If each $MAC_{ij}^t = MAC_{uj}^v$ ($1 \le u \le n, u \ne i$, $1 \le v \le m, v \ne t$) are all hold, the session key K_j is valid, and returns to 1, else, returns to 0 and terminates protocol, or reestablishes the session key.

4 Security and Efficiency Analysis

According to security requirements of the grid system and security goals of group key agreement protocol [22], the security of the proposed scheme is analyzed as follows:

Conclusion 1 (Correctness). The session key K_j that every node obtains from running KeyAgreement $(PW_j^2, V_{j_i}^t, ID_i^t)$ is unique if all of them implement the protocol trustily.

Analysis: During j-th session key agreement, every node $U_i^t \in \{(U_1^1,...,U_{n_1}^1),(U_{n_1+1}^2,...,U_{n_2}^2),...,(U_{n_{m-1}+1}^m,...,U_n^m)\}$ is able to obtain the same K_j:

$$K_j = \prod_{t=1}^m (\prod_{i=n_{t-1}}^{n_t} \hat{e}((V_{j_i}^t \oplus PW_j^2), (H(ID_i^t)P + Pub_t))) = \prod_{t=1}^m (\prod_{i=n_{t-1}}^{n_t} \hat{e}(x_{j_i}^t S_i^t, (H(ID_i^t)P + Pub_t)))$$

$$= \prod_{t=1}^m (\prod_{i=n_{t-1}}^{n_t} \hat{e}(\frac{x_{j_i}^t}{s_t + H(ID_i^t)} P, (H(ID_i^t)P + Pub_t))) = \hat{e}(P,P)^{\sum_{t=1}^m (\sum_{i=n_{t-1}}^{n_t} x_{j_i}^t)}$$

Conclusion 2. Proposed scheme possesses the closeness, that is, for $A \notin \{U_1, U_2, ..., U_n\}$ and any polynomial time algorithm $A(\cdot)$, the probability that A use $A(\cdot)$ to obtain session key is negligible.

Analysis: Assuming that the attacker A want to impersonate legitimate node U_i^t to compute session key K_j, here, $A \notin \{(U_1^1, ..., U_{n_1}^1), (U_{n_1+1}^2, ..., U_{n_2}^2), ..., (U_{n_{m-1}+1}^m, ..., U_n^m)\}$. A must find out the password PW_j^2 or $x_{j_i}^t S_i^t$. Under the assumption that passwords are security, A must obtain $x_{j_i}^t S_i^t$. However, it is computationally unfeasible due to DLP hardness assumption.

Conclusion 3. Proposed scheme is no key control. That is, any participant can't control or predict the values of session keys.

Analysis: In j-th session key agreement, if participants are all implement the protocol trustily, then each U_i^t $(1 \leq i \leq n, 1 \leq t \leq m)$ will contribute same size of secret share $V_{j_i}^t = x_{j_i}^t S_i^t \oplus PW_j^2$, so all of them possess peer status and right to determine K_j.

Conclusion 4. It is computationally unfeasible that any polynomial time adversary learns any information about a session key K_j even if he (she) has learnt the session key K_m $(m \neq j)$.

Analysis: Because every U_i^t $(1 \leq i \leq n, 1 \leq t \leq m)$ chooses at random an ephemeral integer $x_{j_i}^t \in_R Z_p^*$ to computes secret share for every time key agreement, so session keys generated by different session are unlikeness each other. The probability that two session keys are equality is $1/p$.

Conclusion 5. Our scheme is secure against man-in-the middle attacks.

Analysis: Considering j-th session key agreement, for attacker $A \notin \{(U_1^1, ..., U_{n_1}^1), (U_{n_1+1}^2, ..., U_{n_2}^2), ..., (U_{n_{m-1}+1}^m, ..., U_n^m)\}$ and legitimate nodes U_i^a, U_j^b. If A wants to impersonate U_i^a to U_j^b, it must first break the password, and then forge $x_{j_i}^a S_i^a$. However, it is computationally unfeasible due to DLP hardness assumption.

Conclusion 6. Our scheme provides known key secure [22]. That is, it is computational unfeasible that any polynomial time adversary A utilizes session key K_s to learn any information about session $K_t (t \neq s)$. This characteristic is ensured by encrypting mutual information using one-time passwords, and the freshness and security of passwords are guaranteed by password evolutionary mechanism.

Conclusion 7. Our scheme is secure against unknown key-share attacks [22].

To implement such an attack, the adversary is required to learn the private key S_i^t and random number $x_{j_i}^t \in_R Z_p^*$ of some nodes. Otherwise, the attack hardly works. Hence, we claim that our scheme have the attribute of no unknown key-share.

Conclusion 8. Our scheme is secure against key-compromise impersonation attack [22].

Considering very serious attack on our scheme: the adversary A obtains one of the private key S_i^t. In this case, the adversary A is still unable to impersonate anyone of the other nodes in subsequent protocol running since the security of passwords.

Conclusion 9. Our scheme is forward secrecy [22].

We say a protocol is not forward secrecy if the compromise of private keys of one or more nodes allows an adversary to obtain session keys previously established. Our scheme achieves perfect forward secrecy. Indeed, if private keys of all nodes in our system are available to the adversary, it is still hard to obtain a previously established session key from current session key K_j, since session keys are independency.

Conclusion 10. Our scheme is provided property of implicit key authentication.

This characteristic is ensured by the **Conclusion 2.** (detailed definition see [22])

Conclusion 11. Our scheme is an authenticated key agreement protocol [22].

Now we compare the computer costs of our scheme with some existing ID-based group key agreement protocols. We use $\hat{e}$ to denote pairing operation, M_p denote point scalar multiplication in G_1, E denote exponentiation in G_2.

Suppose the length of a point in G_1 is l_1, the length of an element in G_2 is l_2, the length of an element in Z_q^* is l. Table 1 shows the comparison of communication and computation costs.

Table 1. Comparison of communication and computation costs

scheme	M_p	E	$\hat{e}$	The size of the session key
[17]	$3n$	$2n$	1	l_2
[18]	$4n$	0	$2n$	l
[19]	$5n$	0	$3n+1$	l_2
Our scheme	$4n$	0	$2n+1$	l_2

As can be seen from table 1, scheme [17] is most efficient, but it does not provide the function of identity and key authentication.

5 Conclusion

Grid computing is considered as the new network infrastructure of 21-th century and the main trend for IT commercial application in the next ten years. Grid security is the main factor that influences the grid technology application. In heterogeneous and dynamic grid computing environment, keys agreement of different trust domains is one of the key technologies of grid security. In order to develop the grid technology and information industry, it has important significance to research these issues.

References

1. Foster, I., Kesselman, C., Tuecke, S.: The anatomy of the Grid: Enabling scalable virtual Organizations. International Journal on Supercomputer Applications 15(3) (2001)
2. Xu, Z., Feng, B., Li, W.: Computing Grid Technology. Electronic Industry Press, Beijing (2004)

3. Jin, H., Zou, D., Chen, H., Sun, J., Wu, S.: Fault-Tolerant grid Architecture and Practice. Journal of Computer Science and Technology 18(4), 423–433 (2003)
4. Chen, L., Lim, H.W., Mao, W.: User-friendly Grid Security Architecture and Protocols. In: Proceedings of the 13th International Workshop on Security Protocols, pp. 139–156 (2005)
5. Lim, H.W., Robshaw, M.J.B.: A Dynamic Key Infrastructure for GRID. In: Sloot, P.M.A., Hoekstra, A.G., Priol, T., Reinefeld, A., Bubak, M. (eds.) EGC 2005. LNCS, vol. 3470, pp. 255–264. Springer, Heidelberg (2005)
6. Foster, I., Kesselman, C.: Globus: A metacomputing infrastructure toolkit. International Journal of Supercomputing Applications 11(2), 115–128 (1997)
7. Shamir, A.: Identity-Based Cryptosystems and Signature Schemes. In: Blakely, G.R., Chaum, D. (eds.) CRYPTO 1984. LNCS, vol. 0196, pp. 47–53. Springer, Heidelberg (1984)
8. Boneh, D., Franklin, M.: Identity-Based Encryption from the Weil Pairing. In: Kilian, J. (ed.) CRYPTO 2001. LNCS, vol. 2139, pp. 213–229. Springer, Heidelberg (2001)
9. Lim, H.W., Robshaw, M.J.B.: On Identity-Based Cryptography and GRID Computing. In: Bubak, M., van Albada, G.D., Sloot, P.M.A., Dongarra, J. (eds.) ICCS 2004. LNCS, vol. 3036, pp. 474–477. Springer, Heidelberg (2004)
10. Mao, W.: An Identity-based Non-interactive Authentication Framework for Computational Grids. HP Lab, Technical Report HPL-2004-96 (June 2004), http://www.hpl.hp.com/techreports/2004/HPL-2004-96.pdf
11. Lim, H.W., Paterson, K.G.: Identity-Based Cryptography for Grid Security. In: Proceedings of the 1st IEEE International Conference on e-Science and Grid Computing (e-Science 2005), Melbourne, Australia, pp. 395–404. IEEE Computer Society Press, Los Alamitos (2005)
12. Lim, H.W.: On the Application of Identity-Based Cryptography in Grid Security. PhD Thesis, University of London (2006)
13. Wang, L., Wu, C.: Identity Based Group Key Agreement in Multiple PKG Environment. WuHan University Journal of Natural Sciences 11(6), 1605–1608 (2006)
14. Barreto, P.S.L.M., Kim, H.Y.: Fast hashing onto elliptic curves over fields of characteristic 3, Cryptology ePrint Archive, Report 2001/098 (2001), http://eprint.iacr.org/2001/098/
15. Boneh, D., Lynn, B., Shacham, H.: Short signatures from the Weil pairing. In: Boyd, C. (ed.) ASIACRYPT 2001. LNCS, vol. 2248, pp. 514–532. Springer, Heidelberg (2001)
16. Zhang, F., Safavi-Naini, R., Susilo, W.: An Efficient Signature Scheme from Bilinear Pairings and Its Applications. In: Bao, F., Deng, R., Zhou, J. (eds.) PKC 2004. LNCS, vol. 2947, pp. 277–290. Springer, Heidelberg (2004)
17. Li, L., Tsai, Y., Liu, R.: A Novel ID-based Authenticated Group Key Agreement Protocol Using Bilinear Pairings. In: WOCN 2008, pp. 1–5 (2008)
18. Wang, L., Wu, C.: Identity Based Group Key Agreement from Bilinear Pairing. WuHan University Journal of Natural Sciences 11(6), 1731–1735 (2006)
19. Du, X., Wang, Y., Ge, J., Wang, Y.: An Improved ID-based Authenticated Group Key Agreement Scheme. Cryptology ePrint Archive, Report 2003/260 (2003), http://eprint.iacr.org/
20. Cha, J.C., Cheon, J.H.: An identity-based signature from gap Diffie-Hellman groups. In: Desmedt, Y.G. (ed.) PKC 2003. LNCS, vol. 2567, pp. 18–30. Springer, Heidelberg (2003)
21. Cheon, J.H., Kim, Y., Yoon, H.J.: A New ID-based Signature with Batch Verification. Cryptology ePrint Archive, Report 2004/131 (2004), http://eprint.iacr.org/
22. Ateniesey, G., Steiner, M., Tsudik, G.: Authenticated group key agreement and friends. In: ACM Conference on Computer and Communications Security, pp. 17–26 (1998)
23. Okamoto, T., Harada, K., Okamoto, E.: ID-Based Key Agreement Schemes using General Hash Function from Pairing. In: The 2004 Workshop on Information Security Research (2004), http://www-kairo.csce.kyushu-u.ac.jp/WISR2004/presentation07.pdf

Dynamic Path Planning of Mobile Robots Based on ABC Algorithm

Qianzhi Ma and Xiujuan Lei

College of Computer Science of Shaanxi Normal University
Xi'an, Shaanxi Province, China, 710062
zhihui312@163.com
xjlei168@163.com

Abstract. For the global path planning of mobile robot under the dynamic uncertain environment, a path planning method combined time rolling window strategy and artificial bee colony (ABC) algorithm was proposed. To meet the real time requirement, the global path was replaced by local paths within a series of rolling windows. Due to the ability of global optimization, and rapid convergence of artificial bee colony algorithm, it was applied to plan the local path. According to the special environment, a suitable fitness function was designed to avoid dynamic obstacles in artificial bee colony algorithm. The simulation results of proposed method demonstrated that it has great efficiency and accuracy, and it is suitable for solving this kind of problem.

Keywords: Artificial bee colony algorithm; Mobile robot; dynamic path planning.

1 Introduction

Path planning for mobile robot is to find a trajectory from the initial point to the target point which satisfies a certain performance optimal index under some constraints. The quality of path planning usually has an immense impact for the task. A lot of methods have been put forward to the global path planning problem. For example, artificial potential field[1],viewed method[2],Genetic algorithm[3] and so on. These methods are usually used for the problems under the static environment. In fact, the mobile robot may face an even more complex dynamic environment. Therefore, path planning under dynamic complex environment for mobile robot has become necessary. Using the theory of predictive control for reference, this paper presented a path planning method combined time rolling window and artificial bee colony (ABC) algorithm for mobile robot. The dynamic uncertain environment and the strategy of time rolling window were described in detail, and coding method, fitness function, collision detection methods were given when artificial bee colony algorithm was used in rolling time window for local planning. Then the realization principles and procedures of path planning using this algorithm were described. Finally the rationality and validity of the algorithm was analyzed based on the simulation experiments and the results.

F.L. Wang et al. (Eds.): AICI 2010, Part II, LNAI 6320, pp. 267–274, 2010.
© Springer-Verlag Berlin Heidelberg 2010

2 Artificial Bee Colony Algorithm

The development of artificial bee colony algorithm is based on simulation of the for-aging behavior of bee colony. In ABC algorithm[4][5], there are three basic factors: food source, employed bees and unemployed bees. Food source is the search goal of bees. The nectar amount of a food source, called 'profitability', reflect the quality of the food source. Each employed bee works on only one food source. They record the in-formation of food sources and share the information with other bees according to the probability. Unemployed bees include onlookers and scouts. Their main task is to find and exploit new food sources. Onlookers are looking for food sources with high prof-itability by the sharing information from employed bees, and scouts are searching for the new food source near the hive.

To an optimization problem, the position of each food source represents a solution, and the nectar amount of a food source corresponds to the quality of the associated solution. At the beginning, the initial population of *Size* solutions is generated ran-domly. Select half solutions with better function values in the population, and the other solutions represent the position of onlookers. Employed bees are able to search nearby the food source. It is calculated by equation (1) as follow:

$$new\_x_{id} = x_{id} + r(x_{id} - x_{kd}) \tag{1}$$

Where, d is the dimension number of the solutions. r represents uniform random number between 0 and 1. $k \in \{1, 2, \cdots, Size\} - \{i\}$ is generated randomly, which corresponds to any food source except the ith one. As the increasing of iteration number, the value of $x_{id} - x_{kd}$ decreases, which means the search space for bees decreases. It helps algorithm to improve its accuracy.

When the employed bees complete searching in the neighborhood of food source, they will share the profitability information of food sources with onlookers by dancing, then the onlookers choose food source to collect nectar at certain probability. The higher profitability is, the greater the probability of attracting onlookers to follow.

$$P = \begin{cases} \dfrac{fit_i}{\sum\limits_{n=1}^{Size} fit_n} & \max(fit) \\[4ex] \dfrac{\sum\limits_{n=1}^{Size} fit_n - fit_i}{(Size-1)\sum\limits_{n=1}^{Size} fit_n} & \min(fit) \end{cases} \tag{2}$$

The probability can be calculated by following equation (2).Once onlookers select new sources, they have changed into employed bees. They will keep searching in the neighborhood of the food sources. If one solution represented by the position of a food source doesn't change during many iterations, we generate a new solution randomly to represent the behavior that the employed bees give up the current food source.

3 Time Rolling Window Strategy

Reference to the theory of predictive control [6], the method combined time rolling window strategy [7] and local optimization is proposed for dynamic path planning. In the dynamic unknown environment, mobile robot perceives and predicts environmental information within limited time in future by sensors. We call a limited time phase as a time rolling window. As the next sample time coming, the time window will scroll over to the target location. Dynamic path planning can be realized through planning optimal paths in a series of time rolling windows to replace planning the global path planning.

Figure 1 shows a time rolling window W at t moment. Mobile robot's sensors can perceive the environmental information at this moment. Then the change of the information within the future Δt time can be predicted. Through the internal local path planning, the start point of next time rolling window will be found. Repeat this process until the mobile robot gets to the target point. That is the dynamic path planning in the whole environment.

When we plan the local path for each time rolling window, the area outside the current window is seemed as free region which is not restricted by the obstacles' constraints. The local path planning within a time rolling window is to find a local target point of the current window and a feasible path from the start point to the target point. The target point found in this window is also the starting point of the next time rolling window. Take the rolling window at t moment as for example, the start point S' is obtained by planning the prior window. The purpose of path planning in current window is to find the local target point F' and the feasible path point between S' and F'.

At first, view the line $S'F$ between the starting point in current window and the global target point as horizontal axes. The vertical line through the starting point is viewed as vertical axis. Construct the coordinate system. Divide the line $S'F$ into equally parts, and draw the vertical lines of abscissa axis at each point. The points p_i taken from the vertical lines orderly make up a path sequence $S'p1, p2, pi, \cdots, F$. Calculate the robot's position F' at $t+\Delta t$ when it moves along this path. The trajectory that robot moves from S' to F' is the required local path.

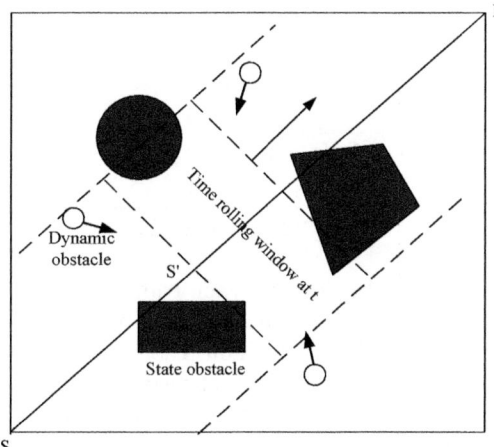

Fig. 1. Time rolling window at t moment

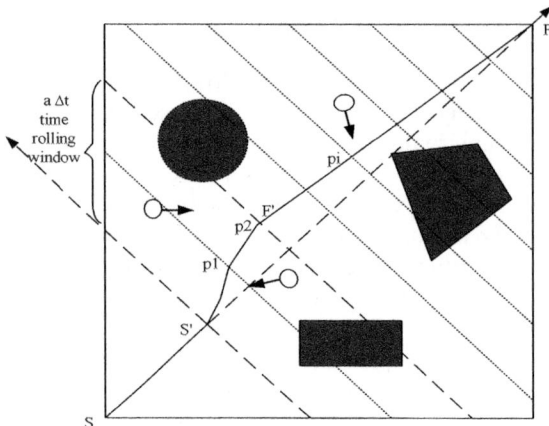

Fig. 2. The schematic diagram of local planning

4   The Design and Process of the Algorithm

4.1   Collision Detection Method

Suppose the robot and the dynamic obstacles are always in uniform state of motion. The obstacles can change the direction of motion. The starting position of the mobile robot R is at (x_{R1}, y_{R1}). The velocity is v_R. At t moment, the position of obstacle B is predicted at (x_{B1}, y_{B1}). The velocity is v_B and the movement direction angle is θ. The position of this obstacle at any moment $t + t'$ within the Δt time window can be calculated as (x_{B2}, y_{B2}). If mobile robot reaches to the location (x_{R2}, y_{R2}) after t' time, The distance of the robot moving is:

$$s = \sqrt{(x_{R2} - x_{R1})^2 + (y_{R2} - y_{R1})^2} \tag{3}$$

$$t' = s / v_R \tag{4}$$

$$k = \tan\theta \tag{5}$$

$$x_{B2} = \frac{1}{2(1+k^2)(2x_{B1} + 2k^2 x_{B1} \pm 2(s^2 + k^2 s^2)^{1/2})} \tag{6}$$

$$y_{B2} = y_{B1} + \frac{k}{2(1+k^2)(2x_{B1} + 2k^2 x_{B1} \pm 2(s^2 + k^2 s^2)^{1/2})} - k x_{B1} \tag{7}$$

Collision detection should be done for each path segment within the time window. The method of detection is to judge whether the robot and the obstacles reach to the same place at the same time and same position. There are two cases to be discussed. One case is that the trajectory of robot does not intersect with the trajectory of obstacles. In this case, collision between the robot and the obstacles will not occur. In the other case, when the trajectory of robot intersects with the trajectory of obstacle, whether a collision occurs can be detected according to the time of the trajectory intersecting. If the centre of trajectories intersect at $O(x_O, y_O)$, $t+t_{B\min}$, $t+t_{B\max}$, $t+t_{R\max}$, $t+t_{R\min}$ are four critical moments of the collision.

$$s_R = \sqrt{(x_{R1} - x_O)^2 + (y_{R1} - y_O)^2} \tag{8}$$

$$t_1 = s_R / v_R \tag{9}$$

$$s_B = \sqrt{(x_{B1} - x_O)^2 + (y_{B1} - y_O)^2} \tag{10}$$

$$t_2 = s_B / v_B \tag{11}$$

$$s_R = t_R + r / v_B \tag{12}$$

$$t_{R\max} = t_1 + r/v_R \quad t_{R\min} = t_1 - r/v_R \quad t_{B\max} = t_2 + r/v_B \quad t_{B\min} = t_2 - r/v_B \tag{13}$$

The condition that collision occurs is shown as equation (14):

$$\begin{cases} If \quad t_{R\min} > t_{B\max} \big| t_{R\max} < t_{B\min} & collision \quad occurs \\ \qquad otherwise & collision \quad doesn't \quad occurs \end{cases} \tag{14}$$

The application of time rolling window reduces the number of obstacles within the planning region. And it also reduces the computing time of collision detection greatly, which is benefit for meeting the demands of real time planning.

4.2   Code Design for Food Source

We use one-dimensional vector to encode the position of a food source. From the starting point of the current planning window S to the global target point F, If $\{S\ p1, p2, pi, \cdots, F\}$ denotes a path, the ordinate of each path point $\{y_s, y_1, y_2, \cdots, y_f\}$ constitute a food source's position.

4.3   Fitness Function

In this dynamic environment, robotic planning path requires that the length of path is as short as possible, and it can avoid both the state and dynamic obstacles effectively. The fitness function of the path is designed as penalty function form like this:

$$f = f_d + \sigma(f_1 + f_2) \tag{15}$$

This function includes the length of planning path f_d and the collision functions with state obstacles and dynamic obstacles f_1, f_2. Where, σ is the penalty coefficient. Assume the target point is at (x_f, y_f). The starting point for mobile robot in some planning window is at $(x_{s'}, y_{s'})$. The line between the starting point and the target point is divided into n parts, and it intersects the window's bounder at $(x_{f'}, y_{f'})$. f_d, f_1 and f_2 will be calculated as following equations:

$$f_d = \sum_{i=1}^{n} \sqrt{(\frac{x_{f'} - x_{s'}}{n})^2 + (y_i - y_{i-1})^2}$$

$$+ \sqrt{(x_f - x_{f'})^2 + (y_f - y_{f'})^2} \tag{16}$$

$$f_1 = f_2 = \sum_{i=1}^{N} L_i \tag{17}$$

$$L_i = \begin{cases} 1 & collide \quad with \quad the \quad ith \quad obstacle \\ 0 & otherwise \end{cases} \tag{18}$$

N is the number of the static or dynamic obstacles. The longer the length of path is and the bigger the time number of the collision occurred is, the greater the value of fitness function is.

4.4 Implementation Steps of the Algorithm

Step 1: Set the duration of the time rolling window Δt, the neighborhood radius of the target point ε, the max iteration number $\max iter$, population scale $Size$ and the max number $Limit$ of the employed bee staying at the same food source.

Step 2: Judge the starting point S' in the current window whether it is within the neighborhood radius of the target point F. If $|S' F| > \varepsilon$, go to Step 3, otherwise, go to Step 7.

Step 3: View line $S' F$ between the starting point S' in current window and the global target point F as horizontal axes. S' is origin point. Construct a new coordinate system. Switch the coordinate information to the new coordinate system.

Step 4: Plan the local path in current window using artificial bee colony algorithm.

a) Set $iter = 0$. Generate $Size$ vectors randomly and calculate the fitness function value. Seem $Size/2$ vectors of better values as food sources, and each food source corresponds to an employed bee. The other vectors denote the onlookers' position. Initialize the flag vector $Bas(i) = 0$ to record the times that the employed bees stay at the same food source.

b) Each employed bee i is searching near the food source. Calculate the fitness function value of the new food source. If the new one is better than the current one, update the old food source and set $Bas(i) = 0$, otherwise $Bas(i) = Bas(i) + 1$.

c) Compute the selection possibility of food source. Then the onlookers select the food source under the possibility and they search and record the better position of food source. Update vector Bas like b).

d) Judge the value of $Bas(i)$ whether it is bigger than. If $Bas(i) > Limit$, the ith employed bee will give up the current food source and change to a scout. The scout will search in the solution space randomly.

e) Record the best position of food source by far.

f) Set $iter = iter + 1$. If $iter > \max iter$, save the coordinate of path nodes on the best feasible path in the current window, then go to Step 5. Otherwise go to c).

Step 5: Switch the coordinate information of the environment back.

Step 6: Connect the path nodes in time rolling windows which have been planned by now. Let the last node as the starting point of the next time rolling window. Update the environmental information of the next duration. Then go to Step2.

Step 7: Connect the starting point in the current window and the final target point.

5   Experiments and Results Analysis

The algorithms were programmed in MATLAB 7.0 and ran on a PC with Intel Core 2 CPU, 1.86 GHz. Set the size of movement environment as 100*100, the starting point at (5, 5) and the target point at (95, 95). The size of population was 10. The dimension number of a food source was 7. The maximum iteration number was 300. There were eight state obstacles and three random dynamic unknown obstacles.

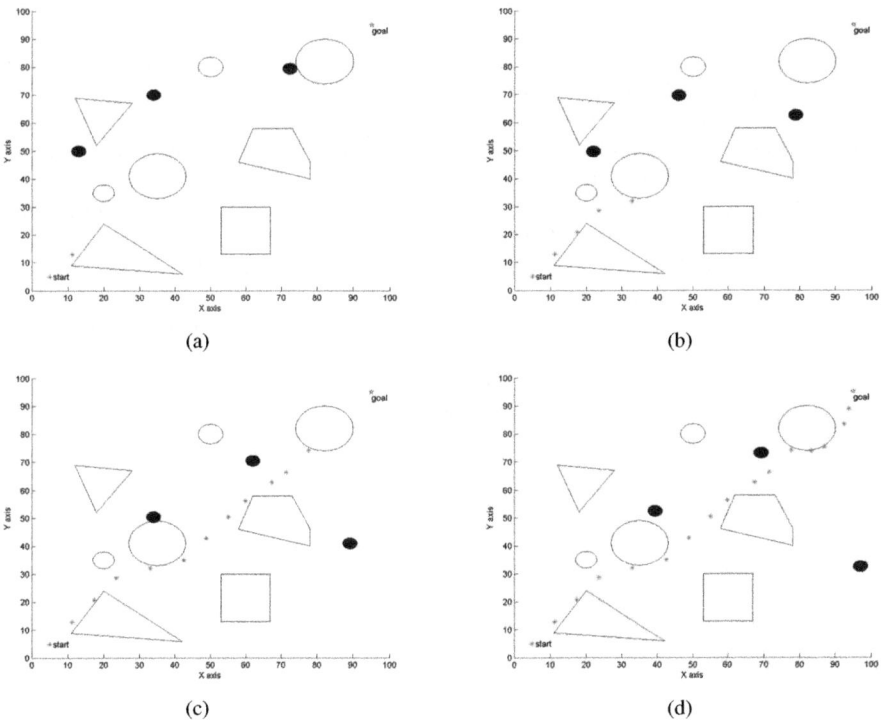

Fig. 3. Dynamic motion process of mobile robot

Four status of in Figure 3 show the dynamic motion process of robot from the origin point to target point by proposed method. The regions enclosed by real lines represent static obstacles and the solid circles are dynamic obstacles. The path robot passed is demonstrated by '*'. From the figures above, it is easily to find that the mobile robot can find the feasible path without collision all the obstacles. So the path planned by proposed method is effectively.

6 Conclusion

In order to plan the path for the mobile robot under the dynamic environment, a novel method of the ABC algorithm and time rolling window strategy for dynamic path planning was proposed. Simulation results showed that the proposed method can avoid the static and dynamic obstacles effectively, and the planning method could satisfy the real time demand. It is suitable for solving dynamic path planning problem.

Acknowledgement. This work was supported by the Natural Science Foundation of Shaanxi Province of China (2010JQ8034) and the Fundamental Research Funds for the Central Universities, Shaanxi Normal University (2009020016).

References

1. Ge, S.S., Cui, Y.J.: New Potential Functions for Mobile Robot Path Planning. IEEE Transactions on Robotics and Automation (May 2000)
2. Huang, H., Chung, S.: Dynamic visibility graph for path planning. In: Intelligent Robots and Systems, 2004, pp. 2813–2818. IEEE, Sendai (2004)
3. Sadati, N., Taheri, J.: Genetic algorithm in robot path planning problem in crisp and fuzzified environments. In: Proceedings of IEEE International Conference on Industrial Technology, vol. (1), pp. 11–14. IEEE, Bangkok (2002)
4. Basturk, B., Karaboga, D.: An Artificial Bee Colony(ABC) Algorithm for Numeric function Optimization. In: IEEE Swarm Intelligence Symposium 2006, USA (2006)
5. Singh, A.: An artificial bee colony algorithm for the leaf-constrained minimum spanning tree problem. Applied Soft Computing 9(2), 625–631 (2009)
6. Sipahioglu, A., Yazicib, A. (eds.): Real-time tour construction for a mobile robot in a dynamic environment. Robotics and Autonomous Systems (56), 289-295 (2008)
7. Cai, X., Li, Y., Wu, T.: Dynamic Path Planning of Mobile Robots in Uncertain Environments Based on PSO and Receding Horizon Optimization. Bulletin of science and technology 24(2), 260–265 (2008)

Urban Arterial Traffic Coordination Control System

Jianyu Zhao[1], Diankui Tang[1], Xin Geng[1], and Lei Jia[2]

[1] School of Control Science and Engineering
University of Jinan, Jinan, China, 250022
cse_zjy@ujn.edu.cn
tangshengli121@126.com
cse_gx@ujn.edu.cn
[2] School of Control Science and Engineering
Shandong University, Jinan, China, 250022
jialei@sdu.edu.cn

Abstract. To optimize urban arterial traffic control, this paper analyzed coordination mechanism of all individual junctions along the road. We set up a traffic control system for urban area network based upon multi-agent technology. Each individual junction and the coordination were considered as agents. Each of them was embodiment of fuzzy neural network. We utilized particle swarm optimization arithmetic to optimize these FNNs. The agent directly talked to each other with FIPA ACL standard language. Compared to the traditional timing control mode, at a junction with moderate traffic volume, the average delay expressed in queue length can be reduced from 120.9(veh./h) to 25.4 (veh./h). Congestion thus significantly relieved.

Keywords: arterial, coordination control, FNN, multi-agent.

1 Introduction

In order to solve the problem of traffic joint control of multi-junction, regional Intelligent Transportation System based on the theoretical framework of multi-agent-based traffic control is increasingly be taken seriously[1]. Multi-agent technology has distributed processing and coordination function, suited to solve the complex and ever-changing system and can solve the traditional traffic control and other intelligent control methods to solve difficult to better coordination and control of regional transportation issues. Feng chen, etc. [2] introduced the concept of multi-agent system to control the whole region. Agent at the junction follow the real-time traffic information on dynamic changes in the density of green time, regional agent optimizes the signal cycle and uses fuzzy control algorithm to achieve the coordination between the agents at different junctions. Regional agents communicate with four-storey information structure. Considering current traffic management system for computational complexity, high cost of the defective hardware, a Multi-agent-based distributed platform for adaptive traffic management system is proposed [3]. The complexity of the traffic control area divided into a number of distributed The task-oriented body of intelligent control, intelligent control of these bodies in accordance with current information to

F.L. Wang et al. (Eds.): AICI 2010, Part II, LNAI 6320, pp. 275–283, 2010.

make a flexible decision-making, signal controllers do not have to take into account all of the control performance, just from the Area Traffic Control Center for appropriate control volume and the implementation of the information provided. Even if the network can not be effectively connected to the control agent, by default agent will also perform basic control operations. Dipti Srinivasan put multi-agent technology into distributed unsupervised control model[4]. Two types of multi-agent system are offered. The first hybrid intelligent system adopts intelligent computing technology, every agent can be graded online learning to establish and update the knowledge base and decision-making. In the second agent system, disturbances will also be integrated into the application of stochastic approximation theory fuzzy neural network.

Compared with above methods, in consideration of the agent characteristics such as autonomy, communication capacity and collaboration skills, this paper presents a new control structure to deal with "green wave band" of arterial and the congestion at the multi-junctions. Specific control structure is given. Coordination principle which is used to reduce congestion when traffic jams occur at the middle section between adjacent junctions is described. This paper is organized as follows: section II analyses the control mechanism of traffic of urban arterial multi-intersections. section III describes the control structure of the entire road network, including intersection control module and coordination control module. The functions of two parts will be described in detail. Section IV will give the specific design features the above two parts. V Section gives simulation results and summary of comments is made by section VI.

2 The Control Mechanism of Traffic Flow of Urban Arterial Multi-intersections

City road capacity is connected with traffic efficiency of urban arterial. According to HCM, adopting arterial traffic coordination control will greatly improve traffic jams during the period of traffic hours. That is the best and the firstly selected method to control urban traffic flows. There are three parameters to be used to design and optimize by current traffic engineering in urban traffic coordination control system[5][6], which can be described as cycle time, green split and offset as follows:

Cycle time: In order to coordinate arterial intersections signals, we usually select the same cycle time for these intersections. For this purpose, we should calculate the cycle of every junction firstly according to method of individual intersection traffic control, and then select the maximum among these cycles as system cycle time.

Green split: In view of the independence of single-junction in the regional road network, each junction used independent control as the main control method to achieve effective control of traffic. So the set of green split of each junction is not same, which is decided by the status of their traffic flow.

Offset: Selecting one from arterial intersections as beginning, turning on green light of the others in a chronological sequence along the arterial, can make vehicles on the road driving smoothly and reducing delay with less or not meeting red light.

3   Arterial Control Structure Based on Multi-agent Technology

Concentrating traffic control scheme of entire road network based on multi-agent technology is that control task to road network can be distributed to single agent under multi-agent technology, adopting a relax-coupling collaboration control to achieve system optimization. Single agent is intelligent, automatic to get task and fulfill the task, which is of ability of sensing, problem solving and communicating with exterior.

The control system should plan as a whole and adjustable control strategy automatically with randomic and fluctuating traffic status. Usually urban traffic control system to coordinate regional intelligence often has multi-level hierarchy, in which each level including many agents that have similar function and structure[7] (Figure 1) . This paper uses two-tier control structure: intersection control module and coordination control module. Its structure is illustrated as Figure 2.

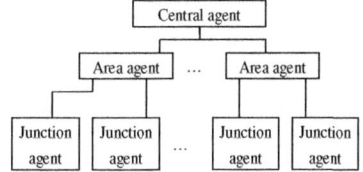

Fig. 1. Structure of multi-agent traffic control

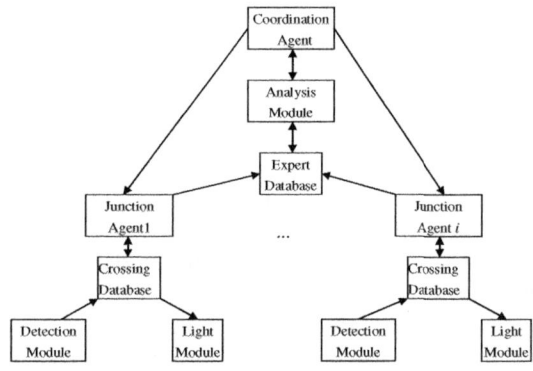

Fig. 2. Control structure of entire road network

Single-junction control module regards the junction agent associated with the junction as control core, and the detection module carry out the collection of information on road conditions, crossing database completes the data pre-processing, intelligent junction agent control intelligent decision-making body with light module to perform the control scheme[8]. It performs light phase of itself and automatically adjusts green split of each phase under coordinated cycle time and offset from coordination agent. Junction agents simultaneously send traffic information to coordination agent, such as phase saturation, traffic flow density, and green split, which is needed by coordination agent.

Coordination control module collects agent input data of all junctions in each cycle, which is selected from all the information in crossing database and expert database does data pre-processing. Coordination agent collects traffic information of current interval and decides cycle and offset of the arterial at next interval. In case of bottle-neck problem, the new cycle is decided by the one of all junctions that has the largest vehicle saturation. The results optimized by coordination agent are sent to junction agents by communication network. When the adjacent junction agents get detection based on a law to have a congestion-related phenomena at the junction, the agents send a request to coordination control module; coordination agent catches the stimulation of collaboration request, expert database call the data into data analysis module, and then decide whether or not to respond to the request to coordinate the decision-making, Once it is necessary to respond co-ordination , various control schemes in different junctions should be modulated according to road condition evaluation[9]. The junction optimized results that have been adjusted are sent to the junction agents from coordination agent through communication network and then become true in various road junctions by light module. It should be noted that: the change of signal cycle should not be too frequent. Frequent adjustments in control scheme, it will be even worse effects of the control, so the general regulation of interval is six cycles of the appropriate signal[10].

4   Design Features of Junction and Coordination Agent

4.1   Design Features of Junction Agent

Individual junction agent as a local control unit achieves the effective control of traffic flow in the intersection. Its design feature emphasizes the ability of flexibility and self-study to dynamic changes of traffic flow. Using real-time sampling traffic information, which is pretreated, the junction agent can get traffic character representing traffic status, such as vehicle density, vehicle queue length at stop line. Then optimizes signal control scheme and accomplishes it by light module, receives cooperation request from the other junction agent and responses to it, and uploads needed information in order for coordination agent to make a whole judgement.

Junction agent in this paper is a fuzzy neural network[11][12], which has 4-level structure with 3 input and 1output(Figure 3). The idea comes from traffic police who directs traffic flow at intersection. FNN controller selects three fuzzy input variants for simulating police control strategy as follows:

E_1 is the error of vehicle queue length waiting to go and expectation; C_1 is error rate that reflects the status of coming-in vehicles at the direction of waiting to go;

E_2 is the error of queue length of going vehicle (current green light) and expectation at this direction.

The Output of FNN described as U represents adjusting time of green light. Setting up 3 language values for each of all three input variants, FNN model can be described as follows:

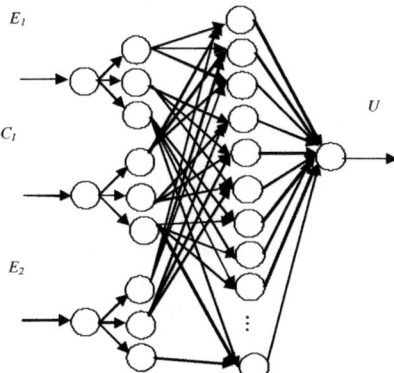

E_1

C_1

E_2

U

Fig. 3. FNN structure of Junction agent

The first level has three nerve cells, corresponding three fuzzy input variants E_1 、 E_2 and C_1. The second level is fitting function of nine nerve cells, corresponding three language values of three fuzzy input variants, which is Gauss function（as $\exp(-\frac{(x_i - m_{ij})^2}{(\sigma_{ij})^2})$）；

The third level comprises twenty-seven nerve cells, representing twenty-seven fuzzy rulers; and the forth level carries out defuzzification of output fuzzy variant.

The parameters in FNN including center of every fitting function m_{ij}, variance σ_{ij} and weight of defuzzification ω_k, are optimized utilizing particle swarm optimization (PSO) arithmetic according to samples from policemens' expert knowledge base .

PSO arithmetic iteration is described as follows:

Step 1: Initialize particle;

Step 2: Calculate fitness value of each particle;

Step 3: If the fitness value is better than the best fitness value (pBest) in history, set current value as the new pBest. Choose the particle with the best fitness value of all the particles as the gBest.

Step 4: Calculate particle velocity according equation (1):

$$v = \omega*v + c1*r1*(\text{pBest-present}) + c2*r2*(\text{gBest-present}). \tag{1}$$

Update particle position according equation (2) :

$$\text{present}=\text{present}+v . \tag{2}$$

Step 5: While maximum iterations or minimum error criteria is not attained, go to step 2.

4.2 Design Features of Coordination Agent

In response to coordination request from the junction agent, Coordination agent analyzes the situation at the junction, and varies the relevant parameters: the signal cycle, offset, to ensure that adjacent sections of the congestion to dissipate until the situation eased.

4.2.1 Design of Signal Cycle of Coordination Agent

We adjust cycle time according to phase saturation x, which can be described as equation (3):

$$x = q / q_c = q / q_s \cdot \lambda \tag{3}$$

Where, q means real volume , q_c indicates traffic capacity of one coming-in lane of a intersection, q_s indicates saturated volume of the lane, and λ means green split.

Adjustment of cycle should meet the saturation of intersection is at about 0.9 for road capacity is biggest at this condition[6][13].when saturation is less than 0.9, cycle time should be reduced for the purpose of enhancing traffic efficiency of intersection; when saturation is more than 0.9, cycle time should be increased. Experience has illuminated that when saturation is bigger than 0.9, traffic congestion will be worse even if with less vehicle increase. So less saturation increase needs more cycle time increase. Conversely, when saturation is less than 0.9, more saturation increase makes less cycle decrease for avoiding bigger traffic disturbance brought by bigger change in control scheme.

The idea of design of light cycle is as follows:

Ruler1: if the saturation of intersection with biggest saturation among arterial is bigger, then delay cycle time.

Ruler 2: if the saturation of intersection with biggest saturation among arterial is less, then shorten cycle time.

Restrict condition: cycle time must not less than the shortest cycle, and not bigger than the biggest cycle [6][13].

Finally we design a FNN to perform this idea.

4.2.2 Design of Offset of Coordination Agent

The offset $\triangle T$ of two adjacent intersections at the same arterial is decided by distance between the two intersections and traffic velocity on it, which can be described as equation (4).

$$\Delta T = L / v \tag{4}$$

Where, L is the distance between two intersections; v is the velocity.

It is very clear that offset is decided by v for L is an invariant, where v might vary with dynamic traffic condition. Density of traffic is relative to the velocity. If density of traffic is high, the velocity is low. FNN method is employed to realize the mapping of density of traffic and the velocity, by which the velocity can be attained, in consequent offset $\triangle T$.

The advantage of using FNN is that FNN can adapt itself to new environment by learning, and track dynamic traffic flow.

Communication between multi-agents is direct communication, which is achieved with FIPA ACL standerd language.

5 Simulation

To simulate coordination control of arterial, we select two junctions, in which one cycle contains east-west and north-south two phases. The simulating idea is as follows just like figure 4.

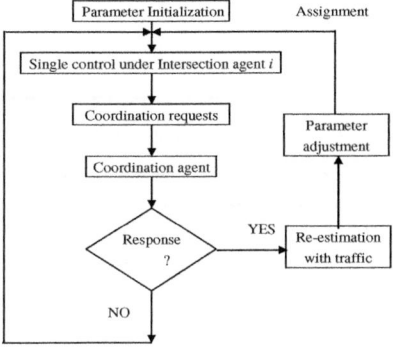

Fig. 4. Algorithm flow chart

Minimum green time is 20S and maximum green time is 120S, which are adopted in FNN adjustment scheme. New cycle, offset, and green split of next interval were adjusted for each 6 cycles. The arriving vehicle meets binominal distribution. The simulation time is 1000 cycles.

The simulating traffic condition is supposed that arterial saturation volume is 3600veh./h and lateral saturation volume is 2500veh./h.Under the condition of lateral volume is 300veh./h, 500veh./h and 800veh./h respectively, vehicle queue length before intersection of arterial was reviewed, in which the simulation results of two methods are showed as Table 1,2 and 3.

As can be seen from Table 1, Table 2 and Table 3, under the same traffic environment, the coordinated control mode based on FNN makes the average delay of vehicles at road junctions fewer than under the current timing control mode. The simulation research indicates that the system can take full advantage of leisure time-space of intersections and make traffic flow pass the intersection with ideal saturation and congestion thus significantly relieved.

Table 1. Lateral traffic volume is 300veh./h

Arterial traffic volume (veh./h)	Average vehicle queue of each cycle (veh./cyc.)	
	Timing control	Coordinated control(FNN)
500	6.1	4.8
1000	20.3	7.1
1500	25.4	12.2
1800	120.9	25.4
2100	*	35.6

Table 2. Lateral traffic volume is 500veh./h

Arterial traffic volume (veh./h)	Average vehicle queue of each cycle (veh./cyc.)	
	Timing control	Coordinated control(FNN)
500	12.1	5.2
1000	22.4	8.4
1500	25.7	13.2
1800	160.8	27.7
2100	*	37.9

Table 3. Lateral traffic volume is 800veh./h

Arterial traffic volume (veh./h)	Average vehicle queue of each cycle (veh./cyc.)	
	Timing control	Coordinated control(FNN)
500	26.5	8.4
1000	42.1	11.2
1500	48.9	27.7
1800	*	54.3
2100	*	*

note : * expresses vehicle queue is long and in congestion

6 Conclusions

In this paper, we proposed a coordination control system for arterial traffic. This system comprises two level agents to realize the knowledge method of "green wave band". Each of them is embodiment of FNN based on PSO. Cycle time, offset and green light were optimized by the multi-agent coordination control system automatically according to dynamic traffic changes. The simulation research indicates that the system can take full advantage of leisure time-space of the intersection and make traffic flow pass through the intersection at ideal saturation. Compared to the traditional timing control mode, at a junction with moderate traffic volume, the average delay expressed in queue length can be reduced from120.9(veh./c) to 25.4 (veh./c). Congestion thus significantly relieved.

References

1. Ou, H., Zhang, W., Zhang, W., Xu, X.: Urban traffic multi-agent system based on RMM and Bayesian learning. In: American Control Conference, Chicago, vol. 4, pp. 2782–2783 (2000)
2. Chen, F., Pang, H.: Study of multi-agent area coordination control for urban traffic. In: 7th World Congress on Intelligent Control and Automation, Chongqing, pp. 4046–4050 (2008)
3. Wang, F.-Y.: Agent-Based Control for Networked Traffic Management Systems. IEEE Intelligent Systems, Tucson 20, 92–96 (2005)
4. Srinivasan, D., Choy, C., Cheu, R.L.: Neural Networks for Real-Time Traffic Signal Control. IEEE transactions on intelligent transportation systems, Parma 7, 261–272 (2006)

5. Zhiyong, L.: Theory and application of intelligent traffic control. Science Press, Beijing (2003) (in chinese)
6. Yongchen, Q.: Urban traffic control. China Communication Press, Beijing (1989) (in chinese)
7. Wang, Y., Yang, Z., Guan, Q.: Novel traffic control system & Its coordination model based on Large-scale systems hierarchical optimization theory. In: Proceeding of the IEEE International Conference on Automation and Logistics, Jinan, vol. 18, pp. 841–846 (2007)
8. Xiaohong, L., Shuhua, R., Lan, S.: A new traffic signal coordinated control method based on mobile technology. In: Proceeding of the 27th Chinese Control Conference, Kunming, vol. 53, pp. 448–453 (2008)
9. Li, Z., He, F., Yao, Q., Wang, F.-Y.: Signal controller design for agent-based traffic control system. In: Proceedings of the 2007, IEEE International Conference on Networking, Sensing and Control, London, pp. 199–204 (2007)
10. Chuiou, S.-W.: An efficient computation algorithm for area traffic control problem with link capacity expansions. Applied mathematics and computation, New York 188, 1094–1102 (2007)
11. Zhao, J., Jia, L., Wang, X.: Fuzzy Control for Traffic Flow of Urban Arterial Roads Intersection. Computer Engineering and Applications 40, 9–10 (2004) (in chinese)
12. Zhao, J., Jia, L., Yang, L., Zhu, W.: RBF neural network traffic flow forecasting model based on particle swarm optimization. Journal of Highway and Transportation Research and Development 23(7), 116–119 (2006) (in chinese)
13. Chuiou, S.-W.: An efficient computation algorithm for area traffic control problem with link capacity expansions. Applied mathematics and computation, New York 188, 1094–1102 (2007)

A Semiparametric Regression Ensemble Model for Rainfall Forecasting Based on RBF Neural Network

Jiansheng Wu

Department of Mathematical and Computer Sciences, Liuzhou Teachers College,
Liuzhou, 545004, Guangxi, China
wjsh2002168@163.com

Abstract. Rainfall forecasting is very important research topic in disaster prevention and reduction. In this study, a semiparametric regression ensemble (SRE) model is proposed for rainfall forecasting based on radial basis function (RBF) neural network. In the process of ensemble modeling, original data set are partitioned into some different training subsets via Bagging technology. Then a great number of single RBF neural network models generate diverse individual neural network ensemble by training subsets. Thirdly, the partial least square regression (PLS) is used to choose the appropriate ensemble members. Finally, SRE is used for neural network ensemble for prediction purpose. Empirical results obtained reveal that the prediction using the SRE model is generally better than those obtained using the other models presented in this study in terms of the same evaluation measurements. Our findings reveal that the SRE model proposed here can be used as a promising alternative forecasting tool for rainfall to achieve greater forecasting accuracy and improve prediction quality further.

Keywords: Semiparametric Regression, RBF neural network, Partial Least Square Regression, Rainfall Forecasting.

1 Introduction

Rainfall prediction is a challenging task in the climate dynamics and climate prediction theory. Accurate forecasting of rainfall information (including the spatial and temporal distribution of rainfalls) has been one of the most important issues in hydrological research, because it can help prevent casualties and damages caused by natural disasters [1]. In general, rainfall forecasting involves a rather complex nonlinear pattern, for example pressure, temperature, wind speed and its direction, meteorological characteristics of the precipitation area and so on [2,3]. Over the past few decades, most of the research carried out in rainfall forecast has used traditional statistical methods, such as multiple linear regression, time series methods.

Recreantly, Neural Network (NN) techniques have been recognized as more useful than conventional statistical forecasting models because they can map any

F.L. Wang et al. (Eds.): AICI 2010, Part II, LNAI 6320, pp. 284–292, 2010.

non–linear function without understanding the physical laws and any assumptions of traditional statistical approaches required [4,5]. Moreover, the results of many experiments have shown that the generalization of single neural network is not unique in the practical application. That is, the neural networks results are not stable. Neural network ensemble is a learning paradigm where a number of neural networks are trained for the same task [6,7].

In this study, a semiparametric regression ensemble (SRE) model is proposed for rainfall forecasting based on radial basis function (RBF) neural network. The rest of the study are organized as follows. The rest of this study is organized as follows. In the next section, describes the building process of the ANNE rainfall forecasting model in detail. For further illustration, this work employs the method set up a prediction model for daily mean field of circulation and daily rainfall in Guangxi are used for testing in Section 3. Finally, some concluding remarks are drawn in Section 4.

2   The Building Process of the Neural Network Ensemble Model

In general, a neural network ensemble is constructed in two steps, i.e. training a number of component neural networks and then combining the component predictions. In this section, the RBF neural network is the basic neural network configuration for rainfall forecasting. Firstly, many individual neural predictors are generated by training RBF neural network. Then an appropriate number of neural predictors are selected from the considerable number of candidate predictors by PLS model. Finally, selected neural predictors are combined into an aggregated neural predictor by SRE model.

2.1   Generating Diverse Individual Neural Network Ensemble

NN are one of the technologies soft computing. It provide an interesting technique that theoretically can approximate any nonlinear continuous function on a compact domain to any designed of accuracy. According to the principle of bias-variance trade-off [8], an ANNE model consisting of diverse models with much disagreement is more likely to have a good generalization [9].

Therefore, how to generate diverse models is a crucial factor. For RBF neural network model, several methods have been investigated for the generation of ensemble members making different errors. Such methods basically depended on varying the parameters of RBF neural networks or utilizing different training sets. In this paper, there are three methods for generating diverse models as follows:

(1) Using different RBF neural network architecture: by changing the numbers of nodes in hidden layers diverse RBF neural networks with much disagreement can be created.

(2) Utilizing different the paraments: through varying the cluster center c of the RBF neural networks and varying the cluster center σ of the RBF neural networks, different RBF neural networks can be produced.

(3) Training neural network with different training sets: by re–sampling and preprocessing data by Bagging technology, diverse RBF neural network models can be produced.

2.2 Semiparametric Regression Model

Parametric regression model which realized the pure parametric thinking in curve estimations often does not meet the need in complicated data analysis. An alternative is a semiparametric regression model with a predictor function consisting of a parametric linear component and a nonparametric component which involves an additional predictor variable. Semiparametric regression can be of substantial value in the solution of complex scientific problems. Semiparametric regression models reduce complex data sets to summaries that we can understand.

Suppose the data consists of n subjects. For subject $(k = 1, 2, \cdots, n)$, Y_i is the independent variable, x_i is the m vector of clinical covariates and z_i is the p vector of gene expressions within a pathway. We assume an output is included in x_i, The outcome y_i depends on x_i and z_i through the following semiparametric regression model

$$Y_i = x_i^T \beta + h(z_i) + \varepsilon_i \tag{1}$$

where β is a m vector of regression coefficients, $h(z_i)$ is an unknown centered smooth function, and the errors e_i are assumed to be independent and follow $N(0, \sigma^2)$. $x_i^T \beta$ is the parametrical part of model for epitaxial forecasting, Its objective is to control the independent variable trend. $h(z_i)$ is the nonparametrical part of model for local adjustment so that it is better to fit responses value. So model contains the effects of parametrical part and the effects nonparametrical part. A solution can be obtained by minimizing the sum of squares equation

$$J(h, \beta) = \sum_{i=1}^{n} (y_i - x_i^T \beta - h(z_i))^2 + \lambda \int_a^b [h''(z_i)]^2 dt, \lambda \geq 0 \tag{2}$$

where λ is a tuning parameter which controls the tradeoff between goodness of fitting and complexity of the model. When $\lambda = 0$, the model interpolates the gene expression data, whereas, when $\lambda = \infty$, the model reduces to a simple linear model without $h(\cdot)$. Based on earlier works [10,11], the semiparametric model involves the following five–step iterative procedures:

1. S_λ is the $n \times n$ positive-definite smoother matrix obtained from univariate cubic spline smoothing, without the parametric terms $x_i^T \beta$. The transformation of an n-vector z to $S_\lambda z$ can be conducted in order of operations.
2. Transform Y to $\tilde{Y} = (I - S_\lambda)Y$, and transform X to $\tilde{X} = (I - S_\lambda)X$. Then calculate the least-squares regression of $\tilde{Y}$ on $\tilde{X}$ with β_λ being the resulting coefficient vector.

$$\beta_\lambda = (\tilde{X}^T \tilde{X})^{-1} \tilde{X}^T (I - S_\lambda)Y \tag{3}$$

3. Compute
$$h_\lambda = S_\lambda(Y - X^T\beta_\lambda) \tag{4}$$

The output vector $\hat{Y}$ is then estimated by

$$\hat{Y} = S_\lambda + \tilde{X}(\tilde{X}^T\tilde{X})^{-1}(I - S_\lambda) \tag{5}$$

4. Select a value for the smoothing parameter λ based on the minimizer of the generalized cross-validation (GCV) criterion

$$GCV(\lambda) = \frac{n(Y - \hat{Y})^T(Y - \hat{Y})}{(n - trH_\lambda)^2} \tag{6}$$

5. Compute $tr\mathbf{H}_\lambda$

$$tr\mathbf{H}_\lambda = trS_\lambda + tr(\tilde{X}^T\tilde{X})^{-1}\tilde{X}^T(I - S_\lambda)\tilde{X} \tag{7}$$

The trace of S_λ in Equation (7) can be computed by in $O(n)$ operations using algorithms from univariate spline smoothing [12].

The resulting estimator is often called a partial spline. It is known because this estimator is asymptotically biased for the optimal λ choice when the components of β depend on t.

2.3   Extraction of Nonlinear Features by Three NNs Methods

The initial data set is first divided into different training sets by used Bagging technology, and then these training sets are input to the different individual ANN models which could be executed concurrently. After training, each individual neural predictor has generated its own result. However, if there are a great number of individual members, we need to select a subset of representatives in order to improve ensemble efficiency. In this paper, the Partial Least Square regression (PLS) technique is adopted to select appropriate ensemble members.

PLS regression is a recent technique that generalizes and combines features from principal component analysis and multiple regressions. It is particularly useful when we need to predict a set of dependent variables from a large set of independent variables (i.e., predictors). In technical terms, PLS regression aims at producing a model that transforms a set of correlated explanatory variables into a new set of uncorrelated variables. The parameter coefficients between the predictor variables and the criterion variable [13,14]. Interested readers can be referred to [15] for more details.

The above-mentioned method can be summed up as follows: firstly, original data set are partitioned into some different training subsets $TR_1, TR_2, \cdots, TR_n$ via Bagging algorithm. Secondly, the individual RBF neural network models with same training data are therefore generated M ensemble individuals. Thirdly, the PLS technique extracts ensemble members. Finally, SRE is used to combine the selected individual forecasting results into a ensemble model. The basic flow diagram can be shown in Fig.1.

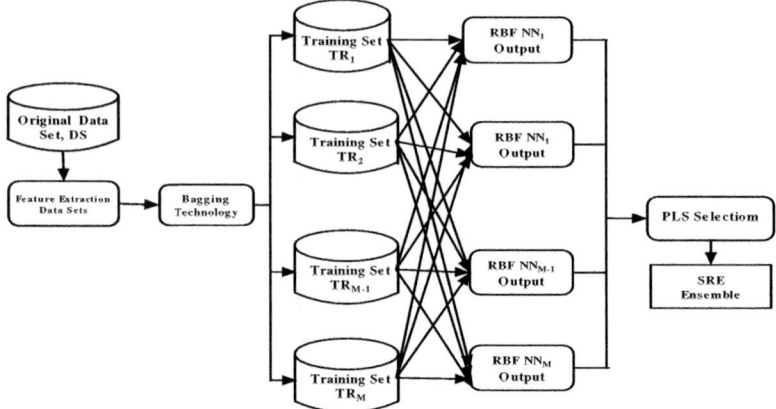

Fig. 1. A Flow Diagram of The Proposed Nonlinear Ensemble Forecasting Model

3   Experiments Analysis

3.1   Empirical Data

Real–time ground rainfall data have been obtained in June from 2003 to 2008 in Guangxi by observing 89 stations, which 144 samples are modeled from 2003 to 2007 in June, other 30 samples are tested modeling in June of 2008. Method of modeling is one-step ahead prediction, that is, the forecast is only one sample each time and the training samples is an additional one each time on the base of the previous training.

Due to the complex terrain of Guangxi and inhomogeneous rainfall, the region has been divided into three regional precipitation based on historical precipitation data by the cluster analysis method to reduce the difficulty of forecasting. Statistics for each district in the average daily precipitation is used as the forecasting object. Fig.2 shows three region maps.

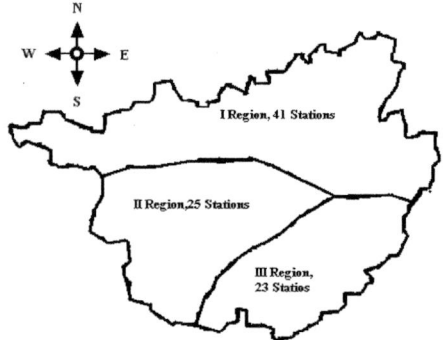

Fig. 2. The Group Average Region Map of Guangxi Rainfall

In the first region as an example to show the process of modeling, it is very important to select the appropriate forecasting factors for model, different climatic variability and its effect have been discussed many times in the literature. In this paper, first of all, the candidate forecasting factors are selected from the numerical forecast products based on 48h forecast field, which includes:

(1) the 17 conventional meteorological elements and physical elements from the T213 numerical products of China Meteorological Administration, the data cover the latitude from 15°N to 30°N, and longitude from 100°E to 120°E, with $1° \times 1°$ resolution, altogether there are 336 grid points.

(2) the fine-mesh precipitation data from the East Asia of Japanese Meteorological Agency, the data cover the latitude from 15°N to 30°N, and longitude from 100°E to 120°E, with $1.25° \times 1.25°$ resolution, altogether there are 221 grid points. We can get 60 variables as the main forecasting factors.

(3) the empirical orthogonal function (EOF) technique [16] is used to integrate the information of forecasting factors from main factors. As comparatively high correlation relationships exist between a large quantity of main factors and the neural network cannot filter factors, it will reduce the ability of having good fitting and prediction. The comprehensive factors can decrease the scale of the modeling and keep it good learning by EOF. We get 6 variables as the predictors by analyzing daily precipitation in the first region.

3.2   The Performance Evaluation of the Model

In order to measure the effectiveness of the proposed method, two types of errors are used in this paper, such as, Normalized Mean Squared Error(NMSE) and Pearson Relative Coefficient(PRC),which be found in many paper. The minimum values of NMSE indicate that the deviations between original values and forecast values are very small. The accurate efficiency of the proposed model is measured as PRC, The higher values of PRC (maximum value is 1) indicate that the forecasting performance of the proposed model is effective, which can capture the average change tendency of the cumulative rainfall data.

According to the previous literature, there are a variety of methods for ensemble in the past studies. For the purpose of comparison, we have also built other three ensemble forecasting models: simple averaging [17], simple MSE approach [18], stacked regression method [19] and variance-based weighting method [19].

3.3   Analysis of the Results

Tab.1 shows the fitting results of 144 training samples for different models. In the two tables, a clear comparison of various methods for the daily rainfall is given via NMSE and PRC. From Tab. 1, the results show that SRE ensemble model better than those of other ensemble forecasting models for the daily rainfall in fitting.

The more important factor to measure performance of a method is to check its forecasting ability of testing samples in order. Tab. 2 shows the forecasting results of 30 testing samples for different models about different measure index.

Table 1. A Comparison of Result of Ensemble Models about Training Samples

Ensemble	Fitting			
Method	NMSE	Rank	PRC	Rank
Simple Averaging	0.2640	3	0.8742	4
Simple MSE	0.2731	4	0.8830	3
Stacked Regression	0.2789	5	0.8543	5
Variance-based weight	0.1880	2	0.9032	2
SRE	0.0517	1	0.9751	1

Table 2. A Comparison of Result of Ensemble Models about Testing Samples

Ensemble	Forecasting			
Method	NMSE	Rank	PRC	Rank
Simple Averaging	0.4274	4	0.8018	5
Simple MSE	0.3988	3	0.8062	4
Stacked Regression	0.4521	5	0.8387	2
Variance-based weight	0.2201	2	0.8341	3
SRE	0.1807	1	0.9780	1

Generally speaking, the forecasting results obtained from the two tables also indicate that the prediction performance of the proposed SRE ensemble forecasting model is better than those of other ensemble forecasting models for the daily rainfall in forecasting.

Subsequently, the forecasting performance comparisons of various models in the first regions. From Tab. 2 in the forecasting of the first region, the differences among the different models are very significant. For example, the NMSE of the simple averaging ensemble model is 0.4274. Similarly, the NMSE of the simple MSE model is 0.3988, the NMSE of the stacked regression ensemble model is 0.4521, and variance-based weight ensemble is 0.2201, however the NMSE of the SRE model reaches 0.1807.

Similarly, for PRC efficiency index, the proposed SRE ensemble model is also deserved to be confident. As shown in Tab. 2, we can see that the forecasting rainfall values from SRE ensemble model have higher correlative relationship with actual rainfall values; As for the testing samples in the first region, the PRC for the simple averaging ensemble model is only 0.8018, for the simple MSE ensemble model it is only 0.8062, for the stacked regression ensemble model PRC is 0.8387 and for variance-based weight ensemble model is 8341; while for the SRE ensemble forecasting models, the PRC reaches 0.9780. It shows that the PRC of SRE ensemble model is close to their real values in different models and the SRE ensemble model is capable to capture the average change tendency of the daily rainfall data.

Furthermore, the same method is used to train precipitation data and predict precipitation at the other two regions. The experimental results also show that SRE ensemble method is better than other methods. From the experiments presented in this paper, the SRE ensemble forecasting model is superior to the other ensemble models for the test cases of daily rainfall.

4 Conclusions

A challenging task for a frequent–unanticipated flash flood region is the provision of a quantitative rainfall forecast to avoid life losing and economic loses. The rainfall data of the Guangxi watershed in southwest of China shows primary rainy season in the June. Therefore, accurate prediction of daily precipitation is very important for the prevention and mitigation of flood disaster. This study proposes we use a SRE forecasting model to predict rainfall based on RBF neural network. In terms of the empirical results, we find that different forecasting models for the forecasting samples of three regions of Guangxi on the base of different criteria, the SRE model is superior to the other ensemble model for the fitting and testing cases of three regions in terms of the different measurement. The results show SRE ensemble model combine components of linear regression model(parametric partly) and nonlinear regression(nonparametric partly), it keeps the easy interpretability of the linear model and retaining some of the flexibility of the nonlinear model. This indicates that the SRE forecasting model can be used as an alternative tool for daily rainfall forecasting to obtain greater forecasting accuracy and improve the prediction quality further in view of empirical results, and can provide more useful information, avoid invalid information for the future forecasting.

Acknowledgment

The authors would like to express their sincere thanks to the editor and anonymous reviewer's comments and suggestions for the improvement of this paper. This work was supported in part by the Natural Science Foundation of Guangxi under Grant No.0832092, and in part by the Department of Guangxi Education under Grant No.200807MS098.

References

1. Lettenmaier, D.P., Wood, E.F.: Hydrology forecasting. In: Maidment, D.R. (ed.) Handbook of Hydrology. McGraw-Hill, New York (1993)
2. Francis, W.Z., Hans, J.S.: On the role of statistics in climate research. Internation of Journal Climatology 24, 665–680 (2004)
3. Marzano, F.S., Fionda, E., Ciotti, P.: Neural–network approach to ground–based passive microwave estimation of precipitation intensity and extinction. Journal of Hydrology 328, 121–131 (2006)

4. Jiansheng, W., Enhong, C.: A novel nonparametric regression ensemble for rainfall forecasting using particle swarm optimization technique coupled with artificial neural network. In: Yu, W., He, H., Zhang, N. (eds.) ISNN 2009. LNCS, vol. 5553, pp. 49–58. Springer, Heidelberg (2009)
5. Jiansheng, W., Long, J., Mingzhe, L.: Modeling meteorological prediction using particle swarm optimization and neural network ensemble. In: Wang, J., Yi, Z., Żurada, J.M., Lu, B.-L., Yin, H. (eds.) ISNN 2006. LNCS, vol. 3973, pp. 1202–1209. Springer, Heidelberg (2006)
6. Jiansheng, W.: A novel Artificial neural network ensemble model based on K–nn nonparametric estimation of regression function and its application for rainfall forecasting. In: 2nd Internatioal Joint Conference on Computational Sciences and Optimization, pp. 44–48. IEEE Computer Society Press, New York (2009)
7. Yu, L., Lai, K.K., Wang, S.Y.: Multistage RBF neural network ensemble learning for exchange rates forecasting. Neurocomputing 71, 3295–3302 (2008)
8. Yu, L., Lai, K.K., Wang, S.Y., Huang, W.: A bias–variance–complexity trade–off framework for complex system modeling. In: Gavrilova, M.L., Gervasi, O., Kumar, V., Tan, C.J.K., Taniar, D., Laganá, A., Mun, Y., Choo, H. (eds.) ICCSA 2006. LNCS, vol. 3980, pp. 518–527. Springer, Heidelberg (2006)
9. French, M.N., Krajewski, W.F., Cuykendal, R.R.: Rainfall Forecasting in Space and Time Using a Neural Network. Journal of Hydrology 137, 1–37 (1992)
10. Speckman, P.: Kernel smoothing in partial linear models. Journal of the Royal Statistical Society: Series B 50, 413–436 (1988)
11. Hall, P., Kay, J.W., Titterington, D.M.: Asymptotically optimal difference-based estimation of variance in nonparametric regression. Biometrika 77, 521–528 (1990)
12. Eubank, R.L.: Spline regression. In: Schimek, M.G. (ed.) Smoothing and regression approaches, computation, and application. Wiley, New York (2000)
13. Pagès, J., Tenenhaus, M.: Multiple factor analysis combined with PLS path modeling. Application to the analysis of relationships between physicochemical variables, sensory profiles and hedonic judgments. Chemometrics and Intelligent Laboratory Systems 58, 261–273 (2001)
14. McIntosh, A.R., Lobaugh, N.J.: Partial least squares analysis of neuroimaging data: applications and advances. Neuroimage 23, 250–263 (2004)
15. Wu, J., Jin, L.: Neural network with partial least square prediction model based on SSA-MGF. Journal of Catastrophology 21(2), 17–23 (2006)
16. Lee, M.A., Yeah, C.D., Cheng, C.H.: Empirical orthogonal function analysis of avhrr sea surface temperature patterns in Taiwan Strait. Journal of marine science and technology 11(1), 1–7 (2003)
17. Bishop, C.M.: Neural networks for pattern recognition. Oxford University Press, Oxford (1995)
18. Krogh, A., Vedelsby, J.: Neural network ensembles, cross validation, and active learning. In: Tesauro, G., Touretzky, D., Leen, T. (eds.) Advances in Neural Information Processing Systems, vol. 7, pp. 231–238. MIT Press, Cambridge (1995)
19. Yu, L., Wang, S.Y., Lai, K.K.: A novel nonlinear ensemble forecasting model incorporating GLAR and ANN for foreign exchange rates. Computers & Operations Research 32, 2523–2541 (2005)

A Modified Particle Swarm Optimizer with a Novel Operator

Ran Cheng and Min Yao

College of Computer Science and Technology, Zhejiang University,
Hangzhou, China
cheng_ran@hotmail.com
myao@zju.edu.cn

Abstract. This paper proposes a simple and effective modified particle swarm optimizor with a novel operator. The aim is to prevent premature convergence and improve the quality of solutions. The standard PSO is shown to have no ability to perform a fine grain search to improve the quality of solutions as the number of iterations is increased, although it may find the near optimal solutions much faster than other evolutionary algorithms. The modified PSO algorithm presented in this paper is able to find near optimal solutions as fast as the standard PSO and improve their quality in the later iterations. Compared with the standard PSO, benchmark tests are implemented and the result shows that our modified algorithm successfully prevents premature convergence and provides better solutions.

Keywords: particle swarm optimization, premature convergence, quality of solutions.

1 Introduction

The particle swarm optimization (PSO) was originally introduced in [1] as a population-based evolutionary technique which was inspired by bird flocking. The PSO is proven to work well when it comes to continues nonlinear function optimization. However, the standard PSO has no ability to perform a fine grain search to improve the quality of solutions as the number of iterations is increased, although it may find the near optimal solution much faster than other evolutionary algorithms [2]. This is considered to be caused by premature convergence [7].

Compared to PSO, other evolutionary algorithms tend to improve the quality of solutions with the increase of iterations [3]. But most of them are time consuming and unstable (e.g. genetic algorithm). So it seems reasonable to build a stable algorithm which is able to fast locate the near optimal solutions in early iterations and improve their quality later. Such attempts have been done by a number of people [3, 4, 5, 6, 7]. Those modified PSO algorithms prevented premature convergence and performed well on improving the quality of solutions, however, as far as we are concerned, they are not simple enough to implement

F.L. Wang et al. (Eds.): AICI 2010, Part II, LNAI 6320, pp. 293–301, 2010.
© Springer-Verlag Berlin Heidelberg 2010

and the improvement on the quality of solutions is not significant. In this paper, we put forward a simple and effective modified particle swarm optimizor with a novel operator named leap operator. In the rest part of this paper, this algorithm is abbreviated as LPSO (Leap-PSO). Compared with the standard PSO, benchmark tests are implemented and the result shows that our modification successfully prevents premature convergence and provides better solutions.

2   Premature Convergence of PSO

In the standard PSO [10], the information of each particle i in the swarm is recorded by the following variables: (i) the current position X_i, (ii) the current velocity V_i, (iii) the individual best position $pbest_i$, and (iv) the swarm best position $gbest$. In each iteration, the positions and velocities are adjusted by the following equations:

$$v_{ij}(t+1) = wv_{ij}(t) + c_1 rand()[p_{ij}(t) - x_{ij}(t)] \\ + c_2 Rand()[p_{gj}(t) - x_{ij}(t)] \tag{1}$$

$$x_{ij}(t+1) = x_{ij}(t) + v_{ij}(t+1) \tag{2}$$

for $j \in 1..d$ where d is the dimension number of the search space, for $i \in 1..n$ where n is the number of particles, t is the iteration number, w is the inertia weight, $rand()$ and $Rand()$ are random numbers uniformly distributed in the range $[0,1]$, c_1 and c_2 are accelerating factors.To control the flying step size of the particles, v_{ij} is constrained in the range $[-v_{max}, v_{max}]$ where v_{max} is commonly set as $10\% - 20\%$ of each search dimension size [9].

Fast convergence is one of the most significant advantages of PSO. However, such convergence always comes too fast for a fine grain search to be performed in the near optimal area. When convergence happens, x_{ij} and v_{ij} stop being modified or just vary in a small range, so that $gbest$ has little chance to be updated which means the quality of solutions is no more improved in the later iterations. Such harmful convergence is called premature convergence. Thus preventing premature convergence is the necessary but not sufficient condition for a high quality of the solutions.

3   Fundamentals of LPSO

Our modified algorithm lies on two fundamental hypotheses:

Hyp. 1. *The worst-fitting particle has the least probability to reach the global optimal solution.*

Hyp. 2. *In the terminal iterations, if the swarm best position gbest is not updated for a number of consecutive iterations, the near optimal area is always located and the search tends to be trapped in premature convergence.*

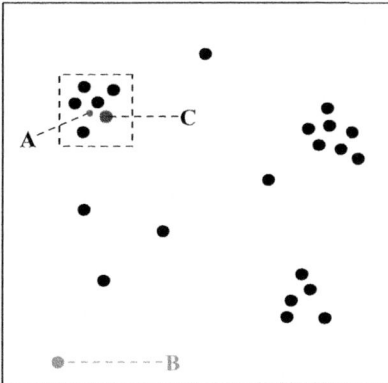

Fig. 1. The situation before the worst-fitting particle's leap

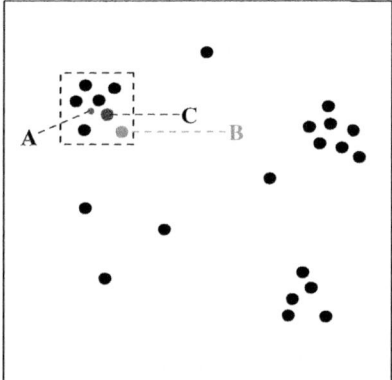

Fig. 2. The situation after the worst-fitting particle's leap

As is mentioned in section 2, when premature convergence happens, x_{ij} and v_{ij} stop being modified or just vary in a small range, so the most express method to prevent premature convergence is to modify x_{ij} and v_{ij}. If they are replaced with random values, the primary convergence is sure to be completely damaged and it makes the PSO method degenerate into an inefficient purely random search method. So our method is to modify them selectively and intentionally. With our method, not only the premature convergence is prevented, but also the primary convergence is not damaged. Since the particles were originally regarded as birds [1], we name the modification of positions and velocities as an intentional *leap*. It involves the following factors:

3.1 Selection of the Particle to Leap

Hyp. 1 is the root for the selection that determines which particle is to leap. According to Hyp. 1, the worst-fitting particle of current iteration is selected. There are two benefits of this selection strategy: (i) In each iteration, at most one particle is selected. It won't damage the distribution of current swarm. (ii) Selecting the worst-fitting particle does not reduce the probability to reach the global optimal position. The position and velocity of the selected particle is presented by $X_l(x_{l1}, x_{l2}, \ldots, x_{ld})$ and $V_l(v_{l1}, v_{l2}, \ldots, v_{ld})$ respectively.

3.2   Condition of the Selected Particle's Leap

Hyp. 2 is the root for the condition which involves two major factors: *terminal iterations* and *a number of consecutive iterations*. In our definition, during a run process of the PSO algorithms, the maximum iteration number is recorded by *maxiter*, t is the current iteration number, if $t \geq \rho * maxiter$ where $\rho \in (0, 1)$, the following iterations are considered to be *terminal*. The *number* in *a number of consecutive iterations* is presented by δ. The number of iterations between two consecutive updates i.e. the *consecutive iterations* is recorded by C. With the declarations above we have the condition of the selected particle's leap:

$$(t \geq \rho * maxiter) \wedge (C \geq \delta) \tag{3}$$

where ρ and δ are thresholds. The first half of (3) determines in which period of a run process leap operations are performed and the second determines the frequency.

3.3   Position After Leap

As is mentioned at the beginning of this section, X_l should be modified intentionally. Our method is to move the selected particle to the near optimal area, as thus the probability to reach the global optimal position is increased. It can be concluded from hyp. 2, the near optimal area is always located in the terminal iterations. As the swarm best position, *gbest* is surely inside the area. So we have:

$$X_l = gbest \tag{4}$$

Unfortunately, since *gbest* is not updated in the terminal iterations, simply replacing X_l with *gbest* is equivalent to making particles gradually gather to the same position. As a result, the search is trapped into another premature convergence and the only difference is that it's inside the near optimal area. The fine grain search is still not performed, although the probability to reach the global optimal position is increased. Enlightened by the mutation operator in genetic algorithm (GA), a stochastic *offset* is added to one of the dimensions:

$$x'_{lk} = x_{lk} + offset \tag{5}$$

where $offset = U(-a, a)$, U is an uniform distribution, $k \in 1..d$. a determines the distribution scope of the leaped particles. In our paper, $a = v_{max}$. k is a random number, which means each dimension has the same chance to be added with an *offset*. Moreover, *offset* obeys the uniform distribution. So, generally, the leaped particles are uniformly distributed in the near optimal area.

3.4   Velocity After Leap

At first, 3 method candidates are designed: (i) Leave V_l as it is, (ii) Re-initialize V_l with random values, (iii) Reset V_l with $\mathbf{0}$. The experiment result shows that candidate (iii):

$$V_l = \mathbf{0} \tag{6}$$

performs the best. Here is a brief analysis: the inertia weight w memorize the velocity in the last iteration, so that for candidate (i), the velocity before leap may have impact on the velocity after leap, however, the position which is already modified by (4) and (5) may not match such a velocity produced by candidate (i); for candidate (ii) , the leaped particle is probably soon be dragged out of the near optimal area in the next iteration since the randomly assigned V_l, which makes (4) and (5) lose effectiveness; candidate (iii) performs the best because with $V_l = \mathbf{0}$, (1) turns out to be:

$$\begin{aligned} v_{lj}(t+1) = 0 &+ c_1 rand()[p_{lj}(t) - x_{lj}(t)] \\ &+ c_2 Rand()[p_{gj}(t) - x_{lj}(t)] \end{aligned} \tag{7}$$

which means $v_{lj}(t+1)$ is determined only by $p_{lj}(t)$ and $p_{lj}(t)$, so that V_l is according to the current environment.

As is shown in Fig. 1 and Fig. 2, the points are the positions of particles in a 2-dementional search space. A is the position of the global optimal solution. B is the position of the worst-fitting particle in current iteration. C is *gbest*. Inside the dashed rectangle is the near optimal area. Fig. 1 presents the situation before leap operation. In Fig. 2, leap operation has been implemented. The particle originally at B has leaped to a position beside C which is inside the near optimal area.

4   Algorithms

Algorithm 1 is the LPSO. In step 5, however, (1) and (2) are not the most effective ones currently. They can be replaced by any other modification, e.g.

Algorithm 1. LPSO(Leap-PSO)

Require: $0 < \delta < maxiter$, $0 < \rho < 1$
1: Initialize a swarm, including random positions and velocities; set parameters δ, ρ, v_{max} etc, $t \leftarrow 0$.
2: Evaluate the fitness of each particle, $t \leftarrow t + 1$.
3: For each particle, compare its fitness with the individual best position *pbest* . If better, update *pbest* with current position.
4: For each particle, compare its fitness with the swarm best position *gbest*. If better, replace *gbest* with current position and $C \leftarrow 0$, else $C \leftarrow C + 1$.
5: Update the velocities and positions with (1) and (2).
6: Find worst-fitting particles and record its index in l, excute **leap operator.**
7: Repeat steps 2–6 until an expected number of iterations is completed or a stop criterion is satisfied.

Algorithm 2. Leap operator

```
 1: if t ≥ ρ * maxiter and C ≥ δ then
 2:    C = 0;
 3:    k = random(1..d);
 4:    offset = random(−v_{max}, v_{max});
 5:    X_l = gbest;
 6:    if x_{lk} + offset ∉ D_k then
 7:       ensure x_{lk} ∈ D_k; {D_k is the domain of dimension k}
 8:    else
 9:       x_{lk} = x_{lk} + offset;
10:    end if
11:    V_l = 0;
12: end if
```

Maurice Clerc's K *(Constrained Factor)* modification in [5] and Y Shi's *adaptive* w modification in [8] etc. Step 6 is the heart of the LPSO which contains a new operator. It's presented by Algorithm 2. Since it's almost an independent operator which can be embedded in any PSO algorithm to form a new LPSO, we name it *leap operator.*

5 Experimental Results

In our experiment, four standard functions for benchmark tests are selected. For each function, the demension number is 30 and for each dimension i, $x_i \in [-100, 100]$. These functions are widely used in genetic and evolutionary algorithms' tests [3, 4, 5, 6, 7] etc. Each function's global optimal solution is 0. The first function is the Sphere(De Jong F1) function given by

$$f_1(x) = \sum_{i=1}^{n} x_i^2 \tag{8}$$

Athough it is a unimodal function, it defferentiates well between good local optimizers and poor local optimizers. The second function is the Rosenbrock function given by

$$f_2(x) = \sum_{i=1}^{n} [100(x_{i+1} - x_i^2)^2 + (x_i - 1)^2] \tag{9}$$

The third function is the generalised Rastrigrin function given by

$$f_3(x) = \sum_{i=1}^{n} (x_i^2 - 10\cos(2\pi x_i) + 10) \tag{10}$$

The fourth function is the generalised Griewank function:

$$f_4(x) = \frac{1}{4000} \sum_{i=1}^{n} x_i^2 - \prod_{i=1}^{n} \cos(\frac{x_i}{\sqrt{i}}) + 1 \tag{11}$$

As is mentioned in section 4, any PSO modification can be regarded as a standard PSO with leap operator embedded in it to form a new LPSO. So we use the modification in [8] as the standard PSO and embed our operator in it.

δ and ρ are parameters in the leap operator. Early experiments have shown the operator works best with $\rho \in [0.4, 0.6]$, so we fix ρ at 0.4. However, δ is a parameter difficult to determine. So we set 2 groups of values ($\delta_1 = 5$, $\delta_2 = 20$) to see its influence on the LPSO. For each group, the population size is set to be 40. In order to see whether the LPSO successfully prevents premature convergence, 5000 iterations are operated in every run (more than commonly 1000–2000 iterations required by PSO). All the other parameter values are suggested in [8] ($0.4 \leq w \leq 0.9$, $c_1 = c_2 = 2$, $v_{max} = 4$) . For each function, 50 trial runs are implemented. The whole experiment is implemented in matlab7.0. The results are in Table 1.

Table 1. Experimental results

Function	Experimental results		
	LPSO		PSO
	δ_1	δ_2	
Sphere(De Jong F1)	0.000000	0.000000	0.000000
	0.000000	0.000000	0.000000
Rosenbrock	0.022905	0.327700	1.513700
	32.188200	33.575200	32.976000
Rastrigrin	0.994960	2.984900	18.904200
	5.074400	12.178300	32.535100
Griewank	0.000000	0.000000	0.000000
	0.008100	0.009000	0.008600

In Table 1, the first value is the best result and the second is the average result of 50 runs. As we can observe, δ_1 perform slightly better than δ_2. On the whole, the LPSO performs much better on f_3 than the standard PSO. For f_1 and f_2, although the average results are just slightly better, the best results show that the LPSO has more potential in finding much better solutions.

Since $\rho * maxiter = 0.4 * 5000 = 2000$, the leap operator is not excuted until the 2000th iteration. Clearly shown by Fig. 3, the LPSO and PSO almost keep the same pace before the 2000th iteration, however, in the later (terminal) iterations, the PSO fails improving the solution's quaility futher more but the LPSO still performs well. It's becuase the LPSO successfully prevents premature convergence.

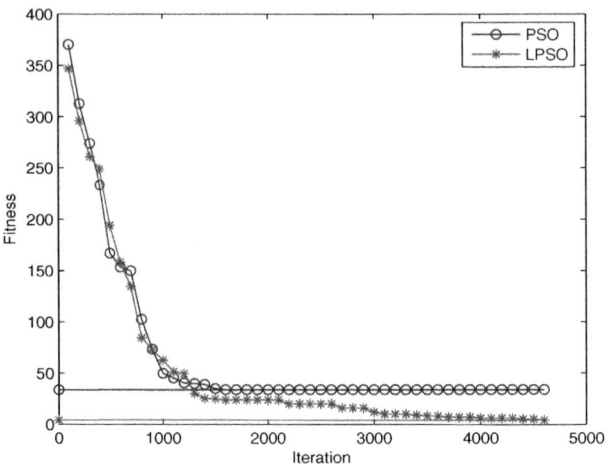

Fig. 3. The 5000 iterations in one typical run $(\delta_1,\ f_3)$.

6   Conclusion

In this paper, we introduced a simple and effective modified PSO algorithm with a novel operator. Experiments have been performed to prove that it successfully prevents premature convergence and improves the quality of solutions.

Even though the results have showed our modification works well, further studies on parameters δ and ρ are still required. Maybe we can develop an algorithm to search for the best values for them. We are currently working on it.

References

1. Kennedy, J., Eberhart, R.C.: Particle swarm optimization. In: Proc. of the IEEE International Conference on Neural Networks, Perth, pp. 1942–1948 (1995)
2. Angeline, P.: Evolutionary optimisation versus particle swarm optimization: Philosophy and performance difference. In: Proc. of Evolutionary Programming Conference, San Diago, USA (1998)
3. Suganthan, P.N.: Particle swarm optimizer with neighborhood operator. In: Proc. of the Congress on Evolutionary Computation, Washington, DC, pp. 1958–1962 (1999)
4. Angeline, P.J.: Using selection to improve particle swarm optimization. In: Proc. of the IEEE Int. Conf. on Evolutionary Computation, Anchorage, pp. 84–89 (1998)
5. Clerc, M.: The swarm and the queen: Towards a deterministic and adaptive particle swarm optimization. In: Proc. of the Congress on Evolutionary Computation, Washington, DC, pp. 1951–1957 (1999)
6. Kennedy, J.: Stereotyping: Improving particle swarm performance with cluster analysis. In: Proc. of the IEEE Int. Conf. on Evolutionary Computation, La Jolla, pp. 1507–1512 (2000)

7. Zhang, Q.-l., Xing, L., Tran, Q.-a. Tran: A modified particle swarm optimization algorithm. In: Proc. of the Fourth International Conference on Machine Learning and Cybernetics, Guangzhou (2005)
8. Shi, Y.H., Eberhart, R.C.: Parameter selection in particle swarm optimization. In: Proc. of the 7th Annual Conf. on Evolutionary Programming, Washington, DC, pp. 591–600 (1998)
9. Eberhart, R.C., Shi, Y.: Particle swarm optimization: developments, applications and recourses. In: Proc. of the IEEE Int. Conf. on Evolutionary Computation, Seoul, vol. 1, pp. 81–86 (2001)
10. EI-Abd, M.: Preventing premature convergence in a PSO and EDA hybrid. In: Proc. of the Congress on Evolutionary Computation, Trondheim, Norway, pp. 3061–3066 (2009)

An AntiCentroid-oriented Particle Swarm Algorithm for Numerical Optimization

Xinchao Zhao[1] and Wenbin Wang[2]

[1] Department of Mathematics, School of Sciences,
Beijing University of Posts and Telecommunications, Beijing 100876, China
xcmmrc@gmail.com
[2] State Key Laboratory of Networking and Switching Technology,
Beijing University of Posts and Telecommunications, Beijing, 100876, China
wwbbupt@gmail.com

Abstract. In order to keep balance of premature convergence and diversity maintenance, an AntiCentroid-oriented particle updating strategy and an improved Particle Swarm Algorithm (ACoPSA) are presented in this paper. The swarm centroid reflects the search focus of the PSA algorithm and its distance to the global best particle (gbest) indicates the behavior difference between the population search and the gbest. Therefore the directional vector from the swarm centroid to the gbest implies an effective direction that particles should follow. This direction is utilized to update the particle velocity and to guide swarm search. Experimental comparisons among ACoPSA, standard PSA and a recent perturbed PSA are made to validate the efficacy of the strategy. The experiments confirm us that the swarm centroid-guided particle updating strategy is encouraging and promising for stochastic heuristic algorithms.

Keywords: particle swarm optimization, swarm centroid, particle updating strategy, evolutionary state, numerical optimization.

1 Introduction

Particle swarm optimization algorithm (PSA) is a swarm intelligence technique originally developed from studies of social behaviors of animals or insects, e.g., bird flocking or fish schooling[1] in 1995. Since then, PSA has gained increasing popularity among researchers and practitioners as a robust and efficient technique for solving complex and difficult optimization problems[2,3,4].

In a standard PSA[5], the velocity of each particle is modified iteratively by its personal best position (i.e., the position giving the best fitness value so far), and the position of best particle from the entire swarm. As a result, each particle searches around a region defined by its personal best position and the position of the population best. This feature of PSA makes it easily get trapped in the local optima when solving complex multimodal problems while keeping satisfiable converging speed. Therefore, accelerating convergence speed and avoiding the local optima have become the two most important and appealing goals in

F.L. Wang et al. (Eds.): AICI 2010, Part II, LNAI 6320, pp. 302–309, 2010.

PSO research. A number of variant PSO algorithms have, hence, been proposed to achieve these two goals[6,7,8,9]. However, it is seen to be difficult to simultaneously achieve both goals[10]. Our aim is try to keep them trade-off.

2   Standard Particle Swarm Algorithm

In essence, the trajectory of each particle is updated according to its own flying experience as well as to that of the best particle in the swarm. In (1), p_i is the position with the best fitness found so far for the ith particle, and p_g is the best position found so far for the entire swarm.

$$v_{i,d}^{k+1} = \omega \times v_{i,d}^k + c_1 \times r_1^k \times (p_{i,d}^k - x_{i,d}^k) + c_2 \times r_2^k \times (p_{g,d}^k - x_{i,d}^k) \qquad (1)$$

$$x_{i,d}^{k+1} = x_{i,d}^k + v_{i,d}^{k+1} \qquad (2)$$

where $v_{i,d}^k$ is the d-th dimension velocity of particle i in cycle k; $x_{i,d}^k$ is the d-th dimension position of particle i in cycle k; $p_{i,d}^k$ is the d-th dimension of personal best (pbest) of particle i in cycle k; $p_{g,d}^k$ is the d-th dimension of the gbest in cycle k; ω is the inertia weight; c_1 is the cognition weight and c_2 is the social weight; and r_1 and r_2 are two random values uniformly distributed in the range of $[0, 1]$.

3   Swarm Centroid-Guided Particle Swarm Algorithm (ACoPSA)

3.1   Evolutionary States and Algorithmic Behaviors

The population distribution characteristics vary not only with the generation number but also with the evolutionary state during the PSA evolutionary process. For example, the particles may be scattered in various areas at an early stage, and, hence, the population distribution is dispersive. As the evolution goes on particles would be attracted together and converge to a locally or globally optimal area. Hence, the population distribution information would be different from that in the early stage. Therefore, how to detect the different population distribution information and how to use this information to estimate the evolutionary state would be a significant and promising research topic in PSO[11]. Among here, the swarm centroid of PSA is an indication of the algorithm's searching interests and its distance to the global best particle implies the difference between the population search and the possible search area of the gbest particle.

3.2   Swarm Centroid

A PSA optimizer maintains a swarm of particles and each individual is composed of three D-dimensional vectors, where D is the dimensionality of the search space.

These are the current position x_i, the previous best position p_i, and the velocity v_i. The current position $x_i = (x_{i,1}, \cdots, x_{i,D})$ can be considered as a set of coordinates describing a point in space. The best solution found so far is stored in $p_i = (p_{i,1}, \cdots, p_{i,D})$. New points are chosen by adding $v_i = (v_{i,1}, \cdots, v_{i,n})$ coordinates to x_i, and the algorithm operates by adjusting v_i, which can be seen as a step size.

Let PSA swarm be constituted with m particle, then the swarm centroid (SC) and the anticentroid-oriented direction vector (ACD) are defined as follows.

Definition 1 [SC]:

$$SC = (sc_1, \cdots, sc_d, \cdots, sc_D), \text{where } sc_d = (\sum_{i=1}^{m} x_{id})/m \qquad (3)$$

Definition 2 [AntiCentroid-oriented Direction, ACD]:

$$ACD = gbest - SC = (p_{g1} - sc_1, \cdots, p_{gd} - sc_d, \cdots, p_{gD} - sc_D) \qquad (4)$$

SC is an overall reflection of the evolutionary states of PSA population and the vector from the swarm centroid to the gbest is a promising direction that many other particles should follow. This effective search direction gives us a lot of information to utilize. However, the population is possible to be trapped if all other particles follows along this direction with a large or moderate step size. So it maybe reach an exploration and exploitation tradeoff[12] if particles search along this direction with a slight step when velocity updating.

3.3   Swarm Centroid and ACD Updating Strategy

Inspired by the new particle updating strategy based on the perturbed global best particle with a micro random *Gaussian* perturbation[6], an anticentroid-oriented direction for global best particle perturbation strategy is proposed as follows, which is also illustrated as Fig.(1), to guide swarm search.

In contrast to conventional approaches, the gbest in ACoPSA is denoted as "possibly at gbest (p-gbest)=$(p_{g,1} \times p_{g,2} \times \cdots, \times, p_{g,D})$", instead of a crisp location. Consequently, the calculation of particle velocity can be rewritten as

$$p_{g,d}^{k\prime} = p_{g,d}^{k} + rand \times ACD_d \times \sigma \qquad (5)$$

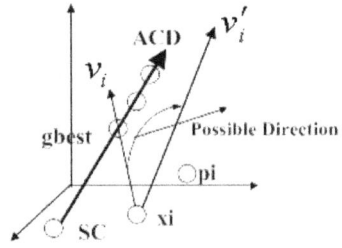

Fig. 1. Search Region of SC&ACD

$$\sigma = p(k) \tag{6}$$

$$v_{i,d}^{k+1} = \omega \times v_{i,d}^k + c_1 \times r_1^k \times (p_{i,d}^k - x_{i,d}^k) + c_2 \times r_2^k \times (p_{g,d}^{k'} - x_{i,d}^k) \tag{7}$$

where $p_{g,d}^{k'}$ is the d-th dimension of p-gbest in cycle k. From (7), it can be observed that the p-gbest is characterized by an oriented micro random perturbation along the direction of ACD, where σ represents the degree of uncertainty about the optimality of the gbest, which is distinct from the normal distribution-based perturbation $N(p_{g,d}^k, \sigma)$[6]. In order to account for the information received over time that reduces uncertainty about the gbest position, σ is modeled as some non-increasing function of the number of cycles as equation (8). For simplicity, $p(k)$ is defined as

$$p(k) = \begin{cases} \sigma_{max}, & k < \alpha \times \text{max\_cycle} \\ \sigma_{min}, & \text{otherwise} \end{cases} \tag{8}$$

where σ_{max}, σ_{min}, and α are manually set parameters.

The perturbed global best updating strategy equations (5-8) should be distinguished from not only the conventional updating operation (1,2), but also the random normal distribution-based perturbing strategy, which applies an ACD-oriented perturbation to the particles. The function of p-gbest is to encourage the particles to explore a region beyond that defined by the search trajectory. By considering the uncertainty associated with each gbest as a function of time, p-gbest provides a simple and efficient exploration at the early stage when σ is large and encourages local fine-tuning at the latter stage when σ is small. Subsequently, this approach helps to reduce the likelihood of premature convergence and guides the search toward the promising search area.

3.4 ACoPSA Algorithm

1: Initialize a population array of particles with random positions and velocities on D dimensions in the search space and other algorithmic parameters.
  2: loop
    3: For each particle, evaluate the desired optimization fitness function in D variables.
    4: Compare particle's fitness evaluation with its $pbest_i$. If current value is better than $pbest_i$, then let $pbest_i$ be the current value, and p_i be the current location x_i in D-dimensional space.
    5: Identify the particle in the neighborhood with the best success so far, and assign its index to the variable g.
    6: Update the velocity and position of the particle according to equations (5-8).
    7. If a criterion is met (usually a satisfied fitness or a maximal number of iterations), exit loop and output the final solution and fitness.
8: End loop

4   Benchmark Tests and Comparisons

In order to validate the necessity and good performance of the proposed oriented perturbed particle updating strategy and ACoPSA algorithm, 6 benchmarks[6] are adopted, and the results are compared with PSO and pPSA[6]. Due to the aim of this paper being nothing more than to illustrate the rationality and necessity of the perturbed updating particle strategy, the parameters fine-tuning process is omitted here.

4.1   Benchmark Functions and Algorithm Configuration

Benchmark functions	Domain	f_{min}
$f_1 = \sum_{i=1}^{n} x_i^2$	$[-100, 100]^n$	0
$f_2 = \max_i\{|x_i|,\ 1 \leq i \leq n\}$	$[-100, 100]^n$	0
$f_3 = \sum_{i=1}^{n}(\lfloor x_i + 0.5 \rfloor)^2$	$[-100, 100]^n$	0
$f_4 = \sum_{i=1}^{n} i x_i^4 + random[0, 1)$	$[-1.28, 1.28]^n$	0
$f_5 = -20 \exp\left[-0.2\sqrt{\frac{1}{n}\sum_{i=1}^{n} x_i^2}\right]$ $-\exp\left(\frac{1}{n}\sum_{i=1}^{n}\cos(2\pi x_i)\right) + 20 + e$	$[-32, 32]^n$	0
$f_6 = \frac{1}{4000}\sum_{i=1}^{n} x_i^2 - \prod_{i=1}^{n}\cos\left(\frac{x_i}{\sqrt{i}}\right) + 1$	$[-600, 600]^n$	0

All the following experimental results are obtained from 30 independent runs. The parameter settings are: dimension number $n = 30$; particle number $Particle = 20$; maximal generations $max\_cycle = 2000$; inertia weight $\omega = 0.9$; $c_1 = 0.5$; $c_2 = 0.3$; $\sigma_{max} = 1.25$, $\sigma_{min} = 0.001$ and $\alpha = 0.5$.

4.2   Statistical Results Comparison and Algorithmic Analysis

Experimental results of three algorithms are given and compared as Table-1 shows. The threshold for reaching the known optima in column *Counts* is set to be 10^{-3}.

Observed from Table-1 we can see that most results of pPSA are better than those of PSO and the results of ACoPSA are much better than those of PSO and pPSA. Both **Best** and **Median** results of ACoPSA are at least 10^3 times better than pPSA as Table-1 indicates. Under the threshold at least a half independent runs of ACoPSA found the global optima as "Counts" column shows. All the above analysis tell us that ACoPSA has very high probability locate the global optima which confirms us the effectiveness of the anti-swarm-centroid along the direction to the global best particle oriented perturbation strategy.

Table 1. Comparison between **PSO**, **pPSA** and **ACoPSA** on the statistic results over 30 independent runs, Where "Best" and "Median" are the best and the median results, "Counts" are the numbers that algorithms converge with a threshold

Fun	Best			Median			Counts		
	PSO	pPSA	ACoPSA	PSO	pPSA	ACoPSA	PSO	pPSA	ACoPSA
1	5.94	6.51e-6	**4.20e-10**	20.55	9.19e-6	**2.46e-9**	0	**30**	26
2	17.80	0.43487	**1.28e-5**	26.94	0.82449	**3.06e-5**	0	0	**17**
3	4.83e2	5	**0**	1.39e3	10	**0**	0	0	**24**
4	0.45788	2.84e1	**2.96e-4**	1.3445	4.81e1	**1.11e-3**	0	0	**13**
5	8.1671	1.778	**2.18e-5**	1.32e1	2.4083	**3.56e-5**	0	0	**24**
6	1.6158	3.62e-7	**5.03e-11**	3.4262	7.39e-3	**1.32e-10**	0	13	**16**

However, ACoPSA sometimes obtained a very unsatisfied result, i.e., ACD particle updating strategy sometimes maybe wrongly guide the population search. For example, there are 26 over 30 times that ACoPSA arrived at 10^{-9} magnitude for function f_1, but the other four results are reaching about 10^3 magnitude. The similar situation happens to function f_3, however, the results of all other functions are all acceptable. That is to say, there are a small chance to be very unlucky when using ACoPSA algorithm. For this situation, it maybe because the population search behavior coincides with that of the global best particle, however, the anticentroid oriented direction deviates from this coincidence. This unfortunate thing does not occur to algorithm pPSA, which illustrates that pPSA is more steady and robust than ACoPSA, although its convergence is inferior to ACoPSA. The next interesting work is to improve the robustness of ACoPSA and the convergence of pPSA to balance the convergence and steadiness[11].

4.3   Further Experiments with Expanded Search Space

In order to verify and compare the performance of ACoPSA and pPSA from another view, the further numerical experiments are made with 100 times magnified search space based on selected functions f_1, f_3, f_4, f_6, whose domains are $[-10^4, 10^4]$, $[-10^4, 10^4]$, $[-128, 128]$ and $[-6 \times 10^4, 6 \times 10^4]$. The parameters are the same to the above experiments except for function f_6 with $max\_cycle = 5000$. The results are listed as Table-2.

Table 2. Comparison between **pPSA** and **ACoPSA** on the statistic results over 30 independent runs with expanded search space

Fun	Best		Median		Counts	
	pPSA	ACoPSA	pPSA	ACoPSA	pPSA	ACoPSA
1	**1.35e-9**	1.95e-9	**3.08e-9**	7.29e-2	**17**	15
3	**0**	**0**	**1.59e3**	5.97e5	**14**	9
4	3.32e-4	**1.50e-4**	1.31e-3	**1.18e-3**	9	**13**
6	**2.36e-11**	3.23e-11	**5.96e-3**	1.86e3	**19**	2

Two algorithms both found the global optima with comparative precision which can be seen from **Best** and **Counts** columns. Algorithm pPSA is more robust than ACoPSA which can be observed from **Median** and **Counts** columns as Table-2 shows. However, all the comparison items of ACoPSA for f_4 are superior to those of pSPA.

5   Conclusion

Inspired by the particle updating strategy based on the perturbed global best particle with a micro random *Gaussian* perturbation, an anticentroid-oriented perturbation particle updating strategy is proposed along the direction of the swarm centroid to global best particle, and an improved particle swarm algorithm (ACoPSA) is presented in this paper. The inherent reason to propose this updating strategy is to utilize the information of population distribution, sharing a similar spirit to the internal modeling in evolution strategies. The swarm centroid of population-based heuristic algorithm reflects the search emphasis of the algorithm and its distance to the best particle indicates the behaviors difference between the population search and the gbest. Therefore the directional vector from the swarm centroid to the gbest implies an effective direction that many particles should follow.

Observed from the algorithm analysis and the simulation experiments we have the following conclusion and indication for further research:

1. ACoPSA has very competitive and encouraging performance for the usual benchmark;
2. ACoPSA is not as robust as pPSA with magnified search space;
3. The oriented perturbation updating strategy is bias in favor of convergence and the random perturbation updating strategy has a better balance in exploration/exploitation than the oriented updating strategy.

Acknowledgements. This research is supported by the Fundamental Research Funds for the Central Universities of China (BUPT2009RC0701).

References

1. Kennedy, J., Eberhart, R.C.: Particle swarm optimization. In: Proc. of IEEE Int. Conf. on Neural Networks IV, pp. 1942–1948. IEEE, Piscataway (1995)
2. Yao, J., Kharma, N., Grogono, P.: Bi-objective Multipopulation Genetic Algorithm for Multimodal Function Optimization. IEEE Trans. on Evolutionary Computation 14(1), 80–102 (2010)
3. Chen, W.-N., Zhang, J., Chung, H.S.H., Zhong, W.-L., Wu, W.-G., Shi, Y.-H.: A Novel Set-Based Particle Swarm Optimization Method for Discrete Optimization Problems. IEEE Trans. on Evolutionary Computation 14(2), 278–300 (2010)
4. Liu, J., Zhong, W.C., Jiao, L.C.: A Multiagent Evolutionary Algorithm for Combinatorial Optimization Problems. IEEE Transactions on Systems, Man and Cybernetics-Part B 40(1), 229–240 (2010)

5. Wu, Q.D., Wang, L.: Intelligent Particle Swarm Optimization Algorithm Research and Application. Jiangsu Education Press, Nanjing (2005)
6. Zhao, X.C.: A perturbed particle swarm algorithm for numerical optimization. Applied Soft Computing 10, 119–124 (2010)
7. Hu, W., Li, Z.S.: A Simpler and More Effective Particle Swarm Optimization Algorithm. Journal of Software 18(4), 861–868 (2007)
8. Hu, J.X., Zeng, J.C.: A Two-Order Particle Swarm Optimization Model. Journal of Computer Research and Development 44(11), 1825–1831 (2007)
9. Ji, Z., Zhou, J.R., Liao, H.L., Wu, Q.H.: A Novel Intelligent Single Particle Optimizer. Chinese Journal of Computers 33(3), 556–561 (2010)
10. Liang, J.J., Qin, A.K., Suganthan, P.N., Baskar, S.: Comprehensive learning particle swarm optimizer for global optimization of multimodal functions. IEEE Trans. Evol. Comput. 10(3), 281–295 (2006)
11. Zhan, Z.-H., Zhang, J., Li, Y., Chung, H.S.-H.: Adaptive Particle Swarm Optimization. IEEE Transactions on Systems, Man and Cybernetics-Part B 39(6), 1362–1381 (2009)
12. Zhao, X.C., Hao, J.L.: Exploration/exploitation tradeoff with cell-shift and heuristic crossover for evolutionary algorithms. Journal of Systems Science and Complexity 20(1), 66–74 (2007)

Comparison of Four Decomposition Algorithms for Multidisciplinary Design Optimization

Peng Wang, Bao-wei Song, and Qi-feng Zhu

Northwestern Polytechnical University, Xi'an, 710072, China
wp970311@163.com

Abstract. Multidisciplinary Design Optimization (MDO) is an effective and prospective solution to complex engineering systems. In MDO methodology, MDO algorithm is the most important research area. Four decomposition algorithms have been proposed for MDO. They are Concurrent subspace optimization (CSSO), Collaborative optimization (CO), Bi-level integrated system synthesis (BLISS) and Analytical target cascading (ATC). On the basis of specific requirements for comparison, a mathematical example is chose and the performances of MDO decomposition algorithms are evaluated and compared, which take into consideration optimization efficiency and formulation structure characteristics.

Keywords: multidisciplinary design optimization, complex system, decomposition algorithm, Comparison.

1 Introduction

Multidisciplinary Design Optimization (MDO) is an effective method to solve complex system design [1-2]. Generally, complex systems are composed of multiple disciplines or subsystems, the traditional design method is difficult to find the optimal solution of the system because of the coupling between disciplines or subsystems, and the design cycle is long. MDO make full use of the interaction between the various disciplines or sub-system synergies, access to the completely optimal solution to the system, and shorten the design cycle through concurrent design.

The main research of MDO covers three major aspects: (1) design-oriented analysis of the various disciplines and software integration; (2) explore effective MDO algorithms, to achieve concurrent design, access to completely optimal solution to the system; (3) MDO distributed computer network environment. Which, MDO algorithm is the most important area and the most active research topic of MDO.

MDO algorithms are usually divided into single-level optimization algorithm and multi-level optimization algorithm two broad categories. Single-level optimization algorithms, including Multidisciplinary Feasible method, (MDF), Individual discipline feasible method, (IDF) and All-At-Once, (AAO).Multi-level optimization algorithm, also known as decomposition algorithms, including the concurrent subspace optimization algorithm (CSSO), collaborative optimization algorithm (CO), Bi-level integrated system synthesis, (BLISS), and Analytical Target Cascading, (ATC) etc. [3].

F.L. Wang et al. (Eds.): AICI 2010, Part II, LNAI 6320, pp. 310–317, 2010.
© Springer-Verlag Berlin Heidelberg 2010

In the MDO algorithms, multi-level optimization algorithm has wider range of applications than the single-level optimization algorithm. Algorithm structure and efficiency optimize decide the usefulness of each algorithm. Scholars at home and abroad have been carried out a number of studies on the efficiency of the MDO optimization algorithms, such as the reference [4-5] compare the MDF, IDF, and CO through the algorithms, in [6] compare the AAO, MDF, IDF, CO, and CSSO algorithm, the reference [7] compare the CSSO, CO, and BLISS algorithm and so on, but it has been a lack of a comprehensive analysis of the structure and efficiency in multi-level optimization algorithm , and serious impact on the choice and application of the algorithm in practice. In this paper, based on he mathematical model , proposed the basic characteristics of the mathematical calculation , described the characteristics and structural systems of four kinds of multi-level optimization algorithms, and conduct a thorough comparison and analysis from the structure and the efficiency of the optimize algorithm.

2 Mathematical Model of MDO

Wherever Times is specified, Times Roman or Times New Roman may be used. If neither is available on your word processor, please use the font closest in appearance to Times. Avoid using bit-mapped fonts if possible. True-Type 1 or Open Type fonts are preferred. Please embed symbol fonts, as well, for math, etc.

Take the two disciplines for example; a complete mathematical model of MDO should be expressed as:

$$
\begin{aligned}
&Find \quad \mathrm{X} = \left[X_1, X_2, X_c \right] \\
&Min \quad \mathrm{F} = \left[F_1, F_2, F_c \right] = \left\{ \begin{array}{l} F_1\left(X_1, X_c, Y_1 \right) \\ F_2\left(X_2, X_c, Y_2 \right) \\ F_c\left(X_1, X_2, X_c, Y_1, Y_2 \right) \end{array} \right\} \\
&S.t. \quad g_1\left(X_1, X_c, Y_1 \right) \le 0 \\
&\qquad\quad g_2\left(X_2, X_c, Y_2 \right) \le 0 \\
&\qquad\quad g_c\left(X_1, X_2, X_c, Y_1, Y_2 \right) \le 0 \\
&\qquad\quad Y_1 = h_1\left(X_1, X_c, Y_2^c \right) \\
&\qquad\quad Y_2 = h_2\left(X_2, X_c, Y_1^c \right)
\end{aligned}
\tag{1}
$$

Which, F is the objective function, including the partial objective function F_1、 F_2 and the sharing of objective function F_c , X is design variables, including local design variables X_1、 X_2 and the sharing of design variables X_c , Y_1、 Y_2 is the state variables, Y_1^c、 Y_2^c is the coupled state variable; g is constraint conditions, including the local constraints g_1、 g_2 , and share constraints g_c ; h_1、 h_2 are corresponding state variables by disciplinary analysis.

Different from the commonly used mathematical model of MDO, in this paper, clearly stated the objective function, design variables and constraints of the MDO all should be divided into two major categories of local and shared for the first time.

3   MDO Multi-level Optimization Algorithms

3.1   CSSO Algorithm

CSSO algorithm is a non-hierarchical two-level multi-disciplinary optimization algorithm [8] proposed by Sobieszczanski-Sobieski in 1998. It contains a system-level optimizer and multiple subsystems optimizer. Each subsystem optimize a set of disjoint design variables Independently, during the optimization , the state variables involved in the subsystem, using the discipline analysis methods to calculate, while the other state variables and constraints are based on Global Sensitivity Equation (GSE)for approximate calculation. Each sub-system is only optimize part of the design variables, the subsystem design variables do not overlap each other, the results of the optimization can joint to form a new design, if the convergence conditions, output the optimal solution, otherwise, as the initial value of the new optimization. The algorithm structure shown in Figure 1:

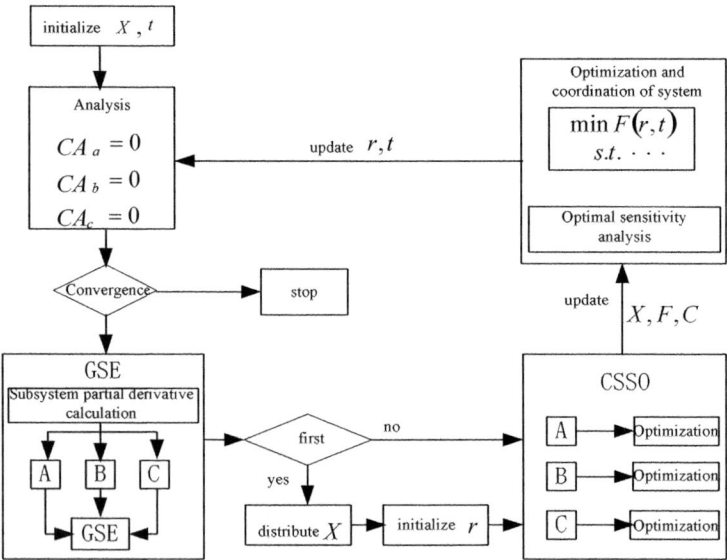

Fig. 1. CSSO Algorithm Structure Diagram

3.2   CO Algorithm

CO algorithm is a hierarchical two-level multi-disciplinary optimization algorithm [9] proposed by Kroo in 1994. CO algorithm divided the whole optimization problem into system-level optimization and several independent parallel sub-system optimizations. The basic idea is that each subsystem in the design optimization without considering the impact of other subsystems, only to meet the constraints and the objective of this sub-optimize is to minimize the differences between the various subsystem design optimization, system-level optimization program and provide targeted programs. We use the system-level optimization to coordinate the inconsistencies of subsystem optimization results, through the multiple iterations between the system-level optimization and the sub- system optimization, and finally find an optimal design consistency. The algorithm structure shown in Figure 2:

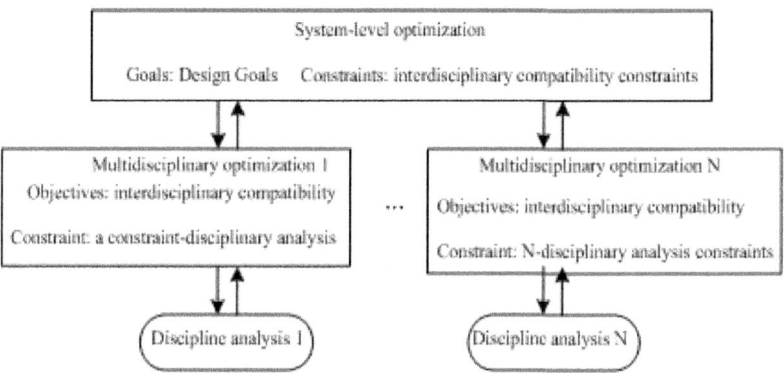

Fig. 2. CO Algorithm Structure Diagram

3.3 BLISS Algorithm

BLISS algorithm is a two-stage multi-disciplinary optimization algorithm [10] proposed by Sobieszczanski-Sobieski in 1998. BLISS algorithm divided the whole optimization problem into system-level optimization and several independent parallel sub-system optimizations. System-level optimization and subsystems optimization linked by the optimum sensitivity derivative, the optimum sensitivity derivatives can be obtained by the Optimum Sensitivity Analysis (OSA). This method conducts a systematic analysis in the beginning of each cycle can to guarantee the feasibility of multi-disciplinary. In addition, the optimization process can be artificially terminated at any time and use the results of the last time as the final result. The algorithm structure shown in Figure 3.

3.4 ATC Algorithm

ATC algorithm is a component-based multi-level optimization algorithm [11] proposed by Michelean in 1999,the series are unrestricted, we can choose the appropriate series, top-down known as the super-system level, system level, the first Class subsystem, the second subsystem. The decomposition is put all the system components as the standard; it appears tree structure after decomposition, called the elements in the tree structure node, including design model and analysis model. Design model use analysis model to calculate the response of the elements, a design model can use multiple analysis models, if the analysis model coupled with each other, you can use other MDO algorithm analysis model integration and coordination. Take the three-layer ATC algorithm as an example, the algorithm structure shown in Figure 4.

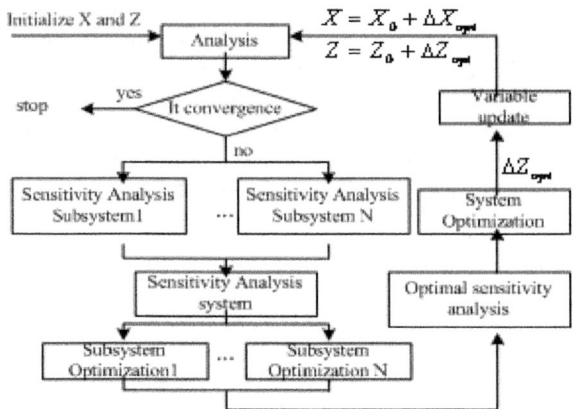

Fig. 3. BLISS Algorithm Structure Diagram

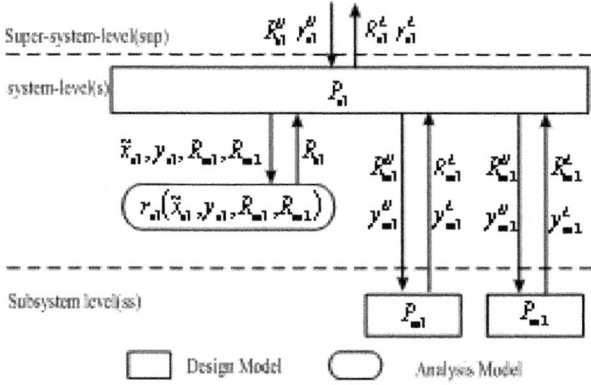

Fig. 4. Algorithm for Three-ATC Chart

4 Basic Characteristics of Mathematical Calculation in the Cases of MDO

According to the mathematical model of MDO, the mathematical examples analyzed by MDO algorithms should possess the following basic characteristics:(1) The subjects must exist disciplines analysis process, in order to achieve the corresponding state variable;(2) coupling state variables must exist;(3) local design variables and shared design variables must be present. In addition, because some MDO algorithms do not consider the shared objective function and shared constraints, so they are not exist in the above-mentioned characteristics.

5 Examples of Analysis and Comparison of Algorithms

According to the basic characteristics of mathematical calculation in the cases of MDO, we select the following multi-disciplinary design optimization examples for MDO algorithm analysis [12], the examples meet the basic features of requirements:

$$Find \quad X=[X_1, X_2, X_3]$$
$$Min \quad F=X_2^2 + X_3 + Y_1 + e^{-Y_2}$$
$$S.t. \quad g_1 = 1 - Y_1/3.16 \leq 0$$
$$g_2 = Y_2/24 - 1 \leq 0 \tag{2}$$
$$Y_1 = X_1^2 + X_2 + X_3 - 0.2Y_2$$
$$Y_2 = \sqrt{Y_1} + X_1 + X_3$$
$$-10 \leq X_1 \leq 10$$
$$0 \leq X_2, X_3 \leq 10$$

Select the initial design points $X = [1,5,2]$, $Y = [10,4]$, use CSSO, CO, BLISS, and ATC algorithm to solve the problem respectively, the results shown in Table 1.

In this paper, multi-island genetic algorithm is used for multi-objective optimal design of UUV shape, and through 1000-step optimization calculating, the optimal solution is finally obtained.

Table 1. Algorithm for Optimizing Results

MDO Algorithm	Optimizing Results						
	X_1	X_2	X_3	Y_1	Y_2	F	N
CSSO	1.9784	0	0	3.16	3.7568	3.1861	1096
CO	1.9776	0	0	3.16	3.7552	3.1833	10621
BLISS	1.9771	0	0	3.15	3.7542	3.1815	270
ATC	1.9776	0	0	3.16	3.7553	3.1834	152

Which N is the total number of iterations at all levels of the system.

As can be seen, ATC algorithm uses fewer numbers of iterations to converge to the exact optimal solution, the optimization results of other algorithms similar to the optimal solution, but a slight deviation, CO algorithm iterations are most.

The additional information used in the optimization process is as follows:

Table 2. Algorithm Needs Additional Information

MDO Algorithm	Additional Information				
	Design variable	Equality Constraints	Analysis	OSA	GSE
CSSO	√	√	√	√	√
CO	√	√	×	√×	×
BLISS	×	×	√	√	√
ATC	√	√	×	√×	×

Which, √ expressed the need for the additional information, × indicated that not need such additional information.

As can be seen, CSSO algorithm needs a maximum of additional information items, and the algorithm structure is complex, ATC and CO algorithm needs a minimum of additional information items, and the algorithm structure is relatively simple.

Combined Table 1 and Table 2, the relationship between the number of iterations and needs of the additional information as shown in Figure 5:

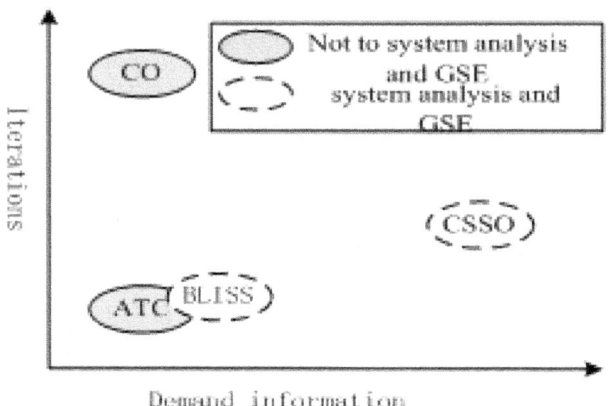

Fig. 5. Iterations and Demand Information

As can be seen, the iterations and demand information of the ATC algorithm is the least, without system analysis and GSE calculation, algorithm structure is simple and has a global convergence, can converge to the original optimal solution [13]; the iterations of BLISS algorithm are relatively small, but need system analysis and GSE calculation, algorithm structure is relatively complex; CSSO algorithm has the most complicated algorithm structure, CO algorithm structure is simple, but the maximum number of iterations, and the obtained solution may not meet the K-T conditions [14].

6   Conclusions

In this paper, take two disciplines for example, give a complete mathematical model of MDO problems, and use it as a basis, propose the basic characteristics of mathematical calculation cases used for the MDO algorithms. We use the actual examples give a comprehensive comparison and analysis of the CSSO, CO, BLISS, and ATC algorithm form both optimize efficiency and algorithm structure, and provide a basis for selection and application of the MDO algorithms in the complex multidisciplinary design optimization systems ,the main conclusions are as follows:

(1) ATC algorithm is less number of iterations, high optimizes efficiency; the algorithm structure is simple and it has a global convergence, so it is the best algorithm in the MDO algorithm;

(2) BLISS algorithm is less number of iterations, high optimizes efficiency, and the algorithm structure is relatively complex, when the system analysis and GSE calculations are easy, it is a good algorithm in the MDO;

(3) CSSO algorithm is more number of iterations, poor optimizes efficiency; the algorithm structure is complex, so it is not conducive to practical application;

(4) CO algorithm is simple in structure, but more number of iterations, poor optimizes efficiency, so it is difficult to the practical application.

References

1. Sobieszczanski-Sobieski, J., Haftka, T.: Multidisciplinary aerospace design optimization: survey of recent developments. Structural Optimization 14, 1–23 (1997)
2. Yu, X.D., Ding, Y.L.: Multidisciplinary design optimization: a survey of its algorithms and applications to aircraft design. Acta Aeronautica et Astronautica Sinica 21, 1–6 (2000)
3. Olivier, D.W., Jeremy, A.: State-of-the-Art and Future Trends in Multidisciplinary Design Optimization. AIAA-2007-1905, Reston, Va., USA (2007)
4. Alexandrov, N.M., Kodiyalam, S.: Initial results of an MDO method evaluation study. AIAA-1998-4884, Reston, Va., USA (1998)
5. Alexandrov, N.M., Lewis, R.M.: Analytical and computational aspects of collaborative optimization for multidisciplinary design. AIAA Journal 40, 301–309 (2002)
6. Balling, R.J., Wilkinson, C.A.: Execution of multidisciplinary design optimization approaches on common test problems. AIAA-96-4033, Reston, Va., USA (1996)
7. Chen, S., Zhang, F., Khalid, M.: Evaluation of three decomposition MDO algorithms. In: Proceedings of 23rd International Congress of Aerospace Sciences, Toronto, Canada (September 2002)
8. Sobieszczanski-Sobieski, J.: A Step from Hierarchic to Non-Hierarchic Systems. NASA-CP-3031. Part1. NASA, Virginia (1989)
9. Kroo, I.: Multidisciplinary optimization methods for aircraft preliminary design. AIAA-94-4325, Reston, Va., USA (1994)
10. Sobieszczanski-Sobieski, J., Agte, J.S., Sandusky, R.: Bi - level integrated system synthesis (BLISS). NASA Langley Research Center, Hampton, Va., USA (1998)
11. Michelena, N.: A System Partitioning and Optimization Approach to Target Cascading [EB/OL] (1999-08-26), http://ode.engin.umich.edu/publications/paper/1999/ICED99.pdf
12. Sell, R.S., Batill, S.M., Renaud, J.E.: Response Surface Based Concurrent Subspace Optimization for Multidisciplinary System Design. AIAA-96-0714
13. Michelena, N., Park, H., Papalambros, P.: Convergence Properties of Analytical Target Cascading. AIAA Journal 41, 897–905 (2003)
14. Alexandrov, N.M., Lewis, R.M.: Analytical and Computational Aspects of Collaborative Optimization. NASA Langley Research Center, Hampton, Va., USA (2000)

Multilevel Image Thresholding Selection Using the Artificial Bee Colony Algorithm

Ming-Huwi Horng and Ting-Wei Jiang

Department of Computer Science and Information Engineering,
National Pingtung Institute of Commerce, PingTung, Taiwan
{horng,mh.horng}@npic.edu.tw

Abstract. Image thresholding is an important technique for image processing and pattern recognition. The maximum entropy thresholding (MET) has been widely applied. A new multilevel MET algorithm based on the technology of the artificial bee colony (ABC) algorithm is proposed in this paper called the maximum entropy based artificial bee colony thresholding (MEABCT) method. Three different methods, such as the methods of particle swarm optimization, HCOCLPSO and honey bee mating optimization are also implemented for comparison with the results of the proposed method. The experimental results manifest that the proposed MEABCT algorithm can search for multiple thresholds which are very close to the optimal ones examined by the exhaustive search method. Meanwhile, the results using the MEABCT algorithm is the best and its computation time is relatively low compared with other four methods.

Keywords: Maximum entropy thresholding, artificial bee colony algorithm, particle swarm optimization, honey bee mating optimization.

1 Introduction

Thresholding is one of the most important techniques for performing image segmentation.. The nonparametric approaches are widely used methods to select for multilevel thresholds. These approaches find the thresholds that separate the gray-level regions of an image in an optimal manner based on some discriminating criteria such as the between class variance, entropy and cross entropy. The popular method, Otsu's method [1], selected optimal thresholds by maximizing the between class variance. However, inefficient formulation of between class variance makes the methods very time consuming in multilevel threshold selection. To overcome this problem, Liao *et al.* [2] proposed a fast recursive algorithm, Fast Otsu's method, along with a look-up-table to implement in the application of multilevel thresholding. Kapur *et al.* [3] proposed a method for gray-level picture thresholding using the entropy of the histogram. Zhang *et al.* [4] adopted the particle swarm optimization algorithm to maximize the entropy for underwater image segmentation. Madhubanti *et al.* [5] proposed a hybrid cooperative-comprehensive learning based PSO algorithm (HCOCLPSO) based on maximum entropy criterion. Yin [6] developed a recursive programming techniques to reduce the order of magnitude of computing the multilevel thresholds and further used the particle swarm optimization (PSO) algorithm to minimize the

F.L. Wang et al. (Eds.): AICI 2010, Part II, LNAI 6320, pp. 318–325, 2010.
© Springer-Verlag Berlin Heidelberg 2010

cross entropy. Horng [7] and Jiang [10] applied the honey bee mating optimization (HBMO) to search for the thresholds of histogram of image.

The artificial bee colony (ABC) algorithm is a new swarm-based approach for optimization, in which the search algorithm is inspired by the foraging behavior of bee colony. Recently, Karaboga et al. [8, 9] had proposed a developed model of artificial bee colony (ABC) algorithm that simulated these social behaviors of honey bees for searching for the numerical optimization problems. In this paper, we applied the ABC algorithm to search for the multilevel thresholds using the maximum entropy (MET) criterion. This proposed method is called the maximum entropy based artificial bee colony thresholding (MEABCT) algorithm. In the experiments of this paper, the exhaustive search method is conducted for deriving the optimal solutions for comparison with the results generated from MEABCT algorithm. Furthermore, the three different methods that are PSO, HCOCLPSO algorithm and HBMO methods are also implemented for comparison.

2   Maximum Entropy Artificial Bee Colony Thresholding Algorithm

The entropy criterion, proposed by Kapur et al [3], had been widely used in determining the optimal thresholding in image segmentation. The original algorithm had been developed for bi-level thresholding. The method can also extend to solve multilevel thresholding problems and can be described as follows.

Let there be L gray levels in a given image **I** and these gray levels are in the range $\{0, 1, 2,..., L\text{-}1\}$. Then one can define as $P_i = h(i)/N$, where

$h(i)$ denotes the number of pixels with gray-level i.

N denotes total number of pixels in the image.

Here, given a problem to select D thresholds, [$t_1, t_2,...., t_D$] for a given image **I**, the objective function f is to maximize:

$$f([t_1, t_2,.....,t_D]) = H_0 + H_1 + H_2 + ... + H_D$$

$$\omega_0 = \sum_{i=0}^{t_1-1} P_i, \qquad H_0 = -\sum_{i=0}^{t_1-1} \frac{P_i}{\omega_0} \ln \frac{P_i}{\omega_0}$$

$$\omega_1 = \sum_{i=t_1}^{t_2-1} P_i, \qquad H_1 = -\sum_{i=t_1}^{t_2-1} \frac{P_i}{\omega_1} \ln \frac{P_i}{\omega_1} \qquad (1)$$

$$\omega_2 = \sum_{i=t_2}^{t_3-1} P_i, \qquad H_2 = -\sum_{i=t_2}^{t_3-1} \frac{P_i}{\omega_2} \ln \frac{P_i}{\omega_2},...$$

$$\omega_D = \sum_{i=t_D}^{t_D-1} P_i, \qquad H_D = -\sum_{i=t_D}^{t_D-1} \frac{P_i}{\omega_D} \ln \frac{P_i}{\omega_D}$$

In this paper, a maximum entropy based artificial bee colony thresholding (MEABCT) algorithm is developed based on the meta-heuristic approach proposed by Karaboga [8]. This proposed algorithm tries to obtain this optimum D-dimensional vector [$t_1, t_2,...., t_D$], which can maximize (1). The objective function is also used as the fitness function for HEABCT algorithm. The details of MEABCT algorithm is introduced as follows.

Step 1. (Generate the initial population of solutions)

Generate the SN solutions z_i ($i = 1, 2, ..., SN$) with D dimensions denoted by matrix Z.

$$Z = [z_1, z_2, ..., z_{SN}], \text{ and } z_i = (z_{i,1}, z_{i,2}, ..., z_{i,D}) \quad (2)$$

where $z_{i,j}$ is the jth component value that is restricted into $[0,...,L]$ and the $z_{i,j} < z_{i,j+1}$ for all j. The fitness of all solutions z_i are evaluated and set cycle=1, meanwhile, the trail number of each solution z_i, $trail_i$, is assigned to 0.

Step 2. (Place the employed bees on their food sources)

In the step 2, each employed bee produces a new solution v_i by using (3) and tests the fitness value of the new solution.

$$v_{ij} = z_{i,j} + \phi_{ij}(z_{i,j} - z_{k,j}) \quad (3)$$

where $k \in \{1, 2, ..., SN\}$ but $k \neq i$ and $j \in \{1, 2, ..., D\}$ are randomly selected indexes. ϕ_{ij} is a random number between $[-1, 1]$. If the fitness of the new one is higher than that of the previous one, the employed memorizes the new position and forgets the old one. Otherwise it keeps the old solution.

Step 3. (Send the onlooker bees on the food sources depending on their nectar amounts)

In this step 3, we first calculate the probability value p_i of the solution z_i by means of their fitness values using (4).

$$p_i = \frac{fit(z_i)}{\sum_{i=1}^{SN} fit(z_i)} \quad (4)$$

An onlooker bee selects a solution to update its solution depending on the probabilities and determines a neighbor solution around the chosen one. The selection procedure for the first onlooker, a random number is produced between $[0, 1]$ and if this number is less than P_1, its solution is selected for updating its solution. Otherwise, the random number is compared with P_2 and if less than that, the second solution is chosen. Otherwise, the third probability of third solution is checked. This process is repeated until all onlookers are distributed onto solutions. The distributed onlooker bee updates its own solution like the employed bees does.

Step 4. (Send the scouts to the search area for discovering new food source)

If the solution z_i does not be improved through the Step 2 and Step 3, the $trail_i$ value of solution z_i will be added by 1. If the $trail_i$ of solution is more than the predetermined "$limit$", the solution z_i is regarded to be an abandoned solution, meanwhile, the employed bee will be changed into a scout. The scout randomly produces the new solution by (5) and then compares the fitness of new solution with that of its old one. If the new solution is better than the old solution, it is replaced with the old one and set its own *trail*$_i$ into 0. This scout will be changed into employed bee. Otherwise, the old one is retained in the memory.

$$z_{ij} = z_{\min, j} + rand(0,1)(z_{\max, j} - z_{\min, j}) \tag{5}$$

where the $z_{\min, j}$ and $z_{\max, j}$ are the minimum and maximum thresholds of the jth component of all solutions, the $rand(0,1)$ is a random number generating function that produces the random number between [0, 1].

Step 5. (Record the best solution)
In this step, we memory the best solution so far and add the cycle by one.

Step 6. (Check the termination criterion)
If the cycle is equal to the maximum cycle number (MCN) then finish the algorithm, else go to Step 2.

3   Expermetal Results and Discussion

We implement the proposed MEABCT algorithm in language of Visual C++ under a personal computer with 2.4GHz CPU, 2G RAM with window XP system. All designed programs are designed by revising the original programs given in the homepage of artificial bee colony algorithm [11]. It is clear from the MEABCT algorithm that there are three control parameters: the number of food sources which is equal to the number of employed bees or onlooker bees *(SN)*, the value of *"limit"* and the maximum cycle number (MCN). In all experiments, we select the colony size *(SN)* 100, MCN 200, and *limit* value 30.   Three images of Fig. 1 named "LENA", "PEPPER", and "BIRD" are used for conducting our experiments.

In order to obtain the consistent comparisons, a popular performance indicator, peak signal to noise ratio (PSNR), is used to compare the segmentation results by using the multilevel image threshold techniques [12].   For the sake of completeness we define PSNR, measured in decibel (dB) as

$$PSNR = 20\log_{10}(\frac{255}{RMSE}) \textbf{(dB)} \tag{6}$$

where the RMSE is the root mean-squared error, defined as:

$$RMSE = \sqrt{\frac{\sum_{i=1}^{M}\sum_{j=1}^{N}(I(i, j) - \hat{I}(i, j))^2}{MN}} \tag{7}$$

Here I and $\hat{I}$ are original and segmented images of size $M \times N$, respectively.

Firstly, we execute the MEABCT algorithm on partitioning the three images. For evaluating the performance of the proposed MEHBMOT algorithm, we have implemented this method on the three test images. Table 4 shows the selected thresholds

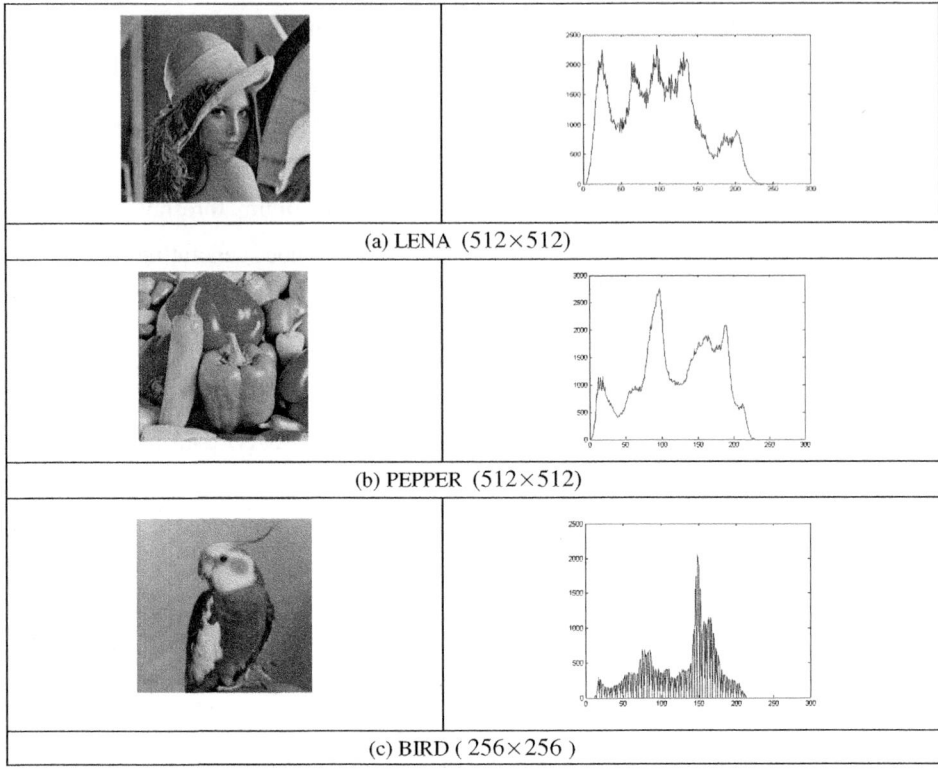

Fig. 1. The test images and corresponding histograms: (a) LENA, (b) PEPPER and (c) BIRD

Table 1. The selection thresholds for three test images by using the MEFFT and the exhaustive search method (k: number of thresholds)

Image (size)	k	Exhaustive		MEABCT	
		Thresholds	Computation time (ms)	Thresholds	Computation time (ms)
LENA	2	80,150	4.89	80,150	1.39
	3	60,109,160	158.49	60,109,160	5.94
	4	56,100,144,182	8290	56,100,144,182	24.39
	5	44,79,114,150,185	451304	44,79,115,148,186	189.35
PEPPER	2	74,146	3.73	74,146	1.45
	3	61,112,164	145.58	61,112,164	5.98
	4	57,104,148,194	7965	57,104,148,194	29.78
	5	42,77,113,153,194	439784	42,77,113,153,194	187.35
BIRD	2	71,138	4.13.	71,138	1.12
	3	70,129,177	132.67	70,129,177	2.89
	4	51,96,139,177	6564	51,94,138,178	17.85
	5	46,74,104,141,178	414789	46,74,105,142,177	109.35

derived by the MEABCT algorithm and the optimal thresholds generated from the exhaustive search method. We find that the selected thresholds of MEABCT algorithm are equivalent or very close to optimal thresholds derived by the exhaustive search methods. Furthermore, we find that the computation times of exhaustive search method grows exponentially with the number of required thresholds. Obviously, the computation needs for the exhaustive search are absolutely unacceptable for $k \geq 4$ (k: number of thresholds). The computation times of the MEABCT algorithm is significantly faster compared to the exhaustive search algorithm. The performance metrics for checking the effectiveness of the method are chosen as the computation time so as to get an idea of complexity, and the PSNR which is used to determine the quality of the thresholded images. Table 2 shows the selected thresholds, computation time, PSNR value and the corresponding fitness value of five test images with different thresholds. This table provides quantitative standard for evaluating. This table shows that the number of thresholds increase, the PSNand the fitness value are enlarged.

The MEABCT and other three multilevel thresholding methods that are MEHBMOT, PSO and HCOCLPSO algorithm are implemented for the purpose of comparisons. Table 3 shows the selected thresholds of the three test images. It is interesting that the selected thresholds by the MEABCT algorithm are equivalent (for 2- or 3-threshold problems) or very close (4- or 5-threshold problem) to the ones MEHBMOT algorithm. The thresholds obtained by PSO algorithms in the segmentation of BIRD image are also distinct from the one of the MEABCT algorithm in 5-level thresholding. It is possible to reveal that the PSO algorithm is unsuitable to search for thresholds. Table 4 shows the computation time and the corresponding PSNR values of the four different multilevel thresholding methods. Several aspects are found in the two tables. The computation time of the MEABCT algorithm is between the MEHBMOT and PSO in the segmentation of LENA, PEPPER and BIRD images. An aspect is found that the HCOCLPSO algorithm is not acceptable because of the heavy need of computation times. Finally, from the corresponding the fitness values of selected thresholds using MEABCT algorithm it appears the fact that the selected thresholds of the MEABCT algorithm can effectively find the adequate solutions based on the maximum entropy criterion.

Table 2. Thresholds, computation times, PSNR values and Fitness values for test images by using MEABCT algorithm.

Image	k	Thresholds	Computation time (ms)	PSNR (dB)	Fitness Value
LENA	2	80,150	1.39	15.46	12.6990
	3	60,109,160	5.94	18.55	15.7658
	4	56,100,144,182	24.39	19.71	18.5875
	5	44,79,115,148,186	189.35	21.68	21.2468
PEPPER	2	74,146	1.45	16.47	12.6348
	3	61,112,164	5.98	18.42	15.6892
	4	57,104,148,194	29.78	19.21	18.5397
	5	42,77,113,153,194	187.35	21.81	21.2830
BIRD	2	71,138	1.12	17.44	11.1647
	3	70,129,177	2.89	18.53	13.8659
	4	51,94,138,178	17.85	20.84	16.4558
	5	46,74,105,142,177	109.35	22.72	18.6961

Table 3. The selected thresholds used the four different image thresholding algorithms

Image	k	Selected thresholds			
		MEABCT	MEHBMOT	PSO	HCOCLPSO
LENA	2	80,150	80,150	80,150	80,150
	3	60,109,160	60,109,160	60,109,160	60,109,160
	4	56,100,144,182	56,100,144,182	56,100,144,182	56,100,144,182
	5	44,79,115,148,186	44,80,115,150,185	43,79,114,150,185	46,83,118,153,187
PEPPER	2	74,146	74,146	74,146	74,146
	3	61,112,164	61,112,164	72,135,193	61,112,164
	4	57,104,148,194	57,104,148,194	58,105,148,194	57,104,148,194
	5	42,77,113,153,194	42,77,113,153,194	43,77,113,153,194	42,77,114,154,194
BIRD	2	71,138	71,138	71,138	71,138
	3	70,129,177	70,129,177	70,129,177	70,130,177
	4	51,96,139,177	51,96,139,177	51,94,138,177	51,96,140,177
	5	46,74,104,141,177	46,74,104,141,177	51,96,139,177,248	44,71,97,139,177

Table 4. The computation times and the corresponding PSNR of the four different multilevel thresholding methods

Image	k	Computation times (ms)/PSNR(dB) (k: number of thresholds)							
		MEABCT		MEHBMOT		PSO		HCOCLPSO	
LENA	2	1.39	15.46	1.45	15.46	1.36	15.46	1.69	15.46
	3	5.94	18.55	6.95	18.55	4.89	18.55	13.58	18.55
	4	24.39	19.71	23.65	19.71	25.69	19.71	169.5	19.71
	5	189.35	21.68	432.6	21.63	137.56	21.61	1158	21.56
PEPPER	2	1.45	16.47	1.87	16.47	1.56	16.47	2.26	16.47
	3	5.98	18.42	6.78	18.42	5.23	17.40	18.43	18.42
	4	29.78	19.21	36.76	19.21	28.43	19.23	219.6	19.21
	5	187.35	21.81	234.9	21.81	154.26	21.39	1086	21.41
BIRD	2	1.12	17.44	1.09	17.44	1.15	17.44	2.10	17.44
	3	2.89	18.53	3.94	18.53	3.17	18.23	15.28	18.34
	4	17.85	20.84	18.65	20.77	19.94	20.73	132.5	20.89
	5	109.35	22.72	106.1	22.65	113.97	20.77	1153	22.20

4 Conclusion

In this paper, we have proposed a method, called MEABCT algorithm, for multilevel thresholds selection using the maximum entropy criterion. The MEABCT algorithm simulates the behavior of honey bee mating to develop the algorithm to search for the adequate thresholds for image segmentation. The MEABCT algorithm is demonstrated that it can rapidly converge. The segmentation results are promising and it encourage further researches for applying the MEABCT algorithm to complex and real-time image analysis problem such as the automatic target recognition and the complex document analysis.

Acknowledgments. Authors would like to thank the National Science council, ROC, under Grant No. NSC 98-2221-E-251-004 for support of this work.

References

1. Otsu: A threshold selection method from gray-level histograms. IEEE Transactions on Systems, Man, Cybernetics 9, 62–66 (1979)
2. Liao, P.S., Chen, T.S., Chung, P.C.: A fast algorithm for multilevel thresholding. Journal of Information Science and Engineering 17, 713–727 (2001)
3. Kapur, J.N., Sahoo, P.K., Wong, A.K.C.: A new method for gray-level picture thresholding using the entropy of the histogram. Computer Vision Graphics Image Processing 29, 273–285 (1985)
4. Zhang, R., Liu, L.: Underwater image segmentation with maximum entropy based on Particle Swarm Optimization (PSO). In: Proceedings of IMSCCS 2006, pp. 360–363 (2006)
5. Madhubanti, M., Amitava, A.: A hybrid cooperative-comprehensive learning based algorithm for image segmentation using multilevel thresholding. Expert Systems with Application 34, 1341–1350 (2008)
6. Yin, P.Y.: Multilevel minimum cross entropy threshold selection based on particle swarm optimization. Applied Mathematics and Computation 184, 503–513 (2007)
7. Horng, M.H.: A multilevel image thresholding using the honey bee mating optimization. Applied Mathematics and Computation 215, 3302–3310 (2010)
8. Karaboga, D., Basturk, D.: On the performance of artificial bee colony algorithm. Applied Soft Computing 8, 687–697 (2008)
9. Karaboga, D., Basturk, B.: A powerful and efficient algorithm for numerical function optimization; artificial bee colony (ABC) algorithm. J. Glob. Opyim. 39, 459–471 (2007)
10. Jiang, T.W.: The application of image thresholding and vector quantization using the honey bee mating optimization. Master thresis, National Ping Rung Institute of Commerce (2009)
11. Karaboga, D.: Artificial bee colony algorithm homepage,
    http://mf.erciyers.edu.tw/abc/
12. Yin, P.I.: Multilevel minimum cross entropy threshold selection based on particle swarm optimization. Applied Mathematics and Computation 184, 503–513 (2007)

Automatic Rule Tuning of a Fuzzy Logic Controller Using Particle Swarm Optimisation

Gu Fang[1], Ngai Ming Kwok[2], and Dalong Wang[2]

[1] School of Engineering, University of Western Sydney, Locked Bag 1797,
Penrith South DC 1797, Australia
g.fang@uws.edu.au
[2] School of Mechanical & Manufacturing Engineering, University of New South Wales,
Sydney NSW, 2052, Australia
{nwkwok,dalong.wang}@unsw.edu.au

Abstract. While fuzzy logic controllers (FLCs) are developed to exploit human expert knowledge in designing control systems, the actual establishment of fuzzy rules and tuning of fuzzy membership functions are usually a time consuming exercise. In this paper a technique, based on the particle swarm optimisation (PSO), is employed to automatically tune the fuzzy rules of a Mamdani-type of fuzzy controller. The effectiveness of the designed controller is demonstrated by the control performance of such an FLC to a nonlinear water tank system with process time delay. The results are compared favourably to a PSO tuned PID controller.

Keywords: Fuzzy logic controller, Automatic rule tuning of fuzzy logic controllers, Particle swarm optimisation, Water tank control.

1 Introduction

Fuzzy logic controllers (FLCs) are developed to exploit human expert knowledge in controlling various systems, in particular those ill-defined, nonlinear systems [1]. However, tuning of FLC to obtain optimal rules and membership functions (MFs) is a time consuming and often frustrating exercise [2].

To overcome these difficulties, various techniques have been reported to automate the tuning process of FLCs. An adaptive network based fuzzy inference system (AN-FIS) was introduced [3], where an adaptive neural network (NN) was used to learn the mapping between the inputs and outputs and a Sugeno-type of fuzzy system could be generated based on the neural network. A quantum NN was also used to learn the data space of a Tagaki-Sugeno-Kang (TSK) fuzzy controller [3]. More recently a hybrid learning algorithm is proposed to utilise particle swarm optimisation (PSO) for training the antecedent part of an ANFIS while the consequent part is trained by an extended Kalman Filter (EKF) [4]. This ANFIS is used as a system identifier.

Evolutionary computation techniques such as the genetic algorithm (GA) and PSO are also attractive candidates in fuzzy controller design. The GA has been used in the automatic design of fuzzy controllers [5, 6] in the areas of mobile robotics where it is used in tuning both the fuzzy MFs and the fuzzy rule bases.

F.L. Wang et al. (Eds.): AICI 2010, Part II, LNAI 6320, pp. 326–333, 2010.
© Springer-Verlag Berlin Heidelberg 2010

GA mimics the evolution of living species while the PSO was inspired by the natural behaviour of animals in forming swarms [7, 8]. Due to its simplicity in implementation, PSO has gained popularities in engineering applications, such as in image processing [9] and in system modelling [10]. A number of publications had also been reported in using PSO to automatically tune the FLC parameters, see for example, [11–14]. These methods were directed at tuning the membership parameters involved in the TS-type fuzzy controllers. In general, the PSO is used to perform the learning tasks that are usually associated with the NN in the TS-FLC. A PSO based fuzzy MF tuning method is also introduced to a fixed point control problem, i.e. parking a car into a predefined garage location [15].

In [16], a micro-GA was combined with PSO to optimise the FLC parameters. Two cases were studied in [16] where the FLC was first assumed to have a fixed number of membership functions while in the second case the MFs are set to be tuneable using the suggested evolutionary computation approaches. In [17], a PSO is used to tune the FLC based on multi-objective optimal functions to achieve best active control outcome for a multi-storey building.

Although there are research results in the area of automatic fuzzy MF tuning [2], to the best of our knowledge, there is no report on using PSO for the Mamdani-type of fuzzy controller tuning that includes the adjustment of not only the MFs but also the fuzzy rule structure. In this paper, we propose to use a PSO to automatically determine the optimal number of rules and the structure of the rules. This FLC is demonstrated in performing tracking control. In particular, we use the proposed FLC to control the water levels of a nonlinear water tank system that involves a time delayed response.

This paper is organized as follows: section 2 briefly explains the PSO method and how it can be used in the FLC rule tuning process. In section 3, the simulation setup and control results are shown to demonstrate the effectiveness of the proposed FLC tuning method. Discussions are also given in section 3 where further comparisons between the proposed FLC controller and a PSO tuned PID controller are given. Conclusions are then provided in section 4.

2   Autonomous FLC Tuning Using a PSO

2.1   Particle Swarm Optimisation

PSO is a non-parametric optimisation method introduced by Kennedy [7, 8]. It is inspired by the formation of swarms by animals such as birds and fish. The principle behind the PSO is that each individual in the swarm, called a particle, will move towards the best performing particle (leader) in the swarm of N particles while exploring the best experience each particle has. In particular, the velocity (v_i) associated with each particle i, ($i = 1, 2, …, N$) at time $k+1$ is calculated as:

$$v_i(k+1) = \eta \times v_i(k) + \mu_1 \times (x_{gb} - x_i(k)) + \mu_2 \times (x_i^{pb} - x_i(k)) \qquad (1)$$

where η is the momentum or inertia factor of the particle, $v_i(k)$ is the velocity of the particle i at time step k, x_{gb} is the global best performing particle up to time step k in the entire population, x_i^{pb} is the best experience that particle i has had up to time step k.

$x_i(k)$ is the current location of particle i. μ_1 and μ_2 are random weighting factors that decides the influences of 'global best' x_{gb} and 'personal best' x_i^{pb} particle to the movement of particle i. In general, these weighting factors μ_1 and μ_2 are chosen according to a uniform probability distribution function, and are within predefined limits. To limit the searching space, $v_i(k+1)$ is also limited to be within a certain range. The new location of particle i can be calculated as:

$$x_i(k+1) = x_i(k) + v_i(k+1) \tag{2}$$

The evaluation of the particle performance is based on a problem specific objective function that decides the 'closeness' of the particle to the optimal solution. For instance, if it is a problem that requires the minimisation of function $f(x(k))$, then the 'global best' performing particle will be decided on the basis of

$$\min_{x_{gb}} f(\mathbf{x}(\tau)), \quad \text{where} \quad \tau = 1,2,\cdots,k. \tag{3}$$

In (3), $\mathbf{x}$ is a vector that represents N particles in the swarm. Similarly, the 'personal best experience' of particle i is determined by:

$$\min_{x_i^{pb}} f(x_i(\tau)), \quad \text{where} \quad \tau = 1,2,\cdots,k. \tag{4}$$

2.2 PSO for FLC Rule Tuning

Fuzzy logic controllers are designed based on expert knowledge that is in the form of rule-based behaviour. In general the FLC rules are expressed in the form:

$$\textit{if input } \mathbf{A} \textit{ is } \mathbf{MF1_A} \textit{ AND input } \mathbf{B} \textit{ is } \mathbf{MF1_B} \textit{ THEN output } \mathbf{C} \textit{ is } \mathbf{MF3_c} \tag{5}$$

where antecedents $\mathbf{A}$ and $\mathbf{B}$ are expressed by membership functions (MFs) $\mathbf{MF1_A}$.and $\mathbf{MF1_B}$. The process that is used to calculate the overall control action in FLC is determined by different type of 'defuzzification' process [2].

Generally fuzzy rules expressed in (5) and the MF can be derived from expert knowledge. However, exact rule numbers and the relationships between the antecedents A and B are difficult to derive. For example, it is difficult, sometimes, to determine if a rule should be "if $\mathbf{A}$ AND $\mathbf{B}$" or "if $\mathbf{A}$ OR $\mathbf{B}$", or "if NOT $\mathbf{A}$ AND $\mathbf{B}$", etc. Furthermore, the MF design that involves the determination of where in the variable space each membership function should locate is also a time consuming process.

The rule bases can be automatically tuned using PSO if the relationship of antecedents and consequences can be expressed using numerical values. In the MATLAB Fuzzy Logic Toolbox the fuzzy rule expressed in (5) is compressed by numerical values as:

$$\mathbf{1\,1,\,1\,(1):3} \tag{6}$$

In (6) the first two 'values' represent the MF numbers associated with the two inputs (negative numbers can be used to represent the NOT function), the 'value' after the comma represents the relationship between the two inputs (1=AND and 2=OR). The value in the bracket is the weighting factor of this rule, while the last number after the colon represents the MF number associated with the output. Therefore, it is possible

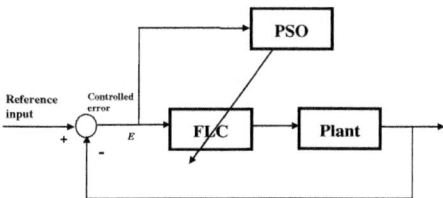

Fig. 1. The proposed PSO based MF tuning method

to use PSO to find the appropriate relationships between the rules and to determine if the number of rules is adequate.

The strategy of using a PSO for rule tuning in FLC can be depicted in Fig. 1. In the proposed PSO process, each particle is formed to represent the rules of the FLC's. As the purpose of the PSO is to minimise the control error of the FLC, the objective function of PSO is defined as:

$$f(\mathbf{x}(k)) = \sum_{t=0}^{T} E^2 \qquad (7)$$

where T is the total running time of the FLC, E is the control error between the reference inputs and actual system outputs.

3   Simulation Studies

3.1   A Water Tank System

To demonstrate the effectiveness of the proposed FLC design based on the PSO tuning method, a nonlinear water tank level control system is used. The water tank system is shown in Fig. 2.

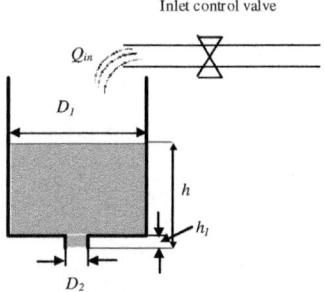

Fig. 2. A Water tank system

The dynamic equation of such a system can be expressed as:

$$\frac{dh}{dt} = (Q_{in} - C_{out}\sqrt{h})/A \qquad (8)$$

where h is the water level of the tank system, Q_{in} is the input flow-rate to the tank, C_{out} is the outflow pipe constant of the tank and A is the cross-section area of the tank.

D_1 and D_2 are the diameters of the water tank at different heights above or below h_1. As there is a certain pipe volume (Δv), between the inlet control valve and the water entry point to the tank, a time delay is also present in the controlled system.

A SIMULINK model that reflects the system behaviour that includes the delay response is built to test the proposed FLC.

3.2 Conventional and PSO Tuned FLC

To control the water tank, a FLC was designed. There are two inputs to the FLC. The first input, labelled 'Level', is the difference between the reference input and the water level in the tank. This input is converted to a voltage signal to reflect the sensor that is to be used. The other input to the FLC, labelled 'Rate', is the information relating to the change rate of the water tank level. The output of the FLC is the voltage change required to operate the valve to achieve desired height.

The initial MFs for the 2 inputs and one output are shown in Fig. 3. The initial FLC rules used are set to have nine (9) rules:

> **1. If (level is high) and (rate is negative) then (valve is no_change)**
> **2. If (level is high) and (rate is none) then (valve is close_slow)**
> **3. If (level is high) and (rate is positive) then (valve is close_fast)**
> **4. If (level is okey) and (rate is negative) then (valve is open_slow)**
> **5. If (level is okey) and (rate is none) then (valve is no_change)**
> **6. If (level is okey) and (rate is positive) then (valve is close_slow)**
> **7. If (level is low) and (rate is negative) then (valve is open_fast)**
> **8. If (level is low) and (rate is none) then (valve is open_slow)**
> **9. If (level is low) and (rate is positive) then (valve is no_change)**   (9)

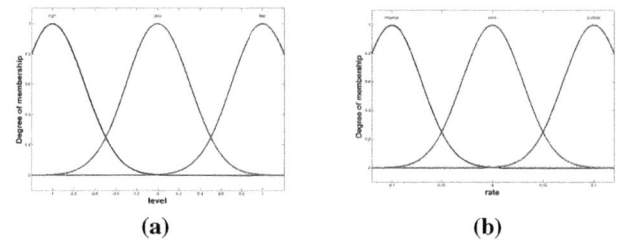 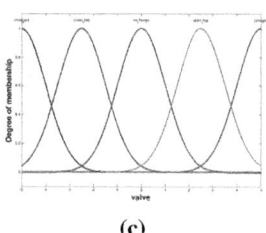

| (a) | (b) | (c) |

Fig. 3. The initial MFs for the FLC inputs (a) and (b) and output (c)

The controller performance of this FLC to the water tank system is shown in Fig. 4. The reference input is a saturated saw signal (the RED line in Fig. 4). The control results are shown in Fig. 4a while the tracking error is shown in Fig. 4b. As expected, the performance of such a controller is not satisfactory as the control errors are in the range of ±4mm (around 6%).

To start the PSO tuning of the FLC rules, it is assumed that the nine rules expressed in (9) are used as the initial rule sets. In addition, the MFs used in this FLC are all of Gaussian forms. There are 5 parameters, as shown in (6), need to be tuned for each rule. This will give 45 parameters to be adjusted for the nine rules. Therefore, in total, each PSO particle has 45 dimensions. It is set that there are 50 particles in the swarm and the total searching iterations are set to 50. It is also defined in the

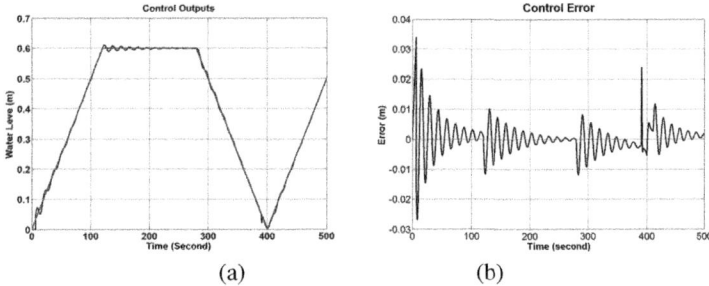

(a)   (b)

Fig. 4. The initial FLC control output

searching process that if the error does not reduce within 10 iterations then the search should be terminated. The inertia factor η was set to be 0.8 and weighting factors μ_1 and μ_2 were set to be 1 and 0.4, respectively.

The objective function that evaluates the fitness of each particle was defined as (7). Therefore, after the proper tuning of the MFs, the FLC will have a minimised control error. When running the PSO, the searching was terminated after 20 iterations when there is no reduction in total control error was observed. At the completion of the PSO tuning, the fuzzy rule base has been reduced to have only 4 rules, as shown in (10).

> **1. If (level is high) and (rate is negative) then (valve is no_change) (1)**
> **2. If (level is not okey) and (rate is positive) then (valve is close_fast) (1)**
> **3. If (level is low) or (rate is positive) then (valve is close_fast) (1)**
> **4. If (level is low) and (rate is none) then (valve is open_slow) (1)**   10)

The control performance of the tunned FLC to the reference signal shown in Fig. 4a is demonstrated in Fig. 5. It can be observed that a marked improvement has been obtained by this automatic FLC tuning process. The maximum error has been reduced from 0.04 *m* to be around 0.012 *m*. To further evaluate the performance of the developed FLC, the reference signals were varied to be a sine wave signal and a step signal. Due to space limitation, only the response and the corresponding tracking error for a sine wave input are presented in Fig 6. These results have further confirmed the benefit of using such an FLC.

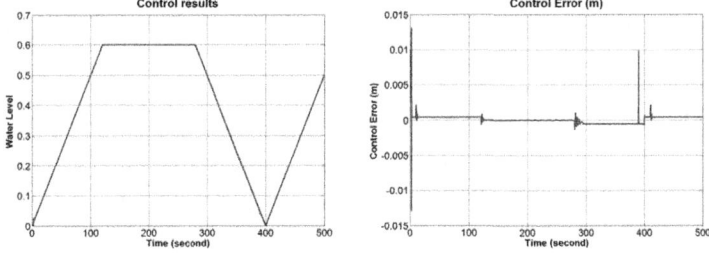

Fig. 5. The tuned FLC control output for a saturated saw reference signal

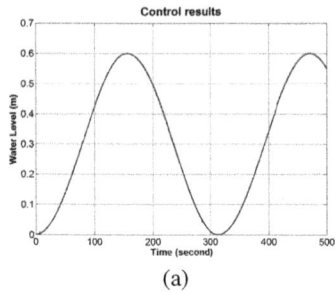 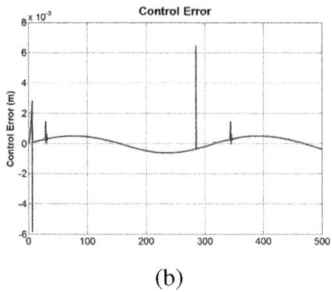

(a)   (b)

Fig. 6. The tuned FLC control output for a sine reference signal

3.3 Discussions

The effectiveness of the proposed FLC controller can be further evaluated where a PID controller is used as a comparison base. It is well known that the PID controller gains K_p, K_i, and K_d are tuneable parameters that affect the performance of the control outputs. In this paper, the PID gain values are also tuned using a PSO as introduced in [2].

The performance of the PID controller is tuned to be best for a step input. The control error for the tuned PID controller for the step input is shown in Fig. 7a. When this PID controller is used in controlling the water tank to follow a sine wave input, as shown in Fig. 6a, the control error is shown in Figure 7b. It can be seen that although the PID has been tuned to follow a step input better than the FLC, its performance in following an alternative reference signal is not as accurate as the FLC.

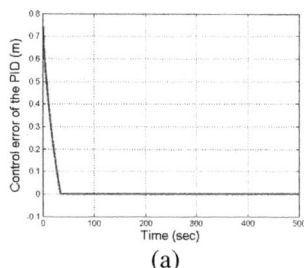 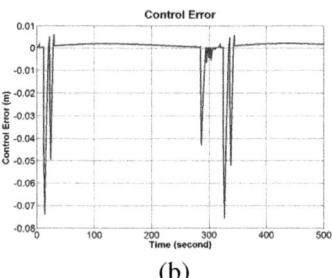

(a)   (b)

Fig. 7. The PSO tuned PID control errors for a step (a) and since (b) reference signals

4   Conclusions

In this paper an automatic tuning method in designing FLC rules is introduced to perform tracking control of a nonlinear system. This method uses PSO to tune the fuzzy rules. Simulation results have shown that the tuned FLC is performing satisfactorily compared with a PID controller even when the PID is tuned to perform in an optimal fashion. The future work will be to use PSO for tuning both the rule base and the MFs simultaneously.

References

[1] Lin, C.T., Lee, C.S.G.: Neural fuzzy systems. Prentice Hall, Inc., Upper Saddle River (1996)

[2] Fang, G., Kwok, N.M., Ha, Q.P.: Automatic Fuzzy Membership Function Tuning Using the Particle Swarm Optimisation. In: IEEE Pacific-Asia Workshop on Computational Intelligence and Industrial Application (PACIIA 2008), Wuhan, China, vol. 2, pp. 324–328 (December 2008)

[3] Jang, J.S.R.: ANFIS: Adaptive-Network-Based Fuzzy Inference System. IEEE Transactions on Systems, Man, and Cybernetics 23(3), 665–685 (1993)

[4] Shoorehdeli, M.A., Teshnehlab, M., Sedigh, A.K.: Training ANFIS as an identifier with intelligent hybrid stable learning algorithm based on particle swarm optimization and extended Kalman filter. Fuzzy Sets and Systems (160), 922–948 (2009)

[5] Pratihar, D.K., Deb, K., Ghosh, A.: A genetic-fuzzy approach for mobile robot navigation among moving obstacles. International Journal of Approximate Reasoning 20(2), 145–172 (1999)

[6] Mucientes, M., Moreno, D.L., Bugarin, A., Barro, S.: Design of a fuzzy controller in mobile robotics using genetic algorithms. Applied Soft Computing 7, 540–546 (2007)

[7] Kennedy, J., Eberhart, R.: Particle swarm optimization. In: Proceedings of 1995 IEEE International Conference on Neural Networks, Perth, Australia, pp. 1942–1948 (1995)

[8] Clerc, M., Kennedy, J.: The particle swarm - explosion, stability, and convergence in a multidimensional complex space. IEEE Transactions on Evolutionary Computation 6(1), 58–73 (2002)

[9] Kwok, N.M., Ha, Q.P., Liu, D.K., Fang, G.: Contrast enhancement and intensity preservation for gray-level images using multiobjective particle swarm optimization. IEEE Trans. Automation Science and Engineering 6(1), 145–155 (2009)

[10] Kwok, N.M., Ha, Q.P., Nguyen, T.H., Li, J., Samali, B.: A novel hysteretic model for magneto rheological fluid dampers and parameter identification using particle swarm optimization. Sensors & Actuators: A. Physical 132(2), 441–451 (2006)

[11] Karakuzu, C.: Fuzzy controller training using particle swarm optimisation for nonlinear system control. ISA Transactions 47, 229–239 (2008)

[12] Niu, B., Zhu, Y., He, X., Shen, H.: A multi-swarm optimizer based fuzzy modeling approach for dynamic systems processing. Neurocomputing 71, 1436–1448 (2008)

[13] Mukherjee, V., Ghoshal, S.P.: Intelligent particle swarm optimized fuzzy PID controller for AVR system. Electric Power Systems Research 77, 1689–1698 (2007)

[14] Lin, C., Hong, S.: The design of neuro-fuzzy networks using particle swarm optimisation and recursive singular value decomposition. Neurocomputing 71, 271–310 (2007)

[15] Esmin, A.A.A., Lambert-Torres, G.: Fitting fuzzy membership functions using hybrid particle swarm optimization. In: Proceedings on 2006 IEEE International Conference on Fuzzy Systems, Vancouver, BC, Canada, pp. 2112–2119 (2006)

[16] Ali, S.F., Ramaswamy, A.: Optimal fuzzy logic controller for MDOF structural systems using evolutionary algorithms. Engineering Applications of Artificial Intelligence (22), 407–419 (2009)

[17] Rao, A.R.M., Sivasubramanian, K.: Multi-objective optimal design of fuzzy logic controller using a self configurable swarm intelligence algorithm. Computers and Structures (86), 2141–2154 (2008)

An Efficient Differential Evolution Algorithm with Approximate Fitness Functions Using Neural Networks

Yi-shou Wang[1], Yan-jun Shi[2,*], Ben-xian Yue[3], and Hong-fei Teng[2,3]

[1] School of Aeronautics and Astronautics, Faculty of Vehicle Engineering and Mechanics,
State Key Laboratory of Structural Analysis for Industrial Equipment,
Dalian University of Technology, Dalian 116024, P.R. China
wangys@dlut.edu.cn
[2] School of Mechanical Engineering, Dalian University of Technology,
Dalian 116024, P.R. China
{shiyj,tenghf}@dlut.edu.cn
[3] Department of Computer Science and Engineering,
Dalian University of Technology, Dalian 116024, P.R. China
yuebenxian@vip.sina.com

Abstract. We develop an efficient differential evolution (DE) with neural networks-based approximating technique for computationally expensive problems, called DE-ANN hereinafter. We employ multilayer feedforward ANN to approximate the original problems for reducing the numbers of costly problems in DE. We also implement a fast training algorithm whose data samples use the population of DE. In the evolution process of DE, we combine the individual-based and generation-based methods for approximate model control. We compared the proposed algorithm with the conventional DE on three benchmark test functions. The experimental results showed that DE-ANN had capacity to be employed to deal with the computationally demanding real-world problems.

Keywords: differential evolution; neural networks; evolutionary algorithms; fitness approximating.

1 Introduction

Evolutionary algorithms (EAs) have had many successful applications in various fields of science and engineering. EAs perform well comparing with the conventional optimization algorithms for the discontinuous, non-differential, multi-model, noisy real-world problems, e.g., spacecraft layout design, aerodynamic design, and sequence-oriented protein design. However, many challenges still arise in the application of EAs to real-world domains. EAs often have to use a large number of fitness evaluations for obtaining a satisfying result. In some extreme cases, the fitness function is too ambiguous to be deterministically evaluated. To deal with such problems, researchers introduced the efficient fitness approximating methods to EAs for reducing the computation time [1-13].

---

[*] Corresponding author.

F.L. Wang et al. (Eds.): AICI 2010, Part II, LNAI 6320, pp. 334–341, 2010.
© Springer-Verlag Berlin Heidelberg 2010

Many fitness approximating methods [1-2] have been proposed for various applications. The popular methods focus on building surrogates based on evaluated points, mainly including instance-based learning methods, machine learning methods and statistical learning methods [2]. Instance-based and machine learning methods include fitness inheritance [3], radial basis function models [4], the K-nearest-neighbor method [5], clustering techniques [6], and artificial neural network (ANN) methods [7]. Statistical learning methods for fitness approximation are called as basically statistical learning models, also known as functional models such as the polynomial models (sometimes called response surfaces) [8], the Kriging models [9], and the support vector machines [10]. These models are also referred to as approximate models, surrogates or meta-models, are all widely used for fitness approximation in EAs. Comparative survey among these methods is presented in the literature [1-2], where approximation levels, approximate model management schemes, model construction techniques are outlined. Artificial neural networks (ANN) have shown to be effective tools for function approximation, and were used in the evolutionary optimization [11]. Therefore, here we also employ ANN as the basis approximating methods in differential evolution (DE).

The use of approximating methods in EAs has received more attention recently [1]. The DE algorithm is a stochastic, population-based, and relatively unknown evolutionary algorithm for global optimization that has recently been successfully applied to many real-world optimization problems [14]. We employ DE in this study because DE can converge quickly, and has demonstrated its efficiency in the computationally demanding real-world problems [15]. Pawan et al [16] presented a computationally effective multi-objective search and optimization technique using coarse-to-fine grain modeling, and combined a GA with ANN as the basic approximating technique for fitness computation.

However, despite the progress made on the approximating techniques in EAs, there is still room for improvement of the computational efficiency of EAs. As far as the knowledge of the authors, little work was done on combining DE with ANN as an approximating technique for the expensive fitness computation. Therefore, we address this issue in this study, develop a DE with ANN-based approximate methods (short for DE-ANN), and make experiments on three benchmark problems to obtain the simulated results.

2 Multilayer Feedforward ANN and Training Algorithms

Multilayer feedforward ANN is one of the most common kinds of ANN to approximate functions. In a multilayer feedforward ANN, the neurons are ordered in layers, starting with an input layer and ending with an output layer. There are many hidden layers between the input and the output layers. Multilayer feedforward ANN include two different phrases [17]: (1) a training phase (also as the learning phrase), and (2) an execution phase. In the first phrase, the ANN is trained on a set of training data samples. After training, the ANN would return a specific output when a specific input is given. In the second phrase, the ANN returns the new outputs according to the new inputs. The above characteristics ensure that the ANN can approximate fitness functions in DE.

Choosing a fast training algorithm is important for DE-ANN when training an ANN with population of DE. The most used algorithm is the backpropagation algorithm, employed to train NSGA-II for approximation in Ref. [16]. But the backpropagation algorithm has some limitations, and performs rather slowly when training. There are many other advanced training algorithms in the literature [18-19]. For one example, the Rprop algorithm [18] proposed by Riedmiller and Braun is one of the best performing first-order training methods for neural networks.

In the Rprop training algorithm, updating each weight is directed by the sign of the partial derivative $\partial E / \partial w_{ij}$, and step-size (the amount of updating a weight) is adapted for each weight individually. The main difference to the backpropagation algorithm is that the step-sizes are independent of the absolute value of the partial derivative. The more benefits of this update scheme in the Rprop algorithm can be found in Ref. [18]. To improve the performance of the Rprop algorithm, Igel et al presented a variant of the Rprop, called iRprop [19]. According to our preliminary test results, the iRprop training algorithm performed better than backpropagation algorithm and Rprop training algorithm when training on the history data of DE. In this study, here we employ the iRprop training algorithm to train the ANN on the population of DE.

3   The Proposed DE-ANN Algorithm

The DE algorithm was introduced by Storn and Price [20]. Since then, several schemes of the DE were proposed [13, 21-22]. The particular version used in this study is the *DE/rand-to-best/1/bin* version, which appears to be the frequently used scheme for complex problems. For minimization problems, i.e., min $f(\vec{x})$, DE works with a population of N candidate solutions. Like other EAs, DE also has the mutation, crossover and selection operations. Unlike other EAs, DE needs less parameters that include population size N, scaling factor F, and crossover constant CR. The main idea of DE is to create new offspring solutions from a weighed difference of parent solutions, and use a greedy selection scheme where the offspring replaces the parent only if it has a better fitness score.

The approximate model can be embedded in almost each part of EAs [1-2], e.g., initialization, recombination, mutation, and fitness evaluations. Because initialization, recombination and mutation are often run randomly, using approximate model in the evolutionary population can reduce the risk of converging to a false optimum. But this reduction of fitness evaluations may be trivial. In most research, the approximate model through the fitness evaluations had received more attentions [1-2, 12, 15].

On approximate fitness functions, Jin et al introduced the individual-based and generation-based evolution control for evolutionary strategy [11]. The individual-based control meant that in every generation, some of the individuals use the approximate model for fitness evaluations, and the others individuals use the original fitness evaluations. This control method can employ a best strategy or a random strategy to select individuals for original fitness evaluations. In the best strategy, we selected the first ranked individuals in the current generation. In the random strategy, we selected the individuals randomly in the current generation. Unlike the individual-based method, the generation-based control meant that in every kth generation, the original fitness function is evaluated, and the data obtained from this generation are used to update the approximate model; in the $(k\text{-}1)$th generations and in the $(k+1)$th generation, the approximate models are used to evaluate the fitness function for evolution. Up to now, there is little literature involving to combine these two methods for the evolution control in DE. Therefore, we address this issue in DE, attempting to obtain the better results.

We propose combing the DE with the multilayer feedforward ANN as the basic approximating technique for fitness function evaluation. Moreover, we employ the iRprop training algorithm to train the ANN on the history data of DE. Furthermore, we combine the individual-based and generation-based methods for approximate fitness evaluations. The overall DE-ANN procedure is shown in Fig. 1.

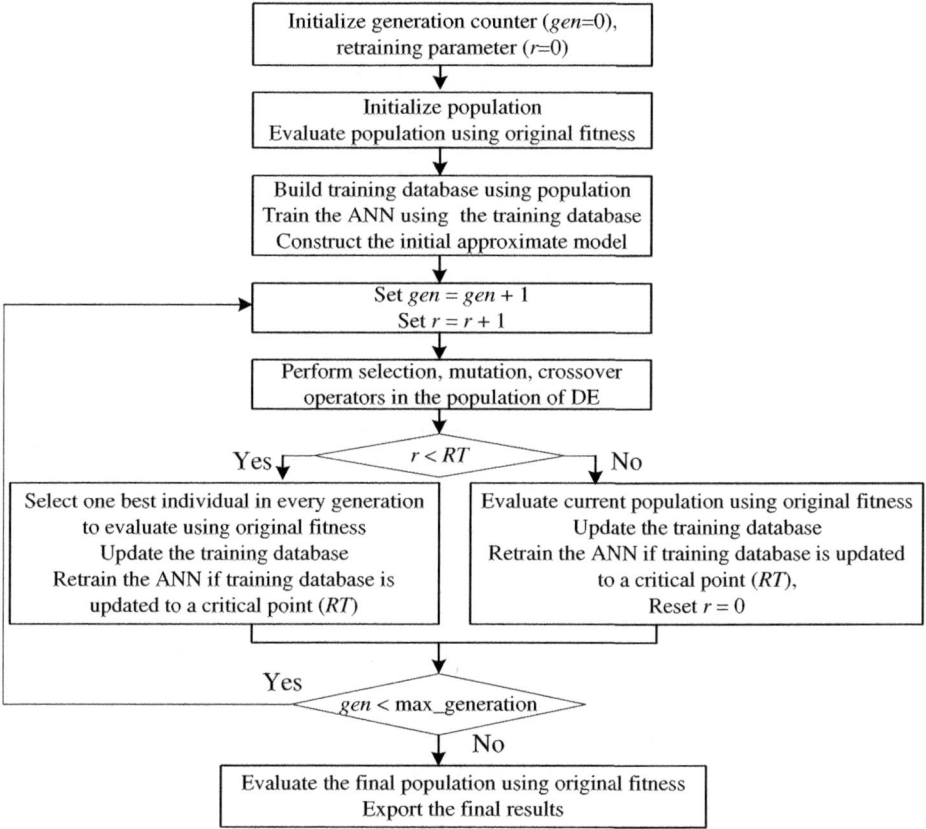

Fig. 1. The procedure of the proposed DE-ANN

It is important to note that the initialized population of DE should always be evaluated using the original fitness function. Thus, we can train the ANN using the training database from original population of DE. Moreover, whenever evaluating the original fitness function, we update the training database using the latest data, and discard the out-of-date data. Furthermore, when the retraining parameter r meets the given critical point RT, we need rebuild the approximate model by retraining the latest database. It is worth mentioning here that the cost time of training the ANN should be added to the overall cost time of evolution. This evolution will take much more time than the conventional DE. To reduce the computation time, we can use a dual processor machine for parallel computing. That is, one processor is used for the ANN training phrase, and the other one is used for the generation of DE.

4 Experimental Studies

To study the proposed DE-ANN algorithms, we used three benchmark functions previously used by Rommel et al for approximate fitness functions in Ref. [11]. These functions and their parameters are listed in Table 1.

Table 1. The benchmark functions and their parameters used in our experimental studies, where n is the dimension of the function, S is the range of variables, and fmin is the minimum value of the function.

Benchmark Functions		n	S	f_{min}
Ellipsoidal	$f(x) = \sum_{i=1}^{n}(i+1)x_i^2$	12	$[-30,30]^n$	0
Rastrigin	$f(x) = \sum_{i=1}^{n}[x_i^2 - \cos(2\pi x_i) + 1]$	12	$[-5.12,5.12]^n$	0
Ackley	$f(x) = 20 + 20e^{-0.2\sqrt{\frac{1}{n}\sum_{i=1}^{n}x_i^2}} + e - e^{\frac{1}{n}\sum_{i=1}^{n}\cos(2\pi x_i)}$	12	$[-1,3]^n$	0

As mentioned above, the DE-ANN and DE has three parameters: (1) the size of the population (N), (2) the crossover constant (CR), and (3) the scaling factor (F). As a result of preliminary test, we use the following values: $N = 80$, $CR = 0.8$, and $F = 0.5$. Recall that the DE-ANN and DE used the *DE/rand-to-best/1/bin* scheme.

About the parameters used for approximate model, we state them as follows: (1) three layers ANN with one hidden layer are used; (2) the input layer has 12 neurons; (3) the output layer has 1 neuron; (3) the hidden layer has 20 neurons; (4) permissible normalized RMS error = 0.02; (5) input and output were scaled in [-1, 1]; (6) the size of the sample data is 600; (7) the size of the selected individual is 1 in individual-based method for evolution control; and (8) the retraining point RT is 0.6*N (population size) generations.

We have run DE-ANN and DE in a fixed amount of fitness evaluations (5000). The simulated results obtained are shown in Table 2 and Figs 2-4. Table 2 provides the statistical analysis of the results of DEANN and DE on three benchmark test functions for 10 runs with different random seeds, where the "Mean" row presents the averaged best value; the "SD" stands for the standard deviation of the best values. Fig.2-4 shows the performance comparison of DE-ANN and DE on the three functions, i.e., Ellipsoidal, Ackley and Rastrigin. Here, we say that algorithm A is more efficient than algorithm B for a given benchmark problem if the mean best value for A is better than that for B. In this opinion, we compared DE-ANN with DE below.

Table 2. Comparison between DE-ANN and DE on the benchmark functions of dimensionality 12

		Ellipsoidal	Ackley	Rastrigin
DE-ANN	Mean	4.39E-3	1.06E-2	4.80E-1
	SD	2.34E-3	4.50E-3	8.13E-1
DE	Mean	2.73E+1	4.23E+0	1.67E+0
	SD	1.08E+1	2.83E-1	3.39E-1

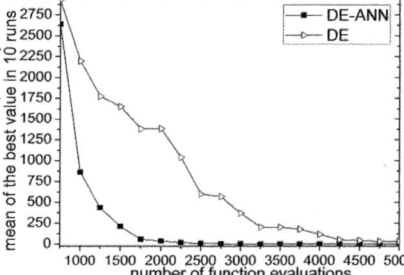

Fig. 2. Performance of DE-ANN and DE on the Ellipsoidal test function.

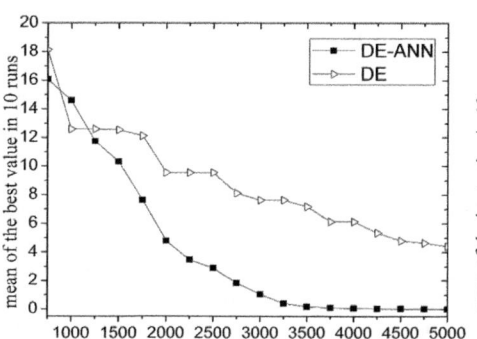

Fig. 3. Performance of DE-ANN and DE on the Ackley test function.

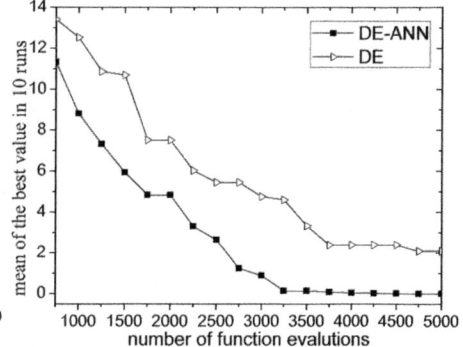

Fig. 4. Performance of DE-ANN and DE on the Rastrigin test function.

Table 2 shows that the DE-ANN outperformed DE in terms of the mean best values on three test functions, especially on the Ellipsoidal function. And Fig.2-4 also show that DE-ANN was better than DE on the performance. Moreover, Fig.2 shows that DE-ANN solved the Ellipsoidal function with higher efficiency than DE in the convergent speed. Fig.2-3 also illustrates that DE-ANN outperformed DE in the convergent precision. Furthermore, Table 2 and Fig. 2-4 show that DE-ANN obtained the near-optimal value of the Ellipsoidal and the Ackley in the fixed evaluations (5000), except for the Rastrigin with lower precision. These simulated results indicate that DE with ANN-based approximate model can reduce the number of the fitness evaluations. This is because DE with ANN-based model captured a coarse approximate model of the original problem, where ANN can direct DE in the right direction, and then help DE to find a near-optimal solution efficiently.

5   Conclusion

We develop an efficient differential evolution with ANN-based approximating technique for computationally expensive problems. The experimental results showed that the DE-ANN outperformed the conventional DE on three benchmark test functions. However, we have to point out that the DE-ANN took more time for evolution than the conventional DE because of the ANN training. Recall that the fitness evaluation of the computationally demanding real-world problems may take much more time than the ANN training. The proposed DE-ANN can be used for this case. In the further work, we will use DE-ANN to deal with the costly real-world problems.

Acknowledgements. This research was supported by the National Natural Science Foundation of China (Grants Nos. 50975039). The work was also supported by the Fundamental Research Funds for the Central Universities and by National Defense Basic Scientific Research Project of PR China (Grant No. B0920060901).

References

[1] Jin, Y.: A Comprehensive Survey of Fitness Approximation in Evolutionary Computation. Soft Computing 9(1), 3–12 (2005)
[2] Shi, L., Rasheed, K.: A Survey of Fitness Approximation Methods Applied in Evolutionary Algorithms. In: Tenne, Y., Goh, C.-K. (eds.) Computational Intel. in Expensive Opti. Prob., ALO, vol. 2, pp. 3–28. Springer, Heidelberg (2010)
[3] Pelikan, M., Sastry, K.: Fitness Inheritance in the Bayesian Optimization Algorithm. In: Deb, K., et al. (eds.) GECCO 2004. LNCS, vol. 3103, pp. 48–59. Springer, Heidelberg (2004)
[4] Ong, Y.S., Nair, P.B., Keane, A.J., Wong, K.W.: Surrogate-Assisted Evolutionary Optimization Frameworks for High-Fidelity Engineering Design Problems. In: Jin, Y. (ed.) Knowledge Incorporation in Evolutionary Computation. Studies in Fuzziness and Soft Computing, pp. 307–332. Springer, Heidelberg (2004)
[5] Takagi, H.: Interactive evolutionary computation. Proceedings of the IEEE, Fusion of the capabilities of EC optimization and human evaluation 89(9), 1275–1296 (2001)
[6] Jin, Y., Sendhoff, B.: Reducing Fitness Evaluations Using Clustering Techniques and Neural Network Ensembles. In: Deb, K., et al. (eds.) GECCO 2004. LNCS, vol. 3102, pp. 688–699. Springer, Heidelberg (2004)
[7] Jin, Y., Hüsken, M., Olhofer, M., Sendhoff, B.: Neural networks for fitness approximation in evolutionary optimization. In: Jin, Y. (ed.) Knowledge Incorporation in Evolutionary Computation, pp. 281–305. Springer, Berlin (2004)
[8] Goel, T., Vaidyanathan, R., Haftka, R.T., et al.: Response surface approximation of Pareto optimal front in multi-objective optimization. Computer Methods in Applied Mechanics and Engineering 196(4-6), 879–893 (2007)
[9] Chung, H.-S., Alonso, J.J.: Multi-objective optimization using approximation model based genetic algorithms. Technical report 2004-4325, AIAA (2004)
[10] Llora, X., Sastry, K.: Goldberg, et al.: Combating User Fatigue in iGAs: Partial Ordering, Support Vector Machines, and Synthetic Fitness. In: Proceedings of the 2005 Conference on Genetic and Evolutionary Computation, pp. 1363–1370 (2005)
[11] Jin, Y., Sendhoff, B.: A Framework for Evolutionary Optimization with Approximate Fitness Functions. IEEE Transactions on Evolutionary Computation 6(5), 481–494 (2002)
[12] Rommel Regis, G., Christine Shoemaker, A.: Local Function Approximation in Evolutionary Algorithm for the optimization of Costly Functions. IEEE Transactions on Evolutionary Computation 8(5), 490–505 (2004)

[13] Zhou, Z.Z., Ong, Y.S., Lim, M.H., et al.: Memetic algorithm using multi-surrogates for computationally expensive optimization problems. Soft Comput. 11, 957–971 (2007)
[14] Storn, R.: System Design by Constraint Adaptation and Differential Evolution. IEEE Transactions on Evolutionary Computation 3(1), 22–34 (1999)
[15] Madavan, N.: Aerodynamic Shape Optimization Using Hybridized Differential Evolution. In: 21st AIAA Applied Aerodynamics Conference, Orlando, Florida, June 23-26. NASA Ames Research Center, Moffett Field, CA, AIAA-2003-3792 (2003)
[16] Pawan, K.S., Nain, D.K.: Computationally effective search and optimization procedure using coarse-to-fine approximation. In: Proceedings of Congress on evolutionary computation (CEC 2003), Canberra, Australia, pp. 2081–2088 (2003)
[17] Hassoun, M.H.: Fundamentals of Artificial Neural Networks. The MIT Press, Cambridge (1995)
[18] Riedmiller, M., Braun, H.: A Direct Adaptive Method for Faster Back propagation learning: The RPROP algorithm. In: Proceeding of the IEEE International Conference on Neural Networks, San Francisco, CA, pp. 586–591 (1993)
[19] Igel, C., Husken, M.: Improving the Rprop Learning Algorithm. In: Proceedings of the Second International Symposium on Neural Computation (NC 2000), pp. 115–121. ICSC Academic Press, London (2000)
[20] Storn, R., Price, K.: DE - A simple and efficient heuristic for global optimization over continuous space. Journal of Global Optimization 11(4), 341–359 (1997)
[21] Ao, Y.Y., Chi, H.Q.: A survey of multi-objective differential evolution algorithms. Journal of Computer Science and Frontiers 3(3), 234–246 (2009)
[22] Chakraborty, U.K.: Advances in Differential Evolution. Springer, Heidelberg (2008)

Evaluate the Quality of Foundational Software Platform by Bayesian Network

Yuqing Lan, Yanfang Liu, and Mingxia Kuang

School of Computer Science and Engineering, Beihang University,
100191 Beijing, China
{lanyuqing,hannahlyf}@buaa.edu.cn,
kuangmingxia@cse.buaa.edu.cn

Abstract. The software quality model and software quality measurement model are the basis of evaluating the quality of the Foundational Software Platform (FSP), but it is quite difficult or even impossible to collect the whole metric data required in the process of the software quality measurement, which is the problem of the FSP quality evaluating. Bayesian networks are the suitable model of resolving the problem including uncertainty and complexity. By analyzing the problem domain of foundational software platform quality evaluation and comparing it with the characteristic domain of Bayesian networks, this paper proposed a method of evaluating the quality of the FSP by Bayesian network. The method includes three parts: node choosing, Bayesian network learning and Bayesian network inference. The results of the experiments indicate a Bayesian network for every quality characteristic should be built in practical quality evaluation of the FSP by the proposed method.

Keywords: Foundational Software Platform; quality evaluation; Bayesian networks; metric; deficiency of data.

1 Introduction

As a result of the trend of platform, network, service-oriented appeared during the process of software development, the software platform, as a kind of software modality, has received more and more attention, especially the Foundational Software Platform (FSP) with operating system as the core, which has gotten a lot of publicity in both the research field and the software industry. The FSP is an application-supporting platform formed by such the general Foundational Software as Operating System, Middleware, Database Management System and Office suite[1], and whether its quality is high or low will strongly affect the quality of its upper application. In the current development of the foundational software industry, the FSP has such problems as usability, reliability, maintainability and so on, because of the lack of the adaptation among the foundational software, which is caused by shortage of the effective quality evaluation of the FSP.

The FSP is a new software form and composed of many foundational software from many different software vendors, so it become quite difficult to collect all the

F.L. Wang et al. (Eds.): AICI 2010, Part II, LNAI 6320, pp. 342–349, 2010.
© Springer-Verlag Berlin Heidelberg 2010

metric data in evaluating the quality of the FSP. In the field of software engineer, it is very essential to propose a method of evaluating the quality of the FSP in the case of deficiency of metric data.

This paper proposes a method to evaluate the quality of the FSP by Bayesian networks, and the method is to build the quality evaluating model by Bayesian networks learning and then to evaluate the given FSP by Bayesian network probabilistic reasoning.

This paper is organized as follows. In section 2, the problem domain of the study is compared with the characteristic domain of Bayesian network, and the method of evaluating the quality of the FSP is proposed. Section 3 explains the proposed method in detail and in section 4 the experiments are conducted. The paper is concluded in section 5.

2   Related Research

A Bayesian network is a graphical representation that depicts conditional independence among random variables in the domain and encodes the joint probability distribution[2]. With a network at hand, probabilistic reasoning can be performed to predict the outcome of some variables based on the observations of others. Bayesian networks are the suitable model for the data mining and uncertainty knowledge representation, and they are mainly used to resolve problems containing uncertainty and complexity.

Research on Bayesian networks includes the learning of Bayesian networks and probabilistic reasoning as follows.

Bayesian networks learning. Bayesian networks learning is to construct Bayesian networks from the observed data and priori knowledge, and there are many algorithms like gradient-based parameter learning algorithm proposed by Russell[3], K2 algorithm proposed by Herskovits that is based on scoring function and hill-climbing algorithm[4], structure Expectation Maximization(EM) algorithm combined EM algorithm with structure search by Friedman[5].

Probabilistic reasoning of Bayesian networks. Bayesian networks probabilistic reasoning is to infer the probability distribution of other objective variables from the given Bayesian network structure and the observed data of some variables and is a process of predicting the probability of the unknown variables by the result of Bayesian networks learning. Bayesian networks probabilistic reasoning contains precise reasoning and approximate reasoning. In theory, the probabilistic reasoning of Bayesian networks is known as a Non-deterministic Polynomial hard problem[6], but practically many inference methods[7] are all valid[8], and even some real-time inference methods of Bayesian networks are proposed for the real-time domain[9]. Generally there are precise algorithms and approximate algorithm for Bayesian networks probabilistic reasoning. Three famous inference algorithms include Belief-Net-Ask, message-passing[10] and variable elimination[11] which are all precise algorithms.

The quality evaluation of the FSP is a non deterministic problem. Comparing its Problem Domain with Feature Domains of Bayesian networks, as shown in Figure 1, this paper proposes evaluating the quality of the FSP by Bayesian networks.

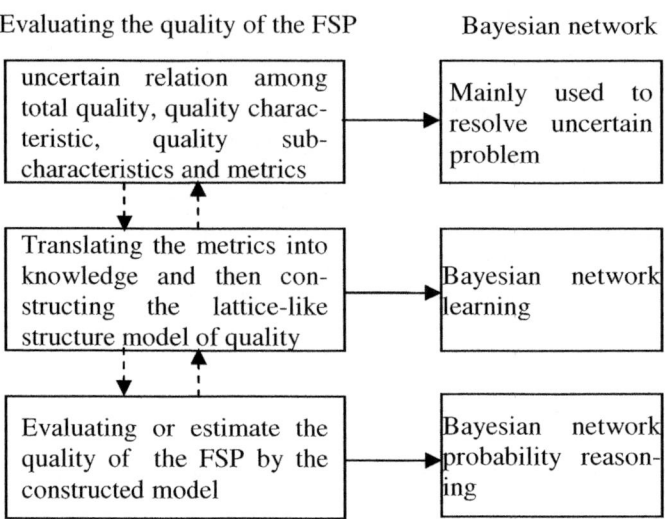

Fig. 1. Comparing the Problem Domain of this paper with Feature Domain of Bayesian networks

3 Method

Under deficient metric data of the FSP, the method of evaluating its quality by Bayesian networks is to collect the existing metric data and knowledge from domain experts, construct Bayesian networks model of this FSP by Bayesian networks learning, and then users can evaluate the quality of the FSP instance according to this model that they have chosen using Bayesian network probabilistic reasoning, as described in Figure 2. Here the process of evaluating the quality of the FSP is divided into three parts: nodes choosing, Bayesian networks learning and Bayesian networks probabilistic reasoning. Node choosing and Bayesian networks learning lay the foundations of Bayesian networks probabilistic reasoning, and the probabilistic reasoning is used to finish inferring the quality of the FSP instances by Bayesian networks Structure and Conditional Probability Table(CPT).4

3.1 Node Choosing of Bayesian Networks

Node choosing is completed by collecting the knowledge of the domain, which is the basis of constructing the structure of Bayesian networks. For the research on evaluating the quality of the FSP by Bayesian networks, node choosing is to collect the index influencing the quality of the FSP, which includes the quality characteristics, quality sub-characteristics and metrics. To collect the knowledge of the domain experts, 50 questionnaires are sent to the experts from such four fields as the FSP developers, the application system integrators, the third part evaluation organizations and the profession customers. After the statistical analysis and the repeated survey, seven quality characteristics and one quality in use are finally extracted. The quality characteristics include functionality, reliability, security, interoperability, manageability, scalability

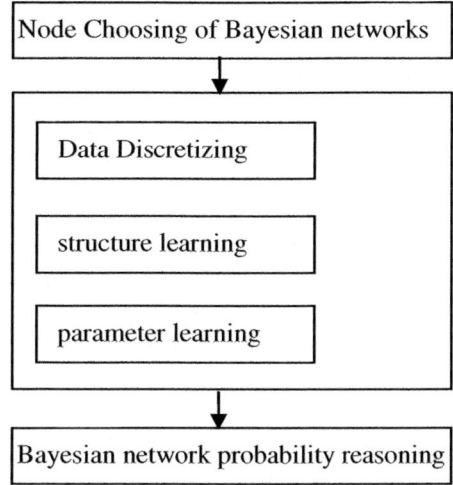

Fig. 2. Process of evaluating the quality of the FSP by Bayesian networks

Table 1. Numbers of external and internal metrics of the FSP quality characteristics

quality characteristics	External metrics	Internal metrics
Functionality	9	7
Reliability	20	8
Security	7	12
interoperability	9	5
manageability	24	25
Scalability	16	12
Efficiency	22	9

and efficiency, and have 107 external metrics and 78 internal metrics. The quality in use has 15 metrics. Limited by pages, just the numbers of external and internal metrics are listed here, as shown in Table 1.Maintaining the Integrity of the Specifications.

3.2 Bayesian Networks Learning

Bayesian networks learning means to construct the Bayesian networks structure needed for evaluating the quality of the FSP using the domain knowledge and lots of the instance of the FSP and compute its CPT. Bayesian networks learning include structure learning and parameters learning of Bayesian networks. This paper adopts K2 searching algorithm by Cooper and Herskovits to finish the Bayesian networks learning of the FSP.

Data Discretizing. The continuous Bayesian networks learning algorithms require data to follow the normal distribution, but now there isn't firm theory to prove the metric data of the FSP to obey the normal distribution. Therefore, the discrete Bayesian network is used for the quality evaluation of the FSP, and the collected metric data need to be discretized. Based on the actual meaning of every metric of the FSP, its value is divided into several ranks. The literature [12] presents the ranking of the metrics of the interoperability and others is similar.

Bayesian networks structure learning. In Bayesian networks structure learning, by analyzing the gathered data set of the FSP case, Bayesian networks structure, which can express statistic characteristic of the data set, is constructed. This paper adopts discrete Bayesian networks learning algorithm-improved K2 searching algorithm to build Bayesian networks structure. In this algorithm, the domain knowledge is introduced and some cause-effect relationships that exist inevitably or don't exist inevitably are defined before finding the parent node in a cycle in K2 algorithm. Limited by pages, just part of Bayesian networks structure for functionality of the FSP is presented as Figure 3.

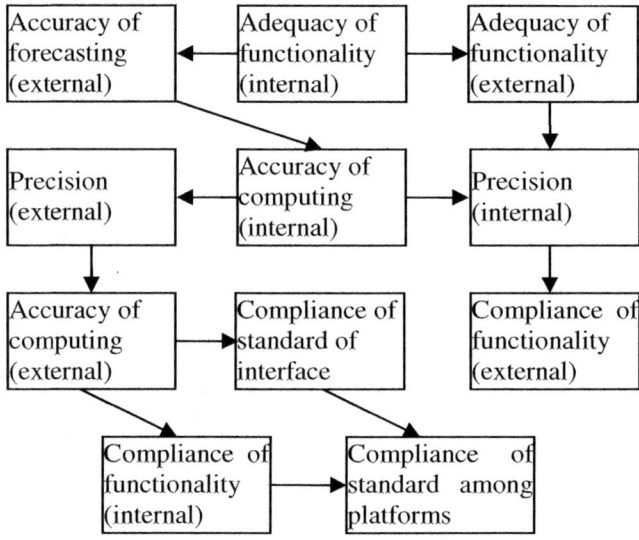

Fig. 3. Bayesian network for functionality

Bayesian networks parameter learning. After constructing the structure of Bayesian networks, the CRT of the built Bayesian network structure is gotten by the algorithm of computing the parameter provided by Cooper and Herskovits.

3.3   Bayesian Networks Probability Reasoning

Bayesian networks probability reasoning is a process of inferring the values of unknown variables in Deficiency data set based on the above Bayesian networks structure and CPT. It is very important that users can evaluate the quality of the FSP under not getting all the metric data by Bayesian networks probability reasoning. In this paper, variable elimination algorithm is used for Bayesian inference, which is the basic method of computing posterior probability. Before describing the algorithm, three definitions are given.

Definition 1. Evidence Variable: In the process of reasoning, the variable, the value of which is known, is called Evidence Variable, and its value is called the value of evidence variable.

Definition 2. Query Variable: It is the variable, the value of which is unknown.

Definition 3. Elimination Sequence: That is a variable sequence including the sequence of inputting variables and the sequence of querying variables.

The algorithm is described as follow:

```
VE(N, E, e, Q, P)
Input of function•
    N: Bayesian network
    E: Evidence variable
    E: Value of evidence variable
    Q: Query variable
    P: Elimination Sequence
Output of function• p(Q | E = e) Conditional
probability of Query variable under Evidence variable
Algorithm:
1 : F← a set of all the Probability Distribution in N
2: assign their values e to the evidence variable in F
3: while (P not null)
4: z← the first variable in P, and then delete z from P
5: F← Elim(F, z)
6: end while
7: all the factors in F are multiplied to obtain a
function h(Q) about Q
8: return h(Q) / sum(h(Q))

Elim(F, z)
Input of function:
    F : a set of functions
    z : variables that will be eliminated
Output of function: another set of function
Algorithm:
1: delete all the functions relating to z from F, de-
fine these function {f1, …, fk}
2: g ← Πfi
3: h ← sum (g)
4: return h to F
5: return F
```

In the variable elimination algorithm, the different elimination sequence leads to the different computation complexity and the elimination sequence that has the lowest total cost is the optimal one, which is proved a NP-hard problem. And in practice, the heuristic rules are used to found out the better but not optimal elimination sequence. This article adopts an algorithm named Maximum Potential Searching to find the elimination sequence, and the algorithm is that all of the nodes in undirected graph g of Bayesian network are numbered in descending with the following rule: in the step i, choosing the unnumbered node with the most numbered adjacent nodes and then numbered it n-i+1, choosing any one if more than one like the above node. After numbering all of the nodes and sort them from small to large, variable elimination sequence is determined.

4 Experiment and Application Analysis

In this section, 5 experiments are conducted to compute the time complexity of the Bayesian networks probability reasoning. In the experiment, we extract n (n = 15, 21, 27, 33, 35) nodes from the chosen 200 metrics to construct Bayesian network and every experiment is finished under only collecting the value of one evidence variable. The time of inferring the values of others that are not evidence nodes by the value of one evidence node is computed and the results is following.

Table 2. Relationship of Bayesian networks probability reasoning and the number of the non-evidence nodes

the Number of Bayesian network nodes	the number of the non-evidence nodes	the consumed time(ms)
15	14	381
21	20	7,892
27	26	436,673
33	32	19,458,525
35	34	82,870,504

The results of experiment in table 2 show that, with the increasing of the evidence nodes, the time of Bayesian networks probability reasoning increase by the exponential growth. In evaluating the quality of the FSP, if all of 200 metrics are used to construct one Bayesian network, Bayesian networks reasoning will not only require large amounts of training data, but it also cost several days or even more time, which is un-practical in the real application.

In this paper a Bayesian network for every quality characteristic is proposed when the quality of the FSP is evaluated. For every Bayesian network, its nodes are the metrics of every quality characteristic and Bayesian network leaning and inferring are all required for every quality characteristic. The quality in use is the same as the quality characteristic. Thus 8 Bayesian networks are constructed for evaluating the quality of the FSP in this paper.

5 Conclusion

The foundational software platform is the new emerging form of software industry, so a practicable and efficient method is urgently required to evaluate its quality to ensure that its quality can meet the demands of users, which is also the requirement of the development and popularity of the FSP.

This paper researches on evaluating the quality of the foundational software platform by Bayesian networks. Firstly, it analyzes the problem of evaluating the quality of the FSP and then compares its problem domain with the characteristic domain of Bayesian networks. Secondly, it proposes a method of evaluating the quality of the FSP by Bayesian networks, including the node choosing of the Bayesian networks, Bayesian networks learning and Bayesian networks inference. Finally, five experiments are conducted and the results show that in the actual quality evaluation, a Bayesian network for every quality characteristic and quality in use of the FSP is constructed.

The proposed method cannot only help users select the FSP of better quality, but also guide the integrators and vendors to improve the quality of the FSP. What is more, it can accelerate development and practical application of the FSP.

Acknowledgment. One of us thanks the National High Technology Research and Development Program of China (863 number: 2009AA01Z406) and the Project of China Standard Software Co.LTD named "Application and Demonstrate of e-government solution at District or Country level based on Chinese Software and Hardware"(number : 8) for support.

References

1. Yuqing, L., Tong, Z., Jing, G., Hui, J., Maozhong, J.: Quality Evaluation of Foundational Software Platform. J. Journal of Software 20, 567–582 (2009)
2. Pearl, J.: Probabilistic Reasoning in Intelligent Systems: Networks of Plausible Inference. Morgan Kaufmann, San Mateo (1988)
3. Russell, S., Binder, J., Koller, D.: Local learning in probabilistic networks with hidden variables. In: 14th International Joint Conferrence on Artificial Intelligence, IEEE Transactions on Software Engineering (1995)
4. Herskovits, E.: Computer-based Probabilistic-Network Construction. Stanford University, USA (1991)
5. Friedman, N.: The Bayesian structure EM algorithm. In: 14th Int'l. Conf., Off Uncertainty in Artificial Intelligence, pp. 125–133. Morgan Kaufmann Publishers, San Francisco (1997)
6. Dagum, P., Luby, M.: Approximating probabilistic reasoning in Bayesian belief networks is NP-hard. J. Artificial Intelligence 60, 51–91 (1993)
7. Russell, S., Norvig, P.: Artificial intelligence: A modern approach, USA. Prentice-Hall Series in Artificial Intelligence (1995)
8. Mitchell, T.M.: Machine Learning. China Machine Press, Beijing (2003)
9. Guo, H., Hsu, W.: A Survey of Algorithms for Real-Time Bayesian Network Inference, http://citeseer.ist.psu.edu/guosurvey.html
10. Darwiche, A.: An introduction to inference in Bayesian networks. MIT Press, Cambridge (1999)
11. Nevin, P., Zhang, L.: Computational Properties of Two Exact Algorithms for Bayesian Networks. J. Journal of Applied Intelligence 9, 173–184 (1998)
12. Yuqing, L., Tong, Z.: Evaluate interoperability of foundational software platform by Bayesian networks. J. Journal of Beijing University of Aeronautics and Astronautics 35, 1148–1151+1160 (2009)

Triangle Fuzzy Number Intuitionistic Fuzzy Aggregation Operators and Their Application to Group Decision Making

Dongfeng Chen, Lei Zhang, and Jingshan Jiao

Department of Aviation Theory, Aviation University of Air Force
Changchun Jilin 130022, China
twodrifters@126.com

Abstract. The method on uncertain multiple attribute group decision making (MAGDM) based on aggregating intuitionistic fuzzy information is investigated.Firstly,some operational laws,score function and variation function of triangle fuzzy number intuitionistic fuzzy sets(TFNIFSs) are proposed. Then,triangle fuzzy number intuitionistic fuzzy weighted geometric (TFNIFWG) operator and triangle fuzzy number intuitionistic fuzzy ordered weighted geometric (TFNIFOWG) operator are studied. Further, a TFNIFWG and TFNIFOWG operators-based approach is developed to solve the MAGDM problems in which the attribute values take the form of TFNIFSs and the expert weights are completely unknown.Finally, some illustrative example is given to verify the developed approach and to demonstrate its practicality and effectiveness.

Keywords: intuitionistic fuzzy sets, triangular fuzzy number, aggregation operator, group decision making.

1 Introduction

Intuitionistic fuzzy sets(IFSs) [1] proposed by Atanassov is a generalization of the concept of fuzzy sets. In 1989,Atanassov and Gargov expanded the IFSs,using interval value to express membership and non-membership[2] function of IFSs. Later,Liu and Wang[3][4] introduced the concept of fuzzy number IFSs as a further generalization of IFSs. Recently,some researchers[4-6] have shown great interest in the fuzzy number IFSs and applied it to the field of decision making.Essentially,such multicriteria decision making method is equivalent to ranking method of fuzzy number IFSs. However, in some cases,the proposed techniques using a score function and an accuracy function cannot give sufficient information about alternatives and may demonstrate the situation of difficult decision or wrong decision. On the other hand, based on the arithmetic aggregation operators, Xu[7] and Wang[4] developed some new geometric aggregation operators, such as fuzzy number intuitionistic fuzzy hybrid geometric(FIFHG) and intuitionistic fuzzy ordered weighted averaging (IFOWA) operator, they also studied the method for group decision making with intuitionistic fuzzy information. Therefor,it is necessary to pay close attention to this issue and develop new ranking and MAGDM methods.

F.L. Wang et al. (Eds.): AICI 2010, Part II, LNAI 6320, pp. 350–357, 2010.

In this paper, a novel score function is presented by taking into account the expectation of the membership and non-membership degree of TFNIFSs.Aimed at the fuzzy number intuitionistic fuzzy information aggregating problems, this paper proposed triangle fuzzy number intuitionistic fuzzy weighted geometric(TFNIFWG) operator and triangle fuzzy number intuitionistic fuzzy ordered weighted geometric(TFNIFOWG) operator. Based on these operators, an approach for solving uncertain multiple attribute group decision making problems is proposed, in which the attribute values are fuzzy number intuitionistic fuzzy numbers and the weights of decision-makers are completely unknown.

2 Ranking of Triangle Fuzzy Number Intuitionistic Fuzzy Sets

2.1 Fuzzy Number Intuitionistic Fuzzy Set

Definition 1. If $\beta = (l, p, q) \in F(D)$, $D \to [0,1]$ then saying β is a triangle fuzzy number of D ,whose membership degree function $\mu_\beta(x): R \to [0,1]$ can be expressed:

$$\mu_\beta(x) = \begin{cases} (x-l)/(p-l), l \leq x \leq p \\ (x-q)/(p-q), p \leq x \leq q \\ 0 \qquad\qquad , other \end{cases} \tag{1}$$

Thereinto: $x \in R$, $0 \leq l \leq p \leq q \leq 1$, p is the barycenter of fuzzy number β ,if $l = p = q$, then β is a real number.

For a triangle fuzzy number β ,its fuzzy mean $E(\beta)$ and standard deviation $\sigma(\beta)$ are defined as[8]:

$$E(\beta) = \frac{l + 2p + q}{4} \tag{2}$$

$$\sigma(\beta) = \frac{3l^2 + 4m^2 + 3n^2 - 4lm - 2\ln - 4mn}{80} \tag{3}$$

Definition 2. Supposing theory field U is a limit set of not full, saying $G = \{(x, \langle \tilde{\mu}_G(x), \tilde{\gamma}_G(x) \rangle) | x \in U\}$ is triangle fuzzy number intuitionistic fuzzy set.

Thereinto: $\tilde{\mu}_G(x) = (\tilde{\mu}_G^1(x), \tilde{\mu}_G^2(x), \tilde{\mu}_G^3(x))$ and $\tilde{\gamma}_G(x) = (\tilde{\gamma}_G^1(x), \tilde{\gamma}_G^2(x), \tilde{\gamma}_G^3(x))$ are triangle fuzzy numbers of $D = [0,1]$,which can express the membership degree and the non-membership degree of x in U ,and fulfill $0 \leq \tilde{\mu}_G^3(x) + \tilde{\gamma}_G^3(x) \leq 1, \forall x \in U$.

Then, $\langle \tilde{\mu}_G(x), \tilde{\gamma}_G(x) \rangle$ is called a triangle fuzzy number intuitionistic fuzzy number(TFNIFN).Let $\tilde{A} = \langle (a_1, b_1, c_1), (l_1, p_1, q_1) \rangle$ and $\tilde{B} = \langle (a_2, b_2, c_2), (l_2, p_2, q_2) \rangle$ be two TFNIFNs, we introduce two operational laws of $\tilde{A}$ and $\tilde{B}$ as follows:

$$\tilde{A} \otimes \tilde{B} = \langle (a_1a_2, b_1b_2, c_1c_2), (l_1 + l_2 - l_1l_2, \ p_1 + p_2 - p_1p_2, q_1 + q_2 - q_1q_2) \rangle \tag{4}$$

$$\tilde{A}^\lambda = \left\langle \left(a_1^\lambda, b_2^\lambda, c_1^\lambda\right), \left(1-(1-l_1)^\lambda, \ 1-(1-p_1)^\lambda, 1-(1-q_1)^\lambda\right)\right\rangle, \quad \lambda \geq 0 \qquad (5)$$

2.2 Ranking Method of Triangle Fuzzy Number Intuitionistic Fuzzy Sets

Next, we propose the ranking method of TFNIFSs by the new score function and variation function, which are defined in the following:

Definition 3. Let $\tilde{G} = \left\{ \left\langle x, \left\langle \tilde{\mu}_G(x), \tilde{\gamma}_G(x)\right\rangle\right\rangle \middle| x \in U \right\}$ is a triangle fuzzy number intuitionistic fuzzy set, then a score function of $\tilde{G}$ can be represented as follows:

$$s(\tilde{G}) = E(\tilde{\mu}_G) \frac{1 + E(\tilde{\mu}_G) - E(\tilde{\gamma}_G)}{2}\left(1 - E(\tilde{\mu}_G) - E(\tilde{\gamma}_G)\right) \qquad (6)$$

Where $s(\tilde{G}) \in [0,1]$, $E(\tilde{\mu}_G)$ and $E(\tilde{\gamma}_G)$ are the fuzzy means of triangle fuzzy number $\tilde{\mu}_G$ and $\tilde{\gamma}_G$ respectively. The larger the score $s(\tilde{G})$, the greater the value of TFNIFS $\tilde{G}$.

Similarly, a variation function of $\tilde{G}$ can be represented as follows:

$$v(\tilde{G}) = \sigma(\tilde{\mu}_G) + \sigma(\tilde{\gamma}_G) \qquad (7)$$

Where $\sigma(\tilde{\mu}_G)$ and $\sigma(\tilde{\gamma}_G)$ are the fuzzy standard deviation of triangle fuzzy number $\tilde{\mu}_G$ and $\tilde{\gamma}_G$ respectively.

Definition 4. Let $\tilde{G}_1$ and $\tilde{G}_2$ are triangle fuzzy number intuitionistic fuzzy sets, we have:

1) if $s(\tilde{G}_1) < s(\tilde{G}_2)$, then $\tilde{G}_1 < \tilde{G}_2$;

2) if $s(\tilde{G}_1) = s(\tilde{G}_2)$ and $v(\tilde{G}_1) = v(\tilde{G}_2)$, then $\tilde{G}_1 = \tilde{G}_2$;if $s(\tilde{G}_1) = s(\tilde{G}_2)$ but $v(\tilde{G}_1) > v(\tilde{G}_2)$, then $\tilde{G}_1 < \tilde{G}_2$.

3 Fuzzy Number Intuitionistic Fuzzy Geometric Aggregation Operators

Definition 5. Let $\tilde{\beta}_j = \left\langle \left(a_j, b_j, c_j\right), \left(l_j, p_j, q_j\right)\right\rangle (j = 1, 2, \cdots, n)$ be a set of TFNIFNs. A triangle fuzzy number intuitionistic fuzzy weighted geometric(TFNIFWG) operator of dimension n is a mapping TFNIFWG: $\Omega^n \to \Omega$,that has an associated vector $w = (w_1, w_2, \cdots, w_n)^T$ such that $w_j > 0$ and $\sum_{j=1}^n w_j = 1$. Furthermore,

$$TFNIFWG_w(\tilde{\beta}_1, \tilde{\beta}_2, \cdots, \tilde{\beta}_n) = (\tilde{\beta}_1)^{w_1} \otimes (\tilde{\beta}_2)^{w_2} \otimes \cdots \otimes (\tilde{\beta}_n)^{w_n} \qquad (8)$$

Especially, if $w = (1/n, 1/n, \cdots, 1/n)^T$,then the TFNIFWG operator is reduced to the triangular fuzzy number intuitionistic fuzzy geometric (TFNIFG) operator.

According to the operational laws (4) and (5),we have:

Theorem 1. Let $\tilde{\beta}_j = \left\langle \left(a_j, b_j, c_j\right), \left(l_j, p_j, q_j\right)\right\rangle (j = 1,2,\cdots, n)$ be a set of TFNIFNs,then their aggregated value by using the TFNIFWG operator is also a TFNIFN, and

$$TFNIFWG_w\left(\tilde{\beta}_1, \tilde{\beta}_2, \cdots, \tilde{\beta}_n\right) = \left\langle \left(\prod_{j=1}^{n} a_j^{w_j}, \prod_{j=1}^{n} b_j^{w_j}, \prod_{j=1}^{n} c_j^{w_j}\right),\right.$$

$$\left.\left(1 - \prod_{j=1}^{n}\left(1 - l_j\right)^{w_j}, 1 - \prod_{j=1}^{n}\left(1 - p_j\right)^{w_j}, 1 - \prod_{j=1}^{n}\left(1 - q_j\right)^{w_j}\right)\right\rangle \quad (9)$$

Where $w = \left(w_1, w_2, \cdots, w_n\right)^T$ is the weighting vector of the FNIFNWG operator, with $w_j > 0$ and $\sum_{j=1}^{n} w_j = 1$.

Definition 6. Let $\tilde{\beta}_j = \left\langle \left(a_j, b_j, c_j\right), \left(l_j, p_j, q_j\right)\right\rangle (j = 1,2,\cdots, n)$ be a set of TFNIFNs. An triangle fuzzy number intuitionistic fuzzy ordered weighted geometric(TFNIFOWG) operator of dimension n is a mapping TFNIFOWG: $\Omega^n \rightarrow \Omega$,that has an associated vector $w = \left(w_1, w_2, \cdots, w_n\right)^T$ such that $w_j > 0$ and $\sum_{j=1}^{n} w_j = 1$. Furthermore,

$$TFNIFOWG_w\left(\tilde{\beta}_1, \tilde{\beta}_2, \cdots, \tilde{\beta}_n\right) = \left(\tilde{\beta}_{\sigma(1)}\right)^{w_1} \otimes \left(\tilde{\beta}_{\sigma(2)}\right)^{w_2} \otimes \cdots \otimes \left(\tilde{\beta}_{\sigma(n)}\right)^{w_n}. \quad (10)$$

Where $\left(\sigma(1), \sigma(2), \cdots, \sigma(n)\right)$ is a permutation of $\left(1,2,\cdots,n\right)$ such that $\tilde{\beta}_{\sigma(j-1)} > \tilde{\beta}_{\sigma(j)}$ for all j .Especially, if $w = \left(1/n, 1/n, \cdots, 1/n\right)^T$,then the TFNIFOWG operator is reduced to the triangular fuzzy number intuitionistic fuzzy geometric(TFNIFG) operator.

Theorem 2. Let $\tilde{\beta}_j = \left\langle \left(a_j, b_j, c_j\right), \left(l_j, p_j, q_j\right)\right\rangle (j = 1,2,\cdots, n)$ be a set of TFNIFNs, then their aggregated value by using the TFNIFOWG operator is also a TFNIFN, and

$$TFNIFOWG_w\left(\tilde{\beta}_1, \tilde{\beta}_2, \cdots, \tilde{\beta}_n\right) = \left\langle \left(\prod_{j=1}^{n} a_{\sigma(j)}^{w_j}, \prod_{j=1}^{n} b_{\sigma(j)}^{w_j}, \prod_{j=1}^{n} c_{\sigma(j)}^{w_j}\right),\right.$$

$$\left.\left(1 - \prod_{j=1}^{n}\left(1 - l_{\sigma(j)}\right)^{w_j}, 1 - \prod_{j=1}^{n}\left(1 - p_{\sigma(j)}\right)^{w_j}, 1 - \prod_{j=1}^{n}\left(1 - q_{\sigma(j)}\right)^{w_j}\right)\right\rangle \quad (11)$$

Where $w = \left(w_1, w_2, \cdots, w_n\right)^T$ is the weighting vector of the FNIFNOWG operator, with $w_j > 0$ and $\sum_{j=1}^{n} w_j = 1$.

Central to this operator is the reordering of the arguments, based upon their values, in particular an argument $\tilde{\beta}_j$ is not associated with a particular weight w_j but rather a weight w_j associated with a particular ordered position i of the arguments.

One important issue of the TFNIFOWG operator is to determine its associated weights.Zeshui Xu[10] reviewed existing main methods, and develop a normal distribution-based method to determine the OWA weights, which is determined by:

$$w_j = \frac{e^{-\left[(j-\mu_n)^2/2\sigma_n^2\right]}}{\sum_{i=1}^{n} e^{-\left[(i-\mu_n)^2/2\sigma_n^2\right]}}, \quad j = 1, 2, \cdots, n \tag{12}$$

Where μ_n is the mean of the collection of $1, 2, \cdots, n$, and σ_n is the standard deviation of the collection of $1, 2, \cdots, n$. μ_n and σ_n are obtained by the following formulas respectively:

$$\mu_n = \frac{1+n}{2} \tag{13}$$

$$\sigma_n = \sqrt{\frac{1}{n} \sum_{i=1}^{n} (i - \mu_n)^2} \tag{14}$$

The method can relieve the influence of unfair arguments on the decision results by weighting these arguments with small values.

4 An Approach to Group Decision Making Based on Intuitionistic Fuzzy Information

Let $A = \{A_1, A_2, \cdots, A_m\}$ and $G = \{G_1, G_2, \cdots, G_n\}$ be the set of alternatives and attributes seperately, and $w = (w_1, w_2, \cdots, w_n)$ is the weighting vector of the attribute G_j, where $w_j > 0$, $\sum_{j=1}^{n} w_j = 1$. Let $D = \{D_1, D_2, \cdots, D_t\}$ be the set of decision makers, $e = (e_1, e_2, \cdots, e_t)$ be the weighting vector of decision makers, with $e_k > 0$, $\sum_{k=1}^{t} e_k = 1$. Suppose that $\tilde{R}_k = \left(\tilde{\beta}_{ij}^{(k)}\right)_{m \times n} = \left(\left\langle \left(a_{ij}^{(k)}, b_{ij}^{(k)}, c_{ij}^{(k)}\right), \left(l_{ij}^{(k)}, p_{ij}^{(k)}, q_{ij}^{(k)}\right) \right\rangle\right)_{m \times n}$ is the intuitionistic fuzzy decision matrix where triangular fuzzy number $\left(a_{ij}^{(k)}, b_{ij}^{(k)}, c_{ij}^{(k)}\right)$ indicates the degree that the alternative A_i satisfies the attribute G_j given by the decision maker D_k, $\left(l_{ij}^{(k)}, p_{ij}^{(k)}, q_{ij}^{(k)}\right)$ indicates the degree that the alternative A_i does not satisfy the attribute G_j given by the decision maker D_k.

We apply the aggregation operators to multiple attribute group decision making based on intuitionistic fuzzy information. The method involves the following steps:

Step 1. Utilize the decision information given in matrix R_k and the TFNIFWG operator which has associated weighting vector $w = (w_1, w_2, \cdots, w_n)$ to aggregate the attribute value of the kth row into the integrated attribute value which is given by the decision-maker D_k:

$$\tilde{\beta}_i^{(k)} = TFNIFNWG_w\left(\tilde{\beta}_{i1}^{(k)}, \tilde{\beta}_{i2}^{(k)}, \cdots, \tilde{\beta}_{in}^{(k)}\right) \tag{15}$$

Step 2. Utilize the TFNIFOWG operator to aggregate all the integrated attribute values given by all the decision-makers into the group integrated attribute value of alternative A_i:

$$\tilde{\beta}_i = TFNIFNOWG_e\left(\tilde{\beta}_i^{(1)}, \tilde{\beta}_i^{(2)}, \cdots, \tilde{\beta}_i^{(t)}\right) \tag{16}$$

Step 3. Calculate the value of score function $S\left(\tilde{\beta}_i\right)$ and variation function $V\left(\tilde{\beta}_i\right)$ to rank all the alternatives A_i $(i = 1, 2, \cdots, m)$, then select the best one(s) in accordance with Definition 4.

5 Illustrative Example

Let us suppose there is an university composed of 4 colleges A_k $(k = 1, 2, \cdots, 4)$, which wants to select the most excellent one. In the process of choosing one of the colleges, three factors are considered—I_1:teaching, I_2: scientific research, I_3:service.In order to evaluate the colleges, a committee composed of three decision makers has been formed. Suppose that the weight vector of $I_i(i=1,2,3)$ is $w = (0.3608, 0.3091, 0.3301)$, but the weights of the three decision makers are completely unknown. The preference information of the colleges A_k $(k = 1, 2, \cdots, 4)$ are represented by the TFNIFNs listed in Table 1 to 3.Then, we utilize the proposed procedure to get the most desirable college(s).

Table 1. The intuitionistic fuzzy decision matrix R1

	I_1	I_2	I_3
A_1	$\langle(0.5,0.6,0.7),(0.1,0.2,0.3)\rangle$	$\langle(0.6,0.7,0.8),(0.1,0.1,0.2)\rangle$	$\langle(0.3,0.4,0.4),(0.2,0.3,0.4)\rangle$
A_2	$\langle(0.4,0.5,0.6),(0.1,0.2,0.3)\rangle$	$\langle(0.5,0.6,0.6),(0.1,0.2,0.3)\rangle$	$\langle(0.5,0.6,0.7),(0.1,0.2,0.3)\rangle$
A_3	$\langle(0.7,0.7,0.8),(0.1,0.1,0.2)\rangle$	$\langle(0.5,0.6,0.7),(0.1,0.1,0.2)\rangle$	$\langle(0.5,0.5,0.6),(0.2,0.3,0.3)\rangle$
A_4	$\langle(0.5,0.6,0.7),(0.1,0.2,0.2)\rangle$	$\langle(0.3,0.3,0.4),(0.1,0.2,0.2)\rangle$	$\langle(0.6,0.7,0.8),(0.1,0.1,0.2)\rangle$

Step 1. Utilize the TFNIFWG operator (8) and (9) to aggregate the attribute value of the kth row into the integrated attribute value $\tilde{\beta}_i^{(k)}(i = 1, 2, \cdots, 4, k = 1, 2, 3)$ which is given by the decision-maker D_k.

Table 2. The intuitionistic fuzzy decision matrix R2

	I_1	I_2	I_3
A_1	$\langle(0.6,0.6,0.7),(0.1,0.2,0.3)\rangle$	$\langle(0.7,0.8,0.9),(0.1,0.1,0.1)\rangle$	$\langle(0.5,0.5,0.5),(0.2,0.3,0.4)\rangle$
A_2	$\langle(0.5,0.6,0.6),(0.2,0.3,0.4)\rangle$	$\langle(0.7,0.7,0.7),(0.1,0.2,0.3)\rangle$	$\langle(0.6,0.6,0.6),(0.1,0.2,0.3)\rangle$
A_3	$\langle(0.8,0.8,0.8),(0.1,0.1,0.2)\rangle$	$\langle(0.6,0.7,0.8),(0.1,0.2,0.2)\rangle$	$\langle(0.5,0.6,0.6),(0.2,0.3,0.3)\rangle$
A_4	$\langle(0.5,0.6,0.7),(0.2,0.2,0.2)\rangle$	$\langle(0.4,0.5,0.6),(0.1,0.1,0.1)\rangle$	$\langle(0.8,0.8,0.8),(0.2,0.2,0.2)\rangle$

Table 3. The intuitionistic fuzzy decision matrix R2

	I_1	I_2	I_3
A_1	$\langle(0.6,0.6,0.7),(0.2,0.2,0.3)\rangle$	$\langle(0.7,0.7,0.7),(0.1,0.1,0.1)\rangle$	$\langle(0.4,0.4,0.4),(0.1,0.1,0.1)\rangle$
A_2	$\langle(0.7,0.8,0.8),(0.1,0.2,0.2)\rangle$	$\langle(0.6,0.6,0.6),(0.1,0.2,0.3)\rangle$	$\langle(0.5,0.6,0.7),(0.1,0.1,0.1)\rangle$
A_3	$\langle(0.7,0.7,0.8),(0.1,0.1,0.1)\rangle$	$\langle(0.7,0.8,0.9),(0.1,0.1,0.1)\rangle$	$\langle(0.6,0.6,0.6),(0.2,0.2,0.2)\rangle$
A_4	$\langle(0.6,0.6,0.6),(0.1,0.1,0.1)\rangle$	$\langle(0.5,0.5,0.5),(0.1,0.1,0.1)\rangle$	$\langle(0.6,0.7,0.8),(0.1,0.1,0.1)\rangle$

Step 2. By (12)、(13) and (14) ,we have $\mu_3 = 2$, $\sigma_3 = \sqrt{2/3}$, $w_1 = 0.2429$, $w_2 = 0.5142$, $w_3 = 0.2429$, then $w = (0.2429, 0.5142, 0.2429)^T$ is the weighting vector of the TFNIFOWG operator; by (10) and (11) ,we obtain the group integrated attribute value of college A_i $(i = 1,2,\cdots,4)$:

$$\tilde{\beta}_1 = \langle(0.582,0.588,0.678),(0.000,0.186,0.292)\rangle$$
$$\tilde{\beta}_2 = \langle(0.477,0.578,0.627),(0.100,0.200,0.300)\rangle$$
$$\tilde{\beta}_3 = \langle(0.588,0.606,0.708),(0.118,0.131,0.221)\rangle$$
$$\tilde{\beta}_4 = \langle(0.486,0.573,0.678),(0.000,0.169,0.200)\rangle$$

Step 3. By (2) and (6),we have

$$s(\tilde{\beta}_1) = 0.771, \ s(\tilde{\beta}_2) = 0.725, \ s(\tilde{\beta}_3) = 0.792, s(\tilde{\beta}_4) = 0.785.$$

Step 4. Rank all the colleges A_k $(k = 1,2,\cdots,4)$ in accordance with the scores $S(\tilde{\beta}_i)$ of the collective overall preference values : $A_3 \succ A_4 \succ A_1 \succ A_2$,thus the most desirable college is A_3 .

6   Conclusion

The traditional aggregation operators are generally suitable for aggregating the information taking the form of numerical values. For the triangle fuzzy number intuitionistic fuzzy information aggregating problems, some new geometric aggregation operators based on TFNIFS are developed in this article. With respect to MAGDM problems in which the decision-maker weights are completely unknown and the attribute values take the form of TFNIFSs,a new group decision making analysis method are developed.Finally,some illustrative example has been given to show the effectiveness of the proposed approach. The work in this paper develops the theories of the OWA aggregation operators,IFSs and TFNIFSs.

References

1. Atanassov, K.T.: Intuitionsitic fuzzy sets. Fuzzy Sets and Systems 20, 87–96 (1986)
2. Atanassov, K., Gargov, G.: Interval-valued intuitionistic fuzzy sets. Fuzzy sets and systems 31, 343–349 (1989)
3. Liu, F., Yuan, X.H.: Fuzzy number intuitionistic fuzzy set. Fuzzy system and mathematics 21, 88–91 (2007)
4. Wang, X.F.: Fuzzy number intuitionistic fuzzy geometric aggregation operators and their application to decision making. Control and Decision 23, 68–73 (2008)
5. Wei, G.: Some induced geometric aggregation operators with intuitionistic fuzzy information and their application to group decision making. Applied soft computing 10, 423–431 (2010)
6. Boran, F.E., Genc, S., Kurt, M., Akay, D.: A multi-criteria intuitionistic fuzzy group decision making for supplier selsection with TOPSIS method. Expert Systems with Applications 36, 11363–11368 (2009)
7. Xu, Z., Yager, R.R.: Some geometric aggregation operators based on intuitionistic fuzzy sets. International journal of general systems, 1–17 (2006)
8. Lee, E.S., Li, R.L.: Comparision of fuzzy numbers based on the probability measure of fuzzy events. Comput. Math. 15, 887–896 (1988)
9. Cheng, C.-H.: A new approach for ranking fuzzy numbers by distance method. Fuzzy sets and systems 95, 307–317 (1998)
10. Xu, Z.: An overview of methods for determining OWA weights. International of intelligent systems 20, 843–865 (2005)

Statistical Analysis of Wireless Fading Channels

Hao Zhang[1], Yong Liu[1], and Junxiang Gao[2]

[1] School of Information and Communication Engineering, Beijing University of Posts and
Telecommunications, Beijing, China
zhanghao19840615@163.com
[2] College of Science, Huazhong Agricultural University, Wuhan, China
bupt124@163.com

Abstract. This paper presents new results on the statistical analysis of wireless
fading channels. Exact closed-form expressions are derived for average Doppler
Shift and average Doppler Spread, Probability density function of received signal's amplitude and phase, level crossing rate and average fading interval, and
probability distribution of fading interval. The utility of the new theoretical
formulas, validated by Monte Carlo simulations, are briefly discussed as well.

Keywords: Doppler Shift, fading channel, level crossing rate, fading interval.

1 Introduction

Rapid fading is an essential issue in mobile propagation and the fading rate depends on
the propagation parameter: the maximum Doppler Shift [1] [2]. Hence studying the
effect of Doppler Shift on wireless fading channel is of significance. The paper first
generally introduces description of wireless channel models, and then examines closer
elementary properties of these models, at last analyses the statistical properties of the
first and second order and the fading intervals of Rayleigh process. Finally simulations
verify the new theoretical formulas.

2 General Descriptions of Rician and Rayleigh Processes

Unmodulated carrier on non frequency selective channel carries signal which can be
regarded as equivalent complex baseband signal with zero mean complex Gauss random process $u(t)$[3]. $u(t)$ includes inphase signal $u_1(t)$ and quadrature signal $u_2(t)$, described by

$$u(t) = u_1(t) + j\, u_2(t) \qquad (1)$$

where $u_1(t)$ and $u_2(t)$ are statistically independent real Gauss random processes.
   Time variant Line of Sight (LOS) component can be described by [4]

$$m(t) = m_1(t) + jm_2(t) = \rho\, e^{\,j(2\pi f\rho t + \theta\rho)} \qquad (2)$$

F.L. Wang et al. (Eds.): AICI 2010, Part II, LNAI 6320, pp. 358–366, 2010.

where ρ, f_ρ and θ_ρ denote the amplitude, the Doppler frequency, and the phase of the line-of-sight component, respectively. One should note about this that, due to the Doppler Effect, the relation $f_\rho = 0$ only holds if the direction of arrival of the incident wave is orthogonal to the direction of motion of the mobile user. Consequently, (2) then becomes a time-invariant component, i.e.,

$$m(t)=m_1(t)+jm_2(t)=\rho\, e^{\,j\theta\rho} \tag{3}$$

At the receiver antenna, we have the superposition of the sum of the scattered components with the line-of-sight component

$$\mu_\rho(t)=\mu_{\rho 1}(t)+j\mu_{\rho 2}(t)=\mu(t)+m(t) \tag{4}$$

with time variant mean value $m(t)$.

So we note that forming the absolute value of $u(t)$ and $\mu_\rho(t)$ leads to Rayleigh process and Rician process, that is,

$$\varsigma(t)=|\mu(t)|=|\mu_1(t)+j\mu_2(t)| \tag{5}$$

$$\xi(t)=|\mu_\rho(t)|=|\mu(t)+m(t)| \tag{6}$$

3 Complementary Characteristics of Rician and Rayleigh Processes

Doppler Power Spectrum Density (PSD) and Autocorrelation function (ACF) of u(t) can be described by[5]

$$S_{\mu\mu}(f)= S_{\mu 1\mu 1}(f) + S_{\mu 2\mu 2}(f) \tag{7}$$

$$r_{\mu\mu}(\tau)=r_{\mu 1\mu 1}(\tau)+r_{\mu 2\mu 2}(\tau) \tag{8}$$

In this paper we discuss two types of Doppler PSD which are Jakes PSD and Gauss PSD [6].

If we define σ_0^2 as the power that $u_i(t)$ carries, or to say, the variance of $u_i(t)$, $i=1,2$ and f_{max} as the maximum Doppler Shift, then Jakes PSD can be described by[6]

$$S_{\mu i\mu i}(f) = \begin{cases} \dfrac{\sigma_0^2}{\pi f_{\max}\sqrt{1-(\dfrac{f}{f_{\max}})^2}}, & f \leq f_{\max} \\[4mm] 0, & f > f_{\max} \end{cases} \tag{9}$$

Using Inver Fourier Transform for $S_{\mu i\mu i}(f)$ we obtain ACF of $u_i(t)$,

$$r_{\mu i\mu i}(\tau)= \sigma_0^2 J_0(2\pi f_{max}\tau),\ i=1,2, \tag{10}$$

Similarly, Gauss PSD and ACF can be described by [6]

$$S_{\mu i\mu i}(f)=\frac{\sigma_0^2}{f_c}\sqrt{\frac{\ln 2}{\pi}}e^{-\ln 2(\frac{f}{f_c})^2},i=1,2,\tag{11}$$

$$r_{\mu i\mu i}(\tau)=\sigma_0^2 e^{-\pi\frac{f_c}{\sqrt{\ln 2}}\tau^2}\tag{12}$$

Since PSD has the same meaning as the probability distribution, the expectation value and variance of PSD can be obtained by

$$B_{\mu i\mu i}^{(1)}:=\frac{\int_{-\infty}^{\infty}fS_{\mu i\mu i}(f)df}{\int_{-\infty}^{\infty}S_{\mu i\mu i}(f)df}\tag{13a}$$

$$B_{\mu i\mu i}^{(2)}:=\sqrt{\frac{\int_{-\infty}^{\infty}(f-B_{\mu i\mu i}^{(1)})^2 S_{\mu i\mu i}(f)df}{\int_{-\infty}^{\infty}S_{\mu i\mu i}(f)df}}\tag{13b},$$

which are also average Doppler Shift and average Doppler Spread. Next, we describe them using autocorrelation function and its first and second order derivatives as follows.

$$B_{\mu i\mu i}^{(1)}=\frac{1}{2\pi j}\frac{r'_{\mu i\mu i}(0)}{r_{\mu i\mu i}(0)},B_{\mu i\mu i}^{(2)}=\frac{1}{2\pi}\sqrt{(\frac{r'_{\mu i\mu i}(0)}{r_{\mu i\mu i}(0)})^2-\frac{r''_{\mu i\mu i}(0)}{r_{\mu i\mu i}(0)}}\tag{14a,b}$$

$$B_{\mu\mu}^{(1)}=B_{\mu i\mu i}^{(1)}=0\ B_{\mu\mu}^{(2)}=B_{\mu i\mu i}^{(2)}=\frac{\sqrt{\beta}}{2\pi\sigma_0}\tag{15a,b}$$

$$B_{\mu\mu}^{(1)}=B_{\mu i\mu i}^{(1)}=0\ B_{\mu\mu}^{(2)}=B_{\mu i\mu i}^{(2)}=\begin{cases}\frac{f_{max}}{\sqrt{2}},JakesPSD\\\frac{f_c}{\sqrt{2\ln 2}},GaussianPSD\end{cases}\tag{16a,b}$$

4   Statistical Characteristics of Rician and Rayleigh Processes

4.1   Probability Density Function of the Amplitude and Phase

Probability Density Function (PDF)s of the amplitude(the absolute value) of Rician and Rayleigh distribution can be described by[7]

$$p_\xi(x)=\begin{cases}\frac{x}{\sigma_0^2}e^{-\frac{x^2+\rho^2}{2\sigma_0^2}}I_0(\frac{x\rho}{\sigma_0^2}),x\geq 0,\\0,x<0\end{cases}\tag{17}$$

$$p_\varsigma(x)=\begin{cases}\frac{x}{\sigma_0^2}e^{-\frac{x^2}{2\sigma_0^2}},x\geq 0,\\0,x<0\end{cases}\tag{18}$$

In Rician fading, the ratio of the power of the line-of-sight component to that of the scattered component $c_R = \rho^2/2\sigma_0^2$ is defined as Rice factor.

Expression of $p_\zeta(r)$ and $p_\varsigma(r)$ tells us that the shape of Doppler Power Spectrum Density $S_{\mu\mu}(f)$ (Jakes or Gauss)has no effect on PDF of complex Gauss random process's amplitude.

Next we focus on the phase of Rician process, $\theta = arg\{\mu_\rho(t)\}$, which and whose PDF can be described by

$$\vartheta(t) = \arctan\{\frac{\mu_2(t) + \rho\sin(2\pi f_\rho t + \theta_\rho)}{\mu_1(t) + \rho\sin(2\pi f_\rho t + \theta_\rho)}\}$$

(19)

$$p_\theta(\theta;t) = \frac{e^{-\frac{\rho^2}{2\sigma_0^2}}}{2\pi}\{1 + \frac{\rho}{\sigma_0}\sqrt{\frac{\pi}{2}}\cos(\theta - 2\pi f_\rho t - \theta_\rho)$$
$$e^{\frac{\rho^2\cos^2(\theta - 2\pi f_\rho t - \theta_\rho)}{2\sigma_0^2}}[1 + erf(\frac{\rho\cos(\theta - 2\pi f_\rho t - \theta_\rho)}{\sigma_0\sqrt{2}})]\}, -\pi < \theta \leq \pi$$

(20)

where erf (.) is called the error function.

Only for the special case that $f_\rho = 0$ ($\rho\neq0$), the phase $\theta(t)$ is a strict-sense stationary process which is then described by the PDF shown in

$$p_\rho(\theta) = \frac{e^{-\frac{\rho^2}{2\sigma_0^2}}}{2\pi}\{1 + \frac{\rho}{\sigma_0}\sqrt{\frac{\pi}{2}}\cos(\theta - \theta_\rho)e^{\frac{\rho^2\cos^2(\theta - \theta_\rho)}{2\sigma_0^2}}$$
$$[1 + erf(\frac{\rho\cos(\theta - \theta_\rho)}{\sigma_0\sqrt{2}})]\}, -\pi < \theta \leq \pi$$

(21)

As $\rho\rightarrow0$, it follows $\mu_\rho(t)\rightarrow\mu(t)$ and, thus, $\xi(t)\rightarrow\zeta(t)$,and (22) becomes the uniform distribution which describes Rayleigh process.

$$p_\theta(\theta) = 1/2\pi, \ -\pi < \theta < \pi$$

(22)

4.2 Level Crossing Rate and Average Fading Interval

Level Crossing Rate (LCR) of Rician process can be described by

$$N_\xi(r) = \frac{r\sqrt{2\beta}}{\pi^{\frac{3}{2}}\sigma_0^2}e^{-\frac{x^2+\rho^2}{2\sigma_0^2}}\int_0^{\frac{\pi}{2}}\cosh(\frac{r\rho}{\sigma_0^2}\cos\theta)$$
$$\{e^{-(\alpha\rho\sin\theta)^2} + \sqrt{\pi}\alpha\rho\sin\theta\cdot erf(\alpha\rho\sin\theta)\}d\theta, r \geq 0$$

(23)

$$\alpha = 2\pi f_\rho/sqrt(2\beta), \beta = \beta_i = -r''_{\mu_i\mu_i}(0), i=1,2$$

(24)

If $f_\rho=0$, and thus $\alpha=0$, when LCR of Rician process with time invariant LOS component becomes

$$N_\xi(r) = \sqrt{\frac{\beta}{2\pi}}\cdot p_\xi(r), r \geq 0$$

(25)

For $\rho\rightarrow0$, it follows $p_\xi(r)\rightarrow p_\varsigma(r)$, and we obtain LCR of Rayleigh process.

$$N_\varsigma(r) = \sqrt{\frac{\beta}{2\pi}} p_\varsigma(r), r \geq 0 \tag{26}$$

Especially for the Jakes and the Gaussian power spectral density, we obtain by using (10), (12) and (24) the result for β.

$$\beta = \begin{cases} 2(\pi f_{max}\sigma_0)^2, Jakes\ PSD \\ \dfrac{2(\pi f_c\sigma_0)^2}{\ln 2}, Gaussian\ PSD \end{cases} \tag{27}$$

For the case when $f_\rho=0$, $r_{\mu1\mu1}(0) = r_{\mu2\mu2}(0)$ but $\beta_1=-r''_{\mu1\mu1}(0)\neq-r''_{\mu2\mu2}(0)=\beta_2$, the expression of LCR is derived as

$$N_\varsigma(r) = \sqrt{\frac{\beta_1}{2\pi}} \frac{r}{\sigma_0^2} e^{-\frac{x^2+\rho^2}{2\sigma_0^2}} \frac{1}{\pi} \tag{28}$$

$$\int_0^\pi \cosh[\frac{r\rho}{2\sigma_0^2}\cos(\theta-\theta_p)]\sqrt{1-k^2\sin^2\theta}d\theta, r \geq 0$$

where k=sqrt((β_1-β_2)/β_1), $\beta_1 \geq \beta_2$.

Next we again obtain the usual relations for Rayleigh processes $\varsigma(t)$ by taking the limit $\rho \rightarrow 0$,

$$N_\varsigma(r) = \sqrt{\frac{\beta_1}{2\pi}} \frac{r}{\sigma_0^2} e^{-\frac{r^2}{2\sigma_0^2}} \frac{1}{\pi} \int_0^\pi \sqrt{1-k^2\sin^2\theta}d\theta, r \geq 0 \tag{29}$$

Furthermore, we are interested in the level-crossing rate $N_\varsigma(r)$ for the case that the relative deviation between β_1 and β_2 is very small, so that,

$$k = \sqrt{\frac{\beta_1-\beta_2}{\beta_1}} = \sqrt{\frac{\varepsilon}{\beta_1}} << 1 \tag{30}$$

holds. Next, using the first two terms of the series for the integral in (29), leads for the level crossing rate $N_\varsigma(r)$ to the approximation

$$N_\varsigma(r) \approx \sqrt{\frac{\beta_1}{2\pi}} \frac{r}{\sigma_0^2} e^{-\frac{r^2}{2\sigma_0^2}} \frac{2}{\pi} \frac{\pi}{2}(1-\frac{k^2}{4}) \tag{31}$$

$$\approx \sqrt{\frac{\beta}{2\pi}} p_\varsigma(r), k << 1, r \geq 0$$

where $\beta=(\beta_1+\beta_2)/2$.

The average duration of fades, i.e., the average length of the duration while the channel amplitude is below a level r, is defined by the quotient of the distribution function of the channel amplitude over the level-crossing rate.

For Rice processes with $f_\rho= 0$ and Rayleigh processes with $\rho=0$, we obtain for the average Fading Interval (AFI)

$$T_{\xi-}(r) = \frac{F_{\xi-}(r)}{N_\xi(r)} = \sqrt{\frac{2\pi}{\beta}} \frac{e^{\frac{r^2}{2\sigma_0^2}}}{rI_0(\frac{r\rho}{\sigma_0^2})} \int_0^r xe^{\frac{r^2}{2\sigma_0^2}} I_0(\frac{r\rho}{\sigma_0^2})dx, r \geq 0 \tag{32a}$$

$$T_{\varsigma-}(r) = \frac{F_{\varsigma-}(r)}{N_\varsigma(r)} = \sqrt{\frac{2\pi}{\beta}} \frac{\sigma_0^2}{r} e^{\frac{r^2}{2\sigma_0^2}}(e^{\frac{r^2}{2\sigma_0^2}} - 1), r \geq 0 \tag{32b}$$

In channel modeling, we are especially interested in the behavior of AFI at low levels r. For this purpose, let $r \ll 1$, so that for moderate Rice factors, we may write $r_\rho/\sigma_0^2 \ll 1$ and, consequently, both $I_0(r_\rho/\sigma_0^2)$ and $I_0(x_\rho/\sigma_0^2)$ can be approximated by one in (32a), since the independent variable x is within the relevant interval $[0, r]$. By this means, it quickly turns out that for low levels r, $T_\xi(r)$ converges to $T_\varsigma(r)$ given by (32b). Furthermore, the relation (32b) can be simplified by using $e^x \approx 1 + x (x \ll 1)$, so that we finally obtain the approximations

$$T_{\xi-}(r) \approx T_{\varsigma-}(r) \approx r\sqrt{\frac{\pi}{2\beta}}, r \ll 1 \tag{33}$$

The above result shows that AFI of Rice and Rayleigh processes are at low levels r approximately proportional to r.

4.3   Statistics of Fading Interval of Rayleigh Process

The PDF of $\varsigma(t)$ is only determined by the variance $\sigma_0^2 = r_{\mu i \mu i}(0)$, the behavior of the autocorrelation function $r_{\mu i \mu i}(\tau)$ at the origin; Besides $r_{\mu i \mu i}(0)$, LCR and AFI are also dependent on $\beta = -r''_{\mu i \mu i}(0)$, the negative curvature of the autocorrelation function at the origin.

If we now ask ourselves which relevant statistical properties are at all affected by the behavior of the autocorrelation function $r_{\mu i \mu i}(\tau)$ $(i=1,2,\tau>0)$, then this leads to the statistical distribution of the fading intervals, where we denote $p_{0-}(\tau_-;r)$ as the probability of that $\varsigma(t)$ crosses a given level r in time interval $(t+\tau_-, t+\tau_- + d\tau)$ upwards for the first time on condition that the last down-crossing occurred within the time interval $(t, t+dt)$. Since an exact theoretical derivation for $p_{0-}(\tau_-; r)$ is very difficult to solve. Fortunately, in [8], Rice derive the probability density $p_{1-}(\tau_-;r)$ as good approximation of $p_{0-}(\tau_-;r)$ for small τ_-. Similarly, $p_{1-}(\tau_-;r)$ describes the case that the Rayleigh process $\varsigma(t)$ crosses the level r in the order mentioned, except that $p_{1-}(\tau_-;r)$ has no information on the behavior of $\xi(t)$ between t and $t+\tau_-$.

$$p_{1-}(\tau_-;r) = \frac{rM_{22}e^{\frac{r^2}{2}}}{\sqrt{2\pi\beta(1 - r_{\mu i \mu i}^2(\tau_-))}} \int_0^{2\pi} J(a,b)e^{-r^2\frac{1 - r_{\mu i \mu i}(\tau_-)\cos\varphi}{1 - r_{\mu i \mu i}^2(\tau_-)}} d\varphi \tag{34}$$

Definitions of parameters α, b and function $J(.)$ can be found in [8].

In the following, we will analyze the statistics of the deep fades. The knowledge of the statistics of the deep fades is of great importance in mobile radio communications, since the bit and symbol error probability are mainly determined by the occurrence of deep fades. Hence, let $r \ll 1$, and (34) becomes

$$p_{1-}(\tau_-;r) = -\frac{1}{T_{\varsigma-}(r)}\frac{d}{du}[\frac{2}{u}I_1(z)e^{-z}] = \frac{2\pi z^2 e^{-z}}{T_{\varsigma-}(r)}[I_0(z)-(1+\frac{1}{2z})I_1(z)] \tag{35}$$

as $r \to 0$, where $z=2/(\pi u^2)$ and $u=\tau/(T_{\varsigma-}(r))$, and $I_\alpha(.)$ represents the αth kind modified Bessel function.

We see that, besides on the level r, $p_{1-}(\tau_-;r)$ only depends on the average duration of fades $T_{\varsigma-}(r)$ and, hence, on $\sigma_0^2 = r_{\mu_i\mu_i}(0)$ and $\beta = -r''_{\mu_i\mu_i}(0)$. Consequently, the probability density of the fading intervals at low levels ($r \ll 1$) is independent of the shape of the autocorrelation function $r_{\mu_i\mu_i}(\tau)$ for $\tau > 0$.

With the help of the expression of $p_{1-}(\tau_-;r)$, the expected value of the fading intervals τ_- can be obtained by

$$E\{\tau_-\} = \int_0^\infty \tau_- p_{1-}(\tau_-;r)d\tau_- = T_{\varsigma-}(r) \tag{36}$$

Meantime, we can also define the fading interval τ_q according to the probability that τ_q includes q percent of all fading intervals.

$$\int_{\tau_q}^\infty p_{0-}(\tau_-;r)d\tau_- = 1 - \frac{q}{100} \tag{37}$$

Developing e^{-z}, $I_0(z)$ and $I_1(z)$ of (35) into a power series and terminating the resulting series after the second term, leads to the approximation usable for our purposes.

$$p_{1-}(\tau_-;r) \approx \frac{\frac{\pi z^2}{2}(3-5z)}{T_{\varsigma-}(r)} \tag{38}$$

Substituting (38) into (37) and we derive an explicit expression for the quantity τq.

$$\tau_q(r) \approx \frac{T_{\varsigma-}(r)}{\{\frac{\pi}{4}[1-\sqrt{1-4(1-\frac{q}{100})}]\}^{\frac{1}{3}}}, r \ll 1 \tag{39}$$

This equation clearly shows that the quantity $\tau_q(r)$ is at deep fades proportional to AFI.

Especially for $\tau_{90}(r)$, $\tau_{95}(r)$, and $\tau_{99}(r)$, we obtain from (39): $\tau_{90}(r) \approx 1.78T_\varsigma(r)$, $\tau_{95}(r) \approx 2.29T_\varsigma(r)$, $\tau_{99}(r) \approx 3.98T_\varsigma(r)$.

Based on the expressions of β in (27), $T_\varsigma(r)$ in (33), we obtain for the quantity $\tau_{90}(r)$ the approximation.

$$\tau_{90}(r) \approx \begin{cases} \dfrac{r}{2\sigma_0 f_{max}}, Jakes\ PSD \\[2ex] \dfrac{r\sqrt{\ln 2}}{2\sigma_0 f_c}, Gaussian\ PSD \end{cases} \tag{40}$$

By means of this result, we see that the quantity $\tau_{90}(r)$ and, hence, the general quantity $\tau_{90}(r)$ ($75 \le q \le 100$) are proportional to r and reciprocally proportional to f_{max} or f_c for low levels r. Hereby, it is of major importance that the exact form of the power spectral density of the complex Gaussian random process, which generates the Rayleigh process, does not have any influence on the behavior of τ_q *(r)*.

5   Simulations and Analysis

To verify the four new crossing rate expressions, Monte Carlo simulations using the spectral method [9] have been conducted. In each simulation, we have generated 100 independent realizations of L iid zero-mean complex Gaussian processes, with 10000 complex samples per realization, over $T = 1$ second.

First the PDF of the phase of Rician process is shown in figure 1, and it is observed that the probability of phase of Rician process symmetrically rounds zero. The larger the Doppler frequency of LOS component is, the phase is near zero more probably. Next Figure 2 tells that LCR first increases and then decreases with level larger from zero. The larger the Doppler frequency of LOS component is, the larger LCR will be. At last figure 3 illustrates that when level is very low(r=0.1), the PDF of fading interval's shape centers on about 0.3 and formula (38) is good approximation of (34).

There is a perfect agreement between the theoretical and simulation results.

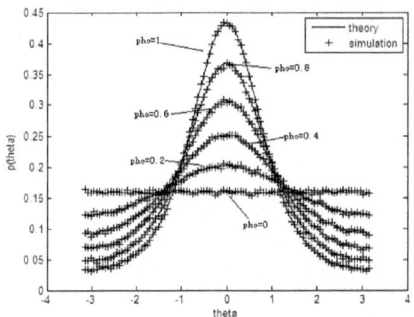

Fig. 1. The PDF of the phase of Rician process

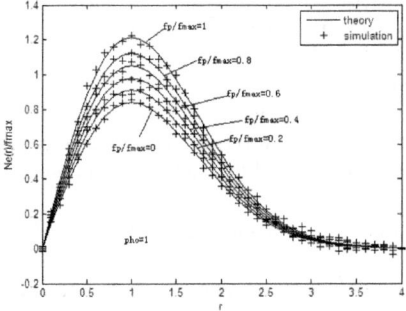

Fig. 2. Variation of LCR against level

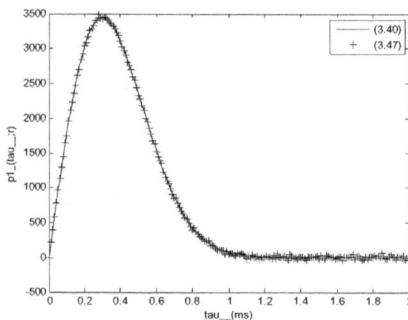

Fig. 3. The PDF of fading interval under Low level r=0.1

6 Conclusions

New results are presented in this paper on the statistical analysis of wireless fading channels. We derive exact closed-form expressions for average Doppler Shift and average Doppler Spread, Probability density function of received signal's amplitude and phase, level crossing rate and average fading interval, and probability distribution of fading interval. At last Monte Carlo simulations validate the utility of the new theoretical formulas.

References

1. Stuber, G.L.: Principles of Mobile Communication, 2nd edn. Kluwer, Boston (2001)
2. Abdi, A., Kaveh, M.: Level crossing rate in terms of the characteristic function: a new approach for calculating the fading rate in diversity systems. IEEE Trans. Commun. 50, 1397–1400 (2002)
3. Akki, A.S.: Statistical properties of mobile-to-mobile land communication channels. IEEE Trans. Veh. Technol. 43(4), 826–831 (1994)
4. Andersen, J.B., Rappaport, T.S., Yoshida, S.: Propagation measurements and models for wireless communications channels. IEEE Commun. Mag. 33(1), 42–49 (1995)
5. Dent, P., Bottomley, G.E., Croft, T.: Jakes fading model revisited. Electronics Letters 29(13), 1162–1163 (1993)
6. Gans, M.J.: A power-spectral theory of propagation in the mobile-radio environment. IEEE Trans. Veh. Technol. 21(1), 27–38 (1972)
7. Brehm, H., Werner, M.: Generalized Rayleigh fading in a mobile radio channel. In: Proc. 2nd Nordic Seminar on Digital Land Mobile Radio Communication, Stockholm, pp. 210–214 (October 1986)
8. Rice, S.O.: Statistical properties of a sine wave plus noise. Bell Syst. Tech. J. 27, 109–157 (1948)
9. Acolatse, K., Abdi, A.: Efficient simulation of space-time correlated MIMO mobile fading channels. In: Proc. IEEE Vehic. Technol. Conf. 2003, pp. 652–656 (2003)

Discretization Method of Continuous Attributes Based on Decision Attributes

Yingjuan Sun[1,2], Zengqiang Ren[3], Tong Zhou[1], Yandong Zhai[1], and Dongbing Pu[3,*]

[1] College of Computer Science and Technology, Jilin University,
Changchun, Jilin Province, China
syj_pyf@sohu.com, cgzhou@jlu.edu.cn, zhaiyd@yahoo.com.cn
[2] College of Computer Science and Technology, Changchun Normal University,
Changchun, Jilin Province, China
[3] College of Computer Science and Information Technology,
Northeast Normal University, Changchun, Jilin Province, China
{renzq,pudb}@nenu.edu.cn

Abstract. The attributes in rough set must be discretized, but the general theory on discretization did not think about the decision attribute adequately during discretization of data, as a result, it leads to several redundant rules and lower calculation efficiency. The discretization method of continuous attributes based on decision attributes which is discussed in this paper gives more attention to both significance of attributes and the decision attributes. The continuous attributes are discretized in sequence according to their significance. The result shows less breakpoints and higher recognition accuracy. The experiment on database Iris for UCI robot learning validates the feasibility of our method. Comparing the result with documents [6] and [11], the method given in this paper shows higher recognition accuracy and much less breakpoints.

Keywords: rough set, significance of attributes, discretization, decision attribute, region division.

1 Introduction

The rough set theory was firstly given by Z. Pawlak, a Poland mathematician, in 1982. It is a mathematic theory mainly used to analyze the indefinite data [1]. The rough set theory is widely applied in pattern recognition, robot learning, data mining, acknowledge achievement, acknowledge discover etc. Its characteristic, which is its primary merit, lies in finding out the relativity among attributes and the law of data finally only from attributes of given data without the characteristics or description of data [2] and [3].

Attributes in a decision system may be continuous or discretized. The rough set theory only can process discretized data. So it is very important for a decision system to descretize its continuous attributes. There are lots of methods of discretization, such as method of equal interval [5], statistics-based method [4], [5] and [6], method

---

* Corresponding author.

F.L. Wang et al. (Eds.): AICI 2010, Part II, LNAI 6320, pp. 367–373, 2010.
© Springer-Verlag Berlin Heidelberg 2010

based on significance of attribute [7] and [8], genetic algorithm and so on [9], [10] and [11]. All of these methods haven't consulted decision attributes during discretizing attributes in a decision system. It can result in impropriety to the discretized region division, or bring out too many rules with much more trivial division, or divide too roughly to recognize classification target. This paper gives a new discretization method of continuous attributes based on decision attributes. Process calculations united with higher significance of attributes during discretizing and pay much more attention to decision attributes. Comparing with other methods, the method given in this paper can create discretized attribute values as little as possible and achieve an optimized rule set on the assumption of insuring the sky-high recognition rate for a decision system.

2 Conception of Discretization

2.1 Discretization Description

The decision table is the knowledge expression system such as $S = (U, A, \{V_a\}, f)$ which owns the condition attribute and the decision attribute. For $\forall x \in U$, there is a list $C(c_1(x),...,c_n(x)), D(d_1(x),...,d_m(x))$, which is called region, where U is a non-null limited set. A is an attribute set defined as a non-null limited set. V_a is a value set where $a \in A$. $f : U \to V_a$ is a single mapping which enables any one of elements in discourse domain U own a unique value in V_a when the attribute of the element is a. $A = C \cup D, C \cap D = \Phi; \{c_1(x),...,c_n(x)\}$ is defined as a condition attribute set. $\{d_1(x),...,d_m(x)\}$ is defined as a decision attribute set. For any one of breakpoint sets $\{(a,c_1^a),(a,c_2^a),...,(a,c_k^a)\}$ in the value set $V_a = [l_a, r_a]$, P_a is one of classifications in V_a, which can be defined by

$$P_a = \{[c_0^a, c_1^a), [c_1^a, c_2^a),..., [c_{k_a}^a, c_{k_a+1}^a)\} \tag{1}$$

l_a and V_a are given by

$$l_a = c_0^a < c_1^a < ... < c_{k_a}^a < c_{k_a+1}^a = r_a \tag{2}$$

$$V_a = \{[c_0^a, c_1^a) \cup [c_1^a, c_2^a) \cup ... \cup [c_{k_a}^a, c_{k_a+1}^a)\} \tag{3}$$

Therefore, we can define a new decision table $S^P = (U, A, V^P, f^P)$ for any $P = \bigcup_{a \in A} P_a$, Where $f^P(x_a) = i \Leftrightarrow f(x_a) \in [c^a{}_i, c^a{}_{i+1})$. For $x \in U, i \in \{0, L, k_a\}$, the old decision system will be replaced by a new one after discretization [2] and [12].

If a condition attribute value set is divided into n regions, every end point of them is a breakpoint and the number of the breakpoint should be $n-1$. The essence of discretization is a process that the condition attribute value set is divided into some regions by selected breakpoints. Each of divided regions is corresponding to a discretized value that is an integer generally. All of the old attribute values that belong to a same region will be combined to a single value, and the old value will be replaced by a same discretized value. Therefore, a process of discretization is a process of selecting breakpoints.

2.2 Significance of Attribute

The degree of relativity between condition attributes and decision attributes reflects the significance of condition attributes. When V_a is a value of condition attribute a, the number of possible value for decision attributes will reflect the significance of condition attribute which is corresponding to them. When a value of the condition attribute a is V_a, a condition attribute value can determinate a decision attribute uniquely on condition that the number of possible value of the decision attributes is unique. That is to say, we need not consider other condition attributes in case the value of the condition attribute a is V_a during a rule generating.

Definition 1. $M_a = \dfrac{1}{n}\sum_{i=1}^{n}\dfrac{1}{l_i}$ is the significance of a attribute in a decision system, where $a \in A$, n is the base number of $V_a \{V_{a,1}, ..., V_{a,n}\}$, l_i is the number of possible values for the decision attribute when the value of the attribute a is $V_{a,i}$.

The above definition shows that bigger value of M_a is in a decision system, stronger the decision capability of the attribute a is.

3 The Algorithm of Discretization for Continuous Attributes Based on Decision Attribute

3.1 Primary Idea of Algorithm

The decision rule generally owns higher relativity with condition attributes, of which the significance is high in a decision system. It means that the higher significance of attribute is stronger in decision capability. Our algorithm is divided into three stages to realize the discretization about condition attributes base on the above idea. The three stages include preparing stage, discretization stage and generating rule set stage. We assume that the non-discretized decision table is S. In the preparing stage, we firstly discretize each continuous attribute in S with the traditional fuzzy clustering algorithm that is called C-mean. The number of clustering dividing is that of decision attribute classifications in the C-mean algorithm. We can get a decision table S' after first discretization. Then we need to calculate the significance of each discretized condition attribute, and order condition attributes by their significance. In the discretization of S stage, we assume that the new discretized decision table is $Snew$ in which all condition attributes are null initially and decision attribute values are same as those in S. Add each discretized attribute value which own the highest attribute value in S' to the corresponding attribute in $Snew$, and then prepare to discretize the next attribute i which owns the second highest value and so on. Then decide whether decision attribute values in $Snew$ are same or not in each line in which condition attribute values are same. If condition attribute values are same, the decision attribute value is unique, then rest continuous attributes in each line that is the same condition attribute value need not to discretize any longer, or else divide all lines that own the same condition value in $Snew$ into a group. We continue to calculate the division region of corresponding attribute i in S within group by each classification decision value. Calculate the union for all divided regions in the end (add a breakpoint for an intersection among divided regions, reference 3.2.1). Merge all regions of each group (reference 3.2.2). We can achieve the divided region of attribute i to realize the discretization for it. Then add the disretized result to $Snew$. We can discretize rest continuous attributes by our idea in significance order. In generating rule set stage, we delete repeat lines in $Snew$ so as to obtain the rule set. The null attribute value in $Snew$ has nothing to do with decision.

3.2   Region Division

The discretization refers to a division of attribute region. If the region is divided too thin, it will lead to thinning of classification rules and increasing of decision rules. On the contrary, if the region is divided too roughly, it will bring out unclear classification along with contrary rules. There are two definitions in this paper named as the divided region and the idle region.

Definition 2. the divided region is a region that owns attribute value on a number line.

Definition 3. the idle region is a region that owns no attribute value on a number line.

3.2.1   Region Division in Group
As we mentioned above, if condition attribute values are same, the decision attribute value is unique, then rest continuous attributes in each line that is the same condition attribute value need not to discretize any longer, or else divide all lines that own the same condition value in $Snew$ into a group. Therefore, the condition attribute value of each line is same from a same group in $Snew$, but the decision attribute value is not identical, that means some inconsistent data existing in $Snew$. We should divide attribute i that owns different decision attribute value into a different region as far as possible. If $Numd_x$ is the number of decision classification in group x, then the number of regions divided by the attribute i in S is at least $Numd_x$. We should be

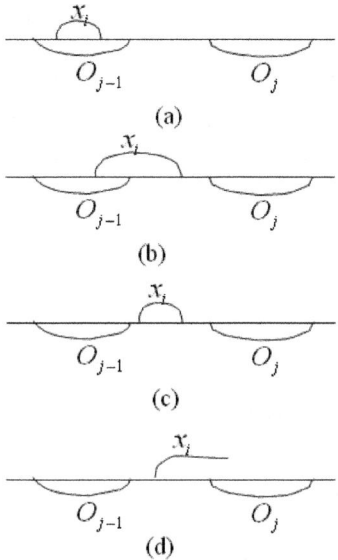

Fig. 1. Region adjust internal group

increased a dividing region if there was an intersection among divided regions. The intersection situation between two divided regions a and b are only the following two situations given by Fig. 1. As a result, the old region division turns to a', b', c'.

3.2.2 Merge Dividing Region of All Groups

Assume the number line O to store the final region division for i. O is null initially. First of all, we divide O with the first region division group, and then merge O with the second region division group and so forth until all of the region division groups have been merged with O. Owing to existing no inconsistent data among groups, we should not increase the division region in O on the assumption of not generating inconsistent data whenever each group merge with O. We empty each updated flag of region in O before it merges with dividing region of each group. The method of merging dividing region of group x with O is the process of merging O with regions of x_1, x_2, L which are sorted by ascending sequence. There are four situations about the relation between $x_i([x_{i,1}, x_{i,2}))$ and O_j, or $x_i([x_{i,1}, x_{i,2}))$ and O_{j-1}, in which is shown Fig. 2. (a) If O_{j-1} is not updated, then mark it with updated flag, or else set $x_{i,1}$ as a new breakpoint in O_{j-1} and divide it into two regions including left region and right region which is marked by updated flag. (b) Move the right end point of O_{j-1} to $x_{i,2}$. If O_{j-1} is already updated, then set $x_{i,1}$ as a new breakpoint in O_{j-1} and divided it into two regions including left region and right region. (c) Move the right end point of O_{j-1} to $x_{i,2}$ if O_{j-1} is not updated, else move the left end point of O_j to $x_{i,1}$ and mark O_j with updated state. (d)Move the left end point of O_j to $x_{i,1}$. If the right end point of x_i is in one region of O, mark the region with updated state.

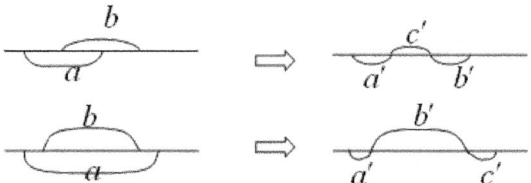

Fig. 2. Attribute i region division

4   Experiment Results

In order to test and verify the feasibility and efficiency of our algorithm, we use Iris as our test data. Iris is a standard data set used for UCI robot learning. There are 150 objects in Iris which includes four continuous condition attributes and three decision classifications. The four continuous condition attributes are SepalLength, SepalWidth, PetalLength and PetalWidth. In experiment, the data set is divided into training sample set and test sample set randomly. The ratio of each classification is in conformity with the old data set so as to obtain an average distribution of sample classification. We use 70% of data in old set as training samples and the rest as test samples. The average correct ratio of our algorithm is 95.44% for 100 running times. The number of average breakpoints for every condition attribute is shown in Table 1. The comparison of experiment result with document [6] and [11] is also shown in Table 1.

Table 1. Iris experiment and comparison with other documents

Attribute	Number of breakpoints		
	Document [6]	Document [11]	This paper
SepalLength	23	5	2.49
SepalWidth	18	3	2.22
PetalLength	8	9	1.94
PetalWidth	7	4	1.6

5   Conclusions

This paper proposes a new discretization method of continuous attributes based on decision attribute and rough set theory. We determinate the attribute discretizating order by their significance. Decision attributes are always the core of discretization. Table 1 shows that the number of breakpoints for our algorithm is simply less than that of document [6] and [11]. At the same time, the algorithm given in this paper can reduce rules greatly except for a higher correct identification ratio. As a result, it improves the efficiency of a decision system.

Acknowledgment. This work was supported by the plan project foundation on science and technology development of Jilin ministry of education under grant No. 172, the Key Science Technology Project of the National Education Ministry of China under grant No.109052, and the Science Technology Development Project of Jilin province under grant No. 20071153.

References

1. Pawlak, Z.: Rough sets. International Journal of Information and Computer Science 11(5), 341–356 (1982)
2. Li, Y.M., Zhu, S.J., Chen, X.H., et al.: Data mining model based on rough set theory. J. T. Singhua Univ. (Sci. & Tech.) 39(1), 110–113 (1999)
3. Yan, M.: Approximate Reduction Based on Conditional Information. Acta Electronica Sinica 35(11), 2156–2160 (2007)
4. Wang, G.Y.: Rough set theory and knowledge acquisition. Xi' an Jiaotong University Press, Xi'an (2001)
5. Jiang, S.Y., Li, X., Zheng, Q.: Approximate equal frequency discretization method. Journal of Jinan University (Natural Science) 30(1), 31–34 (2009)
6. Peng, J.W., Qin, J.W.: Improved heuristic algorithm for discretization. Computer Engineering and Design 29(15), 4003–4005 (2008)
7. Bai, G.Z., Pei, Z.L., Wan, J., et al.: Attribute discretization method based on rough set theory and information entropy. Application Research of Computers 25(6), 1701–1703 (2008)
8. Zhang, L., Lu, X.Y., Wu, H.Y., et al.: Heuristic algorithm used in attribute value reduction of rough set. Chinese Journal of Scientific Instrument 30(1), 82–84 (2009)
9. Wang, F., Liu, D.Y., Xue, W.X.: Discretizing Continuous Variables of Bayesian Networks Based on genetic Algorithms. Chinese J. Computers 25(8), 794–800 (2002)
10. Choi, Y.S., Moon, B.R., Seo, S.Y.: Genetic Fuzzy Discretization with Adaptive intervals for Classification Problems. In: Proceedings of the Genetic and Evolutionary Computation Conference, Washington, DC, USA, pp. 2037–2043 (2005)
11. Xia, Z.G., Xia, S.X., Niu, Q., Zhang, L.: Method of discretization of continuous attributes based on improved genetic algorithm. Computer Engineering and Design 29(16), 4275–4279 (2008)
12. Chen, G.: Discretization method of continuous attributes in decision table based on genetic algorithm. Chinese Journal of Scientific Instrument 28(9), 1700–1705 (2007)

Empirical Research of Price Discovery for Gold Futures Based on Compound Model Combing Wavelet Frame with Support Vector Regression

Wensheng Dai[1], Chi-Jie Lu[2], and Tingjen Chang[3]

[1] China Financial policy Research Centre, Financial School,
Renmin University of China, Beijing 100872, China
daiws@ruc.edu.cn
[2] Department of Industrial Engineering and Management,
ChingYun University
jerrylu@cyu.edu.tw
[3] Statistics School, Central University of Finance and Economics China,
Beijing 100081, China
Metheus.c@gmail.com.tw

Abstract. In theory, a gold futures possesses function of price discovery. However, futures including information must be disclosed by some effective way. This paper proposes a forecasting model which combines wavelet frame with Support vector regression (SVR). Wavelet frame is first used to decompose the series of gold futures price into sub-series with different scales, the SVR then uses the sub-series to build the forecasting model. Empirical research shows that the gold futures has the function of price discovery, and the two steps model is a good tool for making the price information clear and forecasting spot price. further research can try different basis function or other methods of disclosing information.

Keywords: Price Discovery Function, Wavelet Frame, Support Vector Regression, Gold Futures.

1 Introduction

1.1 Background and Brief

Gold always play a most important role in human history either in gold standard era or in credit currency era. As financial crisis develop recently, gold price is soaring. It shows that capital has strong anticipation to hedge against risk. With this background, catching the trend of gold price has important theory and realistic significance.

There are futures and spot gold markets,. Spot price has hysteresis, it is easy to be influenced by product demand and price fluctuated violently. However function of price discovery in future market could just make up this defect. The purpose of this paper is to verify the function of price discovery in gold future with the modern computer techniques, and propose an integrated forecasting model for investors improving their predicted accuracy.

F.L. Wang et al. (Eds.): AICI 2010, Part II, LNAI 6320, pp. 374–381, 2010.
© Springer-Verlag Berlin Heidelberg 2010

The rest will be organized as follows. The second part reviews the research about function of price discovery in future. The third part introduces wavelet frame (WF) and support vector regression (SVR), and the two stage forecasting technique what this paper proposed.

1.2 Literature Review of Price Discovery

Most of researches about function of price discovery in future are focus on two dimensions; one is why does future market have function of price discovery, and the other one is function of price discovery in future market by evidence based test.

There are two thoughts about Function of price discovery in futures price. First holds that futures price is equal to conditional expectation in the due date of futures contracts (Samuelson, 1999). The other viewpoint thinks function of price discovery in future is respondent ability of future market earlier than spot market to new information (Hoffman, 1932). This paper will base on second viewpoint to verify immediateness of future market response information.

There spring many empirical study about price discovery function, researchers refer to dynamic model (Garbade and Silber,1983), regressive analysis (Bigman, 1983), E-G co-integration analysis (Engl and Granger, 1987; Hasbrouck, 1995), ECM and VAR model et al to find and test the relationship between the futures price and spot price to verify the price discovery function of futures. However there is little research in using modern calculation method to study it. It is parts of research to study gold price with machine learning method as neural network, et al. only, but it is confined in forecast of gold spot price or future price. This paper thinks gold future have hiding information which support the function of price discovery, but the information can be disclosed effectively only by modern computer techniques including the wavelet frame method.

2 Methodology

2.1 Wavelet Frame (WF)

Wavelet transform is a signal processing technique and it has been widely applied in image processing, data compression, signal processing, noise removal, object finding and time series analysis, etc [8-11].

In general, multi-resolution analysis (MRA) is the most important concept in the application of wavelet transform. MRA can decompose the whole space of original function   into one approximation space and several detail spaces. Approximation parts can be decomposed again by the iterate process. In other words, one signal can be decomposed to be many components with lower distinguish ability. This process is called wavelet decomposition tree, as Figure 1 showed. In the Figure 1, S represents the original information or time series; Ai is approximation coefficient of ith decomposition level; Di is detail coefficient of ith decomposition level.

The wavelet frame (WF) is one of the most widely applied wavelet transform [12]. It decomposes the original signal S to two parts through high-pass filter and low-pass filter, but it keeps the same length as original signal. So, it is different from those

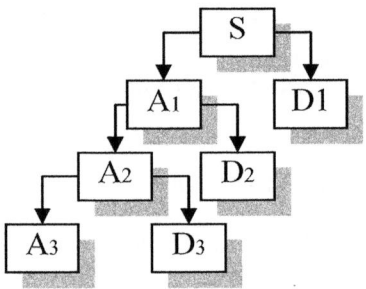

Fig. 1. Wavelet decomposition tree

wavelet transform mostly applied in signal process, data compression and image processing, which usually change the length of signal.

The calculation of WF through convolution is as follows [13].

$$A_{j,l} = \sum_k L_k A_{j-1,l+k} \tag{1}$$

$$D_{j,l} = \sum_k H_k A_{j-1,l+k} \tag{2}$$

where L_k is the coefficients of low-pass filter, H_k is the coefficients of high-pass filter, $A_{j,l}$ is approximation coefficient of the jth level and translation, $D_{j,l}$ is detail coefficient of jth level and translation, when j is zero, it is the original signal.

2.2 Support Vector Regression (SVR)

Support vector regression (SVR) is an artificial intelligent forecasting tool based on statistical learning theory and structural risk minimization principle [3-4, 14]. It has been applied in different kinds of numerical value forecasting problem [3-7].

The SVR model can be expressed as the following equation [3-4]:

$$f(\mathbf{x}) = (\mathbf{w} \cdot \phi(\mathbf{x})) + b \tag{3}$$

Where $\mathbf{w}$ is weight vector, b is bias and $\phi(\mathbf{x})$ is a kernel function which uses a non-linear function to transform the non-linear input to be linear mode in a high dimension feature space.

Traditional regression gets the coefficients through minimizing the square error which can be considered as empirical risk based on loss function. Vapnik et al. [3] introduced so-called ε-insensitivity loss function to SVR. It can be express as:

$$L_\varepsilon(f(\mathbf{x}) - y) = \begin{cases} |f(\mathbf{x}) - y| - \varepsilon & \text{if } |f(\mathbf{x}) - y| \geq \varepsilon \\ 0 & \text{otherwise} \end{cases} \tag{4}$$

Where ε defined the region of ε-insensitivity, when the predicted value falls into the band area, the loss is zero. Contrarily, if the predicted value falls out the band area, the loss is equal to the difference between the predicted value and the margin. The positive and negative signs of difference can be represented by the two slack variables ξ and ξ^* :

$$L_\varepsilon(f(\mathbf{x}) - y) = \begin{cases} |f(\mathbf{x}) - y| - \varepsilon = \xi & \text{if } f(\mathbf{x}) - y \geq 0 \\ |f(\mathbf{x}) - y| - \varepsilon = \xi^* & \text{if } f(\mathbf{x}) - y \leq 0 \\ 0 & \text{otherwise} \end{cases} \tag{5}$$

Where ξ is training error bigger than the margin and ξ^* is training error less than margin.

The SVR uses the minimization of regularized risk function to get the weight and bias, as following equation:

$$R(C) = C\frac{1}{N}\sum_{i=1}^{n} L_r(f(\mathbf{x}_i), y_i) + \frac{1}{2}\|\mathbf{w}\|^2 \tag{6}$$

Where $L_r(f(\mathbf{x}_i), y_i)$ the ε-insensitivity loss is function in equation (5); $C\frac{1}{N}\sum_{i=1}^{n} L_r(f(\mathbf{x}_i), y_i)$ is empirical error; $\frac{1}{2}\|\mathbf{w}\|^2$ is regularization term.

Considering empirical risk and structure risk synchronously, the SVR model can be constructed to minimize the following programming:

$$\text{Min} : \frac{1}{2}\mathbf{w}^T\mathbf{w} + C\sum_i \left(\xi_i + \xi_i^*\right)$$

$$\text{Subject to} \begin{cases} y_i - \mathbf{w}^T\mathbf{x}_i - b \leq \varepsilon + \xi_i \\ \mathbf{w}^T\mathbf{x}_i + b - y_i \leq \varepsilon + \xi_i^* \\ \xi_i, \xi_i^* \geq 0 \end{cases} \tag{7}$$

where $i=1,\ldots,n$ is the number of training data; $\left(\xi_i + \xi_i^*\right)$ is the empirical risk; $\frac{1}{2}\mathbf{w}^T\mathbf{w}$ is the structure risk preventing over-learning and lack of applied universality; C is modifying coefficient representing the trade-off between empirical risk and structure risk. The bigger C value the more importance is attached to empirical risk, while the C is used to represent structure risk.

The equation (7) is a quadratic programming problem. After selecting proper modifying coefficient (C), width of band area (ε) and kernel function, the optimum of each parameter can be resolved though the Lagrange functions.

2.3 The Two-Stage Forecasting Model

The proposed model uses the wavelet frame as a data pre-processed tool to decompose the predicting variable into sub-series, and then uses the sub-series as input variables to construct SVR forecasting model. The frame of the proposed forecasting model can be shown as figure 2.

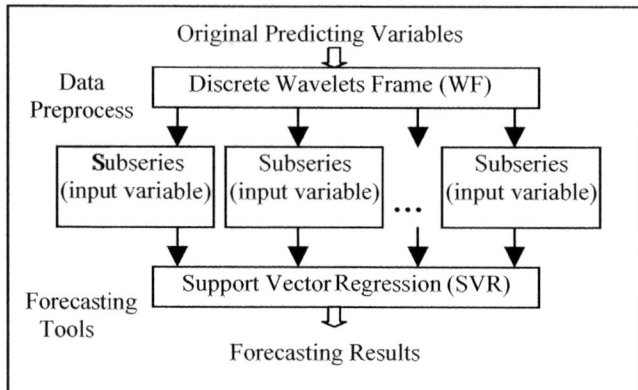

Fig. 2. The frame of the proposed forecasting model

3   Experimental Design

3.1   Data Set

In order to validate the function of price discovery in gold future, we used the model to forecast next day (T+1) of the COMES opening price of gold future, and use forecasting open price of 10 days later (T+10) to be proof.

There are 55 defect data in total. After using simple pruning method to delete it, we get 991 data point. We used 694 data (70%), as training data set and keep the rest 297 data (30%) as testing dada set.

3.2   Parametric Design for the Model

3.2.1   Parameter of Wavelet Frame
To extract hiding information of wavelet frame which most important parameter is the setting of basis function and decomposition order.

Wavelet basis function is kernel of wavelet frame. According to Aussem et la. saying, different kind of Daubechies (Db) model and various selection could build up different model, but research of wavelet transform in financial time series is almost base on single basis function as Haar (Db1) Db2 or Db4 etc. to modeling (Gonghui, 1999; Shin, 2000; Yao, 2000; Yousefi, 2005). The paper uses four basis functions which are Db1 to Db4 to represent wavelet frame.

3.2.2   Parameter of SVR
This two parameter C and ε is the most important in SVR model. The paper is base on sequence searching method of index growth (such as 25, 23,......,2-15) which proposed by Hsu et al. (2003), and combined with parameter setting suggested by Cherkassky and Ma(2004) and Hsu et al. (2003). We use method of Cherkassky and Ma (2004) to estimate training data to get a recommended combination of parameter of SVR (as recommended value of C and ε), and then process index searching in the recommended combination to be able to produce a parameter combination of

minimum mean square error to be optimal combination. Using this method to select parameter of SVR can prevent possible risk of recommended combination; meanwhile it can reduce defects in degree of operation of trial and error too more.

Table 1. Coefficient of low-pass decomposed filter

Basis	Coefficient of low-pass decomposed filter			
Db1	0. 5	0. 5		
Db2	-0. 091506351	0. 158493649	0. 591506351	0. 341506351
Db3	0. 02490875	-0. 060416104	-0. 095467208	
	0. 3251825	0. 570558458	0. 235233604	
Db4	-0. 007493495	0. 023251801	0. 02180815	-0. 132253584
	-0. 019787513	0. 446100069	0. 505472858	0. 162901714

Table 2. Coefficient of high-pass decomposed filter.

Basis	Coefficient of high-pass decomposed filter				
Db1	-0. 5	0. 5			
Db2	-0. 341506351	0. 591506351	-0. 158493649	-0. 091506351	-0. 341506351
Db3	-0. 235233604	0. 570558458	-0. 3251825		
	-0. 095467208	0. 060416104	0. 02490875		
Db4	-0. 162901714	0. 505472858	-0. 446100069	-0. 019787513	
	0. 13225358	0. 02180815	-0. 023251801	-0. 007493495	

3.3 Criteria for Valuating the Model

The paper set three indexes to evaluate the performance of forecasting model and verify function of price discovery. These three indexes are root mean square error (RMSE), mean absolute difference (MAD), and Mean absolute percentage error (MAPE).

4 Experimental Result

Here this paper only reports the best results. As showed in Table 3 and table 4, when C is 2^{13} and ε is 2^{-10} based on Db1 function, the T+1 forecasting can get the best results, while for T+10 forecasting, the model should base on Db4 with C equal to 2^3 and ε equal to 2^{-10}, and the two-stage model can get better forecasting results than the single SVR model whether to T+1 forecasting or to T+10 forecasting.

Table 3. The optimum parameter and criteria for forecasting results of DWF + SVR model

Basis Function	C	ε	Training Sample RMSE	Testing Sample RMSE
The best for T+1: Db1	2^{13}	2^{-10}	0.0002180	0.0001694
The best for T+10: Db4	2^3	2^{-10}	0.000262294	0.000201269

Table 4. Forecasting results of different model.

	RMSE	MAD	MAPE
Single SVR for T+1	12.9173	9.2007	0.972%
Single SVR for T+10	13.43243	9.407204	1.188%
two-stage model combining DWF-SVR:			
DB1 for T+1	11.7290	8.8765	0.856%
DB4 for T+10	12.42453	8.374997	0.974%

The results also show that the gold futures price has indeed the price discovery function, especially when us the modern computer techniques as auxiliary.

5 Conclusions

This paper use modern computing technology to study function of price discovery in gold future, and proposed a two-stage forecasting model by integrating wavelet frame and SVR for financial time series. The paper uses wavelet frame to decompose the gold futures price to be some sub-series for exposing the information hidden in it, and then use SVR tool constructing the predicting model based on those sub-series, thus the article builds up a two-stage forecasting model. This paper study COMEX gold future and spot open price. Empirical results show that it has best forecasting effectiveness to predict open price of next day using DB1 basis function. Even if we predict open price of 10 days later, the result which add forecasting model of price information in future is good than model without future information. Function of price discovery in future is proved. Meanwhile the forecasting effectiveness of model is good enough.

Overall, there are two contributions in this paper. One is using modern computing technology to prove the function of price discovery in gold future, and the other is to develop a two-stage financial time series forecasting model which performs better than a single model and it is proved suitable for forecasting gold spot price. It is different from past research using other forecasting tool as neural network, etc.

It can use different function of WF to do further research in the future, and can introduce other economic variable at one time, and then use other tools such as independent component, etc. to excavate market information further to improve forecasting accuracy.

Acknowledgements

This research was partially supported by programme grant of Key Reaearch Institute of Humanities & Social Sciences, Ministry of Education P.R.C. under Grant Number 2009JJD790049).

References

[1] Aussem, A., Campbell, J., Murtagh, F.: Wavelet-based feature extraction and decomposition strategies for financial forecasting. Journal of Computational Intelligence in Finance 6, 5–12 (1998)

[2] Bjorn, V.: Multiresolution methods for financial time series prediction, computational intelligence for financial engineering. In: Proceedings of the IEEE/IAFE on Computational Intelligence for Financial Engineering, New York, p. 97 (1995)

[3] Cherkassky, V., Ma, Y.: Practical selection of SVM parameters and noise estimation for SVM regression. Neural Networks 17, 113–126 (2004)

[4] Cherkassky, V., Mulier, F.: Vapnik-Chervonenkis (VC) learning theory and its applications. IEEE Transactions on Neural Networks 10, 985–987 (1999)

[5] Drucker, H., Burges, C.J.C., Kaufman, L., Smola, A., Vapnik, V.N.: Support vector regression machines. Advances in Neural Information Processing Systems 9, 155–161 (1997)

[6] Grossmann, A., Morlet, J.: Decomposition of Hardy function into square integrable wavelet of constant shape. SIAM Journal on Mathematical Analysis 15, 736–783 (1984)

[7] Hsu, C.W., Lin, C.C., Lin, C.J.: [J/OL]. A practical guide to support classification (2003), http://www.csie.ntu.edu.tw/~cjlin/papers/guide/guide.pdf

[8] Koike, A., Takagi, T.: Prediction of protein-protein interaction sites using support vector machines. Protein Engineering Design and Selection 17, 165–173 (2004)

[9] Lee, T.S., Chen, N.J.: Investigating the information content of non-cash-trading index futures using neural networks. Expert Systems with Applications 22, 225–234 (2002)

[10] Lee, T.S., Chen, N.J., Chiu, C.C.: Forecasting the opening cash price index using grey forecasting and neural networks: evidence from the SGX-DT MSCI Taiwan Index Futures Contracts. In: Wang, P., Chen, S.S. (eds.) Computational Intelligence in Economics and Finance, pp. 151–170. Springer, Heidelberg (2003)

[11] Li, T., Li, Q., Zhu, S., Ogihara, M.: A survey on wavelet applications in data mining. ACM SIGKDD Explorations Newsletter 4, 49–68 (2002)

[12] Mallat, S.G.: A theory for multiresolution signal decomposition: the wavelet representation. IEEE Transactions on Pattern Analysis and Machine Intelligence 11, 674–793 (1989)

[13] Parisi, F., Vasquez, A.: Simple technical trading rules of stock returns: Evidence from 1987 to 1998 in Chile. Emerging Market Review 1, 152–164 (2000)

[14] Ramsey, J.B.: Wavelets in economics and finance: Past and future. Studies in Nonlinear Dynamics & Econometrics 6, 1–27 (2002)

[15] Rao, R.M., Bopardikar, A.S.: Wavelet Transforms: Introduction to Theory and Applications. Addison Wesley, Boston (1998)

[16] Starck, J.L., Murtagh, F., Bijaoui, A.: Image and Data Analysis: The Multiscale Approach. Cambridge University Press, U.K (1998)

[17] Strang, G., Nguyen, T.: Wavelets and Filter Banks. Wellesley-Cambridge Press, MA (1996)

[18] Van Nevel, A.: Texture classification using wavelet frame decomposition. In: Proceeding of the 1997 Conference Record of the Thirty-First Asilomar Conference on Signals, Systems and Computer, vol. 1, pp. 311–314 (1998)

[19] Vapnik, V.: The Nature of Statistical Learning Theory, 2nd edn. Springer, Berlin (1999)

[20] Yang, Y., Liu, X.: A re-examination of text categorization methods. In: ACM International Conference on Research and Development in Information Retrieval, vol. 22, pp. 42–49 (1999)

[21] Dai, W., Wu, J., et al.: Combining ICA and SVR in time series predication. In: The 3rd International Conference on Risk Management & Global e-Business, Korea, EI (2009)

Author Index